Ninth Edition

Multicultural Education in a Pluralistic Society

DONNA M. GOLLNICK
National Council for the Accreditation of Teacher Education

PHILIP C. CHINN
California State University, Los Angeles

PEARSON

Boston • Columbus • Indianapolis • New York • San Francisco • Upper Saddle River
Amsterdam • Cape Town • Dubai • London • Madrid • Milan • Munich • Paris • Montreal • Toronto
Delhi • Mexico City • São Paulo • Sydney • Hong Kong • Seoul • Singapore • Taipei • Tokyo

Vice President, Editorial Director: Jeffery W. Johnston
Senior Acquisitions Editor: Kelly Villella Canton
Senior Development Editor: Max Effenson Chuck
Editorial Assistant: Annalea Manalili
Executive Marketing Manager: Darcy Betts
Production Editor: Paula Carroll
Editorial Production Service: Electronic Publishing Services Inc.
Manufacturing Buyer: Megan Cochran
Electronic Composition: Jouve
Interior Design: Electronic Publishing Services Inc.
Photo Researcher: Annie Fuller
Cover Designer: Jennifer Hart

Credits and acknowledgments borrowed from other sources and reproduced, with permission, in this textbook appear on the appropriate page within text.

Photo Credits: p. xxiv: © iStockPhoto; p. 36: © Steve Skjold/Alamy; p. 74: © Craig Ruttle/Alamy; p. 108: © Janine Wiedel Photolibrary/Alamy; p. 142: © Zuma Press/Newscom; p. 172: © Robin Nelson/PhotoEdit; p. 206: © Christina Kennedy/PhotoEdit; p. 236: © Shutterstock; p. 278: © Shutterstock; p. 316: © Jim West/Alamy; p. 348: © iStockPhoto

Many of the designations by manufacturers and sellers to distinguish their products are claimed as trademarks. Where those designations appear in this book, and the publisher was aware of a trademark claim, the designations have been printed in initial caps or all caps.

Library of Congress Cataloging-in-Publication Data

Gollnick, Donna M.
    Multicultural education in a pluralistic society/Donna M. Gollnick,
Philip C. Chinn. — 9th ed.
        p. cm.
    Includes bibliographical references and index.
    ISBN-13: 978-0-13-703509-0 (pbk.)
    ISBN-10: 0-13-703509-8 (pbk.)
    1. Multicultural education—United States. 2. Social sciences—Study and teaching (Elementary)—United States. 3. Cultural pluralism—Study and teaching (Elementary)—United States. 4. Social sciences—Study and teaching (Secondary)—United States. 5. Cultural pluralism—Study and teaching (Secondary)—United States. I. Chinn, Philip C. II. Title.
    LC1099.3.G65 2013
    370.117—dc23
                                                                            2011046815

10 9 8 7 6 5 4

ISBN 10: 0-13-703509-8
ISBN 13: 978-0-13-703509-0

To *my parents, Charles D. Kuhn and Kathleen L. Kuhn,*
who instilled in their children the commitment
to equality and human rights.

DMG

To *William J. Gregg and Paul T. Matsunaga,*
whose loyal friendship has always been there
in both the difficult and in the good years.

PCC

ABOUT THE AUTHORS

DONNA M. GOLLNICK is senior consultant for the National Council for the Accreditation of Teacher Education (NCATE), where her primary responsibility is assisting in the creation of a new accrediting organization, the Council for Accreditation of Educator Preparation (CAEP). She has been promoting and writing about multicultural education and equity in teacher education and schools since the 1970s and is past president of the National Association for Multicultural Education (NAME). Dr. Gollnick is the coauthor of *Introduction to the Foundations of American Education, Sixteenth Edition*, and *The Joy of Teaching, Second Edition*.

PHILIP C. CHINN is a professor emeritus at California State University, Los Angeles, where he taught multicultural education, special education, and served as Special Education Division chair. He served as special assistant to the Executive Director for Minority Affairs at the Council for Exceptional Children (CEC), where he coordinated the first national conferences on the Exceptional Bilingual Child and the Exceptional Black Child. He served as vice president of the National Association for Multicultural Education (NAME) and co-editor of *Multicultural Perspectives*, the NAME journal. He co-authored two special education texts. He also served on the California State Advisory Commission for Special Education.

BRIEF CONTENTS

C O N T E N T S

CHAPTER 7: Language 206

CHAPTER 8: Religion   236

SPECIAL FEATURES

Pause to Reflect

Focus Your Cultural Lens: Debate

Critical Incidents in Teaching

PREFACE

The ninth edition of *Multicultural Education in a Pluralistic Society* introduces prospective teachers to the different cultural groups to which students and their families belong. In this time of extensive standardized testing, we must remember that students are the center of teaching. We have to understand and build on their cultures and experiences to help them learn at the highest levels. In this regard, this book provides background on the diversity of the nation's students, explores the social and educational issues faced by teachers in diverse classrooms, and guides the reader to think critically and reflectively about their decisions as a teacher in a multicultural education classroom.

WHAT IS NEW IN THE NINTH EDITION?

NEW! A new chapter, Chapter 5, Sexual Orientation, explores the diverse sexual identities of the population, including lesbians, gays, bisexuals, transgender individuals, queers (LGBTQ), and heterosexuals. Data on harassment of students who are LGBTQ are reviewed, and strategies are identified for confronting and eliminating such harassment. The chapter also discusses how diverse sexual identities can be incorporated into the curriculum and how educators can support LGBTQ students.

NEW! Chapter 6 on exceptionality introduces response to intervention (RTI) and includes a new Critical Incident feature on autism.

NEW! Dual language immersion programs are discussed in Chapter 7.

NEW! Chapter 8 includes a new section on the changing religious landscape of the United States and has updated and expanded its discussion of Islam.

NEW! Regional differences in cuisine, religion, health and well-being, and politics are explored in Chapter 9.

NEW! Gender identities in Chapter 4 have been expanded to include transgender students.

NEW! Discussions of bullying and sexting are now incorporated into Chapter 10, newly titled "The Youth Culture." This chapter also includes a new Critical Incident feature.

NEW! The last section of each chapter, "Digital Resources," includes links to lesson plans, data, and other digital resources to support multicultural teaching.

UPDATED! The discussion of immigration, particularly unauthorized immigration, has been expanded in Chapter 2.

UPDATED! Strategies for meeting the goals of multicultural education are now outlined in Chapter 11.

UPDATED! All tables, figures, and references reflect the latest data and thinking about the issues explored throughout the book.

DIVERSITY IN THE TWENTY-FIRST CENTURY

The United States is a multicultural nation comprised of indigenous peoples, such as the American Indians, Aleuts, Eskimos, and Hawaiians, and those who themselves or whose ancestors arrived as immigrants from other countries. Our students bring different ethnicities, races, classes, religions, and native languages to the classroom. In addition, they differ in gender, sexual orientation, age, and physical and mental abilities. They have come from different parts of the world and now live as part of regional cultures within the United States. As we move further into this century, the population will become increasingly more diverse. By 2020, children of color will comprise half of the school-aged population. As the ethnic diversity of the United States increases, so does the religious landscape as new immigrants bring their religions from Africa, the Middle East, and Asia. They also bring diverse languages, values, and ideas that are reshaping U.S. society.

The culture and the society of the United States are dynamic and in a continuous state of change. Unless teachers are able to understand the role of race, class, gender, and other group memberships in their students' lives, it will be difficult to teach them effectively.

WHAT IMPACT DOES MULTICULTURAL EDUCATION HAVE ON TEACHING?

Education that is multicultural provides an environment that values diversity and portrays it positively. Students' gender, sexual orientation, race, ethnicity, native language, religion, class, or disability should not limit their educational and vocational options. Educators have the responsibility to help students contribute to and benefit from our democratic society. Effective instructional strategies do not evolve solely from the teacher's culture. They are drawn from the cultures of students and their communities. The integration of multicultural education throughout the curriculum helps students and teachers think critically about institutional racism, classism, sexism, ablism, ageism, and homophobia. Hopefully, educators will help their students develop both individual and group strategies to overcome the debilitating effects of these societal scourges.

ABOUT THE NINTH EDITION

Students in undergraduate, graduate, and in-service courses will find this text helpful in examining social and cultural conditions that influence education. It provides the foundation for understanding diversity and using this knowledge effectively in classrooms and schools. Other social services professionals will find it helpful in understanding the complexity of cultural backgrounds and experiences as they work with families and children.

CULTURAL IDENTITY

As in previous editions, the authors approach multicultural education with a broad perspective of the concept. Using culture as the basis for understanding multicultural education, they discuss the groups with which students and their families often identify and the impact those group memberships have on them. These groups are critical in understanding pluralism and multicultural education. Thus, this text examines these groups and the ways in which educators can develop education programs to help all students learn.

EQUITY IN CLASSROOMS

We also emphasize the importance of an equitable education for all students. Educators should not fight against sexism without also fighting racism, classism, homophobia, and discrimination based on abilities, age, religion, and geography. Schools can eradicate discrimination in their own policies and practices if educators are willing to confront and eliminate their own racism, sexism, and other biases. To rid our schools of such practices takes a committed and strong faculty. The ninth edition helps readers develop the habit of self-reflection that will help them become more effective teachers in classrooms that provide equity for all students.

HOW THE TEXT IS ORGANIZED

Multicultural Education in a Pluralistic Society provides an overview of the different cultural groups to which students belong. The first chapter examines the pervasive influence of culture, the importance of understanding our own and our students' cultural backgrounds and experiences, and the evolution of multicultural education. The next nine chapters examine ethnicity and race, class and socioeconomic status, gender, sexual orientation, exceptionality, language, religion, geography (that is, the places we live), and age. The final chapter contains recommendations for using culturally responsive and social justice pedagogies in the implementation of education that is multicultural. The chapters in this edition have been revised and reorganized to reflect current thinking and research in the area. In particular, the first chapter provides the foundational framework that supports our thinking about multicultural education. The final chapter integrates critical pedagogy with research on teaching effectively. Each chapter opens with a scenario to place the topic in an educational setting.

MULTIPLE PERSPECTIVES

We have tried to present different perspectives on a number of issues in the most unbiased manner possible. We are not without strong opinions or passion on some of the issues. However, in our effort to be equitable, we do attempt to present different perspectives on the issues and allow the reader to make his or her own decisions. There are some issues related to racism, sexism, ableism, and so on, that are so important to the well-being of society that we do provide our positions, which we recognize to be our biases.

ATTENTION TO LANGUAGE

Readers should be aware of several caveats related to the language used in this text. Although we realize that the term *American* is commonly used to refer to the U.S. population, we view *American* as including other North and South Americans as well. Therefore, we have tried to limit the use of this term when referring to the United States. Although we have tried to use the terms *black* and *white* sparingly, data about groups often have been categorized by the racial identification, rather than by national origin such as African or European American. In many cases, we were not able to distinguish ethnic identity and have continued to use *black*, *white*, or *persons of color*. We have limited our use of the term *minority* and have focused more on the power relationships that exist between groups. We use *Hispanic* and *Latino* interchangeably to refer to persons with Spanish-speaking heritages who have immigrated from countries as diverse as Mexico, Cuba, Argentina, Puerto Rico, Belize, and Colombia.

FEATURES

Each chapter includes features throughout that illustrate for the reader how concepts and events play out in a multicultural classroom. They also require the reader to stop and reflect about their own views and think about how they would respond to situations in a multicultural classroom.

EXPERIENCE AND APPLY

CHAPTER-OPENING CLASSROOM SCENARIOS

Each chapter opens with a classroom scenario to place the chapter content in an educational setting. Questions at the end of each scenario encourage readers to think about the scenario and guide them to reflect on the decisions they would make.

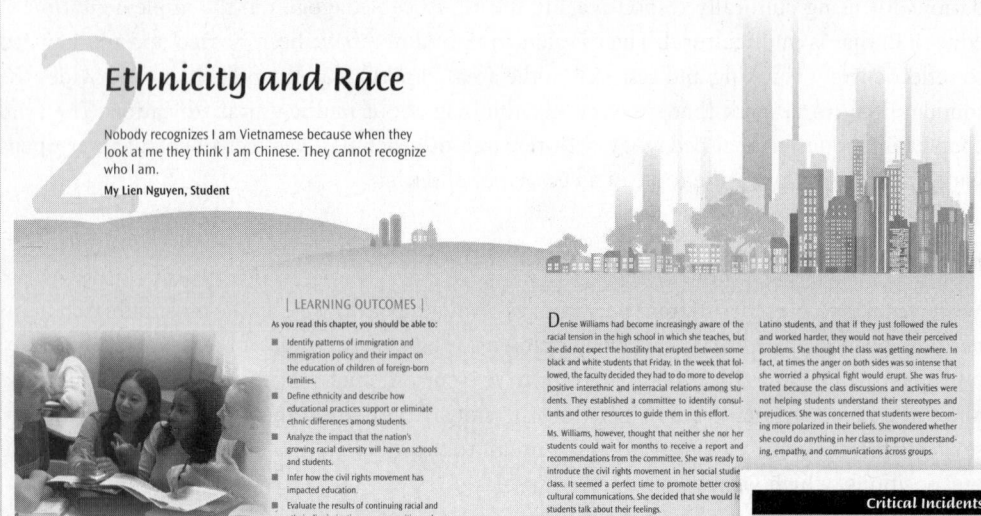

CRITICAL INCIDENTS IN TEACHING

This feature presents both real-life and hypothetical situations that occur in schools or classrooms providing readers with the opportunity to examine their feelings, attitudes, and possible actions or reactions to each scenario. This feature occurs once in each chapter.

EXPLORE YOUR BELIEFS

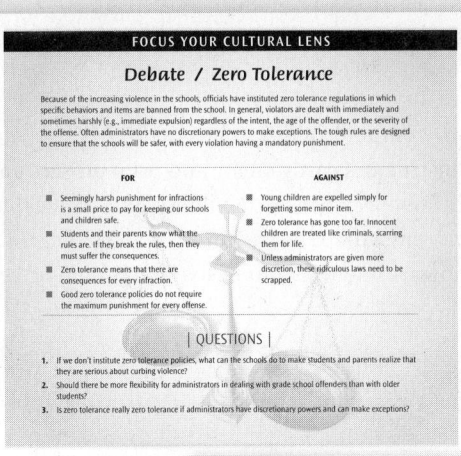

FOCUS YOUR CULTURAL LENS: DEBATE

Located in most chapters, this feature presents a controversial school issue with *for* and *against* statements for readers to consider. Questions guide readers to critically analyze both sides of the issue and encourage them to take a side.

PAUSE TO REFLECT

Located several times in each chapter, this feature encourages readers to reflect on how the issue being discussed relates to their everyday life as teachers. It asks readers to complete an activity, collect data, or it poses questions about the topic.

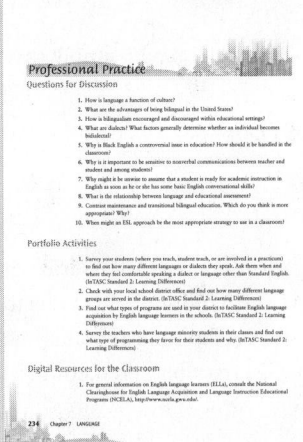

PROFESSIONAL PRACTICE

There are three areas addressed in this section. Questions for Discussion are questions related to sections within the chapter, provided to stimulate classroom discussions of critical issues. Portfolio Activities are suggested activities to enhance the student's learning experiences related to issues raised in the chapter. All are related to one or more of the ten InTASC standards. Digital Resources for the Classroom are suggested websites where additional information related to the chapter can be accessed.

INSTRUCTOR'S MANUAL/TEST BANK

The Instructor's Manual includes a wealth of interesting ideas and activities designed to help instructors teach the course. Each chapter contains learning outcomes, key terms, key concepts, and group activities, as well as a comprehensive test bank containing multiple-choice, true/false, short-answer, and essay questions. (Available for download from the Instructor's Resource Center at www.pearsonhighered.com/irc.)

PEARSON MYTEST

The Test Bank is also available through our computerized testing system, MyTest, a powerful assessment generation program that helps instructors easily create and print quizzes and exams. Questions and tests are authored online, allowing ultimate flexibility and the ability to efficiently create and print assessments anytime, anywhere! Instructors can access Pearson MyTest and their test bank files by going to www.pearsonmytest.com to log in, register, or request access. Features of Pearson MyTest include:

Premium assessment content

- Draw from a rich library of assessments that complement your Pearson textbook and your course's learning objectives.
- Edit questions or tests to fit your specific teaching needs.

Instructor-friendly resources

- Easily create and store your own questions, including images, diagrams, and charts using simple drag-and-drop and Word-like controls.
- Use additional information provided by Pearson, such as the question's difficulty level or learning objective, to help you quickly build your test.

Time-saving enhancements

- Add headers or footers and easily scramble questions and answer choices—all from one simple toolbar.
- Quickly create multiple versions of your test or answer key, and when ready, simply save to Microsoft Word or PDF format and print!
- Export your exams for import to Blackboard 6.0, CE (WebCT), or Vista (WebCT)!

POWERPOINT™ PRESENTATION

Designed for instructors using the text, the PowerPoint™ Presentation consists of a series of slides that may be customized for in-class presentation or used to make handouts or overhead transparencies. The presentation highlights key concepts and major topics for each chapter. Available for download from the Instructor Resource Center at www.pearsonhighered.com/irc.

MYEDUCATIONLAB CORRELATION GUIDE

Available for download from the Instructor Resource Center at www.pearsonhighered.com/irc.

MyEducationLab™ Proven to **engage students**, provide **trusted content**, and **improve results**, Pearson MyLabs have helped over 8 million registered students reach true understanding in their courses. **MyEducationLab** engages students with real-life teaching situations through dynamic videos, case studies, and student artifacts. Student progress is assessed, and a personalized study plan is created based on the student's unique results. Automatic grading and reporting keeps educators informed to quickly address gaps and improve student performance. All of the activities and exercises in MyEducationLab are built around essential learning outcomes.

In Preparing Teachers for a Changing World, Linda Darling-Hammond and her colleagues point out that grounding teacher education in real classrooms—among real teachers and students and among actual examples of students' and teachers' work—is an important, and perhaps even an essential, part of training teachers for the complexities of teaching in today's classrooms.

In the MyEducationLab for this course you will find the following features and resources.

ASSIGNMENTS AND ACTIVITIES Designed to enhance your understanding of concepts covered in class, these assignable exercises show concepts in action (through videos, cases, and/or student and teacher artifacts). They help you deepen content knowledge and synthesize and apply concepts and strategies you read about in the book. (Extensive recommended answers for these assignments are available to the instructor only.)

BUILDING TEACHING SKILLS AND DISPOSITIONS These unique learning units help users practice and strengthen skills that are essential to effective teaching. After presenting the steps involved in a core teaching process, you are given an opportunity to practice applying this skill via analyzing case studies based on real classroom and school situations. Providing multiple opportunities to practice a single teaching concept, each activity encourages a deeper understanding and application of concepts, as well as the use of critical thinking skills.

BOOK SPECIFIC RESOURCES Licensure Test Prep Activities are available in the Book Resources to help you prepare for test taking. Many situations or questions presented provide hints and feedback to better scaffold the student. Flashcards of key terms and concepts are also available.

STUDY PLAN SPECIFIC TO YOUR TEXT MyEducationLab gives students the opportunity to test themselves on key concepts and skills, track their own progress through the course, and access personalized Study Plan activities.

The customized Study Plan—with enriching activities—is generated based on students' results of a pretest. Study Plans tag incorrect questions from the pretest to the appropriate textbook learning outcome, helping students focus on the topics they need help with. Personalized Study Plan activities may include eBook reading assignments and review, practice, and enrichment activities.

After students complete the enrichment activities, they take a posttest to see the concepts they've mastered or the areas where they may need extra help. MyEducationLab then reports the Study Plan results to the instructor. Based on these reports, the instructor can adapt course material to suit the needs of individual students or the entire class.

COURSE RESOURCES   The Course Resources section of MyEducationLab is designed to help you put together an effective lesson plan, prepare for and begin your career, navigate your first year of teaching, and understand key educational standards, policies, and laws.

It includes the following:

- The Lesson Plan Builder, an effective and easy-to-use tool that you can use to create, update, and share quality lesson plans. The software also makes it easy to integrate state content standards into any lesson plan.

- The Preparing a Portfolio module, guidelines for creating a high-quality teaching portfolio.

- Beginning Your Career, which offers tips, advice, and other valuable information on:

  - Resume Writing and Interviewing: Includes expert advice on how to write impressive resumes and prepare for job interviews.

  - Your First Year of Teaching: Provides practical tips to set up a first classroom, manage student behavior, and more easily organize for instruction and assessment.

  - Law and Public Policies: Details specific directives and requirements you need to understand under the No Child Left Behind Act and the Individuals with Disabilities Education Improvement Act of 2004.

CERTIFICATION AND LICENSURE   The Certification and Licensure section is designed to help you pass your licensure exam by giving you access to state test requirements, overviews of what tests cover, and sample test items.

The Certification and Licensure section includes the following:

- **State Certification Test Requirements:** Here, you can click on a state and will then be taken to a list of state certification tests.

- You can click on the **Licensure Exams** you need to take to find:
  - Basic information about each test
  - Descriptions of what is covered on each test
  - Sample test questions with explanations of correct answers

- **National Evaluation Series™** by Pearson: Here, students can see the tests in the NES, learn what is covered on each exam, and access sample test items with descriptions and rationales of correct answers. You can also purchase interactive online tutorials developed by Pearson Evaluation Systems and the Pearson Teacher Education and Development group.

- **ETS Online Praxis Tutorials:** Here you can purchase interactive online tutorials developed by ETS and by the Pearson Teacher Education and Development group. Tutorials are available for the Praxis I exams and for select Praxis II exams.

Visit www.myeducationlab.com for a demonstration of this exciting new online teaching resource.

ACKNOWLEDGMENTS

The preparation of any text involves the contributions of many individuals in addition to those whose names are found on the cover.

We wish to thank Maria Gutierrez for her highly competent assistance in researching and manuscript development. Thanks also to Dr. Ozlem Sensoy, Simon Fraser University, for her thoughtful review and helpful suggestions on the sections on Islam. We also thank Dr. Haywood E. Wyche and Dr. Frances Kuwahara Chinn for their continuous support and assistance throughout the manuscript development. The assistance, patience, encouragement, and guidance of our editors, Max Effenson Chuck and Kelly Villella Canton, are sincerely appreciated.

We wish to thank the following reviewers, whose recommendations were used to improve this edition: Kam Chi Chan, Purdue University, North Central; Corey Marie Hall, Florida Community College, Jacksonville; and Diana Linn, Texas A&M International University. We would also like to thank those who participated in our Advisory Council, providing us with additional feedback during our development process. Participants include: Marie A. Arter, Lourdes University; William P. Austin, The University of Nebraska at Omaha; Berlye I. Baker, Georgia Perimeter College; Ann M. Corfman, Urbana University; Joy Cowdery, Muskingum University; Brian W. Dotts, College of Education, The University of Georgia; Gail T. Eichman, Baldwin-Wallace College; Theresa Garfield Dorel, Texas A&M University, San Antonio; Rick Gay, Davidson College; Corey Hall, Florida State College-Jacksonville; Michele Kahn, University of Houston-Clear Lake; Kimberly Livengood, Angelo State University; Melinda Eudy Ratchford, Belmont Abbey College; Rajeeve Swami, Central State University; and Sharon H. Ulanoff, California State University, Los Angeles.

1

Foundations of Multicultural Education

Equality is the heart and essence of democracy, freedom, and justice.

A. Philip Randolph, Civil Rights Leader, 1942

| LEARNING OUTCOMES |

As you read this chapter, you should be able to:

- Acknowledge the diversity of students in today's schools.

- Examine the role that culture plays in the lives of students and their families.

- Consider whether cultural pluralism is a reasonable and achievable goal in the classroom.

- Recognize why knowing your students is so important to effective instruction.

- Identify the obstacles to creating a just and equal classroom.

- Describe characteristics of multicultural education in the classroom.

You are just beginning your first teaching position in a nearby urban area. Like many new teachers in an urban area, you were offered the job only a few weeks before school started. You had never been to that part of the city but were sure you could make a difference in the lives of students there. You quickly learn that many students have single parents, many of whom work two jobs to make ends meet. Almost all of the students are eligible for free lunch. The families of some students do not speak English at home, but the principal says the students speak English. You are disappointed in the condition of the school, and your classroom in particular, but have been assured it will be repainted during one of the vacation periods.

When students arrive on the first day, you are not surprised that a large proportion of them are from families who emigrated from Central America during the past two decades. The population includes some African American students and a few European American students. You did not realize that the class would include a student who had just moved from Bulgaria and spoke no English and that the native language of two students was Farsi. You have taken a few Spanish courses but know little or nothing about the languages or cultures of Bulgaria and Iran. You wonder about the boy with the black eye but guess that he has been in a fight recently.

| REFLECTIONS |

1. What assumptions about these students and their academic potential did you make as you read this brief description?

2. What kinds of challenges are you likely to confront during the year?

3. What do you wish you had learned in college to help you be a better teacher in this school?

Diversity in the Classroom

Educators today are faced with an overwhelming challenge to prepare students from diverse populations and backgrounds to live in a rapidly changing society and a world in which some groups receive greater societal benefits than others because of race, ethnicity, gender, class, language, religion, ability, geography, or age. Schools of the future will become increasingly diverse. Demographic data on birthrates and **immigration** indicate that the numbers of Asian American, Latino, and African American children are increasing. Over 40% of students in P–12 schools today are students of color (Aud et al., 2010). By 2020, students of color are projected to represent nearly half of the elementary and secondary populations. However, the race and sex of their teachers match neither the student population nor the general population: 83% of the teachers are European American, as shown in Figure 1.1. In elementary schools, 85% of the teachers are female. Teachers at the secondary level, compared with the elementary level, are more likely to be male; female teachers comprise 58% of the teachers at this level (Aud et al., 2010).

In 2008 Latinos, Asian Americans, American Indians, and African Americans already comprised more than half of the public school student populations in Arizona (55.6%), California (72.1%), the District of Columbia (94%), Florida (53%), Hawaii (81%), Louisiana (52%), Maryland (54%), Mississippi (54%), Nevada (58%), New Mexico (71%), and Texas (66%) (Snyder & Dillow, 2011). Students of color represent three of four students in many of the nation's largest school districts (Sable, Plotts, & Mitchell, 2010). Although the U.S. Census Bureau (2010k) reports that only 20% of U.S. children live below the official poverty level, 45% of all public school students are eligible for free or reduced-price lunch programs in the nation's schools (Snyder & Dillow, 2011). African American and Latino students are more likely than other students to be concentrated in high-poverty schools (Aud et al., 2010). The number

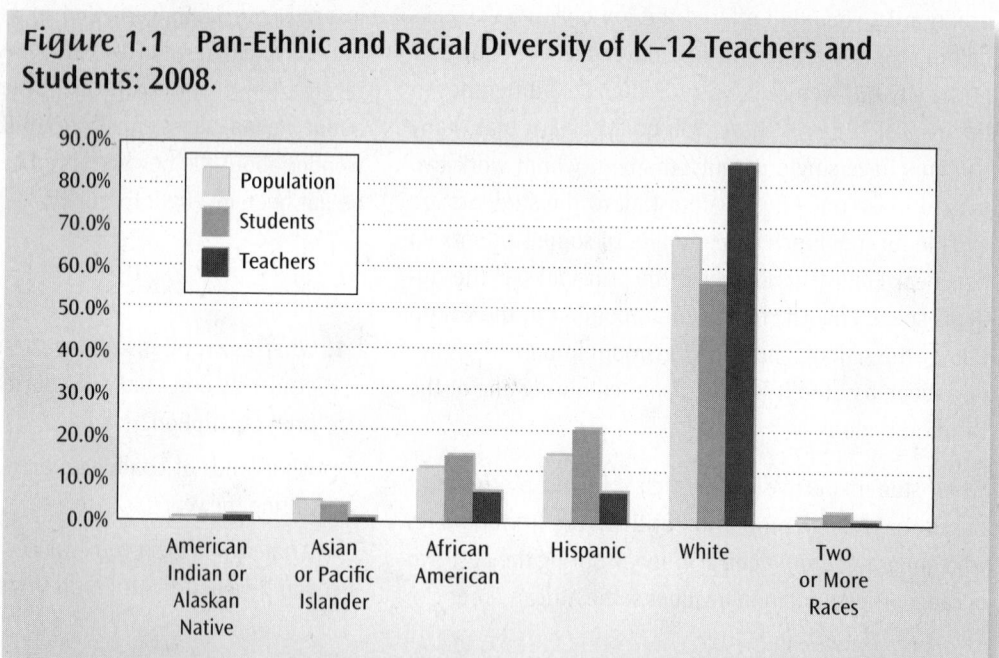

Figure 1.1   Pan-Ethnic and Racial Diversity of K–12 Teachers and Students: 2008.

Source: Aud, S., Hussar, W., Planty, M., Snyder, T., Bianco, K., Fox, M., Frohlich, L., Kemp, J., & Drake, L. (2010). *The condition of education 2010* (NCES 2010-028). Washington, DC: National Center for Education Statistics, Institute of Education Sciences, U.S. Department of Education.

of students with disabilities who are being served by special programs has increased from 4.3 million in 1987 to 6.5 million, or 30% of the school population, in the 2008–09 school year (Snyder & Dillow, 2011).

It is not only ethnic and racial diversity that is challenging schools. During the past 40 years, new waves of immigrants have come from parts of the world unfamiliar to many Americans. With them have come their religions, which seem even stranger to many Americans than the new immigrants. While small groups of Muslims, Hindus, Buddhists, and Sikhs have been in the country for many decades, only recently have they and their religions become highly visible. Even Christians from Russia, Hong Kong, Taiwan, Korea, and the Philippines bring their own brands of worship to denominations that have strong roots in this country. The United States has not only become a multicultural nation, it has also become a multireligious society. In earlier years, most religious minority groups maintained a low and almost invisible profile. As the groups have become larger, they have become more visible, along with their houses of worship.

These religious differences raise a number of challenges for educators. The holidays to be celebrated must be considered, along with religious codes related to the **curriculum,** appropriate interactions of boys and girls, dress in physical education classes, and discipline. Immigrant parents value the importance of education for their children, but they do not always agree with the school's approaches to teaching and learning or accept the public school's secular **values** as appropriate for their family. Values are the qualities that parents find desirable and important in the education of their children, and include areas such as morality, hard work, and caring, often with religious overtones. Working collaboratively with parents and communities will become even more critical in providing education equitably to all students.

Understanding the cultural setting in which the school is located will be very helpful in developing effective instructional strategies that draw on the cultural background and experiences of students and the community. You should help students affirm their own cultures while learning that people across **cultures** have many similarities. In addition, students should become aware of cultural differences and inequalities in the nation and in the world.

Teachers will find that students have individual differences, even though they may appear to be from the same cultural group. These differences extend far beyond intellectual and physical abilities. Students bring to class different historical backgrounds, religious beliefs, and day-to-day experiences that guide the way they behave in school. The cultures of some students will be mirrored in the school culture. For others, the differences between home and school cultures will cause dissonance unless the teacher can integrate the cultures of the students into the curriculum and develop a supportive environment for learning. If the teacher fails to understand the cultural factors in addition to the intellectual and physical factors that affect student learning and behavior, it will be difficult to help students learn.

Multicultural education is an educational strategy in which students' cultures are used to develop effective classroom instruction and school environments. It supports and extends the concepts of culture, diversity, equality, social justice, and democracy into the school setting. An examination of these concepts and their practical applications in schools will lead to an understanding of the development and practice of multicultural education.

Culture

Culture defines who we are. It influences our knowledge, beliefs, and values. It provides the blueprint that determines the way we think, feel, and behave. What appears as the natural and

PAUSE TO REFLECT 1.1

It is normal for people to experience some cultural discontinuity when they visit another country, a new city, or a neighborhood in which the inhabitants are ethnically different from themselves.

■ In what settings have you found yourself where you did not know the cultural norms and were at a loss as to how to fit in?

■ Why did you feel uncomfortable?

■ How were you able to overcome your awkwardness?

only way to learn and to interact with others is determined by our culture. Generally accepted and patterned ways of behavior are necessary for a group of people to live together, and culture imposes order and meaning on our experiences. It allows us to predict how others will behave in certain situations.

Culturally determined norms provide the dos and don'ts of appropriate behavior within our culture. Although we are comfortable with others who share our culture because we know the meanings of their words and actions, we often misunderstand the cultural cues of people from different cultures. Culture is so much a part of us that we fail to realize that not everyone shares our way of thinking and behaving. This may be, in part, because we have never been in cultural settings different from our own. This lack of knowledge often leads to our responding to differences as personal affronts rather than simply cultural differences. These misunderstandings may appear insignificant to an observer, but they can be important to participants. Examples include how loud is too loud, how late one may arrive at an event, and how close one can stand to another without being rude or disrespectful. Teachers may misinterpret the actions and voices of their students if they do not share the same culture.

CHARACTERISTICS OF CULTURE

We learn our culture from the people who are closest to us—our parents or caretakers. The ways that we were held, fed, bathed, dressed, and talked to as babies are culturally determined and begin the process of learning the family's culture. Culture impacts how we dress, what we eat, how we speak, and what we think (Ryan, 2010). The process continues throughout our lives as we interact with members of our own and other cultures.

Two similar processes interact as we learn how to act in society: **enculturation** and **socialization**. Enculturation is the process of acquiring the characteristics of a given culture and becoming competent in its language and ways of behaving and knowing. Socialization is the general process of learning the social norms of the culture. Through these processes, we internalize social and cultural rules. We learn what is expected in social roles, such as mother, husband, student, and child, and in occupational roles, such as teacher, banker, plumber, custodian, and politician. Enculturation and socialization are processes initiated at birth by parents, siblings, nurses, physicians, teachers, and neighbors. They demonstrate and reward children and other adults for acceptable behaviors. We learn the patterns of our culture and how to behave by observing and participating in the culture in which we are raised.

Because culture is so internalized, we tend to confuse biological and cultural heritage. Our cultural heritage is not innately based on the culture into which we are born. For

Our cultures are adapted to the environments in which we live and work. While the environment in rural areas is characterized by space and clean air, urban dwellers adapt to smog, crowded conditions, and public transportation.
© Shutterstock

example, Vietnamese infants adopted by Italian American, Catholic, middle-class parents will share a cultural heritage with middle-class Italian American Catholics rather than with Vietnamese. Observers, however, may continue to identify these individuals as Vietnamese Americans, because of their physical characteristics and a lack of knowledge about their cultural experiences.

Another characteristic of culture is that it is shared. Shared cultural patterns and customs bind people together as an identifiable group and make it possible for them to live together and function with ease. The shared culture provides us with the context for identifying with a particular group. Although there may be some disagreement about certain aspects of the culture, there is a common acceptance and agreement about most aspects. Actually, most points of agreement are outside our realm of awareness. For example, we do not usually realize that the way we communicate with each other and the way we raise children are culturally determined. Not until we begin participating in a second culture do we recognize differences among cultural groups.

Culture is also adaptive. Cultures accommodate environmental conditions, available natural and technological resources, and social changes. For example, Eskimos, who live with extreme cold, snow, ice, seals, and the sea, develop a culture different from that of Pacific Islanders, who have limited land, unlimited seas, and few mineral resources. The culture of urban residents differs from that of rural residents, in part, because of the resources available in the different settings. The culture of oppressed groups differs from that of the dominant group because of power relationships within society.

Finally, culture is a dynamic system that changes continuously. For example, a Japanese American who learned Japanese from his grandparents will be considered old-fashioned when he communicates in Japanese with new immigrants. Some cultures undergo constant and rapid change; others are very slow to change. Some changes, such as a new word or new hairstyle, may be relatively minor and have little impact on the culture as a whole. Other changes have a dramatic impact as occurs when new technology such as the smartphone is introduced into a culture, producing changes far broader than the technology itself. Such changes may also alter traditional customs and beliefs. For example, the use of the computer has led to changes in the way we communicate with each other for business and personal purposes. It has even changed the way some people meet each other. Instead of blind dates, they are matched by a computer dating service with people they may want to meet.

MANIFESTATIONS OF CULTURE

The cultural patterns of a group are determined by how the people organize and view the various components of culture. Culture is manifested in an infinite number of ways through social institutions, lived experiences, and our fulfillment of psychological and basic needs. To understand how extensively our lives are affected by culture, let's examine a few of these manifestations.

Our values are initially determined by our culture. They influence the importance of prestige, status, pride, family loyalty, love of country, religious belief, and honor. Status symbols differ across cultures. For many families in the United States, accumulation of material possessions is a respected status symbol. For others, the welfare of the extended family is of utmost importance. These factors, as well as the meaning of morality and immorality, the use of punishment and reward, and the need for higher education are determined by the value system of our culture.

Culture also manifests itself in nonverbal communication patterns. The meaning of an act or an expression must be viewed in its cultural context. The appropriateness of shaking hands, bowing, or kissing people on greeting them varies across cultures. Culture also determines the manner of walking, sitting, standing, reclining, gesturing, and dancing. We must remind ourselves not to interpret acts and expressions of people from a different cultural group as wrong or inappropriate just because they are not the same as our own. These behaviors are culturally determined.

Language itself is a reflection of culture and provides a special way of looking at the world and organizing experiences that is often lost in translating words from one language to another. Many different sounds and combinations of sounds are used in the languages of different cultures. Those of us who have tried to learn a second language may have experienced difficulty in verbalizing sounds that were not part of our first language. Also, diverse language patterns found within the same language group can lead to misunderstandings. For example, one person's "joking" is heard by others as serious criticism or abuse of power; this is a particular problem when the speaker is a member of the dominant group and the listener is a member of an oppressed group or vice versa.

Although we have discussed only a few daily patterns determined by culture, they are limitless. Among them are relationships of men and women, parenting, choosing a spouse, sexual relations, and division of labor in the home and society. These patterns are shared by members of the culture and often seem strange and improper to nonmembers.

ETHNOCENTRISM

Because culture helps determine the way we think, feel, and act, it becomes the lens through which we judge the world. As such, it can become an unconscious blinder to other ways of thinking, feeling, and acting. Our own culture is automatically treated as innate. It becomes the only natural way to function in the world. Even common sense in our own culture is naturally translated to common sense for the world. Other cultures are compared with ours and are evaluated by our cultural standards. It becomes difficult to view another culture as separate from our own—a task that anthropologists attempt when studying other cultures.

This inability to view other cultures as equally viable alternatives for organizing reality is known as **ethnocentrism**. Although it is appropriate to cherish one's culture, members sometimes become closed to the possibilities of difference. These feelings of superiority over other cultures can become problematic in interacting and working effectively and equitably with students and families of other cultures. Our inability to view another culture through its own cultural lens prevents an understanding of the second culture. This inability can make it impossible to function effectively in a second culture. By overcoming one's ethnocentric view of the world, one can begin to respect other cultures and even learn to function comfortably in more than one cultural group.

Debate / Should Patriotism Be a School Requirement?

What does it mean to be an American? Many schools are revitalizing the teaching of patriotism in elementary schools. First graders in some schools are being taught to love their country along with reading and writing. Greenbriar East Elementary School in Fairfax County outside of Washington, DC, hosts an annual Patriotic Salute in which their diverse student population sings "God Bless America," "This Land Is Your Land," and "We're Glad We Live in the U.S.A." Patriotic programs have included essay contests on the subject of being an American and assemblies to honor veterans. Other schools avoid interjecting patriotism into their curriculum, viewing it as the student's personal responsibility.

At times of crisis such as 9/11 and armed conflicts with other nations, state legislators and school board members are sometimes inclined to require students to recite the Pledge of Allegiance, sing the national anthem, or participate in patriotic activities on a daily or other regular basis. However, these practices begin to infringe on the rights of groups and do not have unanimous support in all communities. For instance, the Supreme Court declared early last century that Jehovah Witnesses students could not be forced to say the Pledge of Allegiance.

Do you think patriotism should be required in schools?

FOR

- Students need to understand what it means to be American.
- Schools have an obligation to help students embrace American democracy.
- Students need to learn to appreciate the United States.

AGAINST

- Civics instruction should be about personal responsibility, not instilling patriotism.
- Democracy is about making informed, thoughtful choices.
- Loving your country is not something that should be indoctrinated.

| QUESTIONS |

1. Why do some school districts feel obligated to push patriotism in their schools?
2. How might schools address issues of good citizenship without offending parents who find the focus on patriotism inappropriate?
3. What do you think is an appropriate balance between helping students be good citizens and overtly pushing patriotism?

Source: **Kalita, S. M. (2004, June 8). A blending of patriotism, native pride: In diverse Fairfax school, civics starts in 1st grade.** *Washington Post,* **p. B.1.**

CULTURAL RELATIVISM

"Never judge another man until you have walked a mile in his moccasins." This North American Indian proverb suggests the importance of understanding the cultural backgrounds and experiences of others, rather than judging them by one's own standards. The principle of cultural relativism is to see a culture as if one were a member of the culture. In essence, it is an attempt to view the world through another person's cultural lens. It is an acknowledgment that another person's way of doing things, while perhaps not appropriate for us, may be valid for him or her. This ability becomes essential in the world today as countries and cultures become more interdependent. In an effort to maintain positive relationships with the numerous cultural groups in the world, we cannot afford to ignore other cultures or to relegate them to an inferior status.

Within our own boundaries are many cultural groups that historically have been viewed and treated as inferior to the dominant culture that has been the basis for most of our institutions. These intercultural misunderstandings occur even when no language barrier exists and when large components of the major culture are shared by the people involved. These misunderstandings often happen because those in one group are largely ignorant about the culture of another group and give the second culture little credibility. One problem is that members of one group are, for the most part, unable to describe their own cultural system, let alone another. These misunderstandings are common among the various groups in this country and are accentuated by differential status based on race, gender, class, language, religion, and ability.

Cultural relativism suggests that we need to learn more about our own culture than is commonly required. That must be followed by study about, and interaction with, other cultural groups. This intercultural process helps one know what it is like to be a member of the second culture and to view the world from that point of view. To function effectively and comfortably within a second culture, that culture must be learned.

THE DOMINANT CULTURE

U.S. political and social institutions have evolved from an Anglo-Saxon or Western European tradition. The English language is a polyglot of the languages spoken by the various conquerors and rulers of Great Britain throughout history. The legal system is derived from English common law. The political system of democratic elections comes from France and England. The middle-class value system has been modified from a European system. Even our way of thinking, at least the way that is rewarded in school, is based on Socrates' linear system of logic.

Formal institutions, such as governments, schools, social welfare, banks, and businesses, affect many aspects of our lives. Because of the strong Anglo-Saxon influence on these institutions, the major cultural influence on the United States, particularly on its institutions, has been white, Anglo-Saxon, and Protestant (WASP). But no longer is the dominant group composed only of WASPs. Instead, many members of the ethnically diverse middle class have adapted traditionally WASP characteristics and values that provide the framework for the dominant culture.

Although most of our institutions still function under the strong influence of their WASP roots, many other aspects of American life have been influenced by the numerous cultural groups that have come to comprise the U.S. population. Think about the different foods we eat, or at least try: Chinese, Indian, Mexican, soul food, Italian, Caribbean, and Japanese. Young people of many cultures choose clothing that is influenced by hip-hop and black culture. But

Members of Congress do not yet represent the diversity of the nation's population.
© Jeff Malet Photography/Newscom

more important are the contributions made to society by individuals from different groups in the fields of science, the arts, literature, athletics, engineering, architecture, and politics.

Although the United States has an agrarian tradition, the population now is primarily located in metropolitan areas and small towns. The country has mineral and soil riches, elaborate technology, and a wealth of manufactured goods. Mass education and mass communication are ways of life. Americans are regulated by clocks and calendars, rather than by seas and the sun. Time is used to organize most activities of life. Most Americans are employees whose salaries or wages are paid by large, complex, impersonal institutions. Work is done regularly, purposefully, and sometimes grimly. In contrast, play is fun—an outlet from work. Money is the denominator of exchange. Necessities of life are purchased rather than produced. Achievement and success are measured by the quantity of material goods purchased. Religious beliefs are concerned with general morality.

The overpowering value of the dominant group is **individualism**, which is characterized by the belief that every individual is his or her own master, is in control of his or her own destiny, and will advance or regress in society only according to his or her own efforts (Bellah, Madsen, Sullivan, Swidler, & Tipton, 2008). This individualism is grounded in the Western worldview that individuals can control both nature and their destiny. Traits that emphasize this core value include industriousness, ambition, competitiveness, self-reliance, independence, appreciation of the good life, and the perception of humans as separate from, and superior to, nature. The acquisition of such possessions as the latest technology gadgets, cars, boats, and homes measures success and achievement.

Another core value is **freedom**, which is defined by the dominant group as not having others determine their values, ideas, or behaviors (Bellah et al., 2008). Relations with other people inside and outside the group are often impersonal. Communications may be very direct or confrontational. The nuclear family is the basic kinship unit, but many members of the dominant group rely more on associations of common interest than on family ties. Values tend to be absolute (e.g., right or wrong, moral or immoral) rather than ranging along a continuum of degrees of right and wrong. Personal life and community affairs are based on principles of right and wrong, rather than on shame, dishonor, or ridicule. Youthfulness is emphasized in advertisements and commercials. Men and women use Botox and have plastic surgery to try to maintain their youthfulness. Many U.S. citizens, especially if they are middle class, share these traits and values to some degree. They are patterns that are privileged in institutions such as schools. They are values to which the dominant society expects all citizens to adhere.

Many groups that immigrated during the twentieth century have become acculturated or have adopted the dominant group's cultural patterns. Although some groups have tried to maintain their original culture, it is usually in vain as children go to school and participate in the larger society. Continuous and firsthand contacts with the dominant group usually result in subsequent changes in the cultural patterns of either or both groups. The rapidity and success of the acculturation process depends on several factors, including location and discrimination. If a group is spatially isolated and segregated (whether voluntarily or not) in a rural area, as is the case with many American Indians on reservations, the acculturation process is very slow. Discrimination against members of oppressed groups can make it difficult for them to acculturate when they choose to do so.

The degree of acculturation is determined, in part, by individuals or families as they decide how much they want to dress, speak, and behave like members of the dominant group. In the past, members of many groups had little choice if they wanted to share the American dream of success. Many people have had to give up their native languages and behaviors or hide them at home. However, acculturation does not guarantee acceptance by the dominant group. Most members of oppressed groups, especially those of color, have not been permitted to assimilate fully into society even though they have adopted the values and behaviors of the dominant group.

Pluralism in Society

Although many similarities exist across cultures, differences exist in the ways people learn, the values they cherish, their worldviews, their behavior, and their interactions with others. There are many reasonable ways to organize our lives, approach a task, and use our languages and dialects. It is when we begin to see our cultural norms and behaviors not just as one approach, but as superior to others, that differences become politicized.

Differing and unequal power relations have a great impact on individuals' and groups' ability to define and achieve their own goals. These differences among and within groups can lead not only to misunderstandings and misperceptions, but also to conflict. Cultural differences sometimes result in political alliances that respond to the real or perceived presence of domination or subordination faced by a group. The result may be strong feelings of patriotism or group solidarity that expand into armed conflicts across nations, tribes, religious communities, or ethnic groups. Feelings of superiority of one's group over another are sometimes reflected in anti-Semitic symbols and actions, cross burnings, gay bashing, and sexual harassment.

Conflicts between groups are usually based on the groups' differential status and value in society. The alienation and marginalization that many powerless groups experience can lead to their accentuating their differences, especially to separate themselves from the dominant group. Groups sometimes construct their own identities in terms of others. For example,

European Americans often do not think of themselves as white, except as it makes them different from Latinos or African Americans. Males define themselves in opposition to females. Many European American men have been socialized to see themselves as being at the center of a world in which they are privileged in relation to women and people of color.

By developing an understanding of differences and **otherness**, we can begin to change our simplistic binary approaches of us/them, dominant/subordinate, good/bad, and right/wrong. We begin to realize that a plurality of truths is appropriate and reasonable. We seek out others for dialogue and understanding, rather than speak about and for them. We can begin to move from exercising power over others to sharing power with them.

ASSIMILATION

Assimilation occurs when a group's distinctive cultural patterns either become part of the dominant culture or disappear as the group adopts the dominant culture. **Structural assimilation** occurs when the dominant group shares primary group relationships with the second group, including membership in the same cliques and social clubs; members of the two groups intermarry; and the two groups are treated equally within society. Assimilation appears to be relevant for voluntary immigrants, particularly if they are white, but does not apply equally to **involuntary immigrants,** who did not choose to emigrate, but were forced to through slavery or other means. Many of these families have been in the country for generations and yet are not allowed to fully assimilate, especially at the structural level.

White European immigrants usually become structurally assimilated within a few generations after arriving in this country. Marriage across groups is fairly common across white ethnic groups and Judeo-Christian religious affiliations, and it is growing across other groups and races. More than two of three Asian Americans and half of Latinos marry outside of their group. However, only 7% of whites and 17% of African Americans were marrying outside their groups in 2008 (Lee & Bean, 2010). If the assimilation process is effective, an immigrant group becomes less distinct from the dominant group and, in the process, changes the dominant group.

Schools historically have promoted assimilation, teaching English and the U.S. culture to new immigrants. Until 30–40 years ago, students of color would have rarely seen themselves in textbooks or learned the history and culture of their group in the classroom. Even today, the curriculum is contested in some communities when families do not see their cultures and values represented. In contrast, school boards in some communities have banned ethnic studies and a focus on any group other than European Americans, which they believe represents the common culture and norms that all students should know and adopt. When national history standards were being developed in the early 1990s, the historians involved proposed a multicultural curriculum that celebrated the similarities and differences of the ethnic groups that comprise the United States. Some very influential and powerful individuals and groups accused the project of promoting differences that would lead to divisiveness among groups and would undermine national unity and patriotism. These traditionalists were so outraged by the proposed multicultural curriculum that the standards were presented to Congress, which condemned them by a vote of 99 to 1 (Symcox, 2002).

CULTURAL PLURALISM

The theory of **cultural pluralism** describes a society that allows multiple distinctive groups to function separately and equally without requiring any assimilation into the dominant society. Some immigrant groups have assimilation as their goal; others try to preserve their native cultures. Refusing or not being permitted to assimilate into the dominant United States culture, many immigrants and ethnic groups maintain their own ethnic communities and enclaves in areas of the nation's cities, such as Little Italy, Chinatown, Harlem, Koreatown, East Los Angeles, and Little Saigon. The suburbs also include pockets of families from the same ethnic group. Throughout the country are small towns and surrounding farmlands where the population comes from the same ethnic background, all the residents being African American, German American, Danish American, Anglo American, or Mexican American. American Indian nations within the United States have their own political, economic, and educational systems. For most American Indians, however, the economic, political, and educational opportunities do not approach equality with the dominant group.

The members of these communities may be culturally encapsulated in that most of their primary relationships, and many of their secondary relationships, are with members of their own ethnic group. Cross-cultural contacts occur primarily at the secondary level in work settings and political and civic institutions. In segregated communities, families may not have the opportunity to interact with members of other ethnic groups, who speak a different language or dialect, eat different foods, or have different values. They may learn to fear or denigrate members of other ethnic groups. Many European Americans live in segregated communities in which they interact only with others who share the same culture. Most people of color are forced out of their ethnic encapsulation to try to achieve social and economic mobility. Many of their secondary relationships are with members of other ethnic groups at work, school, or shopping centers.

MULTICULTURALISM

Multiculturalism allows different cultural groups to maintain their unique cultural identities while participating equally in the dominant culture. Multiculturalism is possible in a nation that acknowledges its cultural diversity and recognizes the advantages of cross-cultural interactions and cooperative organizational processes (Lewis, 2008). People are not required to give up their unique and distinct cultural identities to be successful in the dominant culture. Diversity in the workplace, school, university, or community is valued and affirmatively sought. It allows individuals to choose membership in the cultural and social groups that best fit their identities without fear of ostracism or isolation from either their original or their new group. Lewis (2008) characterizes multiculturalism as liberating "individual and groups from the extremes of homogenized and collective identities," producing "a more open and respectful acceptance of cultural difference, both within and necessarily outside the borders of nation" (pp. 298–299).

A society that supports multiculturalism promotes the retention of diverse ethnic and religious group identities. Some citizens believe that a societal goal should be the integration of diverse groups and the promotion of more equality across groups. Others believe that individuals should be able to maintain their ethnic identities while participating in a common culture. These beliefs are not necessarily mutually exclusive; for example, society could be integrated, but members would not be required to relinquish their ethnic identities. At the same time, an integrated society may lead to greater assimilation in that primary contacts across ethnic groups are more likely.

Identifying the degree of students' assimilation into the dominant culture may be helpful in determining appropriate instructional strategies and providing authentic learning activities that relate to the lived experiences of students. The only way to know the importance of cultural membership in the lives of students is to listen to them. Familiarity and participation with the community from which students come also help educators know students and their families.

Cultural Identity

Groups in the United States have been called **subsocieties** or **subcultures** by sociologists and anthropologists because they exist within the context of a larger society or culture in which political and social institutions are shared (Ryan, 2010). These groups provide the social and cultural identity for their members, allowing them to have distinctive cultural patterns related to their group memberships while sharing some patterns with members of the dominant culture. At the same time, there is no essential or absolute identity such as female or male, American or recent immigrant, or Buddhist or Jew. Our identities in any single group are influenced by our historical and lived experiences and memberships in other groups.

Numerous groups exist in most nations, but the United States is exceptionally rich in the many distinct groups that make up the population. Group identity is based on traits and values learned as part of one's ethnicity, religion, gender, sexual orientation, age, socioeconomic status, native language, geographic region, place of residence (e.g., rural or urban), and abilities or exceptional conditions, as shown in Figure 1.2. Each of these groups has distinguishable cultural patterns shared among all who identify themselves as members of that particular group. Although they share certain characteristics of the dominant culture with most of the

Figure 1.2 Cultural identity is based on membership in multiple groups that continuously interact and influence each other. Identity within these groups is affected by interaction with the dominant group and power relations among groups in society.

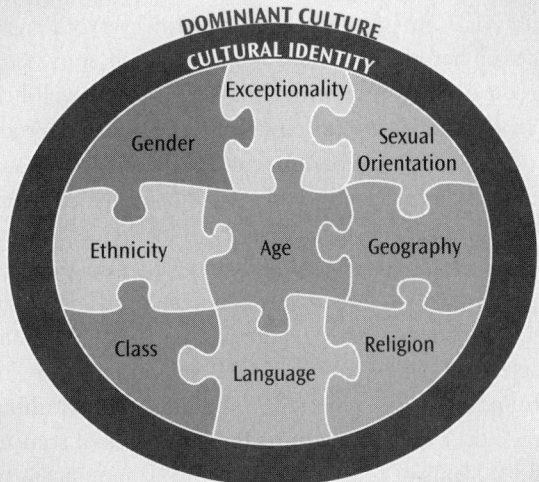

Source: Adapted from Johnson, J. A., Musial, D. L., et al. (2005). *Introduction to the Foundations of American Education* (13th ed.). Boston, MA: Allyn & Bacon. Copyright © 2005 Pearson Education. Reprinted by permission of the publisher.

U.S. population, members of these groups also have learned cultural traits, discourse patterns, ways of learning, values, and behaviors characteristic of the different groups to which they belong.

Individuals sharing membership in one group may not share membership in other groups. For example, all men are members of the male culture, but not all males belong to the same ethnic, religious, or class group. On the other hand, an ethnic group is composed of both males and females from different religious and socioeconomic backgrounds.

The interaction of these various group memberships within society begins to determine an individual's cultural identity. Membership in one group can greatly influence the characteristics and values of membership in other groups. For instance, some fundamentalist religions have strictly defined expectations for women versus men. Thus, membership in the religious group influences, to a great extent, the way a female behaves as a young girl, teenager, bride, and wife, regardless of her ethnic group. One's economic level will greatly affect the quality of life for families, especially the children and elderly in the group.

This interaction is most dynamic across race, ethnicity, class, and gender relations. The feminist movement, for example, was primarily influenced early on by white, middle-class women. The labor movement had an early history of excluding workers of color and women, and their causes. Membership in one group often conflicts with the interests of another, as is the case when people feel forced to declare their primary identity by race rather than gender, class, or sexual orientation.

One cultural group may have a greater influence on identity than others. This influence may change over time and depends on life experiences. We can shed aspects of our culture that no longer have meaning, and we can also adopt or adapt aspects of other cultures that were not inherent in our upbringing. Identity is not fixed. Alternative views of self and culture can be learned as **cultural borders** are crossed.

The degree to which individuals identify with the groups of which they are members and the related cultural characteristics determines, to a great extent, their individual cultural identities. For example, a 30-year-old, middle-class, Catholic, Polish American woman in Chicago may identify strongly with being Catholic and Polish American when she is married and living in a Polish American community. However, other group memberships may have a greater impact on her identity after she has divorced, moved to an ethnically diverse neighborhood, and become totally responsible for her financial well-being. Her femaleness and class status may become the most important representations of her identity, as portrayed in Figure 1.3.

The interaction of these cultural groups within society is also important. Most political, business, educational, and social institutions (e.g., the courts, the school system, the city government) have been developed and controlled by the dominant group. The values and practices that have been internalized by the dominant group also are inherent within these institutions. Members of oppressed groups are usually beholden to the dominant group to share in that power.

Schools "validate, reinforce, and socialize children into many of the values of the larger society" (Hollins, 2011, p. 107). Assimilation policies promote the values of the dominant group, which are reflected in the **hidden curriculum**—the unwritten and informal rules that guide the expected behaviors and attitudes of students in schools. The children of immigrants and students of color are expected to communicate and behave according to the dominant cultural norms and to repress their own cultural identities. In the past, Americanization programs for immigrants not only taught English but also reinforced the meaning of being American. American virtues and being patriotic continue to be reinforced in many schools, especially in times of crisis, such as 9/11 and conflicts with other nations.

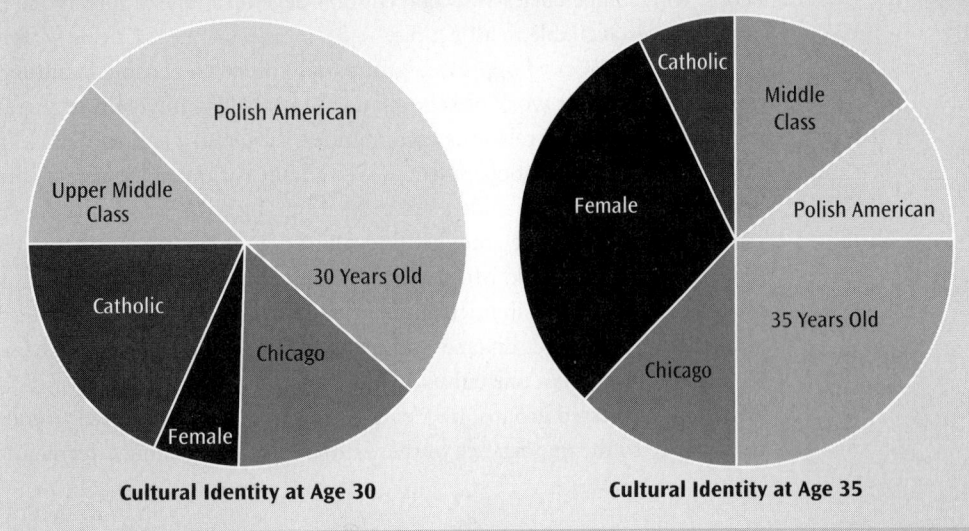

Figure 1.3 Cultural identity is adapted and changed throughout life in response to political, economic, educational, and social experiences that either alter or reinforce one's status or position in society. Some cultural group memberships may take on more importance than others at different periods of life, as shown here for a woman when she was 30 years old and married, and again when she was 35, divorced, and a single mother.

Understanding the importance of group memberships to your identity helps answer the question "Who am I?" An understanding of other groups will help answer the question "Who are my students?" The various groups that educators are likely to confront in a classroom are examined in detail in Chapters 2 through 10.

CULTURAL BORDERS

Each of us belongs to multiple cultures (e.g., ethnic, religious, and socioeconomic groups) that help define us. As long as those differences have no status implications in which one group is treated differently from another, conflict among groups is minimal. Unfortunately, cultural borders are often erected between groups, and crossing them can be easy or difficult. What is valued on one side of the border may be denigrated on the other side. For example, speaking both Spanish and English may be highly rewarded in the community, but speaking Spanish in some schools is not tolerated.

Educators establish cultural borders in the classroom when all activity is grounded in the teacher's culture. As we learn to function comfortably in different cultures, we may be able to move away from a single perspective linked to cultural domination. We may be able to cross cultural borders, bringing the students' cultures into the classroom.

BICULTURALISM

Individuals who have competencies in and can operate successfully using two or more different cultures are border crossers; they are bicultural or multicultural and are often bilingual or multilingual as well. Having proficiencies in multiple cultures allows one to draw on a broad range of abilities and make choices as determined by the particular situation.

Because we participate in more than one cultural group, we have already become proficient in multiple systems for perceiving, evaluating, believing, and acting according to the patterns of the various groups in which we participate. We often act and speak differently when we are in the community in which we were raised than when we are in a professional setting. We behave differently on a night out with members of our own sex than we do at home with the family. People with competencies in several cultures develop a fuller appreciation of the range of cultural competencies available to all people.

Many members of oppressed groups are forced to become **bicultural,** operating (1) in the dominant culture at work or school and (2) in their family culture to participate effectively in their own ethnic and religious communities. Different behaviors are expected in the two settings. Because most schools reflect the dominant society, students are forced to adjust to or act like middle-class white students if they are going to be academically successful. In contrast, most middle-class white students find almost total congruence between the cultures of their family, school, and work. Most remain monocultural throughout their lives. They do not envision the value and possibilities inherent in becoming competent in a different culture.

In our expanding, diverse nation, it is critical that educators be able to participate effectively in more than one culture. Understanding the cultural cues of different ethnic groups, especially oppressed groups, improves our ability to work with all students. It also helps us to be sensitive to the importance of these differences in teaching effectively.

Equality and Social Justice in a Democracy

The United States is a **democracy,** in which people participate in their government by exercising their power directly or indirectly through elected representatives. Schools and the mass media teach us that our democracy is one to be emulated by the rest of the world. A democracy should promote the good of all its citizens. Thus, the Constitution was fashioned with a coherent set of "checks and balances" to limit the systematic abuse of power. **Egalitarianism**—the belief in social, political, and economic rights and privileges for all people—is espoused as a key principle on which democracy is based. All citizens are expected to have a voice. Power should be shared among groups, and no one group should continuously dominate the economic, political, social, and cultural life of the country. Society and government, though not perfect, are promoted as allowing mass participation and steady advancement toward a more prosperous and egalitarian society.

One strength of a democracy is that citizens bring many perspectives, based on their own histories and experiences, to bear on policy questions and practices. Thus, to disagree is acceptable as long as we are able to communicate with each other openly and without fear of reprisal. Further, we expect that no single right way will be forced on us. For the most part, we would rather struggle with multiple perspectives and actions and determine what is best for us as individuals within this democratic society.

At the same time, a democracy expects its citizens to be concerned about more than just their own individual freedoms. In the classic *Democracy and Education,* philosopher and educator John Dewey (1966) suggested that the emphasis should be on what binds us together in cooperative pursuits and results, regardless of the nation or our group alliance and membership.

He raised concern about our possible stratification into separate classes and called for "intellectual opportunities [to be] accessible to all on equitable and easy terms" (p. 88).

The emphasis on individualism in the dominant culture provides a dilemma for educators who promote democratic practice. In many classrooms, individualism is supported through competitive activities in which individual achievement is rewarded. A democratic classroom is designed for students to work together across groups. Responsibility and leadership are shared by students and teachers as students practice being active participants in a democratic setting.

Both individualism and equality have long been central themes of political discourse in a democratic society. The meaning of equality within our society varies according to one's assumptions about humankind and human existence. At least two sets of beliefs govern the ideologies of equality and inequality. The first accepts inequality as inevitable and promotes **meritocracy,** which is a system based on the belief that an individual's achievements are due to their own personal merits. The focus is on individualism and the individual's right to pursue happiness and obtain personal resources. The second set of beliefs supports a much greater degree of equality across groups in society. People who believe in equality and social justice care about those who have fewer resources and develop policies that allow more people to share in the nation's wealth.

This dilemma forces the promotion of some degree of equality while preventing any real equity from occurring. Affirmative action, for example, is viewed by its critics as evidence of group welfare gaining precedence over individual achievement. The outcry against affirmative action suggests that racism no longer exists and that decisions about employment, promotion, and so forth are no longer influenced by racism and sexism. Whites filing reverse discrimination cases believe that their right to an education at a select school, a promotion, or a job should be based solely on their individual achievement. They believe that other factors, such as low income, ethnicity, race, or gender, should not be valued in the process. Even though egalitarianism is an often-espoused goal of democracy in the United States, inequities across groups continue to exist in society and are continually overlooked.

Students do not start life with an equal chance to succeed. Because of family income and wealth, some students have access to resources and experiences in their homes, communities, and schools that are not available to most low-income students.
© Peter Casolino/Alamy

MERITOCRACY

Proponents of meritocracy accept the theories of sociobiology or functionalism or both, in which inequalities are viewed as natural outcomes of individual differences. They believe that all people have the opportunity to be successful if they just work hard enough (Grinberg, Price, & Naiditch, 2009). They give little credit to conditions such as being born into a wealthy family as a head start to success. Members of oppressed groups usually are seen as inferior, and their hardships blamed on their personal characteristics rather than societal constraints or discrimination.

The belief system that undergirds meritocracy has at least three dimensions that are consistent with dominant group values. First, the individual is valued over the group. The individual has the qualities, ambitions, and talent to achieve at the highest levels in society. Popular stories promote this ideology in their descriptions of the poor immigrant who arrived on U.S. shores with nothing, set up a vegetable stand to eke out a living, and became the millionaire owner of a chain of grocery stores. Moving from the bottom of the economic ladder to the top is a rare occurrence. In reality, some individuals and families move up and down the economic ladder one quintile from where they started (Page & Jacobs, 2009). The second dimension stresses differences through competition. IQ and achievement tests are used throughout schooling to help measure differences. Students and adults are rewarded for outstanding grades, athletic ability, and artistic accomplishment. The third dimension emphasizes internal characteristics, such as motivation, intuition, and character, that have been internalized by the individual. External conditions, such as racism and poverty, are to be overcome by the individual; they are not accepted as contributors to an individual's lack of success.

Equal educational opportunity, or equal access to schooling, applies meritocracy to education. All students are to be provided with equal educational opportunities that purportedly will give them similar chances for success or failure. Proponents of this approach believe it is the individual's responsibility to use those opportunities to his or her advantage in obtaining life's resources and benefits. Critics of meritocracy point out that children of low-income families do not start with the same chances for success in life as children from affluent families. Even the most capable of these students do not enjoy equal educational opportunities if the schools they attend lack the challenging curriculum and advanced placement courses typically found in middle-class and affluent communities. Thus, competition is unequal from birth. The chances of the affluent child being educationally and financially successful are much greater than for the child from a low-income family (Page & Jacobs, 2009). Those with advantages at birth are almost always able to hold on to and extend those advantages throughout their lifetimes.

EQUALITY

With the persistence of racism, poverty, unemployment, and inequality in major social systems such as education and health, many have found it difficult to reconcile daily realities with the celebrated egalitarianism that characterizes the public rhetoric. These people view U.S. society as composed of institutions and an economic system that represents the interests of the privileged few rather than the pluralistic majority. Even institutions, laws, and processes that have the appearance of equal access, benefit, and protection are often enforced in highly discriminatory ways. These patterns of **inequality** are not the product of corrupt individuals as such, but rather are a reflection of how resources of economics, political power, and cultural and social dominance are built into the entire political-economic system.

Even in the optimistic view that some degree of equality can be achieved, inequality is expected. Not all resources can be redistributed so that every individual has an equal amount, nor should all individuals expect equal compensation for the work they do. The underlying belief, however, is that there need not be the huge disparities of income, wealth, and power that currently exist. Equality does suggest fairness in the distribution of the conditions and goods that affect the well-being of all children and families. It is fostered by policies for full employment, wages that prevent families from living in poverty, and child care for all children.

Critics decry this perceived socialism as being against the democratic foundations that undergird the nation. They believe that equality of resources and of societal benefits would undermine the capitalist system that allows a few individuals to acquire the great majority of those resources. They warn that equality of results would limit freedom and liberty for individuals.

PAUSE TO REFLECT 1.2

How do you view equality in society and schooling? Check the statements below that best describe your perceptions.

■ The ablest and most meritorious, ambitious, hardworking, and talented individuals should acquire the most, achieve the most, and become society's leaders.

■ The individual is more important than the group.

■ The U.S. economic system represents the interests of a privileged few, rather than those of the pluralistic majority.

■ Huge disparities of income, wealth, and power should not exist in this country.

■ It is the student's responsibility to get as much out of school as possible.

■ External conditions, such as racism and poverty, should be overcome by the individual.

■ Students from all cultural groups can be academically successful.

Which of these statements are most closely related to a belief in meritocracy, and which to a belief in equality?

Equality is more than providing oppressed group members with an equal chance or equal opportunity. One proposal is that equal results should be the goal. These results might be more equal achievement by students of both oppressed and dominant groups and similar rates of dropping out of school, college attendance, and college completion by different ethnic, racial, and gender groups and populations across socioeconomic levels.

Traditionally, the belief has been that education can overcome the inequities that exist in society. However, the role of education in reducing the amount of occupation and income inequality may be limited. School reform has not yet led to significant social changes outside the schools. Equalizing educational opportunity has had very little impact on making adults more equal. Providing equal educational opportunities for all students does not guarantee equal results at the end of high school or college. It does not yet provide equal access to jobs and income across groups. Programs for equal educational opportunity have not overcome the academic and economic disparities that exist among families. Equality in schools would mean that students in impoverished schools would be guaranteed to have teachers who are as highly qualified as the teachers in wealthy school districts. Equality requires financial support for providing quality instruction in environments that are conducive to learning by all students. More, not less, money may be needed to ensure equity in educational results for the children of dominant groups and other groups.

SOCIAL JUSTICE

Social justice is another element of democracy that is based on the expectation that citizens will provide for those in society who are not as advantaged as they are. John Dewey (1966) called for social justice at the beginning of the twentieth century when he said, "What the best and wisest parent wants for his [or her] own child, that must the community want for all of its children. Any other ideal for our schools is narrow and unlovely; acted upon, it destroys our democracy" (p. 3). In schools, social justice requires the critiquing of practices that interfere with equity across groups. Social and economic inequities that prevent students from learning and participating effectively in schools must be confronted.

Enormous disparities exist between the very wealthy and the poor. The very wealthy have accumulated vast resources while the poor are unable to obtain the barest essentials for shelter, food, or medical care. Some suffer from the lack of housing or the lack of heat in the winter and lack of cooling in very hot summers. Every year there are reports of elderly, low-income people who die from exposure to excessive heat or cold. This reality is inconceivable to the many Americans who simply turn their thermostats to the precise temperature that will meet their comfort level. Every day children from low-income families come to school with insufficient sleep because of the physical discomfort of their homes, with inadequate clothing, and with empty stomachs. Tens of thousands suffer from malnutrition and no dental care. When they are sick, many go untreated. Under these conditions, it is difficult to function well in an academic setting.

Civil unrest has almost always been precipitated by the disenfranchised who have no realistic hope of extricating themselves from lives of despair. Children of affluent members of society do not typically form street gangs; they are usually too busy enjoying the good life that prosperity brings. The street gangs of New York, Chicago, and Los Angeles are comprised almost exclusively of young individuals who are poor, embittered, and disenfranchised.

Those who have the power to bring about meaningful change in society are usually the more affluent. They have the resources and connections to make things happen. To bring about truly meaningful change requires paradigm shifts. Even the middle class may be reluctant to make changes if a change in the status quo diminishes their position. Changes are usually supported only if they provide benefits to the dominant group or do not affect them negatively.

Meaningful change in society requires a universal social consciousness. It requires, to some extent, a willingness of the citizenry to explore the means of redistributing some of the benefits of a democratic society. Effective redistribution requires that some who have considerable wealth provide a greater share in the effort to eliminate poverty and its effects. The end result could be a society in which everyone has a decent place to sleep, no child goes to school hungry, and appropriate health care is available to all.

OBSTACLES TO EQUALITY AND SOCIAL JUSTICE

Prejudice, discrimination, and **privilege** stem from a combination of several factors related to power relationships. People who are prejudiced have an aversion to members of a group other than their own. Discrimination leads to the denial of privileges and rewards to members of oppressed groups. Privilege provides advantages and power to groups that have resources and status exceeding those of others.

Prejudice.   Prejudice can result when people lack an understanding of the history, experiences, values, and perceptions of groups other than their own. Members of groups are stereotyped when generalizations are applied to the group without consideration of individual differences within the group. Prejudice manifests itself in feelings of anger, fear, hatred, and distrust toward members of a specific group. These attitudes are often translated into fear of walking in the group's neighborhood, fear of being robbed or hurt by others, distrust of a merchant from the group, anger at any advantages that others may be perceived as receiving, and fear that housing prices will be deflated if someone from that group moves next door.

Some members of all groups possess negative stereotypes of others. For example, many African Americans and Latinos believe that all whites are bigoted, bossy, and unwilling to share power. Some women believe that all men are abusers because that is their experience with men. Feminists become labeled as lesbians because some activists are lesbians. Blue-collar workers are seen as intolerant and bigoted because that is how they have been portrayed in a number of movies. Fundamentalist Christians are labeled as sexist or homophobic because some ministers have preached that message. These negative stereotypes may describe some members of a group, but have been unfairly extended as characteristic of all members of the group.

Although prejudice may not always directly hurt members of a group, it can be easily translated into behavior that does do harm. An ideology based on aversion to a group and perceived superiority undergirds the activities of the neo-Nazis, Ku Klux Klan, skinheads, and other racist groups. A prejudiced teacher may hold high academic expectations for students of one group and low expectations for students of another group. Such prejudice could lead to inappropriate placement of students in gifted or special education programs.

Children who hold biased attitudes toward other groups may simply be reflecting their parents' attitudes, but other implicit messages from peers and the media also affect them (Berk, 2012). Children are influenced by what those around them think, do, and say. Even when parents model tolerance, children may still be exposed to the racist behaviors of others. They may hear older children or adults putting down some groups in jokes or with ethnic slurs. They observe how some individuals do not associate with members of certain groups (Anti-Defamation League, n.d). They may observe how some white teachers associate only with other white teachers in the cafeteria. They may see that a particular teacher's table is filled primarily with teachers of color. Unwittingly, these teachers are modeling behaviors for students.

Children are greatly influenced by the media. They watch television and have easy access to movies on television and those that family members rent. They see pictures in newspapers and in the magazines their parents have in the home. Hardly a day goes by without children being exposed to stereotyping, misinformation, or exclusion of important and accurate information (Anti-Defamation League, n.d).

For the past few years, children have been exposed to the horrors of war in Afghanistan, Iraq, and Libya, as well as bombings in other parts of the world. They have heard or seen reports of American military personnel killed daily by people of color—usually Arabs, whom they assume are Muslims. They continually hear expressions of justifiable anger directed toward terrorists and suicide bombers, who are almost always described by race or religion. The popular media has always had its villains. From the American Indians to the Japanese and Germans in the Second World War, villains of choice have evolved from Communists to Latin American drug lords, and now to Arabs and Muslims. These messages can contribute to children developing prejudicial attitudes about members of a group. This situation is exacerbated by the minimal effort made to show that the majority of the people in these groups are good, law-abiding, loyal Americans.

The Anti-Defamation League (n.d.) suggests that children with poor self-images are prone to develop prejudices. By targeting individuals they can put down, they bolster their own self-worth, making them feel more important and powerful than those they attack. At other times, children may exclude or ridicule other children because they perceive this to be a popular thing to do that will enhance their standing among their peers (Anti-Defamation League, n.d). Because children are cognitively capable of becoming less prejudiced, developing activities that have been shown to reduce prejudice during the early years of elementary school is an appropriate education strategy for teachers.

Discrimination.   Whereas prejudice is based on attitudes, discrimination focuses on behavior. Discrimination occurs at two levels: individual and institutional. Individual discrimination is attributable to, or influenced by, prejudice. Individuals discriminate against members of a group because they have strong prejudicial, or bigoted, feelings about the group, or they believe that society demands they discriminate. For example, realtors, personnel managers, receptionists, and membership chairpersons all work directly with a variety of individuals. Their own personal attitudes about members of a group can influence whether a house is sold, a job is offered, a loan is granted, an appointment is made, a meal is served, or a membership is granted to an individual. The actions of these individuals can prevent others from gaining the experiences and economic advantages that these activities offer.

An individual has less control over the other form of discrimination. Institutional discrimination cannot be attributed to prejudicial attitudes. It refers to inequalities that have been integrated into the systemwide operation of society through legislation and practices that ensure benefits to some groups versus others. Laws that disproportionately limit immigration to people from specific countries are one example. Other examples include practices that lead to a disproportionately large percentage of African Americans being incarcerated; single, low-income mothers being denied adequate prenatal care; and children in low-income neighborhoods suffering disproportionately from asthma as a result of poor environmental conditions.

We have grown up in a society that has discriminated against people of color, low-wage earners, women, and people with disabilities since the first European Americans arrived. We often do not realize the extent to which members of certain groups receive the benefits and privileges of institutions such as schools, Social Security, transportation systems, and banking systems. Because we may think that we have never been discriminated against, we should not assume that others do not suffer from discrimination.

Many argue that institutional discrimination no longer exists because today's laws require equal access to the benefits of society. As a result, they believe that individuals from all groups have equal opportunities to be successful. They fight against group rights that lead to what they perceived to be preferential treatment of the members of one group over others. The government is usually accused of going too far toward eliminating discrimination against historically oppressed groups by supporting affirmative action, contracts set aside for specific groups, special education, and legislation for women's equity. Opponents of these programs charge that they lead to reverse discrimination.

However, the criteria for access to the "good life" are often applied arbitrarily and unfairly. A disproportionately high number of people of color and students with disabilities have had limited opportunities to gain the qualifications for skilled jobs or college entrance or to obtain the economic resources to purchase a home in the suburbs. As businesses and industries move from the city to the suburbs, access to employment by those who live in the inner city becomes more limited. A crucial issue is not the equal treatment of those with equal qualifications, but the equal accessibility to the qualifications and jobs themselves.

The consequences are the same for individual and institutional discrimination. Members of some groups do not receive the same benefits from society as most members of the dominant group. Individuals are harmed by circumstances beyond their control because of their membership in a specific group. The role of teachers and other professional educators requires that they not discriminate against any student because of his or her group memberships. This consideration must be paramount in assigning students to special education and gifted classes and in giving and interpreting standardized tests. Classroom interactions, classroom resources,

women's studies, human relations, special education, and urban education. Let's examine how multicultural education has evolved over the past century.

EVOLUTION OF MULTICULTURAL EDUCATION

Multicultural education is not a new concept. Its roots are in the establishment of the Association for the Study of Negro Life and History. Through their research and books on the history and culture of African Americans, Carter G. Woodson, W. E. B. DuBois, Charles C. Wesley, and other scholars were the pioneers of ethnic studies. Woodson founded the *Journal of Negro History* and the *Negro History Bulletin* to disseminate research and curriculum materials. These materials were integrated into the curricula of segregated schools and historically black colleges and universities, allowing students to be empowered by the knowledge of their own history (J. A. Banks, 2004).

By the 1920s some educators were writing about and training teachers in intercultural education. The intercultural movement during its first two decades had an international emphasis with antecedents in the pacifist movement. Some textbooks were rewritten with an international point of view. Proponents encouraged teachers to make their disciplines more relevant to the modern world by being more issue oriented. One of the goals was to make the dominant population more tolerant and accepting of first- and second-generation immigrants in order to maintain national unity and social control (C. A. M. Banks, 2004). However, issues of power and inequality in society were ignored. The interculturalists supported the understanding and appreciation of diverse groups but did not promote collective ethnic identities, the focus of ethnic studies.

Following the Holocaust and World War II, tensions among groups remained high. Jewish organizations such as the Anti-Defamation League and the American Jewish Committee provided leadership for improving intergroup relations and reducing the anti-Semitic sentiment that existed at the time. National education organizations and progressive educational leaders such as Hilda Taba and Lloyd A. Cook promoted intergroup relations in schools to develop tolerance of new immigrants, African Americans, and other groups of color. Like the earlier intercultural movement, many intergroup educators had the goal of assimilating immigrants and people of color into the dominant society (J. A. Banks, 2004). Some programs focused on understanding the "folk" cultures of these groups. Others were designed to help rid native European Americans of their prejudice and discrimination against other groups. There was disagreement among the supporters of intergroup relations about the degree to which they should promote an understanding of the culture and history of ethnic groups (C. A. M. Banks, 2004). Historian David Tyack (2003) found this movement to be one in which "oppression became reduced to stereotyping and separate ethnic identity was to be dissolved as painlessly as possible" (p. 81).

Although the Supreme Court ruled in 1954 that schools should be desegregated, students in many classrooms today are from the same racial, ethnic, or language group.
© Bob Daemmrich/Alamy

By the 1960s desegregation was being enforced in the nation's schools. At the same time, cultural differences were being described as deficits. Students of color and whites from low-income families were described as culturally deprived. Their families were blamed for not providing them with the **cultural capital** or advantages such as wealth and education that would help them succeed in schools. Programs like Head Start, **compensatory education**, and special education were developed to make up for these shortcomings. Not surprisingly, those classes were filled with students of color, in poverty, or with disabilities—the children who had not been privileged in society and whose cultures seldom found their way into textbooks and school curricula.

In the 1970s the term "cultural deficits" was replaced with the label "culturally different" to acknowledge that students of color and immigrant students have cultures just as do the members of the **dominant group**. One of the goals of this approach was to teach the culturally different to develop the cultural patterns of the dominant society so that they could fit into the mainstream (Sleeter & Grant, 2009). Students with disabilities were still primarily segregated from their able-bodied peers during this period.

The civil rights movement of the 1960s and 1970s brought a renewed interest in ethnic studies, discrimination, and intergroup relations. Racial and ethnic pride emerged from oppressed groups, creating a demand for ethnic studies programs in colleges and universities across the country. Similar programs were sometimes established in secondary schools. However, students and participants in ethnic studies programs were primarily members of the group being studied. Programs focused on students' own ethnic histories and cultures with the objective of providing them with insights into and instilling pride in their own ethnic backgrounds. Most of these programs were ethnic-specific, with only one ethnic group studied. Sometimes the objectives included an understanding of the relationship and conflict between the ethnic group and the dominant population, but seldom was a program's scope multiethnic.

Concurrent with the civil rights movement and the growth of ethnic studies, an emphasis on intergroup or human relations again emerged. Often, these programs accompanied ethnic studies content for teachers. The objectives were to promote intergroup, and especially interracial, understanding to reduce or eliminate stereotypes. This approach emphasized the affective level—teachers' attitudes and feelings about themselves and others (Sleeter & Grant, 2009).

With the growth and development of ethnic studies came a realization that those programs alone would not guarantee support for the positive affirmation of diversity and differences in this country. Students from the dominant culture also needed to learn the history, culture, and contributions of groups other than their own. As a result, ethnic studies expanded into multiethnic studies. Teachers were encouraged to develop curricula that included the contributions of oppressed groups along with those of the dominant group. Textbooks were rewritten to represent more accurately the multiethnic nature of the United States and the world. Students were to be exposed to the perspectives of diverse groups through literature, history, music, and other disciplines integrated throughout the general school program. Curriculum and instructional materials were to reflect multiple perspectives, not just the single master narrative of the dominant group.

During this period, other groups that had suffered from institutional discrimination called their needs to the attention of the public. These groups included women, those with low incomes, people with disabilities, English language learners, and the elderly. Educators responded by expanding multiethnic education to the more encompassing concept of multicultural education. This broader concept focused on the different groups to which individuals belong, with an emphasis on the interaction of race, ethnicity, class, and gender in one's cultural identity. It also called for the elimination of discrimination based on group membership. No longer was it fashionable to fight sexism without simultaneously attacking racism, classism, homophobia, and discrimination against children, the elderly, and people with disabilities.

Critical Incidents in Teaching

Celebrating Ethnic Holidays

Esther Greenberg is a teacher of Asian and African American students in an alternative education class. Ms. Greenberg's college roommate was Chinese American, and she remembers fondly her visit to her roommate's home during the lunar New Year. She remembers how the parents and other Chinese adults had given all the children, including her, money wrapped in red paper, which was a tradition to bring all of the recipients good luck in the New Year. Ms. Greenberg thought that it would be a nice gesture to give the students in her class the red paper envelopes as an observance of the upcoming lunar New Year. Since she was unable to give the students money, she took gold foil–covered chocolate coins (given to Jewish children) and wrapped these coins in red paper to give to her students.

Unfortunately, on the lunar New Year's Day, all of the African American students were pulled out of class for a special meeting. All of the remaining students were her Asian students. When she passed out the red envelopes, the students were surprised and touched by her sensitivity to a cherished custom.

When her administrator was told what Ms. Greenberg had done, he became enraged. He accused her of favoritism to the Asian students and of deliberately leaving out the African American students. When she tried to convince him otherwise, he responded that she had no right to impose Asian customs on African American students. She responded that this was an important Asian custom, and that the Asian students had participated in the observance of Martin Luther King, Jr.'s birthday. However, he continued his attack, saying that this was an Asian superstition bordering on a religious observance. She was threatened with discipline.

| QUESTIONS FOR CLASSROOM DISCUSSION |

- Were Esther Greenberg's actions inappropriate for a public school classroom? If so, why? If not, why not? Was this a violation of the principle of separation of church and state?

- Did Ms. Greenberg create problems for herself by giving out the red envelopes when the African American students were absent from class? Did this create an appearance of favoritism of one racial group over the other?

- How could Ms. Greenberg have handled the situation to make it a pleasing experience for all concerned?

- Was the administrator the one who was out of line, and was Ms. Greenberg simply a victim?

MULTICULTURAL EDUCATION TODAY

The 1990s were characterized by the development of standards, which led to debates between fundamentalists and multiculturalists, especially around the history standards. The fundamentalists argued that the standards should stress what they believed to be the foundations of democracy—patriotism and historical heroes. The multiculturalists promoted the inclusion of diverse groups and multiple perspectives in the standards. In English language arts, groups disagreed about the literature to which students should be exposed, some arguing for multiple perspectives and others arguing that such literature might promote values they could not support.

Multicultural education is sometimes criticized as focusing on differences rather than similarities among groups. Theorists criticize it for not adequately addressing the issues of power and oppression that keep a number of groups from participating equitably in society. At least three schools of thought push multiculturalists to think critically about these issues: critical pedagogy, antiracist education, and critical race theory (Sleeter & Bernal, 2004). Critical pedagogy focuses on the culture of everyday life and the interaction of class, race, and gender in contemporary power struggles. Antiracist education is the strategy used in Canada and a number of European countries to eliminate racist practices such as tracking, inequitable funding, and segregation in schools. Critical race theory focuses on racism to challenge racial oppression, racial inequities, and white privilege (Howard, 2010). Multicultural education as presented in this text attempts to incorporate critical pedagogy, antiracist education, and critical race theory as different groups are discussed. Multicultural education promotes **critical thinking** about these and other issues to ensure that education serves the needs of all groups equitably.

Still, after eight decades of concern for civil and human rights in education, racism persists. Educators struggle with the integration of diversity into the curriculum and provision of equality in schools. Some classrooms may be desegregated and mainstreamed, and both boys and girls may now participate in athletic activities. However, students are still labeled as at risk, developmentally delayed, underprivileged, lazy, or slow. They are tracked in special classes or groups within the classroom based on their real or perceived abilities. A disproportionate number of students from African American, Mexican American, Puerto Rican, American Indian, and Southeast Asian American groups score below European American students on national standardized tests. The number of students of color and low-income students participating in advanced science and mathematics classes is not proportionate to their representation in schools. They too often are offered little or no encouragement to enroll in the advanced courses that are necessary to be successful in college. To draw attention to these inequities, the National Alliance of Black School Educators declared that "education is a civil right" and has called on the country to establish a "zero tolerance policy on illiteracy, dropout and failure" (National Alliance of Black School Educators, 2008, p. 1).

In a country that champions equal rights and the opportunity for the individual to improve his or her conditions, educators are challenged to help all students achieve academically. At the beginning of the twenty-first century, the standards movement focused on identifying what every student should know and be able to do. The federal legislation for elementary and secondary schools, No Child Left Behind (NCLB), requires standardized testing of students to determine a school's effectiveness in helping students learn. It mandates that test scores be reported to the public by "race, gender, English language proficiency, disability, and socio-economic status" (U.S. Department of Education, 2001, p. 10). The goal of NCLB is to improve the academic achievement of all students. Students in low-performing schools may transfer to a higher-performing school to improve their chances of passing tests if their school continues to be low-performing for three years. Congress has begun the process of reauthorizing the Elementary and

Secondary Education Act, which is currently called NCLB, and may have passed it by the time you begin teaching. Although a number of initiatives may change, the emphasis on improving student learning is not likely to decrease.

MULTICULTURAL PROFICIENCIES FOR TEACHERS

States and school districts expect teachers to have **proficiencies**, which include the specific knowledge, skills, and dispositions related to multicultural education, by the time they finish a teacher education program. With NCLB, school districts are obligated to hire teachers who can help low-income students, students of color, English language learners, and students with disabilities meet state standards.

State standards for teacher licensure reflect the national standards in Table 1.1, which were developed by the Interstate Teacher Assessment and Support Consortium (InTASC). Each of the 10 standards is further explicated by statements of the knowledge, dispositions, and performances that teachers should be able to demonstrate before a state license to teach is issued. The InTASC proficiencies related to multicultural education are discussed in this text; others will be addressed in other teacher education courses that you are required to complete. The portions of the InTASC standards (2011) that address multicultural proficiencies state that teachers should:

- Understand the role of language and culture in learning and know how to modify instruction to make language comprehensible and instruction relevant, accessible, and challenging (Standard 1).
- Bring multiple perspectives to the discussion of content, including attention to learners' personal, family, and community experiences and cultural norms (Standard 2).
- Know how to access information about the values of diverse cultures and communities and how to incorporate learners' experiences, cultures, and community resources into instruction (Standard 2).
- Communicate verbally and nonverbally in ways that demonstrate respect for and responsiveness to the cultural backgrounds and differing perspectives learners bring to the learning environment (Standard 3).
- Know how to integrate culturally relevant content to build on learners' background knowledge (Standard 4).
- Facilitate learners' ability to develop diverse social and cultural perspectives that expand their understanding of local and global issues and create novel approaches to solving problems (Standard 5).
- Prepare all learners for the demands of particular assessment formats and make appropriate accommodations in assessments or testing conditions, especially for learners with disabilities and language learning needs (Standard 6).
- Understand learning theory, human development, cultural diversity, and individual differences, and how these impact ongoing planning (Standard 7).
- Know how to apply a range of developmentally, culturally, and linguistically appropriate instructional strategies to achieve learning goals (Standard 8).
- Reflect on one's personal biases and access resources to deepen his or her own understanding of cultural, ethnic, gender, and learning differences to build stronger relationships and create more relevant learning expectations (Standard 9).
- Work collaboratively with learners and their families to establish mutual expectations and ongoing communication to support learner development and achievement (Standard 10).

Table 1.1 InTASC Core Teaching Standards

1. **Learner Development.** The teacher understands how learners grow and develop, recognizing that patterns of learning and development vary individually within and across the cognitive, linguistic, social, emotional, and physical areas, and designs and implements developmentally appropriate and challenging learning experiences.

2. **Learning Differences.** The teacher uses understanding of individual differences and diverse cultures and communities to ensure inclusive learning environments that enable each learner to meet high standards.

3. **Learning Environments.** The teacher works with others to create environments that support individual and collaborative learning, and that encourage positive social interaction, active engagement in learning, and self-motivation.

4. **Content Knowledge.** The teacher understands the central concepts, tools of inquiry, and structures of the discipline(s) he or she teaches and creates learning experiences that make the discipline accessible and meaningful for learners to assure mastery of the content.

5. **Application of Content.** The teacher understands how to connect concepts and use differing perspectives to engage learners in critical thinking, creativity, and collaborative problem solving related to authentic local and global issues.

6. **Assessment.** The teacher understands and uses multiple methods of assessment to engage learners in their own growth, to monitor learner progress, and to guide the teacher's and learner's decision making.

7. **Planning for Instruction.** The teacher plans instruction that supports every student in meeting rigorous learning goals by drawing upon knowledge of content areas, curriculum, cross-disciplinary skills, and pedagogy, as well as knowledge of learners and the community context.

8. **Instructional Strategies.** The teacher understands and uses a variety of instructional strategies to encourage learners to develop deep understanding of content areas and their connections, and to build skills to apply knowledge in meaningful ways.

9. **Professional Learning and Ethical Practice.** The teacher engages in ongoing professional learning and uses evidence to continually evaluate his/her practice, particularly the effects of his/her choices and actions on others (learners, families, other professionals, and the community), and adapts practice to meet the needs of each learner.

10. **Leadership and Collaboration.** The teacher seeks appropriate leadership roles and opportunities to take responsibility for student learning, to collaborate with learners, families, colleagues, and other school professionals, and community members to ensure learner growth, and to advance the profession.

Source: **Interstate Teacher Assessment and Support Consortium. (2011, April).** *InTASC model core teaching standards: A resource for state dialogue.* **Washington, DC: Council of Chief State School Officers, pp. 8–9.**

In working with students who come from different ethnic, racial, language, and religious groups from those of the teacher, the development of dispositions that are supportive of diversity and differences is important. Students quickly become aware of the educators who respect their cultures, believe they can learn, and value differences in the classroom. Examples of dispositions that the InTASC standards expect teachers to have developed include:

- Valuing the input and contributions of families, colleagues, and other professionals in understanding and supporting each learner's development (Standard 1).
- Believing that all children can achieve at high levels and persisting in helping each learner reach his or her full potential (Standard 2).
- Making learners feel valued and helping them learn to value each other (Standard 2).

- Valuing diverse languages and dialects and seeking to integrate them into instructional practice to engage students in learning (Standard 2).
- Realizing that content knowledge is not a fixed body of facts but is complex, culturally situated, and ever evolving (Standard 4).
- Valuing the variety of ways people communicate and encouraging learners to develop and use multiple forms of communication (Standard 8).
- Being committed to deepening understanding of one's own frames of reference (e.g., culture, gender, language, abilities, ways of knowing), the potential biases in these frames, and their impact on expectations for and relationships with learners and their families (Standard 9).
- Respecting families' beliefs, norms, and expectations and seeking to work collaboratively with learners and families in setting and meeting challenging goals (Standard 10).

As a new teacher, you should be able to demonstrate the proficiencies outlined above. The portfolio activities at the end of each chapter will provide opportunities for you to begin to collect artifacts related to these proficiencies for working with a diverse student population and delivering education that is multicultural. Each of these activities indicates the InTASC standard for which the activity may provide evidence of achievement. These artifacts could become part of the portfolio that you are developing in your teacher education program. They may be a valuable part of the portfolio that you present to a future employer, showing that you have developed the knowledge, skills, and dispositions appropriate for working effectively with a diverse student population. Finally, you may be able to further develop and refine these portfolio entries for national certification early in your teaching career.

Most state licensure tests include questions related to diversity in a combination of short-answer and multiple-choice questions. These often include a test of your knowledge of (1) the subject that you plan to teach and (2) pedagogy related to effective teaching. At the end of each chapter of this book you will have the opportunity to practice on a test item that is similar to one that you might find on the licensure test that you will be required to pass before you can teach.

REFLECTING ON MULTICULTURAL TEACHING

Teachers who reflect on and analyze their own practices report that their teaching improves over time. If you decide to seek national board certification after you have taught for three years, you will be required to provide written reflections on your teaching videos. You are encouraged to begin to develop the habit of reflecting on your practice now and to include in that reflection the multicultural proficiencies listed above. From the first day of student teaching, you should begin to reflect on your effectiveness as a teacher. Are you actually helping students learn the subject and skills you are teaching? An important part of teaching is to ask what is working and what is not. Effective teachers are able to change their teaching strategies when students are not learning. They do not leave any students behind. They draw on the experiences and cultures of their students to make the subject matter relevant to them. Self-reflection will be a critical skill for improving your teaching.

You can begin to develop skills for reflection while you are preparing to teach. Many teacher education programs require candidates to keep journals and develop portfolios that include reflection papers. Videotaping the lessons that you teach will allow you to critique your knowledge of the subject matter, interactions with students, and methods of managing a class. The critique could be expanded to address multicultural proficiencies. You may find it valuable to ask a colleague to periodically observe you while you are teaching and provide feedback on your multicultural proficiencies. Honest feedback can lead to positive adjustments in our behavior and attitudes. To get you started, each chapter includes one or two opportunities for you to pause and reflect on issues related to diversity and multicultural education.

Summary

Students from diverse cultural groups will comprise over half of the elementary and secondary school populations by 2020. They come from diverse ethnic, racial, religious, socioeconomic, language, gender, sexual orientation, and ability groups. Understanding cultural diversity and the cultures of students, and knowing how to use that knowledge effectively can help teachers deliver instruction to help students learn.

Culture provides the blueprint that determines the way we think, feel, and behave in society. We are not born with culture, but rather learn it through enculturation and socialization. It is manifested through society's institutions, lived experiences, and the individual's fulfillment of psychological and basic needs. Historically, U.S. political and social institutions have developed from a Western European tradition and still function under the strong influence of that heritage. At the same time, many aspects of American life have been greatly influenced by the numerous cultural groups that make up the U.S. population. The dominant culture is based on its white, Anglo-Saxon, Protestant roots and the core values of individualism and freedom with which many middle-class families identify.

Assimilation is the process by which groups adopt and change the dominant culture. Schools have traditionally served as the transmitter of the dominant culture to all students regardless of their cultural backgrounds. The theory of cultural pluralism promotes the maintenance of the distinct differences among cultural groups with equal power. Multiculturalism allows groups to maintain their unique cultural identities within the dominant culture without having to assimilate.

Cultural identity is based on the interaction and influence of membership in groups based on ethnicity, race, religion, gender, sexual orientation, age, class, native language, geographic region, and ability. Membership in one group can greatly affect one's identity with respect to the others.

A democracy provides social justice for all of its people. Egalitarianism and equality have long been espoused as goals for society, but they are implemented from two perspectives. The emphasis on individualism is supported in a meritocratic system in which everyone is presumed to start out equally, and where the most deserving will end up with the most rewards. Equality, in contrast, seeks to ensure that society's benefits and rewards are distributed more equitably among individuals and groups. Prejudice, discrimination, and privilege continue to be obstacles to equality.

Multicultural education is an educational strategy that incorporates cultural differences and provides equality and social justice in schools. For it to become a reality in the formal school situation, the total environment must reflect a commitment to multicultural education. The diverse cultural backgrounds and group memberships of students and families are as important in developing effective instructional strategies as are their physical and mental capabilities. Further, educators must understand the influence of racism, sexism, and classism on the lives of their students and ensure that these are not perpetuated in the classroom.

Professional Practice

Questions for Discussion

1. How will the changing diversity of the P–12 student population change schools and classroom instruction?

2. What impact does culture have on the behavior of students in the classroom and school? How can students' cultures be integrated into the classroom to validate them and make the curriculum more meaningful to them?

3. What practices in schools could support and promote multiculturalism? What practices support and promote assimilation into the dominant culture?

4. How do ethnicity, gender, and religion interact in determining cultural identity? Why might one's cultural identity change over time?

5. How can a focus on equality and social justice improve the quality of education and the academic achievement of students from diverse groups?

6. Why is multicultural education as important for students of the dominant culture as it is for students of other cultures?

Portfolio Activities

1. Write a reflective paper that describes your cultural identity and the social and economic factors that have influenced it. Identify their importance by drawing a circle similar to Figure 1.3 and indicating the degree of influence each cultural group has on your identity and why. (InTASC Standard 9: Professional Learning and Ethnical Practice)

2. Select one of the schools in which you are observing this semester to develop a case study of the cultural norms prevalent in the community served by the school. In your case study indicate the diversity of the community and the cultural norms that are reflected in the school. Teachers, parents, and students should be interviewed during the development of the case study. Your observations of students should also inform your case. (InTASC Standard 2: Learning Differences)

3. As you progress through your teacher education program, you will be expected to work with students from diverse groups in field experiences, student teaching, and your own classroom. Complete the following checklist to show how close you are to meeting selected InTASC proficiencies related to cultural diversity and multicultural education concepts. Write an accompanying paper on how you will develop the knowledge, skills, or dispositions in which you are not already proficient. (InTASC Standard 1: Learner Development, Standard 2: Learning Differences, and Standard 3: Learning Environments)

Proficiency	Already Proficient	Partially Proficient	Not Proficient
Understand student with exceptional needs, including those associated with disabilities and giftedness.	☐	☐	☐
Understand the role of language and culture in learning.	☐	☐	☐
Know how to apply a range of developmentally, culturally, and linguistically appropriate instructional strategies to achieve learning goals.	☐	☐	☐
Understand that learners bring assets for learning based on their language, culture, family, and community values.	☐	☐	☐
Able to bring multiple perspectives to the discussion of content, including attention to learners' personal, family, and community experiences and cultural norms.	☐	☐	☐
Value diverse languages and dialects and seek to integrate them into your instructional practice.	☐	☐	☐
Believe that all learners can achieve at high levels and persist in helping each learner reach his/her full potential.	☐	☐	☐
Are committed to working with learners, colleagues, families, and communities to establish positive and supportive learning environments.	☐	☐	☐

Digital Resources for the Classroom

1. For resources on the critical aspects of multicultural education, equity, and social justice, go to http://www.edchange.org/multicultural. The website includes quizzes, teacher resources, handouts, speeches, songs, quotations, and links to other resources.

2. To learn more about combating prejudice, visit http://www.adl.org/prejudice/default .asp. A complimentary copy of the booklet 101 Ways to Combat Prejudice can be downloaded.

3. Information on the maintenance of cultures and languages worldwide can be accessed at the website of the United Nations Educational, Scientifics, and Cultural Organization (UNESCO) at http://www.unesco.org/new/en/culture.

4. For more information on becoming a national board certified teacher, visit the website of the National Board for Professional Teaching Standards at www.nbpts.org.

MyEducationLab™

Go to the MyEducationLab (www.myeducationlab.com) for Multicultural Education and familiarize yourself with the topical content, which includes:

- Assignments and Activities, tied to learning outcomes for the course, that can help you more deeply understand course content
- Building Teaching Skills and Dispositions learning units allow you to apply and practice your understanding of how to teach equitably in a multicultural education classroom
- Licensure Test Prep activities are available in the Book Resources to help you prepare for test taking
- A pretest with hints and feedback that tests your knowledge of this chapter's content
- Review, practice, and enrichment activities that will enhance your understanding of the chapter content
- A posttest with hints and feedback that allows you to test your knowledge again after having completed the enrichment activities

A Correlation Guide may be downloaded by instructors to show how MyEducationLab content aligns to this book.

Ethnicity and Race

Nobody recognizes I am Vietnamese because when they look at me they think I am Chinese. They cannot recognize who I am.

My Lien Nguyen, Student

As you read this chapter, you should be able to:

- Identify patterns of immigration and immigration policy and their impact on the education of children of foreign-born families.

- Define ethnicity and describe how educational practices support or eliminate ethnic differences among students.

- Analyze the impact that the nation's growing racial diversity will have on schools and students.

- Infer how the civil rights movement has impacted education.

- Evaluate the results of continuing racial and ethnic discrimination on communities and students.

- Develop strategies for affirming race and ethnicity in classroom.

Denise Williams had become increasingly aware of the racial tension in the high school in which she teaches, but she did not expect the hostility that erupted between some black and white students that Friday. In the week that followed, the faculty decided they had to do more to develop positive interethnic and interracial relations among students. They established a committee to identify consultants and other resources to guide them in this effort.

Ms. Williams, however, thought that neither she nor her students could wait for months to receive a report and recommendations from the committee. She was ready to introduce the civil rights movement in her social studies class. It seemed a perfect time to promote better cross-cultural communications. She decided that she would let students talk about their feelings.

She soon learned that this topic was not an easy one to handle. African American students expressed their anger at the discriminatory practices in the school and the community. Most of the white students did not believe that there was any discrimination. They believed there were no valid reasons for the anger of the African American and Latino students, and that if they just followed the rules and worked harder, they would not have their perceived problems. She thought the class was getting nowhere. In fact, at times the anger on both sides was so intense that she worried a physical fight would erupt. She was frustrated because the class discussions and activities were not helping students understand their stereotypes and prejudices. She was concerned that students were becoming more polarized in their beliefs. She wondered whether she could do anything in her class to improve understanding, empathy, and communications across groups.

| REFLECTIONS |

1. What racial groups are most likely to see themselves represented in the school curriculum?

2. How can a classroom reflect the diversity of its students so that they all feel valued and respected?

3. What were the positive and negative outcomes of the steps taken by Ms. Williams?

Immigration

As people from all over the world joined the American Indians in populating this nation, they brought with them cultural experiences from their native countries. Just because individuals have the same national origins, however, does not mean that they have the same history and experiences. The time of immigration, the places in which groups settled, the reasons for emigrating, individual socioeconomic status, and the degree to which one is affected by racism and discrimination interact to form a new **ethnic group** that distinguishes one from those who came before and those who will come afterward. You will see these differences in schools as students whose families have been in the United States for several generations may not warmly welcome new immigrant students from the same country of origin.

Most groups immigrated to the United States voluntarily to seek freedoms not available in their native countries at the time, to escape dismal economic or political conditions, or to join family members already settled in the country. However, not all people and groups voluntarily immigrated. The ancestors of most African Americans arrived involuntarily on slave ships. Mexicans living in the southwestern part of the country became residents when the United States annexed their lands. The reasons for immigration and the way immigrants were treated after they arrived have had a lasting impact on each group's desire to assimilate into the dominant U.S. society and enjoy equitable access to society's resources.

A BRIEF HISTORY OF THE IMMIGRANT POPULATION

Many people forget that the United States was populated when explorers from other nations arrived on its shores. With the continuing arrival of the Europeans, American Indians were not treated as equal citizens in the formation of the United States. Eventually, most First Americans were forcibly segregated from the European immigrants, and many were forced to move from their geographic homelands to reservations in other parts of the country. This separation led to a pattern of isolation and inequity that remains today. The atrocities and near genocide that characterized the treatment of Native Americans have been ignored in most accounts of U.S. history. Not until 2000 did an official of the U.S. government apologize for the Bureau of Indian Affairs' "legacy of racism and inhumanity that included massacres, forced relocations of tribes and attempts to wipe out Indian languages and cultures" (Kelley, 2000, p. 1).

Five million citizens identify themselves as American Indian or Alaska Native. More American Indians live in California than in any other state, followed by Oklahoma and Arizona (U.S. Census Bureau, 2010k). They are the largest group of color in Alaska, Montana, North Dakota, Oklahoma, and South Dakota. Forty percent of the American Indian population belongs to one of six tribes: Cherokee, Navajo, Latin Native American, Choctaw, Sioux, or Chippewa (U.S. Census Bureau, 2010b).

The 1.1 million Native Hawaiians have experiences similar to those of other **indigenous** populations around the world. In 1894 Queen Liliuokalani of Hawaii was overthrown by a group of white sugar planters in an effort to gain control of the Island and further their interests. The American minister sent to Hawaii by President Grover Cleveland declared the overthrow to be illegal, and the president agreed that the monarchy should be restored. However, the annexationists' interests prevailed, and a white president of the Republic of Hawaii was recognized immediately by the U.S. government. Vital to the interests of the United States,

Hawaii eventually became a territory and, in 1959, the fiftieth state. Today, Native Hawaiians remain near the bottom of the socioeconomic ladder.

Although most of the first European settlers were English, the French, Dutch, and Spanish also established early settlements. After the consolidation and development of the United States as an independent nation, successive waves of Western Europeans joined the earlier settlers. Irish, Swedish, and German immigrants left their home countries to escape economic impoverishment or political repression. These early European settlers brought with them the political institutions that would become the framework for our government. The melding of Northern and Western European cultures over time formed the dominant culture in which other immigrant groups strived or were forced to assimilate.

Africans were also among the early explorers of the Americas and of the foreign settlers in the early days of colonization. By the eighteenth century, Africans were being kidnapped and sold into bondage by slave traders. As involuntary immigrants, this group of Africans underwent a process quite different from that confronting the Europeans who voluntarily **immigrated**. Separated from their families and homelands, robbed of their freedom and cultures, Africans developed a new culture out of their various African, European, and Native American heritages and their unique experiences in this country. Early on, the majority of African Americans lived in the South, where today they remain the majority population in many counties. When industrial jobs in northern, eastern, and western cities began to open up to them between 1910 and 1920, many migrated north—a pattern that was repeated in the 1940s and 1950s. By the beginning of the twenty-first century, the trend had reversed, with a growing number of African Americans from northern states moving south.

Another factor that contributed to African American migration north was the racism and political terror that existed in much of the South at that time. Even today, a racial ideology is implicit in the policies and practices of many of our institutions. It continues to block the full assimilation of African Americans into the dominant society. Although the **civil rights** movement of the 1960s reduced the barriers that prevented many African Americans from enjoying the advantages of the middle class, the number of African Americans, especially children, who live in poverty remains disproportionately high. Schools generally are not yet meeting the needs of African American children. They do not perform as well as most other ethnic groups on standardized tests, and less than half of African American male students are graduating from high school in four years (Howard, 2010).

Mexican Americans also played a unique role in the formation of the United States. Spain was the first European country to colonize Mexico and the western and southwestern United States. In 1848 the U.S. government annexed the northern sections of the Mexican Territory, including the areas currently occupied by Texas, Arizona, New Mexico, and southern California. The Mexican and Native Americans living within that territory became an oppressed minority in the region where they had previously been the dominant population. The labor of Mexicans has been persistently sought by farmers and businesses over the past century. Once the laborers arrived, however, they were treated with hostility and limited to low-paying jobs and a subordinate status. Supremacy theories related to race and language have been used against them in a way that, even today, prevents many Mexican Americans from assimilating fully into the dominant culture.

Although Mexican Americans were involuntary immigrants when they were annexed by the U.S. government, they since have been voluntarily emigrating. They have been joined by other immigrants from Latin America and Spain—a combined group identified as Latino or Hispanic, terms used interchangeably in this book. At the beginning of the twenty-first century, the Latino population became the largest group of color in the United States and is projected to constitute one-third of the population by 2050.

The industrial opening of the West in the mid-1800s signaled a need for labor that could be met through immigration from Asia. Chinese worked the plantations in Hawaii. Chinese, Japanese, and Filipinos were recruited to provide the labor needed on the West Coast for mining gold and building railroads. By 1882 their labor was no longer needed; as a result Congress passed the Chinese Exclusion Act, halting all immigration from China. Japanese American families were arrested and placed in internment camps during World War II, many losing their property and belongings in the process. Because of such bias against the Chinese and Japanese, immigration from Asia was severely limited until 1965. With the changed immigration quotas, Asian Americans have become the second-fastest-growing group in the United States, with the majority being foreign-born or having a foreign-born parent.

At the end of the nineteenth century industries in the nation's cities required more labor than was available. Immigrants from the impoverished eastern and southern European countries were enticed to accept jobs, primarily in midwestern and eastern cities. Into the early twentieth century immigrants continued to arrive from nations such as Poland, Hungary, Italy, Russia, and Greece. The reasons for their immigration were similar to those that had driven many earlier immigrants: devastating economic and political hardship in the homeland and the demand for labor in the United States. Many immigrants came to the United States with the hope of enjoying the higher wages and improved living conditions they had heard about, but found conditions here worse than they had expected. Most were forced to live in substandard housing near the business and manufacturing districts where they worked. These urban ghettos grew into ethnic enclaves in which the immigrants continued to use their native languages and maintain the cultures of their native lands. To support their social and welfare needs, ethnic institutions were established. Many of the racist policies that had been used earlier against African Americans, Mexican Americans, and Native Americans were applied to these immigrants. A major difference was that their offspring were able to assimilate into the dominant culture during the second and third generations.

The immigration rate during most of the past decade has been around 1 million annually (Monger & Yankay, 2011). Over half of the foreign-born population lives in four states: California, New York, Florida, and Texas. One of four California residents and one of five New York residents are foreign-born (U.S. Census Bureau, 2010k). Most immigrants settle in urban areas, constituting more than one of five residents in the cities shown in Figure 2.1. In addition, a growing number of immigrants are moving into suburban and rural areas. Newer immigrants are also increasing the diversity of the Carolinas, Mountain West, Mid-Atlantic, Midwest, and Pacific Northwest regions (Mather, 2009).

THE CONTROL OF IMMIGRATION

Throughout history the U.S. Congress has restricted the immigration of different national or ethnic groups on the basis of the racial superiority of the older, established immigrant groups that had colonized the nation. As early as 1729, immigration was being discouraged. In that year, Pennsylvania passed a statute that increased the head tax on foreigners in that colony. Some leaders, including Benjamin Franklin, worried that Pennsylvania was in danger of becoming a German state. The 1790 Naturalization Act, which allowed only whites to become U.S. citizens, declared that an immigrant could become a citizen after several years of residency.

In the nineteenth century, native-born citizens again worried about their majority and superiority status being threatened by entering immigrant groups. The resulting movement, known

Figure 2.1   Major Cities in Which at Least One of Five Residents Was Foreign Born, 2008.

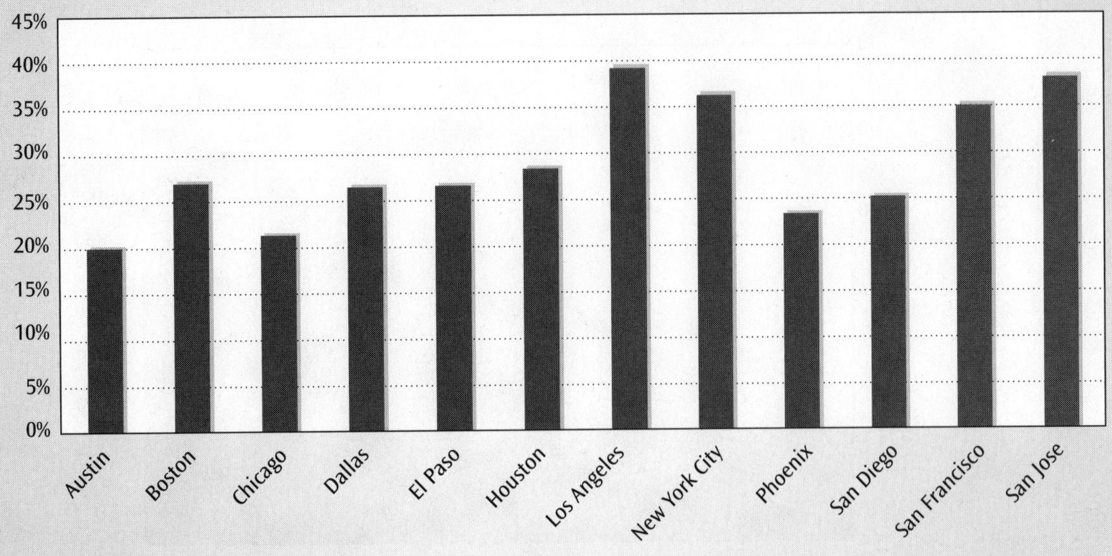

Source: U.S. Census Bureau (2010k). *Statistical abstract of the United States: 2011* (130th ed.). Washington, DC: Author.

as **nativism,** restricted immigration and protected the interests of native-born citizens. This nativism continued into the twentieth century, when the Dillingham Commission recommended, in 1917, that all immigrants be required to pass a literacy test. The nativists received further support for their views when Congress passed the Johnson-Reed Act in 1924, establishing annual immigration quotas that disproportionately favored immigrants from Western European countries. It also stopped all immigration from Japan. The Johnson-Reed Act was not abolished until 1965, when a new quota system was established, dramatically increasing the number of immigrants allowed annually from the Eastern Hemisphere and reducing the number from the Western Hemisphere, which resulted in the changes shown in Figure 2.2.

Congressional leaders and presidential candidates during the 1980s promoted a "get tough" approach to immigration, calling for greater control of the U.S. borders. However, the 1986 Immigration Reform and Control Act actually expanded immigration by allowing visas to people born in countries adversely affected by the 1965 law—Europeans. In the new century, immigration policies are again under attack by citizens who believe that immigration, especially unauthorized immigration, is not being controlled effectively by the federal government.

Today's immigrants enter the United States legally or unauthorized. Legal immigrants come in through four major routes. Family sponsorship is the primary path to immigration, representing approximately 66% of the legal immigrants. Family members who are U.S. citizens can petition the federal government to admit their relatives; there are no caps on the number of visas available for immediate family members. The second-largest group of legal immigrants (14%) have come to the United States at the request of employers. They include workers with "extraordinary ability" in the arts or sciences, professionals with advanced degrees, skilled and unskilled workers, investors, and such special categories as athletes, ministers, and investors. **Refugees** and **asylees** (13%) make up the third group. The fourth group is diversity immigrants (5%), participants in a system that allows people from countries with relatively few immigrants to enter a lottery for 50,000 available slots (Monger & Yankay, 2011).

Figure 2.2 Immigration from Selected Countries and Continents: 1961–2008.

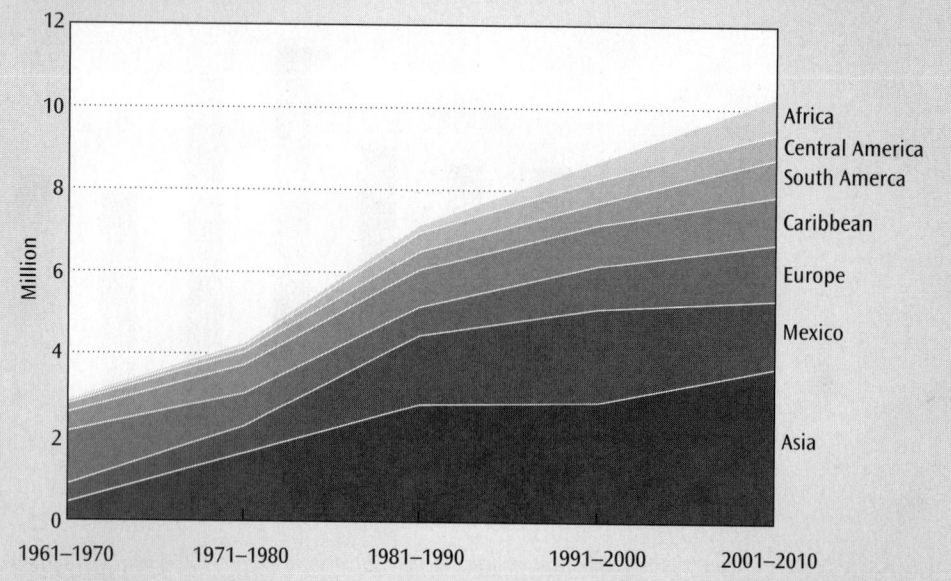

Sources: U.S. Census Bureau (2006). *Statistical Abstract of the United States: 2007* (126th ed.). Washington, DC: Author; Jefferys, K., & Monger, R. (2008, March). *U.S. legal permanent residents: 2007.* Washington, DC: U.S. Department of Homeland Security, Office of Immigration Statistics; Monger, R., & Yankay, J. (2011, March). *U.S. legal permanent residents: 2010.* Washington, DC: U.S. Department of Homeland Security, Office of Immigration Statistics.

As in the past, emotions about immigration policies are dividing restrictionists from immigration supporters. Many citizens value multiculturalism and bilingualism, recalling that their ancestors were immigrants who entered the country with a culture and often a language different from that of the dominant group. Other citizens view the growing cultural and language diversity as dangerous to the continuation of the "American" culture for which they and their ancestors have fought. In some states and school districts, these groups of citizens have led the movement to declare English the nation's official language and oppose the use of bilingual signs and documents, which they see as promoting bilingualism. In some communities they picket places where unauthorized day workers gather to meet potential employers.

In 2006 towns began to pass ordinances to restrict housing and jobs to those who can prove that they are authorized to be in this country. Representing local businesses, the American Civil Liberties Union (ACLU), Latino legal defense funds, and other groups filed suits against these ordinances. Except for a small portion of one of the ordinances, all were struck down in the courts after the towns had paid hundreds of thousands or even several million dollars for representation by their attorneys (Southern Poverty Law Center, 2011).

Proponents of these ordinances argue that unauthorized immigrants are committing crimes, are contributing to overcrowded classrooms and failing schools, and are a burden to taxpayers. In some communities, elected officials demanded that foreign language books and resources be removed from libraries. White residents in some areas demanded immigration papers from Latinos (Southern Poverty Law Center, 2011). Along the U.S.-Mexico border, the Minutemen, the Federation for American Immigration Reform (FAIR), and other nativist groups are actively

Latinos are joined by their allies to protest attacks on immigration rights and anti-discrimination legislation.
© Ellen McKnight/Alamy

patrolling to prevent immigrants from entering the country illegally. The websites of some of these groups encourage citizens to report people they think are unauthorized (Potok, 2011).

In January 2010 a state senator introduced the Support Our Law Enforcement and Safe Neighborhoods Act (Senate Bill 1070) in Arizona, which would require local and state officials to check the immigration status of anyone they suspect might be unauthorized. The bill also made it a crime for an unauthorized person to seek work or trespass on private or public land; also, hiring unauthorized workers from a stopped car would be a criminal act. In late March 2010 a rancher near the Mexican border was killed while helping a person he believed to be an unauthorized immigrant. Many believed the rancher was shot by a Mexican drug smuggler. On April 13, 2010, the Arizona House of Representatives passed Senate Bill 1070, as did the Arizona Senate soon after. When Governor Jan Brewer signed the new law a few days later, thousands of supporters and protestors gathered at the state Capitol. Rallies against the Arizona law were held in cities across the country in the following weeks (Southern Poverty Law Center, 2011). Just before the law was to become effective, a federal judge issued a preliminary injunction against its most controversial provisions. The Ninth U.S. Circuit Court of Appeals in San Francisco upheld the temporary injunction in April 2011.

Although George W. Bush proposed immigration reform during his presidency, Congress took no action. Many Latinos were hopeful that President Barack Obama would push for immigration reform soon after he was inaugurated, but have been disappointed by the inaction of the Obama administration. The Dream Act, intended to allow the children of unauthorized immigrants to attend U.S. colleges, was defeated by Congress in 2010. U.S. citizens are also divided on the action that is needed on immigration. A 2010 Gallup poll found that 50% thought the flow of unauthorized immigrants should be halted and 45% thought that Congress should develop a plan to deal with unauthorized immigrants now in the country (Saad, 2010). No new proposals for immigration reform are expected until after the 2012 national election.

UNAUTHORIZED IMMIGRANTS

Not all immigrants are authorized to be in the country. People from other countries enter the United States as travelers or on student or other special visas. Some of them extend their stay; others never go home. One-third of foreign-born residents are unauthorized (Passel & Cohn, 2011).

Many of these immigrants are later reclassified as legal because they meet the requirements for employment-based visas, they qualify as refugees, or they are sponsored by a family as allowed by law. They may also become legal immigrants through amnesty or similar programs periodically enacted by Congress. Approximately 58% of the unauthorized immigrants are from Mexico and 23% from other Latin American nations, 11% are from Asia, 4% are from Canada and Europe, and 3% are from Africa (Passel & Cohn, 2011). The total number of unauthorized immigrants has decreased since 2007, when it was estimated at 12 million. In 2010 the estimate was 11.2 million, which is 3.7% of the nation's population. Six to 7% of the populations of Nevada, California, Texas, New Jersey, and Arizona is comprised of unauthorized immigrants (Passel & Cohn, 2011).

Eight percent of the births in the United States in 2009 were to unauthorized immigrants (Passel & Cohn, 2011). The children become U.S. citizens because the Fourteenth Amendment grants citizenship to children born in the United States. Unauthorized children have a right to seek a public education under the U.S. Supreme Court decision *Plyler v. Doe* (1982). Educators cannot require students or parents to declare their immigration status, and they cannot make inquiries that might expose such status. For example, parents cannot be forced to provide social security numbers to school districts.

Restrictionists charge that immigrants, especially unauthorized ones, drain the social welfare system as they seek education for their children and medical assistance for their family members. To control the perceived drain on their state budget, Californians passed Proposition 187 in 1994 to deny services to unauthorized immigrants and their families. Although the proposition was later found to be in violation of the ruling in *Plyler v. Doe*, efforts to restrict public services, including education, continue in other states. Some states have passed legislation to provide in-state tuition to children of unauthorized immigrants that increase opportunities for them to attend public colleges and universities (Morse & Birnbach, 2011).

REFUGEES

Refugees are people who are recognized by the federal government as being persecuted in their home countries because of race, religion, nationality, or membership in a specific social or political group. In 2009 nearly 75,000 individuals were admitted as refugees from the countries shown in Figure 2.3. As a result of governmental immigration and refugee policies, the U.S. population from various national and ethnic groups has been controlled but has become increasingly diverse, in part because of the varied countries of origin of the refugees being admitted.

Refugee students may be coping with the stress of the political unrest in their native countries and time spent in refugee camps. They often do not speak English and feel disconnected from their U.S. schools, which could contribute to poor academic performance and high dropout rates. Educators will need to work with the parents of these students to determine their educational goals for their children and to provide the necessary support (Roxas, 2010).

Figure 2.3 **Home Countries of Refugees and Asylees Entering the United States in 2009.**

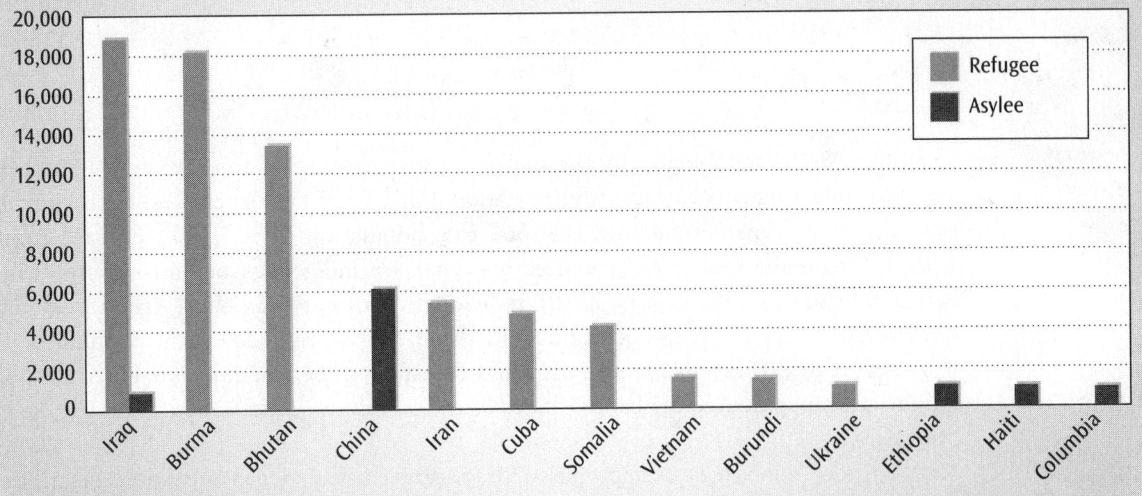

Source: U.S. Census Bureau (2010k). *Statistical abstract of the United States: 2011* (130th ed.). Washington, DC: Author.

EDUCATION OF IMMIGRANTS

The education level of immigrants varies greatly. The percentage of the foreign-born population with bachelor's degrees is nearly equal to the native-born population percentage, 18% and 19%, respectively. Nearly 11% of the foreign-born population have advanced degrees, similar to the case for native-born citizens. At the other end of the scale, 31% of foreign-born adults do not have a high school degree—three times as many as in the native-born population (U.S. Census Bureau, 2010k). Studies of immigrants indicate that those with the social and cultural capital of higher education and higher economic status are more likely to be accepted by the dominant society and allowed to assimilate into the middle class (Portes & Rumbaut, 2001).

Over one of five students in the United Stated has one or more foreign-born parents (U.S. Census Bureau, 2010k). Children of immigrants make up 22% of all children in the United States and are expected to account for one of three children by 2020. The majority of these children are born into Latino (55%) or Asian (16%) families. The southwestern United States is the home of the largest concentration of immigrant children. High concentrations are also found in southern Florida and rural central Washington (Mather, 2009). A key factor in the education success of immigrant children is the level of their parents' education, which of course impacts the economic well being of the family (Mather, 2009).

Parents' ability to speak English well improves their children's chances of academic success (Mather, 2009). One of five students speaks a language other than English at home, but the majority (75%) speak English without difficulty (U.S. Census Bureau, 2010k). English language learners are not performing as well as their white peers on standardized tests in math and reading. Latino immigrant students are more likely to drop out of school than other students, especially if they had limited education in their native countries. Many teachers do not have information or experience that will help them work effectively with immigrant students and foreign-born parents. If the students are lucky, they will attend schools in which the faculty and staff work together to provide them every opportunity possible to achieve academically at high levels.

Ethnicity

The United States is an ethnically and racially diverse nation comprised of nearly 300 **ethnic groups** whose members can identify the national origins of their ancestors. First Americans comprise approximately 1.6% of the total U.S. population (U.S. Census Bureau, 2010b), with 565 federally recognized tribal entities that are **indigenous** or native to the United States (Bureau of Indian Affairs, 2010). Individuals born in Africa, Asia, Australia, Canada, Central America, Europe, Mexico, and South America comprise 12% of the population (U.S. Census Bureau, 2010k). Family members and ancestors of the remaining 86.4% of the population also immigrated to the United States from around the world sometime during the past 500 years.

Many definitions have been proposed for the term *ethnic group*. Some writers describe ethnic identity as one's national origin, religion, and race. Others expand the definition to include gender, class, and lifestyle. The most basic definition focuses on the native country of one's ancestors. Those of us born in the United States belong to one or more ethnic groups, one of them being American. The national origins of our ancestors are reflected in our ethnic identifications such as German American or Chinese American.

A common bond with an ethnic group is developed through family, friends, and neighbors with whom intimate characteristics of living are shared. These are the people invited to baptisms, marriages, funerals, and family reunions. They are the people with whom we feel the most comfortable. They know the meaning of our behavior; they share the same language and nonverbal patterns, traditions, and customs. **Endogamy** (that is, marriage within the group), segregated residential areas, and restriction of activities with the dominant group help preserve ethnic cohesiveness across generations. The ethnic group also allows for the maintenance of group cohesiveness. It helps sustain and enhance the ethnic identity of its members. It establishes the social networks and communicative patterns that are important for the group's optimization of its position in society.

The character of an ethnic group changes over time, becoming different in a number of ways from the culture of the country of origin. Members within ethnic groups may develop different attitudes and behaviors based on their experiences in the United States and the conditions in the country of origin at the time of immigration. Recent immigrants may have little in common

PAUSE TO REFLECT 2.1

Some U.S. citizens trace their roots to the indigenous American Indians; some are first-generation immigrants who were born outside the United States. However, most of the population has lived in the country for generations although their ancestors emigrated from another country.

■ How would you describe your ethnicity? Your race?

■ Do you participate in any ethnic clubs or activities?

■ How assimilated is your family into the dominant culture?

with members of their ethnic group whose ancestors immigrated a century, or even 20 years, before. Ethnic communities undergo constant change in population characteristics, locations, occupations, educational levels, and political and economic struggles, which affects the nature of the group and its members as they become Americans with ethnic roots in another country.

ETHNIC IDENTITY

Developing a healthy and secure ethnic identity helps in developing one's overall identity, providing a sense of belonging, optimism, and self-esteem (Berk, 2012). Among young children, ethnic awareness increases with age. To recognize differences in others, children must be involved in self-identification with these characteristics. By age four they are aware of differences in appearance, language, and names. Soon after, they become aware of religious and cultural distinctions as well (American Academy of Pediatrics, 2011).

One does not have to live in the same community with other members of his or her ethnic group to continue to identify with the group. Many second- and third-generation children have moved from their original ethnic communities, integrating into the suburbs or other urban communities—a move that is easier to accomplish if the person looks white and speaks standard English. Although many Americans are generations removed from immigrant status, some continue to consciously emphasize their ethnicity as a meaningful basis of their identity. They may organize or join ethnic social clubs and organizations to revitalize their identification with their national origin. Such participation is characterized by a nostalgic allegiance to the culture of one's ancestral homeland. As ethnic groups learn English and adopt the cultural behaviors of the dominant group, their ethnicity becomes less distinct and they are less apt to be labeled as ethnic by society, especially if they are white. Their ethnicity becomes voluntary; they can choose to identify with their ethnic group or not.

Ethnic identity is influenced early in life by whether one's family members recognize or promote ethnicity as an important part of their identity. Sometimes, the choice about how ethnic one should be is imposed, particularly for members of oppressed ethnic groups. When the ethnic group believes that a strong and loyal ethnic identity is necessary to maintain group solidarity, the pressure of other members of the group makes it difficult to withdraw from the group. For many members of the group, their ethnic identity provides them with the security of belonging and knowing who they are. Their ethnic identity becomes the primary source of identification, and they feel no need to identify themselves differently. In fact, they may find it emotionally very difficult to sever their primary identification with the group.

The European heritages with which the most U.S. residents identify are German (17%), Irish (12%), English (9%), Italian (6%), Polish (3%), and French (3%) (U.S. Census Bureau, 2010k). Unlike the European groups who emigrated in a wave early in the twentieth century and eventually lost contact with relatives in their

Many individuals and families in the United States maintain ties with their ethnic group by participating in family and cultural traditions.
Jeff Greenberg/PhotoEdit Inc.

Student Conflict Between Family and Peer Values

Wing Tek Lau is a sixth-grade student in a predominantly white and African American Southern community. He and his parents emigrated from Hong Kong four years ago. His uncle was an engineer at a local high-tech company and had encouraged Wing Tek's father to immigrate to this country and open a Chinese restaurant. The restaurant is the only Chinese restaurant in the community, and it was an instant success. Mr. Lau and his family have enjoyed considerable acceptance in both their business and their neighborhood. Wing Tek and his younger sister have also enjoyed academic success at school and appear to be well liked by the other students.

One day when Mrs. Baca, Wing Tek's teacher, called him by name, he announced before the class, "My American name is Kevin. Please, everybody call me Kevin from now on." Mrs. Baca and Wing Tek's classmates honored this request, and Wing Tek was "Kevin" from then on.

Three weeks later, Mr. And Mrs. Lau made an appointment to see Mrs. Baca. When the teacher made reference to "Kevin," Mrs. Lau said, "Who are you talking about? Who is Kevin? We came here to talk about our son, Wing Tek."

"But I thought his American name was Kevin. That's what he asked us to call him," Mrs. Baca replied.

"That child," Mrs. Lau said in disgust, "is a disgrace to our family."

"We have heard his sister call him by that name, but she said it was just a joke," Mr. Lau added. "We came to see you because we are having problems with him in our home. Wing Tek refuses to speak Chinese to us. He argues with us about going to his Chinese lessons on Saturday with the other Chinese students in the community. He says he does not want to eat Chinese food anymore. He says that he is an American now and wants pizza, hamburgers, and tacos. What are you people teaching these children in school? Is there no respect for family, no respect for our cultures?"

Mrs. Baca, an acculturated Mexican American who was raised in East Los Angeles, began to put things together. Wing Tek, in his attempt to ensure his acceptance by his classmates, had chosen to acculturate to an extreme, to the point of rejecting his family heritage. He wanted to be as "American" as anyone else in the class, perhaps more so. Like Wing Tek, Mrs. Baca had acculturated linguistically and in other ways, but she had never given up her Hispanic values. She knew the internal turmoil Wing Tek was experiencing.

| QUESTIONS FOR CLASSROOM DISCUSSION |

- Is Wing Tek wrong in his desire to acculturate?
- Are Mr. and Mrs. Lau wrong in wanting their son to maintain their traditional family values?
- What can Mrs. Baca do to bring about a compromise?
- What can Mrs. Baca do in the classroom to resolve the problem or at least to lessen the problem?

country of origin, the ethnic identity of Latinos is regularly replenished as newcomers from their home countries arrive in their communities with the cultural traditions and native language of their native countries (Jiménez, 2010). Some residents have multiple ancestries, identifying with two or more national origins. They may identify with one ethnic group more than others, or they may view their ethnicity as just American. However, teachers and others with whom students interact may continue to respond to them primarily on the basis of their identifiable ethnicity.

Some families fight the assimilative aspects of schooling that draw children into adopting the dress, language, music, and values of their peers from the dominant culture. Immigrant families, families with origins other than Europe, families who are not Christian, and conservative Christian families may fight **acculturation** and assimilation in an effort to maintain the values, beliefs, and codes of behavior that are important in their cultures.

ACCULTURATION

Many groups that immigrated during the twentieth century have become acculturated, adopting the dominant group's cultural patterns. Continuous firsthand contact with the dominant group usually results in changes to the cultural patterns of either or both groups. The rapidity and extent of the acculturation process depends on several factors, including location and discrimination. If a group is spatially isolated and segregated (whether voluntarily or not) in a rural area, as is the case with many American Indians on reservations, the acculturation process is very slow. Discrimination against members of oppressed groups can make it difficult for them to acculturate when they choose to do so.

The degree of acculturation is determined, in part, by the individuals or families as they decide how closely they want to match the dress, speech, and behavior of members of the dominant group. In the past, members of many groups had little choice if they wanted to share the American dream of success. However, acculturation does not guarantee acceptance by the dominant group. Most members of oppressed groups, especially those of color, have not been permitted to assimilate fully into society even though they have adopted the values and behaviors of the dominant group.

 *Race*

Are racial groups also ethnic groups? In the United States, many people use the two terms interchangeably. Racial groups include many ethnic groups, and ethnic groups may include members of more than one racial group. Race is a concept that was developed by physical anthropologists to describe the physical characteristics of people in the world more than a century ago—a practice that has been discredited. It is not a stable category for organizing and differentiating people. Instead, it is a sociohistorical concept dependent on society's perception that differences exist and that these differences are important. Throughout U.S. history, racial identification has been used by policymakers and much of the population to classify groups of people as inferior or superior to other racial groups, resulting in inequality and discrimination against people of color.

People of Northern and Western European ancestry have traditionally been advantaged in the United States. Until 1952 immigrants had to be white to be eligible for naturalized citizenship. At one time, slaves and American Indians were perceived as so inferior to the dominant group that each individual was counted by the government as only a fraction of a person.

Chinese immigrants in the late nineteenth century were charged an additional tax. When Southern and Eastern Europeans immigrated in the late nineteenth and early twentieth centuries, they were viewed by nativists as members of an inferior race. However, these Europeans were eligible for citizenship because they were white; those from most other continents were not eligible. Arab American immigrants, for example, needed a court ruling that they were white before they could become citizens.

In 1916 Madison Grant's *The Passing of the Great Race* detailed the U.S. racist ideology. Northern and Western Europeans of the **Nordic race** were identified as the political and military geniuses of the world. Protecting the purity of the Nordic race became such a popular and emotional issue that laws were passed to severely limit immigration from any region except Northern European countries. **Miscegenation** laws in many states prevented the marriage of whites to members of other races until the U.S. Supreme Court declared those laws unconstitutional in 1967.

Nativism reappeared in the 1990s in resolutions, referenda, and legislation in a number of states to deny education to unauthorized immigrants, restrict communication to the English language, and limit prenatal care and preschool services that were available to low-income families, who are disproportionately of color. As the nation continues to become more racially and ethnically diverse, nativists call for control of immigration. They worry that the heritage and power of European Americans is being diminished as the population becomes less white.

IDENTIFICATION OF RACE

When race identification became codified in this country, it was acceptable, and even necessary at times, to identify oneself by race. This allows tracking of the participation of groups in schools, colleges, and professional fields to determine the extent of discriminatory outcomes. Federal forms and reports classify the population on the basis of a mixture of racial and pan-ethnic categorizations as shown in Figure 2.4.

A problem with identifying the U.S. population by such broad categories is that they reveal little about the people in these groups. Whether a person was born in the United States or is an immigrant may have significance in terms of how he or she identifies himself or herself. Pan-ethnic classifications impose boundaries that do not always reflect how group members see themselves, as My Lien Nguyen indicated in the quote at the beginning of this chapter. Some students rebel against having to identify themselves in this way and refuse to select a pan-ethnic identity. Puerto Ricans and other Latinos do not generally identify themselves by race, even though the U.S. Census asks Hispanics to identify their race. Their group identity within the United States is primarily connected to their native Spanish language and culture.

Although non-Latino whites are numerically dominant in the United States, they belong to many different ethnic groups. Neither the ethnic identification nor the actual racial heritage of African Americans—which may be a mixture of African, European, American Indian, and other groups—is recognized. Latinos represent different racial groups and mixtures of racial groups, as well as distinct ethnic groups whose members identify themselves as Mexican Americans, Puerto Ricans, Spanish Americans, and Cuban Americans. This category also includes those with roots in numerous Central and South American countries.

The pan-ethnic classification of Asian and Pacific Islander Americans includes individuals whose families have been here for generations and those who are first-generation immigrants. Many have little in common other than that their countries of origin are from the same continent. Asian Americans are immigrants from Bangladesh, Bhutan, Borneo, Burma, Cambodia,

Figure 2.4 Pan-Ethnic and Racial Composition of the United States in 2010.

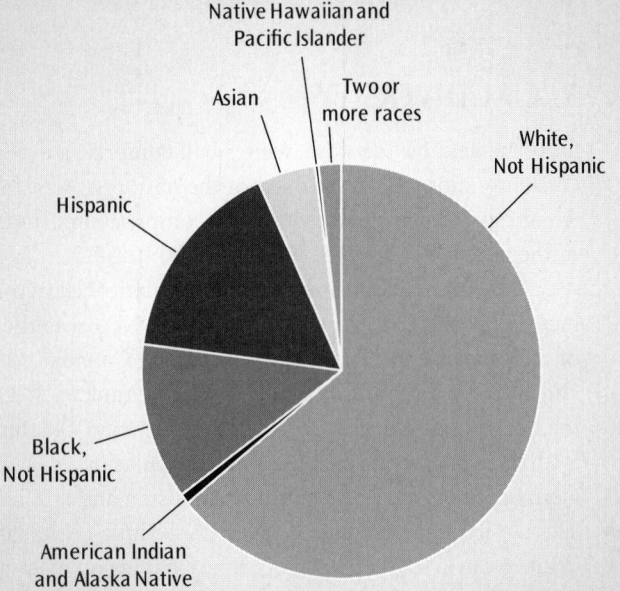

Source: Humes, K. R., Jones, N. A., & Ramirez, R. R. (2011, March). *Overview of race and Hispanic origin: 2010* (2010 Census Briefs). Washington, DC: U.S. Census Bureau.

Chamorro, China, East India, Philippines, Indonesia, Japan, Korea, Laos, Okinawa, Samoa, Sikkim, Singapore, Sri Lanka, Thailand, Vietnam, and other Asian countries.

African Americans have become a single pan-ethnic group because of a common history, language, economic life, and culture developed over centuries of living in the United States. They are a cohesive group, in part, because of the continuing discrimination they experience in the way of racial profiling by police and others, segregated schools and housing, and discriminatory treatment as shoppers, diners, and employees. Just because an individual appears to be African American is not an indication that the person always identifies himself or herself as African American. Some identify themselves as black, others with a specific ethnic group—for example, Puerto Rican or Somali or West Indian. Africans who are recent immigrants may identify themselves ethnically by their nation or tribe of origin, and may not see themselves as members of the long-established African American ethnic group.

The number of people with multiracial backgrounds is growing, with 1.5% of the population claiming "two or more races" in 2009 (U.S. Census Bureau, 2010k). The belief in the racial superiority of whites is reflected in cases of mixed racial heritage. Individuals of black and white parentage are often classified as black, not white; those of Japanese and white heritage usually are classified as Asian American.

Many whites see themselves as raceless. They believe they are the norm, against which everyone else is "other." They can allow their ethnicity to disappear because they do not see it as determinant of their life chances, especially after their family has been in the United States for a few generations. They often deny that racial inequality has any impact on their ability to achieve, believing that their social and economic conditions are based solely on their own individual achievement. They seldom acknowledge that white oppression of people of color around the world has contributed to the subordinate status of those groups. Most whites are unable to acknowledge that they are privileged in our social, political, and economic systems. The study of whiteness exposes the privilege and power it bestows on its members in the maintenance of an inequitable system (Leonardo, 2009; McIntosh, 2010).

RACIAL DIVERSITY

Over the next few decades, whites will comprise a declining proportion of the U.S. population. Currently more than one-third of the nation is African American, Latino, Asian American, or American Indian. These groups will comprise almost 40% of the population by 2020 and 50% of the population by 2042 (Mather, 2009).

Two factors contribute to the population growth of people of color. Of the 2.6 million increase in the U.S. population in 2009, 32% was the result of immigration. Less than 10% of the immigrants came from Europe and Canada; 40% were from Asia, 13% from Mexico, and 13% from the Caribbean (Monger & Yankay, 2011). The second factor is the birthrate. In the baby boom years of 1946 to 1964, the total U.S. fertility rate was 2.9 children per woman, leading to an overall increase in the population. Today that rate is 2.0, as compared to 1.3 in Germany and Japan and 5.7 in Afghanistan and Guinea (Population Reference Bureau, 2010). The differential rate among racial and ethnic groups contributes to distinct growth patterns. White women in the United States are having an average of 2.1 children, Asian Americans and Pacific Islanders 2.0, American Indians and Alaska Natives 1.8, African Americans 2.2, and Latinos 3.0 (U.S. Census Bureau, 2010k).

At the beginning of the twenty-first century, Latinos replaced African Americans as the largest non-European group in the United States. Figure 2.5 shows how the diversity of school-age children and youth has changed over the past 20 years. The majority of the population in

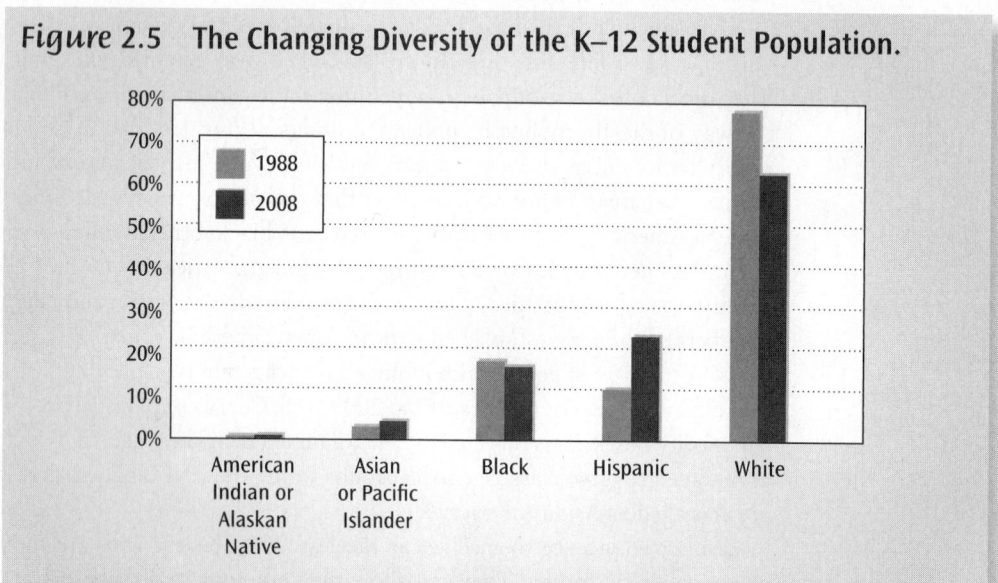

Figure 2.5   The Changing Diversity of the K–12 Student Population.

Source: Aud, S., Hussar, W., Planty, M., Snyder, T., Bianco, K., Fox, M., Frohlich, L., Kemp, J., & Drake, L. (2010). *The condition of education 2010* (NCES 2010-028). Washington, DC: National Center for Education Statistics, Institute of Education Sciences, U.S. Department of Education.

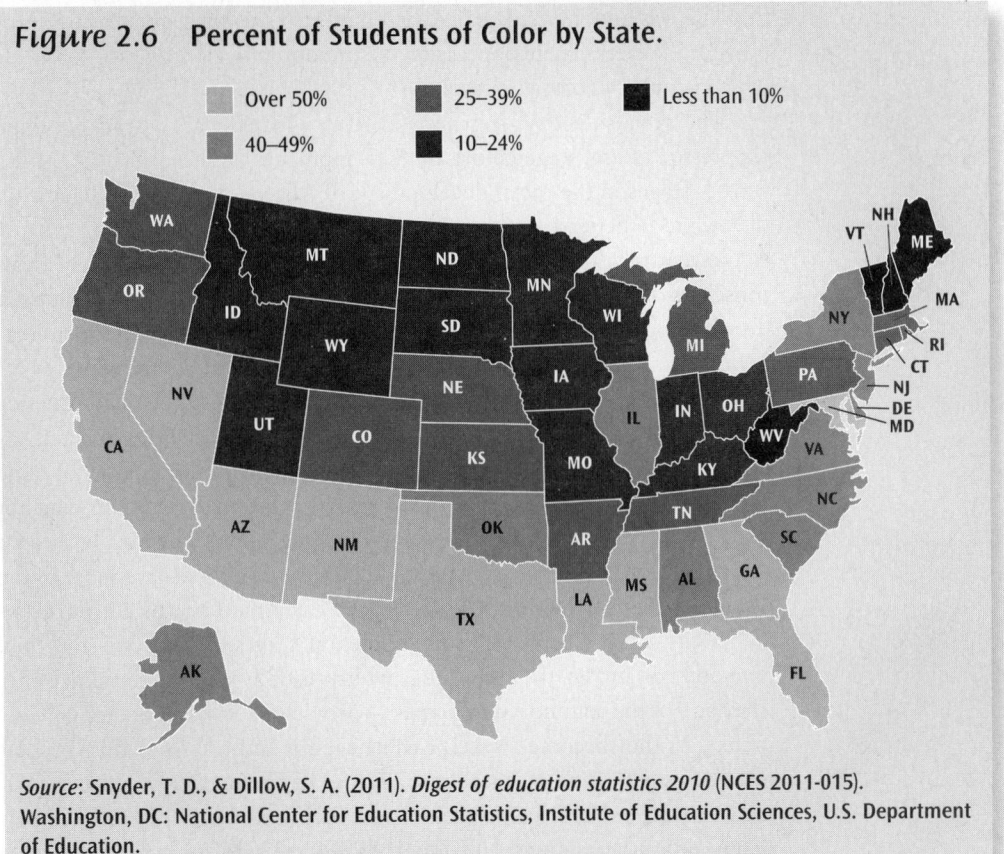

Figure 2.6 Percent of Students of Color by State.

Over 50%   25–39%   Less than 10%

40–49%   10–24%

Source: Snyder, T. D., & Dillow, S. A. (2011). *Digest of education statistics 2010* (NCES 2011-015). Washington, DC: National Center for Education Statistics, Institute of Education Sciences, U.S. Department of Education.

many urban schools is already comprised of students of color, and diversity is growing in many rural areas of the Midwest and the South. White students are projected to represent less than half of the student population by 2023 (Mather, 2009). These demographics obviously will have a profound impact on schools throughout the United States.

Some states and areas of the country are much more diverse than others; for example, the west has the largest concentration (57%) of students of color, the Midwest the lowest (29%). Students of color now comprise over half of the student population in 11 states and the District of Columbia, as shown in Figure 2.6. The highest concentration of African American students is in the South (24%); Latinos are more concentrated in the West, comprising 40% of the student population (Aud et al., 2010).

RACIAL IDENTITY

Racial identity is influenced by one's family and by the people in newspapers, on television, and in movies who share one's identity. How racial groups are stereotyped influences the interactions among members of different racial groups. If a group is seen as aggressive and violent, the reaction of the second group may be fear and protective action. The construct of whiteness by many students of color may be based on a distrust of whites that has grown out of their own or their communities' lived experiences. Unlike most whites, people of color see the privilege of whiteness and, in many cases, have suffered the consequences of their lack of privilege and power in society. Their oppression by the dominant group is often a unifying theme around which people of color coalesce.

The racial identity of groups evolves with education and life experiences, but may be suppressed at any stage before full development. Psychologist William E. Cross (1992) identified six stages in the racial development of African Americans. Black children develop a belief that white is better based on their knowledge of and interaction with the dominant culture. Adolescent youth often experience an event that makes them acutely aware of racism and more conscious of the significance of race in society. During this period, they may be angry about the stereotyping and racism they are experiencing or seeing others experience. Acceptance by their African American peers becomes very important, and **acting white** or hanging with whites is frowned upon. In young adulthood—often in college—an African American develops a "strong desire to surround oneself with symbols of one's racial identity, and actively seek out opportunities to learn about one's own history and culture, with the support of same-race peers" (Tatum, 2003, p. 76). The next stage of development is internalization, in which individuals are secure in their own race and able to develop meaningful relationships with whites who respect their racial identity. In the last stage individuals have a very positive sense of their racial identity and develop a commitment to the issues of African Americans as a group.

Whites also go through developmental stages as they develop their racial identity and abandon racism. At the beginning, whites usually do not recognize the significance of race. They accept the common **stereotypes** of people of color and do not believe that racism pervades society. As they become aware of white racism and privilege, they become uncomfortable and feel guilt, shame, and anger about racism. They begin to recognize that they are prejudiced. In the next stage, they become silent about racism and are frustrated at being labeled a member of a group rather than an individual. As they become more aware of institutional racism, they begin to unlearn their own racism. In this stage they are often self-conscious and feel guilty about their whiteness. The development of a positive white identity allows them to move beyond the role of the victimizer, causing their feelings of guilt and shame to subside. In the last stage, they become an ally to people of color and are able to confront institutional racism and work toward its elimination (Helms, 1990; Tatum, 2009).

Elementary and secondary students will be at various stages in the development of racial identity. They may be angry, feel guilty, be ethnocentric, or be defensive—behaviors and feelings that may erupt in class, as Denise Williams found in the vignette that opened this chapter. Educators must remember that students of color face societal constraints and restrictions that seldom affect white students. Such recognition is essential in the development of instructional programs and schools to effectively serve diverse populations who do not yet share equally in the benefits that education offers.

The Struggle for Civil Rights

Members of oppressed groups sometimes coalesce to fight against the harsh economic and political realities and injustices imposed on them. These movements for democratic rights and economic justice invariably bolster community solidarity based on race or national origins. The fight for civil rights has led to the reduction of the overt discrimination and exclusion that has kept many citizens from having access to the basic necessities and benefits of society. The events that initiated these changes in schools and broader society are outlined in this section.

THE CIVIL RIGHTS MOVEMENT

The fight for civil rights by ethnic and racial groups has a long history in the United States. Native Americans fought to maintain their rights, culture, languages, and lands as foreigners appropriated their homelands. African slaves revolted against their owners. Free blacks decried the discrimination and violence they faced in the North. Martin Delaney led a black nationalist movement in the mid-1800s for black liberation. In the early twentieth century Mexican American miners in Arizona led a strike for better working conditions and pay equal to that of European American miners. Across the Southwest, Mexican Americans established ethnic organizations to fight exploitation and support those who were in dire straits. Chinese and other immigrants used the courts to overturn the 1790 Naturalization Act, which excluded them from citizenship (Takaki, 1993).

Although individuals and groups continued to push the government for civil rights throughout the twentieth century, the movement exploded in the 1950s and 1960s when large numbers of African Americans in the South challenged their oppressed status. Rosa Parks defied authorities in 1955 when she sat in the whites-only section at the front of the bus in Montgomery, Alabama, sparking a boycott of the public transportation system for over a year and leading to the desegregation of the transportation system. Beginning in 1960, students from North Carolina A&T University and other historically black colleges sat at lunch counters designated for whites only, challenging **Jim Crow laws** that forced whites and people of color to use different public accommodations such as water fountains, restrooms, hotels, and restaurants. The Congress of Racial Equality (CORE), the Student Nonviolent Coordinating Committee (SNCC), and the Black Panthers Party organized young people to fight the injustices African Americans faced daily.

Under the leadership of Fannie Lou Hamer, African American Democrats from Mississippi challenged the seating of the all-white delegation at the 1964 Democratic National Convention. Although the African American delegates were not seated, their courage led to the seating of a growing number of ethnically and racially diverse delegates in the years that followed. Facing arrest and beatings, the racially mixed Freedom Riders boarded buses to break the segregation pattern in interstate travel. African Americans, sometimes joined by European Americans, marched for freedom and established Freedom Schools across the South to teach leadership and social activism. The March on Washington in 1963, in which Martin Luther King, Jr. made his famous "I Have a Dream" speech, inspired African Americans to continue the fight for their civil rights. But the violence against them continued. Less than a month after the March on Washington, four girls were killed when a bomb exploded in the basement of their black church in Montgomery, Alabama. Congress finally responded by passing the 1964 Civil Rights Act and the 1965 Voting Rights Act, which banned discrimination in schools, employment, and public accommodations and secured the voting rights of African Americans.

The call for "Black Power" brought attention to the history and contributions of African Americans to society. Black studies and other ethnic studies programs were established in colleges and universities. Educators and textbook publishers were pushed to rewrite books to accurately reflect the multiethnic history of the United States. Yet societal changes did not necessarily follow. Although legislation guaranteed equality for all racial groups, many European Americans continued to fight against the desegregation of schools and other public facilities. Frustration with the dominant group's efforts to impede of progress led African Americans and members of other oppressed groups to identify even more strongly with other members of their ethnic group to fight discrimination and inequality with a unified voice. These struggles continue today, not only in this country but throughout the world.

BROWN V. BOARD OF EDUCATION

Schools have long been at the center of the civil rights movements. At one time children of color were not allowed to attend school. Later they were not allowed to attend schools with white children, leading to a system of desegregated schools in which students of color were delegated to schools without the books and resources to which most white children had access. Desegregation continued in many states until more than a decade after the Supreme Court unanimously declared that separate but equal schooling was not equal in its *Brown v. Board of Education* (1954) decision.

The 1954 decision was the result of four cases before the Supreme Court: *Briggs v. Elliott* in South Carolina, *Davis v. County School Board of Prince Edward County* in Virginia, *Gebhart v. Belton* in Delaware, and *Brown v. Board of Education of Topeka* in Kansas. These cases were addressed together in the 1954 decision of *Brown v. Board of Education*. A fifth case, *Bolling v. Sharpe,* settled a year later, declared that the federal government could not segregate schools in the District of Columbia. The Supreme Court returned to the implementation of *Brown v. Board of Education* in 1955 when it sent all school integration cases back to the lower courts and asked states to desegregate "with all deliberate speed." Later courts called for the desegregation of metropolitan areas, busing students across city lines to ensure integration.

Many segregated school districts and universities took years to integrate their schools. The fierce resistance of many whites in many communities required the use of the National Guard to protect African American students who were entering white schools for the first time. Many whites established private schools or moved to the suburbs, where the population was primarily European American, to avoid sending their children to schools with African American children. Some communities, such as Farmville, Virginia, closed their public schools rather than

The National Guard was required to protect African American students as they desegregated schools in many communities during the 1960s.
© Howard Sochurek/Time & Life Pictures/Getty Images

desegregate them. As public schools became desegregated, many African American teachers and principals lost their jobs. The composition of schools did change in the three decades following the *Brown* decision. In the mid-1960s only 2% of the African American students in the United States attended integrated schools as compared to 37% in the 1980s (Mickelson & Smith, 2010).

Other ethnic groups also used the courts to demand an equitable education for their children. In *Gong Lum v. Rice* in Mississippi in 1927, a Chinese American girl sought the right to attend a white school by arguing that she was not black. The court ruled she was not white, giving the school the authority to determine the racial makeup of their students. A Mexican American student was allowed to attend an integrated school in California in the 1940s as a result of *Mendez v. Westminster*. In 1974 Chinese American students in San Francisco won the right to have their first language used in instruction in *Lau v. Nichols*. The *Brown* decision also served as the precursor for federal laws that supported educational equity for girls and women in Title IX, passed in 1972, and people with disabilities in Section 504 of the Rehabilitation Act of 1973.

POST-*BROWN* TURNAROUND

By the mid-1980s courts had begun lifting the federal sanctions that had forced schools to desegregate, stating that the federal requirements were meant to be temporary to overcome **de jure segregation**. Now that schools were no longer segregated by race, the easing of sanctions allowed school districts to return students to neighborhood schools. Because of **de facto segregation** in communities, the students in many neighborhood schools were overwhelmingly of the same race, returning the status of integration to pre-1970 levels. At the beginning of the twenty-first century, the Civil Rights Project at Harvard University reported that 29% of African American students attended schools in neighborhoods with high poverty, limited resources, social strife, and few, if any, white students. Eighty-six percent of white students attended public schools with limited diversity. Latino students were the most likely to be in segregated schools while Asian American students were most likely to be in integrated schools (Orfield, 2010).

The use of race and ethnicity by a public school or university to promote diversity of its student population was considered by the Supreme Court in *Grutter v. Bollinger* (2003). The court endorsed the arguments of the University of Michigan Law School that it had used race in its admissions policies to increase integration and the need for a diverse workforce. Race was one of a number of factors considered by the school's admission committee. On the same day, the court ruled against the University of Michigan College of Arts and Sciences, which gave bonus points to applicants from specific groups of color.

In 2007 the Supreme Court ruled by a vote of 5 to 4 against programs in Seattle and Louisville that used race in assigning students to schools. The court did not find that either school district could relate its preferred level of diversity in a school to related educational benefits. Chief Justice John G. Roberts wrote that "racial balance is not to be achieved for its own sake" (*Parents Involved in Community Schools v. Seattle School District #1*, 2007). Many educators and commentators claim that the two 2007 Supreme Court rulings against using race to determine where students attend schools have essentially halted the integration of schools. Others see them as "returning to the principle of nondiscrimination" (Wolters, 2008, p. 305) and moving away from the courts' trend of requiring a desired racial mix in schools. The milestones in the desegregation and resegregation of schools are chronicled in Table 2.1.

The goal of desegregation has changed from the physical integration of students within a school building to the achievement of equal learning opportunities and outcomes for all students. Court cases today are examining the unequal access of students of color to qualified teachers, advanced mathematics and science classes, gifted classes, and adequately funded

Table 2.1   Milestones in Desegregating and Resegregating Schools

1896	The Supreme Court authorizes segregation in *Plessy v. Ferguson,* finding Louisiana's "separate but equal" law constitutional.
1940	A federal court requires equal salaries for African American and white teachers in *Alston v. School Board of City of Norfolk.*
1947	In a precursor to the *Brown* case, a federal appeals court strikes down segregated schooling for Mexican American and white students in *Westminster School Dist. v. Méndez.* The verdict prompts California Governor Earl Warren to repeal a state law calling for segregation of Native American and Asian American students.
1950	Barbara Johns, a 16-year-old junior at Robert R. Moton High School in Farmville, VA, organizes and leads 450 students in an anti–school segregation strike.
1954	In a unanimous opinion, the Supreme Court in *Brown v. Board of Education* overturns *Plessy* and declares that separate schools are "inherently unequal."
1955	The Supreme Court rules that the federal government is under the same duty as the states and must desegregate the Washington, DC, schools in B*olling v. Sharpe.* In *Brown II,* the Supreme Court orders the lower federal courts to require desegregation "with all deliberate speed."
1956	Tennessee Governor Frank Clement calls in the National Guard after white mobs attempt to block the desegregation of a high school. The Virginia legislature calls for "massive resistance" to school desegregation and pledges to close schools under desegregation orders.
1957	More than 1,000 paratroopers from the 101st Airborne Division and a federalized Arkansas National Guard protect nine African American students integrating Central High School in Little Rock, AR.
1958	The Supreme Court rules that fear of social unrest or violence, whether real or constructed by those wishing to oppose integration, does not excuse state governments from complying with *Brown* in *Cooper v. Aaron.* Ten thousand young people march in Washington, DC, in support of integration.
1959	Officials close public schools in Prince Edward County, VA, rather than integrate them. Twenty-five thousand young people march in Washington, DC, in support of integration.
1960	In New Orleans, federal marshals shield 6-year-old Ruby Bridges from an angry crowd as she attempts to enroll in school.
1964	The Civil Rights Act of 1964 is adopted. Title IV of the Act authorizes the federal government to file school desegregation cases. Title VI of the Act prohibits discrimination in programs and activities, including schools, receiving federal financial assistance. The Supreme Court orders Prince Edward Country, VA, to reopen its schools on a desegregated basis.
1965	In *Green v. County School Board of New Kent County,* the Supreme Court orders states to dismantle segregated school systems "root and branch." The Court identifies five factors—facilities, staff, faculty, extracurricular activities, and transportation—to be used to gauge a school system's compliance with the mandate of *Brown.*
1969	The Supreme Court declares the "all deliberate speed" standard no longer constitutionally permissible and orders the immediate desegregation of Mississippi schools in *Alexander v. Holmes County Board of Education*.
1971	The Court approves busing, magnet schools, compensatory education, and other tools as appropriate remedies to overcome the role of residential segregation in perpetuating racially segregated schools in *Swann v. Charlotte-Mecklenburg Board of Education.*

1972	The Supreme Court refuses to allow public school systems to avoid desegregation by creating new, mostly or all-white "splinter districts" in *Wright v. Council of the City of Emporia* and *United States v. Scotland Neck City Board of Education.*
1973	The Supreme Court rules that states cannot provide textbooks to racially segregated private schools to avoid integration mandates in *Norwood v. Harrison.*
	The Supreme Court finds that the Denver school board intentionally segregated Mexican American and African American students from white students in *Keyes v. Denver School District No. 1.* The Supreme Court rules that education is not a "fundamental right" and that the Constitution does not require equal education expenditures within a state in *San Antonio Independent School District v. Rodriguez.*
1974	The Supreme Court blocks metropolitan-wide desegregation plans as a means to desegregate urban schools with large minority populations in *Milliken v. Bradley.* The Supreme Court rules that the failure to provide instruction to those with limited English proficiency violates Title VI's prohibition of national origin, race, or color discrimination in school districts receiving federal funds in *Lau v. Nichols.*
1978	A fractured Supreme Court declares the affirmative action admissions program for the University of California Davis Medical School unconstitutional because it sets aside a specific number of seats for African American and Latino students. The Court rules that race can be a factor in university admissions, but it cannot be the deciding factor in *Regents of the University of California v. Bakke.*
1982	The Supreme Court rejects tax exemptions for private religious schools that discriminate in *Bob Jones University v. U.S.* and *Goldsboro Christian Schools v. U.S.*
1986	For the first time, a federal court finds that once a school district meets the Green factors, it can be released from its desegregation plan and returned to local control in *Riddick v. School Board of the City of Norfolk, Virginia.*
1991	Emphasizing that court orders are not intended "to operate in perpetuity," the Supreme Court makes it easier for formerly segregated school systems to fulfill their obligations under desegregation decrees in *Board of Education of Oklahoma City v. Dowell.*
1992	In *Freeman v. Pitts* the Supreme Court further speeds the end of desegregation cases, ruling that school systems can fulfill their obligations in an incremental fashion.
1995	The Supreme Court sets a new goal for desegregation plans in *Missouri v. Jenkins*: the return of schools to local control.
1996	A federal appeals court prohibits the use of race in college and university admissions, ending affirmative action in Louisiana, Texas, and Mississippi in *Hopwood v. Texas.*
2001	White parents in Charlotte, N.C., schools successfully seek an end to the desegregation process, barring the use of race in making student assignments.
2003	The Supreme Court upholds diversity as a rationale for affirmative action programs in higher education admissions, but concludes that point systems are not appropriate in *Gratz v. Bollinger* and *Grutter v. Bollinger.* A federal district court case affirms the value of racial diversity and race-conscious student assignment plans in K–12 education in *Lynn v. Comfort.*
2007	The more conservative Supreme Court strikes down the use of race in determining schools for students in *Parents Involved in Community Schools Inc. v. Seattle School District* and *Meredith v. Jefferson County (Ky.) Board of Education.*

schools. Civil rights groups are asking why students of color are disproportionately represented in nonacademic and special education classes and why the rates for school suspension and dropping out vary among different ethnic groups. As schools become segregated again, educators have a greater responsibility for ensuring that all students learn regardless of the ethnic and racial composition of the school. Teachers will also have the responsibility for helping students understand that the world in which they are likely to work is multiethnic and multiracial, unlike the school they may be attending.

Racial and Ethnic Discrimination

A crucial fact in understanding racism is that many whites see themselves as better than people and groups of color, and as a result exercise their power to prevent people of color from securing the prestige, power, and privilege held by them. Many members of the dominant group do not acknowledge the existence of external impingements that make it much more difficult for people of color to shed their subordinate status than it was for their own European ancestors. They ignore the fact that some people of color have adopted the cultural values and standards of the dominant group to a greater degree than many white ethnic groups. Yet discriminatory policies and practices prevent them from sharing equally with whites in society's benefits. In addition, the opportunities to gain qualifications with which people of color could compete equally with whites have been severely restricted throughout most of U.S. history.

Many whites declare they are not racist. They listen to rap music, dress like black urban youth, and respect African American athletes. They argue that they have never discriminated against a person of color and that they cannot be blamed for events of 40 or 200 years ago. They take no responsibility for society's racism.

INTERGROUP RELATIONS

Interethnic and interracial conflict is certainly not new in the United States, although the intensity of such conflicts has been mild compared to that in many other nations. Oppressed people in this country have a history of resistance, however, as shown by riots after particularly egregious actions of police and strikes by workers. Conflicts between American Indians and whites were common in the European American attempt to subjugate the native peoples.

What are the reasons for continued interethnic conflict? Discriminatory practices have protected the superior status of the dominant group for centuries. When other ethnic groups try to participate more equitably in the rewards and privileges of society, the dominant group must concede some of its advantages. As long as one ethnic or racial group has an institutional advantage over others, some intergroup conflict will occur.

Competition for economic resources can also contribute to intergroup conflict. As economic conditions become tighter, fewer jobs become available. Discriminatory practices in the past have forced people of color into positions with the least seniority. When jobs are cut back, disproportionately high numbers of people of color are laid off. The tension between ethnic groups increases as members of specific groups determine that they disproportionately suffer the hardships resulting from economic depression. Conflict sometimes occurs between oppressed groups when they are forced to share limited societal resources, such as affordable housing and access to quality education programs.

A part of the problem is that whites have little or no experience with being the victims of discrimination and are less likely than other groups to believe that members of other racial groups are discriminated against. In a Gallup poll, 78% of African Americans thought that racism against blacks is widespread in the United States, as compared with 51% of whites and 59% of Latinos (Jones, 2008). Areas in which respondents thought that racial discrimination was a major or minor factor included imprisonment rates (79%), income levels (78%), education levels (72%), and life expectancy (66%). Immediately after the election of the first African American president, Barack Obama, in 2008, 70% of the population thought race relations would improve. A year after the election, 41% thought that race relations had improved, but 61% still believed that they would improve in the future because of Obama's presidency (Saad, 2009). Neither whites nor blacks are overly optimistic about dramatic improvement of race relations; 38% of whites and Latinos and 55% of African Americans believe that race relations will always be a problem (Gallup, 2011).

Whites, blacks, and Latinos have different perceptions of how people of color are treated in society. More than three of five African Americans are dissatisfied with how they are treated; over half of Latinos are dissatisfied with how they are treated. Most whites think that they and people of color have equal job opportunities, but the majority of Latinos and African Americans disagree. Less than half of African Americans believe that their children have as good a chance as white children to receive a good education (Gallup, 2011). When white teachers are unable to acknowledge the discrimination that groups of color know from experience, building trust with students and their families will be more difficult.

During the past 50 years, educational strategies have been developed to reduce and overcome intergroup conflicts. These strategies have focused on training teachers to be effective in intergroup or human relations; on attempting to change the prejudicial attitudes of teachers; on fighting institutional discrimination through affirmative action and civil rights legislation; on encouraging changes in textbooks and other resources to more accurately reflect the multiethnic nature of society; and on attempting to eliminate discriminatory behavior from classroom interactions and classroom practices. All of these strategies are important to combat prejudice and discrimination in the educational setting. Alone or in combination, the strategies are not enough, but that does not diminish the need for professional educators to further develop the strategies. This is not an admission of failure, but a recognition that prejudice, discrimination, and racism are diseases that infect all of society.

HATE GROUPS

White privilege is sometimes taken to the extreme as members try to protect their power by preaching hate against other groups. Since World War II, overt acts of prejudice have decreased dramatically. In the early 1940s, the majority of whites supported segregation of and discrimination against blacks. Today, most whites support policies against racial discrimination and prejudice.

Nevertheless, intolerance of other groups and violence against them continues. The Federal Bureau of Investigation (FBI) defines a hate crime as "a criminal offense committed against a person, property, or society that is motivated, in whole or in part, by the offender's bias against a race, religion, disability, sexual orientation, or ethnicity/national origin" (FBI, 2010). A decade after it was first proposed, Congress passed a federal law in 2009 to protect the population against hate crimes.

Law enforcement agencies reported nearly 7,000 hate crimes in 2008 (National Institute of Justice, 2010). However, many victims do not report hate crimes out of fear of retaliation or the belief that nothing will be done, and an FBI report estimated from victim interviews that approximately 191,000 hate crime incidents occur annually (Harlow, 2005).

While freedom of speech, guaranteed by the First Amendment, is one of the most cherished values in the country, it is also one of the variables contributing to the proliferation of hate groups. The Southern Poverty Law Center reported that hate group chapters in the United States have grown to 1,002, with the majority located east of the Mississippi River (Potok, 2011). These groups include nativist vigilantes who patrol the border with Mexico; antigovernment "patriot" groups; and neo-Nazis, white supremacists, and Aryan groups. Each individual's freedom of speech is guaranteed, and this includes those who express messages of hate in their speeches, in their writings, and now on the Internet.

Recruitment efforts by hate groups often target areas of the country that have experienced economic and racial change, such as factory layoffs or increased diversity in a school as a result of desegregation. Some recruits may be angry about economic conditions that have led to the loss of jobs in their communities. Rather than blaming the corporations, which may be economizing and moving jobs to sources of cheaper labor, they blame African Americans, women, Arabs, Jews, or the government. Hate group organizers convince new recruits that it is members of other groups who are taking their jobs and being pandered to by government programs. A student contact in a school can provide information about any anger in students that might make the school a potential site for recruitment.

Some hate groups have developed sophisticated websites (Potok, 2011) with links intended primarily for school-age youngsters, perhaps featuring cartoons or crossword puzzles for children, all containing a message of hate. Because so many children have become proficient in the use of computers and in surfing the web, it has become imperative for parents and educators to be able to recognize online hate and to minimize the risks to their children and students.

PAUSE TO REFLECT 2.2

Hate groups exist in a number of communities, and schools and colleges can be recruiting grounds for members. Respond to the following questions about conditions in your community that might contribute to recruitment efforts.

	Very	Somewhat	Not at All
1. How prevalent do you think racism is in your college?	☐	☐	☐
2. How prevalent do you think racism is in your home community?	☐	☐	☐
3. How likely is it that a hate group would be established in your home community?	☐	☐	☐

Software that will block or filter hate group websites is available through Internet service providers and software dealers.

Affirming Race and Ethnicity in Classrooms

Race and ethnicity can have a significant impact on how educators perceive students and their behavior and performance in school. Because the cultural background and experiences of teachers may be incongruous with the cultural experiences of students, miscommunication and misperceptions may interfere with learning. Teachers themselves may stereotype students who have a racial or ethnic background different from their own. The majority of teachers are white females who are charged with teaching classes in which the majority of students are students of color. Therefore, it is critical that white teachers become aware of the cultures and experiences of the students in the schools to which they are assigned.

This incongruity may contribute to student perceptions that their cultures and experiences are not reflected or respected in school. More students of color than white students are not actively engaged in their schoolwork, too often dropping out of school, in part because they don't see the payoff from education. Only 82% of 18- to 21-year-olds are high school graduates (U.S. Census Bureau, 2010k). The percentage of students who actually graduate from high school on schedule (i.e., four years after they enter high school) is much lower, ranging from 59% to 62% for American Indians, African Americans, and Latinos, compared to 81% and 89% for European and Asian Americans, respectively (Education Trust, 2009).

ACKNOWLEDGING RACE AND ETHNICITY IN SCHOOLS

Teachers often declare that they are color-blind—that they look past a student's color and treat all students equally regardless of race. The problem is that **color blindness** helps maintain white privilege because it does not recognize the existence of racial inequality in schools (Gallagher, 2010). Teachers do not usually confront issues of race in schools and classrooms, in part because race is not supposed to matter. Teachers' discomfort becomes intertwined with their own uncertainties about race and their possible complicity in maintaining racial inequities.

Race and ethnicity do matter to many students and their families, and do have an impact on communications and interactions with teachers. Students of color are reminded by others of their race almost daily as they face discriminatory practices and attitudes. Rather than pretending that race and ethnicity do not exist, teachers should acknowledge the differences and be aware of ways they can influence learning. Equity does not mean sameness; students can be treated differently, as long as the treatment is fair and appropriate, to accomplish the goal of student learning.

The ethnic communities to which students belong provide the real-life examples teachers should draw on to teach. Knowing students' ethnic and cultural experiences and how subject matter interacts with students' realities are important in designing effective strategies to engage students in learning. Successful teachers ensure that students learn the academic skills needed to compete effectively in the dominant workplace. In the process they acknowledge and respect the ethnicity of their students and the community in which the school is located to prevent students from becoming alienated from their homes, their community, and their culture. A disproportionally large number of students of color are not learning what is needed to perform at acceptable levels on standardized tests. In fact, the achievement of many students of color decreases the longer they stay in school. Educators should do everything possible to ensure that students are achieving academically at grade level or above.

CONFRONTING RACISM IN CLASSROOMS

A first step in confronting racism in schools is to realize that racism exists and that, if teachers are white, they have benefited from it. This is not an easy process, as discussed in the section on racial identity. We often resist discussions of race and racism because we must eventually confront our own feelings and beliefs. Once teachers believe that discrimination exists in society and the school, they are more likely to believe students of color when they report incidents of racism or discrimination. They stop making excuses for the perpetrators or explaining that the action of the perpetrator was not really racist.

Some white students may resist discussions about race and racism, but it is more likely that teachers are the participants who are most uncomfortable with broaching the topic (Singleton & Hays, 2008). Whites are sometimes reluctant to participate in these discussions because they are afraid of offending someone, they worry about becoming angry, or they do not want to be labeled as racist.

Many teachers feel uncomfortable handling students' resistance to the topic of race, in part because they are not confident of their own stance on race. Because students are at different levels in their own racial identity, many of them cannot address these issues as rationally as the teacher might desire. Some will personalize the discussion. Some will be emotional or confrontational. Others will be uncomfortable or silent. Just because the topic is difficult to address does not mean it should be ignored. Teachers should break the silence about race and develop the courage to work at eliminating racism in their own classrooms and schools. One step is to help students think critically about race and social justice for all students.

Teachers should not ignore the racism that is inherent in the policies and practices of their schools. They should intervene when students call each other names that are racist. Students should be helped to understand that racist language and behavior are unacceptable and will not be tolerated in schools. When students use derogatory terms for ethnic group members or tell ethnic jokes, teachers should use the opportunity to discuss attitudes about those groups. Students should not be allowed to express their hostility to members of other groups without being confronted. When teachers allow students to treat others with disrespect, they become partners in the perpetuation of racism. These overt acts can be confronted and stopped, but the more difficult task is to identify and eliminate racist practices in schools.

A teacher's challenge is to seriously confront these issues at a personal level before entering the classroom. If teachers believe that people of color are intellectually inferior, they will find it difficult to harbor high expectations for the academic achievement of those students. In the classroom, you will be in the position to help students grapple with these topics and their own feelings. As you learn to practice antiracism in the classroom, the goal should be to confront racism in the classroom and school as you pursue equal opportunity and academic outcomes for your students. In the practice of antiracist education, teachers reject notions of racial differences, acknowledge that race impacts their students' lives, learn from the knowledge and experience of the communities in which they are teaching, and challenge racial inequality in the classroom, schools, and communities (Pollock, 2008).

RACE AND ETHNICITY IN THE CURRICULUM

The school environment should help students learn to participate in the dominant society while maintaining connections to their distinct ethnicities if they choose. Respect for and support of ethnic differences are essential in this effort. As educators, we cannot afford to reject or neglect students because their ethnic backgrounds are different from our own. We are responsible for making sure all students learn to think, read, write, and compute so that they can function effectively in society. We can help accomplish this goal by accurately reflecting ethnicity and race in the curriculum and using it positively to teach and interact with students.

Traditionally, the curriculum of most schools has been grounded in the dominant culture. It is based on the knowledge and perspective of the West (Northern and Western Europe). The inherent bias of the curriculum does not encourage candid admissions of racism and oppression within society. In fact, it supports the claim of superiority of Western thought over all others and provides minimal or no familiarity with the non-Western cultures of Asia, Africa, and South and Central America. Information on, and perspectives of, other groups is sometimes added as a unit during a school year. Some schools have replaced this traditional curriculum with one based on the culture of students and communities. Multicultural education, on the other hand, encourages a culturally responsive curriculum in which diversity is integrated throughout the courses, activities, and interactions in the classroom.

Ethnic Studies.   Ethnic studies courses introduce students to the history and contemporary conditions of one or more ethnic groups. Many universities and some high schools have ethnic studies programs—such as African American, Asian American, American Indian, and Latino Studies—in which students can major. These courses and programs allow for in-depth exposure to the social, economic, and political history of a specific group. They are designed to correct the distortions and omissions that prevail in society about a specific ethnic group. Events that have been neglected in textbooks are addressed, myths are dispelled, and history is viewed from the perspective of the ethnic group as well as the dominant group. Prospective teachers and other school professionals who have not been exposed to an examination of an ethnic group different from their own should take such a course or undertake individual study.

Traditionally, ethnic studies have been offered as separate courses that students elect from many offerings in the curriculum. Seldom have they been required courses for all students. Although the information and experiences offered in these courses are important to members of the ethnic groups, students from other ethnic groups also need to learn about the multiethnic nation and world in which they live.

Ethnocentric Curriculum.   Some immigrant groups have their own schools, with classes held in the evenings or on Saturdays, to reinforce their cultural values, traditions, and native language. Some ethnic groups have established their own charter or private schools with curriculum that is centered around the history and values of their ethnic group. Some American Indian tribes have established public tribal schools in which the traditional culture serves as the social and intellectual starting point. Although most of these schools are located in rural American Indian communities, some urban areas have created magnet American Indian schools with similar goals.

Some African American communities support an **Afrocentric curriculum** to challenge Eurocentrism and tell the truth about black history. These classes are designed to improve students' self-esteem, academic skills, values, and positive identification with their ethnic group. At the core of this approach is an African perspective of the world and of historical events. These schools are often in urban areas with large African American student populations.

Some parents, educators, and community activists who thought that public schools were not effectively serving their children have established urban, ethnocentric, and grassroots charter schools. These schools place the ethnic culture of the enrolled students at the center of the curriculum; they are Afrocentric, Chicano-centric, or American Indian–centric, emphasizing what is known, valued, and respected from their own cultural roots.

Multiethnic Curriculum. A **multiethnic curriculum** permeates all subject areas at all levels of education, from preschool through adult education, with accurate and positive references to ethnic diversity. The amount of specific content about groups varies according to the course taught, but an awareness and a recognition of the multiethnic population is reflected in all classroom experiences.

Bulletin boards, resource books, and films that show ethnic and racial diversity constantly reinforce these realities. However, teachers should not depend entirely on these resources for instructional content about groups. Too often, people of color are studied only during a unit on African American history or American Indians. Too often, they are not included on reading lists or in the study of biographies, labor unions, or the environment. Students can finish school without reading anything written or produced by females or persons of color. If ethnic groups are included only during a unit or a week focusing on a particular group, students do not learn to view them as integral parts of society. They are viewed as separate, distinct, and inferior to the dominant group. A multiethnic curriculum counteracts the distortion of history and contemporary conditions. Without it, the perspective of the dominant group becomes the only valid curriculum to which students are exposed.

An educator has the responsibility for ensuring that ethnic groups become an integral part of the total curriculum. This mandate does not require the teacher to discuss every ethnic group. It does require that the classroom resources and instruction not focus solely on the dominant group. It requires that perspectives of ethnic groups and the dominant group be examined in discussions of historical and current events. For example, one should consider the perspectives of Mexican and American Indians as well as the dominant group in a presentation and discussion on the westward movement of European Americans in the eighteenth and nineteenth centuries. It requires students to read literature by authors from different ethnic and racial backgrounds. It assumes that mathematics and science will be explored from an American Indian as well as a Western perspective. The contributions of different ethnic groups should be reflected in the books that are used by students, in the movies they view, and in the activities in which they participate.

Multiethnic education includes learning experiences that help students examine their own stereotypes about and prejudice against ethnic and racial groups. These are not easy topics to address, but they should be a part of the curriculum beginning in preschool. At all levels, but particularly in junior high and secondary classrooms, students may resist discussion of these issues. Teachers can create a safe classroom climate by establishing clear guidelines for such discussions.

Development of a multiethnic curriculum requires the educator to evaluate textbooks and classroom resources for ethnic and racial content and biases. Although advances have been made in eliminating ethnic biases and adding information about ethnic and racial groups in textbooks, many older textbooks are still used in classrooms. Biased books should not prevent the teacher from providing multiethnic instruction. Supplementary materials can fill the gap.

The biases and omissions in the texts can be used for discussions of the experiences of groups. None of these instructional activities will occur, however, unless the teacher is aware of and values ethnic differences and their importance in the curriculum.

CLOSING THE ACHIEVEMENT GAP

African American students, as well as Latino and American Indian students, are not meeting standards as measured by the standardized tests required in most states, as shown in Figure 2.7, presenting achievement levels on a national eighth-grade mathematics test. As a result, a disproportionately large number of students of color are not being promoted to the next grade, are not graduating from high school, or are dropping out of school. It is easy to blame the students' lack of interest or active participation in school, the poverty in which they live, or their previous teachers. However, teachers are expected to help all students learn regardless of environmental factors that may make the task challenging. We may think we are being nice to students who have a difficult home life or who are English language learners by making less rigorous academic demands on them than on other students. Instead, students may decide that we do not believe they are capable of learning at the same level as other students and will respond accordingly (Nieto, 2008).

The Role of Assessment.   Schools conduct widespread testing of students to determine if they are meeting the standards established by states. Tests are trumpeted as measures of competence to move from one grade to another, graduate from high school, enter upper-division college courses, earn a baccalaureate, and become licensed to teach. Overwhelmingly, promoters suggest that anyone who cannot pass the appropriate test certainly cannot be qualified to move on to further study. Thus, student performance on state tests has become the primary measure

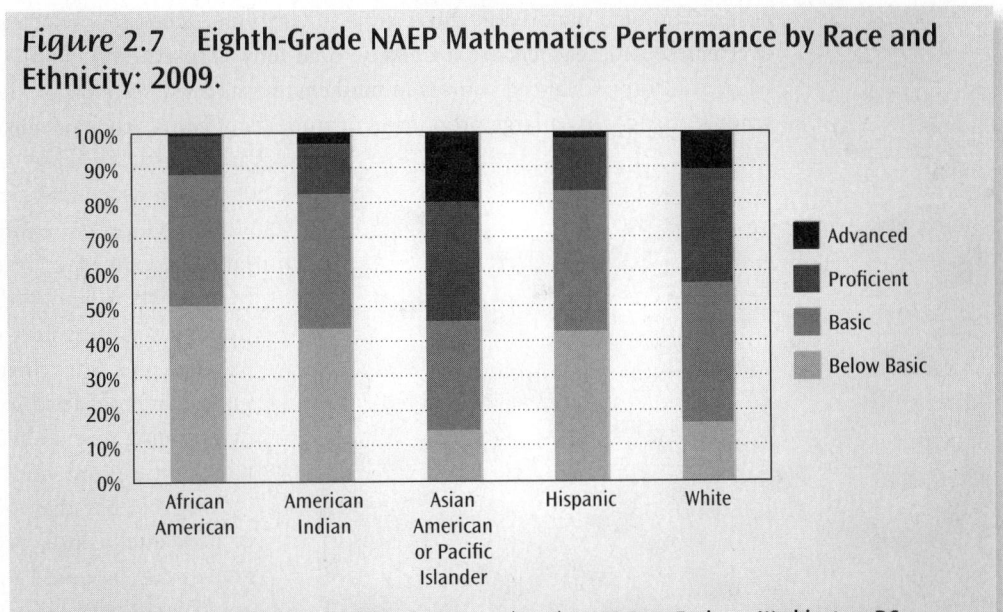

Figure 2.7   Eighth-Grade NAEP Mathematics Performance by Race and Ethnicity: 2009.

Source: National Assessment of Educational Progress. (2011). NAEP Data Explorer. Washington, DC: National Center for Education Statistics, Institute of Education Sciences, U.S. Department of Education. Retrieved on May 27, 2011, from http://nces.ed.gov/nationsreportcard/naepdata/.

of quality in the nation's schools, with sanctions imposed if students are not making **adequate yearly progress** (AYP) or the minimum level of performance required by the federal legislation No Child Left Behind. Teachers and principals can lose their jobs if students do not perform at expected levels. Increasingly, salary increments are based on the degree to which teachers have improved students' performance on tests. In 2011 the *Los Angeles Times* published the value-added ratings for elementary teachers in 470 city schools, ranking them from those whose students showed the most gains to those with the least gains. This focus on student performance on standardized tests has led many teachers to spend much of their instructional time teaching to the test, which has limited their teaching of critical thinking and other skills needed for a twenty-first century workforce.

Between 1970 and 1990, student performance on national tests improved, with the largest gains being made by students of color (Education Trust, n.d.). The progress came to a halt in the 1990s, and the achievement gap between whites and most students of color remains wide. Why do a disproportionately high number of students of color score lower than whites and Asian Americans on standardized tests? Studies indicate

- Students from low-income households and students of color are more likely to be taught a low-level curriculum with low standards for performance (Darling-Hammond, 2010).
- One of three Asian American students completed a calculus-level course, compared to 16% of white, 7% of Latino, 6% of American Indian, and 5% of African American students (U.S. Department of Education, 2007).
- Students in high-poverty and high-minority schools are more likely to be taught by unqualified teachers who are not certified to teach and did not major in the subject they were teaching (Darling-Hammond, 2010).

Should it be a surprise that many students of color do not perform as well as white students when they have not participated in advanced mathematics and science courses or had no teachers who majored in those subjects? In urban schools in which students of color are overrepresented, teachers are less likely to be fully licensed than in schools with middle-class white students. Advanced courses in mathematics and science are not always available in the schools attended by a large proportion of students of color. Students must have access to such courses and qualified teachers so that they can study the content on which they will be tested.

As educators, we must be careful not to label students of color intellectually inferior because their standardized test scores are low. These scores may influence a teacher's expectations for their academic performance. Standardized test scores can help in determining how assimilated into the dominant culture and how affluent one's family may be, but they provide less evidence of how intelligent a person is. Many other factors can be used to provide information about intelligence—for example, the ability to think and respond appropriately in different situations.

What should be the purposes of assessments? Rather than use tests to sort students

Testing is a mainstay of school culture today as students are tested annually to determine if they meet state standards.
© Scott Cunningham/Merrill

on the basis of income, ethnicity, and family characteristics, assessments could be used for student learning to help us understand what students know so that curriculum and activities can be designed to increase their knowledge and skills. Assessments that use observations, portfolios, projects, and essays provide evidence of what students know in many different ways. They are designed to promote complex and engaged learning.

Educators are capable of making valid decisions about ability on the basis of numerous objective and subjective factors about students. If decisions about the capabilities of students of color correspond exactly to the standardized scores, educators should reevaluate their responses and interactions with students. Test results today are making a difference in the life chances for many students, especially those of color and from low-income families. Therefore, educators cannot afford to use assessments in unfair and inequitable ways.

Who Is Responsible for Closing the Gaps?   When students do not achieve at the levels expected, many teachers refrain from taking responsibility. They blame the students, their parents, or the economic conditions of the community rather than seriously reflecting on why students in their classrooms are not learning and what might be changed to help them learn. A number of research studies report that teacher effectiveness is more important in student achievement than a student's race, poverty status, or parents' education (Darling-Hammond, 2010; Sanders & Rivers, 1996). In other words, effective teachers matter. Students who have been assigned the most effective teachers for three years in a row perform at much higher levels than students who were in the classrooms of the least effective teachers for three years. With effective teachers, low-achieving students become high achievers (Education Trust, 2008).

Students are not always active participants in their academic achievement. They are not always engaged with the schoolwork, and they do not always do their homework. However, effective teachers do not allow students to fail. There are many examples of good teachers who have helped students with low test scores achieve at advanced levels. African American and Latino students have performed at the same level as other students in mathematics and other subjects after teachers raised their expectations and changed their teaching strategies.

DESEGREGATION AND INTERGROUP RELATIONS

The most integrated schools today are in rural and small-town areas. The most segregated schools are located in large urban areas and the suburban areas closest to cities. Segregated schools for students of color usually serve impoverished communities and, as before the 1954 Brown decision, are usually providing unequal educational opportunities to their clientele. Charter and private schools tend to be even more segregated than public schools. This segregation guarantees that most white students have little contact with students of color except in the South and Southwest (Orfield & Lee, 2010).

Many middle-class families are very involved in their children's schools, ensuring that they are staffed by highly qualified teachers and offer a challenging curriculum. The problem is that they are less likely to be concerned about the quality of education for other people's children, particularly the children of parents with whom they never interact. However, the courts are beginning to expect states to equalize educational outcomes for all students as they consider cases alleging unequal resources for the education of students of color.

One of the outgrowths of *Brown v. Board of Education* was the need for intergroup relations to assist students and teachers in respecting each other and working together effectively. This need continues today. Even within desegregated schools, students are often segregated in classes, the cafeteria, and activities. To ensure that they interact with students from other ethnic and racial groups, educators have to consciously plan for this outcome. A number of national groups have developed programs to encourage cross-cultural communications. The Southern Poverty Law Center's project Mix It Up at Lunch, for example, challenges schools to mix students from different groups during the lunch hour. More than 3,000 schools are now participating in the project.

Small-group teams and cooperative learning promote both learning and interracial friendships. Students should have equal access to the curriculum, advanced courses, qualified teachers, and activities to develop high-order thinking skills. They should see themselves in the curriculum and in textbooks. Practices such as tracking and pull-out programs are barriers to providing equal access and improving intergroup relations. Engaging parents in school activities and decisions may help decrease the dissonance between school and home. The provision of multicultural education is a critical component in the continued effort to integrate schools and improve intergroup relations.

Summary

The ancestors of the majority of the population voluntarily immigrated to the United States because of economic impoverishment and political repression in their countries of origin and the demands of a vigorous U.S. economy that required a growing labor force. However, the ancestors of many African Americans and the early Mexican residents of the Southwest were involuntary immigrants. Approximately one million people per year continue to immigrate to the United States from all continents of the world.

Ethnicity is a sense of peoplehood based on national origin. Almost from the beginning of European settlement in the United States, the population has been multiethnic, with individuals representing many American Indian and European nations, later to be joined by Africans, Latinos, and Asians. The conditions encountered by different ethnic groups, the reasons they came, and their expectations about life here have differed greatly and have led ethnic groups to view themselves as distinct from each other.

Although no longer useful in describing groups of people, the term *race* continues to be used in this country to classify groups of people as inferior or superior. The popular use of *race* is based on society's perception that racial differences are important—a belief not upheld by scientific study.

People of color have had to fight for their civil rights throughout U.S. history. The efforts of African Americans in the 1950s and 1960s led to the removal of Jim Crow laws, the passage of the 1964 Civil Rights Act and 1965 Voting Rights Act, and the expansion of civil rights for women, Latinos, Asian Americans, American Indians, and people with disabilities. Desegregation is a process for decreasing racial/ethnic isolation in schools. Although early desegregation efforts focused on ensuring that black and white students attended the same schools, increasing numbers of students of color attend predominantly minority schools. Members of oppressed groups continue to experience discriminatory treatment and often are relegated to relatively low-status positions in society.

The school curriculum has traditionally represented the dominant culture as the focus of study. Since the 1970s, ethnic studies have been added to curricula as an extension or special segment that provides in-depth study of the history and contemporary conditions of one or more ethnic groups. Some ethnic groups have established schools or programs in traditional schools that center the curriculum on their ethnicity. A multiethnic approach is broader in scope in that it requires ethnic content to permeate the total curriculum. Educators should examine how they are administering and using standardized tests in the classroom. Too often, testing programs have been used to sort people for education and jobs. If disproportionately large numbers of students of color are scoring poorly on standardized tests, educators should develop different instructional practices to improve academic performance.

The emphasis in desegregation of schools today is on ensuring the academic achievement of all students and eliminating the inequities in educational opportunities. Intergroup activities in schools help students develop cross-cultural communications skills, by providing opportunities to work with students from different ethnic and racial groups.

Professional Practice

Questions for Discussion

1. How different and similar were the immigration patterns of Africans, Asians, Central Americans, Europeans, and South Americans during the past four centuries?

2. Why is membership in an ethnic group more important to some individuals than to others? What characteristics might an educator look for to determine a student's ethnic background and its importance in that student's life?

3. Why does race remain such an important factor in the social, political, and economic patterns of the United States?

4. Why have the changes made during the civil rights movement of the 1950s and 1960s failed to eliminate the income and educational gaps between groups?

5. What are the advantages and disadvantages of the following approaches: ethnic studies, ethnocentric education, and integration of ethnic content throughout the curriculum?

6. Why is the use of standardized tests so controversial? What are the dangers of depending too heavily on the results of standardized tests?

7. Why do school officials seek teachers who believe that all students can learn?

Portfolio Activities

1. Develop a lesson that reflects an integrative approach to incorporating multiethnic content. The lesson should be for the subject and level (e.g., elementary or secondary) that you plan to teach. (InTASC Standard 2: Learning Differences, and Standard 7: Planning for Instruction)

2. As you observe schools, record practices in classrooms, the halls, the cafeteria, extracurricular activities, and the main office that might be perceived as racist by people of color. Write a paper for your portfolio that describes these practices, why they could be considered racist, and how the school could change them. (InTASC Standard 2: Learning Differences)

3. Analyze the performance of students on required standardized scores in your state or one of the schools you are observing. Discuss the results based on the race or ethnicity of students in the school and indicate your conclusions. (Note: Schools are required by the federal legislation No Child Left Behind to disaggregate data by race and ethnicity. For further information on how students of different races and ethnic groups are performing in your state or school district, visit the website of Education Trust at www2.edtrust.org.) (InTASC Standard 6: Assessment)

Digital Resources for the Classroom

1. For education resources related to diversity, check the Anti-Defamation League's website at http://www.adl.org/main_Education/default.htm.

2. Resources for teaching tolerance and free subscriptions to the magazine *Teaching Tolerance* can be found at http://www.splcenter.org/what-we-do/teaching-tolerance.

3. Go to http://www.tolerance.org/mix-it-up to learn more about the Southern Poverty Law Center's Mix It Up at Lunch program.

4. See hundreds of stories of bigotry in Responding to Bigotry: Speak Up! at http://www.tolerance.org/sites/default/files/general/speak_up_handbook.pdf. People in Baltimore, MD, Columbia, SC, Phoenix, AZ, and Vancouver, WA, talk about their encounters in stores and restaurants, on streets, and in schools.

5. For information and resources on combating hate, go to the Anti-Defamation League's website at http://www.adl.org/combating_hate/.

6. A curriculum for teaching students to engage in civil discourses in the classroom is available at http://www.tolerance.org/sites/default/files/general/TT_Civil%20Discourse_whtppr_0.pdf.

MyEducationLab™

Go to the MyEducationLab (www.myeducationlab.com) for Multicultural Education and familiarize yourself with the topical content, which includes:

- Assignments and Activities, tied to learning outcomes for the course, that can help you more deeply understand course content

- Building Teaching Skills and Dispositions learning units allow you to apply and practice your understanding of how to teach equitably in a multicultural education classroom

- Licensure Test Prep activities are available in the Book Resources to help you prepare for test taking

- A pretest with hints and feedback that tests your knowledge of this chapter's content

- Review, practice, and enrichment activities that will enhance your understanding of the chapter content

- A posttest with hints and feedback that allows you to test your knowledge again after having completed the enrichment activities

A Correlation Guide may be downloaded by instructors to show how MyEducationLab content aligns to this book.

3 Class and Socioeconomic Status

I'm not stupid, I'm just poor. People don't seem to get the difference.

Anonymous

While he was still in college, Tomas Juarez decided he wanted to work with children from low-income families. He began his teaching career, however, in a culturally diverse suburban school. The school had been built only a few years before and included state-of-the-art science labs. Students were proficient with computers; they even helped Mr. Juarez develop his skills. Most of the students participated in extracurricular activities, and their parents were active in school affairs. More than 90% of the previous graduating class had enrolled in postsecondary programs. It was a pleasure to work with a team of teachers who planned interesting lessons based on a constructivist approach, engaged students in the content, and developed higher-order thinking skills.

After a few years, Mr. Juarez decided he was ready to take on the challenge of an inner-city school where most students were members of oppressed groups. As soon as he stepped into his new school, he realized that he had been spoiled in the suburbs.

First, the smell wasn't right and the halls were dirty, even though it was the beginning of the school year. The room that was to be his classroom did not have enough chairs for all of the students who had been assigned to the class. Not only did the room look as if it had not been repainted for 20 years, but numerous ceiling tiles were missing. His first thought was that both he and the students would be exposed to asbestos and lead poisoning. Outside, the playground was uninviting. There was no grass, the stench from local factories was overpowering, and the football field did not even have goalposts.

During Mr. Juarez's first few weeks, he found that the students were terrific. They were enthusiastic about being back in school. He had only enough textbooks for half the class, however, and no money in the budget to purchase more. Supplies were limited, and most of the school's audiovisual equipment had been stolen the previous year and not replaced.

| REFLECTIONS |

1. Why were conditions at Mr. Juarez's new school so much different from those in the suburban school?

2. What are the chances of Mr. Juarez's students being academically successful at the same level as his students in the suburban school?

3. Why are students in the urban school more likely to drop out, become pregnant, and not attend college?

Class

"**Class** is a system that differentially structures group access to economic, political, cultural, and social resources" (Andersen & Collins, 2010, p. 71). It determines the schools we attend, the stores in which we shop, the restaurants at which we eat, the community in which we live, and the jobs to which we have access. Class is socially constructed by society and its institutions, determining the relationships between families and people who have little or limited financial resources and those who are wealthy.

Two views of equality in the United States suggest different class structures. One view accepts the existence of different socioeconomic levels or classes in society. It also strongly supports the notion that a person can be socially mobile and move to a higher class by finishing college and working hard. An individual who has not yet achieved upper-middle-class status is often viewed as less capable. The hardships faced by low-income families are blamed on their lack of middle-class values and behaviors. The individual is at fault for not moving up the class ladder—a phenomenon called "blaming the victim."

In the second view of U.S. society, distinct class divisions are recognized. Those individuals and families who own and control corporations, banks, and other means of income production comprise the privileged **upper class**. The professional and managerial elite have not only accumulated wealth; they also are able to ensure that their needs are supported by legislative officials they have helped elect (Hacker & Pierson, 2010). People who earn a living primarily by selling their labor make up the middle and working classes. Another class includes those people who are unable to work or who can find work only sporadically. Although some individuals are able to move from one class level to another, opportunities for social mobility are limited. Those who control most of the resources and those who possess few of the resources are dichotomous groups in a class struggle.

Most people are caught in the socioeconomic strata into which they were born; the political-economic system helps keep them there. Certainly for some individuals it is possible to be socially and economically mobile. Stories about athletes, coaches, movie stars, and singers are recounted during sporting events and in newspaper and television reports. Few people, however, have abilities that translate into the high salaries of elite stars of the entertainment world. A college education is the most effective path for moving from low-income to middle-class or higher status.

Family background accounts for a large part of the variation in educational and occupational attainment. The opportunity to participate equally in the generation of wealth is thwarted before one is born. Individuals born into a wealthy family are likely to achieve wealth; individuals born into a low-income family will have much more difficulty achieving wealth no matter how hard they try. Families usually do everything possible to protect their wealth to guarantee that their children will maintain the family's economic status. The barriers that exist in society often lead to the perpetuation of inequalities from one generation to the next.

CLASS IDENTITY

Most people, if asked, can identify themselves by class, which for most people is probably the **middle class**. They may not strongly vocalize their identification with a specific class, but they participate socially and occupationally within a class structure. Their behavior and value system may be based on a strong ethnic or religious identification, but that specific identification is greatly influenced by their economic circumstances. The first generation of a group that has moved to the middle class may continue to interact at a primary level with friends and relatives who remain in the **working class**. Differences in friends, communities, and jobs, however, often lead to the disappearance of those cross-class ties over time.

Most U.S. citizens exhibit and articulate less concern about class consciousness than do many of their European counterparts. However, many, including teachers, have participated in class actions such as strikes or work stoppages to further the interests of the class to which they belong. Class consciousness, or solidarity with others at the same socioeconomic level, has become more pronounced since the recession began in 2008. Many middle- and working-class people have lost the jobs that allowed them to live comfortably at their class level. Actions taken by state and local governments to control spending have led to rallies by teachers and other public workers who worry about job losses, reductions in salary and benefits, and loss of collective bargaining rights. In the past, the dominant cultural values and belief systems held the individual personally responsible for his or her class position, including keeping a job.

SOCIAL STRATIFICATION

Social stratification ranks individuals and families on the basis of their **income**, education, occupation, wealth, and power in society. Many people accept and follow the dictates of socially defined behavior based on their occupation, race, gender, and class. However, civil rights organizations, including women's groups, strive to combat the institutionalized acceptance and expectation of unequal status across groups.

Inequality results, in part, from differential rankings within the division of labor. Different occupations are evaluated and rewarded unequally. Some jobs are viewed as more worthy, more important, more popular, and more preferable than others. People who hold high-ranking positions have developed a common interest in maintaining their positions and the accompanying power. They have established policies and practices to restrict others' chances of obtaining the same status—a key to establishing and maintaining a system of stratification.

Many people in the United States receive high or low rankings in the social stratification system on the basis of characteristics over which they have no control. Women, people with disabilities, the elderly, children, and people of color often are granted little prestige. Some of the groups to which we belong are assigned at birth because they are the ones to which our parents belong; we have no choice about our membership. If we have been born into

PAUSE TO REFLECT 3.1

Think about the community in which you grew up and about the class of your family and other members of the community.

- How would you describe the socioeconomic status of your family?

- What was the socioeconomic status of the majority of students in your high school?

- How did your family's socioeconomic status influence your educational aspirations and those of your high school peers?

higher-ranking socioeconomic positions, we will have advantages and privileges over children who were born in lower-ranking groups. Although white, able-bodied, Christian men are supposed to be advantaged in society because of their race and religion, they do not all enjoy high-ranking status. They appear at all levels along the continuum, from a homeless person to a billionaire, but these individuals and their families remain overrepresented at the highest levels. Conversely, members of most oppressed groups fall at all levels of the continuum, with just a few at the top of the socioeconomic scale.

Socioeconomic Status

How is economic success or achievement measured? The economic condition of a person or group is measured using a criterion called **socioeconomic status (SES)**. It serves as a composite of the economic status of a family or individual on the basis of occupation, educational attainment, and income. Related to these three factors are wealth and power, which also help determine an individual's SES but are more difficult to measure.

These five determinants of SES are interrelated. Although inequality takes many forms, these factors are probably the most salient for an individual because they affect how one lives. A family's SES is usually readily observable—in the size of their home and the part of town in which they live, the schools their children attend, and the clubs to which the parents belong. Many educators place their students at specific SES levels on the basis of observations about their families, the way students dress, the language they use, and their eligibility for free or reduced-price lunch.

INCOME

Income is the amount of money earned in wages or salaries throughout a year. One way to look at income distribution is by dividing the population into fifths; the lowest one-fifth has the lowest income, and the highest one-fifth has the highest income. Figure 3.1 shows the percentage of total income earned and the total wealth controlled by each fifth of the population. The top fifth of the population earned 50% of the total income, whereas the bottom fifth earned 3% of the total income. High incomes are reserved for the privileged few. The 5% of U.S. families with the highest incomes earned 22% of the total income of all families (U.S. Census Bureau, 2010k). And the wealthiest families are becoming even wealthier. Between 2001 and 2006, the top 1% of income earners received 53% of the income gains (Hacker & Pierson, 2010).

Many people view this income inequity as a natural outcome of the American way. Those people who have contributed at high levels to their professions or jobs are believed to deserve more pay for their effort. People at the lower end of the continuum are either unemployed or work in unskilled jobs and thus are not expected to receive the same economic rewards. The distance between the two ends of this continuum can be quite large, however. Chief executive officers (CEOs) of the largest 500 U.S. companies earned an average annual compensation of $8.5 million in 2009, which was 263 times the average earnings of their employees. The CEOs at the 50 companies that laid off the most workers since the onset of the economic crisis had average earnings of nearly $12 million in 2009 (Anderson, Collins, Pizzigati, & Shih, 2010). At the other end of the scale, people earning the minimum wage

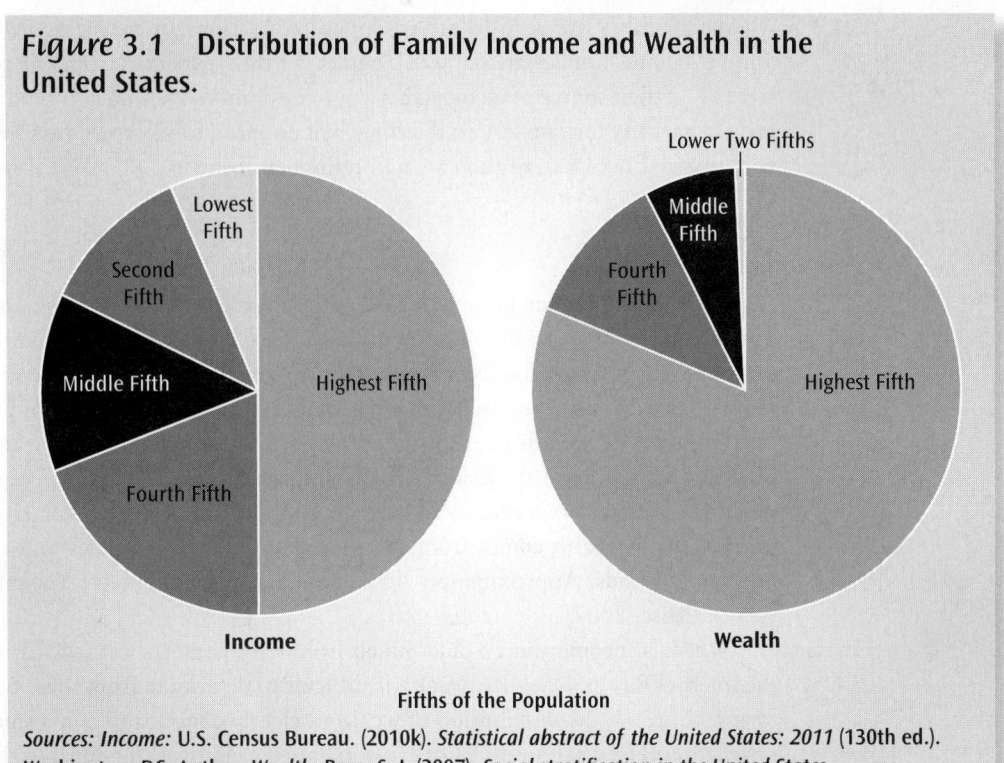

Figure 3.1 Distribution of Family Income and Wealth in the United States.

Sources: Income: U.S. Census Bureau. (2010k). *Statistical abstract of the United States: 2011* (130th ed.). Washington, DC: Author. *Wealth:* Rose, S. J. (2007). *Social stratification in the United States.* New York: New Press.

receive $15,060 annually. International studies report that the gap between high and low wage earners is greater in the United States than in most other industrialized countries. This situation is exacerbated by the lack of tax structures to adjust the disparities; in fact, the rich are paying less in taxes than in 1961 (Goldberg, Collins, Pizzigati, & Klinger, 2011). When these disparities are noted at the political level, some conservatives accuse the other side of encouraging class warfare.

Between World War II and 1973, the growth of the U.S. economy allowed the incomes of workers at all levels to increase at a faster rate than expenditures. Many middle-income families were able to purchase homes, cars, boats, and luxuries for the home; money was sometimes also available for savings. During this period, the annual **median income** of all people 14 years of age and older nearly tripled. The standard of living for most of the population was markedly better in 1973 than in 1940. Beginning in 1973, however, the cost of living (i.e., the cost of housing, utilities, food, and other essentials) began to increase faster than incomes. Except for the wealthy, all families felt the financial pressure. No longer did they have extra income to purchase nonessentials. No longer was one full-time worker in a family enough to maintain a reasonable standard of living. The 1990s saw another upswing in the economy. By 2008, the median annual income of a family had reached $61,521. When both husband and wife worked, the median income of a couple was $86,621 (U.S. Census Bureau, 2010k).

Income sets limits on the general lifestyle of a family, as well as on their general welfare. It controls the consumption patterns of a family—the amount and quality of material possessions, consumer goods, and luxuries, and it influences savings, housing, and diet. It determines whether families are able to afford college educations or new cars. Most low-income and middle-income families are barely able to cover their expenses from one paycheck to the next. If they lose their source of income, they could be homeless within a few months. Higher incomes provide security for families, so that they will not need to worry about paying for the essentials and will have access to health care and retirement benefits.

WEALTH

Although the difference in income among families is great, an examination of income alone does not reveal the vast differences in the way families live. Income figures show the amount of money earned by a family for their labors during one year, but the figures do not include money earned from investments, land, and other holdings. They do not present the **net worth** of a family. The **wealth** of a family includes savings accounts, insurance, corporate stock ownership, and property. Wealth provides a partial guarantee of future income and has the potential of producing additional income and wealth. However, for most families, the majority of their wealth comes from the equity value of their homes and the residual value of household goods. Approximately 40% of U.S. households have virtually zero or negative wealth (Rose, 2007).

Whereas income can be determined from data gathered on federal income tax forms by the Internal Revenue Service, wealth is difficult to determine from these or any other standard forms. However, the distribution of wealth is clearly concentrated in a small percentage of the population. The wealthiest 1% of the population held over one-third of the nation's wealth in 2004, with an average of $15 million per person (Page & Jacobs, 2009). Figure 3.1 shows how wealth is distributed across fifths of the population.

The wealthiest nations in the world are the United States, Canada, and countries in Western Europe, but inequities across groups continue to exist in these countries. The world's wealth is held by a few people. For example, the richest 1% of the people in the world have combined incomes equal to over half (57%) of the incomes of the world population (Smith, 2008). The sales revenues of large corporations such as Wal-Mart, Hewlett Packard, Toyota, and General Motors exceed the gross national income of many countries of the world, as do the profits of ExxonMobil (Smith, 2008). The difference between the economic lives of populations in the wealthiest and poorest countries in the world is shocking in its magnitude. The annual income per person in the richest country is 100 times more than in the poorest country (Smith, 2008). These differences affect quality of life, health, and life expectancy.

Wealth ensures some economic security for its holders even though the degree of security depends on the amount of wealth accumulated. It also enhances the power and prestige of those who possess it. Great wealth attracts power, provides an income that allows luxury, and creates values and lifestyles that are very different from those characterizing the rest of the population. Wealth also gives great economic advantages to the children in such families, who can attend the best private schools, travel widely, and not have to worry about medical and health needs.

OCCUPATION

Income, for most people, is determined by their occupation. Generally speaking, income is a fair measure of occupational success—both of the importance of the occupation to society and of one's skill at the job. In addition to providing an income, a person's job is an activity that is considered important. Individuals who are unemployed often are stigmatized as noncontributing

Differences in Socioeconomic Status

The middle school in a rural community of 9,000 residents has four school-sponsored dances each year. At the Valentine's dance, a coat-and-tie affair, six eighth-grade boys showed up in rented tuxedos. They had planned this together, and their parents, who were among the more affluent in the community, thought it would be "cute" and paid for the rentals. The final dance of the year is scheduled for May, and it too is a coat-and-tie dance. This time, rumors are circulating around school that "everyone" is renting a tux and that the girls are getting new formal dresses. The parents of the three boys are, according to the grapevine, renting a limousine for their sons and their dates. These behaviors and dress standards are far in excess of anything previously observed at the middle school.

Several students, particularly those from lower-income backgrounds, have said they will boycott the dance. They cannot afford the expensive attire, and they claim that the ones behind the dress-up movement have said that only the nerds or geeks would show up in anything less than a tux or a formal gown.

| QUESTIONS FOR CLASSROOM DISCUSSION |

■ How can schools ensure that the cost of attending school affairs is not prohibitive for some of its students?

■ Should school administrators intervene in the plans being made by the more advantaged students? What could they do to control the situation?

■ Why could the actions of these advantaged students be disruptive to the school climate?

members of society who cannot take care of themselves. Even individuals with great wealth often hold jobs although the additional income is unnecessary. Just over half of today's workforce is comprised of **white-collar** workers—people who do office work. The percentage of service workers is growing, although the percentage who are private household workers continues to decline. Between now and 2018, the 10 fastest-growing occupations are expected to fall in the health and computing fields (U.S. Census Bureau, 2010k):

1. home health aides
2. personal and home care aides
3. computer software engineers and application specialists

4. medical assistants
5. network systems and data communications analysts
6. dental assistants
7. dental hygienists
8. medical scientists (except epidemiologists)
9. physician assistants
10. veterinary technologists and technicians

A number of the jobs on this list require on-the-job training, but no postsecondary preparation (e.g., home health aides, dental assistants, and medical assistants). Others require an associate or bachelor's degree. A doctoral degree is required for medical scientists (U.S. Census Bureau, 2010k). The difference in income among these jobs will vary greatly.

The type of job one holds is the primary determinant of income received, providing a relatively objective indicator of a person's SES. The job usually indicates one's education, suggests the types of associates with whom one interacts, and determines the degree of authority and responsibility one has over others. It accounts for differing amounts of compensation in income and differing degrees of prestige in society.

Occupational prestige is often determined by the requirements for the job and by the characteristics of the job. The requirements for an occupation with prestige usually include more education and training. Job characteristics that define the prestige of an occupation are rooted in the division between mental and manual labor. When the prestige of an occupation is high, fewer people are able to gain entry into that occupation. When the prestige of an occupation is low, employees are allotted less security and income, and accessibility is greater. Occupations with the highest prestige generally have the highest salaries.

EDUCATION

The best predictor of occupational prestige is the amount of education required for the job. Financial compensation is usually greater for occupations that require more years of education. For example, medical doctors and lawyers remain in school for several years beyond a bachelor's degree program. Many professionals and other white-collar workers have completed at least an undergraduate program. Craft workers often earn more money than many white-collar workers, but their positions require specialized training that often takes as long to complete as a program leading to a college degree.

A great discrepancy exists among the incomes of people who have less than a high school education and those who have completed professional training after college. In 2008 the median annual income of a male who had not completed high school was $20,845; for a male who had attained a bachelor's degree, it was $57,278. The differential for a female was $11,904 versus $36,294 (U.S. Census Bureau, 2010k). Women do not earn as much as men, no matter what education level they have achieved.

Education is rightfully viewed as a way to enhance one's economic status. However, impressive educational credentials are more likely to be achieved as a result of family background than because of other factors. High school graduates whose parents have bachelor's degrees or higher are more likely to enroll in postsecondary education. The higher the socioeconomic level of a student's family, the greater the student's chances of finishing high school and college. The rate of students who enrolled in college soon after high school graduation ranged in 2009 from 59% of those from families with annual incomes less than $36,080 to 90% of those from families with incomes of more than $108,284. College graduation rates ranged from

The types of jobs one holds impacts one's socioeconomic status. Low-wage jobs make it difficult if not impossible to move into the middle class.
© Laima Druskis/PH College

8% for students in the bottom quartile of family income to 82% for the top income level, as shown in Figure 3.2 (Family Income and Educational Attainment, 2010).

The conditions under which low-income students live can make it difficult for them to go to school as an alternative to going to work. The colleges that students attend are influenced more by the SES of the family than by the academic ability of the student. Many students simply cannot afford to attend private colleges and instead choose community colleges or state colleges and universities. To add to the problems faced by low-income students contemplating college, the cost of tuition has risen continuously over the past decade (Baum & Ma, 2010). Thus, a student's socioeconomic origins have a substantial influence on the amount and type of schooling available and, in turn, the type of job obtained.

POWER

Individuals and families who are at the upper SES levels exert more power than those at any other level. These individuals are more likely to sit on state or local policy boards, boards of colleges and universities, and boards of corporations. They determine who receives benefits and

Figure 3.2 High School Graduation, College Enrollment, and College Completion by Family Income.

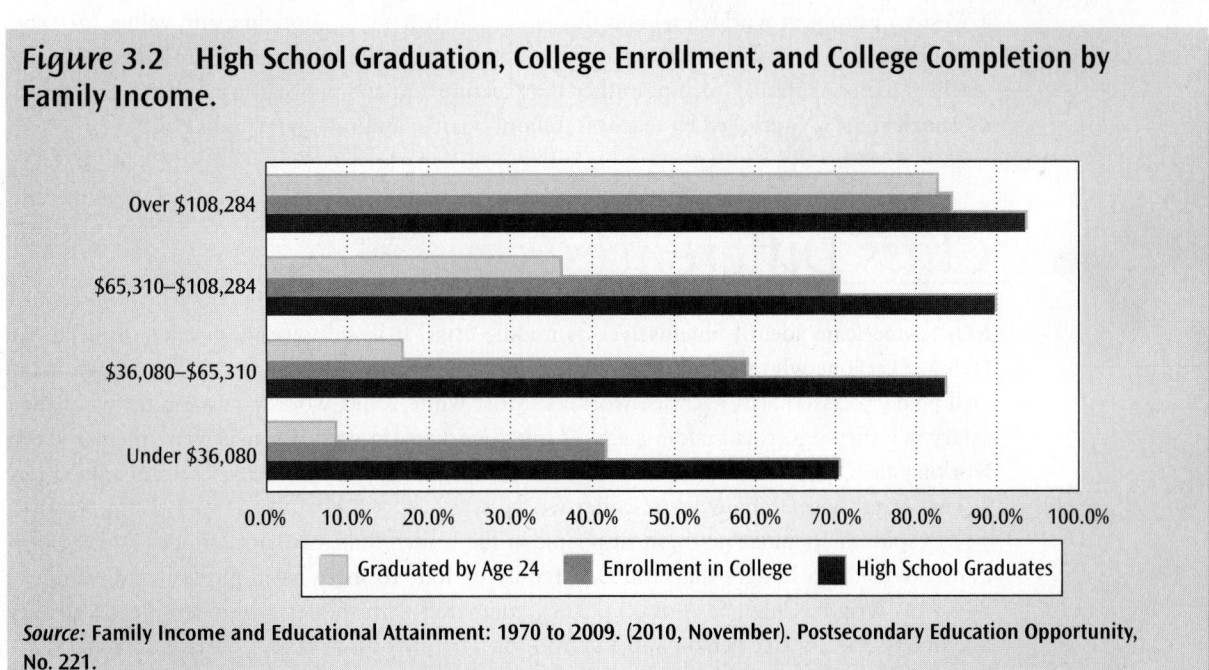

Source: Family Income and Educational Attainment: 1970 to 2009. (2010, November). Postsecondary Education Opportunity, No. 221.

rewards in governmental, occupational, and community affairs. Groups and individuals with power control resources that influence their lives and the lives of others. Groups or individuals with little power do not have the means to get what they need or the access to the people who could influence their interests. They continually obtain a lower share of society's benefits, in part because they lack access to sources of power.

People with higher incomes are more likely to participate in national and local politics. They are also much more likely to vote in presidential elections. In the 2008 national elections 25% of the voters had incomes of $100,000 or more even though that group comprises only 16% of the population (Soss & Jacobs, 2009). Contributing financially to political candidates provides power to influence election outcomes. The American Political Science Association (APSA) reported that "citizens with lower or moderate incomes speak with a whisper that is lost on the ears of inattentive government officials, while the advantaged roar with a clarity and consistency that policymakers readily hear and routinely follow" (2004, p. 1). This power translates to legislative action that benefits people, families, and corporations with money. APSA reports that "recent research strikingly documents that the votes of U.S. senators far more closely correspond with the policy preferences of each senator's rich constituents than with the preferences of the senator's less-privileged constituents" (p. 14).

Education is not exempt from the exercise of power. Wealth and affluence can create an uneven playing field for many students as parents with larger incomes use their power to ensure that their children have access to the best teachers, advanced placement courses, gifted and talented student programs, and private schools. Parents are able to financially contribute to the hiring of teachers for programs such as music and art, which many school districts can no longer afford. They will not tolerate the hiring of unqualified or poor teachers. On the other end of the income spectrum are families with little input into decisions concerning the education of their children and who cannot afford to contribute the resources to maintain a full and desirable curriculum.

Power relationships also exist between teachers and students. Teachers and administrators wield power over students by controlling the knowledge dispensed (predominantly grounded in a Western European worldview) and the acceptable behaviors, thoughts, and values for experiencing success in schools. Few teachers today are totally **authoritarian**; a growing number of teachers use cooperative learning rather than lecture and competitive strategies. Nevertheless, the curriculum is controlled by teachers, school boards, and national standards.

Class Differences

Many Americans identify themselves as middle class. It is an amorphous category that can include everyone who works steadily and is not a member of the upper class. It ranges from well-paid professionals to service workers. Most white-collar workers, no matter what their salary, see themselves as middle class. Manual workers, in contrast, may view themselves as working class rather than as middle class, even though their incomes and cultural values may be similar to those of many white-collar workers.

Despite the popular myth, most people in the United States are not affluent by U.S. standards. A medium budget that allows a family of four to meet basic requirements is above $44,100 (Wright, Chau, & Aratani, 2011), compared with the federal government's poverty line of $10,956 for one person and $21,954 for a family of four (U.S. Census Bureau, 2010k). In 2008 more than one in three U.S. families earned less than $44,100 (U.S. Census Bureau,

2010c), which corresponds to the category of low income. Many of these individuals identify themselves as middle class, but they may be unable to obtain the material goods and necessities to live comfortably. In this section we will explore the different classes and socioeconomic levels of the population.

THE UNEMPLOYED AND HOMELESS

The portion of the population who suffers the most from the lack of a stable income or other economic resources is the unemployed and homeless. The long-term poor fall into this group, but most others are temporarily at this level, moving in and out of poverty as they work off and on at low wages. More than half of the population will have lived below the poverty line at least once by the time they turn 75 years old (Pimpare, 2008). Children suffer the most from persistent poverty. A study by the Urban Institute (Ratcliffe & McKernan, 2010) found that 10% of U.S. children spend at least half of their childhood in poverty. "Children who are poor at birth are significantly more likely to be poor as an adult, drop out of high school, and have a teen nonmarital birth than those not poor at birth" (p. 6). And the longer the period in their childhood during which they stay poor, the greater their chances of experiencing these outcomes as adults.

Families and people in poverty have been socially isolated from the dominant society. They usually are not integrated into, or welcome in, the communities of the other classes. Recommendations to establish low-income housing, homeless shelters, or halfway houses in middle-class communities are often met with vocal outrage from the residents. Some analysts think this lack of integration has exacerbated the differences in behavior between members of the underclass and those of other classes.

The number of unemployed individuals has almost doubled since the 2008 recession. Nearly 14 million people, or 9% of the civilian workforce, in April 2011 were classified as unemployed; another 2.5 million unemployed people had given up looking for work and were not included in the government's report of the unemployed (U.S. Bureau of Labor Statistics, 2011a). Because of the 2008 recession, the number of homeless individuals and families has continued to increase. Children and families live on the streets of our cities, comprising a large portion of today's homeless population as shown in Figure 3.3, but homelessness is not limited to cities. About 9% of the homeless live in rural areas in cars, campers, or substandard housing with relatives (National Coalition for the Homeless, 2009). Because almost all cities report having more homeless people than shelter space, the number housed nightly in shelters undercounts the actual number of homeless people. The National Law Center on Homelessness and Poverty (2010) reports that 3 million people have been homeless at some time during the previous year, and 1.3 million of them are children. Many of the homeless work, but at such low wages they are unable to afford housing.

Why are people homeless? Poverty, a lack of jobs, and a lack of affordable housing are the primary reasons for homelessness. The federal definition of affordable housing is rent equal to 30% of one's income. To afford a two-bedroom apartment in most parts of the country, a person who makes the minimum wage will require one or more additional minimum-wage earners in the household. Half of low-income families with children are spending 63% or more of their income on housing, leaving little to cover expenses such as health care, child care, and other basic necessities. At the beginning of the 2008 recession, 16% of households were spending more than half their income on rent or a mortgage. Over half of the households with incomes in the bottom quartile are spending more than half of their income on rent. Because of job losses and reductions in working hours, a growing number of people are

Figure 3.3 Who Are the Homeless in Our Cities?

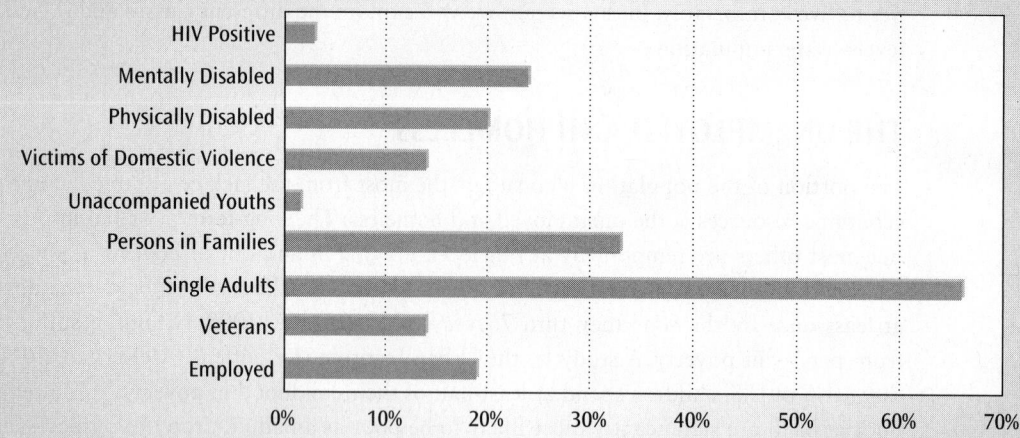

Source: United States Conference of Mayors. (2010). *Hunger and homelessness survey: A status report on hunger and homelessness in American cities*. Washington, DC: Author.

unable to pay their rent or mortgage, ending up homeless (Joint Center for Housing Studies of Harvard University, 2010).

Domestic violence is another cause of homelessness; women who are escaping violent relationships do not always have someplace else to go. Other homeless people are without a place to stay because the number of facilities to care for people with mental disabilities is limited. Some people who are dependent on drugs or alcohol have lost their jobs, can't keep a job that earns enough to pay for their housing, or have become estranged from their families. Some teenagers leave home because of family problems, economic problems, or residential instability, often ending up homeless on city streets.

Between 500,000 and 1.5 million children and youth are homeless at some point during a given year (Paquette, 2010; National Center on Family Homelessness, 2010). Some homeless students do not attend school for extended periods of time and are not as healthy as other children. Many have not received immunizations that are expected in childhood. They experience higher rates of asthma, respiratory infections, ear infections, stomach problems, and obesity than other children. They have more emotional and behavioral problems, show delayed development, and have learning disabilities. They are often hungry or lack adequate nutrition. Further, they are more likely to have been abused or neglected by parents and other adults (National Center on Family Homelessness, 2010).

The **McKinney-Vento Homeless Assistance Act,** passed by Congress in 1987, requires public schools to recognize the educational rights of and provide protection for homeless children and youth, including students who are living with relatives or friends because they have lost their housing. The law requires school districts to provide transportation for homeless students to keep them in their schools of origin if requested by their parents or guardians. A school cannot deny enrollment to homeless students because they do not have school records, immunization records, proof of residency, or other documents. The McKinney-Vento Act ensures that homeless students have access to schooling and are not denied services because of circumstances beyond their control. The school district's liaison for homeless students should serve as an advocate for them, assisting them in accessing available services in the school system and

An increasing number of homeless adults, families, and children are found in communities around the country.
© Laima Druskis/PH College

community. This legislation has made a difference. Before it was passed, 25% of homeless students were in school, compared to 85% today (Murphy & Tobin, 2011).

The unemployed and homeless suffer from economic insecurity and from social, political, and economic deprivation. When they do hold full-time jobs, they are of the lowest prestige and income levels. The jobs are often eliminated when economic conditions tighten or the jobs move to the suburbs, again resulting in unemployment. The work for which they are hired is often the dirty work—not only physically dirty but also dangerous, menial, undignified, and degrading. Most people who are living in poverty want a job, not charity (Pimpare, 2008). They want work that will help move them out of poverty.

Many stereotypical notions about the poor need to be overcome for teachers to effectively serve students from low-income families. Some Americans believe that people are poor because of their moral failings or that they simply do not want to work. They are often treated with condescension, not as equals (Pimpare, 2008). Students from these families should not be blamed if they show acceptance of, resignation to, or even accommodation to their poverty as they learn to live with their economic disabilities.

Some anthropologists and sociologists who have studied the relationship between cultural values and poverty status have proposed the theory of a culture of poverty. They assert that the poor have a unique way of life that has developed as a reaction to their impoverished environment. This thesis suggests that people in poverty have a different value system and lifestyle that is perpetuated and transmitted to future generations. Critics of the culture of poverty thesis believe that the cultural values of this group are much like those of the rest of the population but have been modified in practice because of situational stresses (Gorski, 2008). This explanation suggests that the differences in values and lifestyles are not passed from one generation to the next, but rather are their adaptations to the experience of living in poverty.

THE WORKING CLASS

The occupations pursued by the working class are those that require manual work, for which income varies widely, depending on the skill required in the specific job. The factor that is most important in defining the working class is the subordination of members to the capitalist control of production. These workers do not have control of their work. They do not give orders; they take orders from others. They have been hurt the most because of job losses resulting from technological advances, the movement of jobs to other countries, and the recent recession.

Blue-collar workers are engaged primarily in manual work that is routine and mechanical. The level of education required for most of these jobs is not as high as for white-collar jobs, which are not mechanical and are less routine. Without additional training, it becomes difficult to move into a higher-level position. Blue-collar workers generally perceive themselves as hardworking and honest, and as performing important work for society. They want to be successful and commonly hope that their children will not have to spend their lives in the same kind of job. Of the employed population, 38.5% have the blue-collar jobs shown in Figure 3.4 (U.S. Census Bureau, 2010k).

The income of these workers varied in 2009 from a median weekly wage of $398 in food services to $781 for installation, maintenance, and repair occupations (U.S. Census Bureau, 2010k), which provide different standards of living. Although the income of the working class is equal to and sometimes higher than that of white-collar workers, these workers generally have less job security. Work is more sporadic, and unemployment is unpredictably affected by the economy. Jobs are uncertain because of displacement as a result of technology. Fringe benefits available to these workers are often not as good as those offered to other workers. Vacation time is usually less, health insurance more typically unavailable, and working conditions more dangerous.

Over the past few decades, jobs have shifted from the manufacturing sector to jobs in protective services (police and firefighters), food services, health services, cleaning services, and personal services (hairdressers and early childhood assistants). The number of temporary, part-time, and contract jobs is expanding. Most of these jobs provide low wages and limited, if any, health care or retirement benefits.

People at the low end of the wage scale are the working poor. They do the jobs that most people with more education refuse to do or can't afford to do. Although many work one or more jobs at the minimum wage of $7.25 per hour, they can't pull themselves out of poverty. A number of state and local jurisdictions have set a minimum wage that is higher than the federal level. The working poor are more likely than other workers to hold part-time jobs and to be women, to be African American or Hispanic, and to lack a high school degree. Thirteen percent of workers in the service occupations have earnings below the poverty level from jobs that pay minimum wage or less and may be supplemented by tips. Service workers account for one in

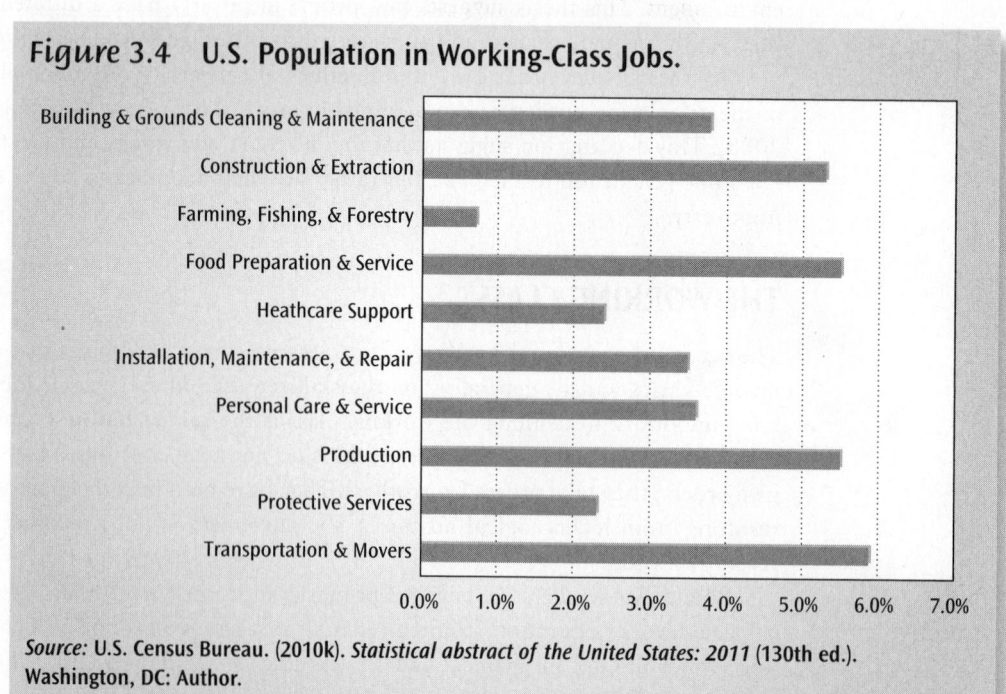

Figure 3.4   U.S. Population in Working-Class Jobs.

Source: U.S. Census Bureau. (2010k). *Statistical abstract of the United States: 2011* (130th ed.). Washington, DC: Author.

three of the working poor (U.S. Bureau of Labor Statistics, 2011b). Although union workers generally receive higher incomes and enjoy negotiated health care and retirement benefits, many low-income workers do not join unions or they work in states or companies that aggressively discourage union membership.

THE MIDDLE CLASS

The incomes of Americans who consider themselves middle class vary greatly. These include members of the working class, managers, and professionals who do not see themselves as either poor or rich. It includes families from all ethnic and racial groups, and both immigrant and native families. To move into the middle class and maintain that status often requires two wage earners. For the purpose of this discussion, families are classified as middle class if they fall in the third or fourth quintile of income earners in the country, which includes 60% of the population. The income range is $39,000 to $100,240 (U.S. Census Bureau, 2010k), which leads to different lifestyles at the two ends of the continuum. Although some members of the middle class have comfortable incomes, many have virtually no wealth. Many live from paycheck to paycheck, with little cushion against the loss of earning power through catastrophe, recession, layoff, wage cuts, or old age. Some fall into poverty for brief periods over their life cycle.

The jobs held by the middle class differ greatly, especially in income compensation. Overall, middle-class workers earn a median income above that of most blue-collar workers, but there is a great deal of crossover. For example, the median income of sales workers was $34,580 in 2009; workers who provide administrative support in offices earned less, at $31,824. Teachers and other educators had a median income of $46,496 (U.S. Census Bureau, 2010k). As a group, white-collar workers have greater job security and better fringe benefits than many blue-collar workers, but these benefits are being eroded under the current economic constraints.

Some white-collar jobs are as routine and boring as many blue-collar jobs; others are highly interesting and challenging. Still others are extremely alienating in that employees cannot control their environments. Some employees perceive their work as meaningless, are socially isolated from co-workers, and develop low levels of self-esteem. The type of job and the environment in which it is performed vary greatly among workers with white-collar jobs. Members of this class appear to believe strongly in the Protestant work ethic. They generally adhere to a set of beliefs and values that are inherent in the good life. Although they are only slightly better off economically than their blue-collar counterparts, they have or try to maintain a more affluent lifestyle.

Thirty years ago, sociologists suggested that the middle class was beginning to disappear (Mooney, 2008). At that time blue-collar workers were losing their manufacturing jobs; many of the replacement jobs paid lower wages, making it difficult to maintain their lifestyles. Today's middle-class families face stagnant salaries, part or all of which many are forced to use to pay for their health insurance and retirement planning (Hacker & Pierson, 2010)—benefits that their parents' companies covered. Reporter Nan Mooney (2008) concluded that "today's middle class is struggling to redefine itself in an era in which education and employment no longer guarantee you much of anything" (p. 21).

THE UPPER MIDDLE CLASS

Professionals, managers, and administrators are the elite of the middle class. They represent the status that many upwardly mobile families are trying to reach. Their income level allows them to lead lives that are, in many cases, quite different from those of white-collar and blue-collar workers. They are the group that seems to have benefited most from the nation's economic growth. Although they lie at a level far below the upper class, the **upper middle class** are the affluent members of the middle class.

The professionals who best fit this category are those who must earn professional or advanced degrees and credentials to practice their professions. One of every five workers has a professional or related job. Judges, lawyers, architects, physicians, college professors, teachers, computer programmers, and scientists are the professionals. Excluding teachers and social services occupations, most professionals earn far more than the median income of $54,288 reported in the census for this category (U.S. Census Bureau, 2010k). Generally, these members of the upper middle class are among the top 5% of income earners, with annual salaries over $180,000. They usually own a home and a couple of cars and are able to take vacations (Mooney, 2008).

This group also includes managers and administrators, who make up 20% of the employed population. They are the successful executives and businesspeople, a very diverse group that includes the chief executive officers of companies, presidents of colleges, and owners of local businesses. Those who are the most affluent make up the middle and upper management positions in financing, marketing, and production. The gap between men's and women's earnings is greater for managers and administrators than for professionals. As reported earlier in this chapter, the administrators of large corporations earn salaries far above this level; their salaries and fringe benefits place them in the upper class.

The incomes and opportunities to accumulate wealth are higher for this group compared with other members of the middle class because they have enough money to invest and earn additional income. Members of this class play an active role in civic and voluntary organizations. Their occupations and incomes give them access to policymaking roles within local, state, and national organizations. They actively participate in the political process when possible.

The occupations of the people in this group play a central role in their lives, often determining their friends as well as their business and professional associates. Their jobs allow autonomy and a great amount of self-direction. Members of this group tend to view their affluence, advantages, and comforts as universal rather than as unique. In the past, they believed in the American dream of success because they had achieved it. However, this dream now appears to be working primarily for college graduates who choose careers in the financial and corporate world. College graduates who choose fields such as reporting, teaching, social work, and other human services professions do not appear to be eligible for the opportunities for upper economic and social mobility available to earlier generations (Mooney, 2008; Hacker & Pierson, 2010).

THE UPPER CLASS

High income and wealth are necessary characteristics for entering the upper class as well as being accepted by those who are already members. Within the upper class, however, are great variations in the wealth of individual families. This income level is comprised of two groups. One group includes the individuals and families who control great inherited wealth; the other group includes top-level administrators and professionals. Prestige positions, rather than great wealth, allow some families to enter or maintain their status at this level. The upper class includes individuals with top-level, highly paid positions in large banks, entertainment companies, and industrial corporations. It also includes those who serve as primary advisors to these positions and government leaders—for example, corporate lawyers.

The disparity in income and wealth between members of this class and members of other classes is astounding. In 1980, for example, chief executive officers earned about 42 times as much as the average worker in their companies. In 1990 the pay ratio reached 107:1. By 2009 it had increased to 263:1 (Anderson et al., 2010). The number of people reporting incomes of more than a million dollars has grown dramatically since the 1980s. This increase in the size of the upper class has occurred, in part, because of the growing incomes of CEOs. The richest hundredth of a percent (i.e., 0.01%) of the population includes around 15,000 families with average annual incomes of $35 million, responsible for 6% of the national income (Hacker & Pierson, 2010). For the first time, in 2005, all of the richest 400 Americans on the Forbes Magazine list were billionaires. The wealthiest families have been able to increase their share of income and wealth consistently over the past 30 years, whereas low-income families saw almost no gain and middle-class families saw only a modest gain (Hacker & Pierson, 2010).

Wealth and income ensure power. The extremely small proportion of the population who hold a vastly disproportionate share of the wealth also benefit disproportionately in resource distribution. The power possessed by these people allows them to protect their wealth. The only progressive tax in this country is the federal income tax, in which a greater percentage of the income is taxed as the income increases. Loopholes in the tax laws provide benefits to those whose unearned income is based on assets. What does this mean in terms of advantage to the rich? Tax laws in the 1980s were regressive, resulting in a decline in the taxes of higher-income families. The 1990s saw a more progressive structure in which the taxes of higher-income families rose in comparison to the taxes of low-income families. The tax cuts of 2001 reduced taxes for everyone, but more so for high-income families. The debate about taxes continues today, with one side arguing that the rich should be taxed more and the other side arguing that taxes should be cut for the wealthy because they believe such cuts will stimulate the economy.

Although families with inherited wealth do not represent a completely closed status group, they do have an overrepresentation of Anglo, Protestant members who were born in the United States. They tend to intermarry with other members of the upper class. They are well educated, although a college degree is not essential. The educational mark of prestige is attendance at elite private prep schools and prestigious private colleges and universities. Greater assimilation of lifestyles and values has occurred within this class than in any other. Although diversity exists among them, members of the upper class may be the most homogeneous group, and they are likely to remain so as long as their cross-cultural and cross-class interactions are limited.

Economic Inequality

Income inequality is higher in the United States than in all other industrialized countries except Mexico and Turkey. International studies report that the United States has the highest poverty rate and institution of social policies that limit opportunities for moving out of poverty. Low-income workers in the United States earn less than low-income workers in other industrialized countries. Other countries have stronger unions, higher minimum wages, and more generous benefits, including more vacation days. The policies of other countries provide a social safety net for families through maternity leave, family leave, universal health care, and child care for its children (Organisation for Economic Co-operation & Development, 2008). As a result of the world-wide recession, which began in 2008, many European countries are being forced to reduce their safety nets, leading to marches against the government by outraged citizens.

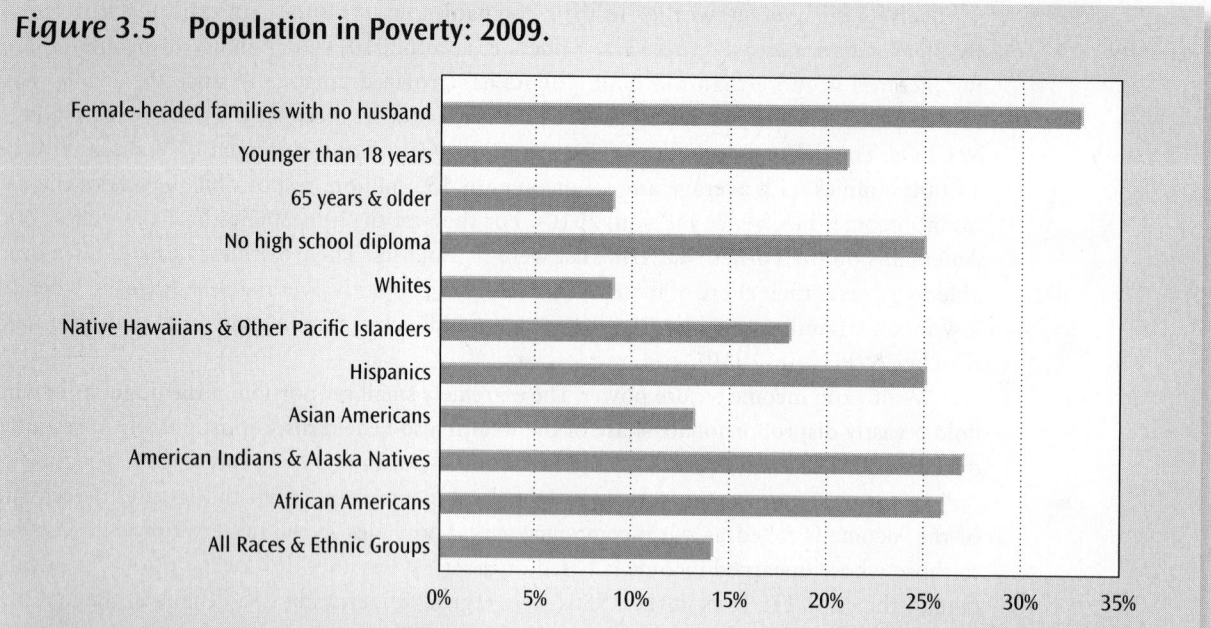

Figure 3.5 Population in Poverty: 2009.

Source: DeNavas-Walt, C., Proctor, B. D., & Smith, J. C. (2010). *Income, poverty, and health insurance coverage in the United States: 2009* (Current Population Reports, P60-238). Washington, DC: U.S. Census Bureau.

Nearly 44 million people, or 14.3% of the population and 11.1% of all families, were living in poverty by federal standards in 2009 (U.S. Census Bureau, 2010k). Poverty is most likely to be a condition of the young, people of color, women, full-time workers in low-status jobs, and the illiterate, as shown in Figure 3.5.

The poor are a very heterogeneous group. They do not all have the same values or lifestyles. They cannot be expected to react alike to the conditions of poverty. To many, their ethnicity or religion is the most important determinant of the way they live within the economic constraints of poverty. To others, the devastating impact of limited resources is the greatest influence in determining their lifestyles, which are limited severely by the economic constraints that keep them in poverty.

RACIAL AND ETHNIC INEQUALITY

Although equality is an important American value, we have not yet reached equality in incomes across ethnic and racial groups. African American families earned 61% ($39,879) of the median income of white families ($65,000), Latinos 60% ($40,466), and Asian American and Pacific Islander families 113% ($73,578) in 2008 (U.S. Census Bureau, 2010k). One of the reasons for these differences is that people of color are more likely to be concentrated in low-paying jobs, as shown in Figure 3.6. The percentage of African Americans in the higher-paying and higher-status jobs is much lower than for whites. Although both absolute and relative gains in the occupational status of African Americans have been made during the past 40 years, they and Latinos are still heavily overrepresented in the semi-skilled and unskilled positions.

Although more whites are in poverty than any other group (18.5 million), the percentage of whites in poverty is smaller compared with other groups except for Asian Americans.

Of the white population, 9% fall below the poverty level, compared with 26% of African Americans, 25% of Latinos, and 12% of Asian Americans (DeNavas-Walt, Proctor, & Smith, 2010). Considerable diversity exists among Asian Americans as with other groups. For example, some Asian Americans—primarily families from the second wave of Southeast Asian immigrants—are much more likely to live in poverty than most other Asian Americans.

This inequitable condition is perpetuated by several factors. People in poverty are more likely not to have graduated from high school. Students of color drop out of school in greater proportions than white students, limiting their income potential. Dropout rates are also related to family income. High school graduation rates range from 70% for those from families earning less than $36,080 annually to 94% for those from families earning more than $108,284 (Family Income and Educational Attainment, 2010).

A job is necessary to earn income, and fewer people have jobs now than before the 2008 recession. The employment rate for all groups has more than doubled since 2005, but a greater percentage of whites and Asian Americans retained their jobs or found new ones. Less than 9% of the white and 7% of the Asian American population were unemployed in 2009, compared with 15% of African Americans and 12% of Latinos (U.S. Census Bureau, 2010k). Continuing discrimination against African Americans and Latinos contributes to lower academic achievement and educational attainment, which results in lower-status jobs and periodic unemployment.

The historical experiences of ethnic groups have had a great impact on their gains in SES. For example, the absolute class position (income, occupation, rate of employment) of

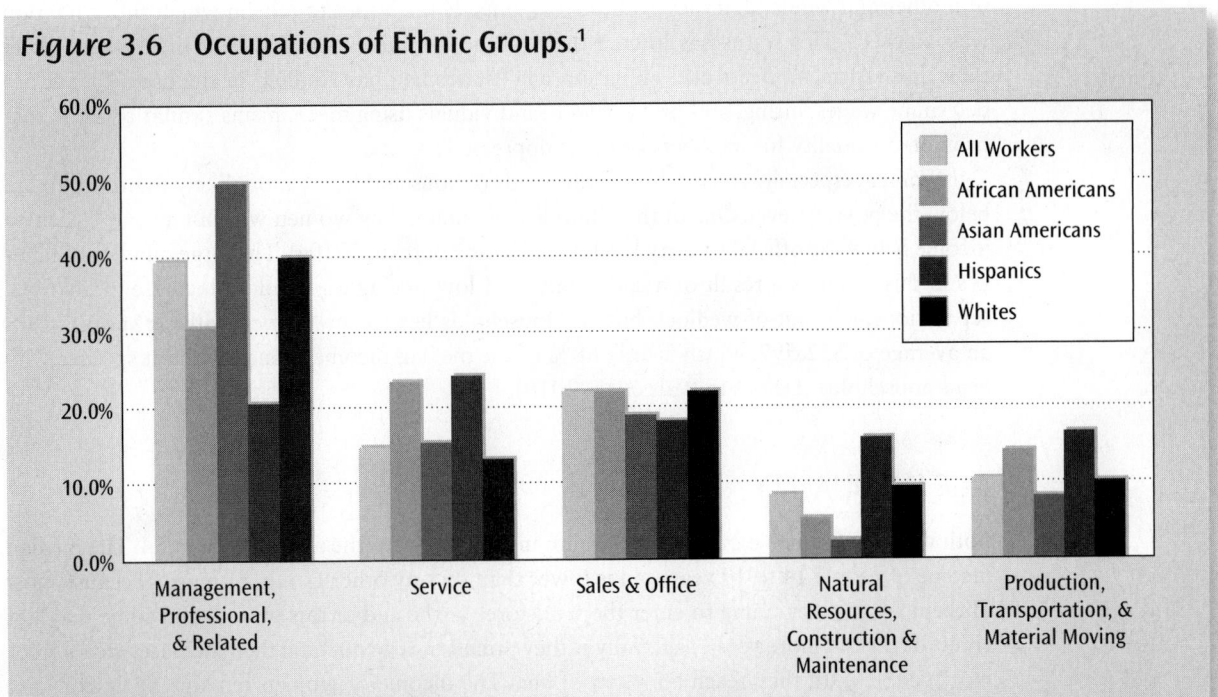

Figure 3.6 Occupations of Ethnic Groups.[1]

[1]The figure shows the percentages of all workers from a specific ethnic group who are working in a job category (e.g., 31.5% of all employed African Americans work in management, professional, and related occupations).

Source: U.S. Census Bureau. (2010k). Statistical abstract of the United States: 2011 (130th ed.). Washington, DC: Author.

African Americans improved as a result of their migration to America's large cities where they could find jobs paying higher wages during the first half of the twentieth century. Their educational attainments have narrowed the formerly enormous gap between blacks and whites with regard to completion of high school; median number of school years completed; and, to a lesser degree, standardized test scores and prevalence of college attendance. Even though the gaps in educational attainment have narrowed, less than 50% of African American males graduate from high school within four years after entering as freshmen, reducing their income potential dramatically.

Other oppressed groups with a disproportionately low SES have had different historical experiences from African Americans but suffer similarly from discrimination. Mexican Americans are highly overrepresented as farm laborers, one of the lowest-status occupations. Many American Indians have been isolated on reservations, away from most occupations except those lowest in prestige, and the numbers of such positions are limited. Asian Americans, who as a group have a high educational level and a relatively high SES, often reach middle-management positions but then face a glass ceiling that prevents them from moving into upper management.

GENDER INEQUALITY

As a group, women earn less and are more likely to suffer from poverty than any other group, with women of color suffering the greatest oppression. The origins of such inequality, however, are very different from inequality based on race and ethnicity. Institutional discrimination based on gender began in a patriarchal society in which women were assigned to the traditional roles of mother and wife and, if they had to work outside the home, to jobs in which subordination was expected. This status has limited their job opportunities and has kept their wages lower than those of men. Overt discrimination against women has resulted in the use of gender to determine wages, hiring, and promotion of individuals using mechanisms similar to those that promote inequality for members of other oppressed groups.

Women, especially those who are the heads of households, are more likely than men to fall below the poverty level. One of three families maintained by women without a spouse earn an income below the official poverty level (U.S. Census Bureau, 2010g). The large number of families in this group is a result of a combination of low-paying jobs and an increase in divorces, separations, and out-of-wedlock births. Households headed by women without spouses earn an average of $32,597, which is only 68% of the median income of men without spouses who head households (DeNavas-Walt et al., 2010).

AGE INEQUALITY

Both women and men earn their maximum income between the ages of 45 and 54. The median income of people 14 to 19 years old is lower than for any other group, primarily because most of them are just beginning to enter the workforce at the end of this period, and some may not enter for several more years, especially if they attend college. Income then increases steadily for most people until they reach 55 years of age. The income of women remains fairly constant throughout much of their working lives, whereas the income for a large percentage of men increases dramatically during their lifetimes.

The highest incidence of poverty occurs for young people, as shown in Figure 3.7. Children's class status depends on their families, leaving children little or no control over their destiny

Figure 3.7 People in Poverty by Age, Race, and Ethnicity: 2008.

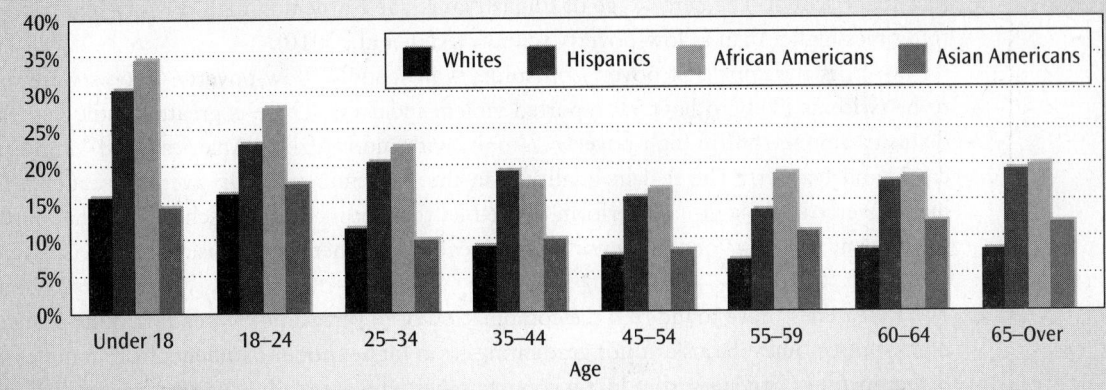

Source: **U.S. Census Bureau. (2010k).** *Statistical abstract of the United States: 2011* **(130th ed.). Washington, DC: Author.**

during their early years. Since the economic recession began in 2008, which is the year for the data in Figure 3.7, an increasing number of children are from families who have fallen into poverty. One-fifth of the nation's children live in families that are officially considered poor. One of 10 children lives in extreme poverty, meaning that the family income is $10,025 or less, which is half of the official poverty level. If we accept the categorization that families earning twice the poverty level are low-income in that they barely make ends meet, nearly two of five children live in low-income families (Wright et al., 2011).

A higher percentage of children in the United States are in poverty than in other industrialized countries (Organisation for Economic Co-operation & Development, 2011). The degree of child poverty varies across states, with Arkansas, the District of Columbia, Kentucky, Mississippi, and New Mexico having the highest rates, exceeding 25%. Poverty rates are much higher for most children of color. Thirty-six percent of African American, 33% of Latino, and 34% percent of American Indian children live in families who fall below the official poverty level, compared to 12% of white and 15% of Asian American children. Children in immigrant families are more likely than children with native-born parents to live in poverty, with rates of 27% and 19%, respectively (Wright et al., 2011).

In schools poverty is tracked by the number of students eligible for free or reduced-price lunches (FRPL). Children who are eligible for free meals are in families with incomes that are 130% of the poverty level, which was $28,665 or below for a family of four in 2011. If they are in families with incomes between 130% and 185% of the poverty level ($40,793), they are eligible for a reduced-price meal. In the 2008–09 school year, 45% of U.S. students were eligible for this program (Snyder & Dillow, 2011). Overall the percentage of white students on FRPL is less than half that for other students with the exception of Asian Americans. In city schools 82% of Hispanic, 80% of African American, 67% of American Indian, 45% of Asian American, and 31% of white students were eligible for FRPL. Families with schoolchildren in the nation's towns are low-income at about the same rate as in cities. Fewer low-income families with children are found in the suburbs and rural areas (Aud et al., 2010).

In low-poverty schools less than 25% of the students are eligible for FRPL; in high-poverty schools more than 75% of the students are eligible. Seventeen percent of the nation's schools were high-poverty in the 2007–08 school year; these schools were more highly concentrated in cities. African American and Hispanic students were 8 times more likely than white students to attend a high-poverty elementary school and 15 times more likely to attend a high-poverty secondary school. The percentage of English language learners in high-poverty schools was 6 to 8 times higher than in low-poverty schools (Aud et al., 2010).

What is the impact of poverty on students in schools? Low-poverty schools were found to be twice as likely to have no reported violent incidents. There is greater ethnic and racial diversity among staff in high-poverty schools, with more African American and Latino principals and teachers. The real inequality is in the academic area. On average, students from high-poverty schools do not perform as well as their peers in other schools on the National Assessment of Educational Progress (NAEP) reading, mathematics, music, and art assessments (Aud et al., 2010).

Researchers have found that the combination of poverty and low reading skills place children at three times the risk of not graduating from high school as students from families with higher incomes. Students from low-income families who are reading at a proficient level in the third grade have a much better chance of completing high school (Hernandez, 2011). However, 17% of low-income students were reading at the proficient or advanced level in the fourth grade in 2009 compared to 45% of higher-income students. Only 10% of African American and 11% of Hispanic low-income students were at the proficient level, as shown in Figure 3.8 (National Assessment of Educational Progress, 2011). A number of factors contribute to this low performance. For example, students from low-income families are more likely to be absent from school, which is associated with lower academic performance. Research also finds that students' reading proficiency level drops over the summer unless they are engaged in reading (Hernandez, 2011).

Figure 3.8
Performance on Fourth-Grade Reading Tests by Students in Low-Income Families: 2009.

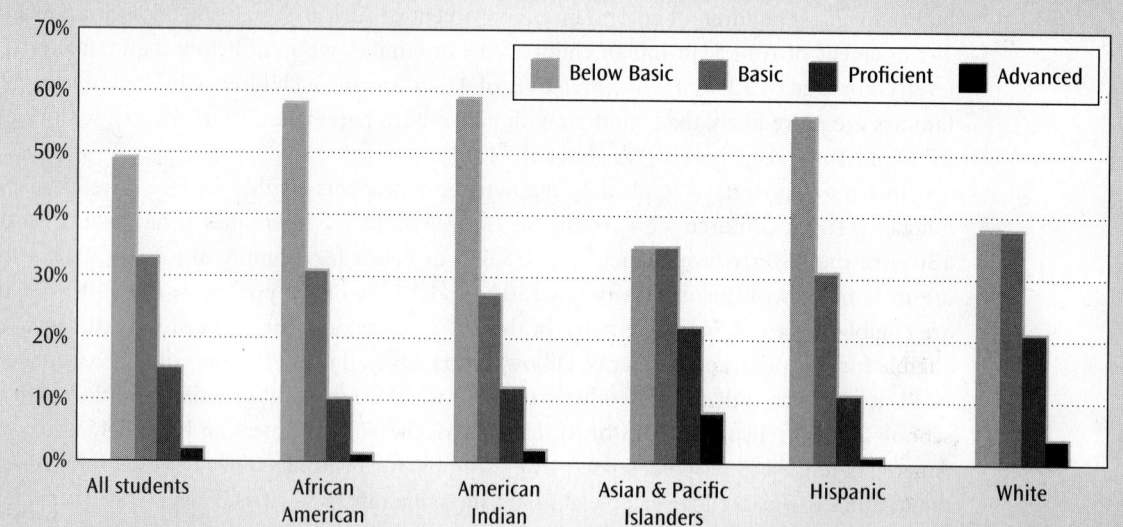

Source: National Assessment of Educational Progress. (2011). NAEP Data Explorer. Washington, DC: National Center for Education Statistics, Institute of Education Sciences, U.S. Department of Education. Retrieved on May 27, 2011, from http://nces.ed.gov/nationsreportcard/naepdata/.

Students from low-income families often begin kindergarten with lower cognitive skills than their peers in families with middle and high incomes (Berk, 2012). To compound the problem, many kindergartners in low-income families begin their schooling in high-poverty public schools with low-quality teaching and discriminatory practices such as ability grouping (Darling-Hammond, 2010). These children will be disadvantaged in developing their adult earning power by inferior schooling, an oppressive financial environment, and poor health.

Teaching for Equality

Many social reformers, educators, and parents view education as a powerful device for achieving social change and reducing poverty. From the beginning of the public school movement in the early nineteenth century, low incomes and immorality were believed to result from inadequate education. Thus, children from low-income families were encouraged to attend charity schools and public common schools to learn the Christian values that would help them develop the discipline for working.

As of the 1960s, many students from low-income families still were not achieving academically at the same levels as their more economically advantaged peers and were still dropping out of school at higher rates. As part of President Lyndon Johnson's War on Poverty, the federal government attempted to decrease poverty through the establishment of Head Start, Title I (compensatory education), Upward Bound, Job Corps, Neighborhood Youth Corps, and other educational programs. However, test scores of students from low-income groups have not improved as much as expected nor has economic equality of families been realized.

This lack of progress in overcoming the effects of poverty on students should not be taken as evidence that educational reforms are not worthwhile. Some changes make schooling more attractive to students and even increase the achievement of many students. In a number of states educational resources have become more equitably distributed as a result of court cases. Nevertheless, the initial goal of programs aimed at increasing income equity and eliminating poverty has not been realized. More than school reform will be needed to raise the academic achievement of low-SES students. The social and economic conditions of their lives must be improved through higher wages and social policies that support low-income families (Rothstein, 2008).

Different sociohistorical interpretations of education are presented to explain the role of schools in society and the degree to which this goal and others are being met. In one view schools are an agent of social reform that can improve the chances of economic success for its graduates. The second view posits that schools exist as agents of the larger social, economic, and political context, with the goal of inculcating the values necessary to maintain the current socioeconomic and political systems.

Supporters of the first view are much more benign in their description of the role of schools in helping students become socially mobile. They are optimistic that social reform can be achieved by providing low-income students with more effective schools. The other view sees schools as preparing students to work efficiently at their jobs in corporate organizations. The needs of business and industry are met by preparing students from low-income families for low-wage jobs that will be managed by college graduates from middle- and high-income families.

Rather than provide equal educational opportunity, many schools perpetuate existing social and economic inequities in society. In this section, we examine four areas that influence inequities in schools: teacher expectations, tracking, curriculum, and funding.

TEACHER EXPECTATIONS

The students in many schools are from lower- and middle-income families. Some teachers' academic expectations of students are based on the family SES. Students from middle-class families may be viewed as more able to achieve at high academic levels. Students from low-income families are harmed by such expectations. In contrast, students from upper-middle-class families are generally advantaged by such teacher judgments because they are expected to perform better in school, are treated more favorably, and do perform at a higher level in most cases.

Students from low-income families typically take fewer courses in mathematics and science, which contributes to later disparities in college enrollment and vocational choices. In many schools with large numbers of low-income students, advanced courses in these subjects may be offered, but they lack the academic rigor of the more advantaged schools. Thus, low-income students who are achieving at a level equal to students from higher-income families are stifled in their attempts to move to higher levels in the advanced courses available at their schools. It is no wonder that they don't score as high on standardized assessments. They lack the opportunity to take the same high-level courses as their middle-class peers.

Ethnographic studies of schools document how students are classified, segregated, and taught differently, starting with their first days in school. Most teachers can identify the personal characteristics of students that will lead to academic success. They then develop instruction and interactions with their students to ensure that the students will, in fact, behave as the teachers expect—a phenomenon called the **self-fulfilling prophecy**. The kindergarten teacher who divides her class into three reading and mathematics groups by the third week of school has limited knowledge about the academic abilities of the students. Too often, the groups are organized according to nonacademic factors. Students in the highest group may be dressed in clean clothes that are relatively new and well pressed. They interact well with the teacher and other students, are quite verbal, and use standard English. Students in the lower two groupings may be poorly dressed and use a dialect or be English language learners. Their families may appear to be less stable than those of students in the highest group. If the teacher's goal is to spend time with students in the lower group to ensure that they develop the language and reading skills they will need to be successful in the first grade, and that they develop the skills to make them less distinguishable from students in the higher groups, this grouping strategy may be successful. The problem is that many teachers do not expect the students who are in the lower academic group at the

Suburban schools are more likely than inner-city schools to have the technology, resources, extracurricular activities, and attractive playground space that make a school welcoming to students.
© H. Mark Weidman Photography/Alamy

beginning of the year to perform at high levels by the end of the year. The result is that students in the highest group continue to perform better academically and to behave in a more acceptable manner than students in the other two groups. As the teacher had projected, these students are more successful throughout their schooling than students from lower socioeconomic levels.

When teachers make such judgments about students, they are taking the first step in preventing students from having an equal opportunity for academic achievement. Rather than ensure that students have access to an egalitarian system, such classification and subsequent treatment of students ensures the maintenance of an inequitable system. This action is not congruent with the democratic belief that all students should be provided equal educational opportunities. All students can learn, including those in the lower-ability group; they can learn at the same level as many other students with the assistance of effective teachers.

In helping to overcome the stigma of poverty, educators must consciously review their expectations for students. Students' feelings of low esteem should not be reinforced by teachers. Seeing students as individuals, rather than as members of a specific socioeconomic group, may assist educators in overcoming the **classism** that exists in the school and the community. Information about a student's family background can be used in understanding the power of environment on a student's expression of self; it should not be used to rationalize stereotypes and label students. Educators should become aware of any prejudices they themselves hold against members of lower socioeconomic groups and work to overcome their biases. Otherwise, discriminatory practices will surface in the classroom in the form of self-fulfilling prophecies that harm students and perpetuate societal inequities.

Inner-city schools are populated by many low-income and working-class students whose environment outside the school is very different from that of students in most suburban schools. For many students, schools are safe places compared to the atmosphere of abuse and crime that may be part of the daily lives of students in a neighborhood characterized by poverty. These students have strengths that are not recognized or supported by many educators. Many are very resilient under conditions that present obstacles to their well-being and academic achievement. Although it is essential to ensure that all students learn the subject matter, how these skills are taught should vary depending on the environment in which students live—a factor greatly dependent on the family's SES. Helping students achieve academically in schools that serve students from low-income families requires competent educators who know the subjects they are teaching as well as believing that all students can learn.

How can the development of negative and harmful expectations for students be prevented? Teachers, counselors, and administrators can unconsciously fall into such behavior because they have been taught that poverty is the fault of the individual. As a result, students are blamed for circumstances beyond their control. Instead, educators should see as a challenge the opportunity to provide these students with the knowledge and skills to overcome poverty. Educators should select approaches they would use for the most gifted students. The goal should be to improve the educational experience for students who previously would have been tracked into the low-ability classes. Too many teachers blame the students, their families, and their communities for students' failure to learn rather than examining and changing their own teaching practices to improve student learning. Effective teachers do make a difference (Darling-Hammond, 2010).

Equality in student achievement could be increased by raising the level of instructional content and instructional discourse in all courses at all levels. Achievement is improved when teachers help students interact with the academic content through discussion and **authenticity**—relating the content to students' prior experiences and real-world applications. These strategies work for all students, not just those in the advanced placement and honors courses.

TRACKING

Tracking students into different groups or classes based on their intellectual abilities is a common educational practice. Teachers often divide the class into smaller groups for instructional purposes. These groups could have a heterogeneous makeup, with each group containing girls and boys from different ethnic groups and students who are currently high and low achievers. In these groups students could help each other. In other cases, teachers may assign students to a group based on their perception of the students' academic abilities, which may be based on students' latest standardized test scores. Teachers may use different instructional strategies in these groups and have different expectations for learning outcomes.

Tracking occurs when students are assigned to courses based on their perceived intellectual abilities or other characteristics, such as speaking a language other than English or having a disability. Middle and high school students either choose or are assigned to college preparatory, vocational, general, and advanced courses based, in great part, on how their teachers or counselors judge their future potential. Some students are placed in gifted courses or programs, and others in courses that are clearly meant for low-ability students.

Supporters of tracking argue that separating students based on their perceived academic abilities allows teachers to better meet the needs of all students. Critics argue that tracking and homogeneous grouping based on ability is discriminatory and prevents many students from developing their intellectual and social potential.

Tracking is an area in which class matters. High ability appears to be more closely related to race and class than to intellectual potential (Burris, Wiley, Welner, & Murphy, 2008). Students whose families are already privileged benefit the most from tracking. Students in the gifted and advanced programs are academically challenged in their courses, with enrichment activities that encourage them to develop their intellectual and critical thinking skills. At the other end of the learning spectrum, the learning environment is often uninviting, boring, and not challenging. Rather than preparing these students to move to higher-level courses, these courses keep them at the lowest levels of academic achievement.

Being in the low-ability group diminishes student achievement. Students in this group have limited access to rigorous courses and to rich and creative experiences that will enhance opportunities for learning (Darling-Hammond, 2010). Critical thinking tasks are reserved for the high-ability groups. Oral recitation and structured written work are common in low-ability groups. Students are exposed to knowledge at a slower pace than their peers in higher-ability groups, and the knowledge is low in status, helping them fall further behind in subjects like mathematics, foreign languages, and sciences.

Teachers in low-ability classrooms spend more time on administration and discipline and less time actually teaching. As one might expect, student behavior in low tracks is more disruptive than in higher-level groups. However, this probably happens, in part, because students and teachers have developed behavioral standards that are more tolerant of inattention, and not because of students' individual abilities. To compound the problem, the more experienced and more successful teachers are disproportionately assigned to the higher-ability groups. Unfortunately, many teachers generally view high-track students positively and low-track students negatively.

Disproportionately large numbers of students from lower socioeconomic levels are assigned to low-ability groups beginning very early in their school careers. Even more tragic is the fact that the number of students from low-income families who are classified as being mentally challenged is disproportionately high. This inequitable classification places students of color in double jeopardy because they also disproportionately suffer from poverty.

In many schools with diverse student populations, students are segregated based on race, class, and language into separate tracks within the school. White middle-class students have disproportionately high representation in gifted and talented programs while African Americans, Latinos, students from low-income families, and English language learners comprise the majority of the students in low-ability classrooms. For the most part, the courts have agreed with the plaintiffs that tracking students into low-ability courses and programs is a discriminatory practice that limits their educational opportunities and their potential for later occupational and economic success. Even when students and parents are encouraged to choose courses, a school district may be liable for discriminatory action if parents have not been appropriately informed of the prerequisites for advanced courses. Other discriminatory practices that are being reviewed by courts today are the inadequate preparation of low-income students and students of color to pass standardized tests and the assignment of unqualified teachers to the schools in which these students are concentrated.

Some courts have ordered school districts to detrack their schools (Welner, 2002). Other schools have voluntarily made this decision to improve the education of students who have traditionally been assigned to the low tracks. However, dismantling tracking systems in schools is not an easy undertaking. Some teachers fight detracking, in part because they do not believe that heterogeneous groupings contribute to the learning of all students. They may believe that gifted students will suffer if they are integrated with students who do not perform at the same academic level.

Middle-class parents, especially upper-middle-class parents, sometimes fight efforts to detrack schools and integrate their children with students who they think are not as smart or deserving of the best educational resources (which are often limited to gifted and talented students). Many of these parents believe that their success should be passed on to their children by ensuring that they receive the highest-quality education possible. To prevent detracking, these parents employ strategies to hold on to the privilege that their children can gain from education. They use their power to force administrators to respond to their demands. They have been known to threaten to remove their children from public schools and to hold out for other special privileges for their children. At times, they co-opt parents from the middle class to support their stand. Nevertheless, some schools have been able to detrack their programs with the goal of improving the education of all students regardless of the socioeconomic level or race of their parents.

CURRICULUM FOR EQUALITY

The curriculum should reflect accurately the class structure and inequities that exist in the United States. The existence of nearly half the population is not validated in the curricula of most schools. Curriculum and textbooks usually focus on the values and experiences of a middle-class society. They highlight the heroes of our capitalist and political system, who were primarily white males of economically privileged families. They usually ignore the history and heroes of the labor struggle in this country, in which laborers resisted and endured under great odds to improve their conditions. They do not discuss the role of the working class in the development of the nation. The inequities based on the income and wealth of one's family are usually neither described nor discussed. In classrooms, students should learn of the existence of these differences. They should understand that the majority of the population does not live the middle-class myth.

Debate / Detracking

Data in many schools show that the children of upper-middle-class families are overrepresented in high-ability programs for the gifted and talented and underrepresented in low-ability special education and general education courses. School officials are being pushed by the courts to change their practices that segregate students by SES or race. One of the remedies for eliminating these discriminatory practices is detracking, or dismantling tracks for students based on ability as determined by standardized tests or teachers' perceptions. Some teachers and middle-class parents resist the move to a single track in which students from different ability groups are mixed.

Opinions about these strategies differ. Some people believe that detracking will provide greater equality of opportunity across economic and racial groups; opponents believe that it will lead to a lower quality of education overall. Some pros and cons of detracking are listed next.

FOR	AGAINST
■ Eliminates discrimination against students from low-income families and students of color.	■ Is not fair to high-ability students, who need to be challenged at advanced levels.
■ Integrates students from different ability levels.	■ Makes it more difficult for teachers to provide appropriate instruction for all students, whose abilities differ greatly.
■ Encourages classroom instruction that is challenging and interesting for low-income as well as upper-middle-class students.	■ May lead to pressure from upper-middle-class parents, who may withdraw their children from public schools.
■ Supports a classroom environment in which high-ability students learn while assisting peers who may not be at the same academic level.	■ Waters down the curriculum for high-ability students.
■ Provides low-SES students greater access to good teachers, improving their chances for learning at higher levels.	■ Prevents high-ability students from participating in gifted and talented programs and advanced-level courses that will give them the advantage needed to be admitted to elite colleges and universities.

| QUESTIONS |

1. How do schools ensure that the voices of low- and middle-income families are included in discussions about detracking and the provision of educational equity in schools?
2. How does detracking schools contribute to the provision of equal educational opportunity?
3. What other steps could school officials take to provide low-income students greater access to advanced courses?
4. What are your reasons for supporting or not supporting detracking strategies in schools?

Often overlooked are the experiences that students bring to the classroom. School is not the only place where students learn about life. Differences in school behavior and learning among students from dissimilar socioeconomic levels are strongly dependent on the knowledge and skills needed to survive appropriately in their community environments. Most low-income students, especially those in urban areas, have learned how to live in a world that is not imaginable to most middle-class students or teachers. Yet the knowledge and skills they bring to school are not always valued. Educators should recognize the value of the community's informal education in sustaining its own culture and realize that formal education is often viewed as undermining that culture.

Students need to see some of their own cultural experiences reflected in the curriculum. They need to see ordinary working people depicted as valued members of society. These students and their families need to be helped to see themselves as desirable and integral members of the school community, rather than as second-class citizens who must learn the ways of the more economically advantaged to succeed in school.

Educators should become familiar with the activities, films, and books used in class. If students never see their communities in these instructional materials, their motivation and acceptance may be limited. All students should be encouraged to read novels and short stories about people from different socioeconomic levels. When studying historical or current events, they should examine the events from the perspective of the working class and people in poverty, as well as from the perspective of the country's leaders. Teaching can be enhanced by drawing examples from experiences with which students are familiar, especially when the experiences are different from the teacher's own.

All students, no matter what their SES, should be helped to develop strong and positive self-concepts. Many students do not realize the diversity that exists in this country, let alone understand the reasons for the diversity and the resulting discrimination against some groups. Middle-class children tend to believe that most people live like their families. Educators are expected to expand their students' knowledge of the world, not to hide from them the realities that exist because of class differences. In a classroom in which democracy and equity are important, low-income students should receive priority time from teachers and have access to the necessary resources to help them become academically competitive with middle-class students.

Finally, all students should be encouraged to be critical of what they read, see, and hear in textbooks, through the mass media, and from their parents and friends. The curriculum should

PAUSE TO REFLECT 3.2

New teachers are often assigned to teach in schools with large numbers of students from low-income families. Think about how you could help these students see themselves represented in the curriculum.

- How will you ensure that your low-income students will not be marginalized in the curriculum?

- What projects might your students engage in to learn more about equality and inequality based on socioeconomic differences?

- What courses have you taken that can help you understand the inequities in society? What did they address?

encourage the development of critical thinking and problem-solving skills. Although teachers traditionally talk about the democratic vision, they generally are unwilling to model it. Students and teachers who become involved through the curriculum in asking why the inequities in society exist are beginning to think critically about our democracy.

SCHOOL FUNDING

At the beginning of this chapter, Mr. Juarez found great differences in the conditions of schools in the inner city versus the suburbs. The problem is greatly exacerbated by the fact that the current system for funding schools mirrors these inequities. Education is financed by local, state and federal sources, but primarily by local and state sources at 43.5% and 48.3%, respectively; federal support is around 8% (Zhou, 2010). Property taxes are the primary source of local funding for schools, which contributes to the disparities in education from one community to another. Communities with high-income families will generate much more in property taxes than low-income communities to support their schools.

The average per-pupil expenditure for the United States was $10,297 in 2008, but the amount varied greatly across states, ranging from $3,886 in Utah to $11,572 in New York (Zhou, 2010). Although the nation spends more per pupil that most other countries, a larger portion of school revenues are received from private sources than in any country other than Korea. Regardless of the greater per-pupil expenditures, class sizes are higher in the United States than in most other countries, teacher salaries represent a lower proportion of the GDP per capita, and the teaching load is higher (Organisation for Economic Co-operation & Development, 2011).

Researchers and policymakers disagree as to how much money is needed by schools to improve academic achievement. Some researchers suggest that higher per-pupil expenditures, better teacher salaries, more educated and experienced teachers, and smaller class and school sizes are strongly related to improved student learning. If we agree that more money would help reduce the inequities across groups in schools and that greater resources are needed in low-wealth school districts, what areas would provide the greatest payoff for improving student achievement, especially for students from low-income families? Among the recommendations from researchers and educators are smaller class sizes, prekindergarten programs for four-year-olds, tutoring for students having difficulty, cooperative learning, family support systems, more qualified teachers, and extensive staff and teacher development for delivery of effective programs.

Summary

Socioeconomic status (SES) is a composite representing the economic status of a family or of unrelated individuals, based on income, wealth, occupation, educational attainment, and power. Families range from the indigent poor to the very rich. Where a family falls along this continuum affects the way its members live, how they think and act, and the way others react to them. Although a family may actively participate in other cultural groups centered around ethnicity, religion, gender, exceptionality, language, or age, the class to which a family belongs is probably the strongest factor in determining how one lives.

Social stratification is possible because people occupy different levels of the social structure. People of color, women, the young, the elderly, and individuals with disabilities are disproportionately represented at the low end of the social stratification system.

The United States can be divided into classes based on income and occupation. Individual choice is most limited for those who are in poverty and who can barely meet essential needs. People of color and women who head families are overrepresented at the lowest SES level. Class consciousness is strongest among the upper classes, whose members know the value of solidarity in the protection and maintenance of their power and privilege.

Disproportionately large numbers of students from lower SES levels are tracked in low-ability groups in their early school years. Too often, low-income students are placed in remedial programs because of discriminatory testing and placement. Educators should consciously review their expectations for students and their behavior toward students from different SES levels to ensure that they are not discriminating. In addition, the curriculum does not serve students well if it reflects only the perspective of middle-class America. Low-income students need to see some of their own cultural experiences reflected in the curriculum. Financial support for more equitable funding of schools, no matter where they are located or which students attend them, is likely to reduce the achievement gap between groups of students. The current property tax system for supporting schools gives the advantage to families with high incomes.

Professional Practice

Questions for Discussion

1. How does social stratification affect students in schools?

2. What is the relationship of low-, middle-, and high-income status to power in society? How does access to power influence equal educational opportunity for students from low-income families?

3. As a teacher, how do you determine the economic level and class of the families of your students? How does this knowledge sometimes influence instruction in the classroom?

4. How do class and race interact to maintain economic inequities in society and in schools?

5. What role does education play in maintaining or changing the SES of the population? How can a teacher level the playing field for students from different economic backgrounds?

Portfolio Activities

1. Visit a school in an economically depressed area of your community or a nearby city, and another school in a community in which students are primarily from the upper middle class. Record the differences you find in the physical environment, aesthetics, school

climate, resources for students, and attitudes of faculty and students. Write a paper comparing the two schools and analyzing the reasons for the differences you have observed. (InTASC Standard 3: Learning Environments)

2. Locate the most recent Kids Count data on the Internet and examine the data for your state or the state in which you plan to teach. Write a paper that describes the findings and how the state compares to other states. Discuss what these data suggest for your future teaching. (InTASC Standard 2: Learning Differences)

3. Volunteer to tutor at a homeless shelter or after-school program for students from low-income families, and record your feelings about the children and the settings as journal entries. Your entries could include your feelings on going to the shelter or program for the first time, the strengths of the children with whom you work, and what you've learned about the obstacles students face outside of school. (InTASC Standard 2: Learning Differences and Standard 10: Leadership and Collaboration)

Digital Resources for the Classroom

1. The National Coalition for the Homeless includes lesson plans for different grade levels at http://www.nationalhomeless.org/factsheets/index.html#other.

2. The Homeless Resource Center includes facts and videos about being homeless, including a 2011 video about homeless LGBTQ youth. It can be accessed at http://homeless.samhsa.gov/Resource/Larkin-Street-Stories-The-Homeless-LGBT-Experience-Episode-1-51012.aspx.

3. Information on the McKinney-Vento Homeless Assistance Act and resources for implementing it are available at http://center.serve.org/nche/briefs.php. The site also includes best practices for working with homeless students.

4. The website of Teaching for Change provides resources for teaching equality, including podcasts and videos. It can be accessed at www.teachingforchange.org/.

5. Rethinking Schools was initiated by a group of Milwaukee teachers in 1986 to improve education in their own classrooms and work for the reform of schools committed to equity and to the vision that public education is central to the creation of a humane, caring, multiracial democracy. Articles by teachers fill its quarterly magazine, *Rethinking Schools,* providing ideas about teaching for equality. Check it out at www.rethinkingschools.org.

MyEducationLab™

Go to the MyEducationLab (www.myeducationlab.com) for Multicultural Education and familiarize yourself with the topical content, which includes:

- Assignments and Activities, tied to learning outcomes for the course, that can help you more deeply understand course content
- Building Teaching Skills and Dispositions learning units allow you to apply and practice your understanding of how to teach equitably in a multicultural education classroom
- Licensure Test Prep activities are available in the Book Resources to help you prepare for test taking
- A pretest with hints and feedback that tests your knowledge of this chapter's content
- Review, practice, and enrichment activities that will enhance your understanding of the chapter content
- A posttest with hints and feedback that allows you to test your knowledge again after having completed the enrichment activities

A Correlation Guide may be downloaded by instructors to show how MyEducationLab content aligns to this book.

4 Gender

No person shall, on the basis of sex, be excluded from participation in, be denied the benefits of, or be subjected to discrimination under any education program or activity receiving federal financial assistance.

Title IX (Education Amendments, 1972)

| LEARNING OUTCOMES |

As you read this chapter, you should be able to:

- Understand differences between males and females and how these differences impact schooling.

- Analyze the role of gender identification in how people view themselves and are viewed by others.

- Explore how the women's movement contributed to gender equity in society.

- Characterize the negative results of sexism and gender discrimination.

- Evaluate strategies used by educators to provide equitable education for boys and girls.

"What made me think that I wanted to spend my days with middle schoolers?" thought Ms. Carson. "They are driving me crazy today. Jack keeps bothering Jason, who is trying to read his assignment. In fact, all of the boys are fidgety. The girls seem to like the story they are reading and are anxious to discuss it. The boys, on the other hand, seem to want nothing to do with it."

"Why do we have to read this story?" Jason blurted out. "It's only about some sissy girl who thinks she can hit a baseball. Why don't we play baseball? The boys against the girls. That'll show who can play baseball."

Ms. Carson was frustrated. "What am I to do? I selected this story so that the girls could see themselves as athletes who can be competitors. Now the boys don't see themselves in the story. Maybe boys and girls should be taught in separate classrooms."

| REFLECTIONS |

1. Why is Ms. Carson concerned about how girls are portrayed in the literature that her middle-schoolers read?

2. Characterize the difference between the girls' and boys' behavior in this classroom.

3. What could Ms. Carson do to engage both the girls and boys in the same literature lesson?

Male and Female Differences

How different are males and females? We can fairly easily distinguish the two by their physical appearance alone. Girls tend to have lighter skeletons and different shoulder and pelvic proportions than boys. In the womb, there were major differences in hormonal levels of estrogen and testosterone, which controlled the physical development of the two sexes. Soon after birth, boys and girls have similar hormonal levels and are similar in physical development, a state of affairs that lasts through the early years of elementary school. The onset of puberty again brings major changes in the hormonal levels of the two sexes. At this time, the proportion of fat to total body weight increases in girls and decreases in boys. The differences in physical structure generally contribute to the male's greater strength, greater endurance for heavy labor, greater ease in running or overarm throwing, and lesser ability to float in water. However, the extent of these physical differences can also be influenced by environment and culture. They can be altered with nutrition, physical activity, practice, and behavioral expectations. Some of the differences between the two sexes are outlined in Table 4.1.

Table 4.1 Differences Between Males and Females

Males	Females
In early life, mature more slowly and are sick more often	Around puberty, confidence drops, interest in math and science slips, and interest in beauty grows
Not prone to eating or other psychological disorders	Fewer learning and behavioral disorders
Less likely to have mastered the language, self-control, and fine motor skills necessary for a successful start in school	Less likely to participate in group sports activities
Fewer problems caused by teen pregnancy	Fewer discipline problems
Attention-getting classroom behavior	Higher academic performance
Higher mathematics and science test scores	Higher reading and writing test scores
Higher SAT test scores for admission to college	Higher educational aspirations
More likely to earn a degree in engineering or computer technology	More likely to graduate from high school and college
More likely to have a high-prestige and higher-paying job	Less likely to have incomes equal to their male counterparts
More likely to die in accidents or be victims of violent crime	More likely to be sexually assaulted
More likely to commit suicide	More likely to attempt suicide

Sources: Gurian, M. (2001). *Boys and girls learn differently! A guide for teachers and parents.* San Francisco: Jossey-Bass; Eliot, Lise. (2009). *Pink brain, blue brain: How small differences grow into troublesome gaps—and what we can do about it.* Boston: Mariner, Houghton Mifflin Harcourt.

Most researchers have found little evidence that our brains are hardwired to make us behave differently (Eliot, 2009; Fine, 2010; Jordan-Young, 2010). Why, then, do we see differences in behavior between the two sexes? Women and men often segregate themselves at social gatherings. They dress and groom differently. The topics of their conversations often differ. They participate in sex-specific leisure activities. In classrooms, students are sometimes segregated by sex for school activities. Boys tend to be more rambunctious in their play. Girls and boys often choose different games at recess, where girls are seen jumping rope and boys throw balls at each other. These choices extend into adulthood; many men are fascinated with sports, not missing a game of their favorite college or professional team and managing their own fantasy teams. They may arrange a game of touch football or pick-up basketball with friends. Women, on the other hand, are more likely to watch ice skating or gymnastics on a different channel.

Are these behaviors and choices due to one's being male or female? What makes us behave differently? Do we learn our male and female behaviors through socialization patterns based on sex? Are we born to behave, think, and act differently (i.e., nature) or do we learn these differences (i.e., nurture)? How can understanding these differences help us support, protect, and provide fair treatment to boys and girls as they grow up and move through school? Let's begin by looking at what we know about the differences between the two sexes.

DIFFERENCES BASED ON NATURE

Research on biological differences between the sexes has led to contrasting conclusions about the role of biology after birth in defining female and male differences. The X and Y chromosomes that determine our sex represent a very small proportion of our total gene pool; males and females share roughly 99.8% of their genes (Eliot, 2009). The differences in psychological traits (e.g., empathy, ambition, compassion, aggressiveness, and being responsible) and academic abilities between the average female and male are quite small. The differences are much greater within the male and female populations than between males and females in general (Eliot, 2009). In spite of these research findings, many parents and educators believe that there are innate differences between boys and girls, which can lead to stereotypes and the development of different expectations for their behavior, academic achievement, and future occupations.

These researchers conclude that speaking, reading, mathematics, mechanical ability, and interpersonal characteristics such as aggression, empathy, risk taking, and competitiveness are learned, not innate (Eliot, 2009). Rather than explaining our differences primarily by nature, we are learning that the environment has a great influence on our genes. Girls and boys can learn to use both hemispheres of the brain so that they can effectively develop the full range of skills. Developing the characteristics that are identified with each sex depends on immersion in our cultures and what we learn from our parents and teachers.

Prior to the twentieth century, intelligence was equated with the size of the brain. Because men's brains are larger than women's, scientists of the time concluded that women were not as intelligent as men and, thus, were inferior to them. Today we know that brain size is related to body size, not to intelligence (Eliot, 2009). When Alfred Binet developed the first intelligence test at the beginning of the twentieth century, no differences were found in the general intelligence level between females and males. However, many studies have found gender differences in mathematical and reading skills, with females performing at higher levels on the National Assessment of Educational Progress (NAEP) reading tests and males performing better on NAEP assessments of mathematics (Corbett, Hill, & St. Rose, 2008).

The right hemisphere of the cerebral cortex controls spatial relations, and the left hemisphere controls language and other sequential skills. Some researchers have found that females generally favor the left hemisphere, which is associated with speaking, reading, and writing, while males generally have greater right-hemisphere specialization, which is connected to spatial visualization, mathematics, and science (Eliot, 2009). Psychologist Michael Gurian and physician Leonard Sax attribute these differences to the two sexes being biologically programmed to behave differently. They assert that the two sexes are born with different aptitudes that lead to boys being less verbal and outperforming girls in mathematics and science. They conclude that most classrooms are girl-friendly, causing boys to lag behind in academic achievement (Cleveland, 2011). These reported differences have led to recommendations for segregated classrooms that better fit the respective behaviors and aptitudes of the two sexes (Cleveland, 2011). Some school districts are establishing separate schools for boys and girls based on this research.

Not all scientists agree with Gurian and Sax. For instance, neuroscientist Lise Eliot (2009) argues that these conclusions are based on studies of adult brains, and any differences in verbal ability between the two sexes are "subtle and pertain to very specific language tasks only" (p. 187). In her study of the research on differences in the brains of females and males, she and other scientists—for example, Rebecca M. Jordan-Young (2010)—found no evidence that mental and emotional abilities are hardwired by sex. She recommends that the current achievement gaps be eliminated by effectively teaching verbal skills to boys, and mathematics, science, and spatial skills to girls, in coeducational classrooms.

Researchers on both sides of the argument recommend that different types of classroom activities are needed to engage boys and girls in the academic areas in which they are not performing proficiently. Boys need more "one-on-one verbal engagement, literary immersion, and opportunities for physical play, hands-on learning, and exploration of all types" (Eliot, 2009). Girls need to be engaged in similar activities to develop their mathematics, science, and spatial skills at higher levels. Expectations for both girls and boys need to be high, no matter the subject area. Excuses that they are not performing well because of their sex are no longer acceptable in an educational environment in which schools are expected to ensure that all students perform at their grade level.

SOCIALLY CONSTRUCTED DIFFERENCES

Although nature determines our sex at the beginning of life, it does not have to limit our abilities to the stereotyped roles of male or female. How children spend their time and what they are taught can help them either live the stereotypes or break out of the parameters that privilege one group over another. The recreational and interpersonal differences between girls and boys are much greater than their cognitive and academic differences (Eliot, 2009). Schools are designed to teach subjects such as mathematics, language arts, reading, and science. They do not generally teach students how to express their emotions or take risks to reduce the gap between males and females. This gap, however, can be reduced by parents and teachers.

Parents, other significant adults such as religious leaders and teachers, siblings, and peers teach newborns, toddlers, students from preschool through college, and other adults the meaning of femaleness and maleness. As soon as we know a baby's sex, we begin to choose clothes, furniture, toys, and planned activities based on that factor alone. No matter how hard some parents may try not to reinforce the stereotypes, society is working against them. Appropriate gender behavior is reinforced with gender-specific toys and by the actions of girls and boys on the pages of children's books and magazines, on television, and on the Internet as well as in play with their peers. In this socialization process, children develop social skills and a sense of self in

Culture determines the appropriate activities in which boys and girls should participate.
© Larry Fleming/PH College

accordance with socially prescribed roles and expectations. Appropriate gender behavior is reinforced throughout the life cycle by social processes of approval and disapproval and reward and punishment by children's friends and the adults closest to them.

The Influence of Media on Perceptions of Gender Roles.

Television is one of the primary perpetuators of gender stereotyping. By high school graduation, the average child will have spent more hours in front of the television than in a classroom. On television, a woman's beauty can count for more than intelligence. Adult working women are commonly portrayed, but strong, intelligent, working-class women are generally invisible. Neither female heroines nor male heroes are social workers, teachers, or secretaries. They may be superhero crime fighters or CSI lab technicians, but few women on television today are the full-time, stay-at-home mothers who populated the sitcoms of earlier days. A growing number of women are news anchors, although they are often paired with a male anchor on local news shows. Women's sports can be found on television, but the range of coverage is minuscule compared to men's football, basketball, and baseball.

A number of men's and women's magazines portray the two sexes stereotypically. Many magazines are designed for one or the other group at specific age categories. Most newspapers have style pages that include articles on fashion, food, and social events—pages specifically aimed at what are believed to be the interests of women. The sports pages are written with men as the primary target and with an emphasis on competition and winning; news about women's sports seldom makes the front page. Women's magazines often focus on women who are successful professionals while exhibiting the feminine attributes of beauty, caring, and housekeeping. Working mothers are supermoms who not only work, but are devoted mothers who meet the needs of their children in much the same way as stay-at-home mothers do. Most magazines for young women focus on celebrities, fashion, and attracting men (Douglas, 2010). Sex and sports are the focus of most men's magazines (Kimmel, 2008). Articles on being a good father or husband seldom find their way into these magazines.

Children are not immune to the influence of the media. Cartoon characters, children's movies, and toys help determine their gender identities, which are reinforced by their same-sex peers. For example, many preschool girls are enamored with the princesses of the Disney movies, convincing their parents to purchase the gowns, shoes, jewelry, and makeup of their favorite character. Not only do they play dress-up at home, they dress as princesses for preschool and when they attend the Disney movies. Toys, games, books, and activities continue to be sorted into the traditional pink for girls and blue for boys. Retailers have learned how to market their products for the appropriate sex and reinforce stereotypical roles and expectations. Girls are pretty and sweet; boys are active and aggressive (Orenstein, 2011).

Socialization Patterns in School.

When a child enters school, educators usually continue the socialization patterns initiated by parents that reinforce the stereotyped behaviors associated with males and females. The attitudes and values about appropriate gender roles are embedded in the curriculum of schools. Elementary schools are sometimes accused of imitating the mothering role, with a predominance of female teachers and an emphasis on obedience and conformity (Kimmel, 2008). In classrooms, boys and girls receive different feedback and encouragement for their work. Boys often control classroom conversations by answering questions quickly. Teachers are more likely to praise boys for their intellectual responses. At the same time, boys are more likely to be publicly criticized by teachers when they break a rule (Sadker, Sadker, & Zittleman, 2009).

Children are also active participants in the socialization process. Play groups are often determined by the sex of the children, especially in the elementary and middle grades (Orenstein, 2011). Even when girls and boys play the same game, they often play it differently, with the boys being more aggressive. However, not all boys and girls follow the socially acceptable ways of their sex. Not all boys participate in large-group activities and are aggressive. The forgotten boys whose voices have been silenced and marginalized may follow behavior patterns generally associated with girls, but they risk being labeled as sissies and can become isolated from other boys. The same is true for girls. Everyone has probably known a tomboy who chose to play with the boys rather than the girls. This segregated play is extended into classrooms as students line up to march to the cafeteria or when girls are pitted against boys in academic competitions.

School playgrounds reflect the importance placed on male as opposed to female activities. The space required to play baseball, soccer, basketball, and kickball is much greater than that necessary for girls' jump rope, foursquare, and bar tricks. Some girls may play the boys' sports with them, but almost no boys join the girls' games. When boys do engage in girls' games like jump rope, it is usually to disrupt the game, not to be equal participants. If they choose to join the girls' games as equals, they are likely to be teased or called a "sissy" or "gay" by their male peers. Girls who choose to join the boys' games do not usually face negative labels of the sort that boys save for each other.

Combating Gender Stereotypes in the Classroom.

Critics of elementary classrooms indicate that instruction is designed around the behaviors, interests, and needs of girls to the detriment of boys. Teachers should consciously ensure that classroom activities do not favor one group over another. Both boys and girls can learn the skills and attitudes that seem to be more natural to the opposite sex through participating in the preferred activities of the other group. Cooperative projects in classrooms in which girls and boys work together can undermine sexual opposition if the students share the work rather than one group always dominating. Teachers need to pay attention to the leadership in these small groups, and may sometimes have to assign girls to the leadership role to guarantee that both boys and girls are developing leadership skills. As girls participate in boys' activities that require more movement, their brains begin to adapt the skills needed for better performance in spatial tasks.

Whereas adults read newspapers, magazines, and books, children spend much of their reading time with textbooks. How do the genders fare in terms of the resources used in classrooms across the nation? Studies show that great improvements have been made over the past 30 years. Textbooks are not as racist and sexist as in the past, and perspectives are better balanced. However, teachers still need to be cognizant of the gender and ethnicity of the authors being read by students. The non-sexist literature read by children and young people tends to show girls with masculine traits appropriate for a protagonist. Male protagonists do not normally reflect feminine characteristics (Fine, 2010). What can teachers do when classroom resources primarily reflect stereotyped portrayals and perspectives of females and males? They have to identify other resources for their students. The Internet may be helpful in identifying different role models for students, games for boys and girls to develop skills at which the other sex is generally more adept, and interesting readings that provide different perspectives from those in the textbook.

Gender Identity

Generally, sex is used to identify an individual as male or female based on biological differences. If we believe, as most research shows, that we are not hardwired for the differences between the sexes that we see in society, the major biological differences are that women can bear children and men have penises. The differences we observe are based primarily on **gender** or the cultural differences of men and women, which define the characteristics behind the meaning of being a female or male. These are usually defined as femininity and masculinity, which are culturally determined and learned through socialization.

Traditionally, women have been equated with nature and men with culture, which controls and transcends nature (Shaw & Lee, 2007). Being associated with nature denotes childbearing, child rearing, and child nurturing, which in the past kept women near the home, where those activities occurred. Men had the freedom to move beyond the home to hunt and seek resources to support the family, becoming the traditional breadwinner for the family. These patterns of women's and men's work evolved into the current cultural patterns in which women are the predominant workers in the home and in nurturing professions while men are overrepresented as corporate leaders, engineers, and construction workers.

Most of us take our gender identity for granted and do not question it because it corresponds to our sex. One's recognition of the appropriate gender identity occurs unconsciously early in life. It becomes a basic anchor in the personality and forms a core part of one's self-identity. Children begin selecting toys associated with their gender by the time they start walking. By the age of three years, they realize that they are either boys or girls and have begun to learn their expected behaviors (Eliot, 2009). By the time they enter school, children have clear ideas about gender. Most children know that girls and boys are supposed to behave differently. When they don't follow the rules for their gender behavior, they are often reminded by parents or their peers, and sometimes their teachers. Many are prepared to strive for conformity with these gender-stereotyped roles. However, not everyone's gender identity matches that person's sex. Some identify themselves as of the opposite sex, sexless, or somewhere in between. Some are **transgender** individuals who cross-dress or have surgery to physically alter their sex to match the one with which they identify.

MASCULINITY AND FEMININITY

Most cultures value masculinity over femininity. Masculinity is often measured by a man's independence, assertiveness, leadership, self-reliance, and emotional stability. "Real" men are supposed to be tough, confident, and self-reliant as well as aggressive and daring (James & Thomas, 2009). Femininity is stereotypically characterized as emotional, dependent, compliant, empathetic, and nurturing. As a result, men have been bestowed with greater power than women, leading to their being identified as the superior sex. When these differences became translated into the work environment, women were tracked into the nurturing fields of teaching, health care, and social services. They were supervised by men with assertive leadership skills and higher incomes. This pattern may be economically viable for families where both the wife and husband work, but it lands many single mothers and their children in poverty.

Few people fall solely at one or the other end of the feminine-masculine continuum. Most of us possess some characteristics of each. However, culture and society often expect us to mirror the gender behaviors associated with our sex, which could be detrimental to how we see ourselves and to fulfilling our potential in the work that we select. Generally, females are allowed more flexibility in their gender identification than males. Even young girls receive positive reinforcement for acting like boys by being physically active, participating in sports, and rejecting feminine stereotypical behavior. However, males are particularly susceptible to society's pressure. As a result, they sometimes go overboard in proving their masculinity.

Many of us do not fit the stereotypical profile associated with our sex. Many men are empathetic and caring, and many women are tough and assertive. People show different feminine and masculine characteristics depending on the circumstances, as shown by recent presidents and congressmen who cry and yet are tough and assertive when needed. Some conservatives argue that men are losing their masculinity and are being harmed as they become more feminine.

Life is not easy for young men, as supported by statistics indicating they are much more likely than girls to commit suicide, binge-drink, use steroids, suffer from undiagnosed depression, and be killed by gunfire or in a car crash (Kimmel, 2008). However, these problems cannot be attributed to boys becoming more feminine. Boys hold each other to a culturally determined gender identity, with little room for divergence (Dowd, 2010). Psychologist William Pollack calls this the boy code, which appears to apply across cultures. The boy code involves the following expectations (Neu & Weinfeld, 2007):

1. Don't cry.
2. Don't run from danger.
3. Don't ask for help or let anyone know that you need help.
4. Don't seek comfort from another person.
5. Don't show your emotions.
6. Don't hug your friends.
7. Don't show tenderness and love.

According to Michael Kimmel, who has interviewed thousands of high school and college men across the country, the boy code is translated into the guy code as boys become young men. The guy code is "bros before hos," confirming masculinity as "the relentless repudiation of the feminine" (Kimmel, 2008, p. 45). Above all else, they want to be seen as masculine by their peers, fathers, brothers, and coaches. Among the worst thing that can happen to a young man is to be called a "sissy," a "wuss," or "gay"—the clear sign that one is not masculine enough. Many young men do not really accept this code; they think it is stupid and mean, but they are more afraid of not being validated as masculine than they are motivated to rebuke the system (Kimmel, 2008). Although men have more power than women, they often see themselves as powerless but are unable to align with other powerless groups (Dowd, 2010).

We are living in an era of changing norms in which old, unequal roles are being rejected by many people. These changes are resulting in new uncertainties where the norms of the gender role are no longer so distinct. As new norms develop, more flexible roles, personalities, and behaviors are evolving for both females and males. You are likely to see adolescents struggling with their gender identity, especially in the middle and high school years.

TRANSGENDER IDENTITY

Gender identity in some cultures and societies is not limited to male and female. "Two-souled" or "berdache" people appear in the ethnographic literature of indigenous cultures in the southwestern part of the United States (Connell, 2009). They have male bodies, act more like women, and have spiritual powers. Javanese society includes "banci" people, with male bodies in women's dress. These identities are sometimes considered a third gender (Connell, 2009).

Some individuals are born with the biological trappings (such as a vagina or penis) of one sex, but think and behave like the other sex. For example, a child may be born in a boy's body but be a girl in every other aspect of life; such a child is a transgender. In some cases, transgender individuals have surgery or use hormones to transform their bodies to match the sex with which they identify—a process called sex or gender reassignment.

When someone's identity, appearance, or behavior falls outside the conventional gender norms, they are described as transgender (American Psychological Association, 2006). Many of these individuals are transvestites, people who cross-dress. Transgender students may choose a name that denotes their identity rather than their sex. The protocol is to interact with a transgender student as if the student is of the sex with which he/she identifies. In other words, you would interact with a male student who identifies as female by using the female pronoun, "her," and interacting with her as you would with other females in your class.

Transgender students often face sexual harassment similar to that faced by many gay students. Educators should be aware of possible harassment and intervene appropriately to protect the legal rights of these students and ensure a safe environment in their classrooms.

INFLUENCE OF ETHNICITY AND RELIGION

The degree to which a student adheres to a traditional gender identity is influenced by the family's ethnicity, class, and religion. For many women of color, racial discrimination has such an impact on their daily lives and well-being that gender is often secondary in their identity. In some religions, gender identity and relations are strictly controlled by religious doctrine. Thus, gender inequality takes on different forms among different ethnic, class, and religious groups. The degree to which traditional gender roles are accepted depends, in large part, on the degree to which the family maintains the traditional patterns and the experiences of their ethnic group in this country. Families that adhere to traditional religious and cultural patterns are more likely to encourage adherence to rigid gender roles than are families that have adopted bicultural patterns.

Women in African American families have developed a different pattern. Historically, they have worked outside the home and are less likely to hold strict traditional views about their roles. They have learned to be both homemakers and wage earners. Unlike many middle-class European American women, middle-class African American women do not necessarily perceive marriage as a route to upward mobility or a way out of poverty.

Women of color, no matter their socioeconomic status, have current and historical experiences of discrimination based on their race and ethnicity. Identification with one group may be prevalent in one setting but not another. It is often a struggle to develop an identity that incorporates one's gender, ethnicity, race, sexual orientation, class, and religion into a whole with which one feels comfortable and self-assured. Most students of color are likely to identify themselves by their ethnic or racial group rather than by their sex or gender. Developing cross-cultural relationships based on gender can be difficult in some school settings, with the possible exception of some organized sports activities.

Religions generally recognize and include masculine and feminine expectations as part of their doctrines. Regardless of the specific religion, rituals sometimes reflect and reinforce systems of male dominance. The more conservative religious groups usually support a stricter adherence to gender-differentiated roles. Their influence extends into issues of sexuality, marriage, and reproductive rights. They may have successfully organized politically to control state and federal policies on family and women's affairs. On the other hand, the more liberal religious groups may support the marriage rights of gays and lesbians and the right of a woman to choose abortion, and may encourage both males and females to lead their congregations. Religious perspectives on the appropriate roles of females and males can conflict with the school culture in designating the ways girls and boys are allowed to interact with each other in the classroom and hallways. Requirements for the dress of girls and young women in physical education classes may clash with religious dictates. Educators should be alert to religious perspectives as they discuss gender issues in classrooms, plan lessons on sexuality, and interact with females and males in the classroom.

Students with physical disabilities may face challenges in meeting the traditional expectations for masculinity and femininity as well. They may be unable to participate in athletics, which is one of the social expectations for males. Today some students and adults with physical disabilities are able to compete in wheelchair basketball, tennis, and marathons. Special Olympics provide another opportunity for students with disabilities to participate in athletic events. Females with certain disabilities may also face challenges, with society's emphasis on "the body beautiful, body whole" affecting perceptions of their femininity.

Struggles for Gender Equity

Most major changes in society do not occur quietly. Throughout most of history (and still in many parts of the world today), women were not considered equal to men. In fact, most were subordinate to men. They were dependent on them for financial well-being as their daughters and their wives. For women on their own, jobs were neither plentiful nor well-paying. With some education, they could be hired as teachers if they could convince school authorities that they were moral, upstanding young women. Once they married, they could not teach; they became the responsibility of their husbands. Without laws that provided them autonomy from their spouses or fathers, women could not file for divorce, own property, or apply for men's jobs. Is it any wonder that some women wanted to change their circumstances? The desire for independence and equal rights has fired the struggles of women and their male allies for gender equity since the Seneca Falls Convention in 1848.

THE EARLY STRUGGLES

During the mid-nineteenth century, women activists were part of the antislavery movement. They also were trying to raise the public's awareness about women's issues, including the right to divorce, own property, speak in public, prevent abuse by husbands, work, and vote. At the Seneca Falls Convention women organized to fight against their oppression. This effort involved some male supporters, including Frederick Douglass and white abolitionists who were fighting against slavery and for human and civil rights of all people. However, even most women did not support the women's movement at that time. They did not view their conditions as oppressive and accepted their roles as wives and mothers as natural.

Later in the century, protective legislation for women and children was enacted to make some manual jobs inaccessible to women because of the danger involved. The legislation also

The gains in the equality of women over the past four decades are due to the battles fought by women in the 1970s and earlier.
© NCJ/TOPIX MirrorPixNewscom

limited the number of hours women could work and the time at which they could work, much like today's child labor laws. Such legislation did little, however, to extend equal rights to women. During this period, the members of women's groups were predominantly European Americans. They segregated their fight for equal rights from the struggles of other oppressed groups and refused to take a stand against Jim Crow laws and other violations of the civil rights of ethnic and racial groups. It was 50 years after the passage of the Fifteenth Amendment, which granted African American men the right to vote, before women would be granted the right to vote following hard-fought battles that included organizing, picketing, arrests, hunger strikes, and forced feedings in jail.

THE SECOND WAVE

The most comprehensive advances in the status of women were initiated in the 1960s when **feminists** were able to gain the support of more women and men than at any other time in history. As in the previous century, this movement developed out of the struggle for civil rights being waged by African Americans. The 1963 Equal Pay Act required that men and women receive equal pay for the same job, but did not prevent discrimination in hiring. In an attempt to defeat the Civil Rights Bill in Congress, a Southern congressman added the words "or sex" to Title VII, declaring that discrimination based on "race, color, national origin, or sex" was prohibited. This legislation, which passed in 1964, was the first time that equal rights had been extended to women. Soon afterward, President Lyndon Johnson signed an executive order that required businesses with federal contracts to hire women and people of color, creating the first affirmative action programs.

By 1983 political leaders were no longer disposed to extend full equal rights to women. Women's groups pushed for passage of the Equal Rights Amendment (ERA), which read, "Equality of rights under the law shall not be denied or abridged by the United States or by any state on account of sex." Although Congress passed the one-sentence Equal Rights Amendment, conservative groups concerned about family values lobbied state legislatures to reject the amendment. Although two-thirds of the U.S. population supported the ERA, it was not adopted by the required number of states.

Women's movements have traditionally been dominated by middle-class white women. Limited to women's issues, the movement in the early days was not open to the prospect of broader civil rights for all oppressed groups. This focus prevented the widespread involvement in the movement of both men and women of color. Support from the working class was also limited because the needs of neither these women nor women on welfare were reflected in the agenda. Lesbians and bisexuals did not feel that the women's movements addressed or highlighted their issues, leading to the establishment of separate groups to meet their needs.

The 1990s ushered in a change in the feminist movement toward broader support for the civil rights of all groups rather than just women. As an example, the nation's largest feminist organization, the National Organization for Women (NOW), today includes in its agenda fighting racism and supporting welfare reform, immigrant rights, and affirmative action. A growing number of articles and books on equity by modern feminists, sociologists, and critical theorists address the interaction of race, gender, and class in the struggle for equity for all groups.

TODAY'S CHALLENGES

Equal rights for women, men, gays, and lesbians continue to be contested. Feminists fight for equality in jobs, pay, schooling, responsibilities in the home, and the nation's laws. They believe that women and men should have a choice about working in the home or outside the home, having children, and acknowledging sexual orientation. They believe that women should not have to be subordinate to men at home, in the workplace, or in society. They fight to eliminate the physical and mental violence that has resulted from such subordination by providing support groups and shelters for abused women and children, as well as by pressuring the judicial system to outlaw and severely punish such violence. In addition, they promote shared male and female responsibilities in the home and the availability of child care to all families.

PAUSE TO REFLECT 4.1

Both males and females can support women's rights and fight together for equality. Think about your knowledge of women's issues.

- Do you consider yourself a feminist? Are there feminist issues you support?

- How have you been exposed to feminism and women's issues?

- What was the last magazine you read? Was the content of the magazine focused specifically on either women's or men's issues?

Many citizens think that equity for the sexes has already been achieved. Many young women and men take for granted the rights that have been won. In 1978, for example, nearly four of five high school women in a prestigious prep school identified themselves as feminists. A decade later, less than half of them did. Women are now the presidents of major corporations. They have run for president of the United States, beginning in 1972, with Shirley Chisholm. Geraldine Ferraro and Sarah Palin were candidates for vice president. The last two secretaries of state have been women, interacting with leaders from around the world. The cabinets of the past four U.S. presidents have included a number of women. It might seem to some observers that women are in many positions of power and are able to compete equally with men for any job. However, females make up 52% of the population but comprise only 17% of the U.S. Senate and are presidents of only a few global corporations. Legislation that supports equality has been enacted by one Congress and taken away by another. For example, the inclusion of Title IX, which is the major legislative action for sexual equality in schools, is rigorously debated each time Congress meets to reauthorize the Elementary and Secondary Education Act.

Some critics of feminism have identified a "boy crisis" in schools as the outcome of feminists' reform of schools to advantage girls and disadvantage boys (Dowd, 2010; Berg, 2009). Peg Tyre (2010), author of *The Trouble with Boys*, reports that boys in the United States "are retained at twice the rate of girls, are identified as having learning disorders and attention problem[s] at three times the rates of girls, and get more C's and D's and do less homework than girls" (p. ix). Blaming feminists' fight for equality for the poorer performance of boys creates opposition between girls and boys (Kimmel, 2008). It suggests that the changes in schools that have contributed to greater equality for girls have provided a poorer education for boys. It is not white middle- and upper-income male students who are dropping out of school and not enrolling in college. The problem is that schools are not effectively serving working-class, African, and Latino boys (Kimmel, 2008; Berg, 2009).

Much has been accomplished over the past four decades, but inequality continues to be a problem. The current movement is more inclusive, addressing the civil rights of women of color, women in poverty, and elderly women. However, a number of social issues have still not been embraced by political leaders. Thus, feminists continue to lobby for universal child care, safety nets for the nation's children, better health care for women and children, and other laws and practices that support females. They also continue to fight to maintain the rights that have been won.

PAUSE TO REFLECT 4.2

Many students report that they have been sexually harassed in school. However, not all teachers and school officials believe them. Think about your own experiences.

- Have you ever been a victim of sexual harassment? If so, how did you feel at the time? Whom did you tell about it?

- Have you observed someone being sexually harassed? Did you intervene? Why or why not?

- What can teachers do to help stop harassment among students?

The Cost of Sexism and Gender Discrimination

Sexism is the belief that males are superior to females. Often, it occurs in personal situations of marriage and family life where the husband or father "rules the roost." It also occurs in the workplace when women hold lower-status jobs, work for men, and receive lower wages than men for the same work.

When physical strength determined who performed certain tasks, men conducted the hunt for food while women raised food close to home. With industrialization, the pattern of men working away from home and women working close to home was translated into labor market activity for men and non–labor market activity for women. Men worked specific hours and received pay for their work. By contrast, women worked irregular and unspecified periods in the home and received no wages for their work. Women's work at home was not as valued as the work of men, who contributed to labor market production.

Only a century ago, most women could not attend college, had no legal right to either property or their children, could not initiate a divorce, and were forbidden to smoke or drink. Because these inequities no longer exist and laws now protect the rights of women, many people believe that men and women are today treated equally in society. However, society's deep-rooted assumptions about how men and women should think, look, and behave can lead to discriminatory behavior based on gender alone.

Many of us discriminate on the basis of gender without realizing it. Because we were raised in a sexist society, we think our behavior is natural and acceptable, and we often don't recognize discrimination when it occurs. Women may not be aware of the extent to which they do not participate equally in society, and men may not acknowledge the privilege that maleness bestows on them—signs that the distinct roles have been internalized well during the socialization process. Most parents do not directly plan to harm their sons and daughters by teaching them to conform to stereotyped roles. For example, some young women are encouraged to seek fulfillment through marriage rather than by their own achievement and independence, which may prevent them from achieving social and economic success at the same levels as men. Parents may be unaware that their sons may never learn to be compassionate and empathetic if they are taught they must always meet the masculinity standard.

Many individuals outside the family also practice gender discrimination. The kindergarten teacher who scolds the girl for playing in the boys' corner is discriminating. Not allowing boys to show their emotions may prevent their full development as human beings. The personnel director who hires only women for secretarial positions and only men as managers is discriminating on the basis of gender. Educators have the opportunity to help students break out of group stereotypes and provide them with opportunities to explore and pursue a wide variety of options in fulfilling their potential as individuals. They can help girls and young women develop some of the traits traditionally labeled as masculine and help boys and young men be caring and compassionate.

Gender discrimination not only is practiced by individuals but also has been institutionalized in policies, laws, rules, and precedents in society. These institutional arrangements benefit one gender over the other, as described in the following sections.

JOBS

Historically, the sexual division of labor has been fairly rigid, with the roles of women being limited to reproduction, child rearing, and homemaking. When women did work outside the home, their jobs were often similar to their roles in the home—caring for children or the sick. Jobs were stereotyped by gender. As recently as 2008, women represented more than 90% of the traditional female occupations and less than 10% of the traditional male jobs, as shown in Table 4.2. Even though more young women are finishing high school and college than their male peers, they are still not making inroads into many traditional male jobs. The jobs in which women predominate are accompanied by neither high prestige nor high income. People in the category of professionals, such as teachers and nurses, do not compete in income or prestige

Table 4.2 **Occupations in Which Women Are Most Likely and Least Likely to Participate**

Occupation	Women's Participation (%)	Occupation	Women's Participation (%)
Speech-language pathologists	98.1	Brickmasons, blockmasons, and stonemasons	0.4
Dental hygienists	97.7	Tool and die makers	1.0
Preschool and kindergarten teachers	97.6	Electricians	1.0
Dental assistants	96.3	Logging workers	1.0
Secretaries and administrative assistants	96.1	Carpenters	1.5
Occupational therapists	95.9	Aircraft mechanics and service technicians	1.7
Child care workers	95.6	Automotive body repair	2.1
Medical records and health information technicians	95.0	Aircraft pilots and flight engineers	2.6
Licensed practical nurses	93.3	Construction laborers	3.1
Receptionists and information clerks	93.6	Crane and tower operators	3.7
Word processors and typists	92.9	Firefighters	4.8
Registered nurses	91.7	Surveying and mapping technicians	4.9
Teacher assistants	91.7	Truck drivers	4.9
Bookkeeping, accounting, and auditing clerks	91.2	Grounds maintenance workers	6.1
Hairdressers and cosmetologists	90.6	Engineering managers	6.3
Payroll and timekeeping clerks	90.1	Mechanical engineering	6.7

Source: **U.S. Census Bureau. (2010). Statistical abstract of the United States: 2011 (130th ed.). Washington, DC: U.S. Author.**

with architects and engineers. Women continue to be overrepresented as clerical and service workers and underrepresented as managers and skilled workers.

It has been difficult for women to enter administrative and skilled jobs. These jobs have fewer entry-level positions than the less prestigious ones. The available jobs for many women are those with short or no promotion ladders, few opportunities for training, low wages, little stability, and poor working conditions. Clerical and sales positions are examples of such jobs, but even professions such as teaching and nursing offer little opportunity for career advancement. To earn the comfortable living that is the American Dream requires a woman to seek either a traditionally male job or a husband with a good income.

When men enter traditionally female fields, they typically do not hold the same positions as women. In 2009 men comprised less than 3% of preschool and kindergarten teachers and 18% of public elementary and middle school teachers (U.S. Census Bureau, 2010b), but represented 41% of elementary school principals (Aud et al., 2010). Forty-one percent of public high school teachers and 71% of secondary principals were men (Aud et al., 2010). Male social workers are more often community organizers than group workers or caseworkers. Although the percentage of men participating in traditionally female jobs has increased, males have become overrepresented in the higher-status, administrative levels of these occupations. For example, 77% of preschool through grade 12 teachers are women, as compared with 49% of college and university faculty who are women (U.S. Census Bureau, 2010k).

Sixty-five percent of women between the ages of 16 and 64 were working in the civilian workforce in 2009, as compared with 73% of the men in the job categories identified in Figure 4.1 (U.S. Census Bureau, 2010a). Regardless of their race and ethnicity, women participate in the labor

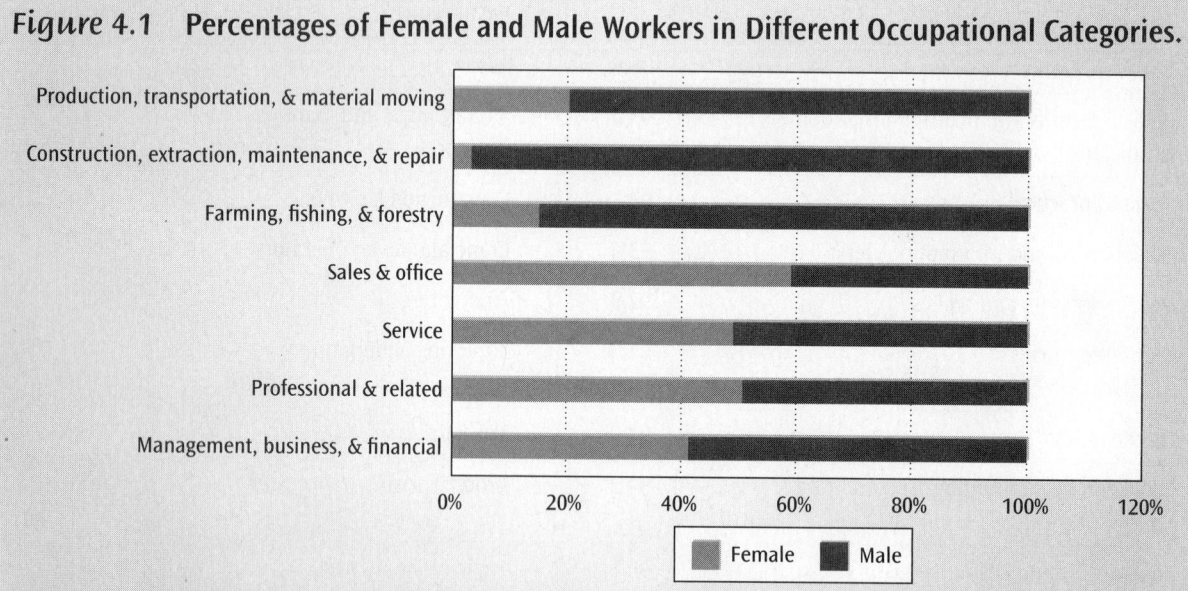

Figure 4.1 **Percentages of Female and Male Workers in Different Occupational Categories.**

Source: U.S. Census Bureau. (2010). 2005–2009 American community survey. Washington, DC: Author. Retrieved on January 2, 2011, from http://factfinder.census.gov/servlet/DatasetTableListServlet?_ds_name=ACS_2009_5YR_G00_&_type=table&_program=ACS&_lang=en&_ts=312166909367.

force at rates between 54% and 67%. Latina and American Indian/Alaskan Native women are less likely to work than women from other groups.

The participation gap between men and women in a number of high-prestige professions has narrowed over the last few generations but has not been eliminated. Women are still underrepresented in mathematics, science, and technology fields. In 1950 only 6.5% of all physicians were women; in 2009, 32% were women. The percentage of female lawyers has increased from 4% to 32%, but only 10% of all engineers and 25% of architects are women (U.S. Census Bureau, 2010k). The number of women in some professional jobs should continue to rise because women are receiving an increasing number of degrees in these fields. While the gap for women is closing in many fields, they still earn only 17% of the bachelor's degrees in engineering and 18% of those in computer science. Men completing bachelor's programs are seriously underrepresented in the fields of family and consumer sciences (12%), public administration and social services, the health professions (15%), education (21%), and psychology (23%) (Aud et al., 2010).

What do these trends suggest to educators? First, schools have prepared a growing number of young women who see themselves as professionals and have prepared themselves with the knowledge and skills to pursue those fields. At the same time, a limited number of young men are pursuing jobs that are traditionally female. Why are they not choosing those fields? These figures also clearly indicate that young women are either not preparing themselves for the higher-paying and prestigious jobs in engineering and computer science or are not choosing to pursue those fields after high school. What educational strategies would equalize the number of males and females pursuing the fields in which the respective groups currently have limited representation?

INCOME

Regardless of their education, men are expected to work. Most women today also work, but the decision to work is not always a choice. It may be a necessity because they are single parents, unmarried, or widowed. Although almost as many women as men work outside the home, women do not earn as much as their male counterparts. To maintain an adequate or desirable standard of living today, both husband and wife in many families must work. The percentages of married women and white women in the workforce increased dramatically in the last half of the twentieth century. Only 16.7% of all married women worked outside the home in 1940. By 2009, 61% did. Seventy percent of all married women with children between 6 and 7 years old were employed in 2010 (U.S. Census Bureau, 2010k). The difference that an additional income makes in the way a family lives is obvious.

Incomes of women continue to differ by race, with Asian American and white women having the highest incomes, following the same pattern as men, as shown in Figure 4.2. The income difference between men and women in the same ethnic group was higher among whites and Asian Americans than among African Americans and Latinos, but Asian American and white women earned more than African American and Latino men. This inequality is due to differences in levels of educational attainment and the types of jobs held by members of these groups, which in turn is partly due to the lingering racism in a society that has not provided the same educational and societal resources to all ethnic and racial groups. For example, nearly half of the Asian American population over 25 years old have a baccalaureate degree or higher, compared to 13% of the Latino, American Indian, and Native Alaskan populations. Although the gap between the incomes of all men and all women continues to shrink, the income of white women has grown the most over the past 40 years (U.S. Bureau of Labor Statistics, 2010b).

Figure 4.2 Median Incomes of Females and Males by Race.

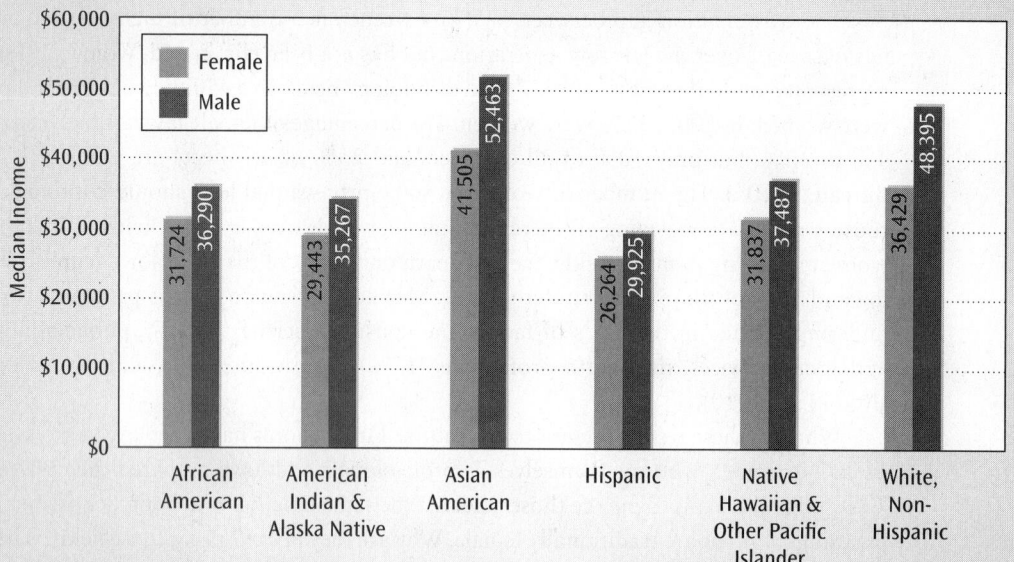

Source: U.S. Census Bureau. (2010). 2005–2009 American community survey. Washington, DC: Author. Retrieved on January 2, 2011, from http://factfinder.census.gov/servlet/DatasetTableListServlet?_ds_name=ACS_2009_5YR_G00_&_type=table&_program=ACS&_lang=en&_ts=312166909367.

Figure 4.3 Income of Year-Round, Full-Time Workers by Age and Gender in 2007.

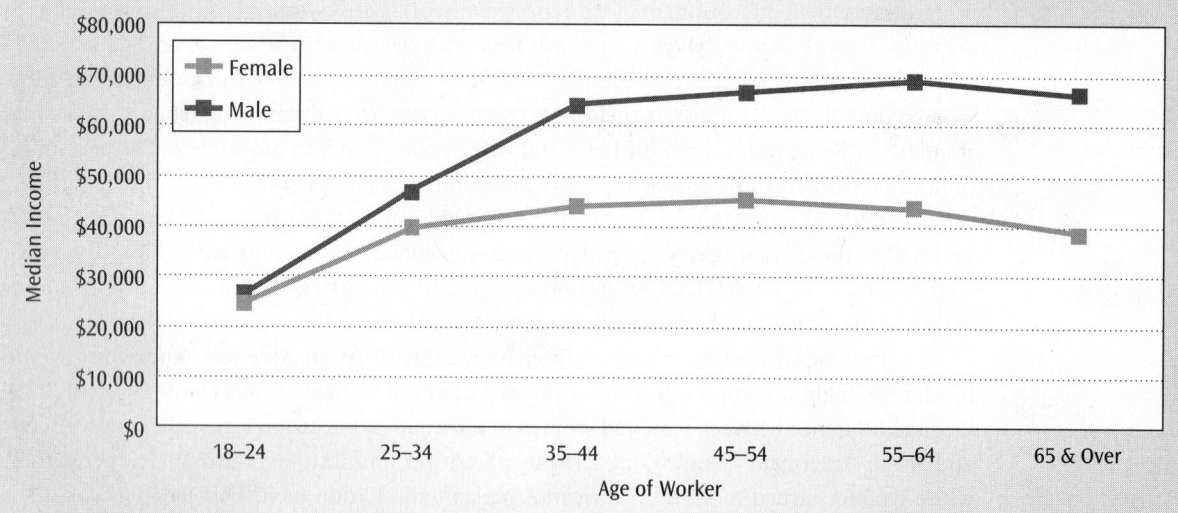

Source: U.S. Census Bureau. (2010). *Statistical abstract of the United States: 2011* (130th ed.). Washington, DC: Author.

The difference in income between men and women generally increases with age, as shown in Figure 4.3. Discrepancies in income are in part a result of the types of jobs held by the two groups. Figure 4.1 shows the uneven distribution of men and women in various occupational categories. Women are underrepresented in jobs in management, business, finance, construction,

Table 4.3 Comparison of Women's and Men's Salaries in Various Types of Jobs in 2009

Occupation	Women's Median Salary	Men's Median Salary	Women's Salaries as Percentage of Men's
Management, business, and financial operations	$51,438	$71,730	72
Professional and related	$47,576	$66,204	72
Services	$22,084	$30,600	72
Sales and office	$31,734	$43,517	73
Farming, fishing, and forestry	$18,692	$23,953	78
Construction, extraction, maintenance, and repair	$36,157	$39,294	92
Production, transportation, and material moving	$25,206	$36,654	69

Source: U.S. Census Bureau. (2010). 2005–2009 American community survey. Washington, DC: Author. Retrieved on January 2, 2011, from http://factfinder.census.gov/servlet/DatasetTableListServlet?_ds_name=ACS_2009_5YR_G00_&_type=table&_program=ACS&_lang=en&_ts=312166909367.

production, and natural resources (e.g., farming, fishing, and forestry). They hold the majority of jobs in the service, office support, and professional (e.g., teaching and nursing) fields.

Even within the same occupation groups, salaries between women and men differ. Table 4.3 compares salaries for selected jobs. In 2009 the weekly earnings of women working full-time was 80% of men's (U.S. Bureau of Labor Statistics, 2010). At the same time, the gap between low-income and high-income groups has led to growing inequality among women. Both men and women at the bottom of the income scale are losing ground. Women who enter traditionally male jobs with low-paying income are not increasing their chances of moving into the middle class. Highly educated women are the ones who have made absolute wage gains during this period.

More women (57%) were enrolled in higher education than men (46%) in 2010. Compared to males, females are earning more degrees at all levels. In 2009 they received 57% of the bachelor's degrees, 60% of the master's degrees, and 52% of the doctorates. Women with bachelor's degrees or beyond have median incomes that are only 67% of the income earned by males with the same education. Women with bachelor's degrees earned $35,972, compared to men's $54,091, in 2009. Men with professional degrees earned $102,392, while such women earned only $60,259 (U.S. Census Bureau, 2011).

Although the difference in the salaries of women and men in working-class jobs has decreased, many of these jobs do not pay enough to allow one to live much above the poverty threshold. Wages for these jobs have remained rather stagnant for men as well as women, not increasing at the same rate as jobs at the top end of the labor market (Boys in K–12 Education, 2011). Such discrimination greatly affects the quality of life for men and women, particularly those who are single heads of households, and their children.

Both men and women need jobs that provide an income adequate to support themselves and their families. No longer are factory jobs available that provide an income for life. This trend will require young people to become more engaged in learning and to attend college at higher rates than today. Educators will need to work more effectively with parents and the community to eliminate the high dropout rate, especially among young men of color.

SEXUAL HARASSMENT

Sexual harassment is a form of sex discrimination that has long existed in the workplace, where women have been the recipients of unwanted and unwelcome sexual behavior. Sometimes the perpetuator is in a position of power over the woman and uses that power to secure favors or to make sexual advances. In other cases, it is a co-worker who makes unwanted advances. As in other areas related to gender socialization, schools mirror society in the perpetuation of sexual harassment. Both boys and girls report receiving unwanted sexual attention in schools (Gruber & Fineran, 2008).

Sexual harassment occurs in the halls and classrooms of our schools, often while other students watch. Perpetrators of sexual harassment include male and female teachers, school administrators, janitors, and coaches as well as other students. It is not only boys who harass others; girls are also guilty, but less often. The harassment can be verbal (e.g., making insulting remarks or jokes, spreading sexual rumors), visual (e.g., sharing naked pictures, making obscene gestures), or physical (e.g., pinching, fondling, or flashing). At worst, the victim is sexually abused or raped. Teachers who offer an A to a student for sexual favors or dates are sexual harassers. If actions by another student or adult are unwelcome by the victim and make him or her uncomfortable, scared, or confused, they constitute harassment (Equal Rights Advocates, 2011).

Sexual harassment can be very damaging to its victims, having an impact on their emotions and subsequent behavior. They may feel self-conscious, embarrassed, afraid, and confused (Legal Momentum, 2008). It can also affect students' school performance. They may participate less in classrooms and find it difficult to pay attention. They may skip school to avoid facing the harasser (National Women's Law Center, 2007).

Elementary school boys and adolescent males are also victims of sexual harassment. They frequently challenge each other to prove their masculinity. They harass new students; haze the rookies on the basketball, football, or other sports teams; and initiate new members of a fraternity through drinking rites and sexual games that can be dangerous to their health and well-being. These young men operate on a code that denigrates females, gays, lesbians, and anybody else who they feel threatens their privileged gender role (Kimmel, 2008). They do everything possible to prove they are masculine and not sissies or gay, even if that requires harassing females and each other. Those boys who do not meet these gender expectations try to avoid settings in which they may be bullied, beat up, or humiliated; these settings could include school or another place in which students congregate. While some boys do stand up to these pressures, many practice a code of silence where they watch their peers bully others without intervening or reporting incidents to a teacher or parent. Young men between 16 and 24 years old suffer from the emotional stress that these actions elicit, resulting in a suicide rate that is higher than that of any other age group (Kimmel, 2008).

Educators and parents alike may explain away sexual harassment on grounds such as "boys will be boys" and attribute the behavior to the perennial school bullies. Young men may be confused by accusations of sexual harassment, in part because the behavior has long been viewed as typical for male adolescents. Many principals and teachers either don't know that

The Boys' Code

"Assault in the Locker Room" was the headline in the newspaper, surprising most members of the Clarke High School community. Clarke High School was not an inner-city school; it was located in an affluent community with a secret. Its basketball team had been a powerhouse for the last decade. What had gone wrong?

The family of a freshman student reported to the school administration that their son had been abused in the locker room by the three star players. On one occasion, they caught him coming out of the shower, duct-taped his genitals to his body, taped him to the wall, and brought in his former girlfriend to have a look. And the abuse did not stop there. He and another rookie on the reserve team were harassed by older teammates on the bus returning from an away game last month. They were punched, called "faggots," and used as the objects of simulated sex. While only two of the players were the direct perpetrators of the abuse, others cheered them on.

In the investigation that followed, the basketball players denied the abuse. They said the older players were just horsing around. They didn't mean anything by it. All rookie athletes were initiated into their sports this way and had been for years. Their parents said it was just "boys being boys." They had gone through the same type of hazing when they were in high school, and they turned out all right. Why was this kid suing the school? Why was he ruining the school spirit that was at an all-time high with an outstanding basketball season?

The three star players were suspended with three games left in the season—games that, if won, probably would have guaranteed the school's best season ever. The coach was under investigation. What did he know about these initiation rites? Adults in the community were asking, "What has gone wrong in our school?" Why did other players maintain a code of silence about the abuse? Why did the ex-girlfriend not report the abuse? How can the community recover?

| QUESTIONS FOR CLASSROOM DISCUSSION |

- What action should school administrators have taken when the freshman first reported the abuse?
- If you were the basketball coach, what would you have done to prevent this type of abuse in the locker room and on the bus?
- How will you help students have an honest discussion about this incident?

harassment is occurring in their schools or ignore it. Most students say they are not comfortable reporting incidents to teachers or other school personnel. They usually tell a friend, but many, especially boys, tell no one. However, harassment and sex discrimination are social justice issues and are included under civil rights laws. Students who have suffered from such harassment are beginning to fight back through the courts. They assert that the harassment was reported to teachers, counselors, or administrators, but no action was taken to stop it.

School officials are no longer allowed to ignore the sexual harassment and abuse of students and may be forced to pay damage awards if they do. An educator most likely will be fired if found to be harassing a student, and the educator's actions are likely to be reported on the local evening news. Schools and school districts are legally required to protect students from sexual harassment by **Title IX** (more on that later in the chapter). Any school receiving federal financial assistance must have an anti-discrimination policy and grievance procedures that address sex discrimination, including sexual harassment. According to the National Women's Law Center (2007, p. 4), teachers should:

- Act quickly when confronted with sexual harassment.
- Ensure that they report any instances of harassment of which they are aware to the person designated by the school to handle such complaints.
- Strategize with students about improving the classroom environment.
- Enlist the support of parents.
- Make certain the classroom is a welcoming environment for all students.

Policies and practices within schools may need to be revised, but discussions should involve the broader community of students and parents.

Educators can assist in the elimination of harassment, bullying, and other youth violence. They can start by modeling appropriate behavior by avoiding sexual references, innuendoes, and jokes. They should monitor their own behaviors to ensure that they are not using their power as an authority figure to harass students.

Educators can also encourage students to form or join school leadership groups that work to educate others about and prevent sexual harassment. Educators can help young men feel empowered enough to resist being bystanders to sexual harassment and other bullying. The positive attributes of masculinity and femininity such as honor, respect, integrity, ethics, and doing the right thing should be reinforced in schools. They can help both female and male students be resilient, especially when they do not meet the stereotyped expectations of their gender. Based on his research of young men who have suffered from harassment, Kimmel (2008) reported, "To a man, they all spoke of at least one adult who made a difference, 'someone who believed in me and stood by me'" (p. 271). A teacher, coach, counselor, or principal can be the person who makes a difference to students who have been victimized or are trying to do the right thing.

Bringing Gender Equality to the Classroom and Beyond

Education is a key to upward mobility and financial security in adulthood. The occupational roles that individuals pursue will influence the way they are able to live in the future. Students' chances to pursue postsecondary education are greatly influenced by their education in elementary and secondary schools. By the time students are in high school, they have made their choices, or have been placed in a track that will determine their chances of going to college.

Girls appear to take better advantage of education than their male peers. They are less likely to drop out of high school, be in fights, or be diagnosed with a disability. They score higher than boys on tests of reading and verbal skills, are ranked higher in classes, and achieve more honors (Kimmel, 2008). Young women enroll in college at higher rates than their male counterparts (U.S. Census Bureau, 2010k). Although males generally end up with better jobs and higher salaries, not all males are served well by schools. The number of boys diagnosed as emotionally disturbed is four times the number of girls. Boys are six times more likely to be classified as having ADHD (attention deficit and hyperactivity disorder) (Kimmel, 2008).

High-stakes testing and other forms of assessment allow teachers to identify gaps in student learning, allowing them to develop strategies that build on the prior experiences of students. Some types of assessment, such as observation and project-based assessment, show teachers the students' progress throughout the year. Tests are also used to make high-stakes decisions that may dramatically affect a student's future. Differences between the test scores of females and males have narrowed over the past few decades, but girls remain slightly ahead in reading and writing and boys in mathematics. Males tend to do better than females on college admission examinations, in part because multiple-choice tests favor boys, who take less time to guess when they do not know the answer (Sadker et al., 2009). If the tests included more essay questions, the gap between the sexes would be reduced even further. The most recent data on test performance show that

- At grades 4 and 8, girls on average score seven to nine points higher than boys on national assessments of reading (Aud et al., 2010).
- At grades 4 and 8, boys on average score two points higher than girls on national assessments of mathematics (Aud et al., 2010).
- Males score higher than females on both the verbal and mathematics sections of the SAT (Corbett et al., 2008).
- On the ACT, males perform better on the math and science sections, but females score higher than males on the English and reading sections (Corbett et al., 2008).

The data indicate some differences in the academic achievement of females and males that might be eliminated if educators improved male performance in literacy and female performance in mathematics and science. There is not common agreement, however, on how to accomplish this goal. Some researchers have proposed that teachers develop classroom environments that take advantage of the learning styles of boys and girls. Professional development programs on gender equity focus on changing the content of curriculum and the behavior of teachers toward students. Teachers, counselors, teacher aides, coaches, and principals all have roles in eradicating the inequities that result from sexism. Let's examine some of the approaches supporting gender equity in schools.

TITLE IX

Title IX of the 1972 Education Amendments addresses the differential, stereotypical, and discriminatory treatment of students on the basis of their gender. It protects students and employees in virtually all public school systems and postsecondary institutions in the United States. The law prevents gender discrimination in (1) the admission of students, particularly to postsecondary and vocational education institutions; (2) the treatment of students; and (3) the employment of all personnel.

The number of women who participate in sports has increased dramatically since Title IX was passed in 1972, but the law has also had a great impact on the lives of girls in today's schools.
© Bettmann/Corbis

Title IX makes it illegal to treat students differently or separately on the basis of gender. It requires that all programs, activities, and opportunities offered by a school district be equally available to males and females. All courses must be open to all students. Boys must be allowed to enroll in family and consumer science classes, and girls allowed in technology and agriculture courses. Regarding the counseling of students, Title IX prohibits biased course or career guidance; the use of biased achievement, ability, or interest tests; and the use of college and career materials that are biased in content, language, or illustrations. Schools cannot assist any business or individual in employing students if the request is for a student of a particular gender. There can be no discrimination in the type or amount of financial assistance or eligibility for such assistance.

Membership in clubs and other activities based on gender alone is prohibited in schools, with the exceptions of YWCA, YMCA, Girl Scouts, Boy Scouts, Boys' State, Girls' State, Key clubs, and other voluntary and tax-exempt youth service organizations that have traditionally been limited to members of one gender who are 19 years of age or younger. Rules of behavior and punishment for violation of those rules must be the same for all students. Honors and awards may not designate the gender of the student as a criterion for the award.

The most controversial section of Title IX concerns athletic programs. Provisions for girls to participate in intramural, club, or interscholastic sports must be included in the school's athletic program. The sports offered by a school must be coeducational, with two major exceptions: (1) when selection for teams is based on competitive skill and (2) when the activity is a contact sport. In these two situations, separate teams are permitted but are not required. Although the law does not require equal funding for girls' and boys' athletic programs, equal opportunity in athletics must be provided. The courts apply the following three-part test to determine equal opportunity:

1. The percentage of male and female athletes is substantially proportionate to the percentage of females and males in the student population.
2. The school has a history of expanding opportunities for females to participate in sports.
3. A school fully and effectively meets the interest and abilities of female students even if it may not be meeting the proportionate expectation of the first requirement.

Participation in sports provides physiological and psychological benefits to participants. Research has shown that sports help girls and boys become more confident, develop higher self-esteem, and build a better body image compared with their peers who do not participate. In addition, they are less likely to become pregnant, use drugs, and drop out of high school (Hanson, Guilfoy, & Pillai, 2009; National Coalition for Women and Girls in Education, 2008). Therefore, ensuring an equal opportunity to play sports is important in equity.

When Title IX was passed in 1972, 294,015 young women participated in high school sports. Around 40 years later, that number has increased more than tenfold, with nearly 3.2 million females now participating in high school sports (National Federation of State High School Associations, 2010). Female athletes now comprise 42% of all high school athletes. The number of women in intercollegiate athletics has increased by 456%, to 166,728 (National Collegiate Athletic Association, 2009). Equality of participation across women's groups differs based on membership in other groups. Women of color, women with disabilities, and lesbians participate in sports at lower rates than their white classmates (National Coalition for Women and Girls in Education, 2008).

The law alone has not changed the basic assumptions and attitudes that people hold about appropriate female and male roles, occupations, and behaviors, but it has equalized the rights, opportunities, and treatment of students within the school setting. Experience has shown that once discriminatory practices are eliminated and discriminatory behavior is altered, even unwillingly, changes in attitudes often follow. Equal treatment of students from preschool through college will encourage all students to explore available career and life options.

IMPROVING ACADEMIC ACHIEVEMENT

The achievement test scores of 9- and 13-year olds have increased since the National Assessment of Education Progress (NAEP) began testing in 1970, but the performance of 17-year-olds has not. The problem is that the majority of these students, female and male, are not performing at a proficient level. Students from the United States are performing in the middle of the pack or lower on international tests. In fact, students in most industrialized countries outperform U.S. students. The real gap in achievement in the United States is not between boys and girls, but among white, African American, and Hispanic students.

Girls are currently participating in mathematics and science courses at about the same level as boys. In fact, girls are more likely to complete advanced academic courses in science and mathematics than boys (U.S. Department of Education, 2007) but are less likely to select science, technology, engineering, and mathematics (STEM) areas as college majors, and thus are less likely to have jobs in these fields, which have higher salaries than the traditional female professions. What can teachers do to increase the interest of girls in the STEM fields? One strategy is to help female students develop the right hemisphere of their brains. Beginning in preschool, teachers could encourage girls to build things. At all levels, girls should be encouraged to be more physically active, including participating in organized sports. The more hands-on mathematics and science work can be, the more interested both girls and boys will be in the subjects (Eliot, 2009).

While girls may be less accomplished in math and sciences, boys trail girls in reading and language arts tests. To help balance the playing field, teachers should develop strategies for engaging boys in reading and language arts. Boys may need a greater focus on phonics than girls (Eliot, 2009). Selecting books that will hold the interest of the boys is important, as shown in the scenario that began this chapter. In addition to finding books to hold the interest of boys, teachers may want to divide students into different reading or work groups. There may be other art and music projects that would engage boys and girls with words that contribute to the development of their literacy skills.

Girls and boys use computers and the Internet at home and at school at about the same rate. However, there are differences in the way they use technology. Boys play more computer games and begin playing them at an earlier age. They are also more interested in programming and designing, and leave high school with a greater interest in computers (Abbott et al., 2007).

This interest in computers can translate into a job in one of the fastest-growing occupations with some of the highest salaries. Women are not preparing for jobs in this field at the same rate as men; they account for less than one of three students in postsecondary programs in computer and information sciences (U.S. Census Bureau, 2010k). One of the challenges for educators is increasing the interest of girls in computers.

Different approaches to schooling and teaching may increase the participation rates of females. Both male and female students today use technology in different ways than most of their teachers. They are constantly engaged with social networking. Their cell phones keep them connected 24/7. They stay in contact with friends and families through texting and tweeting. They are able to multitask and multiprocess. They learn with many activities going on around them. They prefer constructing their own knowledge and being actively engaged in their learning (Abbott et al., 2007). They want to use technology to learn. The challenge for teachers is to figure out how to use these tools effectively in the classroom.

NONSEXIST EDUCATION

Nonsexist education is designed to ensure that the two sexes are treated fairly and equitably in the curriculum, their interactions with teachers, and instructional and extracurricular activities. To promote nonsexist classrooms, teachers require readings that include women authors as well as male authors. Males and females should appear on bulletin boards and in teacher-prepared materials in non-stereotypical jobs and roles. Male students learn to participate in stereotypically female activities and vice versa.

Portrayal in the Curriculum.   All students should be exposed to the contributions of women as well as men throughout history. History courses that focus primarily on wars and political power tend to focus more on men; history courses that focus on the family and the arts more equitably include both genders. Science courses that discuss all of the great scientists often forget to discuss the societal limitations that prevented women from being scientists. (Women scientists and writers of the past often used male names or turned their work over to men for publication.) Because teachers control the information and concepts taught to students, it is their responsibility to present a view of the world that includes women and men and their wide ranges of perspectives.

Students are bombarded by subtle influences in schools that reinforce the notion that boys are more important than girls. This unplanned, unofficial learning—the hidden curriculum— has an impact on how students feel about themselves and others. The curriculum is infused with traditional male norms (Dowd, 2010). Sexism is often projected in the messages that children receive in the illustrations, language, and content of texts, films, and instructional materials. When boys are stereotypically portrayed as more active, smarter, more aggressive, and exerting more control over their lives than girls, girls are assigned more passive characteristics that may not serve them well in the future. Boys who are always expected to behave in stereotypically masculine ways also suffer.

Incorporating Student Voices.   One of the goals of nonsexist education is to allow girls and young women to be heard and to understand the legitimacy of their experiences. Girls are often silenced as they enter adolescence and take on their more feminine roles, being less assertive and letting boys control discussions in the classroom. Young men are not often encouraged to break out of the expected masculine role, with its own rules of what is required to be a man.

They may become depressed and have lower self-esteem as they try to conform to the rules (Cleveland, 2011).

Young men should have the opportunity to explore their role in our inequitable society. They should learn to speak for the equity of girls and women. Teachers will not find accomplishing this an easy task. Many students resist discussions of power relations and how they stand to benefit or lose within those relations. However, the value to students and society is worth the discomfort that such discussion may cause students, and perhaps teachers. The classroom may be the only place in which students can confront these issues and be helped to make sense of them.

Interacting with Students. An area over which all educators have control is their own interactions with students. Consistently, researchers find that educators treat boys and girls differently in the classroom, on the athletic field, in the hall, and in the counseling office (Sadker et al., 2009). While teachers may not think they respond differently to boys and girls, when they critically examine their interactions, most find that they do, in fact, respond differently based on a student's gender. To overcome the common problem of letting boys respond more often to questions, teachers should focus on making sure that they give equal voice to female students in the classroom. Also, teachers should pay attention to the type of feedback they provide to female and male students, including how much time they take to provide oral feedback and encouragement to female versus male students.

One of the goals of a nonsexist education is to eliminate the power relationships based on gender in the classroom. Teachers can monitor the tasks and activities in which students participate in the classroom. Males often receive more attention because of their misbehavior than for their academic performance (Sadker et al., 2009). Female and male students should share the leadership in classroom activities and discussions. Girls and young women may need to be encouraged to participate actively in hands-on activities, and boys may need encouragement in reading and writing activities.

Learning Together. If left alone, many girls and boys choose to sit with members of the same sex and participate in group activities with members of the same sex (Orenstein, 2011). To ensure that boys and girls work together in the classroom, the teacher may have to assign seats and groups. Small, heterogeneous, cooperative work groups reduce the emphasis on power relationships that characterize competitive activities. These activities can be designed to provide all students, even those who are often marginalized in the classroom, with the opportunity to participate at a more equitable level.

Nonsexist education does not ignore gender in the classroom. It does not require that boys and girls be treated the same in all cases. Gender may need to be emphasized at times to ensure equity. Instructional strategies should be varied to engage both girls and boys with the subject matter, as discussed earlier. Girls may be more comfortable than boys with cooperative group work, reading, listening, and seat work. Engaging more boys in the subject matter may require the use of spatial and graphic aids such as manipulatives in mathematics. Team competition, physical exercise, art, and music can also be used for instructional purposes to draw males into the subject (Gurian & Stevens, 2005). A wide repertoire of instructional strategies should include some that are more engaging to girls, others to boys, and others to both groups. Girls and boys will learn to operate in one another's cultural spheres, and the teacher can avoid the disengagement of one group that typically results with the use of only instructional strategies that are geared to the other group.

Debate / Separate Education for Boys and Girls

Editorials in the community in which your school is located are calling for the school district to create an all-boys middle school and high school that will provide parents an alternative to the coeducational schools that exist across the city. The editorial writers argue that too many young men in the city are not graduating from high school in four years and are not attending college at the rates they should. They say local employers report that many of the high school graduates are not prepared for the jobs that are available. They think that an all-boys school can more effectively develop the self-esteem and the academic and vocational skills of the young men who are currently not being served well by the schools.

The leaders of your local neighborhood organization have asked you to discuss the educational advantages and disadvantages of schools that are segregated by sex. They also want you to make a recommendation on where they should stand on the issue as the school district develops a proposal for these schools.

FOR

- The classroom can address the needs and learning styles of boys, which are very different from those of girls, without doing a disservice to the girls in the classroom.

- The instruction in a segregated setting can focus on fulfilling boys' academic potential because girls will not be there to distract them from the subject matter.

- Because the teachers in the all-boys school will be primarily male, these young men will have positive role models who can more effectively prepare them for manhood.

- The single-sex environment will encourage young men to more openly discuss issues that are critical to their social and academic development.

AGAINST

- Research shows little or no difference in the achievement of boys or their attitudes toward the subject whether they are in boys-only or coeducational courses.

- Single-sex courses reinforce gender stereotypes.

- This approach lets the teachers in coeducational schools off the hook when the school system should be helping all teachers provide an equitable education for boys and girls.

- When the boys go to college or enter the workforce, they most likely will be working with both men and women. A course with boys only does not mirror the real world.

| QUESTIONS |

1. What reasons for establishing a boys-only middle school and high school are the most compelling to you?

2. Even though the research on single-sex schools generally does not show significant improvement in the achievement of boys or girls, are there other reasons that the approach may be viable? Why or why not?

3. What will be your recommendation to your neighborhood organization? Why?

THE BOY CRISIS

Educators are faced with outcries about a "boy crisis" in schools. Concerned observers indicate that boys have been shortchanged as schools turned their focus to improving the academic performance of girls in the 1970s and 1980s. Teachers reportedly have become so impatient with boys' loud, disorderly behavior that they are not teaching them. Teachers should be vigilant that they are not favoring one group over another. Attention to establishing a developmentally appropriate classroom will ensure that the needs of both boys and girls are being met. Having more male teachers in classrooms, especially in early childhood and elementary schools, would provide additional models for male behavior (Eliot, 2009).

Nonsexist education is reflected in the school setting when students are not sorted, grouped, or tracked by gender in any aspect of the school program, including special education, which includes a disproportionately high number of boys. The teacher can develop a curriculum that does not give preferential treatment to boys over girls or girls over boys; that shows both genders in aggressive, nurturing, independent, exciting, and emotional roles; that encourages all students to explore traditional and nontraditional roles; and that assists them in developing positive self-images about their sexuality.

SINGLE-SEX EDUCATION

Single-sex schools focus on developing the confidence, academic achievement, and leadership skills of young women or men by using their unique learning styles and cultural experiences. Although most single-sex schools are for females, some private schools are for boys only. Schools in some urban areas have been established for young African American men. These schools often make African American culture the center of the curriculum with the goal of developing self-esteem, academic achievement, and leadership of students who often confront a hostile environment.

Early in U.S. history, education for girls and boys was segregated, but by 1850 public schools had quietly become coed (Tyack, 2003). Since then, most single-sex schools and colleges have been private. Over time, the courts have required public men's colleges to open their doors to women. One of the most recent examples was the Virginia Military Institute, which admitted women for the first time in 1997. Public schools have also not been allowed to segregate schools or classes by sex. However, when the No Child Left Behind Act was passed by Congress in 2001, public schools were allowed greater flexibility in experimenting with single-sex education to improve the achievement of both girls and boys. A number of public schools and academies have now been established. A more common and expedient way to offer single-sex environments is to establish segregated courses within a coeducational school. Hundreds of schools have now incorporated or are experimenting with this approach (Sadker et al., 2009).

Some research shows that girls are more likely to participate in advanced mathematics and science courses when they are in single-sex classes. Girls in single-sex schools report being more valued and supported (Sadker et al., 2009). Teachers are more likely to use strategies such as cooperative teaching. However, little is known about whether the instruction in single-sex courses and schools differs from that in coeducational settings. Reviews of the research show that students in single-sex settings do have generally higher self-esteem than their peers in coeducational settings. However, little or no difference in achievement and attitudes about the academic subject have been found (Sadker et al., 2009). A study of female-only courses in mathematics and science found positive differences in performance and persistence in taking additional mathematics and science courses (Shapka & Keating, 2003). Similar positive findings have been found for some male-only courses (Gurian & Stevens, 2005). Opponents to single-sex classes and schools argue that they are more likely to reinforce traditional, stereotypic gender roles.

WOMEN'S STUDIES

Women's studies programs are similar to ethnic studies programs in their attempt to record and analyze the historical and contemporary experiences of a group that has traditionally been ignored in the curriculum. Courses in women's studies include concepts of consciousness raising and views of women as a separate group with unique needs and disadvantages in schools and other institutions. They examine the culture, status, development, and achievement of women as a group.

Women's studies have evolved in high schools, colleges, and universities as units in history, sociology, and literature courses; as separate courses; and as programs from which students can choose a major or minor field of study. Similar to the ethnic studies programs, the experiences and contributions of women and related concepts have been the focus.

Women's studies provide a perspective that is foreign to most students. Historical, economic, and sociological events are viewed from the perspective of a group that has been subordinate to men throughout history. Until students participate in such courses, they usually do not realize that 51% of the population has received so little coverage in most textbooks and courses. These programs allow students to increase both their awareness and their knowledge base about women's history and the contributions of women. In some of these courses, women are taught skills for competing successfully in a man's world or for managing both a career and a family. In addition, many women's studies programs assist in developing a positive female self-image. Psychological and career assistance to women is also a part of some programs.

Although the content of women's studies is needed to fill the gaps of current educational programs, it is usually an elective course. Thus, the majority of students may never integrate the information and concepts of women's studies into their academic work. The treatment of women as a separate entity also subtly suggests that the study of women is secondary to the study of a world that is controlled by males. All students should learn about a world in which the contributions of both males and females are valued.

Summary

Our sex is determined by biology. Some researchers have reported that the brains of males and females are hardwired differently, causing the differences between the two sexes. However, other researchers find that these differences are primarily socially constructed and can be learned through culture and education.

Our gender identity is based on our feminine or masculine characteristics. The degree to which an individual adheres to a traditional gender identity varies as a result of past socialization patterns, which are influenced by the family's ethnicity, race, and religion.

Sexism and gender discrimination have kept women in less prestigious and lower-paying jobs than men. Even the amount of education obtained by a woman does little to close the gap between the earnings of men and women—now at 80 cents for every dollar earned by a man. Such discrimination greatly affects the quality of life for families, single mothers, and children.

The federal legislation Title IX makes it illegal for schools to discriminate against girls and women in any educational program, including athletics. One of the goals for gender equity is to eliminate the gender differences in academic achievement. Nonsexist classrooms in P–12 education incorporate curricula that include females as well as males, and support the learning of both sexes. A number of private schools, including colleges, enroll only female students, and a number of public school systems have established single-sex schools to meet the different learning styles and perceived needs of females and males. Women's studies programs in schools and universities allow men and women to study the history, culture, and psychology of women. These programs have promoted research on girls and women that support a gender equity agenda.

Professional Practice

Questions for Discussion

1. In what ways are differences between the sexes culturally, rather than biologically, determined? How might the differences be reinforced or changed in classrooms?

2. What roles do masculinity and femininity play in one's gender identity?

3. How has the women's movement changed the status of girls and the way they are treated in schools? What were the major legislative actions that contributed to these changes?

4. Explain how gender discrimination has disproportionately affected women.

5. How can you, as an educator, help increase the participation of females and other underrepresented groups in computer science, mathematics, and science careers?

Portfolio Activities

1. Collect data on the numbers of boys and girls in mathematics, science, or technology courses in the schools you are observing. Describe the course-taking patterns by the level of the course (for example, general education and advanced placement). What, if any, differences exist between the course taking of girls and boys? (InTASC Standard 2: Learning Differences, and Standard 3: Learning Environments)

2. Observe the differences between how boys and girls act in classrooms and interact with teachers. Analyze the differences and discuss how the teacher may reinforce or try to change stereotypical gender behavior. Describe teachers' responses to students that are most supportive of learning. Discuss how these responses differ for boys and girls. (InTASC Standard 3: Learning Differences, and Standard 8: Instructional Strategies)

3. Observe classes using cooperative learning and other instructional strategies. Record the engagement of boys and girls in the different instructional approaches. Analyze your findings based on gender. Discuss whether the differences could be generalized to the sex of the students or whether the differences exist within the same sex. (InTASC Standard 3: Learning Differences, and Standard 8: Instructional Strategies)

Digital Resources for the Classroom

1. For tutorials on sex discrimination and remedies, visit http://www.hunter.cuny.edu/gendertutorial/tutorial1.html#

2. Video clips of women scientists, students, and professors at Hunter College (New York) explaining how and why they pursued science and encouraging other young women and girls to enter the field of science can be accessed at http://www.hunter.cuny.edu/genderequity/science-career-video.html

3. Want to know how girls are faring in other countries? Visit the website for the United Nations Girl's Education Initiative at www.ungei.org, which includes papers on and descriptions of projects from around the world.

4. The website of the National Coalition for Women and Girls in Education has information and resources on Title IX for educators and parents at http://www.ncwge.org.

5. For lesson plans on teaching high school students about sexual harassment, visit http://www.discoveryeducation.com/teachers/free-lesson-plans/sexual-harassment.cfm.

MyEducationLab™

Go to the MyEducationLab (www.myeducationlab.com) for Multicultural Education and familiarize yourself with the topical content, which includes:

- Assignments and Activities, tied to learning outcomes for the course, that can help you more deeply understand course content
- Building Teaching Skills and Dispositions learning units allow you to apply and practice your understanding of how to teach equitably in a multicultural education classroom
- Licensure Test Prep activities are available in the Book Resources to help you prepare for test taking
- A pretest with hints and feedback that tests your knowledge of this chapter's content

- Review, practice, and enrichment activities that will enhance your understanding of the chapter content
- A posttest with hints and feedback that allows you to test your knowledge again after having completed the enrichment activities

A Correlation Guide may be downloaded by instructors to show how MyEducationLab content aligns to this book.

5 Sexual Orientation

Human rights apply to everyone, no matter who they are or whom they love.

Secretary of State, Hillary Rodham Clinton, on the Affirmation That Human Rights Applies to Gay and Lesbian Rights by 85 Countries at the United Nations' Human Rights Council Meeting in Geneva, March 2011

| LEARNING OUTCOMES |

As you read this chapter, you should be able to:

■ Describe the diversity of sexual orientation and the stages through which people move to clarify their sexual identity.

■ Identify the discrimination historically faced by lesbian, gay, bisexual, transgender, and queer (LGBTQ) people and the struggles they have made for equality in the United States.

■ Analyze the toll that heterosexism takes on LGBTQ youth and educators in the nation's schools.

■ Develop strategies for ensuring that future classrooms and schools value sexual diversity among students and support LGBTQ students in having positive and successful experiences in schools.

Jason Cunningham had been teaching for five years when his school district adopted a comprehensive policy on its commitment to gay students. It stated, "Ideals related to anti-homophobia and sexual orientation equity will be reflected in all aspects of organizational structures, policies, guidelines, procedures, classroom practices, day-to-day operations, and communication practices." Jason's principal decided that their high school would become the model for the district. To initiate the process, he required teachers and other school professionals to attend four diversity training sessions during the year.

Although Jason believed that all students should be treated equally, he was worried about what he would be required to teach. He knew nothing about sexual orientation other than that Congress had repealed the "Don't Ask, Don't Tell" policy, which would allow gays and lesbians in the military to be open about their sexual orientation. He was not so sure that was a good idea. He couldn't think of one gay adult he knew. Besides, most of the people he knew thought of homosexuality as wrong, even sinful. He had shared many jokes and innuendos about gays with his friends over the years.

Jason wondered whether this would be another workshop telling him that he is part of the problem and must change what he is teaching. He wasn't sure he could talk to his students about homosexuality, especially because deep down he believed that gays had made a bad choice about their lifestyle. He knew that some of his students verbally harassed students they thought were gay, but he didn't see a need to get involved in their business.

| REFLECTIONS |

1. What does Jason's school district's sexual orientation policy suggest for teachers' work?

2. What issues should be addressed in the diversity training to help Jason become a partner in making his high school a model for sexual orientation equity?

3. If you were a teacher in this school, how would you respond to the school district's directive that classroom practices be anti-homophobic and provide sexual orientation equity?

Sexual Identity

The fact that the population is not solely heterosexual is much more obvious today than at any time in the past. Although not all lesbian, gay, bisexual, transgender, and queer (**LGBTQ**) individuals are out, their visibility as a group is higher than ever. Issues of the LGBTQ community are now common in the news. A **gay** Episcopal priest was selected bishop of New Hampshire in 2003, leading to a division in the church. Gays are being prosecuted and executed in Uganda for their homosexuality. The military has eliminated its "Don't Ask, Don't Tell" policy. Gay and **lesbian** couples are marrying. Days of silence, **gay-straight alliances** (GSAs) in schools, and court cases against school districts for not protecting LGBTQ students from harassment have highlighted the plight of LGBTQ students in the nation's schools. At the same time, local communities, religious congregations, and state and national policymakers continue to debate sexual diversity and the rights of individuals who are not heterosexuals.

Many people have little knowledge about **sexual orientation** other than heterosexuality. Perhaps you have never thought about it, which means that you are probably heterosexual and see it as the norm. Others know that their sexual orientation is not heterosexual. What is sexual orientation? The American Psychological Association (APA) (2008) defines it as an "enduring pattern of emotional, romantic, and/or sexual attractions to men, women, or both sexes" (p. 1). The APA (2008) further indicates that different sexual orientations are normal forms of human bonding.

After personal interviews about the sexual behavior of more than 11,000 white adults in the 1940s and 1950s, zoologist Alfred Kinsey reported that 10% of the male population and 2% to 6% of the female population were predominantly homosexual (Kinsey Institute, 2011). The figure of 10% continues to be commonly used to designate the percentage of gays and lesbians in the population. However, recent data indicate that 3.5% of the population identify themselves as lesbian, gay, **bisexual**, or **transgender** (Keen, 2011).

DIVERSE SEXUAL ORIENTATIONS

Most of the population do not think about their sexuality except in terms of the opposite sex and the stages their families expect them to progress through—dating, getting married, and having children. For most young people, no other options for their sexuality exist. They have not chosen to be heterosexual, and they have always been attracted to the opposite sex. They may not have known that other people experience a different sexual orientation than their own and have little or no knowledge about other sexual orientations.

The term "homosexuality" first appeared in Leipzig, Germany, in 1869 and had become accepted in the professional literature by 1880. Over the next 100 years, the terms "homosexual" and "heterosexual" became identified with the sex of two persons who were sexually attracted to each other. Many people at this time viewed homosexuality as a sin, a moral failure, a sickness, or a crime. Until 1973 the American Psychiatric Association classified it as a mental illness.

No one questions heterosexuality; it has been the only accepted norm with any other sexual orientation being identified as abnormal or even deviant. Therefore, one of the common questions asked is why some people are not heterosexual. A common approach to answering this question is to use science to prove that gays do not choose their sexual orientation but are born with it. In pursuit of this scientific proof, researchers have explored genes, the brain, hormones, and prenatal chemistry to explain why some people are LGB. In the July 1993 issue of *Science*, molecular biologist Dean Hamer reported finding a DNA marker (Xq28) on the X chromosome of women. Hamer connected that marker to male sexual orientation, but his research has not been replicated, calling into question the existence of a "gay gene." Hormonal differences, especially concerning the role of testosterone, have been investigated, but the great majority of LGB individuals have hormonal levels that match the heterosexual population. Some researchers believe that the hypothalamus—a small mass of cells at the base of the brain—has something to do with it. Others have found evidence that there is a higher incidence of homosexuality in some families than the general population, suggesting that it is hereditary. Environmental influences such as child rearing have also been proposed as a contributing factor to one's sexual orientation, but research has not confirmed this theory (LeVay, 2011; Wilson & Rahman, 2008).

One perspective within the LGB community is that the reason one is gay or straight should not make a difference. The focus on finding a biological explanation could undermine social justice initiatives, such as equity and the right to be gay without being abused, which are important in the community (Lehr, 2007). Identifying a genetic link could have negative impacts on the LGB community if, for example, insurance companies refused to cover people with that gene because they may have a greater chance of having AIDS.

Many people continue to believe that biology has something to do with sexual orientation, and it may well play an important role. However, heritability is much more complicated than a single gene. Researchers will continue to try to find an answer while the LGB community addresses the social justice issues that affect their daily lives.

DIVERSITY OF SEXUAL ORIENTATIONS

Terms to describe sexual identity differ depending on the context and individual. Heterosexual, straight, homosexual, gay, lesbian, bisexual, transgender, and queer are terms commonly used today. However, some youth don't like any of the current labels for describing their own sexuality; instead they are developing their own terms to describe themselves. Educators should know the terms in current use, but they should not themselves apply labels to students. Students and colleagues must have the freedom to determine their own sexual identities using the terms that have the most meaning for themselves.

The majority of the population is heterosexual, sometimes referred to as straight, which is defined as being sexually attracted to members of the opposite sex. Persons who are sexually attracted to members of the same sex have been labeled as homosexuals. However, that term has the stigma of being associated with mental illness (Savage & Harley, 2009), which historically was how homosexuality had been classified by the American Psychiatric Association. Today that term has largely been replaced with "lesbian," "gay," or "bisexual." Although "gay" refers to men who are sexually attracted to other men, it is also used as a general term that applies to all LGB persons, and it is sometimes used in this textbook for that purpose. "Lesbian" refers to women who are sexually attracted to other women, and "bisexual" refers to people who are sexually attracted to both men and women.

Sexual orientation includes not only the gender to whom one is sexually attracted, but also gender diversity such as transgender or **intersex**. Transgender persons have a psychological sense of being of the gender (male or female) that does not match their genetic sex (for example, a biological woman identifies herself as a man or vice versa). It sometimes applies to those who do not conform to their assigned gender roles (Eaklor, 2008). Transgender youth and adults may change their social gender by dressing and behaving like the other sex. However, this broad category also includes **transvestites** (cross-dressers) and **transsexuals,** who surgically change their genitals and alter other characteristics to match their gender identity. Transgenders are included in **LGBTIQ** because many of the issues and obstacles that they face in society are similar to those encountered by gays, lesbians, and bisexuals (Savage & Harley, 2009).

Intersex individuals have been born with an atypical anatomy that does not clearly identify their sex (American Psychological Association, 2008). For example, they may have one testis and one ovary, or testes and some female genitalia, or ovaries and male genitals. In the past, medical doctors and parents sometimes determined what the sex of an intersex child would be, resulting in surgery to make the genitals conform to that decision. In some notable cases, the gender identity of these children later in life did not match the sex that had been chosen for them.

The Q in LBGTIQ stands for **questioning** or **queer**. The questioning category includes individuals who are wondering about their sexuality, who are not sure of their sexual orientation, or who are not ready to claim a label for their identity (Savage & Harley, 2009). "Queer" is a term applied by some members of the LGBTIQ community to anyone who is not heterosexual. Queerness allows fluidity across categories, is political, challenges the status quo, and rejects assimilation into mainstream society (Whitlock, 2007). Younger people view the term as more empowering than other terms that describe them, but some members of the LGBTIQ community remember "queer" as a derogatory term used against them in the past, which leads them to reject the term (Savage & Harley, 2009). Nevertheless, educators should be aware of the terms and be able to figure out the communities in which "queer" and other terms are acceptable.

As a response to essentialism, **queer theory** has evolved to guide the exploration of sexual orientation. "It questions taken-for-granted assumptions about relationships, identity, gender, and sexual orientation" (Meyer, 2007, p. 15). It challenges the binary categories of man/woman, masculine/feminine, student/teacher, and gay/straight, pushing educators and others to think about the world differently (Meyer, 2007). Thus, you see discussions of "queering the curriculum" or "queering straight teachers," encouraging a perspective that does not see one sexual orientation (i.e., heterosexuality) as the norm against which others are measured and evaluated.

The idea that sexual orientation plays out along a continuum is not new. In his famous study of sexual behavior over 70 years ago, Alfred Kinsey used a 7-point scale between absolute heterosexuality and absolute homosexuality to categorize his interviewees. Some people are bisexuals and are in the middle of the scale. Others have been attracted to or had sexual relationships with people of the same sex at some time, but are not exclusively gay or lesbian. Others were exclusively heterosexual. A number of young people who are communicating online reject labels and are finding new ways to describe themselves across that continuum (Crowley, 2010).

SELF-IDENTITY

Our sense of sexuality or sexual orientation identity is based on sexual attractions, related behaviors, and a connection with others with the same orientation (American Psychological Association, 2008). It is about how people decide to identify themselves. Most researchers agree that sexual orientation is established early in life. As early as six years old, some boys and girls have a sense that they are sexually different from their peers. With the onset of puberty, they are likely to be attracted to a peer of the same or different sex. Young people are identifying themselves as LGBTQ as early as middle school.

Similar to racial and ethnic groups, **LGBT** individuals appear to move through stages of development as they become comfortable with their sexual identity. Because heterosexuals are in the privileged sexual identification category in our society, they may not identify their sexuality unless they become aware of their privilege or become an LGBT ally. The first step for LGBT students is the realization that they are sexually attracted to same-sex individuals, which distinguishes them from most of their peers. Their feelings may confuse them and lead them to question the reality of their developing sexual identity. The next stage often includes exploration and experimentation as they determine whether they are LGBT, which could include testing relationships with those of the opposite sex. Eventually they begin to identify themselves with a label or decide that none of the current labels describe them. When they feel comfortable with their sexual identity and are willing to face the possible discrimination and alienation that can accompany their disclosure as LGBT, they come out to others. The last stage of the process allows them to develop pride in their sexual identity (Joyce, O'Neil, & McWhirter, 2010). New research suggests that identity develops along different trajectories rather than in these distinct stages depending on the individual, their contexts, and the support they elicit from family, peers, and members of the broader LGBTQ community (Joyce et al., 2010).

During the stages of struggling with their identity, some LGBTQ individuals may feel depressed, isolated, and not valued. The messages that they receive from others may indicate that they are abnormal and making choices that will not serve them well in the future. They may not know that professional organizations such as the American Psychological Association have declared that multiple sexual orientations are "normal forms of human experience" (American Psychological Association, 2008, p. 3). Though many LGBTQ students are happy, well adjusted, and liked by others, some students who are LGBTQ, or are perceived to be, are harassed by other students in schools. These pressures to be different from who they are contribute to LGBTQ students missing school, underperforming academically in school, dropping out of school, and attempting suicide at a higher rate compared with heterosexual students.

The classroom teacher is likely to find students falling at different points along the gender and sexual identity continuum, both in their beliefs about female and male roles and in their actual behavior. Lesbian and gay adolescents are struggling with their sexual identity and its meaning in a heterosexist climate. Heterosexual students also struggle with issues about their sexuality and how to express it appropriately, often receiving mixed messages from their parents, their peers, and the media. Understanding the influence of students' cultural memberships will be important as teachers try to open up the possibilities for all of them, regardless of their gender and sexual identity. Having teachers who are supportive of LGBTQ students and intervene on their behalf contributes greatly to successful school experiences for these children and youth.

Some religious groups have identified homosexuality as a sin or disease that can be eliminated or cured. They believe that people choose their sexual orientation. Antigay activists and parents may push youth and adults into programs designed to make them "normal" by denouncing their LGBTQ identity, and choosing to be heterosexual. Organizations such as the American Psychological Association, American Psychiatric Association, and American Academy of Pediatrics do not support "reparative or conversion therapy" (American Psychological Association, 2008). These organizations report that such therapy reinforces negative stereotypes about gays and lesbians and contributes to an unsafe climate for them.

Most LGBTQ youth and adults are very resilient and have established happy and fulfilling lives. In a survey of 553 gays and lesbians, only 1% of the respondents indicated that there was nothing positive about their sexual orientation. Coming out, which requires disclosing one's

Coming out is much easier for students when they have the support of family members and other students.
© Jim West/Alamy

sexual identity to others, was a critical step in developing a positive identity. Three of five participants in this survey reported that their families had been supportive as they clarified their sexual identity. Having a supportive gay and lesbian community in which they can participate was seen as a positive aspect of being gay or lesbian. Coming out often requires a great deal of personal insight and reflection as these individuals struggle with who they are and develop the courage to share their identity with others. Some gays and lesbians find that going through this process has strengthened them, made them more empathetic to other oppressed groups, and increased their activism for social justice. The other reported positive outcome of being gay and lesbian was the freedom they felt from the gender-specific roles often expected of women and men (Riggle, Whitman, Olson, Rostosky, & Strong, 2008). These findings demonstrate the importance of schools' creating safe places for young people to come out and realize their full human potential.

INTERACTION WITH RACE, ETHNICITY, AND RELIGION

All of us have multiple identities that influence our membership in different cultural groups. Because of racism within the gay community, LGBTQ people of color may not receive the needed support from the larger gay community (Jamil & Harper, 2010). Conversely, the **heterosexism** that exists in some religious, ethnic, and racial groups can lead to intolerance and exclusion of LGBTQ members. Family members and other respected adults and peers from these communities may be unwilling to accept an LGBTQ identity and unwilling to provide the support that LGBTQ youth need during this period. As a result, these young people have to learn about gay culture from other sources—their peers, mass media, and the Internet (Jamil & Harper, 2010)—which may not provide accurate information and may also pose a threat to their well-being. When they can't explore their identity under the watchful eye of a caring adult such as a teacher, they may be forced to seek information in other places, where they may encounter adult predators (Macgillivray, 2008).

In many schools, students' membership in multiple groups has an impact on their relationships with other students and their treatment by these students. Compared to white LGBTQ students, LGBTQ students of color are more likely to be harassed and assaulted because of both their sexual identity and their race or ethnicity, a situation that is intensified if they are in schools in which their racial or ethnic group is in the minority. Multiracial, African American, and Asian/Pacific Islander LGBTQ students are more likely than other groups to feel unsafe because of their race or ethnicity. Native American students also experience harassment because of their religion (or perceived religion) in addition to the other factors (Diaz & Kosciw, 2009). However, LBGTQ students do not have to face discrimination and harassment in schools. When schools have policies against such harassment and apply them effectively, such abuse will be reduced and eventually eliminated. LGBTQ students are helped with their identity struggles and societal obstacles by supportive educators and peers.

Struggles for Sexual Equity

Until World War II most gay and lesbians hid their sexual identities in the communities in which they grew up, often marrying someone of the opposite sex, having children, and living as heterosexuals. States had laws that criminalized gays, allowing them to be arrested in their homes as well as public places. Gays and lesbians were often not allowed to teach because it was believed that they would have a negative impact on children and youth.

When Alfred Kinsey released his books on male sexuality in 1948 and female sexuality in 1953, it was self-affirming for many gays and lesbians as they realized they were not the only ones whose sexual orientation did not match societal expectations. Kinsey's conclusions were widely attacked. Most people had believed that few people were homosexual, and they now worried that the culture would be destroyed by them. Politicians and religious leaders became even more overt in their condemnation of those who deviated from the heterosexual model.

FIGHTING FOR SEXUAL EQUITY

Between 1927 and 1967, the state of New York banned what it called "sexual perversion" as a dramatic theme in plays. Similar bans were placed on movies. Noted writers ignored the ban, continuing to include gays and lesbians in their books and screenplays. The rock 'n' roll era that began in the 1950s with artists such as Elvis Presley, Chuck Berry, and Little Richard celebrated sensuality and rebellion against society's rules, but it was predominantly within a heterosexual context. However, literature and music did become sources of expression for the youth who broke the sexual norms. The Beats were young men, and a few young women, "who wrote prose and poetry of their disillusionment with the materialism and moral dictates of the fifties" (Eaklor, 2008, p. 82). Sexual freedom and the celebration of their gayness were hallmarks of this subculture. One of the most famous works during this period was the poem *Howl* by Allen Ginsberg, which references drugs and gay sex. The poem became known to the broader public when the owner of the bookstore that was publishing it was charged with obscenity (Eaklor, 2008).

In the 1950s Evelyn Hooker began to question the pathological explanations for homosexuality as a result of her study of gay men. Using standard psychological research tools, she found that gay men were as well adjusted as straight men, and sometimes more so (Eaklor, 2008). Her findings set the stage for gays and their allies to fight popular psychiatric treatments that often involved electroshock therapy. Although Dr. Hooker presented her findings at a 1956 meeting of the American Psychological Association, it took nearly two decades for the American Psychiatric Association to remove homosexuality from its list of mental illnesses.

The Lavender Scare. A period known as the Lavender Scare (or Pink Scare) began in the 1950s when homosexuals were thought to be more of a threat to national security than Communists were (Johnson, 2004). The U.S. Senate called for a purge of homosexuals from the government. Within a year, the Federal Bureau of Investigation (FBI), under Director J. Edgar Hoover, had identified 406 individuals so designated (Miller, 2006). When Congress passed the Immigration and Nationality Act (McCarran-Walter Act) in 1952, it banned homosexual immigrants from entering the country. In 1953 President Eisenhower signed an Executive Order to dismiss homosexuals from the government—a practice that was followed into the 1970s. Lesbians and gays also were being dismissed from the military at a rate that rose to 3,000 annually in the early 1960s.

In addition to losing their jobs, gays and lesbians were arrested by the hundreds in bars, parks, and theaters as well as at parties in their own homes. In some communities, citizens were summoned to call out their homosexual neighbors and work colleagues. Many citizens confused homosexuality with pedophilia and child molestation and feared the recruitment of others into their ranks. Homosexuals' demands for justice were ignored by most of the population. Civil rights groups did not intervene to support gays and lesbians who were losing their jobs or being harassed in other settings. To support each other and their struggles for acceptance and equity in society, gays and lesbians began organizing in cities such as San Francisco, Detroit, Philadelphia, New York, and Washington, D.C. (Eaklor, 2008). One of their goals was to eliminate the pathological diagnosis that was prevalent in the dominant culture.

Movement for Gay Rights.   The 1950s marked the beginning of the civil rights revolution led by African Americans. Soon after the March on Washington on August 28, 1963, which rallied a quarter of a million people for human, civil, and economic rights, critical legislation for civil rights was passed by Congress, including the Civil Rights Act of 1964 and the Voting Rights Act of 1965. Other oppressed groups, including the LGBTQ community, followed with calls for the recognition of their civil rights. The counterculture and antiwar movements increased the questioning of the norms, values, and assumptions of mainstream society. This was the era in which gays and lesbians began picketing government agencies, including the White House, the United Nations, the Pentagon, and the State Department.

On June 27, 1969, the gay rights movement was born when police raided New York City's Stonewall Inn in Greenwich Village. Stonewall Inn was a refuge for gays, who were not welcome in other bars. Its patrons were mostly males and drag queens of different ages and economic levels. Police arrived around 1:00 a.m. the next morning to close the bar, purportedly because it was operating without a license, but raids on gay bars were not unusual. The bar was closed, employees arrested, and patrons pushed outside. As those arrested were placed in police wagons, the ousted patrons and the crowd that had gathered began throwing coins, bottles, and bricks at police. It soon escalated into a riot, with everything in the bar being destroyed. This initial riot lasted only a few hours, but the crowd had fought back against the police. Crowds reconvened the following night at the Inn and on the street outside. They began shouting for "gay power" and cheering for gay liberation. It took police hours to disperse the crowd, which reassembled to battle the police for the next four nights (Eaklor, 2008). Within a few months, the radical Gay Liberation Front (GLF) was formed.

Gays had rioted earlier in Los Angeles and San Francisco against police raids, but those riots had been carefully organized by gay leaders. Stonewall Inn was different. Participants were gays who were rejected not only by society, but by more conservative gays who lived as if they were heterosexual. At Stonewall the riot was spontaneous, full of emotion, and bloody. It became the symbol for the fight against the inequities faced by LGBTs. Soon afterward the number of LGBT groups grew from 50 to over 800.

As shown in Table 5.1, progress for gay rights and the elimination of discrimination against gays has been made since 1969, although numerous obstacles periodically forestalled significant changes. After the Stonewall riot, it became somewhat easier for gays and lesbians to openly admit their homosexuality, especially if they lived in cities. A number of gay activists turned to the establishment of organizations concerned with law and policy to attack discrimination. In 1973 the National Gay Task Force and the Lambda Legal Defense and Education Fund were created. The National Gay Task Force was renamed the National Gay and Lesbian Task Force within a few years, with the goal of politically fighting the antigay backlash. Lambda Legal began to fight the federal government's antigay policies in the courts. It has continued to be

Table 5.1 Milestones in the Movement for Gay Rights

June 28, 1969	Police raided Stonewall Inn, which was subsequently followed by a riot in Greenwich Village of New York City.
1970	The National Institute of Mental Health study group recommended civil rights protection for gays. Thousands marched in a New York gay parade to celebrate the anniversary of the Stonewall Inn riot.
1970s	Civil Service Commission lifted its ban on employment of homosexuals. Police stopped raiding bars but continued to arrest gays in other areas. Gay and lesbian caucuses were formed in professional associations. The Save Our Children campaign initiated by former Miss America Anita Bryant worked to repeal protection for gays. A California proposal, the Briggs Initiative, would have banned gay teachers and their supporters from public schools. It was defeated.
1979	100,000 gay men and lesbians participated in the March on Washington to call for gay rights.
1980	The Moral Majority organized to oppose homosexuality. Gay men with a mysterious illness began appearing in emergency rooms. The disease was later identified as AIDS, which provided a unifying cause for the gay community through the 1980s. Wisconsin passed a gay civil rights law, which was introduced by an openly gay legislator.
1987	The second gay and lesbian March on Washington included spreading out AIDS quilt on the Mall. ACT UP (AIDS Coalition to Unleash Power) was founded in New York City.
1989	Massachusetts passed a gay civil rights law sponsored by an open lesbian and closeted gay man.
1993	The third gay and lesbian March on Washington protested the military ban against gays and lesbians.
1996	U.S. Supreme Court ruled that states could not ban protection of gay rights outright in *Rohmer v. Evans*.
2000	Vermont approved civil unions between gays and lesbian couples. The U.S. Supreme Court ruled 5–4 in *Boy Scouts of American v. Dale* that a private organization has a right to discriminate against homosexuals.
2003	U.S. Supreme Court ended laws against sodomy in *Lawrence v. Texas*.
2004	Gay and lesbian couples were allowed to marry in Massachusetts.
2005	Connecticut approved civil unions.
2006	New Jersey approved civil unions. Anti-gay Federal Marriage Amendment failed in Congress.
2007	New Hampshire legalized civil unions.
2008	Connecticut legalized same-sex marriage. Proposition 8, banning same-sex marriage in California, passed.
2009	Iowa, New Hampshire, and Vermont legalized same-sex marriage.
2010	A federal district judge in California found Proposition 8 unconstitutional; the decision is being appealed. Congress repealed "Don't Ask, Don't Tell," allowing lesbians and gay men to serve openly in the military.

at the center of legal cases related to AIDS, domestic partnership, and other civil rights issues (Eaklor, 2008).

LGB politicians began to run in and to win elections in the 1970s. Allan Spear was elected to the Minnesota state senate and Barney Frank to the Massachusetts House in 1972, but neither of them had come out at that time. In the following two years, Gerry Studds (D-MA) and Robert Bauman (R-MD) were elected to the U.S. House of Representatives. Harvey Milk was among the first openly gay citizens to win an election when he was voted into the San Francisco Board of Supervisors in 1977. The number of elected LGBTQ legislators has increased over the past three decades at the local, state, and national levels.

A Backlash and a Disease. The 1980s saw a backlash against the feminist and LGBTQ gains achieved over the previous decade. Conservative Christians began to influence politics, calling for a return to "family values," which they believed should be built on the nuclear family and marriage between a male and a female. Feminists and gays were blamed for the destruction of the family as they fought for the equal rights of women, lesbians, and gays, which many conservatives blamed for the increasing number of divorces and immoral behaviors to which they did not want their children exposed. Beginning in the 1970s, these groups organized to defeat the Equal Rights Amendment, which would have outlawed discrimination based on sex. These differences between conservatives, feminists, and LGBT individuals fueled the "culture wars" in society. Activists on both sides rallied to their causes and lobbied Congress and state legislatures for change. The Human Rights Campaign Fund was established as the first political action committee (PAC) to lobby on behalf of gays and lesbians (Eaklor, 2008).

A report of the National Centers for Disease Control (CDC) on June 5, 1981, reported that young men in a number of large U.S. cities had contracted a type of pneumonia that was usually found in cancer patients. The victims in all of the reported cases were gay. As the story spread across the country, rumors and theories also spread about the disease being contagious and propagated by gays with multiple partners. It was another year before researchers determined that the condition was an infection, designated it as AIDS (Acquired Immunodeficiency Syndrome), and reported that it was not spread by casual contact. In 1984 scientists discovered the virus that was responsible for AIDS. Within two years the virus was labeled the human immunodeficiency virus (HIV), and scientists had developed a blood test to determine if an individual was HIV positive. They learned that the virus was spread through the exchange of bodily fluids during sexual activity, needle sharing by drug users, and blood transfusions. Between 1981 and 1986, 12,000 deaths from the disease had been reported (Eaklor, 2008). Even after non-gays had been diagnosed with the disease, the general public continued to identify it as a gay disease. Three decades after these first young men began seeking care, AIDS had become a global disease that was disproportionately affecting women (Eaklor, 2008).

During this period, the LGBT community mobilized against AIDS and the growing **homophobia** in society (Eaklor, 2008). They engaged in raising awareness about the disease, lobbying for funds to support research about it, and raising funds to care for the growing number of people suffering from the disease. Members of one of the best-known anti-AIDS organizations, ACT UP (AIDS Coalition to Unleash Power), became angry at the inaction of the government and other groups to find a cure for AIDS. They were known for their tactics to disrupt or shut down businesses or government offices, including Wall Street and the National Institutes of Health (NIH). In San Francisco a group began a project to memorialize those who had died of AIDS by designing 3′ × 6′ panels, one for each victim, and joining them into the AIDS Memorial Quilt. When the quilt was first displayed on the National Mall in Washington, DC, in 1987, it had 1,920 panels; by 2006 it had 45,000 panels (Eaklor, 2008).

One Step Forward and One Step Backward.   Not all members of the LGBT community agreed on the tactics and direction for their activism. Lesbians often felt neglected in the work. The place of bisexuals in the movement was not clear, and transgender individuals were forming their own groups, usually based on their gender identity (e.g., male-to-female or female-to-male). Although groups and individuals within them may have disagreed on strategies, they generally agreed that they should be fighting to protect LGBT people from discrimination, counter antigay legislation, and repeal sodomy laws in the states (Eaklor, 2008). Progress was being made in the 1980s. Wisconsin passed the first bill to ban discrimination based on sexual orientation. Six states and a number of cities and communities passed similar legislation soon after (Eaklor, 2008). Sexual orientation was included in the Hate Crimes Statistics Act signed by George H. W. Bush in 1990. In addition, a growing number of gays and lesbians were being elected to public offices at the local and state levels as well as being appointed by government officials (Eaklor, 2008).

The culture wars continued to influence school policies throughout the end of the twentieth century and into the twenty-first. Books about lesbians and gays were removed from school libraries. In 1992 antigay activists and some parents in New York City contested the school district's adoption of the "Rainbow Curriculum," which supported diversity, including gays and lesbians (Eaklor, 2008). When the curriculum was finally adopted, the references to books on lesbian and gay families had been removed. A number of college and universities eliminated ROTC programs and refused to allow recruiters from the military on campus because of their "Don't Ask, Don't Tell" policy. At the same time, a number of higher-education institutions continued to refuse to allow students to establish gay and lesbian groups on campus.

The LGBT community was optimistic that the political landscape would change with the election of Bill Clinton as president. Clinton was the first president who had solicited their support in his election and indicated that he would lift the ban on homosexuality in the armed services. Faced with strong resistance to lifting the ban by military officials, Clinton compromised by establishing a "Don't Ask, Don't Tell" policy, by which gays and lesbians could serve in the military if they remained closeted. The hopes of the LGBT community were again crushed as their right to be open about their sexual identity would be denied if they wanted to serve in the military. The "Don't Ask, Don't Tell" policy remained in effect until December 2010, when it was repealed.

On another front, marriage between same-sex individuals was being tested. Many religious communities already performed marriages or blessing ceremonies between same-sex couples, but they had no legal standing (Eaklor, 2008). Other religions would not recognize same-sex relationships or the sexual identity of their LGBT members. Three same-sex couples in Hawaii sued for the right to receive marriage licenses in 1991 but lost their case. However, the Hawaii Supreme Court later found that the denial of marriage licenses to these couples was discriminatory on the basis of sex (Miller, 2006) and called on the state to demonstrate a reason for excluding these couples from marriage. The state legislature responded quickly by defining marriage as taking place between a man and woman only, a decision that led to another suit. Rather than wait for the Hawaii case to be resolved, Congress passed the Defense of Marriage Act (DOMA) in 1996 to oppose same-sex marriages. The voters of Hawaii ratified the legislature's definition of marriage in 1998. At the same time, Alaskan voters approved a constitutional amendment restricting marriage to a man and woman.

Prior to the 2004 national elections, 11 more states passed anti–gay marriage legislation (Miller, 2006). By 2006, 40 states had passed similar amendments (Johnson, 2006). As part of the 2008 national elections, California voters approved by a 52% to 48% margin Proposition 8, overturning the California Supreme Court's ruling that same-sex couples have a constitutional right to marry. An analysis of the characteristics of the people who voted in favor of Proposition 8 found that by large margins they were Republican, were conservative, attended a religious service weekly, and were over 65 years old (Eagan & Sherrill, 2009). Proposition 8 was overturned by a Federal District Court judge in 2010, but an appeal was pending in 2011.

Although 41 states had defined marriage as limited to a man and woman by March 2011, other states were taking different action. In 2000 the Vermont legislature approved civil unions between gay and lesbian couples that would allow them the benefits and responsibilities of marriage without sanctioning marriage. Connecticut followed suit in 2005. The movement for gay marriage received a boost when the Massachusetts Supreme Judicial Court in November 2003 declared that gay and lesbian couples had a right to marriage. By 2004 gay and lesbian couples were marrying in San Francisco, Portland (OR), and a few other cities. However, state legislators intervened, eventually declaring those marriage licenses void. On May 17, 2004, gays and lesbians were married in Massachusetts for the first time. Congress considered an amendment to the U.S. Constitution to ban same-sex marriages, but the Senate failed to adopt it in July 2004. By 2011 six states (Connecticut, Iowa, Massachusetts, New Hampshire, Vermont, and New York) plus Washington, DC, and the Coquille Indian Tribe in Oregon allowed same-sex couples to marry. Other countries, particularly in Europe, have been more open to gay marriages. These marriages are legally recognized in Argentina, the Netherlands, Belgium, Canada, and Spain; France, Germany, Finland, and Iceland have partnership laws that extend legal rights to same-sex couples.

Debates about civil unions and marriage between gays continue in both the religious and secular arenas, but the public is becoming more accepting of gay and lesbian relationships. A Gallup poll in May 2011 found that the majority of Americans now view gay relationships as morally acceptable (Jones, 2011b). However, 45% of the public still oppose gay marriages. Liberals, moderates, Democrats, and independents are more likely to accept gay marriages (Jones, 2010a).

CONTINUING CHALLENGES FOR EQUITY

Even though a growing number of gays and lesbians are open about their sexual identity, many continue to fear reprisal from employers, neighbors, or friends. In many areas of the country and in many classrooms, gays are harassed and abused if they openly acknowledge their sexual

LGBTQ groups and their allies periodically join together to protest discrimination, harassment, and antigay legislation and politics.
© Scott Houston/Alamy

identity. A number of families, religious leaders, and teachers not only reject them, but label them as immoral and deviant. Unlike one's racial identity, which can be easily identified by others, gays and lesbians can hide their identities from a hostile society. As a result, many of them suffer loneliness and alienation by not being able to acknowledge their sexuality.

A number of policy and political advances have been made over the past two decades, but these changes have in large part been limited to a few communities or states. Many employers include sexual orientation in their nondiscrimination policies, and an increasing number offer domestic partnership benefits to unmarried couples. Lesbians and gays are parents to more than 4% of all adopted children (Human Rights Campaign, 2011). At the same time, antigay legislation continues to be enacted in many states. Many of the rights and benefits available to heterosexuals are not available to LGBTQ persons. Gays and lesbians are often denied access to their partners' hospital rooms and decision-making power related to after-death benefits and inheritances that would be freely available to heterosexual spouses. Gays and lesbians in some states cannot adopt children, or they lose custody of their natural-born children when they enter a relationship with someone of the same sex.

As more people come to recognize and accept gay relations and gay rights over the coming years, antigay legislation should gradually be overturned. Current LGBTQ organizations will be supported in moving their agenda forward by other civil rights and social justice organizations as those groups become more inclusive in their membership and issues.

Heterosexism's Toll on Students and Adults

A TARGETED MINORITY

Heterosexuality is the privileged **sexual orientation** or sexual identity in U.S. society and in the world. In the past, laws were written to prohibit any other sexual behavior or identity. When the Supreme Court ruled in *Lawrence v. Texas* that all sodomy laws were unconstitutional, 13 states still had them on their books (Stein, 2010). Many regions of the country do not have legislation or policies to prevent discrimination against LGBTQ persons. LGBTQs are frequently not admitted to "straight" clubs and are vulnerable to attacks on city streets and country roads.

An antigay movement is being promoted by some evangelical Christian leaders through organizations such as the American Family Association and Family Research Council (Schlatter, 2010). Some African American ministers have identified "the so-called 'homosexual agenda'— not poverty, racism, gang violence, inadequate schools, or unemployment—as the No. 1 threat facing black Americans today" (Mock, 2007, p. 19). These religious leaders generally believe that people are not born LGBTQ, but learn it from others. They believe that religion can help "save" their children from this plight. When a religious congregation declares that homosexuality is immoral, its members may have a difficult time going against the authority of leaders to accept LGBTQs as equals.

LGBTQs are now victimized by hate crimes more than any other group in the United States. FBI data show that they are twice as likely to be violently attacked as Jews or African Americans, 4 times more likely than Muslims, and 14 times more likely than Latinos (Potok, 2010). Gay bashing ended in a violent death when transgendered Brandon Teena was raped and murdered in 1993 in Nebraska upon discovery that he was biologically female; two men killed gay college student Matthew Shepard in Wyoming in 1998, leaving him tied to a fence to die; and a student shot Lawrence King in his California junior high school in 2008 because he was gay.

Authority figures also contribute to the policing and enforcing of heterosexuality. A recent study of longitudinal data on adolescent health found that gay and lesbian teenagers are about 40% more likely to be punished by schools, police, and the courts than their heterosexual peers. Lesbian teens are more than two to three times more likely than straight girls to be punished (Himmelstein & Brückner, 2011).

LGBTQ youth may experience invisibility and isolation in their homes, communities, and schools (Savage & Harley, 2009). They do not see positive images of LGBTQ people in their schools. The school and local library may not have books or other information on LGBTQ issues. They learn that they are not "normal" and are often hated by others. When LGBTQ identities are included in the school curriculum, the focus is often on negative contexts that indicate all of the problems with being LGBTQ (Savage & Harley, 2009). They do not learn that different sexual orientations are a normal part of a society (American Psychological Association, 2008), that LGBTQ people have contributed to the history and culture of the nation, and that their predecessors have struggled for decades for equality and the elimination of antigay policies and practices.

LGBTQ students do not always conform to society's heterosexual expectations for behaviors and appearance. They are often very proud of being different and nonconforming.
© QS Select/Queerstock, Inc./Alamy

Feeling positively about one's sexual identity fosters well-being and mental health (American Psychological Association, 2008). However, many LGBTQ young people and adults worry incessantly about "coming out" or being open with friends, family, and colleagues about their sexual orientation. They may worry about being thrown out of their homes, losing friends, being harassed or physically attacked, or facing discriminatory actions such as losing a job or being expelled from a club. Because urban areas are usually more tolerant of sexual diversity than rural areas, gays and lesbians are more likely to be open about their sexual identity in metropolitan areas where social outlets and support services exist. As acceptance of sexual diversity increases in society, the need to hide one's sexual identity should decrease.

THE SCHOOL CLIMATE

Heterosexism can lead to harassment in schools, which is more common than most educators would like to admit. The 2009 National School Climate Survey by the Gay, Lesbian, and Straight Education Network (GLSEN) found that LGBT students face violence, bias, and harassment in schools (Kosciw, Greytak, Diaz, & Bartkiewicz, 2010). Two of five LGBT 13- to 21-year-old students in the survey reported that they have been pushed or shoved at school. Half of that group had been punched, kicked, or injured with a weapon by another student. The majority of the students felt unsafe in school and sometimes just didn't go to school to avoid the harassment. Verbal abuse in which students are called names or are threatened was the most common form of harassment. "That's so gay" may be one of the most common phrases used in the nation's schools; 9 of 10 LGBT students report frequently hearing it or other negative uses of "gay" by classmates. Three of four say they often hear names such as "faggot" or "dyke" (Kosciw et al., 2010). One does not necessarily have to be LGBT to be harassed; students who are perceived to be gay, whether or not they are, are also the targets of these remarks.

A rash of suicides at the beginning of the 2010–11 school year brought public attention to the problem of bullying, especially of LGBTQ students (Rudolph, 2010). Fifteen-year old Billy Lucas hung himself in Greensburg, Indiana, after being constantly picked on because he was perceived as gay. Other students had told him he should kill himself. Seth Walsh, a 13-year-old California student, hung himself after relentless harassment by his peers for his perceived sexual identity. Another 13-year-old, Asher Brown, shot himself after being bullied for two years at Hamilton Middle School on the outskirts of Houston. Justin Aaberg, a 15-year-old student in the Anoka-Hennipin School District, which is northwest of Minneapolis, hung himself after being tormented with antigay bullying. Three other students in this school district who were gay or perceived as gay had also committed suicide during the previous year. An openly gay senior at Shioctom High School in Wisconsin, Cody Barker took his own life. Finally, Raymond Chase, an openly gay sophomore at Johnson and Wales University, hung himself in his dormitory room (LGBTQ Nation, 2010).

Harassment is not always face-to-face. Over half of the students in the GLSEN study reported being harassed or threatened by classmates through electronic means such as text messages, e-mails, and postings on the Internet (Kosciw et al., 2010). One of the most famous cases of cyber-bullying was Tyler Clementi, a freshman at Rutgers University, who jumped off the George Washington Bridge after his roommate posted his sexual encounter with a male on the Internet in 2010.

These seven suicides within a three-week period received a great deal of media attention, leading to declarations from the secretaries of the U.S. Department of Education and the U.S. Department of Health and Human Services that action in support of LGBTQ students would

Debate / Sexual Orientation in the Curriculum

Educators are struggling with how best to incorporate sexual orientation into the curriculum, eliminate bullying based on sexual orientation, and provide support for their LGBTQ students. Although the population is becoming more accepting of gays and lesbians, not all communities are supportive of the recognition of sexual orientation in their schools. In fact, some parents and religious leaders actively fight against any discussion of it at any grade level.

Concern about the inclusion of sexual orientation in the school curriculum has not been limited to the local school district level. State legislators are becoming involved in deciding what should be taught about gays and lesbians in schools and at what age, and they disagree. A few states have passed legislation to ban any discussion of sexual orientation other than heterosexuality in their schools. Legislation is pending in one state to prevent discussion in grades K–8 of the fact that some people are gay. Another state has passed legislation requiring incorporation of the history of homosexuality into social studies.

Do you think sexual orientation should be incorporated into the curriculum of the nation's schools?

FOR	AGAINST
■ LGBTQ students should see themselves in the curriculum to help them develop positive identities.	■ Discussion of sexual orientation in the curriculum will encourage more students to become LGBTQ.
■ Children and youth at all ages should be taught to be accepting of others, including individuals whose sexual identity is not heterosexual.	■ Students at all levels should learn the gender roles that are appropriate for their sex.
■ Young children should learn that families are very diverse, including some with same-sex parents.	■ Introducing positive images of same-sex couples and LGBTQs will lead students to think it is acceptable to be LGBTQ, which is an inappropriate role for schools.
■ Bullying against LGBTQ students could be greatly reduced with curriculum that incorporates LGBTQ content.	■ Students should learn that bullying against any student is inappropriate. This approach can be successful without promoting differences in sexual orientation in the school curriculum.

| QUESTIONS |

1. How would you respond to the question? What rationales support your response?
2. How will you know whether the community in which you are teaching is supportive of the inclusion of sexual orientation issues, history, and experiences in the curriculum?
3. If you are teaching in a very conservative community, what strategies would be appropriate in providing support for LGBTQ students in the school?

be forthcoming. Syndicated columnist and author Dan Savage initiated the project "It Gets Better," in which people were encouraged to send messages of hope to LGBTQ youth. Hoping for 100 videos, the project received over 10,000 within six months, including videos from a number of celebrities in which they encourage youth to be strong and to understand that life will be better in the future.

Where are school officials during these attacks on students? LGBT students reported that only 15% of the teachers or other school professionals regularly intervened when other students made homophobic remarks in front of them. Most LGBT students do not report incidents of harassment or assault to school officials because they think that nothing will be done or it will make the situation worse. In one of three cases reported to officials, students reported that the action taken was effective or very effective, leaving two of three cases being ignored or not effectively handled (Kosciw et al., 2010).

Hostile climates for LGBT students affect their academic performance, college aspirations, and psychological well-being. When school officials and teachers are supportive of LGBT students, the students feel safer in school, miss fewer days of school, and are more likely to attend college (Kosciw et al., 2010). The problem is that the number of staff members who are supportive of gay students in a school is small. Almost all of the LGBT students in the GLSEN study could identify one supportive staff member in their school, and just over half of the students could identify six or more supportive staff. The study also found that LGBT students were safer in schools that had adopted policies against bias, violence, and harassment of LGBT students. Less than one-fifth of students reported that the school had a comprehensive policy that included sexual orientation or gender identity. Victimization of LGBT students was also reduced when the school had student clubs such as Gay-Straight Alliances to provide support for and be allies to LGBT peers. However, less than half of the students reported that such a club existed in their schools (Kosciw et al., 2010).

Professional educators have the responsibility to provide a safe and inclusive environment at school by eliminating homophobia in the school climate. High school is a difficult time for many adolescents, but it is particularly stressful for gays and lesbians as they struggle with the knowledge that they are members of one of the most despised groups in society. They have few, if any, support systems in their schools or communities. They are often alone in making decisions about acknowledging their sexual orientation and facing attacks by others. Educators must not limit the potential of any student because of her or his sexual orientation or gender identity. Teachers and administrators should confront colleagues and students who engage in name calling and harassment. The courts agree. In *Nabozny v. Mary Podlesny, William Davis, Thomas Blauert, et al.* (1996), a Wisconsin court awarded a gay student $1 million in damages for the physical abuse and verbal harassment he endured as school administrators looked the other way. Six gay students won a similar settlement in 2004 after a California school system did not protect them against harassment (Savage & Harley, 2009).

LGBTQ TEACHERS

Teachers have always been expected to be positive role models for students, which requires them to be very careful about their social activities and relationships. Single teachers were often warned about sharing residences with adults of the same sex, or of the opposite sex if they were not married. Such behavior could be declared immoral and could lead to dismissal from a job, especially teaching. In a 1932 education foundations textbook, *The Sociology of Teaching*, the author told teacher candidates that homosexuality was a "deviant, contagious, and dangerous disease" (Renn, 2010). Teachers whose LGBT identity was discovered could be fired in many school districts. During the Civil Rights movements of the 1960s and 1970s, teachers who had been fired began to fight back in the courts, which usually sided with school districts that used immoral behavior as the reason for the firing (Eckes & McCarthy, 2008). The tide began to turn with the California case of *Morrison v. Board of Education* (1969), when the judges found a teacher's sexual orientation a valid reason for dismissal only if it contributed to poor job performance.

Many gay and lesbian educators separate their personal and professional lives for fear of losing their jobs. They worry that they might be accused of molestation or touching students inappropriately, charged with recruiting their students into being homosexual, or caught in a homosexual liaison. In addition, they worry about threats; harassment; vandalism to their cars and homes; and violence by students, parents, colleagues, and other members of the community. Although courts usually protect their jobs, they cannot provide the security and comfort that is needed by teachers who openly acknowledge their homosexuality (Biegel, 2010). Just as in the military, a "don't ask, don't tell" policy operates in many schools.

When lesbian and gay teachers are silent about their sexual identity, they serve neither as role models for gay and lesbian students nor provide the support needed by students whose needs may be ignored by school officials. Heterosexual teachers who are willing to support gay and lesbian students also may face discriminatory retaliation by others.

In the last two decades of the twentieth century, lawyers argued against the dismissal of gay and lesbian teachers by drawing on the constitutional protections of an educator's lifestyle (Eckes & McCarthy, 2008). The Fourteenth Amendment's Due Process and Equal Protection Clauses provided the primary support for these cases when teachers could prove that their dismissal was based solely on their sexual identity. The landmark case *Lawrence v. Texas* (2003), in which the U.S. Supreme Court found that homosexuals have a right to privacy in their sexual lives, and the 1969 California case *Morrison v. Board of Education* provided the precedents that would generally favor teachers. As a result, the courts began to rule in favor of LGBTQ teachers unless a school district could successfully make the argument that the teacher's private sexual behavior had a negative impact on his or her effectiveness as a teacher (Eckes & McCarthy, 2008).

More recent court cases are focusing on working conditions related to a teacher's sexual orientation (Eckes & McCarthy, 2008). For example, a New York teacher sued the school district because the principal did not respond to the teacher's complaints of harassment by students. In *Lovell v. Comsewogue School District* (2002), the court used the Fourteenth Amendment to hold school officials responsible for protecting teachers from harassment by students, parents, and colleagues no matter what the teacher's sexual identity was. In *Schroeder v. Hamilton School District* (2002) in Wisconsin, the court ruled in favor of the school district because it had taken some minimal action to discipline the students. The findings of courts have also differed when teachers have been dismissed because they surgically changed their gender. A California school district was allowed to provide a substantial financial settlement for a teacher to resign. Educators in Illinois and New York were allowed to retain their positions after such surgery (Eckes & McCarthy, 2008). Until federal laws specifically protect LGBTQ educators, court decisions are likely to vary across the country.

Even today, gay and lesbian teachers do not feel welcome in a number of school districts, which is likely to lead to the loss of some very competent teachers. Even in schools in which sexual diversity is accepted, teachers have to determine when, how, and whether to share their sexual identity with school administrators, colleagues, parents, and students. For LGBTQ students, knowing that a teacher has the same sexual identity as theirs could be very helpful.

Some LGBTQ teachers choose and are honored to provide support to LGBTQ students who are struggling with their own identity. The teacher publication *Rethinking Education* includes a number of articles by gay, lesbian, and transgender teachers who have decided to be open to their students about their sexual identity. The book *One Teacher in 10: LGBT Educators Share their Stories* (2005), edited by the former executive director of GLSEN, Kevin Jennings, also includes teacher stories about being open about their sexual identity.

Schools That Value Sexual Diversity

Schools have a very important role in promoting a nation's culture and its values. Educators accomplish this task through the formal curriculum that they teach and through the informal curriculum of value-laden rules that guide the daily activities of a classroom and a school. Both the formal and informal curricula usually reinforce the values of the dominant culture, which is white, middle class, heterosexual, English speaking, able-bodied, and Christian. When it comes to the diversity of sexual identity, heterosexuality has historically been the identity that is most valued and visible in schools.

Think of the ways that heterosexuality is supported in the informal curriculum. The system approves of dating between boys and girls, and it sponsors dances in which boys and girls dance together. A queen and king are often elected for the springtime prom. Girls and boys may be allowed to hold hands in the hallways or at school events. Nuclear families with a mother and father are depicted on bulletin boards and discussed in units on the family in primary grades. What if you are a LGBTQ student? Will the school system allow you to hold hands with a person of the same sex or dance with a person of the same sex at a school-sponsored dance? Would the school system allow the student body to elect two kings or two queens for the prom? How often would you see a photo or illustration of children with same-sex parents? How comfortable would same-sex parents feel when they attended a school event?

As a teacher, you may receive resistance from some parents and school officials once you begin to recognize the sexual diversity of students in a positive and accepting way or you begin to incorporate content about LGBTQs in the curriculum. You should know that your students are likely to be at very different places in the acceptance of sexual diversity. With the existence of these types of obstacles to reflecting sexual diversity in your classroom, why should teachers tackle this project? Longtime educator Elizabeth J. Meyer (2010) identifies the following four reasons for taking on this challenge:

1. **Student safety.** Bullying and harassment are often gendered in nature, directed at students who are gay or perceived to be gay and students who do not conform to the heterosexual behavioral expectations associated with their biological sex, including boys who are effeminate and girls who are tomboys. In a school that values sexual diversity, students would respect and support each other regardless of their sexual identities.
2. **Physical and emotional health.** LGBTQ students often feel ostracized and isolated in schools because teachers and other students do not see them as normal. They may be hiding their sexual identity because they fear possible harassment as a result of their being open about their sexual identity. Consequently, they are more likely than their heterosexual peers to engage in high-risk sexual behaviors or drug and alcohol abuse.
3. **Diversity and equity.** Although most schools now have incorporated diversity into the curriculum, that diversity seldom includes sexual identity. LGBTQ students feel excluded from

textbooks, the curriculum, and class discussions. Their issues are usually not addressed even when they are receiving national news coverage.

4. **Student engagement and academic success.** Students need to be engaged in classroom work to achieve academic success, which will be critical to their future education, jobs, and earnings. Students who have to worry about the hostile environment of a school may disengage by cutting classes and skipping school—acts that have a negative impact on their academic achievement. Dropout rates for LGBT students are also higher than those of their peers.

QUEERING THE CURRICULUM

Although research indicates that the incorporation of LGBTQ issues in the curriculum promotes feelings of inclusivity and safety (Meyer, 2010; Kosciw et al., 2010), only 12% of LGBTQ students report that they are taught anything about their culture or identity (Kosciw et al., 2010). If sexual identity is discussed at all in schools, it is usually in health and sex education class (Meyer, 2010). It is generally a part of class discussions of HIV, in which gays are sometimes blamed for the spread of the disease. Sex education programs may become embroiled in controversy between families and school officials, especially when the curriculum includes discussion of LGBTQ identity. In many districts, parents can request that their children be excused from sex education classes when topics such as sexual orientation and birth control are discussed.

In schools that value sexual diversity, educators incorporate factual information on sexual identity in the curriculum. The focus is not on what causes LGBTQ identity, but on the factors that contribute to heterosexism and homophobia that make it so difficult for people who are LGBTQ to cope with their sexual identity. LGBTQ students should be able to see themselves not only in textbooks, but in the topics that are discussed. Sexual identity should not be a taboo

PAUSE TO REFLECT 5.1

Imagine you are teaching a high school class. You are leading a discussion about current events, and today's topic is AIDS. After several minutes of give-and-take discussion among students in the class, the following dialogue occurs:

Teacher: Who can tell me what AIDS stands for?
Student: Homo
Teacher (ignoring the student's remark): AIDS stands for acquired immunodeficiency syndrome. What is HIV?
Student: Homo

The class continues with the teacher talking and students making homophobic remarks throughout the lesson.

- If you were the teacher of this class, how would you have responded to the students' homophobic remarks?

- How would you have engaged the students in a discussion about AIDS and HIV that would have expanded the discussion beyond AIDS as a gay problem?

Based on a study reported in Meyer, E. J. (2010). *Gender and sexual diversity in schools.* **New York: Springer.**

Same-Sex Parents

Maureen Flynn is a third-grade teacher in a suburban public school. Each year, she looks forward to Parents' Night, when she can meet the parents of her students. As she inspects her room one final time, the door opens and two nicely dressed women appear. "Good evening," they say, almost in unison.

"Good evening. Welcome to the third grade. I'm Maureen Flynn."

"We're Amy Gentry and Kirsten Bowers. We're Allison Gentry-Bowers's mothers."

"Oh," says Ms. Flynn, trying not to show any surprise. "Let me show you some of Allison's artwork and where her desk is."

The rest of the evening is routine. Ms. Flynn introduces herself, welcomes the parents, and asks them to introduce themselves. As the parents exchange names and greetings, there are a few questioning looks as Allison's two mothers introduce themselves. Ms. Flynn explains what the class is currently doing and what the goals and activities are for the remainder of the year. The parents and Ms. Flynn exchange pleasantries and then all go home.

The next morning as class begins, Colleen Burke blurts out, "Miss Flynn, my mommy said that Allison has two mommies. How can that be? How can anyone have two mommies? Everyone is supposed to have a father and a mother." All of the students look to Ms. Flynn for her response.

| QUESTIONS FOR CLASSROOM DISCUSSION |

- How should Maureen Flynn respond to Colleen's question?
- How could Ms. Flynn use this opportunity to discuss diverse family structures?
- How should she plan to interact with Allison's and Colleen's parents in the future?

subject in the classroom. Teachers should be able to help students develop greater awareness and understanding of it when the topic arises.

Finding themselves in the curriculum helps to increase the self-esteem and feelings of affirmation of LGBTQ students (Savage & Harley, 2009). Inquiry-based activities encourage students to explore topics individually and in small groups as they prepare to share their findings with the full class. This approach can allow for multiple perspectives on topics being studied, including the perspectives of LGBTQs (Meyer, 2010). Involving students in developing their own auto-ethnographies will allow them to explore their identities and the privileges they may have as a result of their identity (Meyer, 2010).

Middle School and Secondary Curriculum.   Social studies could explore the privilege of heterosexuality in society and include a study of the history of LGBTs and their struggles for equality. Social studies also provides the opportunity to discuss current events at the local, state, and national levels related to LGBTQ issues, such as same-sex marriage, antigay laws, and adoption by gays and lesbians. In these discussions students can learn to do research on a topic, think critically about the issues, and participate in the political process. These discussions and respectful debates should also attend to the intersection of sexual identity with race, ethnicity, socioeconomic status, gender, and religion (Meyer, 2010).

Language arts and literature courses should include books and short stories by gay and lesbian authors as well as authors of color and with native languages other than English. As the teacher, you should not be afraid to identify the sexual identity of the author and talk about how it may have influenced the author's writing (Savage & Harley, 2009). Fiction and nonfiction with LGBTQ characters can help students understand the meaning of diversity, the damage of discrimination, and the strengths of LGBTQs. The contributions of gays and lesbians to society could be highlighted in these courses as well as in courses in art, music, the sciences, and physical education.

Teachers of mathematics and science also can find opportunities to include LGBTQs in their curriculum. For example, the study of graphs, charts, and statistics could report data related to the experiences of LGBTQ students in schools or society. Word problems could be checked for their **heteronormativity**, which is the assumption that heterosexuality is normal and any other identity is abnormal. Biology could address "information related to reproduction, chromosomal and hormonal influences on embryonic development, as well as how biological sex informs and is related to social norms related to gender" (Meyer, 2010, p. 70).

Early Childhood and Elementary Curriculum.   Queering the curriculum is not limited to middle and secondary schools. Two areas in which related issues could be introduced in early childhood and elementary education are gender role expectations and families (Meyer, 2010). Units on families are common at this level, and gender roles are taught and reinforced through the informal curriculum of preschool and elementary schools. Gender identity becomes important very early in life. Young children learn very quickly the "right" clothes to wear and the appropriate toys and games to play based on their biological sex. Preschool classrooms often have a boys' corner separate from the girls' corner, and the two groups are not generally encouraged to integrate their play. In fact, children may be redirected if they select a toy, book, or game that is more directly identified with the opposite sex. One of the problems with this approach is that it reinforces gender stereotypes. Another is that it limits students' opportunities to read stories, engage in play activities, and pursue friendships with children of the opposite sex whom they may prefer and enjoy (Meyer, 2010).

In lessons on families and family relationships, teachers do not have to limit pictures and discussions to nuclear families with a heterosexual mother and father. They should include families in which the parents are two males, two females, or grandparents; they should include families headed by a single parent. The families should be racially or ethnically diverse and from around the world to emphasize the diversity of families who successfully raise children. The value of diversity can also be captured in the variety of children's books now available that show this diversity of families in a positive light. Some of the children in a class may have

LGBTQ parents, who should be respected and treated as equal members of the school's support system.

CONFLICT ABOUT LGBTQ-INCLUSIVE CURRICULUM

Although the inclusion of LGBTQ information is generally legal in almost every state under First Amendment principles, a few Southern states limit how it is incorporated into sex education classes (Biegel, 2010). Seven states (Alabama, Arizona, Mississippi, Oklahoma, South Carolina, Texas, and Utah) prohibit the positive portrayal of LGBTQs in the school curriculum. Texas and Alabama require that they be presented negatively (Meyer, 2010). Under current law, educators and school districts have the right to incorporate LGBTQ content in the curriculum (Biegel, 2010), although the way they do it may be limited in the states listed above.

Not all parents and communities view the diversity of sexual identity as positive. The argument used most often against it is that the positive portrayal of LGBTQs promotes homosexuality among children. Teachers have been attacked for incorporating information and resources on LGBTQ people and issues in the curriculum. Opponents raise their concerns in local newspapers and at school board meetings, but they seldom win a court case against the inclusion of LGBTQ materials (Biegel, 2010). In *Morrison v. Board of Education of Boyd County, Kentucky*, for example, conservative religious parents sued the school district for requiring students to participate in diversity training and not allowing parents to remove their children from the training sessions. They were concerned that LGBTQ content was positively presented, and that they were not allowed to provide their view of homosexuality. The Kentucky court did not find that the students' constitutional rights had been violated and indicated that parental permission to attend the training was not needed for middle and high school students (Biegel, 2010).

SUPPORTING LGBTQ STUDENTS

Teachers can provide an environment for critically examining the dominant cultural norms that denigrate LGBTQs. They can encourage an understanding of sexual diversity through the presentation of facts, facilitation of discussions, and staging of democratic debates in which everyone's opinion is respected. When homophobic name calling by students occurs, teachers could follow up with a teachable moment to provide facts and correct myths about LGBTQs. If educators ignore homophobic remarks made by students or other adults, children and youth are quick to conclude that something is wrong with gays and that they can be treated disrespectfully.

Teachers should learn to present information on LGBTQs without embarrassment or condemnation. To be respected by LGBTQ and other students, teachers must guarantee respectful treatment of all students. This may be difficult for some teachers. How can educators move to this level of acceptance of and comfort with sexual diversity? First, they should become familiar with the history, culture, and current concerns of LGBTs by reading or attending lectures and films about them. Second, they should create a safe and equitable classroom environment for all students.

In addition to helping all students correct the myths they have learned about gays and lesbians, educators should promote the healthy development of self-identified LGBTQ youth in the school setting. Key to this approach is breaking the silence that surrounds the discussion of homosexuality. The classroom and school should provide a safe and supportive climate for children and adolescents who identify their sexual orientation. They should learn that they are not alone in figuring out their sexual orientation and sexuality.

Supporting LGBTQ students is not always easy for a school district. Some students, usually supported by their parents, take steps to interfere with the rights of LGBTQ students. In 2001 Minnesota high school student Elliot Chambers wore a sweatshirt with "Straight Pride" on the front and a man and woman holding hands on the back. This triggered a heated debate at a meeting of a student Christian group about homosexuality. The principal asked the student to remove the shirt because a number of students had complained, and he was worried that physical fights among students might occur. Based on the student's First Amendment rights to free speech, a judge ruled in favor of the student. He also acknowledged the school's work to create an environment of tolerance and respect for diversity and suggested that schools, parents, and the community "work together so that divergent viewpoints, whether they be political, religious, or social, may be expressed in a civilized and respectful manner" (*Chambers v. Babbitt*, 2001). In a suburban Chicago school, the court ruled in favor of the school district in a case where the text on the student's T-shirt was a negative reference to being gay (*Nuxoll v. Indian Prairie School District*, 2008).

Safe School Policies.   Parents and communities generally think that schools should be safe for students. The overall goal for a school should be to treat all students with equal respect and dignity (Biegel, 2010). Many school districts developed policies related to bullying after the shootings at Columbine High School in 1999. However, those policies were not always comprehensive in that they did not include sexual orientation or gender identity among the groups to be protected. Comprehensive safe school policies provide faculty and staff guidance for intervening when students are using homophobic language. Students in schools with comprehensive policies report hearing fewer homophobic remarks and are more likely to report harassment and abuse to school officials (Kosciw et al., 2010).

Twenty-eight states have developed generic safe school laws to protect students from bullying and harassment. Fifteen states and the District of Columbia have taken an additional step by actually prohibiting discrimination and harassment based on group membership, including sexual and gender identity. Schools in states with the more comprehensive policies are almost twice as likely to have gay-straight alliances than schools in states without a comprehensive policy. They also have a higher number of school personnel who support LGBTQ students (Kosciw et al., 2010).

Following the Title IX model, the Student Non-Discrimination Act was reintroduced on March 10, 2011, in the U.S. Congress by Senator Al Franken (D-MN) and Representative Jared Polis (D-CO). This legislation, if passed, would prevent any federally funded school program or activity from discriminating based on actual or perceived sexual orientation or gender identity.

Even with the safe school policies, schools are not always enforcing them as effectively as they should. Some gay and transgendered students have sued school districts for not protecting them from constant abuse from other students, and courts generally rule in favor of the students. School districts could face litigation if they do not take affirmative steps to prevent harassment and bullying of LGBTQ and other students.

A number of schools have established safe zones or safe spaces for LGBTQ students—usually a specific classroom. The safe space in a school may be marked by a pink triangle or other LGBTQ symbol. In these places students can be themselves and feel free to discuss issues related to their gender identity (Biegel, 2010, p. 126).

Gay-Straight Alliances. Students in the GLSEN study feel safer when they are in a school with a Gay-Straight Alliance (GSA), which is a student-initiated club of LGBTQ and straight students that provides a safe place for students to discuss issues and meet others with similar interests (Meyer, 2010). When a school has a GSA, LGBTQ students report hearing fewer homophobic remarks, and school personnel are more likely to intervene when homophobic remarks are made. Forty-five percent of the students reported that a GSA existed in their school (Kosciw et al., 2010). LGBT students of color were less likely to have a GSA in their schools. Only 33% had an LGBT club or GSA in their school, but over half of the students participated in the GSA when one was available (Diaz & Kosciw, 2009).

The Federal Equal Access Act of 1984 requires that student clubs be established and managed by students. Teachers and other school personnel may serve as advisors to the group. Macgillivray (2007), a former GSA advisor, recommends that the LGBTQ students and their allies not be treated as victims. The goal should be to help students realize their strengths and accomplishments as they develop into young adults.

If you are the GSA advisor, remember that sexual identity may not be the primary group identification for all of the members; it could be religion, race, ethnicity, or exceptionality. Many GSAs are initiated by young white females as allies of LGBTQ students. These students may not be adept at supporting LBGTQ students of color, and may establish a club in which male students and students who do not share their culture do not feel welcome (McCready, 2010). The club should provide students "opportunities to celebrate who they are, no matter what their primary identification" (Macgillivray, 2007, p. 29).

Students who initiate a GSA may need assistance from their advisor in determining the purpose of the group. Initially, many GSA clubs try to make the student body and teachers aware of antigay discrimination and provide training on safety and tolerance. They may seek approval from school administrators to organize events around National Coming Out Day (October 11), the Day of Silence (April 1), and National History Month (October). Over time, club members may want to explore how the curriculum, school policies, and school practices privilege heterosexuals and ignore other sexual identities (Macgillivray, 2007).

In some communities parents or religious groups may raise objections about students establishing a GSA club. They may think that the school is promoting or encouraging homosexuality. They may argue that the GSAs are sex clubs in which all that students care about and talk about is sex or that they are for recruiting students to become LGBTQ. They may worry that it will cause a disruption within the school or that it will undermine their message that homosexuality is wrong. They also argue that the GSAs will force teachers and students to accept homosexuality as normal (Macgillivray, 2007). Some groups have sued school boards to stop students from initiating a GSA club, but they have not been successful in overturning the school board's decision. Based on the federal Equal Access Act, courts have ruled that if the school district allows students to establish other clubs, it must allow the formation of a GSA club (Biegel, 2010).

LGBTQ students and their allies establish Gay-Straight Alliance clubs in schools to support each other.
© Marmaduke St. John/Alamy

Summary

Although a number of researchers have looked for a biological cause of homosexuality, no definitive link has yet been found. Sexual orientation includes both sexual identity as a gay, lesbian, bisexual, or heterosexual and gender identity. LGBTQ youth go through developmental stages similar to other groups as they clarify and become comfortable with their sexual orientation and identity. Membership in the LGBTQ community can be greatly influenced by membership in racial, ethnic, or religious groups that may or may not provide support for LBGTQ members.

In the 1950s homosexuals were under attack, purged from government and military employment and arrested in their homes, parks, and bars for being gay. In the riot at Stonewall Inn in 1969, gays began to publicly resist harassment and began to fight more aggressively for their civil rights in the courts. By the 1980s gays were facing setbacks as conservative Christians fueled culture wars against feminists, lesbians, and gays as gay men began to be diagnosed with AIDS. The culture war in schools led to the removal of books on gays and lesbians from school libraries and bans on teaching about homosexuality unless it was from a negative perspective. Not far into the twenty-first century (2004) the "Don't Ask, Don't Tell" policy continued to prevent LGBTQs from coming out in the military. By the end of 2006, 40 states had legislative mandates or voter amendments against same-sex marriage. By 2011, six states, the District of Columbia, and the Coquille Indian Tribe had extended marriage to same-sex couples and "Don't Ask, Don't Tell" had been repealed by Congress.

Laws in most states do not currently prevent discrimination against LGBTQs, who are the primary victims of hate crimes in the United States. The majority of LGBTQ students feel unsafe in schools; they are harassed and sometimes physically abused by other students. LGBTQ students are more likely to attempt and commit suicide than their peers. Courts are upholding the rights of teachers to be LGBTQ; they cannot legally be fired because of their sexual orientation. School districts are also required to protect LGBTQ teachers from harassment by students, parents, and colleagues.

Incorporating LGBTQ content into the curriculum will help increase the self-esteem and feelings of affirmation of LGBTQ students. Educators have the right to include LGBTQ content in the curriculum, but some states limit the way that content can be taught. Comprehensive safe school policies that specifically include protection based on sexual orientation and gender identity are providing support to LGBTQ students by helping reduce harassment against them. Student-initiated Gay-Straight Alliances (GSAs) for LGBTQ students and their allies provide a safe place for students to discuss issues affecting their lives and teach others about tolerance and safety.

Professional Practice

Questions for Discussion

1. What is meant by sexual diversity? Why is "queer" a popular term used by young people to refer to their sexual identity?

2. How would you characterize the progress made by LGBTQs since the 1950s to promote equality for people of diverse sexual identities?

3. Why does harassment against LGBTQ students continue to exist at such high rates in the nation's schools? What do you think could be done to dramatically reduce the incidents of harassment in schools?

4. How would you incorporate LGBTQ content into the subjects that you plan to teach or with the age groups that you plan to teach?

5. Why would or why wouldn't you volunteer to serve as the advisor to a Gay-Straight Alliance club?

Portfolio Activities

1. Assess the climate in one or more schools that you are observing for incidents of LGBTQ harassment in hallways and classrooms. How often do you hear homophobic remarks? How do teachers or other school personnel respond to students' homophobic remarks? In your paper on this topic, include demographics of the students in the school(s) that you are observing, indicate the nature of the school's or school districts' policy on safety for LGBTQs, present the data that you have collected on homophobic remarks and teachers' responses, and discuss your analysis of the data and your conclusions. (InTASC Standard 3: Learning Environments)

2. Using the Internet and interviews with teachers in the school or schools you are observing, determine what LGBTQ content is being included in the curriculum. Check the state's and district's requirements or limitations related to the incorporation of LGBTQ content. Analyze the cultural and political climate of the community in which the schools are located to determine the support for an inclusive curriculum. In the paper that you prepare on these topics, indicate the support that you would have from the community and school administrators to queer the curriculum that you plan to teach. (InTASC Standard 7: Planning for Instruction)

3. Determine what schools in your area have Gay-Straight Alliances or other LGBTQ clubs, and select one of the schools to visit and collect additional information about their purposes, activities, and perceived differences they have made in the school climate. Identify the faculty adviser for the group and interview him or her. Ask for permission to observe

a club meeting and/or interview selected members. Prepare a summary of your findings and your potential role in supporting LGBTQ students when you begin teaching. (InTASC Standard 1: Learner Development)

Digital Resources for the Classroom

1. *Bullied: A Student, a School, and a Case that Made History* is a documentary by the Southern Poverty Law Center that follows the Wisconsin student who sued his school district for not stopping the harassment and abuse he received as a gay student. Educators can order a free copy at www.tolerance.org/bullied.

2. The U.S. Department of Education website http://www.stopbullying.gov/ provides resources for students and teachers on stopping bullying, including comprehensive guidelines for anti-bullying laws and policies.

3. GLSEN's website, http://www.glsen.org, provides lesson plans, recommendations for creating safe schools, and other resources for teachers and students.

4. The website for the Parents, Families, and Friends of Lesbians and Gays (PFLAG), http://www.pflag.org, includes resources for teachers, including tools for creating safe schools.

5. *Assault on Gay America: The Life and Death of Billy Jack Gaither* explores the roots of homophobia, homosexuality in the Bible, the debate about a "gay gene," and the meaning of gay and straight. The series by the Public Broadcasting Service (PBS) can be accessed at http://www.pbs.org/wgbh/pages/frontline/shows/assault/.

6. The It Gets Better project is described at http://www.itgetsbetter.org/pages/about-it -gets-better-project/. Educators could guide students to this site to view videos from over 10,000 people that may be helpful to them in getting through the difficult period of being a LGBTQ teenager.

7. The curriculum package Welcoming Schools by the Human Rights Campaign provides suggestions to elementary teachers for talking about gender and sexual diversity with students. It is available at www.hrc.org/welcomingschools.

8. Lesson plans, current events, law, history, and social issues related to LGBTQs can be accessed at www.safeschoolscoalition.org/RG-lessonplans.html. Lesson plans are available for elementary, middle-level, and secondary classrooms.

MyEducationLab™

Go to the MyEducationLab (www.myeducationlab.com) for Multicultural Education and familiarize yourself with the topical content, which includes:

- Assignments and Activities, tied to learning outcomes for the course, that can help you more deeply understand course content
- Building Teaching Skills and Dispositions learning units allow you to apply and practice your understanding of how to teach equitably in a multicultural education classroom

- Licensure Test Prep activities are available in the Book Resources to help you prepare for test taking
- A pretest with hints and feedback that tests your knowledge of this chapter's content
- Review, practice, and enrichment activities that will enhance your understanding of the chapter content
- A posttest with hints and feedback that allows you to test your knowledge again after having completed the enrichment activities

A Correlation Guide may be downloaded by instructors to show how MyEducationLab content aligns to this book.

Exceptionality

No otherwise qualified handicapped individual in the United States . . . shall, solely by reason of his [or her] handicap, be excluded from the participation in, be denied benefits of, or be subjected to discrimination under any program or activity receiving federal financial assistance.

Section 504, P.L. 93-112 (Vocational Rehabilitation Act, 1993)

| LEARNING OUTCOMES |

As you read the chapter, you should be able to:

- Explain what an exceptional student is.

- Explain the significance of the 1954 Supreme Court case *Brown v. Board of Education* and how this case impacts children with disabilities.

- Discuss how Public Law 94-142, the Education for All Handicapped Children Act of 1974, changed the face of U.S. education forever. Explain what the provision "free and appropriate education in the least restrictive environment" means.

- Explain how and why some exceptional groups form their own disability cultural groups.

- Cite the primary issues regarding the overrepresentation and underrepresentation of some ethnic/racial groups in special education classes and possible contributing factors.

- Discuss some of the basic needs of exceptional children.

Guadalupe "Lupe" Gutierrez, a third-grade teacher at the Martin Luther King Elementary School, has been asked to see the principal, Erin Wilkerson, after the students leave. Dr. Wilkerson explains that the school is expanding their full inclusion program in which special education children, including those with severe disabilities, are fully integrated into general education classrooms. Congruent with school district policy, King Elementary is enhancing its efforts to integrate special education students into general education settings. Gutierrez's classroom is one of four general education classrooms in which special education students will be placed in the next few weeks. "What this will involve, Lupe, is two students with severe disabilities. One is a child with Down's syndrome who has developmental disabilities, which is characterized by severe delays in the acquisition of cognitive, language, motor, and social skills. He has some severe learning problems. The other child has normal intelligence but is nonambulatory, with limited speech and severe cerebral palsy.

"You will be assigned a full-time aide with a special education background. In addition, Bill Gregg, the inclusion specialist, will assist you with instructional plans and strategies. What is important is that you prepare your students and the parents so that a smooth transition can be made when these students come into your class in January, just two and a half months from now. I'd like you and Bill to map out a plan of action and give it to me in two weeks."

| REFLECTIONS |

1. What should Gutierrez and Gregg's plan of action include?

2. When students with severe disabilities are integrated into general education classrooms, do they detract from the programming of nondisabled students?

3. Are the students with disabilities potentially a disrupting influence in the classroom?

4. Do general education teachers like Lupe Gutierrez have adequate training and background to accommodate students with disabilities in their classrooms?

5. Should they be integrated, regardless of their degree of disability?

Students with Disabilities and Those Who Are Gifted and Talented

A significant segment of the population in the United States is made up of exceptional individuals. The Centers for Disease Control and Prevention (CDC, 2010) reports that, according to the U.S. Census Bureau, there are over 54 million individuals in the United States with some type of disability. Hallahan, Kauffman, and Pullen (2012) report that approximately 10% of students (over 6 million) receive special education services. The National Center for Education Statistics (2008) reports a proportion of approximately 6.7%, or 3.2 million, gifted and talented students, although not all receive special education services. Educators continuously come in contact with exceptional children and adults. They may be students in our classes, our professional colleagues, our friends and neighbors, or people we meet in our everyday experiences.

Exceptional people include individuals with disabilities and gifted individuals. This fact alone makes the subject of exceptionality very complex. Some, particularly persons with disabilities, have been rejected by society. Because of their unique social and personal needs and special interests, many exceptional people become part of a cultural group composed of individuals with similar exceptionalities. For some, this cultural identity is by ascription; they have been labeled and forced into enclaves by virtue of the residential institutions where they live. Others may live in certain communities or neighborhoods by their own choosing. This chapter will examine the exceptional individual's relationship to society. It will address the struggle for equal rights and the ways the treatment of individuals with disabilities often parallels that of oppressed ethnic minorities.

Definitions of exceptional children vary from one writer to another, but Heward's (2009, p. 9) is typical:

> Exceptional children differ from the norm (either below or above) to such an extent that they require an individualized program of special education and related services to fully benefit from education. The term exceptional children includes children who experience difficulties in learning as well as those whose performance is so superior that modifications in curriculum and instruction are necessary to help them fulfill their potential. Thus, exceptional children is an inclusive term that refers to children with learning and/or behavior problems, children with physical disabilities or sensory impairments, and children who are intellectually gifted or have a special talent.

This definition is specific to this category of school-age children, who are usually referred, tested to determine eligibility, and then placed in special education programs. Included in the process is the labeling of the child. At one end of the continuum are the **gifted and talented** children, who have extraordinary abilities in one or more areas. At the other end are children with disabilities (some of whom may also be gifted). Students with disabilities are labeled as having **intellectual disabilities** (ID, previously referred to as mental retardation), learning disabilities, speech impairment, visual impairment, hearing impairment, emotional disturbance (or behavioral disorders), or physical and health impairments.

If you completed a public school education within the past 15 to 20 years, there is a high likelihood that you experienced having a person with a disability in one or more of your classes.

LABELING

The categorizing and labeling process has its share of critics. Opponents characterize the practice as demeaning and stigmatizing to people with disabilities, with the effects often carried through adulthood, where they may be denied opportunities as a result. Some individuals, including many with learning disabilities and intellectual disabilities (ID), were never considered to have disabilities prior to entering school. Individuals with ID often have problems in intellectual functioning and in determining socially appropriate behaviors for their age group. The school setting, however, intensifies their academic and cognitive deficits. Many, when they return to their homes and communities, do not seem to function as individuals with disabilities. Instead, they participate in activities with their neighborhood peers until they return to school the following day, where they may attend special classes (sometimes segregated) and resume their role in the academic and social structure of the school as students with disabilities. The labels carry connotations and perhaps stigmas. Some researchers have found that general education classmates often display negative attitudes toward peers with intellectual disabilities and socially reject or neglect them (Siperstein, Parker, Bardon, & Widaman, 2007).

Some disabilities are more socially acceptable than others. Visual impairment stimulates public empathy and sometimes sympathy. The public has long given generously to causes for the blind, as evidenced by the financially well-endowed Seeing Eye Institute, which is responsible for training the well-known guide dogs. The blind are the only group with a disability who are permitted to claim an additional personal income tax deduction by reason of their disability. Still, the general public perceives blindness to be one of the worst afflictions that could be imposed on a human being. In contrast, ID and to some extent emotional disturbance are often linked to lower socioeconomic status and individuals of color. These are among the least socially acceptable disabilities and are perhaps the most stigmatizing. This is, in part, because of the general public's lack of understanding of these disabilities and the debilitating impact they can have on the family structure.

Learning disability, one of the newest categories of exceptionality, is one of the more socially acceptable disability conditions. Whereas intellectual disabilities are often identified with lower socioeconomic groups, those with learning disabilities may have middle-class backgrounds. Regardless of the level of general acceptance, middle-class parents more readily accept learning disabilities than intellectual disabilities as the cause of their child's learning deficits. This may also be the case with emotional disabilities or behavioral disorders as compared with **attention deficit hyperactive disorders (ADHD)**. The former tends to be more stigmatizing while ADHD may have more social acceptance. What has been observed is a reclassification of some children from having intellectual disabilities to being learning disabled. It has been said that one person's intellectual disability is another's learning disability and still another's emotional disturbance. The line that distinguishes one of these disabilities from another can be so fine that an individual could be identified as a student with emotional disturbance by one school psychologist and as a student with learning disabilities by another.

Although the labeling controversy persists, even its critics often concede its necessity. Federal funding for special education is predicated on the identification of individuals in specific disabling conditions. These funds, with $12.32 billion appropriated for the 2009–10 school year (New America Foundation, n.d.), are so significant that many special education programs would all but collapse without them, leaving school districts in severe financial distress. Consequently, the labeling process continues, sometimes even into adulthood, where university students may have to be identified with a disability to receive necessary accommodations to their learning needs. Vocational rehabilitation counselors often use labels more indicative of their clients' learning problems than of their work skills. If their work peers become aware of these labels, the result could be stigmatizing and lead to social isolation.

HISTORICAL ANTECEDENTS

The plight of persons with disabilities has, in many respects, closely paralleled that of oppressed ethnic groups. The history of the treatment of those with disabilities does not reveal a society eager to meet its responsibilities. Prior to 1800, with a few exceptions, those with intellectual disabilities, for example, were not considered a major social problem in any society. Those with more severe intellectual disabilities were killed, or they died early of natural causes (Drew & Hardman, 2007).

The treatment and care of people with intellectual and physical disabilities have typically been a function of the socioeconomic conditions of the times. In addition to attitudes of fear and disgrace brought on by superstition, early nomadic tribes viewed individuals with disabilities as nonproductive and as a burden draining available resources. As civilization progressed from a less nomadic existence, individuals with disabilities were still often viewed as nonproductive and expendable (Drew & Hardman, 2007).

They were frequently shunted away to institutions designated as hospitals, asylums, or colonies. Many institutions were deliberately built great distances from the population centers, where the residents could be segregated and more easily contained. For decades, American society did not have to deal with its conscience with respect to its citizens with severe disabilities. Society simply sent them far away and forgot about them. Most Americans did not know of the cruel and inhumane treatment that existed in many facilities. Today, due to urban sprawl, many of these institutions are now close to or within population centers.

Individuals with mild disabilities were generally able to be absorbed into society, sometimes seeming to disappear, sometimes contributing meaningfully to an agrarian society, often not even being identified as having a disability. As society became more industrialized and educational reforms required school attendance, the academic problems of students with disabilities became increasingly more visible. Special schools and special classes were designated to meet the needs of these children. Thus, society segregated these individuals, often in the guise of acting in their best interests.

Society's treatment of some groups with disabilities, such as those with intellectual disabilities, has frequently been questionable with respect to their civil rights. Although many Americans find the old miscegenation laws prohibiting intermarriage between different ethnic groups abhorrent, few realize that as recently as the latter part of the twentieth century, nearly half of the states had miscegenation laws that prohibited marriage between individuals with intellectual disabilities.

In some instances, individuals with mild intellectual disabilities were released from state institutions into society under the condition that they submit to eugenic sterilization (Edgerton, 1967). The prospect of marriage prohibitions and eugenic sterilization for persons with intellectual disabilities raises serious social and ethical issues. The nondisabled segment of society, charged with the care and education of individuals with disabilities, apparently views as its right and responsibility to control those matters dealing with sexual behavior, marriage, and procreation. In a similar way, educators determine the means of communication for the deaf individual, either an oral/aural approach or a manual/total communication approach. Such decisions have profound implications because they determine not only how these individuals will communicate but also, to a great extent, with whom they will be able to communicate. Too often, society seeks to dehumanize people with disabilities by ignoring their personal wishes, making critical decisions for them, and treating them as children throughout their lives.

While the remainder of this chapter will focus on the litigation that led to legislation for exceptional children and youth, the focus will be on children with disabilities. The focus on children with disabilities is not meant to diminish the importance of gifted and talented (G/T) students. They are equally important in their own right, but space limitations for this chapter preclude a lengthy treatment of the G/T students. The vast majority of litigation, legislation, funding, and programming involves children with disabilities. In addition, children with disabilities have historically suffered rejection and blatant discrimination by both educators and society, which the gifted and talented have generally not had to endure.

Litigation

Educational rights of individuals with disabilities were not easily gained. In many respects, the struggle for these rights paralleled the struggles of ethnic minorities for the right to education. These rights were not handed to children with disabilities out of the concern or compassion of educators. Many educators were reluctant to extend educational rights to children with disabilities, and when they finally did so, it was because the children's rights had been won in the courts and the education community was ordered to provide for these students.

Some of the court decisions and many of the arguments that advanced the rights of African Americans and other oppressed groups were used by the advocates of children with disabilities. However, in reality, the battles and the rights gained by the disability rights advocates came years after similar rights were won by ethnic minority groups.

Attorneys for the children with disabilities and their parents utilized case law to fight their court battles. **Case law** is the published opinions of judges, which interpret statutes, regulations, and constitutional provisions. The U.S. legal system relies on the value of these decisions and the legal precedents they established. Few cases result in published opinions and those that are published take on great importance.

BROWN V. BOARD OF EDUCATION

As with African American students, the initial struggles for children with disabilities involved the right to, or the access to, a public education. One of the most famous and important court decisions was the Supreme Court decision in *Brown v. Board of Education of Topeka* (1954). Historically, the Supreme Court of the United States had sided with the Louisiana District Court in *Plessy v. Ferguson* in 1896, which upheld the constitutionality of Louisiana's Separate Car Act, providing for separate but equal transportation facilities for African Americans. The *Plessy* verdict became a part of case law and set a precedent, segregating blacks from whites in transportation, public facilities, schools, restaurants, and so on. This decision "legitimized" the establishment and maintenance of racially segregated "Jim Crow" schools, which were supposed to be separate but equal. As history clearly shows, these schools were inherently unequal. This was the setting for the *Brown* case.

In 1950 Topeka student Linda Brown had to ride the bus to school five miles although a school was located just four blocks from her home. Linda met all of the requirements to attend the nearby school, but was prohibited from doing so because she was African American. Linda Brown's parents and 13 other black families filed suit against the Topeka Board of Education because of the district's refusal to admit their children to its all-white schools. Linda Brown's name was the first name listed in the suit, and the case became known as *Brown v. Board of*

Education. The case eventually found its way to the United States Supreme Court and became a major part of U.S. history.

The U.S. Constitution mandates that all citizens have the rights to life, liberty, and property. They cannot be denied these without due process. *Brown* determined that education was a property right. Although there is no constitutional guarantee of a free public education, in *Brown* the U.S. Supreme Court found that if a state undertakes the provision of free education for its citizenry, the property right of an education is established. The property (education) rights of Linda Brown and the other African American children had been taken without due process, a clear violation of the Fourteenth Amendment to the U.S. Constitution. The *Brown* decision overturned *Plessy* with regard to education (some of the other rights were not clearly gained until the Civil Rights Act of 1964) and began the integration of all children of color into American schools.

Brown did not involve children with disabilities, but the precedent it set in guaranteeing equal educational opportunity for ethnic minority children extended to students with disabilities. It would take another 16 years, however, before the concept of equal opportunity would actually be applied to children with disabilities. The Court had essentially ruled that what the Topeka School District had provided Linda Brown and the other African American children was not appropriate. Not only have the courts supported rights of students with disabilities to have a free education, but legislation has also sought to ensure them the right to an appropriate education.

The *Brown* decision found "separate but equal" education to be unequal. Separate education denied African American students an equal education. The Court mandated a fully integrated education, free from the stigma of segregation. Chief Justice Warren stated that segregation "generates a feeling of inferiority as to their (children's) status in the community that may affect their hearts and minds in a way unlikely ever to be undone."

Throughout the history of special education in the United States, children with disabilities have faced a continuous uphill struggle to gain the right to attend public schools. Eventually some programs were instituted, but until the mid-1970s certain children, particularly those with moderate to severe disabilities, were routinely excluded from public education. One of the arguments to deny admission to children with moderate or severe intellectual disabilities was that they could not learn to read, write, or perform arithmetic in the same manner as nondisabled students. Learning these academic skills is education, it was argued. Since they were not educable, they did not belong in schools.

Parents and supporters of these children countered, arguing that learning self-help skills and other important life skills was indeed learning, and this was education. These children, along with children with severe physical disabilities could learn, particularly if support services were provided.

PARC V. THE COMMONWEALTH OF PENNSYLVANIA

In 1971 the Pennsylvania Association for Retarded Children (PARC) brought a class action suit against the Commonwealth of Pennsylvania for the failure to provide a publicly supported education to students with intellectual disabilities. The attorneys for the plaintiffs argued the following:

- Education cannot be defined as only the provision of academic experiences for children.
- All students with intellectual disabilities are capable of benefiting from programs of education and training.
- Having undertaken a free public education for the children of Pennsylvania, the state could not deny children with intellectual disabilities the same opportunities.

- The earlier the students with intellectual disabilities were provided education, the greater the amount of learning that could be expected.

The Federal District Court ruled in favor of the plaintiffs, and all children ages 6 to 21 were to be provided a free public education. The court stipulated that it was most desirable to educate children with intellectual disabilities in programs like those provided to their peers without disabilities (Murdick, Gartin, & Crabtree, 2007; Yell, 2012).

MILLS V. BOARD OF EDUCATION

Following the PARC decision, another class action suit, *Mills v. Board of Education*, was brought before the Federal District Court for the District of Columbia, on behalf of 18,000 out-of-school children with behavior problems, hyperactivity, epilepsy, intellectual disabilities, and physical problems. The court again ruled in favor of the plaintiffs and mandated that the District of Columbia schools provide a publicly supported education to all children with disabilities. In addition, the court ordered the following (Murdick et al., 2007; Yell, 2012):

- The district is to provide due process procedural safeguards.
- Clearly outlined due process procedures must be established for labeling, placement, and exclusion.
- Procedural safeguards include right to appeal, right to access records, and written notice of all stages of the process.

While these two high-profile cases were being played out in their respective communities, other states were finding similar challenges. PARC was a state chapter of the National Association for Retarded Children (NARC, now the Association for Retarded Citizens). NARC and other national organizations, such as the Council for Exceptional Children, actively supported disability advocates throughout the country in preparing court briefs and in offering other means of support. Armed with their victories and case law favorable to their cause, parent groups in other states began taking on their legislatures and school districts and winning. Over 46 cases were filed on behalf of children with disabilities in the first two and a half years following the *PARC* and *Mills* decisions (Yell, 2012). Fresh with many court victories, disability advocates in the early 1970s were busy preparing for their next battleground, the U.S. Congress.

PAUSE TO REFLECT 6.1

It took the legal actions of concerned and frustrated parents and the support of competent and caring professionals to finally bring the end of segregation and injustice to children with disabilities, who had been disenfranchised from a meaningful and appropriate education.

- How does this compare with the plight of African American children in the history of United States education?
- Would children with disabilities still be segregated had legal action not been taken?
- Why does it so often take legal action against American educators to ensure that society does what is right?

Legislation

Following critical court victories (e.g., *PARC* and *Mills*) for children with disabilities in the early 1970s, Congress began passing key civil rights legislation for individuals with disabilities. Not surprisingly, much of the legislation was patterned after the civil rights legislation for ethnic minorities. These new laws would forever change the way individuals with disabilities would be treated in the United States and served as a model for much of the world. Today it is inconceivable that school could be inaccessible to students in wheelchairs, that elevators could have floor buttons not marked with Braille, or a that four-story university building could be built without an elevator. Toilet stalls and aisles in restaurants were often too narrow to provide access for individuals in wheelchairs. These situations were commonplace as recently as the mid-1970s.

SECTION 504

In 1973 Congress enacted **Section 504 of Public Law 93-112** as part of the Vocational Rehabilitation Act. Section 504 was the counterpart to Title VI of the Civil Rights Act of 1964. The language was brief, but its implications are far reaching: "No otherwise qualified handicapped individual in the United States . . . Shall, solely by reason of his (or her) handicap, be excluded from the participation in, be denied the benefits of, or be subjected to discrimination under any program or activity receiving federal financial assistance."

Section 504 prohibits exclusion from programs solely on the basis of an individual's disability. A football coach, marching band director, or a university admissions officer cannot deny a student participation solely on the basis of a disability. However, if a learning disability prevents a student from learning marching band formations even with accommodations, if the student's test scores are clearly below the university admissions standards and indicative of likely failure, and if ID inhibits a student's ability to learn football rules and plays, then exclusion can be justified. If denial of participation is unjustified, the school or agency risks the loss of all federal funds, even in programs in the institution that are not involved in the discriminatory practice (Murdick et al., 2007; Yell, 2012).

PUBLIC LAW 94-142

In 1975, **Public Law 94-142, the Education for All Handicapped Children Act**, was signed into law. This comprehensive legislation provided individuals age 3 to 21 with the following:

- A free and appropriate education for all children with disabilities
- Procedural safeguards to protect the rights of students and their parents
- Education in the least restrictive environment
- Individualized Educational Programs
- Parental involvement in educational decisions related to children with disabilities
- Fair, accurate, and nonbiased evaluations

These provisions forever changed the face of American education. Every child with a disability is now entitled to a free public education, which is to be appropriate to his or her needs. The education is to be provided in the least restrictive environment, which means that the student is to be educated in a setting as close to a general or regular education class as is feasible. Parents are now to have an integral role in their child's education, and are to be involved in the

Parents have, by law, a significant voice in their special education child's education.
© Lisa F. Young/Fotolia

development of the education program and to share in other decisions relating to their child. When appropriate, the student is also to be involved. There are procedural safeguards the schools must follow to ensure that the rights of the students and parents are observed. Each student must have an **Individualized Education Program (IEP)**, which is designed to meet the student's unique needs. The identification and evaluation process is to be nondiscriminatory and unbiased, with multifactored methods used to determine eligibility and placement (Murdick et al., 2007; Yell, 2012).

Prior to the passage of P.L. 94-142, nearly half of the nation's 4 million children with disabilities were not receiving a publicly supported education. Furthermore, more than 3 million students with disabilities admitted to schools were not receiving an education appropriate to their needs (Yell, 2012). Many of the students who were in special education were often isolated in the least desirable locations within the schools. In the first two special education teaching assignments (both prior to P.L. 94-142) experienced by one of the authors of this text, this was very much the case. In the first, all three special education classes were located in the basement of the junior high school, isolated from the other students. In the second school, there were two lunch periods to accommodate the large student body. The special education students were required to eat in the school cafeteria between the two lunch periods, and were expected to exit the facility before any other students entered. When a new school building was completed next to the old, outdated facility, the special education class remained in the old facility while the rest of the school moved.

AMERICANS WITH DISABILITIES ACT

President George H. W. Bush signed Public Law 101-336, the **Americans with Disabilities Act (ADA)**, into law on January 26, 1990. ADA was the most significant civil rights legislation in the United States since the Civil Rights Act of 1964. ADA was designed to end discrimination against individuals with disabilities in private-sector employment, public services, public accommodations, transportation, and telecommunications.

Among the many components of this legislation, the following are a sampling of the efforts to break down barriers for individuals with disabilities (Murdick et al., 2007; Yell, 2012):

- Employers cannot discriminate against individuals with disabilities in hiring or promotion if they are otherwise qualified for the job.
- Employers must provide reasonable accommodations for an individual with a disability, such as attaching an amplifier to the individual's telephone.

- New buses, bus and train stations, and rail systems must be accessible to persons with disabilities.
- Physical barriers in restaurants, hotels, retail stores, and stadiums must be removed; if this is not readily achievable, alternative means of offering services must be implemented.
- Companies offering telephone services to the general public must offer telephone relay services to those using telecommunication devices for the deaf.

INDIVIDUALS WITH DISABILITIES EDUCATION ACT (IDEA)

Congress passed Public Law 101-476, the **Individuals with Disabilities Education Act (IDEA)**, in 1990 as amendments to Public Law 94-142. Key components of this amendment included the addition of students with autism or traumatic brain injury as a separate class entitled to services. A **transition plan** was an added requirement to be included in every student's IEP by age 16. The transition plan includes a needs assessment and individual planning to transition the student with a disability successfully into adulthood. In addition to substituting the term "disability" for "handicap," a far-reaching change in the new legislation included changed language to emphasize the person first and the disability second. The title of the legislation included "Individuals with Disabilities," and not "disabled individuals." Nearly all of the newer literature uses the language "children with intellectual disabilities, students with learning disabilities, individuals with cerebral palsy, and people with hearing impairments." Individuals with disabilities are people or individuals first. Their disability is secondary and at times inconsequential to their ability to perform the tasks they undertake (Murdick et al., 2007; Yell, 2012).

IDEA AMENDMENTS

The 1997 IDEA Amendments (P.L. 105-17) reauthorized and made improvements to the earlier law. It consolidated the law from eight to four parts and made significant additions, including the following (Murdick et al., 2007; Yell, 2012):

- Strengthened the role of parents, ensured access to the general education curriculum, and emphasized student progress by changing the IEP process
- Encouraged parents and educators to resolve their differences through nonadversarial mediation
- Gave school officials greater latitude in disciplining students by altering some procedural safeguards
- Set funding formulas

In 2004 Congress passed another amendment to IDEA (P.L. 108-446), referred to as IDEA 2004 or the **Individuals with Disabilities Education Improvement Act.** IDEA 2004 added new language about "academic and functional goals." IEPs must now include "a statement of measurable annual goals, including academic and functional goals. . . ." The amendment also required the use of instructional strategies and practices grounded in research and most likely to produce positive student outcomes (Cook, Tankersley, & Landrum, 2009). Another requirement of IDEA 2004 aligned IDEA with the No Child Left Behind requirement of "highly qualified teachers." Under IDEA requirements, emergency or provisional certificates do not qualify an individual (Weishaar, 2007; Yell, 2012). All students deserve highly qualified teachers. However, there has been and still is a shortage of fully certified or credentialed special education teachers in most states, and a mandate for highly qualified teachers will not make them suddenly appear for school districts to employ.

Despite the shortages, school districts can no longer employ individuals with only emergency licensure. School districts must find ways to compensate for the lack of trained personnel by qualifying those previously hired under emergency licensure using creative new categories, such as internships, or in creative instructional staffing for students with disabilities.

Some school districts have created co-teaching arrangements utilizing qualified special education teachers with qualified general education teachers. In some other instances qualified special education teachers provide consultation to general education teachers. These arrangements may provide benefits of inclusion for students with disabilities.

The mandate requires the district to notify parents if their child's teacher does not meet the appropriate standards. Individuals hired without full licensure must show progress toward completion. This provision, while not immediately solving the problem of shortages, is holding school districts accountable and may, in the future, provide better-qualified teachers for children with special needs. IDEA 2004 has brought some additional changes, and these can be accessed on the web.

The 2004 reauthorization of the Individuals with Disabilities Education Act includes a new initiative in the pre-referral and identification of children with learning disabilities. This process is referred to as **response to intervention (RTI)** and is based on a multi-tiered approach to meeting the needs of children. Usually associated with learning disabilities, RTI has as its primary aim to provide intervention to students who are not achieving at comparable rates with their peers. The core concepts involve research-based intervention, measuring student response, and data-based instructional decisions (Kavale & Spaulding, 2008). RTI includes various levels of support in the general education setting prior to a referral to special education services. Only if students are not responding to research-based quality instruction in general education will they be referred to special education (Hallahan et al., 2012). While policy makers and practitioners have expressed considerable interest in RTI, research results are not yet available to validate the effectiveness of the process (Smith & Tyler, 2010).

IDEA FUNDING

When Congress passed Public Law 94-142 in 1975, it mandated services for children with disabilities. This required states and school districts to provide extensive and often expensive services to these children. Congress set a goal to fund the mandate at 40% of the cost to educate children with disabilities. Often the classes for these children are smaller and many require additional staffing with aides, which increases the cost to the schools. Parents empowered by this mandate have rightfully insisted that their children receive the services to which they are entitled. From 1995 to 2009, Congress's appropriations for IDEA increased from $3,253,000,000 to $12,579,677,000 (Committee on Education Funding, 2010). While this is a very significant increase, special education programs have expanded, and as recently as 2009 Congress's IDEA funding has barely reached the 16.8% level, less than half of what had been promised (Committee on Education Funding, 2010). This leaves school administrators in a difficult quandary, trying to provide the mandated appropriate services to all children using the underfunded resources of IDEA. This situation is further complicated by the economic downtown in the United States since 2007, which has resulted in severe budget cuts for education.

The federal mandates requiring a free and appropriate education for all children with disabilities have been viewed by some as both a blessing and a curse. For millions of children who would have been disenfranchised from a meaningful education, IDEA has guaranteed their rightful access to education. However, the failure of Congress to fully fund its 40% promise of fiscal support while it holds school districts to full compliance may be viewed as a curse by some school districts that are desperately trying to balance their diminishing budgets.

Many parents of children with disabilities are fully aware of the legal rights of their children. They may fight to secure the best possible education for their children regardless of the district's financial ability to provide expensive services (e.g., residential schools, long-distance transportation). In these situations the cost of providing service may greatly exceed funding from state and federal sources and may be far greater than the average budgeted costs for the typical student. These situations may add to a district's financial distress and may require the use of funds from general education to provide special education services.

In other situations, school districts have been said to abuse their federal and state funding and to use these funds for their general education purposes. With more than $12 billion flowing into states and local school districts, there is the chance for inappropriate use of funds unless adequate accountability measures are put into place (Cox, 2011; Biddle, 2009).

POST–P.L. 94-142 LITIGATION

Even with over 30 years of legislation, amendments, and refinements, there are many aspects of special education law that remain unclear to the children, their parents and advocates, and school district personnel. The laws are extremely precise in some areas and deliberately vague in others. In addition, there are many other variables that exacerbate the problem of interpreting and implementing the various laws and regulations.

Congress itself is part of the problem. It has mandated extensive provisions for children with disabilities. Many of these are time and staff intensive, and expensive to implement. Congress, moreover, has failed to meet its fiscal obligations to make IDEA fully viable. Yet school districts are required to implement expensive mandates without the promised fiscal support. Thus, when many states and school districts are experiencing budget shortfalls, special education can be a challenge for educators to find the necessary resources. Staffing is another serious problem facing most states. Even when school districts are committed to full compliance with the laws, the acute national shortage of qualified special education and related services personnel may preclude their ability to do so. Parents who are aware of the law's requirement of an appropriate education are often angry and may feel that the schools have betrayed the best interests of their children, and they have often successfully addressed their frustrations by taking legal action against the schools. In some cases the schools are at fault for deliberately ignoring the IDEA requirements, but their situation is often exacerbated by lack of funding or the lack of qualified teachers.

Because IDEA does not provide a substantive definition of a "free and appropriate education," the issue has often been left to the courts. Parents, as might be expected, typically view an appropriate education as the best possible education for their child. In 1982 *Hendrick Hudson School District v. Rowley* became the first case related to "an appropriate education" for a student with a disability to reach the U.S. Supreme Court. Amy Rowley was a student with a hearing impairment who was placed in a regular education kindergarten class. Several of the school personnel learned sign language to enable them to communicate with Amy. A teletype machine was placed in the school office to facilitate communication with Amy's parents, who were also deaf. Amy was provided with a hearing aid by the school, and a sign language interpreter was assigned to her class. Amy completed kindergarten successfully and was found to be well adjusted and making better-than-average progress.

Following the kindergarten year, as was required by P.L. 94-142, an IEP was developed for the upcoming school year. The plan specified that Amy was to continue her education in a regular classroom. She was to continue the use of the hearing aid, and she would receive speech and language therapy three hours a week. In addition, she was to receive instruction an hour daily from a tutor who specialized in children with hearing impairments.

The parents disagreed with the IEP; they believed that Amy should have a qualified sign language interpreter for all academic classes. The school district, however, concluded that a full-time interpreter was unnecessary and denied the request. As was their right under P.L. 94-142, the parents requested and were granted a due process hearing. The parents prevailed, and the case found its way through the lower courts until it finally reached the U.S. Supreme Court.

The Court, noting the absence in the law of any substantive standard for "appropriate," ruled that Congress's objective was to make a public education available to students with disabilities. The intent was to guarantee access on appropriate terms, but not to guarantee a particular level of education. The Court ruled that schools were not obligated to provide the best possible education, but a "basic floor of opportunity." It found that a free and appropriate public education (FAPE) standard could be determined only from a multifactorial evaluation on a case-by-case basis. This case essentially ensured the continuation of litigation to resolve "appropriate education" disputes (Murdick et al., 2007; Yell, 2012).

This case was significant in that it was the first case related to P.L. 94-142 to reach the Supreme Court. It set a standard for "appropriate education" to require more than simple access to education but less than the best possible educational program. The Court also focused attention on the rights of parents and guardians, giving them full participation at every stage of the process (Conroy, Yell, Katsiyannis, & Collins, 2010). It became part of case law, setting a precedent for similar cases that would follow (Murdick et al., 2007; Yell, 2012). Consequently, when a school can demonstrate that a student is making satisfactory progress (this too is open for debate), the district's position tends to prevail.

The courts have had to rule on other provisions of the law. For example, the courts have also ruled in favor of the child when parents have sought non-physician support services necessary to sustain the student's ability to function in school (e.g., *Irving Independent School District v. Tatro*). Through the years a developing body of case law provides both parents and advocates and school personnel with a better understanding of how the law should be implemented.

Public Law 94-142 provided students with disabilities their legal educational rights. However, school districts too often have been found out of compliance, either deliberately or due to the negligence of personnel. Over the past 30 years there have been numerous court decisions (e.g., Chandra Smith Consent Decree, Los Angeles Unified School District and Felix Consent Decree, Hawaii Department of Education) resulting in massive judgments that cost districts far more in legal fees and staff time than they would have expended if they had initially complied with the law.

More than ever, children and adults with disabilities are an integral part of the nation's educational system and are finding their rightful place in society. Although the progress in recent years is indeed encouraging, society's attitudes toward individuals with disabilities have not always kept pace with the advancement of legal rights. As long as people are motivated more by fear of litigation than by moral and ethical impulses, we cannot consider our efforts in this arena a complete success.

LAWS AND FUNDING FOR GIFTED AND TALENTED STUDENTS

Currently there may be as many as 3 million academically gifted students in the United States. In addition, there are students who are considered talented and who could benefit from special educational programming. While the importance of gifted and talented education cannot be overstated, it unfortunately is often overlooked. Gifted and talented individuals are a country's potential leaders, innovators, and researchers who may someday enhance the quality of our lives. While there is permissive legislation for the gifted and talented (laws that allow gifted and talented programming to take place), there are no federal or state mandates for the education of this group. Funding for gifted and talented children is extremely limited and does not begin to approach that provided by IDEA for children with disabilities.

The Javits Gifted and Talented Students Education Act, passed by Congress in 1988, is the only federal program dedicated specifically to gifted and talented students. It does not fund local gifted education programs. The act is designed to support scientifically based research, and to provide demonstration projects and innovative strategies to enhance the ability of schools to meet the educational needs of these students. Unfortunately, the funding for this act is very limited, and in recent years has declined from $9,600,000 in 2006 to $7,460,000 in 2009. As of 2011 there are proposals to eliminate funding entirely.

Most educators understand the importance of special education for the gifted and talented. Legislators, however, are faced with diminishing fiscal resources partially related to the mandated funding for children with disabilities. Some may believe that children with disabilities must have special programming to survive, whereas gifted and talented students are more able to fend for themselves. While there is some truth to this belief, failure to provide for this group's educational needs amounts to the waste of a valuable resource. These are the individuals who have the potential to find a cure for cancer or Alzheimer's disease, to solve the nation's fiscal crises, or to develop alternative energy sources never before imagined. While external funding may not be available to support programs for these students, schools need to commit themselves to develop their own programming for these students within their fiscal confines.

Exceptional Individuals and Society

Even in modern times, the understanding and treatment of any type of deviance have been limited. Society has begun to accept its basic responsibilities for people with disabilities by providing for their education and care, but social equality has yet to become a reality.

Society's view of people with disabilities can perhaps be illustrated by the way the media portrays this population. While the media in recent years has shown increasing sensitivity toward individuals with disabilities, there is much room for improvement. In general, when the media wishes to focus on persons with disabilities, they are portrayed as (a) children, often with severe intellectual disabilities and obvious physical stigmata, or (b) persons with crippling conditions who are either in wheelchairs or on crutches. Thus, society has a mindset regarding who people with disabilities are. They are often viewed as children or childlike, and they have severe disabilities—intellectually, physically, or both.

Because society often views those with disabilities as childlike, they are denied the right to feel like nondisabled individuals.

Many religious groups now provide interpreters for individuals with deafness and other services for individuals with disabilities.
© Patrick White/Merrill

Teachers and other professional workers can often be observed talking about individuals with disabilities in their presence, as if the individuals are unable to feel embarrassment. Their desire to love and be loved is often ignored, and they are often viewed as asexual, without the same sexual desires as the nondisabled.

Contemporary American society places great emphasis on physical beauty and attractiveness. Individuals who deviate significantly from physical norms are subject to possible rejection, even if their physical deviations do not interfere with their day-to-day functioning.

In their classic book, Gliedman and Roth (1980) suggest that nondisabled individuals perceive those with disabilities as individuals who seldom hold good jobs, seldom become heroes in our culture, and are seldom visible members of the community. They further suggest that society systematically discriminates against many capable individuals with disabilities. They indicate that the attitudes of society, which views disability as incompatible with adult roles, parallel racism. They state that society perceives a "handicapped person as mentally or spiritually inferior because he is physically different or that 'people like that' have no business being out on the streets with 'us regular folks'" (p. 23).

Although society must remain vigilant, circumstances for individuals with disabilities have improved substantially in the past decade. Smith and Tyler (2010) suggest that years of activism, improved attitudes, and increased community presence have all contributed to a distinct change in how we respond to individuals with disabilities.

Gliedman and Roth (1980) suggest that, with respect to discrimination, individuals with disabilities are in some ways better off than African Americans in that they face no overt discrimination, no organized brutality, no lynch mob "justice," and no rallies by supremacist groups. In some ways, however, people with disabilities are worse off. African Americans and other groups have developed ethnic pride. It is probable that no one has ever heard a "cerebral palsy is beautiful" cry, however. Society opposes racism with the view that African Americans are not self-evidently inferior, but at the same time it takes for granted the self-evidently inferior status of those who have disabilities.

As we stereotype individuals with disabilities, we deny them their rightful place in society. The disability dominates society's perception of the person's social value and creates an illusion of deviance. Individuals with disabilities are viewed as vocationally limited and socially inept.

Persons with disabilities may be tolerated and even accepted as long as they maintain the roles ascribed to them. They are often denied basic rights and dignity as human beings. They are placed under the perpetual tutelage of those perceived as more knowledgeable and more capable than they. They are expected to subordinate their own interests and desires to the goals of a program decreed by the professionals who provide services to them.

The general public may be required by law to provide educational and other services for individuals with disabilities. The public is prohibited by law from practicing certain aspects of discrimination against citizens with disabilities. No one, however, can require the person on the street to like those with disabilities and to accept them as social equals. Many will not accept a person with a disability. Just as racism leads to discrimination or prejudice against other races because of the belief in one's own racial superiority, ableism leads to stereotyping of, and discrimination against, individuals with disabilities because of the attitude of superiority held by some nondisabled individuals.

Society tends to place behavioral expectations on both men and women. Males have specific masculine roles they are expected to fulfill. Boys are usually expected to be athletic. Physical impairments, however, may preclude athletic involvement. Unable to fulfill this role, the young paraplegic male may develop a sense of devalued self-worth or a feeling that he is less than a man. Feminine roles are also assigned, and women with physical disabilities who are unable to assume these roles may suffer from feelings of inadequacy. With the increased participation of women in athletics, and the success of the American women in recent Olympic competition, some females may also suffer the frustration of being unable to participate in athletic or other physical programs.

EXCEPTIONAL CULTURAL GROUPS

Because of insensitivity, apathy, or prejudice, many of those responsible for implementing and upholding the laws that protect individuals with disabilities fail to do so. The failure to provide adequate educational and vocational opportunities for individuals with disabilities may preclude the possibility of social and economic equality. These social and economic limitations are often translated into rejection by nondisabled peers and ultimately into social isolation.

Not unlike many ethnic minority groups who are rejected by mainstream society, individuals with disabilities often find comfort and security with each other, and in some instances they form their own enclaves and social organizational structures. Throughout the country one can find cohesive groups of individuals, such as those who have visual or hearing impairments and those who have intellectual disabilities. In some instances, they congregate in similar jobs, in the same neighborhoods, and at various social settings and activities.

Near Frankfort Avenue in Louisville, Kentucky, three major institutions provide services for individuals who have visual impairments. The American Printing House for the Blind, the Kentucky School for the Blind, and Kentucky Industries for the Blind are all in close proximity. The American Printing House for the Blind, the leading publisher of materials for individuals with visual impairments, employs a number of individuals who are blind. The Kentucky School for the Blind is a residential school for students with visual impairments, and it also employs a small number of individuals with visual impairments, including teachers. Kentucky Industries for the Blind operates as a sheltered workshop for individuals who are blind. With the relatively large number of persons who are blind employed by these three institutions, it is understandable that many individuals with visual impairments live in the surrounding residential area.

Settling in this area allows them to live close enough to their work to minimize the potential transportation problems related to their visual limitations. It also provides a sense of emotional security for the many who, in earlier years, attended the Kentucky School for the Blind and lived on its campus and thus became part of the neighborhood. The neighborhood community can also provide social and emotional security and feelings of acceptance. A few years ago, a mailing was sent from the Kentucky School for the Blind to each of its alumni; 90% of the addresses on the mailings had the same zip code as the school.

Individuals with visual impairments or hearing impairments are among the most likely to form their own cultural groups. Both have overriding factors that contribute to the need for individuals to seek out one another and to form cultural groups. Some of the blind have limited mobility. Living in cultural enclaves allows them easier access to one another. They share forms of communication—oral language, Braille, and talking books. Social and cultural interests created partly as a result of their physical limitations can often be shared. The hearing impaired may have communication limitations within the hearing world. Their unique means of communication provides them with an emotional as well as a functional bond. Religious programs and churches for individuals with hearing impairments have been formed to provide services to assist in total communication and social activities.

Individuals with physical disabilities may or may not become a part of a cultural group related to the disability. Some function vocationally and socially as part of the mainstream society. Given adequate cognitive functioning and adequate communication patterns, normal social interaction is possible. Socialization, however, may depend on the degree of impairment and the individual's emotional adjustment to the disability. Some individuals with physical disabilities may function in the mainstream world and also maintain social contacts with others with similar disabilities. Social clubs for individuals with physical disabilities have been formed to provide experiences commensurate with members' functional abilities, as well as a social climate that provides acceptance and security. Athletic leagues for competition in sports, such as wheelchair basketball and tennis, have been formed. Many racing events (e.g., the Boston Marathon) now include competition for wheelchair entries.

Many of the individuals with mild intellectual disabilities live independently or in community-based and community-supported group homes. The group homes provide a family-like atmosphere, and house parents supervise them. Most of the individuals with moderate intellectual disabilities who do not live in institutions tend to live at home. Many individuals with severe and profound intellectual disabilities, and some with moderate intellectual disabilities, are institutionalized and thus forced into their own cultural group or enclave, isolated from the rest of society.

The gifted and talented usually do not experience the same type of discrimination and social rejection that many individuals with disabilities experience. Yet, like individuals with disabilities, they may suffer isolation from mainstream society and seek others with comparable abilities to gain a feeling of acceptance as well as intellectual or emotional stimulation. The existence of Mensa, an organization whose membership prerequisite is a high score on an intelligence test, attests to the apparent need of some gifted individuals to be with others of their own kind.

Rejection of the gifted and talented may differ from that of individuals with disabilities because the roots may stem from a lack of understanding or jealousy, rather than from the stigma that may relate to certain disabilities.

Disproportionate Placement in Special Education

For over four decades, the overrepresentation of culturally and linguistically diverse students in special education classes has been a controversial issue for education. In the 1960s and 1970s, leaders in the field of special education such as Dunn (1968) and Mercer (1973) began to highlight the issue of disproportionate placement of minority students.

Disproportionality is defined as "the representation of a group in a category that exceeds our expectations for that group, or differs substantially from the representation of others in that category" (Skiba et al., 2008, p. 264).

Overrepresentation of ethnic minority students in special education is clearly a major issue in education. While overrepresentation in special education does not necessarily equate with inappropriate placement, it is indicative of problems either within the educational system or in society in general. It is possible that there are actually more children of color in need of special education than their numbers or percentages in the general school population might suggest. If

The overrepresentation of students of color in special education classes is a major problem in education.
© Anne Vega/Merrill

a child legitimately qualifies for special education services and is in need of such, it would be a disservice to him or her not to provide special education services because the percentages do not match. We are discussing the lives and education of children, and wrong decisions can have a lasting impact on their future. However, there are inappropriate placements, resulting in overrepresentation.

At least three major problems with overrepresentation have been identified by researchers: the negative effects of labeling, placement in isolated and restrictive settings, and the ineffectiveness of services in some special education settings (Waitoller, Artiles, & Chaney, 2010). Artiles and Bal (2008) further suggest that minority students, who confront significant inequities in such areas as school quality and funding, are further disadvantaged by placement in programs that may not produce positive long-term outcomes.

In 1968 the Office of Civil Rights (OCR) began its biannual survey of student placement in special education classes. The data also provided racial backgrounds of the students using the broad categories of white, black, Asian/Pacific American, American Indian, and Latino. While the actual percentages have varied from survey to survey, one finding has remained consistent. African American students, particularly males, have been greatly overrepresented in classes for students with intellectual disabilities and serious emotional disturbances. In some states Latino students are overrepresented in classes for students with mild intellectual disabilities. Another consistent finding is that African American, American Indian, and Latino students are greatly underrepresented in classes for the gifted and talented.

REPORTING BY COMPOSITION AND INDIVIDUAL RISK

There are two valid means of reporting data related to the placement of students of color in special education classes: **composition index** and **risk index** (Skiba et al., 2008). The composition index compares the percentage of a group in a program with the percentage that group represents in the population. It gives us the answers to two questions: What is the percentage of African American students in classes for students with intellectual disabilities, and what is the percentage of African Americans in the school-age population? If a particular group's percentage in a program is substantially higher than its percentage of the school-age population, this would indicate overrepresentation (Smith & Tyler, 2010). While African American students represent only 17% of the school-age population, they account for 33% of students identified as intellectually disabled (Skiba et al., 2008). The Office of Civil Rights reports special education enrollments by composition.

The risk index measures the percentage of a group in a program compared to the percentages of other groups (Skiba et al., 2008). It provides the answer to the question: What percentage of African American students are in classes for students with intellectual disabilities as compared to white students? In the entire United States, it was found that 2.64% of all African

American students were placed in classes for students with intellectual disabilities, as compared to 1.18% of white students (Skiba et al., 2008).

With 2.64% of African American students having been placed in these classes, the figures may appear to be small. However, it is problematic when we realize that the percentage of African Americans who are in classes of students with intellectual disabilities is nearly five times greater than that of Asian/Pacific American students and twice that of white students. Also important is the fact that one-third of African American students are *not* intellectually disabled, as one might mistakenly assume from the OCR composition data. Rather, a little less than one-third of those in classes for students with intellectual disabilities are African American. This is a very important concept to understand.

CONTRIBUTING VARIABLES

While the majority of students in special education have most likely been carefully diagnosed and placed, educators and child advocates have raised concerns that it is also highly likely that many children are inappropriately placed in special education. The variables that contribute to the disproportionate special education placement are multifaceted. Some of the problems that contribute to the placement of these students are rooted in the social structure of the country. Other problems may be related to medical and genetic causes, particularly for moderate and severe forms of disability, and may be beyond the ability of educators to remediate.

Poverty. Dunn's (1968) findings that large percentages of students in classes for individuals with intellectual disabilities were from backgrounds of poverty remain applicable to this day. Artiles and Bal (2008) assert that poverty and racial minority status are correlated and that significant developmental deficits requiring special education services may be the result of poverty. Twenty-five percent of African Americans and 22% of Hispanics are classified as poor, compared to 11% of the white population (Smith & Tyler, 2010). Poverty contributes to a significant number of problems. Pregnant women in poverty are provided less than optimal care during the prenatal period, as well as the period during and after birth. Physicians who provide medical care through government clinics are often burdened with excessive case loads and are unable to provide the quality of care that women are afforded from private physicians and managed-care medical facilities. Appropriate nutrition and dietary supplements may be less available both to expectant mothers and to their children. Poverty may necessitate working late into term, even where it is advisable to stop working and rest.

Children born preterm (those under normal gestation and less than 5 lb., 8 oz. [2500 g]) may be at risk of developing cognitive and sensory disabilities (Drew & Hardman, 2007). Though more closely aligned with socioeconomic factors, preterm births have been associated with ethnicity. Younger women having children are more likely to have preterm babies, crack babies, and fetal alcohol syndrome children (Drew & Hardman, 2007), and teen births are disproportionately high among the poor.

Lead Poisoning. Nationally, about 250,000 children between the ages of 1 and 5 have elevated lead levels in their blood, according to the Centers for Disease Control and Prevention (CDC, 2010). Lead poisoning can contribute to behavior problems, coma, seizures, and even death (Davis, 2007; CDC, 2010).

The primary sources of lead exposure to children in the United States are (1) house dust contaminated by lead paint and (2) soil contamination. Both the residue of lead paint and decades of industrial and vehicular emissions have contaminated the soil. Lead paint was in wide use in the 1940s, declined in use in the 1950s and 1960s, and was banned from residential use in 1978. However, older homes built before the ban are potentially hazardous to children. CDC reports that, according to a study, the children at greatest risk of lead poisoning are those living in pre-1946 homes with a prevalence of 8.6% with elevated lead levels. The high lead prevalence rate for children living in homes built between 1946 and 1973 was 4.6%, and dropped to 1.6% for children in homes built after 1973. The study found that the prevalence among low-income children was 16.4% as compared to children from middle-income (4.1%) and high-income families (0.9%) (Davis, 2007).

In recent years, millions of toys, including some well known brands were recalled due to excessive amounts of lead in their paint. Parents and educators must be vigilant in the selection of toys and educational materials, particularly those manufactured in other countries.

Overreferrals. The individuals who are placed in classes for students with mild intellectual disabilities and severe emotional disturbances are disproportionately male, African American, and from lower socioeconomic backgrounds. The first step in special education placement is the referral process. Anyone (parents, doctors, educators) can make referrals. Teachers make most referrals in the elementary school years. These teachers are overwhelmingly female, white, and middle-class. There is often incongruity between educators and culturally diverse students with respect to cultural values, acceptable behaviors in the school, and educational expectations. This may result in overreferrals to classes for students with disabilities and underreferrals to classes for the gifted and talented. In overreferrals, teachers tend to make excessive referrals of students of color for placement in special education classes for students with disabilities. In underreferrals educators fail to recognize potential giftedness and do not make referrals for placement in classes for gifted students. Ford (2011) suggests that underrepresentation of African American students in gifted programs is consistently around 50%. Davis, Rimm, and Siegle (2011) strongly advocate a multidimensional approach in identifying gifted and talented minority students, one that looks beyond IQ scores. Gifted education is clearly not exempt from the many problems that plague education. Experts say that although approximately 3 million students are identified as gifted, 80% of these students never receive specialized instruction (Rivera, 2008).

Racial Bias. There are numerous stories that can be told of students of color being automatically placed in low academic tracks or in special education, particularly prior to the advent of IDEA.

Both ethnicity and gender are among the most consistent predictors of intellectual disabilities and serious emotional disturbance identification by the schools. OCR surveys have revealed persistent overrepresentation of students of color in certain disability categories (and underrepresentation in the gifted and talented). We have already discussed the overrepresentation of African American children in classes for students with intellectual disabilities. While the disproportionate placement of African American males in classes for students with emotional disturbances is not to the extent found in classes for individuals with intellectual disabilities, it is nevertheless at a troubling level. The placement percentage nationally of students in classes for students with emotional disturbances was 0.85%, while the percentage of African Americans in these classes was nearly 1.5% (50% higher than the general school population). Twenty-nine percent of the students in classes for students with emotional disturbances were African American (U.S. Department of Education, 2006).

Assessment Issues. Assessment of students of color is also a major concern as a contributing variable to the overrepresentation of these students in special education classes. Litigation in the 1970s (e.g., *Diana v. State Board of Education*, 1970, language minority Latino students; and *Larry P. v. Riles*, 1979, African American students) demonstrated the dangers of **biased assessment** instruments and procedures. Assessments that favor certain cultural groups and discriminate in content are considered biased. It is clear that some students in special education have central nervous system damage and that others have visual, auditory, orthopedic, and speech disabilities. There is no dispute regarding the appropriateness of the special education placement of these individuals. However, inappropriate placement of students of color in the judgmental categories of mild intellectual disabilities and severe emotional disturbance must be addressed if we are to have true equity in our educational system.

Unexplained Issues. The differences in special education placement between Latino and African American students and between male and female African American students cannot readily be explained by either social background or measured ability. The poverty rates between Latinos and African Americans have been similar for a number of years. As previously stated, poverty is often listed as a variable that contributes to disability. However, we lack a clear explanation as to why placement rates for Latinos in disability special education classes are relatively low compared to African American student rates. We also lack a clear understanding of why black males and females have such disparate placement percentages when they come from the same socioeconomic backgrounds.

One possibility is the fact that males and females are socialized differently regardless of racial or ethnic background. Perhaps the socialized behaviors of African American males have a higher level of incongruity with educators' values than do those of African American females, and they elicit more negative attention.

In observing the placement differences between African Americans and Latinos, it might be noticed that some Latino students have more educational options open to them, including **bilingual education** and English as a Second Language (ESL) programs. Bilingual education, which utilizes both the home language and English in the instructional process, is designed to meet the needs of language minority students. ESL programs utilize only English with these students with the primary intent to teach them English.

NEED FOR DISAGGREGATED DATA

While national data show trends for the various racial/ethnic groups, the data are often confusing because of the failure to disaggregate the various groups. For example, Asians and Pacific Americans are consistently shown to be underrepresented in disability categories and overrepresented in gifted and talented classes. There is considerable diversity within this category, as it includes Asian groups such as the Chinese, Japanese, Koreans, Indians, and Vietnamese, while also including Pacific Americans such as Hawaiians, Samoans, and Tongans. There are considerable cultural differences between Asian groups and even greater differences between the Asians and Pacific Americans. Japanese Americans and Tongan Americans have little in common culturally. Yet they are grouped together for U.S. government reporting purposes. The same is true among Latinos. There are considerable cultural differences between Cuban Americans living in Miami and Central American immigrants living in East Los Angeles. They are also reported as one group.

PAUSE TO REFLECT 6.2

The overrepresentation of students of color is one of the most problematic issues facing special educators today. We have the knowledge and the ability to all but eradicate this problem.

- What steps would need to be taken to significantly reduce the problem of overrepresentation of students of color in special education?

- Do our educators and our legislators lack the will and the concern to take the necessary steps to ameliorate the problem?

When disaggregating data by states, or by ethnic groups, we often find considerable differences compared to national data. For example, data from the Hawaii State Department of Education shows that Hawaiian students are overrepresented in some categories of special education such as intellectual disabilities. Yet this cannot be determined from analyzing national data. Latinos or Hispanics are underrepresented in classes for students with intellectual disabilities and emotional disturbance in the OCR national data. Yet in some states they are overrepresented, and Artiles, Rueda, Salazar, and Higareda (2002) found sixth- through twelfth-grade English language learners in 11 predominantly Latino urban school districts to be overrepresented in special education.

The inequities in special education raise concerns about the inequities in other areas of education and raise the prospect that there may be a relationship in these problematic issues. Special education overrepresentation often mirrors the overrepresentation seen in other categories and viewed by some as problematic: dropouts, low-track placements, corporal punishment, suspensions, and involvement in the juvenile justice system.

The problem has persisted for decades and will not be easily ameliorated. It will take a concerted effort to eliminate all bias from the assessment process, a restructuring of teacher education curricula, and a commitment of the wealthiest nation to eliminate the insidious effects of poverty on our children.

CALIFORNIA PROPOSITION 227 AND SPECIAL EDUCATION

California's voters passed **Proposition 227** in 1998. This proposition, now a California law, requires all language minority students to be educated in sheltered English immersion programs, normally not intended to exceed one year. Sheltered English immersion is an instructional process for young children in which all or nearly all classroom instruction is in English. One aspect of this policy will be addressed in this chapter. The proposition, which intended to dismantle bilingual education, sent waves of panic through California's bilingual education community. Those working with special needs students had even greater concerns because many believed that they were prohibited from using the home language with limited and non-English-speaking students. They were also concerned that the new law would require them to transition the students into general education classrooms after one year. Proposition 227 is a state law, and there is a similar proposition in Arizona and a similar law in Massachusetts. The federal law, IDEA, always takes precedence over a state law, however. Therefore, if the student's IEP requires bilingual education, it must be provided for as long as indicated.

Teaching Children with Exceptionalities

The educational implications for working with exceptional individuals are numerous and entire chapters could be devoted to each type of exceptionality. Educators should remember that exceptional children, those with disabilities and those who are gifted, are more like than unlike normal children. Their basic needs are the same as all children's. Abraham Maslow's theory on self-actualization is familiar to most students in education. To be self-actualized, or to meet one's full potential, Maslow (1954) theorized, one's basic needs must be fulfilled. That is, to reach self-actualization, one's physiological needs, safety needs, belongingness or love needs, and esteem needs must first be met. Although many individuals with disabilities may never match the accomplishments of their nondisabled peers, they can become proficient at whatever they are capable of doing. Educators can assist them by helping to ensure that their basic needs are met, allowing them to strive toward self-actualization.

Teachers must be constantly cognizant of the unique needs of their exceptional children. The exceptional adult may choose, or may be forced by society, to become part of a cultural group. The interactions between educators and the exceptional child may not change what will eventually take place. Even if exceptional adults are part of a cultural group, they also will interact with the mainstream society on a regular basis. Efforts on the part of the educator to meet the needs of the child may ultimately affect the exceptional adult's interaction with society.

Teachers of children with physical and other health impairments may find it advantageous to check the student records carefully to determine potential problem situations with these students in the classroom. If a child has particular health problems that may surface in the classroom, the child's teachers need to be prepared so that they will know precisely what to do should the child have, for example, an epileptic seizure. The parents will most likely be able to provide precise instructions, and the school nurse could provide additional recommendations. If the children are old enough to understand, they too can be a valuable source of information. Ask them what kinds of adaptations, special equipment, or teaching procedures work best for them. Teachers should not be afraid of their own uncertainties. They should feel free to ask the students when they prefer to have or not have assistance. Teachers should treat their students with disabilities as normally as is feasible, neither overprotecting them nor doing more for them than is needed or deserved. Allowing them to assume responsibility for themselves will do much to facilitate their personal growth.

Many variables affect the learning, cognition, and adjustment of individuals with disabilities. This is particularly evident for culturally and linguistically diverse learners who must cope with issues of language, culture, and values.

The range and variety of experiences imposed on, or withheld from, persons with disabilities may result in undue limitations. Too often, parents and teachers assume that a child's visual limitation precludes the ability to approximate the typical everyday experiences of sighted children. Children who are blind may not be able to see the animals in a zoo, but they can smell and hear them. They may not be able to enjoy the scenes along a bus route, but they can feel the stop-and-go movements, hear the traffic and people, and smell their fellow travelers. The child who is deaf may not be able to hear the sounds at the symphony or the crowd's roar at a football game. Both events, however, offer the possibility of extraordinary sensory experiences to which the child needs exposure. The child with cerebral palsy needs experiences such as going to restaurants, even if the child has difficulty using eating utensils in a socially acceptable manner.

Well-adjusted individuals with a sensory disability usually attain a balance of control with their environment. Individuals who depend completely on other members of the family and on friends may develop an attitude of helplessness and a loss of self-identity. Individuals with disabilities who completely dominate and control their environment with unreasonable demands sometimes fail to make an acceptable adjustment and could become selfish and self-centered.

It is critical to remember that children who are exceptional are, first and foremost, children. Their exceptionality, though influencing their lives, is secondary to their needs as children. Following are three types of needs for parents and educators to keep in mind for children with disabilities: communication, acceptance, and the freedom to grow. They may also be applicable to some gifted students.

COMMUNICATION NEEDS

Exceptional children are far more perceptive than many adults give them credit for being. They are sensitive to nonverbal communication and hidden messages that may be concealed in half-truths. They, more than anyone else, need to deal with their exceptionality, whether it is a disability, giftedness, or both. They need to know what their exceptionality is all about so that they can deal with it. They need to know how it will affect their lives in order to adjust appropriately, to make the best of their lives, and to reach their full potential. They need straight, honest communication tempered with sensitivity.

ACCEPTANCE NEEDS

The society in which we live often fails to provide the exceptional child with a positive and receptive environment. Even the educational setting can be hostile and lacking in acceptance. The teacher can facilitate the acceptance of a child in a classroom by exhibiting an open and positive attitude. Students tend to reflect the attitude of the teacher. If the teacher is hostile, the students will quickly pick up these cues. If the attitude is positive, the students are likely to respond and provide a receptive environment for their classmates with disabilities.

Jeff, a first-grade student who suffered from a hearing loss, was fitted with a hearing aid. When he came to school wearing the hearing aid, the students in the class immediately began whispering about the "thing" Jeff had in his ear. After observing the class behavior, with the permission of Jeff's parents the teacher privately assisted Jeff in a show-and-tell preparation for the next day. With the teacher's assistance and assurances, Jeff proudly demonstrated his hearing aid to the class, showing them how he could adjust it to allow him to hear even some things they could not. By the end of the demonstration, Jeff was the envy of the class, and all further discussion of the hearing aid was of a positive nature.

FREEDOM TO GROW

Students with disabilities need acceptance and understanding. Acceptance implies freedom for the exceptional child to grow. At times, it may seem easier to do things for a child rather than to take the time to teach the child. A number of years ago, one of the co-authors lived and worked at a residential state school for the blind. Recounted next are two actual events that took place at the school.

Sarah (the name has been changed) was a nine-year-old girl who was blind and had an orthopedic disability and who studied at the state residential school for the blind. She wore leg braces but had a reasonable amount of mobility with the use of crutches. To save time and effort, fellow students or staff members transported her between the cottage where she lived

New Student with Autism Who Has Musical Talent

With the full inclusion policies or efforts that some school districts have implemented, more teachers are finding children with autism placed in their general education classrooms.

Since 1995 there has been a dramatic increase in students identified with Autism Spectrum Disorder (ASD), which includes three related developmental disorders: autism disorder ("classic autism"), Asperger's syndrome, and pervasive developmental disorder not otherwise specified (atypical autism). At this time, no cause of ASD has been identified. There are no racial/ethnic links to this condition, but it is more prevalent in males than females. The condition is lifelong, but as children grow older, the symptoms can become less severe with appropriate training. Prevalence may be as high as 1 in 110 births in the United States (CDC, n.d.1; CDC. n.d.2).

Children with autism are the most common ASD students in the schools. Numerous characteristics tend to set these children apart from their normal peers. Communication problems may include a delayed or lack of language development, the inability to maintain a social conversation, or the use of gestures instead of words. Others may find some autistic children annoying because of continuous word or sentence repetition or nonsense utterances.

Their socialization skills typically reflect a lack of interest in peer relationships and an inability to maintain appropriate eye contact or to show empathy. They may be or appear to be withdrawn. Some find behaviors of children with autism to be unacceptable, with acting up behaviors or tantrums, perseverating, overactive or passive behaviors, aggressiveness, and repetitive body movements common (Brown, Gerber, & Oliva, 2011).

When Tracy Harris, a third-grade teacher in Albuquerque, was advised by her principal, Ms. Guerrero, that she would soon have a nine-year-old student with autism, Jerome Santos, placed in her class, she was assured that an inclusion specialist would assist in the transition. In speaking to Jerome's mother, the inclusion specialist and Ms. Harris learned that in spite of Jerome's awkwardness and lack of social skills, he had reasonably good musical skills—a phenomenon found in some children with autism. He loved playing the piano, having taken lessons for four years, and he had learned to play over twenty songs well from memory. Jerome's first impression on the class would be important to his acceptance by his classmates.

| QUESTIONS FOR CLASSROOM DISCUSSION |

- Can Ms. Harris and the inclusion specialist utilize Jerome's musical ability in introducing him to the class?

- Should they consult Jerome and his parents before they mention his music skills and ask their permission to request that Jerome play for his new classmates?

- Should they arrange to have Jerome demonstrate his piano playing skills on the first day?

- Are there other things that should be taken into consideration to facilitate Jerome's transition into his new class?

Centers for Disease Control and Prevention (n.d.1) Autism Spectrum Disorders (ASDs), Facts About ASDs, Retrieved April 25, 2011, http://www.cdc.gov/ncbddd/autism/data.html

Centers for Disease Control and Prevention (n.d.2). Autism Spectrum Disorders (ASDs), Data and Statistics, Retrieved April 25, 2011, http://www.cdc.gov/ncbddd/autism/data.html

National Institute of Mental Health (n.d.). Autism Spectrum Disorders (Pervasive Developmental Disorders). Retrieved April 25, 2011, http://www.nimh.nih.gov/health/publications/autism/complete-index.shtml

National Institutes of Health, Autism Spectrum Disorders (ASDs), Retrieved April 25, 2011, http://www.nichd.nih.gov/health/topics/asd.cfm

and the classroom building in a wagon. One day her teacher decided she needed to be more independent in her travel to and from her cottage. To Sarah's surprise, the teacher informed her after school that she would not ride back in the wagon but that he would walk her back. Angered, she denounced him as cruel and hateful. She complained bitterly the full 30 minutes of their walk back to the cottage. After a few days the complaining subsided and the travel time was curtailed. Within a few weeks Sarah was traveling on her own in 10 minutes or less with a newfound independence and self-respect.

At other times, it may be tempting for teachers and parents to make extra concessions for the exceptional child. Often, these exceptions hinder the emotional growth of the child and may later cause serious interpersonal problems.

Jimmy was a seven-year-old boy who was blind, and he attended the same state institution as Sarah. He was a favorite of the staff members because of his pleasant personality and overall adjustment. On a Sunday afternoon he was assisting a staff member in making holiday cards. The conversation turned to Christmas and Jimmy's wish for a transistor radio. (This incident took place in 1960, when transistor radios were new on the market and very expensive.) Since Jimmy had already made this request to his parents, the staff member was confident that the parents would not deny this child his wish. To the surprise of the staff, Jimmy returned after the holidays without a radio. He explained to the staff that the radios were so expensive that had his parents granted his wish, it would come at the expense of the other children in the family. Weeks later, when Jimmy returned from his birthday weekend at home, he entered his cottage with a transistor radio in hand, but in tears. He informed the staff that he and his younger brother Ralph had been fighting in the car on the way to the school and his parents were going to take away their favorite toys. When a staff member went out to greet Jimmy's parents, Ralph was also crying because he didn't want his toy taken away.

Jimmy's family had a modest income. Although their child's disability created adjustment problems for everyone, they had resolved to treat him as an equal in the family. As such, he shared all of the family privileges. He also suffered the same consequences for inappropriate behavior. This attitude on the part of the parents was probably a primary factor in Jimmy's excellent adjustment to his disability.

NORMALIZATION AND INCLUSION

Much effort is directed today toward the concept of normalization. **Normalization** means "making available to all persons with disabilities or other handicaps, patterns of life and conditions of everyday living which are as close as possible to or indeed the same as the regular circumstances and ways of life of society" (Nirje, 1985, p. 67). Understanding normalization helps us understand what has led us to the current educational movements for children with disabilities.

Normalization was expanded and advocated in the United States by Wolfensberger (1972). He has subsequently suggested a rethinking of the term "normalization" and introduced the concept of **social role valorization**—giving value to individuals with intellectual disabilities (Wolfensberger, 1983, 2000). He suggests that the "most explicit and highest goal of normalization must be the creation, support, and defense of valued social roles for people who are at risk of social devaluation" (1983, p. 234).

Drew and Hardman (2007) suggest that normalization has brought about an emphasis on deinstitutionalization, whereby individuals from large residential facilities for people with intellectual disabilities are returned to the community and home environments. They add that the concept is not limited to movement away from institutions to a less restrictive environment; it also pertains to those individuals living in the community for whom a more "normal" lifestyle may be an appropriate goal.

The principles of normalization as it was introduced were developed with individuals with intellectual disabilities (mental retardation) as the target group. In more recent years, the concept has broadened so that all categories of individuals with disabilities are now targeted.

The term "mainstreaming" has given way to **"inclusion,"** suggesting that a natural evolutionary process from the concept of normalization has taken place. Turnbull, Turnbull, and Wehmeyer define inclusion as allowing "students with disabilities to learn in general education classes and have a sense of belonging in these classes" (2010, p. 42). Mastropieri and Scruggs (2007) differentiate between inclusion and **full inclusion,** with the latter serving students with disabilities and other special needs entirely within the general classroom. This is an important difference, as students in full inclusion do not receive any of their education in segregated settings.

Initially inclusion was intended for students with mild disabilities. The more current movement, full inclusion, seeks to provide

With the passage of Public Law 94-142, education is to take place in the least restrictive environment. Increased awareness and acceptance of full inclusion has facilitated placement in general education classrooms.
© Krista Greco/Merrill

children with moderate to severe disabilities with similar opportunities. Although resistance to inclusion of students with mild disability is far less intense than it once was, it is still felt from some educators. The arguments against integrating children with severe disabilities have often centered on the presumed inability of nondisabled children to accept their peers with disabilities. In reality, some of the reservations may be more a reflection of educators who themselves are unable or unwilling to accept the dignity and worth of individuals with severe disabilities.

Historically, special education in the United States has offered a full continuum of placements for students with disabilities. These services have ranged from the most restrictive placements, such as residential schools and special schools, to the least restrictive settings, such as full inclusion in the general education classroom.

Federal special education law (IDEA) does not require inclusion. The law does require the least restrictive environment for students with disabilities. Herein lies the basis for considerable controversy in special education. The controversy is often fueled within special education itself, as educators are not in complete agreement regarding what is the least restrictive environment. **Least restrictive environment (LRE)** means that children with disabilities are to be educated with nondisabled children whenever possible, in as normal an environment as possible. Few special educators would argue against the concept of inclusion. However, disagreement focuses on whether full inclusion is appropriate for every child regardless of the type or the severity of the disability.

To some, and perhaps to many of the advocates of full inclusion, the issue is not the efficacy of general education placement. Rather, it is a moral and ethical issue. Opponents of inclusion use many of the same arguments that segregationists used more than 50 years ago. Most Americans today would consider it unconscionable to segregate children in schools on the basis of race or ethnicity. This, we can agree, is morally and ethically wrong. Advocates for full inclusion find it equally repugnant to segregate children on the basis of a disability.

In reality, most if not all children with disabilities could be served in a general education classroom if adequate resources and supports were made available. Therein lies a primary problem. There is seldom an adequate supply of certified or credentialed personnel in special education and related services (e.g., school psychologists). General educators have many issues and concerns to address in the area of inclusion:

- The special needs student may detract from the attention normally provided other students.
- What kind of reception will the nondisabled students give to the students with disabilities?
- If educators are not provided with appropriate training to accommodate students with disabilities, they will not be able to provide appropriate instructional services.
- The younger students and those with more severe disabilities will require greater attention.
- The promises of support in terms of classroom personnel and other resources may not be kept.

A pragmatist would argue that there are not enough fiscal resources to provide the support necessary for successful full inclusion of all children. The courts will not accept an excuse such as, "We don't do it because there are inadequate resources." The courts may accept the argument that a particular program or service is not in the best interests of the student, but it must be clearly supported and documented. However, if full inclusion is warranted, the courts will order the schools (as they have consistently done) to "get the resources and do it."

Those who question aspects of full inclusion may argue that some children are so disruptive and dangerous to themselves and to other students that they cannot be provided for in general education. Supporters of full inclusion can reply that given adequate resources, students can be taught to stop disruptive and dangerous behaviors. There has been a progressive trend toward greater inclusion in the nation's schools. Prior to the 1984–85 school year, only about a

Debate / Is Full Inclusion Feasible for All Children with Disabilities?

The Individuals with Disabilities Education Act is a federal law that requires the placement of students with disabilities in the least restrictive environment. This means that these students should be placed in or as close to a general education setting as is feasible for them. What is the least restrictive setting for a child with a disability? Is it feasible to place every child with a disability in a general education setting? Are there adequate resources to do this? Do we have the skill and the will to make it work?

FOR

- Full inclusion for all children with disabilities is a moral and ethical issue. It is as immoral to segregate a child because of his or her disability as it is to segregate children because of the color of their skin.

- The least restrictive environment that is feasible for every child is a general education classroom. We have the know-how to deliver quality educational services for every child in an inclusive general education classroom.

- The fact that we do not have adequate fiscal resources is not the fault of the child with a disability. If we don't have the resources, then we need to find ways to get them.

AGAINST

- Full inclusion may work for some students with disabilities, but it makes no sense to insist on it for every student regardless of the disability or the degree of impairment.

- Some students with disabilities lack the maturity, the cognitive ability, the social skills, or appropriate behaviors to function in general education.

- Until the federal government makes good on its commitment to fully fund IDEA, there will never be adequate resources to successfully implement full inclusion for all children with disabilities.

- Even if the fiscal resources were there, there simply are not enough professionally prepared personnel to provide the types of services needed for successful inclusion of every child.

| QUESTIONS |

1. Are there some students who should never be considered for general education placement?

2. If the federal government mandates special education for all children, commits itself to funding 40% of the cost, and continues to renege on the full funding, should school districts be forced to fully implement IDEA?

3. Is excluding children with disabilities from full inclusion in general education morally and ethically comparable to excluding children because of race?

fourth of the students with disabilities spent a significant part of their day in general education classrooms. By the 1998–99 school year, nearly half of the students were involved in general education for most of the school day (Turnbull, Turnbull, & Wehmeyer 2010). Some general conclusions can be drawn:

- As long as Congress fails to meet its financial obligations to fully fund IDEA, school districts will continue to have difficulty in providing adequate resources for special education.
- Segregating students with disabilities from general education classes without justification is morally and ethically wrong.
- The debate over inclusion and full inclusion continues and is not likely to be fully resolved in the immediate future.

It is important for us as educators to see the parallels and differences between the current debate regarding this group of students and the issues that *Brown* addressed more than 50 years ago. The two situations have similarities, but the groups are different. It is important that as educators we maintain open minds so that we ourselves perhaps can be educated.

The legal mandates do not eliminate special schools or classes, but they do offer a new philosophical view. Instead of the physical isolation of individuals with disabilities, efforts must be made to enable students with disabilities to assume a more appropriate place in the educational setting. Still, many children with disabilities may not benefit appreciably from an inclusive setting and may be better educated in a special setting. As attitudes become more attuned to the laws, people with disabilities may have more options to participate in the decision to be a part of the mainstream or to be segregated into their own cultural groups.

PAUSE TO REFLECT 6.3

Students with disabilities are sometimes forced into segregated settings for reasons beyond their control. For example, Kevin was a student who lived with his family on the side of a mountain in Appalachia. Kevin was blind, with no travel vision. A hike of nearly a third of a mile down the side of the mountain was necessary to reach the school bus stop. Kevin had good mobility skills and could negotiate the trail to and from the bus stop when weather conditions were good. The school was able to provide appropriate special education and general education services for him. During the winter, however, when snow covered the ground for the entire season, he could not get his bearings with his long cane and was unable to negotiate the trail. There was no one who could help him get to and from the bus stop, so during the winter he stopped going to school. The only school that could meet his needs apparently was the state school for the blind, which could provide him with residential services. The state residential school, however, represents the most extreme form of a segregated setting for students with disabilities.

- Is segregating Kevin from his nondisabled peers inappropriate? Immoral? Unethical?

- Is the issue of full inclusion for students with disabilities similar to the issue of desegregation of all students of color into integrated classroom settings?

- Some educators say they want a full continuum of services for students with disabilities that would permit inclusion for some and segregated classrooms for others, or even institutionalization. Is this a moral and ethical way to educate America's students? Is this an excuse for educators to discriminate against some?

Summary

The concerns related to the disproportionate placement of ethnic minorities, males, and students from low-income families in special education programs focus on a long-standing educational problem. The issues raised are not meant to question that there are students with intellectual disabilities, serious emotional disturbances, and other disabilities in both majority and minority groups. Rather, they are raised to call attention to problems in referral and assessment, as well as to the problems associated with poverty.

Adults with disabilities often become part of a cultural group of individuals with disabilities by ascription or by individual choice. They do not choose to have a disability, and they may be unable to experience full acceptance or integration into the world of those who are perceived to be physically, socially, and intellectually normal. Their adjustment to their environment may be in part a function of the way they are perceived, treated, and accepted by educators. Consequently, teachers and other educators may have a greater influence on children with disabilities than they realize.

The Education for All Handicapped Children Act (EHA, P.L. 94-142), the Individuals with Disabilities Education Act (IDEA, P.L. 101-476), Section 504 of the Vocational Rehabilitation Act Amendments of 1973 (P.L. 93-112), and the Americans with Disabilities Act (ADA, P.L. 101-336) guarantee all exceptional children the right to a free and appropriate education and freedom from discrimination related to their disability. While thousands of children with disabilities are experiencing inclusive education in general education classes, many others are excluded because of bias, prejudice, or lack of understanding. Despite the mandates, equality still eludes millions of individuals with disabilities in this country. Until the federal government fulfills its fiscal commitment to fully fund IDEA, full inclusion will continue to be a problematic and controversial issue for educators.

Insensitivity, apathy, and prejudice contribute to the problems of those with disabilities. Because of prejudice, institutionalization, or the perceived necessity of meeting their own needs, some exceptional individuals form their own cultural groups and some their own enclaves where they live and socialize with one another. The laws can require services for individuals with disabilities, but only time and effort can change public attitudes.

Professional Practice

Questions for Discussion

1. What are some of the objections to labeling children with disabilities?

2. Why was *Brown v. Board of Education* (1954) important to special education?

3. What are the major implications of P.L. 94-142, IDEA, Section 504 of P.L. 93-112, and the Americans with Disabilities Act?

4. How do individuals with disabilities sometimes become a part of an exceptional cultural group?

5. Explain the difference between reporting placement in special education classes by composition and by risk.

6. What are some of the variables that contribute to the overrepresentation of students of color in special education classes?

7. What are the educational implications of California's Proposition 227 for students with disabilities?

8. What are some of the needs of exceptional children?

9. Explain the concepts of normalization and social role valorization, and trace their evolution to the concepts of inclusion and full inclusion.

10. What are the problems with providing full inclusion to all children with disabilities?

Portfolio Activities

1. Examine an entire building on your campus to determine its accessibility to individuals with wheelchair mobility. Answer the following:
   a. Do curbs leading to the building allow wheelchair access?
   b. Is the entrance to the building accessible by wheelchair? Is it ramped?
   c. Are restrooms equipped with larger stalls to accommodate wheelchairs?
   d. Is the building multilevel, and if so, how does the student access the different floors?
   e. Are there Braille signs in appropriate places? (InTASC Standard 2: Learning Differences, and Standard 3: Learning Environments)

2. Examine your campus to determine if it is accessible to visually impaired individuals. Determine if there are hazards on the campus, which endanger individuals who are blind (e.g., holes in the ground, posted metal sign at face height). (InTASC Standard 2: Learning Differences, and Standard 3: Learning Environments)

3. Determine the percentage of students of color in the school in which you are working or student teaching. Determine the percentage of students of color in this same school who have been placed in special education classes and determine if there is some degree of overrepresentation. This information is for your own use and possibly for university classroom discussion. If you are a student teacher in the school, it may not be in your best interest to make an issue of overrepresentation with the school administration. (InTASC Standard 2: Learning Differences, and Standard 3: Learning Environments)

Digital Resources for the Classroom

1. General information on exceptional children is available at the Council for Exceptional Children's website, http://www.cec.sped.org/am/template.cfm?section=Home

2. For additional general information on exceptional children, including fact sheets and facts and questions, access the ERIC Clearinghouse on Disabilities and Gifted Children at http://www.hoagiesgifted.org/eric/index.html.

3. For a summary of the Supreme Court decisions related to exceptional children, go to http://www.wrightslaw.com/caselaw.htm.

4. For general information on gifted and talented children from the Association for the Gifted, visit http://www.cectag.org/.

5. For the U.S. Department of Justice's Guide to Disability Rights Law, go to http://www.ada.gov/cguide.htm, providing a summary of federal laws that protect the rights of individuals with disabilities.

MyEducationLab™

Go to the MyEducationLab (www.myeducationlab.com) for Multicultural Education and familiarize yourself with the topical content, which includes:

- Assignments and Activities, tied to learning outcomes for the course, that can help you more deeply understand course content

- Building Teaching Skills and Dispositions learning units allow you to apply and practice your understanding of how to teach equitably in a multicultural education classroom

- Licensure Test Prep activities are available in the Book Resources to help you prepare for test taking

- A pretest with hints and feedback that tests your knowledge of this chapter's content

- Review, practice, and enrichment activities that will enhance your understanding of the chapter content

- A posttest with hints and feedback that allows you to test your knowledge again after having completed the enrichment activities

A Correlation Guide may be downloaded by instructors to show how MyEducationLab content aligns to this book.

7 Language

To devalue his [or her] language or to presume Standard English is a better system is to devalue the child and his [or her] culture and to reveal a naiveté concerning language.

Joan Baratz, 1968

| LEARNING OUTCOMES |

As you read the chapter, you should be able to:

- Recognize why a French-speaking kindergarten student in Los Angeles may be accorded higher status and respect by teachers and in society than a Spanish-speaking kindergarten student.

- Explain the relationship of language to culture by discussing how the word *time* is viewed differently by various cultural groups.

- Differentiate between accents and dialects.

- Articulate the difference between contact and noncontact cultures and how that impacts how teachers differentiate instruction.

- Distinguish between the role of first language (L1) in second language (L2) acquisition and the ways instructors can accommodate English language learners and second language learners.

- Differentiate between bilingual education and ESL programs.

Theresa Roberts, a kindergarten teacher at Mokumanu Elementary School in Honolulu, had just finished welcoming her new class and introducing herself. As she wrote her name and the school's on the chalkboard, she felt a slight tug on the back of her skirt and heard a faint voice just above a whisper say, "Teacha, I like go pee." Turning around, she saw the pleading face of Malia Kealoha. "What did you say?" Ms. Roberts responded disgustedly. In a slightly louder voice, Malia repeated herself, "I like go pee." With classmates beginning to giggle, Ms. Roberts exclaimed, "You will go nowhere, young lady, until you ask me in proper English. Now say it properly." "I no can," pleaded Malia. "Then you can just stand there until you do." With the students still giggling and Malia standing as ordered, Ms. Roberts proceeded with her lesson.

A few minutes later, the occasional giggle exploded into a chorus of laughter. As Ms. Roberts turned to Malia, the child was sobbing as she stood in the middle of a large puddle of urine on the classroom floor.

| REFLECTIONS |

1. Do teachers have the right to expect and demand Standard English from their students?

2. How important is it for students to be able to speak Standard English?

3. If a student is able to communicate well enough in his or her non–Standard English for others to understand, why should educators be concerned about non–Standard English usage?

Language and Culture

The preceding incident took place in a school in Hawaii many years ago. Malia (not her real name) described the incident as one of the most painful and humiliating in her life. When she entered school, she was unable to speak **Standard English** (language considered proper in a community); she could speak only pidgin English (a creole of English with words and phrases from Hawaiian, Chinese, Japanese, etc.). The teacher knew precisely what the child was trying to say. The teacher's insensitivity, however, resulted in lasting emotional scars on Malia as a child, and now as an adult. This type of insensitivity, unfortunately, is not an isolated phenomenon. Individuals in southeastern New Mexico have described similar incidents involving non-English-speaking Mexican American students entering school for the first time.

Language is a system of vocal sounds and/or nonverbal systems by which group members communicate with one another. It is a critical tool in the development of an individual's identity, self-awareness, and intellectual and psychological growth. It makes our behavior human. It can incite anger, elicit love, inspire bravery, and arouse fear. It binds groups of people together. Language and dialect serve as a focal point for cultural identity. People who share the same language or dialect often share the same feelings, beliefs, and behaviors.

Language provides a common bond for individuals with the same linguistic heritage. It can play a key role in providing a national sense of identity. Language may also be the means by which one group of people stereotypes another. Language and accents can usually be altered, whereas racial and physical appearance generally cannot. Through changing the style of one's language or even the language itself, individuals can shape others' impression of them.

Most students enter school speaking what is considered Standard English. Others speak little or no English. Some are bilingual; some speak a **nonstandard dialect** (the same language but a different pronunciation from what is considered standard, e.g., Black English). Some students with hearing impairments may use sign language to communicate. As the scene changes from school to school, the languages and **dialects** (which are usually determined by region or social class) spoken also change. The scene, however, is indicative of the multilingual nature of the United States, a result of its multicultural heritage. Because some students speak one or more languages, as well as dialects of these languages, they are part of another cultural group. Of course, not all African American children speak **Black English** (a vernacular or dialect of the majority of Black Americans), nor do all Hispanics or Latinos speak Spanish. Within most cultures, members vary greatly in language or dialect usage.

Eurocentrism and Eurocentric curricula place Europeans and European Americans as the focus of the world with respect to culture, history, economics, values, lifestyles, world views, and so forth. Because U.S. society has such strong Eurocentric roots, European languages and accents may be given higher status than those from non-European countries. French and German languages may be viewed as more academic, more sophisticated, and more prestigious in some segments of society. Children from these linguistic backgrounds may be viewed with greater esteem than immigrant children from Third World countries. Society and educators may stigmatize bilingual students, especially those from limited English backgrounds, which are often identified with poverty. They may perceive them to be low in status and educationally at risk. Too often some students from immigrant and language minority backgrounds have been discouraged by their teachers from seeking a college education.

Rather than value and promote the use of two or more languages, some educators expect students to replace their native languages with English. Unfortunately, some students lose the home language in the process. Movements to establish English-only policies and practices may further devalue the immigrant student's home language.

Individuals who have limited English proficiency frequently suffer institutional discrimination as a result of the limited acceptance of languages other than English. Adger, Wolfram, and Christian (2007) assert that students in this group are frequently at great risk for school failure, despite the fact that they may not necessarily be categorized as disadvantaged.

LANGUAGE AS A SOCIALIZING AGENT

Language is much more than a means of communication. It is used to socialize children into their linguistic and cultural communities, where they develop patterns that distinguish one community from another. Thus, the interaction of language and culture is complex but central to the socialization of children into acceptable cultural patterns. Although there are many theories regarding the development of language, exactly how a language is learned is not completely understood. Almost all children have the ability to learn one or more native languages. In part through imitating older persons, children gradually learn. They learn to select almost instinctively the right word, the right response, and the right gesture to fit the situation. By age 5, children have learned the syntax of their native language, and they know that words in different arrangements mean different things. This suggests that within their own communities, children develop impressive language skills, although these skills may vary greatly from school requirements (Adger et al., 2007). At an early age, children acquire the delicate muscle control necessary for pronouncing the words of the native language, or for signing naturally if the child is deaf. As the child grows older, it becomes increasingly difficult to make the vocal muscles behave in the new, unfamiliar ways necessary to master a foreign language. This tends to inhibit people from learning new languages and encourages them to maintain the one into which they were born.

Native speakers of a language unconsciously know and obey the rules and customs of their language community. Society and language interact constantly. A wrong choice in word selection may come across as rude, crude, or ignorant. Individuals who are learning a new language or who are unfamiliar with **colloquialisms**, the informal or conversational speech in a community, may make wrong choices or even be surprised when the use of certain words is incongruous with their perceptions of what is proper. For example, an Australian exchange student attending a Texas university was shocked when a young woman at his church responded to his query of what she had been doing during the summer: "Oh, just piddling around." Her response was meant to convey the message that she had been passing her time in idle or aimless activities. From his frame of reference, however, the Australian student understood her to say that she had been urinating. It is important for classroom teachers to recognize that students who are new to a language may not always be able to make appropriate word selections or to comprehend the meaning of particular dialects or colloquialisms. Although the United States is primarily an English-speaking country, many other languages are spoken here. Spanish, Chinese, French, German, Tagalog (Filipino), Vietnamese, and Italian are the most commonly used languages other than English.

In the 1930s Fiorello La Guardia was the mayor of New York City. La Guardia, of Jewish and Italian ancestry, was fluent in **Yiddish**, Italian, German, and French as well as the New

The United States has become increasingly diverse linguistically, as evidenced by the various business signs we see in our communities.
© Shutterstock

York dialect of English (NYC Mayors, 2011; Jewish Virtual Library, 2011). La Guardia was known to vary not only the language, but his speech style with each ethnic group. For example, when speaking to Italian audiences, he used broad, sweeping gestures characteristic of the people of southern Italy. When speaking to Jewish audiences, he used the forearm chop identified with many Eastern European Jews. With some Jewish groups he spoke in Yiddish. The example of La Guardia suggests not only that different ethnic groups have different communication styles but also that individuals adjust their communication style, whenever possible, to suit the needs of the intended audience.

LANGUAGE DIVERSITY

Among English-speaking individuals are numerous dialects—from the Southern drawl to the Appalachian white dialect to the Brooklyn dialect of New York. Each is distinctive, and each is an effective means of communication for those who share its linguistic style. There were approximately 55 million non-English-speaking individuals living in the country in 2007 (U.S. Census Bureau, 2010e). This figure does not include the millions of English-speaking individuals whose dialects are sometimes labeled as nonstandard. The U.S. Census Bureau identified 381 languages spoken in the United States in 2007 (U.S. Census Bureau, 2010e).

The advantage to being bilingual or multilingual is often overlooked because of our ethnocentrism, or belief in the superiority of our own ethnicity or culture. In many other nations, children are expected to become fluent in two or more languages and numerous dialects, enabling them to communicate with other groups and to appreciate language diversity. In a world that is becoming increasingly global, it has become evident to more and more U.S. educators and parents that there are distinct advantages to bilingual or multilingual skills.

PAUSE TO REFLECT 7.1

In many countries in Europe, Asia, and other parts of the world, students are required to learn other languages other than the official language of their country. In the United States, except for our foreign-born students or those whose parents have immigrated from other countries, few of our students learn other languages.

■ Why do you think bilingualism and multilingualism do not receive the same support in the United States?

■ Are there advantages to being fluent in more than one language in the United States? If yes, what are they? Are there any disadvantages? If yes, what are they?

The Nature of Language

There is no such thing as a good language or a bad language from a linguistic point of view. All languages have developed to express the needs of their users. In that sense, all languages are equal. It is true that languages do not all have the same conventions of grammar, phonology, or semantic structure. It is also true that society places different levels of social status on the different language groups. These judgments are based not on linguistic acceptability, but on social grounds (Adger et al., 2007). Hudley and Mallison (2011) suggest that language is always changing and variation is inherent. They further suggest that standardized English is influenced or determined by powerful individuals and institutions that have political, social, and cultural status, enabling them to determine what is socially acceptable and prestigious. Standardization is deliberately and artificially imposed; there is no linguistic reason a standardized variety of English should be considered inherently better than any other variety of English. All languages meet the social and psychological needs of their speakers and, as such, are equal.

CULTURAL INFLUENCES

Language usage is culturally determined. In addition to influencing the order of words to form phrases, language influences thinking patterns. "Time" is described differently from culture to culture. Western societies view time as something that can be saved, lost, or wasted; punctuality is highly valued. In other societies, time assumes different values. In Japan, time usage may be a function of the status of relationships. People with higher status may be accorded the courtesy of more waiting time for their arrival than a person of lower status (Samovar, Porter, & McDaniel, 2010).

Individuals from the southern United States may be accustomed to exchanging pleasantries and what they may consider "small talk," prior to substantive or business conversation. Chatting first about Saturday's football game or the spring flowers in bloom may be considered a polite way to lead into the real issues that need to be discussed. To do otherwise might be considered rude by some individuals. Others, unaccustomed to Southern ways, may consider this behavior a waste of time.

Some Asians tend to be indirect in their speaking patterns. They may not speak directly to the point initially, but provide background information on what they are trying to convey. One reason for this manner of speaking is the feeling that, for one to understand and appreciate the point to be made, a foundation or background must be fully laid out. In this manner, the point of the discussion is placed clearly in proper context. For others who are more accustomed to getting directly to the issue at hand, the main point could be lost in the indirect presentation of the concept.

For effective communication to take place, it is important that there be enough cultural similarities between the sender and the receiver for the latter to decode the message adequately. Even when one is familiar with a word or phrase, comprehension of the intended meaning may not be possible unless there is some similarity or understanding of the cultural background.

In certain cultural groups, words and phrases may assume a different meaning. "Bad" among some adolescent groups takes on the opposite meaning from its usual one and may denote the "best." **Argot** is a more or less secretive vocabulary of a co-culture group. "Turning a trick," is an example of argot used by a prostitute to indicate that he or she has or had a customer. **Co-cultures** are groups of people who exist and function apart from the dominant culture. Users of argot include prisoners, homosexuals, gang members, sporting groups, and prostitutes (Samovar et al., 2010).

PAUSE TO REFLECT 7.2

Today, so many of our students are immigrants from countries other than the United States. As families become increasingly mobile, students move from one region of the country to another and bring with them unique speech patterns. Sit down with a group of your peers.

- Does anyone have a noticeable accent? How would you characterize it?

- Have you ever judged others on the basis of a dialect or an accent? If yes, when and how? Where was the person from?

- What kind of dialect do the people of your hometown have?

Language is very much cultural. It, together with dialect, is usually related to one's ethnic, geographic, gender, or class origins. Speakers from a particular background often downgrade the linguistic styles of others. For example, easterners may be critical of the speech of southerners, citing the latter's use of slow, extended vowels and the expression "y'all." Southerners, on the other hand, may be critical of the speech and language patterns of some individuals from areas in New York, who they think "speak through their noses" and use such phrases as "youse guys." An eastern dialect of English is appropriate in the eastern United States, the southern dialect is appropriate in the South, and Black English, or **Ebonics,** the dialect of the majority of Black Americans, is appropriate in many African American communities.

Language systems are dynamic like most other cultural features. They change constantly as society changes. Language change is inevitable and rarely predictable. For example, an elderly third-generation Japanese American born and raised in Maryland learned Japanese from both his grandparents and parents. On his first trip to Japan he spoke to the locals in what he considered his fluent Japanese. While he had no difficulty communicating, he was surprised that they were amused at his speech, which they found archaic and representative of the early 1900s. The Japanese he had learned from his family was indeed the Japanese language of nearly a hundred years earlier. In some areas, language change is so gradual that it goes unnoticed. In other circumstances, changes are easily noted. Expressions and words tend to be identified with a particular period. Sometimes language is related to a particular culture and a certain period. For example, slang words and terms such as "24/7," "airhead," and "iffy" may be a part of our language for a time, to be replaced by other expressions.

Language Differences

Literally thousands of languages are known in the world today. Lewis (2009) has identified 6,909 living languages. Vyacheslav Ivanov of the University of California, Los Angeles, indicates that there are at least 224 identified languages in Los Angeles County. In addition, many of these languages have different dialects (for example, Chinese Mandarin, Cantonese, Taiwanese, etc.). Professor Ivanov estimates that publications are locally produced in about 180 languages. There are 92 languages that have been specifically identified among students in the Los Angeles Unified School District (Los Angeles Almanac, 2011).

Social variables also contribute to language differences. Both class and ethnicity reflect differences in language. The greater the social distance between groups, the greater the tendency toward language differences. Upwardly mobile individuals often adopt the language patterns of the socially dominant group because it may facilitate social acceptance.

BILINGUALISM

Language diversity in the United States has been maintained primarily because of continuing immigration from non-English-speaking countries. In its relatively short history, the United States has probably been host to more linguistically diverse individuals than any other country. As new immigrants enter the country, they bring with them their own culture, values, and languages. As their children and grandchildren are born in this country, these immigrants witness with ambivalence the loss of their home language in favor of English.

One aspect of **bilingualism**, the ability to speak two languages, in the United States is its extreme instability, for it is often a transitional stage toward **monolingualism** (the ability to speak only one language) in English. Many children who are bilingual in their homes eventually lose the ability to utilize the home language in favor of the dominant language. In this way they become monolingual, with the ability to function in just one language. Schools have assisted in this process. Prior to World War I, native languages were used in many schools where a large number of ethnic group members were trying to preserve their languages. In the United States, the maintenance and use of native languages other than English now depend on the efforts of members of the language group through churches and other community activities. Now our bilingual education programs are primarily designed to move students quickly into English-only instruction. However, a review of the research suggests that bilingual education in the United States may be far more effective than a strictly monolingual approach. August, Goldenberg, and Rueda (2010) advocate dual-language competency in promoting reading achievement in English. They cite studies suggesting that English learners instructed in two languages demonstrate greater English literacy skills.

Early language policies throughout this country were extremely narrow in focus, failing to take into account the sociocultural problems inherent in language and learning. The acquisition of a second language is important when it serves one's own social and economic needs. Without English language skills, immigrants are often relegated to the menial, lowest-paying, and sometimes most dangerous jobs in society.

People hold different opinions about the degree of fluency required to be considered bilingual. Whereas some maintain that a bilingual individual must have native-like fluency in both languages, others suggest that measured competency in two languages constitutes bilingualism. There are two types of bilingualism: **subtractive bilingualism** and **additive bilingualism**. Subtractive bilingualism occurs when a second language replaces the first. Additive bilingualism is the development of a second language with no detriment to the first (Herrera & Murry, 2011). The latter has the more positive effect on academic achievement, as the learner is able to acquire a high level of proficiency in both languages.

ACCENTS

An **accent** generally refers to the way an individual pronounces words. Because some monolingual Japanese speakers do not have the *l* sound in their language, many tend to pronounce English words that begin with the letter *l* as if they began with the letter *r*. Thus, the word "light" may be pronounced as if it were "right," and "long" as if it were "wrong." An accent differs from the standard language only in pronunciation. Teachers should be aware that persons who speak with an accent often speak Standard English but, at this level of their linguistic development, are unable to speak without an accent.

DIALECTS

In the United States, English is the primary language. Numerous English dialects are used throughout the country, however. There is no agreement on the number of dialects of English spoken in the United States. There are several regional dialects, such as eastern New England, New York City, western Pennsylvania, Middle Atlantic, Appalachian, Southern, Central, Midland, North Central, Southwest, and Northwest. While Southern speech, or drawl, is frequently denigrated in other parts of the country, the South is likely the largest dialect area. More Americans speak variations of a "Southern" dialect than speak any other regional dialect in the United States. Powerful Southern politicians (e.g., Jimmy Carter, Trent Lott, Lindsey Graham) and popular television personalities (e.g., Paula Deen) have increased the exposure and acceptance of Southern speech.

Dialects are language rule systems used by identifiable groups that vary in some manner from a language standard considered ideal. Each dialect shares a common set of grammatical rules with the standard language and should be considered structurally equivalent (Adger et al., 2007). Theoretically, dialects of a language are mutually intelligible to all speakers of the language; however, some dialects enjoy greater social acceptance and prestige.

Certain languages are sometimes improperly referred to as dialects. Examples are African languages labeled as African dialects or the languages of the American Indians as Indian dialects. This improper practice is similar to labeling French and German as dialects spoken in the different regions in Europe.

Regional Dialects.   Dialects differ from one another in a variety of ways. Differences in the pronunciation of vowels are a primary means of distinguishing regional differences, whereas consonant differences tend to distinguish social dialects. Regional and social dialects cannot be divorced from one another, however, because an individual's dialect may be a blend of the two. In northern dialects, for example, the *i* in words such as "time," "pie," and "side" is pronounced with a long-*i* sound, which is a rapid production of two vowel sounds, one sounding like *ah* and the other like *ee*. The second sound glides off the first so that "time" becomes *taem*, "pie" becomes *pae*, and "side" becomes *saed*. Southern and related dialects may eliminate the gliding *e*, resulting in *tam* for "time," *pa* for "pie," and *sad* for "side" (Adger et al., 2007).

Social Dialects.   In social dialects, consonants tend to distinguish one dialect from another. Common examples of consonant pronunciation differences are found in the *th* sound and in the consonants *r* and *l*. In words such as "these," "them," and "those," the beginning *th* sound may be replaced with a *d*, resulting in *dese*, *dem*, and *dose*. In words such as "think," "thank," and "throw," the *th* may be replaced with a *t*, resulting in *tink*, *tank*, and *trow*. Adger and colleagues (2007) suggest that middle-class groups may substitute the *d* for *th* to some extent in casual speech, whereas working-class groups make the substitution more often.

In some groups, particularly the African American working class, the *th* in the middle or at the end of a word is not spoken. The *th* in "author" or "tooth" may be replaced with an *f*, as in *aufor* and *toof*. In words such as "smooth," a *v* may be substituted for the *th*, resulting in *smoov*. In regional and socially related dialects, *r* and *l* may be lost, as in *ca* for "car" and *sef* for "self."

Grammatical Differences.   Among dialects, differences in various aspects of grammatical usage can also be found. Adger and colleagues (2007) suggest that nonstandard grammar tends to carry with it a greater social stigma than nonstandard pronunciation.

A common example of grammatical differences in dialect is the absence of suffixes from verbs where they are usually present in standard dialects. For example, the *-ed* suffix to denote past tense is sometimes omitted, as in "Yesterday we play a long time." Other examples of grammatical differences are the omission of the *s* used in the present tense for agreement with certain subjects. "She have a car" may be used instead of "She has a car." The omission of the suffix has been observed in certain Native Indian communities, as well as among members of the African American working class. In the dialect of some African American working-class groups, the omission of the *s* in the plural form of certain words and phrases, as in "two boy" rather than "two boys," has been observed. "Two" is plural, and adding an *s* to show that "boy" is plural is viewed as redundant. Also often omitted in these dialect groups is the possessive *'s*, as in "my friend car" instead of "my friend's car."

Other Differences. Variations in language patterns among groups are significant when compared by age, socioeconomic status, gender, ethnic group, and geographic region (Adger et al., 2007). For example, individuals in the 40- to 60-year age group tend to use language patterns different from those of teenage groups. Teenagers tend to adopt certain language patterns that are characteristic of their age group. Slang words, particular pronunciations of some words, and certain grammatical contractions are often related to teenage and younger groups.

Social factors play a role in the choice of language patterns. The more formal the situation, the greater the likelihood that more formal speech patterns will be used. The selection of appropriate speech patterns appears to come naturally and spontaneously. Individuals are usually able to "read their environment" and select, from their large repertoire, the language or speech pattern that is appropriate for the situation.

Adger and colleagues (2007) also indicate that although the evidence is not conclusive, the range between high and low pitch used in African American communities is greater than that found in white communities. Such differences are the result of learned behavior. African American males may tend to speak with raspiness in their voices. American women, it has been suggested, may employ a greater pitch distribution over a sentence than do men.

BIDIALECTCALISM

Certain situations, both social and professional, may dictate adjustments in dialect. Some individuals have the ability to speak in two or more dialects, making them **bidialectal**. By possessing the skills to speak in more than one dialect, an individual may have some distinct advantages and may be able to function and gain acceptance in multiple cultural contexts. For example, a large-city executive with a rural farm background may quickly abandon his Armani suit and put on his jeans and boots when visiting his parents' home. When speaking with the hometown friends, he may put aside the Standard English necessary in his business dealings and return to the regional dialect, which validates him as the local town person they have always known.

Likewise, a school psychologist in New Orleans who speaks Standard English both at home and at work may continue to speak Standard English in her conference with working-class parents at the school. However, there may be an inflection or local variation of speech that she uses to develop rapport and credibility with certain parents. At times this may happen spontaneously with no deliberate planning or thought. This may convey to the parents that although she is highly educated and may be dressed professionally, she is still a local person and understands their needs and those of their children.

Children tend to learn adaptive behaviors rapidly, a fact that is often demonstrated in the school. Children who fear peer rejection as a result of speaking Standard English may choose to use their dialect even at the expense of criticism by the teacher. Others may choose to speak with the best Standard English they know in dealing with the teacher but use the dialect or language of the group when outside the classroom.

Educators must be aware of children's need for peer acceptance, and balance this need with realistic educational expectations. Pressuring a child to speak Standard English at all times and punishing him or her for any use of dialect may be detrimental to the overall well-being of the child.

PERSPECTIVES ON STANDARD ENGLISH

There are actually several dialects of Standard American English (Adger et al., 2007). Although Standard English is often referred to in the literature, no single dialect can be identified as such. In reality, however, the speech of a certain group of people in each community tends to be identified as standard. Norms vary with communities, and there are actually two norms: informal standard and formal standard. The language considered proper in a community is the **informal standard**. Its norms tend to vary from community to community. **Formal standard** is the acceptable written language that is typically found in grammar books. Few individuals speak formal Standard English.

As stated earlier, individuals or institutions that enjoy power and status determine what is considered to be standard. Teachers and employers are among those in such a position. These are the individuals who decide what is and what is not considered standard and what is acceptable in the school and in the workplace. Thus, people seeking success in school and in the job market often try to use that which is deemed standard. Generally speaking, Standard American English is a composite of the languages spoken by the educated professional middle class.

PERSPECTIVES ON BLACK ENGLISH

Black English, sometimes referred to as Vernacular Black English, **African American English**, African American Vernacular English (AAVE), or Ebonics, is one of the best-known dialects spoken in the United States. It becomes controversial when schools consider using it for instruction. Its use is widespread, and it is a form of communication for the majority of African Americans. It is a linguistic system used primarily by working-class African Americans within their speech community (Adger et al., 2007).

Although there has been much debate regarding its nature and history, Black English is considered by most linguists and African Americans to be a legitimate system of communication. It is a systematic language rule system of its own and not a substandard, deviant, or improper form of English. Although differences are found between Black English and Standard English, they both operate within a set of structural rules like any other language or dialect. Adger and colleagues (2007) assert that when comparing the linguistic characteristics of Black English and Standard English, we find far more common language features than distinctive ones. They dispute the theory by some linguists that Black English is increasingly evolving in a divergent path from other vernacular English dialects. In fact, there is considerable overlap among Black English, Southern English, and Southern white nonstandard English. Much of the distinctiveness of the dialect is in its intonational patterns, speaking rate, and distinctive lexicons.

Teacher bias against Black English is common among majority-group educators and among some African American educators as well. Although Black English is an ethnically related dialect, it is also a dialect related to social class. Dialects related to lower social classes, such as Appalachian English and Black English, are typically stigmatized in our multidialectal society.

Attitudes Toward Black English

Cesar Plata is the principal of Jackie Robinson Middle School. An appointment has been made with him by Ms. Ruby Norton, the mother of a sixth-grader. She has declined to give Plata's secretary any information about her reasons for wanting to see him. Plata exchanges the customary greeting and then asks Ms. Norton what he can do for her. At this point, she calmly tells Mr. Plata that his teachers need to stop being racist and to start respecting the culture of African American students.

Mr. Plata is feeling defensive and tries to maintain his composure as he inquires about the nature of the complaint. "This white teacher of Trayson says to my son to stop talking this Black English stuff because it is bad English and he won't allow it in his classroom. He says it's a low-class dialect, and if Trayson keeps talking like that, he ain't never going to amount to nothing, will never get into college, and won't never get a good job. That's just plain racist. That's an attack against all black folk. His granddaddy and grandmother talk that way. All my kinfolk talk that way. I talk that way. You mean to tell me that this school thinks we're all low-class trash? Is that what your teachers think of black folk?"

| QUESTIONS FOR CLASSROOM DISCUSSION |

- How should Mr. Plata respond to Ms. Norton?
- Should he arrange a meeting between Ms. Norton and Aaron Goodman, Trayson's teacher?
- What should be the school's position on Ebonics, or Vernacular Black English?
- Is this a school district or an individual school issue?
- Is Mr. Goodman wrong to tell Trayson that his speech is a low-class dialect?
- Is Mr. Goodman wrong to tell Trayson that if he speaks only Black English it will have negative educational and vocational consequences?

Unfortunately, many people attach relative values to certain dialects and to the speakers of those dialects. Assumptions are made regarding the intelligence, ability, and moral character of the speakers, and this can have a significant negative impact (Adger et al., 2007). As a result, the use of these dialects without the ability to speak Standard American English leaves the speaker with a distinct social, educational, and sometimes occupational disadvantage. The refusal to acknowledge Black English as a legitimate form of communication could be considered another example of Eurocentric behavior. Insofar as teachers endorse this rejection, they are sending a message to many of their African American students that the dialect of their parents, grandparents, and significant others in their lives is substandard and unacceptable. The rejection of Black English as a legitimate form of communication is viewed by some educators as detrimental to the academic development and achievement of students.

Requiring only a Standard American English dialect in the schools is both insensitive and controversial. Because of the close relationship between ethnic minority groups and dialects that are often considered nonstandard, this issue may also have civil rights implications.

Some argue that the school has the responsibility to teach each student Standard English to help him or her to better cope with the demands of society. There is little doubt that the inability to speak Standard English can be a decided disadvantage to an individual in certain situations, such as seeking employment.

Many individuals have distinct preconceived notions about non–Standard-English-speaking individuals. If teachers and other school personnel react to students in a manner that is grounded in these preconceptions, the consequences could be serious. Students who are perceived and treated as less intelligent because of their speech may respond as such and become part of a self-fulfilling prophecy, functioning below their ability. In cases where children are tracked in schools, they may be placed in groups below their actual ability level. This problem surfaces in the form of disproportionately low numbers of African American and Latino children being placed in classes for the gifted and talented (Ford, 2010). School administrators cite the inability to appropriately identify these gifted and talented ethnic minority children as one of their biggest challenges. Teachers who harbor negative attitudes toward children with nonstandard dialects may be less prone to recognize potential giftedness and may be less inclined to refer these children for possible assessment and placement.

Educators have several alternatives for handling dialect in the educational setting. The first is to accommodate all dialects on the basis that they are all equal. The second is to insist that only a standard dialect be allowed in the schools. This alternative would allow for the position that functional ability in such a dialect is necessary for success in personal, as well as vocational, pursuits. The third alternative is a position between the two extremes, and it is the alternative most often followed. Native dialects are accepted for certain uses, but Standard English is encouraged and insisted on in other circumstances. Students in such a school setting may be required to read and write in Standard English because this is the primary written language they will encounter in this country. They would not be required to eliminate their natural dialect in speaking. Such a compromise allows students to use two or more dialects in the school. It tends to acknowledge the legitimacy of all dialects while recognizing the social and vocational implications of being able to function using Standard English.

SIGN LANGUAGE

Some languages do not have a written system. Individuals who are deaf are not able to hear the sounds that make up oral languages and have developed their own language for communication. **American Sign Language (ASL)** is a natural language that has been developed and used by persons who are deaf. Just in the past 30-plus years, linguists have come to recognize ASL as a language with complex grammar and well-regulated syntax. A growing number of colleges and universities accept fluency in ASL as meeting a second-language requirement. The majority of adults who are deaf in Canada and the United States use ASL. Individuals who are deaf use it to communicate with each other. Like oral languages, different sign languages have developed in different countries.

Children who are deaf are able to pick up the syntax and rhythms of signing as spontaneously as hearing children pick up their oral languages. Both children who hear and children who are deaf who are born into deaf families are usually exposed to ASL from birth. Many children who are deaf, however, have hearing parents and do not have the opportunity to learn ASL until they attend a school program for the deaf, where they learn from both their teachers and peers.

ASL is the only sign language recognized as a language in its own right, rather than a variation of spoken English. With its own vocabulary, syntax, and grammatical rules, ASL does not correspond completely to spoken or written English (Heward, 2009; Smith & Tyler, 2010). To communicate with the hearing, those who are deaf often use signed English, a system of signing that parallels the English language. Rather than have its own language patterns like ASL, **signed English** is a system that translates the English oral or written word into a sign. When one sees an interpreter on television or at a meeting, it is usually signed English that is being used.

Sign language is one component of the deaf culture that sets its users apart from the hearing world. Because of the residential school experiences of many individuals who are deaf, a distinct cultural community has developed. As a cultural community, they are highly endogamous, with a very high rate of in-group marriages involving individuals who are deaf. Although ASL is the major language of the deaf community, many individuals are bilingual in English and ASL.

Nonverbal Communication

Although most people think of communication as being verbal in nature, nonverbal communication can be just as important in the total communication process. Because it is so clearly interwoven into the overall fabric of verbal communication, nonverbal communication often appears to be inseparable from it.

Nonverbal communication can serve several functions. It conveys messages through one's attitude, personality, manner, and even dress. It augments verbal communication by reinforcing what one says: A smile or a pat on the back reinforces the positive statement made to a student. It contradicts verbal communication: A frown accompanying a positive statement to a student sends a mixed or contradictory message. Nonverbal communication can replace a verbal message: A finger to the lips or a teacher's hand held in the air may communicate "Silence" to a class.

The total meaning of communication includes not only the surface message as stated (content) but also the undercurrent (emotions or feelings associated with that content). The listener should watch for congruence between the verbal message and the message being sent nonverbally.

How we appear to others is a form of nonverbal communication and can, therefore, be considered as a part of our communication or language. Research has supported the contention that definite prejudices are based on physical characteristics. For example, physical attractiveness plays a part in the way we perceive other people. If one has a bias against a particular group (e.g., overweight or short), individuals from that group could be perceived as unattractive and can suffer from social rejection based on the perceptions and bias in the work situation (Huget, 2011). One's skin color, attire, posture, body movements, gestures and facial expression all tend to communicate and send messages to others, much like the spoken word (Samovar et al., 2010).

Cultural differences have profound implications on how individuals interact nonverbally. Some cultural groups are more prone to physical contact than others. Latinos and Native Hawaiians, for example, tend to be among the contact cultures. Consequently, one can often observe Latinos or Hawaiians greeting each other with a warm embrace. This is true among the men from these groups. As they meet their friends, it is certainly not uncommon to see these

There is often as much or more communicated nonverbally as there is verbally.
© Monkey Business Images/Shutterstock

men embracing one another. On the other hand, it might be surprising to see Asian men embracing one another. Of course, the more acculturated Asian American men are likely to observe behaviors typical in the general society.

The distance individuals prefer to maintain between themselves and another person is approximately 2 feet or 0.64 meter (Cloud, 2009). If the distance is much greater than this, individuals may feel too far apart for normal conversation using a normal voice level. Individuals of other cultural groups, such as Arabs, Latin Americans, and Southern Europeans, are accustomed to standing considerably closer when they talk. In contrast with these contact cultures, Asians and Northern Europeans have been identified as noncontact cultures and may maintain a greater distance in conversation. Students maintain differential distances in cross-cultural relationships. White Americans tend to maintain a greater distance when conversing with blacks than when conversing among themselves. Women tend to allow a tighter conversational space than do men. Straight individuals may distance themselves more from conversational partners they perceive to be gay.

Educators need to be aware that different cultural groups have different expectations when it involves contact with a teacher. The differences may have implications for educators. Some groups may view a pat on the head of a child as a supportive gesture. However, some Southeast Asians believe that the individual's spirit resides in the head, and a pat on the head of a child may very well be viewed as offensive by both the parents and the child. Some Asian students may distance themselves in sitting or standing next to a teacher as a sign of deference or esteem (Samovar et al., 2010).

Other nonverbal issues may involve the facial expressions or behaviors of the student. American teachers typically expect a child to look at them while they are having a conversation. However, some groups consider it disrespectful for the child to look directly into the eyes of the teacher. Consequently, as a sign of respect, the child may look at the floor while either speaking to the teacher or being spoken to. The teacher, however, may view the behavior in the opposite manner than intended, and demand that the child look her or him in the eyes.

Some nonverbal gestures can have significantly different meanings across cultures. The thumbs up gesture, which generally conveys a message of "perfect," "good," or "well done" in most Western countries, has essentially the same meaning in Egypt and China. However, when a teacher wanting the parents of immigrant students from Thailand, Iran, or Iraq to know that she approves of a student's performance signals them with a thumbs up from across the room, there can be unpleasant consequences. The thumbs up gesture is considered obscene in those countries.

Any discussion of nonverbal behavior has inherent dangers. As examples are given, you must realize that these are generalizations and not assume that any given behavior will immediately be interpreted in a certain way. Nonverbal communications are often a prominent part of the context in which verbal messages are sent. Although context never has a specific meaning, communication is always dependent on context.

Second Language Acquisition

With the arrival of new immigrants annually into the United States, the result is the addition of more language minority students in our schools. In 1990, 1 in 20 K–12 public school students was an **English language learner (ELL)**. By 2008 the presence of ELL students had increased to 1 in 4. An ELL student is one who does not speak English or whose English limitations preclude the child's ability to fully participate in mainstream English instruction. There were 5,346,673 ELL students in P–12 schools in the United States in 2009 (Swanson, 2009). Table 7.1 shows the growth of ELL programs between 1998 and 2009. Table 7.2 lists the five states with the largest ELL enrollments.

School districts with the largest ELL enrollments in 2006 included Los Angeles Unified (293,711), New York (136,089), and Chicago (66,479). The Los Angeles metropolitan area had an ELL enrollment of 675,000 students, while the New York metropolitan area had 216,000 (Swanson, 2009).

Table 7.1 **Elementary and Secondary Enrollment of ELL Students in the United States, 1998–99 to 2008–09**

School Year	Total Enrollment	Growth Since 1997–98	Total ELL Enrollment	ELL Growth Since 1997–98
1998–99	46,153,266	0.00%	3,540,673	0.0%
1999–2000	47,356,089	2.61%	4,416,580	24.74%
2000–01	47,665,483	3.28%	4,584,947	29.49%
2001–02	48,296,777	4.64%	4,750,920	34.18%
2002–03	49,478,583	7.20%	5,044,361	42.47%
2003–04	49,618,529	7.51%	5,013,539	41.60%
2004–05	48,982,898	6.13%	5,119,561	44.59%
2005–06	49,324,849	6.87%	5,074,572	43.32%
2006–07	49,863,427	7.89%	5,218,800	47.40%
2007–08	49,914,453	7.98%	5,297,935	49.63%
2008–09	49,487,174	7.22%	5,346,673	51.01%

Source: U. S. Department of Education, Office of English Language Acquisition, Language Enhancement, and Academic Achievement for Limited English Proficient Students (OELA), http://www.ncela.gwu.edu/files/uploads/9/growingLEP_0708.pdf.

Table 7.2 States with the Largest ELL Enrollments

	ELL Enrollment	Percentage of U.S. ELL Enrollment
California	1,512,122	28.28%
Texas	713,218	13.34%
Florida	257,776	4.82%
New York	229,260	4.29%
Illinois	208,839	3.91%

Source: National Clearinghouse for English Language Acquisition, http://www.ncela.gwu.edu/faqs/view/4.

ENGLISH LANGUAGE LEARNER CHARACTERISTICS

It is often a surprise to many educators to learn that most of the ELL students are born in the United States, although 80% of their parents are born outside of the country. Coming from 400 different language backgrounds, 70–80% are Spanish speakers, and 12.6% are from Asian and Pacific Island backgrounds. While the most common ELL languages are Spanish, Vietnamese, Chinese, Korean, and French, the most common non-English language varies by state. In Alaska, the most common non-English language is Eskimo-Aleut; in Hawaii, Ilicano (Filipino dialect); in Montana, Navajo; in South Dakota, German; and in Vermont, French (Swanson, 2009; Goldenberg, 2008).

ELL students are often at a socioeconomic disadvantage compared to their non-ELL peers. A disproportionate number live in poverty. Most parents of ELL students have less education than the parents of non-ELL students. Slightly over 40% of the parents of ELL students have not completed high school, as compared to only 9.3% of the parents of non-ELL students. The parents of ELL students, especially those from Mexico and Central America, do not compare favorably with the parents of non-ELL students in other areas of education, employment, and income. Thirty-five percent of ELL students are foreign born, but 48.4% are second-generation Americans, meaning that at least one parent was born in the United States. Seventeen percent are third-generation Americans with both parents born in the United States (Swanson, 2009). Asian language immigrants, the second largest ELL group, do not experience the overall poverty issues that the Spanish speaking groups face. Over 87% of Asian parents have high school diplomas, but there is a high level of diversity within groups, particularly when Southeast Asians are compared to the other Asian groups. Among some of the Cambodian and Laotian immigrants, there is a high level of poverty (Goldenberg, 2008).

Nationwide, one-fourth of ELL students are failing to make progress toward English language proficiency, according to reporting states. Half are making progress or have attained proficiency. The graduation rate for ELL students was 64% as compared to 80.1% of all students in 2006 (Swanson, 2009).

The acquisition of English skills serves both social and economic needs. Motivation is usually high. Without linguistic acculturation, assimilation into mainstream society may be impossible. This, in turn, effectively keeps non-English speakers out of many job markets. In the future educators can anticipate increasing numbers of students whose primary language is other than English.

THE ROLE OF FIRST LANGUAGE IN SECOND LANGUAGE ACQUISITION

Most children acquire their first language naturally through constant interaction with their parents or significant others. Knowledge of their first language plays an important role in the process of acquiring and learning a second language. Some concepts acquired through learning their first language (e.g., Spanish) can be transferred to a second language (e.g., English) when a comparable concept in the second language is encountered. However, English speakers should not think of Spanish, French, Chinese, or any other language as consisting of words that, if translated, basically transform into English. There are words and concepts in all of these languages for which there is no English equivalent. There may be no exact English translation to convey the exact same meaning. For example, "heung" in the Chinese Cantonese dialect is translated into English as "fragrant." However, "heung" has no exact English translation. The Chinese have a very distinctive meaning that conveys not only fragrance but a multisensory experience. When Cantonese speakers say that food that they have placed in their mouths is "heung," it may imply that it tastes, smells, and feels very special.

The failure of schools to build on a child's first language during these early years may have serious consequences in the learning process. The implications of these observed language behaviors suggest that ELL children should be allowed to develop a firm grasp of basic concepts in their home language prior to instruction of academic concepts in an English-only environment. Research demonstrates that when children are provided a strong educational foundation in their native language, they gain both knowledge and literacy, and this powerfully supports English language development (Crawford & Krashen, 2007).

Language Proficiency.   James Cummins (1996), a preeminent researcher in language acquisition, found that many ELL students failed academically after completing English as a second language (ESL) training and being placed in monolingual English class settings. Many of these students were subsequently referred and placed in special education classes. In carefully studying the language characteristics of these students, Cummins found that in two years these students are able to acquire adequate English communication skills to suggest to their teachers that they were prepared to function in a monolingual English class placement. Cummins also found, however, that the basic language skills, which he labeled **"basic interpersonal communicative skills" (BICS)**, are adequate everyday conversational skills, but are inadequate to function in high-level academic situations. An example of BICS is "playground English," which relies on nonlinguistic cues and context and is used to facilitate communication (for example, gestures and other nonverbal cues). BICS, he indicates, is primarily social rather than intellectual. It requires less knowledge of the language, and utilizes simpler syntax and a more limited vocabulary than is needed in academic settings.

Although two years of teaching is adequate for everyday conversational usage, an additional five to seven years of school training is essential to develop the higher levels of proficiency required in highly structured academic situations. Cummins (1984) labeled this higher level of proficiency **"cognitive academic language proficiency" (CALP)**. Professors who were themselves ELL students in their earlier years have shared with the authors their experiences in making professional presentations in foreign countries. For example, a Chinese American professor who was born in China and whose first language is Chinese can carry on fluent conversations in both Mandarin and Cantonese dialects. However, this individual insists on translators for her presentations in China because she does not consider herself proficient in academic Chinese. Other colleagues from non-English-speaking backgrounds have shared similar experiences.

This may have some similarities to BICS-level students who have not yet developed academic-level English competence and are thrust into English-only academic situations. Unfortunately, these students are not in a position to insist on translators.

Cummins's framework for conceptualizing language proficiency has been widely adopted by many ESL and bilingual special education programs and has profound implications for language minorities. Cummins (2000) suggests that there are two reasons it takes much longer for ELL students to learn academic language than it does to learn basic conversational language. First, academic language is the language of technical subject matter (e.g., science, math), literature, journals, and other scholarly materials. It is very different from conversational language.

As students progress through successive grades, they encounter words that Cummins characterizes as "low-frequency" words. These are words with Greek and Latin derivations. In addition, they are exposed to more complex syntax (for example, passive) and abstract expressions that are seldom if ever heard in everyday conversation. Second, academic language is what educators develop among native English speakers who are already fluent in conversational English when they enter school. Therefore, the ELL student is learning conversational English while classmates are at a higher level, learning academic English.

Cummins believes that sociocultural determinants of school failure for these students are more significant than linguistic factors. Schools must counteract the power relations that exist in society, removing the racial and linguistic stigmas of being a minority group child. Cummins suggests that power and status relationships between majority and minority groups influence the school performance of these students. Lower-status groups tend to have lower expectations for academic achievement.

OFFICIAL ENGLISH (ENGLISH ONLY) CONTROVERSY

In 1981 U.S. Senator S. I. Hayakawa, a harsh critic of bilingual education and bilingual voting rights, introduced a constitutional amendment to make English the official language of the United States. The measure sought to prohibit federal and state laws, ordinances, regulations, orders, programs, and policies from requiring the use of other languages. Hayakawa's efforts were made not only in support of English but also against bilingualism. Had the amendment been adopted, Hayakawa's proposal would have reversed the efforts that began in the 1960s to accommodate linguistic minorities in this country. The English Language Amendment died without a hearing in the 97th Congress.

In 1983 Hayakawa helped found the organization U.S. English and began lobbying efforts that resulted in a reported 1.8 million–member organization and an annual budget in the millions of dollars (U.S. English, 2011). This movement, also referred to as **Official English** or **English Only**, supports only the limited use of bilingual education and has mounted a major effort to lobby the U.S. Congress to pass legislation to make English the official language of the United States. As of 2010 English as the official language has been adopted in the form of statutes and state constitutional amendments in 31 states (U.S. English, 2011). The organization favors **sheltered English immersion,** and it maintains its position that ELL students should be transitioned completely out of bilingual education and into mainstream English usage within a maximum of one or two years.

Official English has become a polarizing issue. For supporters of the English Only movement, English has always been the common language in the United States. Supporters of the English Only movement believe that it is a means to resolve conflict in a nation that is diverse in ethnic, linguistic, and religious groups. They also believe that English is an essential tool for social mobility and economic advancement.

Crawford (2007) maintains that attempts to restrict the use of languages other than English are never only about the language. He suggests that it also indicates a negative attitude toward the speakers of other languages.

Differentiating Instruction for All Language Learners

Language is an integral part of life and an integral part of our social system. The diversity and richness of the language systems in this country are a reflection of the richness and diversity of American culture. The ability of U.S. educators to recognize and appreciate the value of different language groups will, to some extent, determine the effectiveness of our educational system.

Projections by the Pew Research Center suggest that the U.S. population will reach 438 million by 2050. Of that number 67 million may be immigrants, including 50 million children and grandchildren. Nearly 20% of U.S. residents will be immigrants, and this means increased numbers of ELL students (Passel & Cohn, 2008).

All children bring to school the language systems of their cultures. It is the obligation of each educator to ensure the right of each child to learn in the language of the home until the child is able to function well enough in English. This may suggest the use of ESL or bilingual programs for ELL children. Research demonstrates that encouraging the development of students' native languages can provide excellent support in helping them to acquire literacy and academic skills in English (August et al., 2010). Equally important, especially for educators, is the responsibility to understand cultural and linguistic differences and to recognize the value of these differences while working toward enhancing the student's linguistic skills in the dominant language. Although it is important to appreciate and respect a child's native language or dialect, it is also important that the teacher communicate the importance and advantages of being able to speak and understand Standard English in certain educational, vocational, and social situations.

LANGUAGE AND EDUCATIONAL ASSESSMENT

Few issues in education are as controversial as the assessment of culturally diverse children. The problem of disproportionate numbers of ethnic minority children in special education classes for children with disabilities have historically resulted from such assessment. The characteristics of language are directly related to the assessment of linguistically different children. One of the dangers of assessment tests is that they measure intelligence by those things that are valued within the dominant group and tend to exclude things that are culturally specific to minority children. Pence and Justice (2008) further caution that some students are misidentified as having language disorders because of tests that were developed for Standard American English monolingual speakers. The introduction of standards-based instruction has resulted in an even more complex assessment process (Faltis, 2006). Refusal to acknowledge the value of linguistic differences has resulted in inadequate services and the inappropriate placement of children through highly questionable assessment procedures.

Historically tests were normed primarily "with" or "on" white middle class children. This means that the values and scores of ethnically and linguistically diverse children were not equitably factored in when standards were determined. Each year millions of standardized tests are administered worldwide. After years of criticism regarding the bias in tests, test developers and publishers have been diligently attempting to create unbiased instruments. However, ethnic and linguistic minority children are just that—a minority, and their numbers in a target audience sample may be smaller. As a result, the test norms may still be biased against them. There is an expectation of cultural and linguistic uniformity in the development of assessment tests (Adger et al., 2007). Therefore, such tests are often considered biased against the student who is not proficient in English or who speaks a nonstandard dialect.

Most intelligence tests rely heavily on language. Yet little attempt may be made to determine a child's level of proficiency in the language or dialect in which a test is administered. For example, a Latino child may be able to perform a task that is called for in an intelligence test, but may not be able to adequately understand the directions given in English. Even if a Spanish translation is available, it might not be in a dialect with which the child is familiar. Using an unfamiliar Spanish dialect may place a student at an extreme disadvantage and may yield test results that are not a true indication of the student's ability. If the psychologist or psychometrist speaks in Castilian Spanish and the student speaks Spanglish, there is a linguistic disconnect, and the student may be at a considerable disadvantage.

The same may be true for Asians, African Americans, and Native Americans being tested. Rather than accurately testing specific knowledge or aptitude, all too often intelligence tests measure a student's competence in standard forms of the language (Adger et al., 2007). It is unlikely that there are any completely unbiased assessment instruments being used to test achievement or intelligence.

Several successful class action lawsuits have been brought against school boards or school districts on behalf of children placed in special education classes on the basis of low scores on IQ tests. Typically the suits argue that biased and inappropriate test instruments were used on language minority students, which resulted in inappropriate special education placement. Among the cases often cited is *Guadalupe Organization, Inc. v. Tempe Elementary School District No. 3, 587 F.2d 1022, 1030 (9th Cir. 1978)*, which was a suit filed in Arizona that resulted from the disproportionately high placement of Yaqui Indian and Mexican American children in classes for students with mental retardation (ID). *Diana v. State Board of Education* was a suit brought on behalf of children of Mexican immigrants placed in classrooms for students with intellectual disabilities on the basis of low IQ scores on tests argued to be discriminatory.

BILINGUAL EDUCATION

The National Association for Bilingual Education defines **bilingual education** as "use of two languages in school—by teachers or students or both—for a variety of social and pedagogical purposes" (National Association for Bilingual Education, n.d.). Bilingual education has been supported, in part, by federal funds provided by the Bilingual Education Act of 1968, reauthorized in 1974, 1978, and 1984. The federal legislation views bilingual education more broadly, allowing and even encouraging instructional methodology other than the use of two languages.

Children who speak little or no English cannot understand English-speaking children or lessons that are presented in English. Not only are these children faced with having to learn new subject matter, but they must also learn a new language and often a new culture. It is likely that many of these children will not be able to keep up with the schoolwork and will drop out of school unless there is appropriate intervention. The school dropout rate for Latino students is disproportionately high. The high school dropout rate for Latino immigrants was 18.3% in 2008, versus 4.8% for whites and 9.9% for African Americans. The dropout rates for Native

American students are also high. Although language differences may not be the sole contributor to the academic problems of these children (poverty has a strong correlation as well), they are considered by many to be a major factor.

Lau v. Nichols. In 1974 a class action suit, *Lau v. Nichols* (1974), on behalf of 1,800 Chinese children was brought before the U.S. Supreme Court. The plaintiffs claimed that the San Francisco Board of Education failed to provide programs designed to meet the linguistic needs of those non-English-speaking children. The failure, they claimed, was in violation of Title VI of the Civil Rights Act of 1964 and the equal protection clause of the Fourteenth Amendment. They argued that if the children could not understand the language used for instruction, they were deprived of an education equal to that of other children and were, in essence, doomed to failure.

The school board defended its policy by stating that the children received the same education afforded other children in the district. The position of the board was that a child's ability to comprehend English when entering school was not the responsibility of the school, but rather the responsibility of the child and the family. In a unanimous decision, the Supreme Court stated, "Under state imposed standards, there was no equality of treatment merely by providing students with the same facilities, textbooks, teachers, and curriculum; for students who do not understand English are effectively foreclosed from any meaningful education" (*Lau v. Nichols*, 1974). The Court did not mandate bilingual education for non-English-speaking or limited-English-speaking students. It did stipulate that special language programs were necessary if schools were to provide an equal educational opportunity for such students. Hence, the *Lau* decision gave considerable impetus to the development of bilingual education as well as ESL programs.

In 1975 the Education for All Handicapped Children Act (amended in 1990 as the Individuals with Disabilities Education Act [IDEA]) required each state to avoid the use of racially or culturally discriminating testing and evaluation procedures in the placement of children with disabilities. It also required that placement tests be administered in the child's native language. In addition, communication with parents regarding such matters as permission to test the child, development of individualized education programs (IEPs), and hearings and appeals must be in the native language. The IEP specifies the programming and services that children with disabilities will receive and requires the participation of the parents in its development.

Throughout the 1970s the federal government and the state courts sought to shape the direction of bilingual education programs and mandate appropriate testing procedures for students with limited English proficiency. The *Lau* remedies were developed by the U.S. Office of Education to help schools implement bilingual education programs. These guidelines prescribed transitional bilingual education and rejected ESL as an appropriate methodology for elementary students. With a change of the federal administration in 1981, a shift to local policy decisions began to ease federal controls. Emphasis was placed on

A million new immigrants enter the United States annually. Many will be students in our schools who will need specialized instruction to help them acquire English skills.
© Anne Vega/Merrill

making the transition from the native language to English as quickly as possible. The methodology for accomplishing the transition became the choice of the local school district. Thus, ESL programs began to operate alongside bilingual programs in many areas. Although the future level of federal involvement in bilingual education is uncertain, there is little doubt among educators that some form of bilingual education is needed.

Transitional Programs.   The primary goal of bilingual education is not to teach English or a second language per se, but to teach children concepts, knowledge, and skills in the language they know best and to reinforce this information through the use of English. Most bilingual education programs today are **transitional programs,** which emphasize bilingual education as a means of moving from the culture and language most commonly used for communication in the home to the mainstream of U.S. language and culture. It is an assimilationist approach in which the ELL student is expected to learn to function effectively in English as soon as possible. The native language of the home is used only to help the student make the transition to the English language. The native language is gradually phased out as the student becomes more proficient in English.

Bilingual educators strongly support the use of bicultural programs even within the transitional framework. A bicultural emphasis provides students with recognition of the value and worth of their families' culture and enhances the development or maintenance of a positive self-image.

Dual-Language Immersion Programs.   Dual-language immersion programs, sometimes referred to as two-way bilingual immersion programs, have grown in the past few years from a few hundred to over 1,000 programs across the United States. California and Texas are the leading states implementing these programs, which involve a type of bilingual education programming. California had 228 programs in 100 school districts in 2008. The Glendale Unified School District in Los Angeles County, for example, offers programs in Italian, German, Spanish, Armenian, Japanese, and Korean (Watanabe, 2011). Instruction in the Glendale programs is, for example, 90% in Italian and 10% in English in kindergarten and first grade. Language usage is 50-50 by the fifth grade. The goals of the dual language program are:

- Bilingualism, oral proficiency in two languages
- Biliteracy, reading and writing in two languages
- Achievement at or above grade level
- Multicultural competencies (Watanabe, 2011)

Dual-language immersion programs include students with an English background and students with one other language background. Ideally, half the class will consist of students whose home language is Japanese, for example. The other half of the students in the class will come from English speaking families. Students are expected to stay in the program throughout elementary school.

While bilingual education has a negative connotation for some, dual-language immersion has become an accepted niche and may not face the attacks from the bilingual education opponents that the other bilingual programs have had to deal with. It has been embraced by some parents, who want these programs to give their children an edge in an increasingly global world. In California, parents must sign waivers of consent prior to placement in two-way language immersion programs in compliance with Proposition 227 mandates. Research suggests that by late elementary school or middle school, students in dual language programs perform at levels comparable to or higher than peers in English-only programs (Watanabe, 2011).

Advocates of bilingual education see the advantages in being bilingual. Although bilingual education programs have been established primarily to develop English skills for ELL students, some offer opportunities for English-speaking students to develop proficiency in other languages. In addition, bilingualism provides an individual with job market advantages. As the United States becomes less parochial, the opportunity for business and other contacts with individuals from other countries increases, providing decided advantages to bilingual individuals. Crawford (2007) reminds critics of bilingual education that the United States has always been linguistically diverse. He further suggests that given that language diversity is common throughout the world, Americans are at a distinct disadvantage if they embrace a monolingual philosophy. In a global economy, the United States clearly stands to benefit from increased proficiency in other languages.

Bilingual education as it currently exists has many problems and many critics. Research has provided evidence that well-developed and well-delivered bilingual education programming can deliver positive results. Critics have also provided ample evidence that some children in bilingual education programs have fared poorly and many have dropped out of school. What should be recognized is that there has been an acute national shortage of qualified bilingual educators. Being bilingual does not necessarily qualify an individual as a bilingual educator. Many who have filled bilingual education positions have not been fully qualified in their preparation and training. When these individuals fail to deliver desired results, bilingual education is often unfairly characterized as being programmatically unsound.

ENGLISH AS A SECOND LANGUAGE

English as a second language (ESL) is a program often confused with bilingual education. In the United States, learning English is an integral part of every bilingual program. But teaching English as a second language in and of itself does not constitute a bilingual program. Both bilingual education and ESL programs promote English proficiency for ELL students. The approach to instruction distinguishes the two programs. Bilingual education accepts and develops native language and culture in the instructional process. Bilingual education may use the native language, as well as English, as the medium of instruction. ESL instruction, however, relies exclusively on English for teaching and learning. ESL programs are used extensively in this country as a primary medium to assimilate ELL children into the linguistic mainstream as quickly as possible. Hence, some educators place less emphasis on the maintenance of home language and culture than on English language acquisition, and they view ESL programs as a viable means for achieving their goals.

In some school districts there may be ELL students from several different language backgrounds, but too few in some groups to warrant a bilingual education class (e.g., Cantonese, Farsi, Russian). In such a situation, an ESL may be the most logical approach to providing appropriate services for these students.

California's Proposition 227. U.S. English members have vigorously supported California's **Proposition 227**, a state ballot initiative that passed in 1998 by a margin of 61% to 39%. This law was intended by its supporters to put an end to bilingual education in the state. This proposition is often referred to as the Unz initiative after its co-author, Ron Unz. Operating under the organization One Nation, Unz and his supporters cite numerous examples of bilingual education failures. The proposition requires all language minority students to be educated in sheltered English immersion programs, not normally intended to exceed one year. Sheltered English immersion or structured English immersion involves a classroom where

English language acquisition is accomplished with nearly all instruction in English, but with the curriculum and presentation designed for children who are learning the language. During this time, ELL students are temporarily sheltered from competing academically with native English-speaking students in mainstream classes. At the completion of the year, the students are transferred to English language mainstream classrooms (Unz & Tuchman, 1998). The law allows parents to seek waivers, and, if granted, the child's education may continue in a bilingual classroom. If schools or teachers fail to implement a child's education as prescribed by the law, they may be sued.

As might be expected, supporters of bilingual education have vigorously attacked the proposition with concern that the Unz initiative will spread to other states. Proposition 227 opponents argue that the Unz initiative was not backed by research or scientific data. Rather, they argue, it was based on observations of the high failure and dropout rates of ELL students, primarily Latino. It was also based on Unz's presumption that most ELL students are able to grasp the fundamentals of speaking English in a year. They support their arguments against the proposition by citing research (e.g., Cummins, 1984) suggesting that only basic conversational skills can be acquired in such a limited time, but not the necessary academic language skills, which take years to develop adequately. Opponents of Proposition 227 contend that the law is a "one size fits all" approach to educating students and that it cannot have lasting benefits. Obtaining waivers is often problematic for parents, especially if their English skills are limited and they have difficulty communicating with school personnel. There are also concerns that the law intimidates teachers and administrators and inhibits them from doing what they know is educationally appropriate for students.

A year after the implementation of Proposition 227, achievement test scores for ELL students in the Oceanside Unified School District, which had faithfully followed the mandates of the Proposition, showed an 11 percentage point increase. The achievement test scores the following year were also positive, providing validation for Proposition 227 supporters.

Subsequent research (e.g., Hakuta, 2001a, 2001b; Hakuta, Butler, & Bousquet, 1999; Orr, Butler, Bousquet, & Hakuta, 2000) found that in the first two academic years of testing (1998–99 and 1999–2000), achievement test scores improved somewhat across the board in the state. Scores rose for ELL students in both English-only classrooms and bilingual education classrooms. These researchers found that some school districts that had maintained various forms of bilingual education experienced similar increases to that of Oceanside Unified District. They strongly suggested that a statistical phenomenon known as **regression to the mean** had been in operation for the Oceanside students. Regression to the mean implies that scores at the extreme ends of the statistical distribution move toward the population average (mean), with low scores moving higher and high scores moving lower. They also point to class size reduction, which had just taken place in California schools, as contributing to the improved scores. While the test scores for ELL students had improved, they were still low.

By 2001 the Oceanside School District's percentile scores for ELL students had evened out and in some instances dropped. That year, ELL third-grade reading scores were one percentage point below the state's ELL percentile score. District-wide, ELL test scores in more than half the schools had declined compared to the previous year, contrary to the rising state ELL test scores.

While data regarding improved educational outcomes as a result of Proposition 227 are inconclusive, it is clear that there is still an achievement gap between English learners and their peers who enter school proficient in English (Wentworth, Pellegrin, Thompson, & Hakuta, 2010).

One result of Proposition 227 is conclusive. Unz's goal to dismantle bilingual education in California was mostly successful. In the 1997–98 academic year, there were 409,897 ELL students enrolled in bilingual education programs in California schools. By the 2005–06 academic-year, the number had dropped to 95,155.

Other Efforts to Dismantle Bilingual Education.

English language learners are often caught in the middle of politics. Both sides of the English Only movement believe strongly that their positions are best for language minority immigrant students. Ron Unz and his supporters continue their efforts to bring what they consider a success in California (both the passage of Proposition 227 and the educational results) to other parts of the country. In 2000 Arizona voted into law Proposition 203. This law required English-only instruction in the public schools. By 2004 enrollment in bilingual programs in Arizona dropped from 32% of ELLs to 5%. Studies since the passage of Proposition 203 indicate that ELLs in Arizona still suffer from an achievement gap (Mahoney, MacSwan, Haladyna, & Garcia, 2010).

In 2002 Massachusetts voted into law Chapter 386, which mandated sheltered English immersion programs as the method of instruction for ELLs. This effectively ended transitional bilingual education in the state. While Massachusetts has not completed a thorough evaluation of the impact of Chapter 386, Mahoney et al. (2010) report that dropout rates for ELLs increased, as did the academic achievement gap.

In November 2002 Colorado voters rejected Ron Unz's anti–bilingual education, English immersion Amendment 31 (Escamilla, Shannon, Carlos, & Garcia, 2003). This was Unz's first defeat in his four statewide efforts to dismantle bilingual education.

Opponents of the English Only movement readily agree on the importance of learning English. However, they view their adversaries as individuals trying to force Anglo conformity by ending essential services in foreign languages. They view the attacks on bilingual education as unjustified because good bilingual education has been shown to be effective. Bad bilingual education, they concede, is ineffective and is seldom bilingual education, except in name. Opponents of bilingual education, they argue, have seen to it that these programs fail by giving inadequate support or resources, by staffing programs with unqualified personnel, by obtaining faulty test results on bilingual education students, by testing all students in English, and by other means that cast a negative light on bilingual education.

PAUSE TO REFLECT 7.3

In spite of research by respected scholars showing its effectiveness when properly implemented, bilingual education has been attacked from many sides, including high-ranking individuals in state and federal government.

- What is the attitude toward bilingual education in your state?

- What lessons can be learned from the results of achievement test scores?

Debate / Curtailing Bilingual Education

With the Supreme Court decision in the *Lau v. Nichols* case in 1974, bilingual education came to the forefront in American education and was given a greater sense of legitimacy. While *Lau v. Nichols* did not mandate bilingual education, it required schools to address the linguistic needs of their students from diverse backgrounds.

Over the past 35-plus years, the road for bilingual education has often been bumpy. Although some researchers continue to affirm its value, others conclude that while not harming students, bilingual education provides no particular advantage (Krashen & McField, 2005). Some critics have attacked it as a colossal failure, and advocate for English immersion classes and the discontinuation of bilingual education. Under the George W. Bush administration, the name of the U.S. Office of Bilingual Education and Minority Language Affairs was renamed as the Office of English Language Acquisition, Language Enhancement, and Academic Achievement for Limited English Proficient Students (OELA).

FOR	AGAINST
■ Opponents of bilingual education advocate sheltered English immersion limited to one year, yet they have no research to back the efficacy of what they propose.	■ Over 400,000 California students began the school year as non–English proficient, prior to Proposition 227, and at the end of the school year, only 5% had learned English.
■ Research by Cummins and Hakuta has clearly shown that ELL students cannot become proficient in English for academic purposes in one year's time.	■ Prior to California's Proposition 227, English language learners studied grammar, reading, writing, and all other academic subjects in their own native languages—almost always in Spanish—while receiving only small amounts of English instruction.
■ The problems with bilingual education are rooted in the lack of qualified personnel trained in bilingual education techniques, the lack of adequate resources, and the lack of commitment at both the federal and state levels.	■ Achievement test scores for immigrant children are low and dropout rates are high.
■ Research has clearly demonstrated that bilingual education, properly implemented, is highly effective.	■ Bilingual education in California, Arizona, and Massachusetts has been reduced to a fraction of what it used to be. The same should happen throughout the United States.

| QUESTIONS |

1. What should programmatic decisions (e.g., on the type of program that should be offered for ELL) be based on?

2. Are the attacks on bilingual education justified?

3. What has the research shown with respect to language acquisition and ELL?

From http://onenation.org/unz101997.html and http://faculty.ucmerced.edu/khakuta/research/publications/(2000)%20-%20HOW%20
LONG%20DOES%20IT%20TAKE%20ENGLISH%20LEARNERS%20TO%20ATTAIN%20PR.pdf.

In spite of their differences, the majority of the individuals who support bilingual education, as well as those who are opposed to it, are well-intentioned individuals who want to enhance the educational opportunities for immigrant children. If all interested parties would be less concerned with the politics of the issue and would base their programmatic preferences on sound, well-documented research, the students would be the ultimate winners.

Summary

As discussed earlier in this chapter, cultural differences in nonverbal communications between students and teachers can be very frustrating to both. To begin to overcome such differences, a teacher must try to analyze particular nonverbal communications when students, especially those from a different cultural background, are not responding as the teacher expects. What the teacher perceives as inattention on the part of the students, interruptions by the students at times considered inappropriate by the teacher, or even a tendency on the part of the students to look away from the teacher while being addressed may, in fact, be due to cultural differences.

In most school settings, students from subordinate groups are expected to become bicultural and adopt the nonverbal communication patterns of the dominant group while in school. A more sensitive approach is for teachers also to learn to function biculturally in the classroom.

Teachers should reflect on what is occurring in the classroom when communications are not as expected. The first step is to become more aware of the nature of the difficulty. In the school setting, students should sometimes have access to teachers, counselors, or administrators who are from a culturally similar background. Teachers can make an effort to learn about the cultural cues of students and to react appropriately. A more effective approach, however, is to analyze what is happening in the classroom and to respond on the basis of what is known about the student and his or her cultural background.

The *Lau* decision of 1974 ensures non-English-speaking children the right to an appropriate education that meets their linguistic needs. Even with a legal mandate, appropriate services may not always be delivered because of lack of tolerance or insensitivity to languages or dialects that are not considered Standard English. Because nonstandard dialects tend to have a negative stigma attached to them, some educators may refuse to view them as legitimate forms of communication. Although they may indeed be legitimate forms of communication and may serve the speaker well in certain contexts, nonstandard English dialects may preclude certain social and vocational opportunities.

Bilingual education has both its supporters and its detractors. Through proper educational programming, however, children with limited English proficiency can receive the education to which they are entitled. Our responsibility as educators is to recognize the linguistic diversity of our nation's students, and to recognize the value of the family's unique cultural and linguistic background. As students become bilingual and bidialectal, they will find themselves in the position of being able to navigate through a greater variety of social, academic, and vocational settings.

Professional Practice

Questions for Discussion

1. How is language a function of culture?
2. What are the advantages of being bilingual in the United States?
3. How is bilingualism encouraged and discouraged within educational settings?
4. What are dialects? What factors generally determine whether an individual becomes bidialectal?
5. Why is Black English a controversial issue in education? How should it be handled in the classroom?
6. Why is it important to be sensitive to nonverbal communications between teacher and student and among students?
7. Why might it be unwise to assume that a student is ready for academic instruction in English as soon as he or she has some basic English conversational skills?
8. What is the relationship between language and educational assessment?
9. Contrast maintenance and transitional bilingual education. Which do you think is more appropriate? Why?
10. When might an ESL approach be the most appropriate strategy to use in a classroom?

Portfolio Activities

1. Survey your students (where you teach, student teach, or are involved in a practicum) to find out how many different languages or dialects they speak. Ask them when and where they feel comfortable speaking a dialect or language other than Standard English. (InTASC Standard 2: Learning Differences)
2. Check with your local school district office and find out how many different language groups are served in the district. (InTASC Standard 2: Learning Differences)
3. Find out what types of programs are used in your district to facilitate English language acquisition by English language learners in the schools. (InTASC Standard 2: Learning Differences)
4. Survey the teachers who have language minority students in their classes and find out what type of programming they favor for their students and why. (InTASC Standard 2: Learning Differences)

Digital Resources for the Classroom

1. For general information on English language learners (ELLs), consult the National Clearinghouse for English Language Acquisition and Language Instruction Educational Programs (NCELA), http://www.ncela.gwu.edu/.

2. The U.S. Office of English Language Acquisition, Language Enhancement, and Academic Achievement for Limited English Proficient Students (OELA) provides additional information on English language learners at http://www2.ed.gov/about/offices/list/oela/index.html.

3. The Center for Applied Linguistics (CAL) http://www.cal.org/, provides general information on linguistics including English language learners, dialects, etc. and provides publications without charge.

4. The National Association for Bilingual Education (NABE) is the largest organization which supports bilingual education: http://www.nabe.org/.

5. U. S. English is a primary force behind anti-bilingual education legislation. Its goal is to make English the official language of the U. S.: http://www.us-english.org/.

MyEducationLab™

Go to the MyEducationLab (www.myeducationlab.com) for Multicultural Education and familiarize yourself with the topical content, which includes:

- Assignments and Activities, tied to learning outcomes for the course, that can help you more deeply understand course content
- Building Teaching Skills and Dispositions learning units allow you to apply and practice your understanding of how to teach equitably in a multicultural education classroom
- Licensure Test Prep activities are available in the Book Resources to help you prepare for test taking
- A pretest with hints and feedback that tests your knowledge of this chapter's content
- Review, practice, and enrichment activities that will enhance your understanding of the chapter content
- A posttest with hints and feedback that allows you to test your knowledge again after having completed the enrichment activities

A Correlation Guide may be downloaded by instructors to show how MyEducationLab content aligns to this book.

Religion

Congress shall make no law respecting an establishment of religion, or prohibiting the free exercise thereof; or abridging the freedom of speech, or of the press; or the right of the people peaceably to assemble, and to petition the Government for a redress of grievances.

First Amendment to the United States Constitution, 1791

| LEARNING OUTCOMES |

As you read this chapter, you should be able to:

- Provide examples of how an educator will find different religious settings in the various regions of the country.

- Discuss and provide examples of how religion is important to a large percentage of Americans.

- Provide some specific examples of how the religious landscape of the United States has been changing in recent years.

- Contribute to a discussion on the basic beliefs and focus of evangelical Christians and how they have influenced the political process in the United States.

- Examine how religious beliefs related to gender roles can have an effect on everyday expectations and attitudes related to women and men in society.

- Characterize the concept of separation of church and state and how it impacts what can and cannot legally take place in American schools.

The teachers and administrators of the Edison Onizuka Middle School near San Francisco had put the finishing touches on their plans for the school's honors convocation. They had selected Ramakrishnan Patel and Rebecca Rose, who were tied with the highest grades in the eighth grade, to be recognized in a convocation ceremony. Each student was asked to make a 7- to 10-minute speech on the value of an education. Because the faculty and Dr. Hovestadt, the principal, wanted the district superintendent to be part of the ceremony, they had agreed to schedule the event at 3:00 p.m. on the fourth Saturday in May, the superintendent's only available time.

Dr. Hovestadt called the Patel and Rose families to inform them of their children's selection as convocation speakers. As expected, both sets of parents were delighted at the news of their son's and their daughter's accomplishments and selection. Mr. Rose indicated, however, that Saturday was quite impossible because it was the Sabbath for their family, who were Orthodox Jews. The Sabbath, a day of religious observance and rest among Jews, is from sundown on Friday until sundown on Saturday. Orthodox Jews are a conservative branch of Judaism who strictly observe religious law. The event had to be rescheduled for any other day but the Sabbath. It was impossible, Dr. Hovestadt pleaded. All the plans were made, and no satisfactory alternative dates were available. "Would you plan the event on a Sunday?" Mr. Rose exclaimed. "I would not ask you to. Then why do you schedule it on our Sabbath? You must change the day." With the two at an impasse, Dr. Hovestadt knew he had to come up with an alternative plan in a hurry.

| REFLECTIONS |

1. Is Mr. Rose being unreasonable?

2. What if the event in question took place in a homogeneous community that was primarily Christian and the Rose family were one of only two Jewish families in the community? In a democracy, does the majority always rule?

3. How would you feel if you were a Christian living in a non-Christian community, and a major event that you were expected to attend was scheduled on Christmas Day?

4. Do the rights of every individual have to be considered?

Religion and Culture

In the early treatment of multicultural education, religion was seldom if ever addressed as one of the prominent microcultures influencing a student's perceptions and behaviors. Religion is likely as important in shaping an individual's persona as gender, class, or ethnicity. The purpose of this chapter is to assist you in understanding how religion can be an important part of the cultural makeup of an individual, rather than to provide a comparative review of all religions. We will briefly examine the larger religious groups within the United States and a few of the smaller ones. It is impossible to address every religious group or sect in a single chapter. Our decision to limit the groups or denominations discussed is not to suggest that some lack importance. All religions and religious groups are important, especially to those who belong to them. We will discuss here some of the most common religious groups educators may see in their schools. Considerable coverage in this edition will be devoted to evangelical Christians because of their current influence on the political process and the efforts of some within the evangelical movement to influence educational systems.

In this edition, as in the previous edition, there will also be a focus on Islam. The events of September 11, 2001, the conflicts in Afghanistan and Iraq, and the growth of Islam in the United States and throughout the world are some of the obvious reasons for our focus on this religion.

RELIGIOUS COMPOSITION OF SCHOOLS

The religious pluralism of the school in which one teaches will be determined, in great part, by the school's geographic region of the United States. Immigration and migration patterns result in different ethnic and religious groups settling in different parts of the country. The perspectives of the religious community often influence what parents expect from the school. If the religious values of the parents are incongruous with the objectives of a school, serious challenges for educators are likely. A look at the religious composition of schools in various sections of the country will provide a sense of the diversity to be found in our schools.

As one visits various schools across the United States, distinctive patterns are apparent. In some regions, schools are greatly influenced by religious groups in the community. In these communities, the members of the school board, the appointment of the school administrative leadership, and the curriculum may be shaped by the dominant religious groups. In other regions, religion may have little if any influence on the nature of the schools.

- A rural high school in the South may be comprised primarily by students from conservative Protestant backgrounds such as Southern Baptist and the Church of Christ. Some students may be members of United Methodist or other less conservative churches. In such a district, local churches serve as the primary social institution for many of the students. The curriculum and textbooks may be carefully scrutinized by the school board for what it considers objectionable subject matter, such as sex education, evolution, and alternative lifestyles.
- In Ohio, Indiana, Pennsylvania, Iowa, or Ontario, Canada, a visitor may find some students from Amish or Mennonite families. The Amish students can be identified by their distinctive attire, and the students from Mennonite groups also dress conservatively. The Amish students remain in school until they complete the eighth grade. In accordance with their beliefs, they will then leave school and work on their family farm, which uses neither electricity nor motorized equipment. Most Mennonite students will complete school, and some will go on to higher education and face no prohibitions against the use of electricity or motorized vehicles.

- In Utah and some communities in Idaho, a visitor to the public schools may find that most of the students are members of the Church of Jesus Christ of Latter Day Saints (LDS), also known as Mormons. Religion cannot be and is not taught in the public schools, but church values may still be reflected in everyday school activities. In many of the predominantly LDS communities, students in secondary schools are given release time from their schools to attend seminaries, which are adjacent or in close proximity to their public schools. The seminaries provide religious training by instructors employed by the LDS church. Upon completion of high school, many of the male students and a few of the female students will serve for two years on church missions.

- In another U.S. community one encounters a wide range of religious backgrounds. Some students are Roman Catholic, some are Baptists, some are Jewish, while others are Muslim, Hindu, and Buddhist. A few are atheists and some are agnostics. The atheists believe that there is no God, while the agnostics argue that we do not and cannot know whether in fact God or gods exist. While religion may be important to some of the students and their families, it does not heavily influence the curriculum or daily life in the schools in this community.

These examples suggest that communities in the United States, Canada, and some other countries are religiously very diverse and that the religious makeup of some communities may be influential in the overall culture of the schools.

Like other institutions in the United States, most schools have a historical legacy of white Protestant domination. Such influence has determined the holidays, usually Christian holidays such as Christmas, celebrated by most public schools. Moreover, the dominant Protestant groups have determined many of the moral teachings that have been integrated into the public schools.

The First Amendment and the Separation of Church and State

The First Amendment clearly states that Congress is prohibited from making laws establishing a religion or prohibiting religious worship. This has been consistently interpreted by the courts as affirming the principle of separation of church and state. One of the most valued parts of our Constitution, this provision is also one of the most controversial. Throughout the history of this country, various individuals and groups have tended to interpret this amendment to meet their own needs and interests. For some, religious emphasis is appropriate in the public schools as long as it is congruent with their own religious persuasion. These same people, however, may be quick to cite the constitutional safeguards for separation of church and state if other groups attempt to infuse their religious dogmas. Equity and propriety are often in the eye of the beholder, and one's religious orientation may strongly influence one's perception of what constitutes objectivity, fairness, and legality.

Since the removal of prayer from the schools by a 1963 Supreme Court decision, parent groups have continued to fight to restore prayer in the schools through state and federal legislation. Parent groups have also fought on religious grounds to prevent the teaching of sex education and evolution. Parents from different religious backgrounds have fought verbally and even physically over what books their children should read in literature courses and what curriculum should be used in social studies and science classes. Members of more liberal Protestant, Catholic, and Jewish denominations often argue that they want their children exposed to the perspectives of different religious and ethnic groups. Members of the more conservative groups may argue that they do not want their children exposed to what they consider the immoral perspectives and language inherent in such instructional materials. They object to **secular humanism** in the curriculum, which they believe emphasizes respect for human beings and de-emphasizes the role God.

Community resistance to cultural pluralism and multicultural education has, at times, been led by individuals associated with conservative religious groups. Because cultural pluralism inevitably involves religious diversity, multicultural education is sometimes viewed as an impediment to efforts to maintain the status quo or to return to the religious values of the past. In fact, some of those who object to multicultural education see it as a bedfellow of the secular humanist movement and other movements that detract from basic moral values. Multicultural education, however, provides a basis for understanding and appreciating diversity and minimizes the problems related to people being different from one another.

Of all the microcultures examined in this book, religion may be the most problematic for educators. If the educator is from a religious background that is different from that prevalent in the community or has a perspective about the role of religion that differs from that of the community, misunderstanding and conflicts may arise that prevent effective instruction. If an educator does not understand or ignores the role of religion in the lives of students, it may be difficult to develop appropriate instructional strategies, or even retain one's job.

This chapter examines religion's impact on a student's life, some of the prevalent religions in the United States, and the educational implications of religion.

Religion as a Way of Life

Many religions are particularistic, in that members believe that their own religion is uniquely true and legitimate and all others are invalid. Other religious groups accept the validity of distinct religions that have grown out of different historical experiences.

THE IMPORTANCE OF RELIGION IN OUR LIVES

In the United States, 84% of the population claim to have a preference for some religious group and about 42% of adults attend a church or synagogue in an average week, as shown in Figure 8.1. Sixty-three percent of Americans reported membership in a church or synagogue, while 36% reported no such membership.

Down from a high of 67% in 1999, 58% of Americans in 2010 indicated they believed that religion could solve all or most of today's problems (Gallup, 2010). Religiosity, the degree to which one is religious, appears to be a function of culture. Age, gender, geographical background, and political affiliation influence the religious nature of a person, as we will find in other sections of this chapter.

Religion is clearly an important aspect of the lives of many people. As shown in Figure 8.2, 54% indicate that religion is very important in their lives (Gallup, 2010). Although it may have little impact on the lives of some, it influences the way many other people think, perceive, and behave. The forces of religious groups are far from quiescent. They can influence the election of school board members as well as the curriculum and textbooks used in schools. Principals, teachers, and superintendents have been hired and fired through the influence of religious groups.

While the United States may be a religious nation, it is not among those considered the most religious. Six countries report 99% or more of their residents indicate that their religion is important in their daily lives. These six countries—Bangladesh, Niger, Yemen, Indonesia, Malawi, and Sri Lanka—are considered among the world's poorest. The United States ranks in

Figure 8.1 Weekly or Near Weekly Attendance at U.S. Churches and Synagogues.

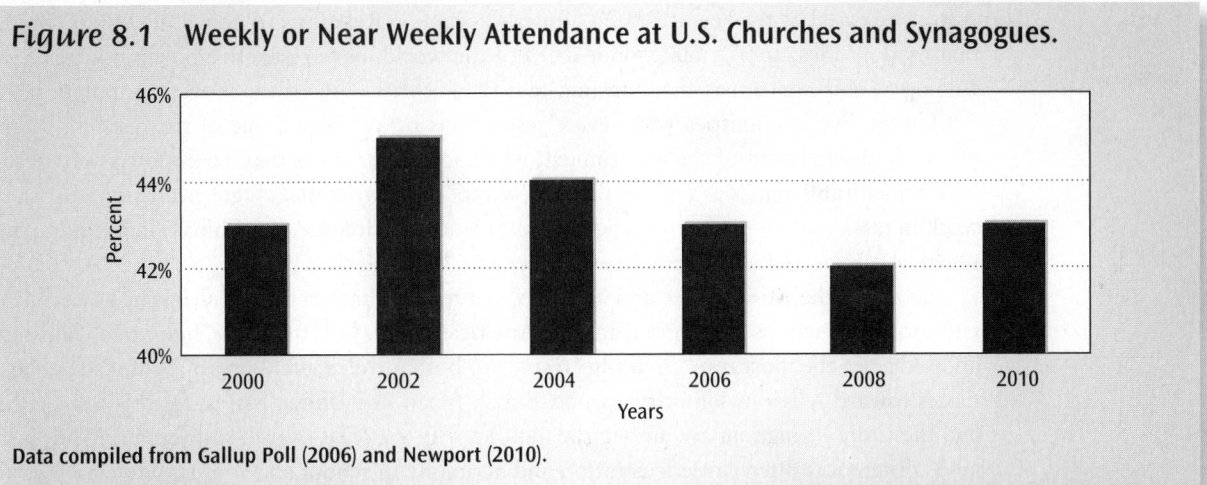

Data compiled from Gallup Poll (2006) and Newport (2010).

Figure 8.2 Americans Indicating Religion as Very Important in Their Lives.

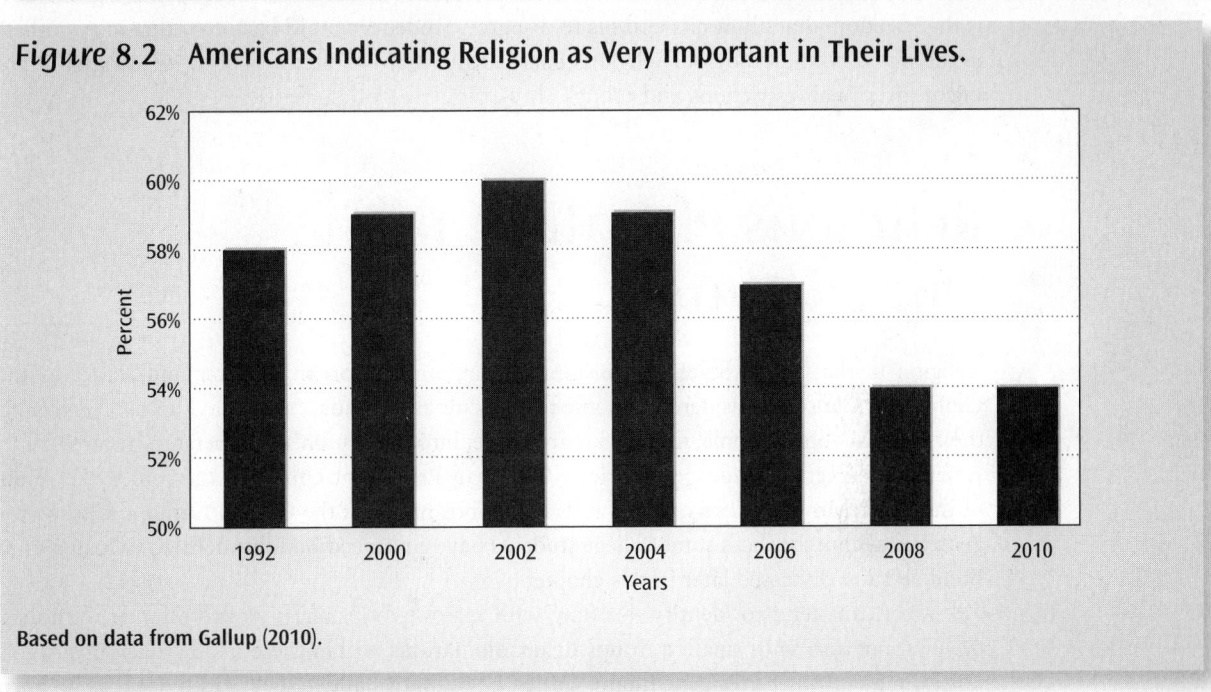

Based on data from Gallup (2010).

the middle of the bottom half of the nations surveyed, with 81% of Americans claiming that their religious beliefs are very important or fairly important to them in their daily lives. Some of the countries ranking at the bottom include the United Kingdom, Japan, Denmark, and Sweden, which are among the world's wealthiest (Crabtree, 2010). These findings may suggest that the families of children who live in poverty find comfort and support in religion, while families who are from more affluent backgrounds may be less inclined to turn to religion in their daily lives. This could have implications for the students educators work with in their schools.

FREEDOM OF RELIGIOUS EXPRESSION

As countries such as the United States and Canada pride themselves in the fundamental rights of religious freedom for all of their citizens, individuals in other countries are not as fortunate.

A study released by the Pew Research Center's Forum on Religion & Public Life (2009a) found that 64 countries, approximately one-third of the world, have restrictive policies on religion. Adding to this concern is the alarming fact that nearly 70% of the world's population, or 6.8 billion, live in countries with severe restrictions on religion. Some of the restrictions are primarily the function of the government, while social hostilities may be imposed on citizens with unfavorable religious ties. At times, Pew reports, restrictions by government and society work in tandem. Government restrictions on religion predominate in China and Vietnam, but social hostilities toward religious groups there are low or moderate.

Globally, the Middle East and North Africa tend to have the most stringent government and social restrictions on religion, and the Americas the least. Iran, Egypt, Indonesia, Pakistan, and India are the most restrictive with respect to both governmental pressures and social hostilities toward religious minority groups. Brazil, Japan, the United States, Italy, South Africa, and the United Kingdom are among the nations with the least overall restrictions. While religious differences often cause frustration and acrimony in school and society, one who lives in a country such as the United States often takes freedom of religious expression for granted. It is that freedom that allows its citizens to disagree. Students should be taught that many others in the world do not enjoy our religious liberties and that we ourselves need to be vigilant that unconstitutional restrictions and rulings are not imposed on our citizenry.

Religious Pluralism in the United States

Religion in the United States is constantly changing. A Korean minister and leader of the **Unification Church** (considered by some to be a cult and an adaptation of Christianity) has led thousands of young people, many who are white, into his church's membership. Some African Americans have left traditional African American Protestant churches and joined the ranks of the Black Muslims. Tens of thousands of Latinos have left the Roman Catholic Church for Pentecostal churches, and some college students have embraced Buddhism. (Black Muslims and Buddhism are discussed later in this chapter.)

Americans tend to identify not only with major groups, such as Protestants, Catholics, or Jews, but also with smaller groups or denominations within these major religious groups. For example, former President Jimmy Carter, a Southern Baptist, identifies himself as a **"born again"** Christian. Others may identify themselves as charismatic Catholics. Within each major group is considerable heterogeneity.

Religious demographic data are often problematic. The U.S. Census Bureau does not gather information on religious membership or preferences. However, it is important to note that most denominations have remained in their traditional regional strongholds, with Catholics in the Northeast, liberal and moderate Protestants in the Northeast and Midwest, and conservative Protestants in the South. Some groups, however, have expanded their base considerably. For example, Episcopalians, Presbyterians, and members of the United Church of Christ are no longer as concentrated in the Northeast as they once were; some numerical base shifts have been made into the Sun Belt, primarily the southern and southwestern regions. Conservative Protestants, such as the Southern Baptists, are growing in all regions, including the Northeast and the West. Mormons have extended their influence far beyond the borders of Utah, Idaho, and Nevada.

Their presence is felt in every state, as well as in many other countries. The Jewish population tends to be located in metropolitan areas throughout the country, with large concentrations in the mid-Atlantic region.

The data that are available are often self-reported by each religious group, and are sometimes of questionable accuracy, but some figures are listed in Table 8.1. The groups that do report do not always do so regularly. Of the U.S. population, 72% identify themselves as belonging to Protestant, Catholic, Orthodox, or Jewish churches or synagogues (Gallup, 2010). Until early in the twentieth century, however, Protestantism was by far the dominant religious force in the country. As of 2010 Protestants are the largest religious group in the United States, with 47% of the population; 22% of the population identify themselves as Catholic, 2% as Jewish, 1% as Orthodox, 13% as having no religious affiliation (Gallup, 2010), and 0.6% as Muslim (Kosmin & Keysar, 2009). The numerical estimates of Muslims living in the United States vary considerably, from around 1,349,000 (Kosmin & Keysar, 2009) to as many as 7 million, with Islamic organizations providing the higher estimates. Islam, in recent years, has grown rapidly in the United States, more than doubling in adherents since 1990. Although Judaism has decreased numerically and as a percentage of the U.S. population, it is still routinely listed as one of the three major religious groups. This may be due to the fact that Judaism has been a driving force for such a long period of U.S. history, and because Jewish individuals have provided so much leadership in the cultural, economic, and political landscape of the country.

Some denominational differences have their origins in ethnic differences. The English established the Anglican (Episcopalian) and Puritan (later Congregational) churches here; the Germans established some of the Lutheran, Anabaptist, and Evangelical churches; the Dutch, the Reformed churches; the Spanish, French, Italians, Poles, and others, the Roman Catholic churches; and the Ukrainians, Armenians, Greeks, and others, the Eastern Orthodox churches. Over time, many of these separate ethnic denominations have united or expanded their membership to include other ethnic groups.

Although religious pluralism has fostered the rapid accommodation of many American religious movements toward acceptability and respectability within society, groups such as Jehovah's Witnesses have maintained their independence. The smaller groups that maintain their distinctiveness have historically been victims of harassment by members of mainstream religious groups. Christian Scientists, Jehovah's Witnesses, Children of God, and the Unification Church are minority groups that have been subjected to such treatment.

Conflict among the four major faiths (Protestantism, Catholicism, Judaism, and Islam) has also been intense at different periods in history. Anti-Semitic, anti-Muslim, and anti-Catholic sentiments are still perpetuated in some households and institutions. Although religious pluralism in our past has often led to conflict, the hope of the future is

Table 8.1 Religious Identification in the United States

Christian	72%
Protestant	47%
Catholic	22%
Mormon	2%
Orthodox	1%
Jewish	1.2–2.0%
Atheist or agnostic	1%
Buddhist	0.07%
Muslim	0.06%
Hindu	0.04%
No affiliation	13%

Data compiled from the Pew Forum on Religion and Public Life— Religious Landscape Survey (2008) and Gallup (2010).

that it will lead to a better understanding and respect for religious differences. In the following sections, we examine in greater detail four major faiths and a few others that the educator may find in various U.S. schools.

A CHANGING RELIGIOUS LANDSCAPE

While the United States has remained primarily a Christian nation, with strong Protestant influence, the country has seen slow but steady changes in the last few decades. The American Religious Identification Survey (Kosmin & Keysar, 2009) revealed some interesting trends that may be alarming to some religious groups.

Between 1990 and 2008, there were significant changes in how Americans identified themselves religiously. The percentage of individuals who identified as Christians declined by approximately 10%; those who identified as non-Christians increased by slightly more than a half a percentage point, to 3.9%; and those identifying as atheist or agnostic almost doubled, reaching 15%.

Nearly all Protestant denominations declined in membership. The greatest declines were found among churches referred to as Mainline Protestant: Methodist, Lutheran, Presbyterian, Episcopalian, and United Church of Christ. However, some of these declines were countered with slight increases among those identified as nondenominational Christians.

Mormon percentages held steady; Jewish percentages declined; Muslim percentages remained relatively low, but doubled; and Asian or Eastern religions also remained low but doubled during the 1990 to 2008 period.

The survey findings suggest that Americans are possibly becoming less religious, with nearly twice as many (almost 20%) choosing no religious identification in 2008 compared with 1990. While the decline in identification may or may not reflect a decline in spirituality among Americans, it is nevertheless of concern to religious conservatives and fuels their call for the infusion of religious values into the schools (Kosmin & Keysar, 2009).

The Pew Religious Landscape Survey (2008) also found some revealing information regarding the religious characteristics of the U.S. population. A majority (62%) of Americans over the age of 70 were Protestant, while a minority (43%) of young adults between the ages of 18 and 29 belonged to Protestant congregations. In addition, a larger portion of the younger group (25%) indicated no religious affiliation as compared to just 8% of the older Americans. While religious preferences may change as individuals age, these statistics provide us with a glimpse of what the future may hold for religion in the United States.

The Pew survey also found that the Protestant and Jewish populations are older than most other religious groups, which could potentially result in further percentage declines. Mormon and Muslim families are often larger than those of many other religious groups, which could contribute to their relative growth.

Another finding from the Pew survey may be surprising to some. A wide majority of Mainline Protestants (moderate to liberal), Catholics, and Jews along with a slight majority of Muslims believe that salvation or eternal life can be attained through religions other than their own.

THE END OF CHRISTIAN AMERICA?

In April 2009 the feature article in *Newsweek* was entitled "The End of Christian America." The findings of the American Religious Identification Survey (Kosmin & Keysar, 2009) sent shockwaves across the country's religious communities. The declines in religiosity in the Northeast, considered the foundation or the home base of American religion, are seen as especially troubling to some (Meacham, 2009). The increasing numbers of individuals identifying themselves as **"unchurched"** may or may not be a function of these individuals turning away from religion. Some may choose not to identify a church membership as a backlash to what they perceive as the increasingly conservative views of their former churches. Some of these individuals may continue to maintain their spirituality in their own ways independent of an organized religious body. However, the number of individuals who describe themselves as atheists or agnostics has increased from 1 million in 1990 to 3.6 million in 2009.

The term "post-Christian" is being used by some to describe the possible demise of Christian America. With a drop of 10% in individuals self-identifying as Christian in the past two decades and with more than two-thirds of the population (68%) believing that religion is losing influence in American society, this has been a wake-up call for religious conservatives. Some conservatives feel that they are losing the battle over issues related to school prayer, abortion, and same-sex marriage. They are fearful of what they perceive as non- Christian religious influences brought into the country by immigrants. Concerned that the country may be moving toward a Europe-like secular state, they seek to return the country to their vision of a Christian America (Meacham, 2009).

As contemporary Christianity evolves in U.S. society, there is an apparent dichotomy between the conservative Christian community and the liberal/moderate Christians and non-Christians. Some conservatives choose to home-school their children to shelter them from what they view as objectionable elements in society. They may tend to avoid those who do not share their conservative values. Even some who have conservative religious values have expressed their concern about the actions of other conservatives who they feel are not conservative enough. Kinnaman and Lyons (n.d.) write critically about contemporary Christianity from within the faith. Kinnaman, president of the Barna group (a Christian research organization), provided the research data for their article. Lyons is the founder of Q, another Christian organization. They suggest that contemporary Christianity has an image problem, plagued by a variety of unflattering perceptions.

The research found that many outside the faith feel that today's Christians are un-Christian, or un-Christ-like, in their behavior and have little esteem for the Christian lifestyle. One-fourth of them believe that the Christian faith has changed for the worse. Their perceptions of contemporary Christianity are as follows:

Perception	Outsiders Ages 16–29
Anti-homosexual	91%
Judgmental	87%
Hypocritical	85%
Sheltered (old-fashioned, out of touch with reality)	78%
Too political	75%
Proselytizers (insensitive to others, not genuine)	70%

These findings have implications for both educators and students. Educators who share conservative values, even if in keeping with majority community values, are professionally obligated to respect the religious values of all of their students, even when they have personal concerns regarding their students' religious or spiritual life. Educators also need to be vigilant for students who demonstrate religious intolerance toward others. Some religious groups emphasize the importance of proselytizing to win non-believers to their faith. Although it is their right to hold these beliefs, it is not their right to impose them on others in the public school setting.

PROTESTANTISM

The Western Europeans who immigrated to this country in large numbers brought with them their various forms of Protestantism. While claiming 47% of the population (Gallup, 2010), Protestants in the United States no longer constitute the dominant numerical majority as in previous decades, but continue to influence society and institutions.

To illuminate the differences within Protestantism, which are often reflected in the classroom, the faith may be divided into two broad categories—liberal and conservative. **Liberal Protestants** (sometimes referred to as Mainline Protestants) stress the right of individuals to determine for themselves what is true in religion. They believe in the authority of Christian experience and religious life rather than the dogmatic church pronouncements and interpretations of the Bible. They are likely to support and participate in social action programs because of their belief that what individuals become depends greatly on an environment over which they have little control. They may or may not believe in the virgin birth of Jesus, and they may not share their conservative counterparts' belief in the inerrancy of the Bible. Some may not accept the miracles cited in the Bible as factual. The United Church of Christ and Episcopalian churches are examples, although the degree of liberalism depends on the individual congregation. Methodists and Disciples of Christ represent more moderate denominations within this category.

Conservative Protestants generally believe that the Bible is inerrant, that the supernatural is distinct from the natural, that salvation is essential, and that Jesus will return in bodily form during the Second Coming. They emphasize personal morality rather than social ethics. Southern Baptists are the largest group in this category.

Effect of Protestantism on Education. Protestants have a long history of involvement in both public and private educational programs. Differences in beliefs among Protestants have resulted in many court cases to determine what can or cannot be taught to or asked of students in the public schools. In addition to efforts by some **fundamentalist Christians** to institute the teaching of creationism, there has been other litigation. Jehovah's Witnesses have had confrontations with schools because some of their children have refused to salute the flag. The Amish have fought in courts to remove their children from public schools after they have completed the eighth grade. Some religious groups continue to fight against the 1963 Supreme Court decision that disallowed prayer in school.

Ten Connecticut clergymen founded Yale, the nation's third oldest university, in 1701. Now considered as a nonsectarian institution, Yale still maintains some religious influence with its prestigious Yale Divinity School. Baylor University (Southern Baptist), Southern Methodist University (United Methodist), Goshen College (Mennonite), and Centre College (Presbyterian) are a few examples of the hundreds of Protestant institutions of higher education in the United States that have educated and influenced the lives of millions of American and international students.

Evangelicals. Evangelical Christians are a key component because of their influential presence in U.S. society and their frequent efforts to influence education in U.S. schools. Evangelical Christianity is not new. Evangelicals have been part of the religious landscape of the United States since the mid 1700s. Billy Graham and his ministry is one of the best known-examples of contemporary evangelical Christianity. Evangelicals are conservative Christians, primarily Protestants, who insist on the necessity of a conversion or "born again" experience, acceptance of the authority of the Bible, and of the birth, miracles, and resurrection of Jesus as supernatural events (Hemeyer, 2010; Corrigan & Hudson, 2010). Estimates suggest that between 34% (Kosman & Keysar, 2009) and 40% (Gallup, 2010) of the U.S population identify themselves as evangelicals. If these percentages are accurate, approximately 120 million Americans could be considered evangelicals.

By the end of the 1970s some of the Mainline Protestant denominations were seeing declining memberships due in part to the loss of older members, the inability to attract comparable numbers of young members, and the leadership of these groups possibly moving toward the moderate left politically and toward theologies viewed as ethically centered. Some of these mainline churches did not embrace the evangelical movement, which may have contributed to their difficulty in maintaining their congregations.

The evangelical movement may have been the beneficiary of the membership declines of the mainline churches. In recent years, there has been phenomenal growth in evangelical churches. Some have become mega-churches, with weekly attendance of 2,000 or more, and with some exceeding 10,000 or 20,000.

Evangelicals strongly support the nuclear family and place great emphasis on individual morality and responsible personal behavior. Pro-choice policies are in direct conflict with their beliefs. Marsden (2006) states that by the early 1980s, opposition to abortion had become the centerpiece of the Catholic-Protestant alliance for militants. Hundreds if not thousands of crisis pregnancy centers have opened throughout the country. Often they open next to planned-parenthood centers or are even located in the same building to counter the work of the pro-choice advocates.

Homosexuality goes against the values of the evangelicals, who strongly believe that one can overcome what they believe is a sin by being converted and by abstaining and even changing their behavior with the help of God and the religious community. Evangelicals strongly believe that humanity was established in God's image and see the heterosexual relationship as God's model. Both abortion and gay rights are contrary to what evangelicals believe is God's intention for humanity (Corrigan & Hudson, 2010).

Evangelicals cast a broad umbrella, forming a very diverse group of individuals who often have different beliefs and agendas. In recent years there has been an increasing division between conservative or fundamentalist evangelicals and their moderate counterparts. Some moderate evangelicals have taken a more conciliatory approach to gays and lesbians. While continuing their opposition to homosexuality, the teaching of evolution, and the pro-choice agenda, many of the moderate evangelicals have expressed compassion and less actively attacked these issues than the more conservative groups. Some moderates, tiring of the divisive politics of religion, are embracing a wider-ranging agenda, with an emphasis on reaching out to the poor and disenfranchised, and focusing on other social and human rights issues. While these evangelical moderates tend to lean more toward the middle both politically and religiously than their fundamentalist evangelical counterparts, they are typically far more conservative than most mainline Protestants.

Marsden (2006) contends that fundamentalists are militant evangelicals who are waging battles on two fronts. They are struggling against the theological modernism in mainline denominations. Fundamentalists are also fighting against what they view as alarming changes in culture, involving issues such as gender, sexuality, and the family. They are distressed over changing sexual standards, the ordination of women, birth control, divorce rates, the decline in family authority, the ban on prayer in schools, and the teaching of biological evolution. Marsden also notes that while fundamentalists typically believe that church leaders and public spokespeople should be male, women in the fundamentalist movement defend their subordinate roles and exercise considerable influence in the movement.

With evangelicals assuming a major role, religion has become even more central to many local and national elections and has in some instances helped shape public policies. Joining with conservatives from Jewish and Catholic groups, they have been influential in the outcomes of some presidential elections (e.g., George W. Bush) as well as the 1994 and 2010 midterm elections. In addition, they have had an impact on state and local elections, direct and indirect influences on the composition of school boards, and a say in judicial appointments. Their support in electing conservative Presidents has resulted in the appointment of conservative federal justices, whose interpretation of the law will have a lasting effect for decades to come.

Evangelicals and Education.

Evangelical Christians also have differing views on education. Some of the more conservative evangelicals prefer to send their children to private Christian schools, while others prefer to home-school their children. Some believe it is their responsibility to take over the schools and to infuse the curriculum with a Christian orientation.

Fundamentalist evangelicals are distressed by what they view as the negative influence of secular humanism. They are concerned about the hiring of homosexual and lesbian teachers, and also with the modern curriculum, which they view as harmful to America's children because it lacks a Christian influence.

School prayer remains an important issue among many of the evangelicals. Tuition tax credits are another issue that is often raised, especially among those individuals who have removed their children from the public schools in favor of private Christian schools. These issues are addressed later in this chapter.

The majority of evangelical parents and other concerned citizens see their role in relation to the schools as just being there to offer support and providing a positive influence by their behaviors. Many do not criticize the public schools but focus on the failings of the family in not meeting the responsibility of instilling morality and values. Some do support the schools instilling a common core of values and morality, a policy most in the country would support. They want the schools to focus on basic academics—reading, writing, and mathematics—rather than social concerns (e.g., poverty, human rights violations, gender equity, ethnic studies). They are concerned with what they view as unfair discrimination against religious studies in the schools such as creation science or intelligent design.

Today a significant number of Americans continue to reject Charles Darwin's view of evolution. Newport (2006) found that 46% of Americans surveyed believe that God created humans about 6,000 years ago in essentially their current form. This finding should give educators a clear understanding of why the teaching of evolution has often come under attack in the schools and why some parents insist that other theories of the origins of man be provided in the schools.

Evangelicals are firmly behind the movement to either rid the schools of evolution in the curriculum or to establish alternative theories. The most often cited alternative theory is **creation science**. Creation science accepts the creation of all living things in six days, literally as presented in the Bible (Corrigan & Hudson, 2010; Hemeyer, 2010). As might be expected, opponents of creation science suggest that it is not a science, but a theory based on a story told in the Bible.

A third theory has been proposed: **intelligent design**. Supporters of intelligent design suggest that only an intelligent being could have created a natural world that is so complex and so well ordered. Some scientists and evolutionists suggest that intelligent design is creationism veiled in a relatively new term (Corrigan & Hudson, 2010; Carlson, 2005). It is important for educators to understand that supporters on both sides of the issue are often passionate in their beliefs and opinions.

Evangelicals may not be a numerical majority in the United States, but they are an influential force in our society. Their efforts affect politics, our judicial system, our legal system, and our schools. Those who disagree with their beliefs, their practices, and their efforts to bring change to the country may resent them. Whether educators agree or disagree with their views and practices, it may be helpful to understand that what evangelicals ultimately want for the country is no different from what other religious persuasions seek. They envision a safer, more moral America, one free of the drugs, crime, and violence that now plague our schools and our streets. While some educators may not share the values of the evangelicals or agree with how they intend to accomplish their goals, it may be helpful to understand who they are and what they seek to achieve. This can help you in being respectful of their values and may minimize the likelihood of conflict over curriculum and student assignments.

Political Influence of Protestants and Other Religious Groups. The political leadership in the country often reflects the influence of various religious groups. In 2011, as in the past, Protestants led in representation in Congress with 56.65%, as compared to the 51.3% of the general population who indicated they were Protestants that year. **Roman Catholics** followed with 29.2%, which is higher than the Gallup finding of 23.9% for the general population. Jewish congressional members made up 7.3% of the House and Senate seats, which is considerably higher than their 1.2% to 1.7% proportion of the general population. The Mormon presence in Congress was 2.8%, also higher than their 1.7% presence in the overall population (Pew Forum, 2011).

Members of more liberal churches (e.g., Episcopalians, Presbyterians) and Jewish members may be disproportionately overrepresented in Congress because, historically, they have felt a responsibility toward social issues. Another likely factor is the social class of members of these various denominations. Because seeking political office can be quite costly, religious groups whose members are typically upper middle class tend to be overrepresented in political offices. Political races have become extremely expensive, as evidenced by mayoral, gubernatorial, and congressional races where tens of millions of dollars have been spent on campaigns. In the 2009 and 2010 elections, two candidates for mayoral and gubernatorial office, respectively, each spent well over $100 million of their own funds (Williams, 2011). The personal fortunes of the 10 wealthiest members of Congress range from $188 million down to $46 million (Brown, 2010).

While the American electorate has shown its willingness to send significant numbers of Jewish individuals, and smaller numbers of Muslim and Buddhist individuals, to Congress, there are no individuals in Congress who have indicated a lack of religious affiliation. Sixteen percent of the overall U.S. population claim no religious affiliation.

Protestantism remains the major religious influence not only on society but also on political leadership. Because Protestants continue to represent such a large segment of the population, such influence is to be expected.

CATHOLICISM

Although the doctrine and pattern of worship within the Catholic Church are uniform, individual parishes differ to some extent according to the race, ethnic background, and social class of their members. Individual dioceses also may differ in keeping with the conservative or liberal (progressive) views of the presiding bishop. Unlike the Protestant faith, however, which includes denominational pluralism, the **Catholic** faith is a single denomination under the Pope, who has authority over all Catholics throughout the world.

With approximately 22% of the U.S. population identifying with the Roman Catholic Church (Gallup, 2010), the American Religious Identification Survey (Kosmin & Keysar, 2009) reported U.S. Catholic Church membership to be 57,199,000.

Today, the Catholic Church in the United States is the wealthiest national church in the Roman Catholic world and contributes approximately half of its income to the Church in Rome. The increasing numbers of American cardinals and American priests appointed to important posts in Rome attest to the growing importance of the Catholic Church in the United States (Corrigan & Hudson, 2010).

Diversity Among Catholics. The movement toward conservatism has not been limited to Protestants. In many instances, conservative Catholics have joined forces with conservative Protestants on such issues as abortion and sexual morality. Some Catholics have even abandoned their traditional support of the Democratic Party to support conservative Republican candidates. On the other end of the continuum, some Catholics have protested the conservative position of their church regarding the limited participation of women in leadership roles, and some support the pro-choice movement. Some Catholics ignore their church's position on certain forms of birth control, while others continue to have large families.

Membership in U.S. Catholic churches involves many different ethnic groups. Some parishes are predominantly Irish, while others are predominantly Italian, Polish, Mexican, Puerto Rican, or other ethnic groups. A parish may choose to conduct services in the predominant language group of its parishioners or may have individual masses for different language groups. Cultural events of the ethnic groups may be incorporated into the daily activities of the particular parish (for example, Quinceniera for Latino females reaching the age of 15).

Effect on Education. In addition to its phenomenal numerical growth, the Roman Catholic Church in the United States has developed the largest private educational system in the world. In many communities, Catholic parochial schools offer quality educational options to both Catholic and non-Catholic students at a lower cost than most other private institutions.

With thousands of elementary and secondary schools from Vermont to Hawaii and such internationally recognized universities as Notre Dame, Creighton, and Loyola, Roman Catholic schools and universities have educated millions of Americans and greatly influenced the culture of the country.

Political Influence. In 1928 Alfred Smith, a Democrat, became the first Roman Catholic to run for the office of President. Attacks were made against Smith's religion, claiming that if elected he would make Catholicism the national religion. In the 1960 presidential election, similar attacks were made against John F. Kennedy and his Catholic background.

By becoming a uniquely American church, members of the Catholic Church have not rejected the belief that they belong to the one universal church. Instead, they have accepted the fact that U.S. society is intrinsically pluralistic and that their religion is one of the four major faiths practiced today together with Protestantism, Judaism, and Islam.

JUDAISM

Judaism is one of the oldest religions known to humanity and also provides the historical roots of both Catholicism and Protestantism. Primarily as a result of Jews from many countries amalgamating under the identification of Jewish American, Judaism has become one of the major faiths in this country. While the Jewish population in the United States is relatively small, the contributions of Jewish Americans to the fields of medicine, science, academia, business, economics, entertainment, and politics in the United States have been profound.

In the nineteenth century, large numbers of Jews emigrated from Germany and many began moving from Jewish enclaves along the East Coast to other parts of the country. Religious persecution in countries such as Russia and Germany brought additional Jewish refugees to the United States in the twentieth century.

Kosmin and Keysar (2009) estimated the U.S. Jewish population to be approximately 2,680,000, or 1.2% of the total U.S. population (as compared to the 2010 Gallup estimate of 2%). Compared with the Protestant and Catholic populations, the Jewish population has decreased significantly numerically and in percentage of the general population over the last 50 years, partly as a result of intermarriage and low birth rates. Yet, as a group, they remain a distinctive, identifiable religious minority whose social standing and influence are disproportionate to their numbers. Education, including higher education, has played an important role in the Jewish community by advancing young people from the working class into white-collar and professional positions.

Diversity within Judaism.   There is no Jewish race. Jewish identity is a blend of historical, religious, and ethnic variables. Early Jewish settlers in the United States found it difficult, if not impossible, to practice Judaism in the traditional ways that they had observed in Europe. Jewish religious practices and patterns were modified to meet the needs of the immigrants and in ways that made them characteristically American.

While some Jewish families have maintained their ties to Orthodox and Conservative Judaism, the majority of American Jews are now affiliated with Reform Synagogues. Reform Jews represent the more liberal end of the continuum. According to Jewish law, one who is born to a Jewish mother or who converts to Judaism is considered a Jew. Reform Jews also accept children born to non-Jewish mothers as Jews. At the other end of the continuum from the Reform Jews are the Orthodox Jews. They tend to hold firm to Jewish law, including rules on diet and dress. Conservative Judaism represents the moderates in Judaism. They are more conservative than the members of Reform congregations and often more liberal than the Orthodox Jews. "Conservative" indicates the group's attempt to conserve traditional Judaism rather than to reform. It does not indicate political conservatism. Some Conservative Jews observe **Kosher** dietary laws, while others do not. Both Reform and Conservative Judaism allow women to be ordained as rabbis.

A thirteen-year-old Jewish male observes his Bar Mitzvah by reading from the Torah in Hebrew. The event marks his entry into religious adulthood.
© iStockPhoto

In addition to differences in religious adherence to traditional Jewish law, American Jews come from diverse backgrounds. There are two major groups of Jews who immigrated to the United States. The Ashkenazim came from Jewish communities in central and Eastern Europe. The Sephardim were Jews from Spain, Portugal, and other Mediterranean countries and the Middle East. Other groups of Jews include those from Jewish communities in Ethiopia and India. These different groups brought much of the culture of their countries of origin when they immigrated to the United States. Some of the Sephardic Jews from Spain settled in Hispanic communities in areas such as New Mexico. Many have blended in with their Hispanic neighbors and become an integral part of their communities.

Although most Jews identify with their religion, the Jewish practice of religion is relatively loose regarding synagogue attendance and home religious observance. Nevertheless, the U.S. synagogue is the strongest agency in the Jewish community. Although they may not attend services regularly, a large percentage of Jews retain some affiliation with a synagogue. Attendance on High Holidays, such as Rosh Hashanah, Yom Kippur, and Passover, however, is usually high. The synagogue in the United States serves not only as a place of religious worship but also as a primary base for Jewish identity and cultural survival.

Effect on Education.   The majority of Jewish children attend public K–12 schools. Many of the Reform Jewish temples or synagogues throughout the country operate private preschools and kindergartens. In some of the larger Jewish communities, particularly among the Orthodox groups, yeshivas, or private religious schools, provide instruction in both academics and in-depth religious studies. Jewish universities such as Yeshiva University in New York and Brandeis University in Massachusetts have made significant contributions to higher education in the United States.

For decades American schools have observed the Christian holiday of Christmas. In the last 30 or 40 years, educators have become increasingly sensitive to the diversity of the students in their schools. December is also the time of the year when Jewish families observe Chanukah (Hanukkah), an eight-day Jewish holiday commemorating a historical event in Jewish history. Many schools, in the spirit of inclusiveness and sensitivity, now refer to the holiday vacation period as the December school recess and December school parties as holiday parties. The families choosing to do so can maintain religious observances at home.

Political Influence.   While the Jewish population in the United States is relatively small, the group's political influence and representation in political office is significant. In early 2011 there were 13 Jewish U.S. senators, 30 Jewish representatives to Congress, and a significant number of Jewish individuals working in leadership positions in the Obama administration. Numerous Jewish individuals have served as state governors, and as U.S. ambassadors and cabinet members under different administrations.

Anti-Semitism.   Jews in the United States and throughout the world have been the targets of prejudice and discrimination, sometimes leading to attempted annihilation of the population. During World War II the Jewish Holocaust resulted in the deaths of millions of European Jews. The civilized world ignored the overwhelming evidence of the Nazi atrocities and did nothing to intervene. Now, in the twenty-first century, neo-Nazis, the President of Iran, and others suggest that the Jewish Holocaust was a myth that never happened. Other attempts at genocide persist in various places in the world. It is the responsibility of educators to help their students understand that, even today, genocides are taking place in Europe, the Middle East, Africa, and other parts of the world.

Anti-Semitism is rooted in Jewish-Gentile conflicts that have existed for centuries. In the United States, Jews and Catholics were also targets of the Ku Klux Klan, especially in the 1920s and 1930s, when anti-Semitic newspapers and radio commentators proliferated (Johnstone, 2007). Discrimination has occurred in both occupational and social life. In some instances, Jews have been denied high-level corporate management positions and had limited access to or been barred from membership in social clubs (Hemeyer, 2010). Periodic synagogue burnings and defacement are reminders that anti-Semitic sentiments still exist.

ISLAM

As a religious term, **Islam** means to surrender to the will or law of God. Islam is one of the major religions of the world, with over 1 billion adherents worldwide. Islam is also one of the fastest-growing religions in the United States. Kosmin and Keysar (2009) estimate the U.S. Muslim population at 1,349,000 (1.2% of the total population). The Pew Forum (2010b) reports that while there were 1,209 mosques located throughout the United States in 2000, the number increased significantly to 1,897 mosques in 2010. While many Americans think Islam is primarily a Middle Eastern religion, only a small portion of the world's Muslims live in that region. Indonesia, Pakistan, and India all have larger Muslim populations than any Middle Eastern country does. There are more Muslims in China than in Syria, while Russia has more Muslims than Jordan and Libya combined (Pew Forum, 2009b).

More than a hundred years ago, a group of immigrants from the Middle East settled in Cedar Falls, Iowa. They were among the first Muslims to settle in this country. The descendants of these immigrants have maintained the religion of their ancestors, built a new mosque, and become an integral part of their community. As everyday citizens, business people, and professionals, they dress, talk, and act like any other American. Only their religion distinguishes them from their Christian and Jewish neighbors.

Islamic Beliefs. Those who practice Islam are **Muslims**. Islam is both a belief system and a way of life for individuals and entire societies. Islam is based on the holy writings of the **Qur'an** (or **Koran**). Muslims believe that the Qur'an consists of the exact words that were revealed by God through the Angel Gabriel to the prophet Muhammad (A.D. 570–632). The Qur'an's basic theme is the relationship between God and His creatures. It provides guidelines for a society that is just, with proper human conduct, and an economic system that is equitable. Muslims believe that Islam began with Adam and continued through the line of prophets including Abraham, Moses, Jesus, and Mohammad. The basic tenets of Islam include:

1. *Faith:* Belief in one God (**Allah**) and in Mohammad as his last messenger.
2. *Prayer:* Five times daily, facing Mecca.
3. *Charity:* Contributing to the poor.
4. *Fasting:* No food or water from sunrise to sunset during Ramadan (ninth month of the Islamic year).
5. *Pilgrimage:* A visit to Mecca once in one's lifetime (the Hajj) (Ellwood & McGraw, 2009).

The pilgrimage to Mecca is an obligation for those who are physically and financially able. Muslims worship the same God (Allah) as do Christians and Jews. Christian Arabs also refer to God as Allah (Denny, 2011; Ellwood & McGraw, 2009).

Islam and the West. The tragic events of September 11, 2001, which resulted in the loss of thousands of lives, focused world attention on Muslim extremists. Since then, the United States has been in almost continuous conflict with Muslim extremists in Afghanistan and Iraq. Around the world, in

Educators will continue to see increasing numbers of religious minority group students in their classrooms, reflecting the religious diversity of the United States.
© Anne Vega/Merrill

Who Is an American?

Nadar Hoseini is a third-grader in a suburban community in northern Virginia. Nadar's parents, Iranian by ethnicity, emigrated from Great Britain in the mid-1990s and are now naturalized citizens. Nadar was born in Virginia, where his father is a chemist for a large manufacturer. He and his family are practicing Muslims and have never hidden that fact. During recess Ms. Nash, Nadar's teacher, notices that Nadar is sitting alone and is visibly upset. After some probing, she learns that Nadar's friends have shunned him.

"Michael told everyone that now that they got Bin Laden, his father says all those Muslims are going to get it too. We are going to drive all of them out of the country," he tells Ms. Nash. "Michael said that his father told him, 'Your friend Nadar is one of them Muslims, and you had better not let me catch you playing with him again. We're going to ship all of them Muslims back where they came from!'"

Protesting, Nadar insists that he was born in the United States and that he and his family are American. The protest falls on deaf ears as Nadar's classmates join Michael in ostracizing him. Ms. Nash is determined to help Nadar's situation but at the moment is at a loss as to how she will approach the problem.

| QUESTIONS FOR CLASSROOM DISCUSSION |

- What should Ms. Nash say to Nadar?
- How can she change the perceptions of the boys without seeming to attack Michael's father?
- What sensitivity activities can she conduct in the class?

countries such as Spain, the Philippines, Great Britain, and Indonesia, hundreds of lives have been lost at the hands of Islamic extremists.

The continuing conflicts in both Iraq and Afghanistan and the ongoing strained relations with Iran have drawn daily attention to Islamic extremists. By the official beginning of troop withdrawals from Iraq in August 2010, more than 4,700 coalition servicemen and women, the vast majority American, had lost their lives in Iraq, with tens of thousands more wounded. In 2009 the Afghanistan casualties began to increase dramatically (CNN, 2010; Iraq Coalition Casualty Count, 2010).

It is clear that in the United States and in other parts of the Western world, many individuals are uncomfortable with and suspicious of Muslims. It is also true that there are individuals in the Muslim world, including those who are not extremists, who either dislike the United States and other Western nations or, at best, have a negative perception of us.

Since the events of 9/11, 49% of Americans indicate that they have an unfavorable opinion of Islam, and 31% believe that mainstream Islam encourages violence (Roberts, 2010). Various incidents and the resultant attitudes have left many in the Western World with what Kincheloe, Steinberg, and Stonebanks (2010) refer to as Islamaphobia. The researchers suggest that Muslims have been inaccurately defined by the media and politicians, resulting in a trickle-down effect into the communities and the schools. There certainly have been horrendous acts of violence committed by some individuals in the name of Islam. These individuals and these acts should be denounced and condemned. It is important, however, that these individuals and their behaviors be recognized as the exception rather than the rule, so that an entire religion and its adherents are not victimized.

In 2010 the CBS program *60 Minutes* aired a segment with correspondent Leslie Stahl (2010). She interviewed a group of university-educated Muslim students from Pakistan and found that approximately a third of them believed that it is U.S. government policy to destroy Islam. Even more shocking was the belief among some of the students that the U.S. government was actually behind the 9/11 attacks, which were intended to justify the invasion of Iraq. They believed that the United States (and presumably other Western countries) invaded Iraq and Afghanistan out of hatred of Islam. This belief, held by radical extremists and by other Muslims, is referred to as the Narrative.

Some noted Christian evangelists have been outspoken critics of Islam, and their comments, including those referring to Islam as an evil religion, have been well publicized. More recently the controversies related to the proposed Islamic centers in Murfreesboro, Tennessee, and in New York City have generated anger and conflict on both sides. Radio and television talk shows fuel the fire for both sides daily. The much-publicized threat to burn the Qur'an, the most sacred book in Islam, by a Florida minister enraged Muslims around the world and sparked riots and further anger toward the United States. These controversies are reported in media around the world such as Al Jazeera, the Arab media network, which broadcasts throughout the Arab world and in other countries.

The history of conflict between Christianity and Islam is long and in many instances has been extremely brutal. Heinous acts have been documented on both sides. What is important to understand is that even in the best of circumstances, where peaceful co-existence prevails, there is some element of discomfort and at times distrust. It only takes a few well-publicized actions or statements on either side of the controversy to incite anger, distrust, or worse.

Diversity within Islam.   Believers are of two major groups. Sunni Muslims, who comprise 85% of Islam, believe that the rightful leadership began with Abu Bakr and that the succession has passed to caliphs, or political leaders. Shi'i or Shi'ite Muslims are a smaller but highly visible group. Shi'ite Muslims believe that Muhammad intended the succession of leadership to pass through the bloodline of his cousin and son-in-law, 'Ali. Shi'ite Muslims have attracted considerable world attention in recent years because of their insistence of adherence to Islamic law by their countries' governments (Denny, 2011; Hopfe & Woodward, 2009).

Some religious/political Shi'ite leaders view Western culture as antithetical to Islam and have strongly resisted U.S. and other Western influences on their countries. Saddam Hussein, who led Iraq for many years, was a Sunni Muslim. He and his Sunni followers dominated the numerically superior Shi'ites in his country by force and at one time waged war with the Shi'ite government in Iran. The sectarian violence within Iraq, which the United States has sought to control, has involved these two warring factions.

Black Muslims.   While U.S. **Black Muslims** have primarily aligned themselves with the Sunni form of Islam, they form a unique identity of their own.

Elijah Poole (1875–1975), who became known as Elijah Muhammad, led the Nation of Islam into national visibility. In the early 1960s Malcolm X (1925–1965) became the most articulate spokesperson for the Nation of Islam (Ellwood & McGraw, 2009; Fisher 2011).

Malcolm X and other Black Muslims sought to use the Nation of Islam to engage African Americans in economic nationalism and to instill in them a sense of pride and achievement. This was accomplished through the rejection of Christianity, which they taught was a symbol of white oppression in America.

Wallace Deen Muhammad became the leader of the Nation of Islam after the death of his father, Elijah Muhammad, in 1975. Under his leadership, the Nation of Islam embraced traditional Sunni Islam and changed its name to the American Muslim Mission. "During the 1970s and 1980s, W. D. Muhammad, as he is known, slowly dispensed with the racist rhetoric of his sect's past and led his followers toward orthodox Koranic Islam" (Kosmin & Lachman, 1993, p. 136). As a result, the group often supports conservative causes such as the free market. Hard work, personal responsibility, and family values are expected of members (Fisher, 2011; Kosmin & Lachman, 1993).

The well-known leader of the Black Muslims, Louis Farrakhan, led a splinter movement in the 1980s that resumed the use of the original name, Nation of Islam, and the black separatist position. He continues to receive considerable attention from the press and political leaders because of his sometimes inflammatory rhetoric as well as his appeal to non-Muslim African Americans. This influence was demonstrated in his ability to mobilize an interfaith coalition that drew nearly 1 million African American men together for the One Million Man March in Washington, D.C., in 1996. Members have become role models in many inner cities as they establish businesses. They often serve as visible neighborhood guardians against crime and drug abuse, and have assumed an important role in the rehabilitation of individuals released from prison (Fisher, 2011; Johnstone, 2007).

Effect on Education.   The vast majority of Muslim students in the United States and Canada attend public schools. The September 11, 2001, attacks enhanced concerns of some Muslim students in U.S. schools for their personal safety and concerns that the wearing of traditional attire (e.g., head covering for women) could draw unfavorable attention to them. Taggar (2006) interviewed Muslim high school students and the majority reported that Muslims had been labeled in stereotypical ways and were particularly concerned with the media's portrayal of their culture and religion. Taggar urges culturally responsive teaching requiring educators to examine their own attitudes and beliefs before they attempt to educate their students. Taggar further urges the creation of a school environment that is emotionally and physically safe for all students.

In the United States, about 15,000 students attend 200 Islamic schools. These schools are designed to provide full-time educational programs "to help a child grow into an Islamic personality with the ideals and images which can help him and her achieve the best in this world and the best in the Hereafter" (Johnstone, 2007). Many of these schools are located in Islamic centers throughout the country. In addition, some Muslim students attend weekend religious training in Islamic schools.

As a group, U.S. Muslims may be better educated than the average American. Twenty-five percent obtain college degrees, compared to 19.1% for the general population, and another 10% of American Muslims go on to graduate studies (Roberts, 2010; U. S. Census Bureau, 2010l).

BUDDHISM

Buddhism is one of the world's major religions, with estimates ranging from a quarter of a billion to a third of a billion members worldwide. Immigration of Asians each year from countries such as China, Taiwan, Korea, Thailand, Japan, and Tibet brings thousands of additional Buddhists into the United States, further changing the religious landscape of the country. Estimates of 1,189,000 Buddhists in the United States (Kosmin & Keysar, 2009), representing 0.7% of the U.S. population (Pew Forum, 2008) appear to be conservative given the fact that there are now more than 12 million Asians in the country, with over half having immigrated from predominantly Buddhist countries.

The Fo Kuang Shan Hsi Lai Temple in Hacienda Heights, California, is the largest Buddhist temple in the Western Hemisphere.
© Shutterstock

With Buddhists coming from so many regions of the world, there are invariably different forms of Buddhism practiced. Buddhist schools of thought or belief are united in a twofold orientation toward existence: a fundamental negative attitude toward life and a pessimistic approach to ordinary existence. Buddhists view existence itself as the problem with life. As long as there is existence, there is suffering. The second common orientation of all Buddhists is that Buddha provides a solution to the frustrations of life. Each school of Buddhism provides a pathway to overcome the meaninglessness of life. Buddha is the solution to life's dilemma (Fisher, 2011; Young, 2010).

Buddhism teaches that the path to enlightenment is neither through a life of luxury nor through self-deprivation, but through the middle way, away from the extremes. The key to salvation is to let go of everything. Salvation and enlightenment occurs when one realizes his or her place of nonself in the world. Nonexistence is the reality and self-extinction is the key. With enlightenment comes the state of nirvana, meaning "blown out" (Hopfe & Woodward, 2009; Young, 2010).

Chinese, Japanese, Korean, and Vietnamese individuals are often influenced by Confucian philosophy, which guides daily behaviors in much the same way that a religion does. Thus, some individuals may be Buddhist (or Christian or some other religion) with a strong philosophical overlay of Confucianism. The commitment to academic excellence and respect for parents, elders, and authority are characteristics often found among these groups of Asian students. Many of these cultural traits can be directly or indirectly attributed to the Confucian philosophy deeply instilled into many Chinese, Japanese, Korean and Vietnamese students from an early age.

HINDUISM

Hinduism is the major religion of India and the world's third largest religion after Christianity and Islam. There are approximately 837,000,000 adherents in the world, representing 13% of the world's population. The number of Hindus in the United States ranges from 766,000 to 1,100,000, or an estimated 0.4% of the U.S. population (Pew Forum, 2008). Generally regarded as the world's oldest organized religion, it differs from Christianity and other Western religions in that it does not have a single founder (Robinson, 2010b). Hinduism has no central organization. Hinduism is credited with influencing the development of both Buddhism and Jainism (Hopfe & Woodward, 2009).

Like most other religions, Hinduism has basic beliefs about divinities, life after death, and how followers should conduct their lives. Unlike Judaism, Christianity, and Islam, Hinduism does not limit itself to a single book or writing. Several sacred writings contribute to the basic beliefs of Hinduism.

Teachings of Hinduism. Hinduism teaches that the soul never dies. When the body dies, the soul is reincarnated. The soul may be born into an animal or another human being. The law of karma states that every action taken by an individual influences how he or she will be reincarnated. Those who live a good life will be reincarnated into a higher state. Those who do evil will be reincarnated in lower forms such as a worm. Reincarnation continues until a person reaches spiritual perfection. The soul then enters a new level of existence, referred to as moksha, from which it never returns (Ellwood & McGraw, 2009).

OTHER DENOMINATIONS AND RELIGIOUS GROUPS

In addition to the four major faiths in the United States, there are several other religions an educator might encounter in a community. They include Christian religious groups and others that do not fall into the discrete categories of Protestantism, Catholicism, Judaism, or Islam.

Latter-Day Saints. The Church of Jesus Christ of Latter-Day Saints (LDS or Mormon) is a rapidly growing group that is neither Catholic nor Protestant. In the early 1830s Joseph Smith founded the LDS Church in western New York State. By his own account, Smith was instructed to translate a history of ancient inhabitants of North America written on tablets of gold, which had been stored in a nearby hillside. The translations were published in 1830 as the Book of Mormon, which together with the Old and New Testaments and some of Smith's later revelations, became the sacred scripture of Mormonism (Hemeyer, 2010).

Smith and his followers met strong opposition from established Protestant groups, and they were harassed and violently driven out of various communities. The Mormon practice of polygamy (the Church discontinued the practice of plural marriage in 1890) exacerbated their unacceptability to other groups, and in 1844 Smith and his brother were killed by a mob in Carthage, Illinois. With the death of Smith, Brigham Young became the new leader of the group and led them to Utah, now the religious center of the Mormons. The Mormons aggressively proselytize and as a result have grown to a membership of 3,158,000 in the United States (Kosmin & Keysar, 2009) and 11.7 million worldwide (Young, 2010).

Eastern Orthodoxy. The Eastern Orthodox Church is another Christian religion that does not fall into the two major groupings of Protestant and Roman Catholic. Eastern Orthodoxy probably claims about one-fourth of all Christians worldwide. One reason that the Eastern Orthodox Church is lesser known in this country may be that its members, from Syria, Greece, Armenia, Russia, and the Ukraine, only immigrated during the last century. Although they split with the Roman Catholic Church in 1054 over theological, practical, jurisdictional, cultural, and political differences, to many outsiders they appear very similar to the pre–Vatican II Catholic church.

Worldwide, the Eastern Orthodox Churches together have an estimated combined membership of 214,000,000 to 300,000,000 (Robinson, 2006a). There are 15 self-governing Orthodox Churches worldwide, each with its own Patriarch, Metropolitan, or Archbishop as its spiritual leader (Fisher, 2011). The Pew Forum (2008) estimates Orthodox membership at 0.6% (approximately 1,800,000) of the U.S. population.

Christian Science and Unitarian Universalists.   At least two other religions have a Christian heritage but seem to fall through the cracks of discrete categorization because of their precepts: the Christian Scientists and Unitarian Universalists.

The Christian Scientists, with probably fewer than half a million members, believe that all that God creates is good, as a good God would not create that which is not good. They rely on the power of God to heal rather than traditional medicine. Adherents are not prohibited from utilizing traditional care, though reliance on the power of God is encouraged, as they believe that the cause and cure of illness is spiritual. Believing that the body is the temple of the Holy Spirit, Christian Scientists advocate healthy habits including exercise, good nutrition, and abstaining from alcohol and tobacco use. Many are vegetarians. Their publication, *Christian Science Monitor,* is a highly respected online newspaper (Hemeyer, 2010).

The second group that defies categorization are the Unitarian Universalists, a church that connotes liberalism to most people. Their membership has included several U.S. presidents (e.g., Thomas Jefferson, John Adams) and noted writers such as Henry Wadsworth Longfellow, and this helped make the church an influence in the founding years of this country.

The Unitarian Universalist Association was created by a merger between the American Unitarian Association and the Universalist Church of America. Young (2010) states, "Among its (Unitarians) principal teachings were a commitment to interpret the Bible rationally, a dedication to follow the example of Jesus, but not assert that he is God, and a strong devotion to serve humanity and right the wrongs of society."

Young (2010) suggests that Unitarian Universalism supports free and open search for the truth, with the recognition that the truth can be found in all religious traditions. The goal is to create a world community of justice and peace.

Native American Religions.   Native Indian religions are among the most difficult to describe or characterize, as there are 314 federally recognized tribes or groups, and each is likely to have its own distinctive views on religion. Many Native Americans are Christians, so that the number of practitioners of Native American religion is relatively small. Because there are so few adherents to Native American religions, their numbers have not shown up in the recent surveys such as the 2008 American Religious Identification Survey or the 2010 poll results provided by the Gallup organization. The American Religious Identification Survey provided an estimate of 145,363 adherents in 2004 (Adherents.com, 2011). There are a few general characteristics that tend to transcend tribal boundaries. Traditional Native American religions recognize three levels of spiritual beings—a supreme god, nature spirits, and ancestor spirits.

Shamans are spiritual leaders or medicine men or women with special gifts that enable them to mediate between the spirit world and the earthly world. They are considered holy men or women who, through their contacts with the spirit world, heal, provide spiritual renewal, and see into the future for others (Hartz, 2009).

Sikhism.   Sikhism was founded in the fifteenth or sixteenth century B.C.E. in India. Sikhism draws elements from Hinduism and Islam, stressing a universal single God. Union with God is accomplished through meditation and surrender to divine will. Sikhs believe in reincarnation, karma, and the destruction and rebuilding of the universe. Male Sikhs are initiated into a religious brotherhood called the Khalsa, and vow to never cut their hair or beard and to wear special pants, an iron bangle, a steel dagger, and a comb. Male Sikhs are readily observable with their turbans. There are an estimated 490,000 Sikhs in North America (Hopfe & Woodward, 2009; Ellwood & McGraw, 2009).

Baha'ism. Baha'ism, or Bahai, was founded in Persia (Iran) in the mid-nineteenth century. Its founder, Baha'ullah, claimed to be the divine manifestation of God and the last of a line of divine figures including Zoroaster, Buddha, Christ, and Muhammad. Bahai emphasizes the principles of equality of the sexes and races, and religious adherence. Bahai believers advocate for peace, justice, racial unity, economic development, and education. There are an estimated 300,000 or more members in the United States (Corrigan & Hudson, 2010; Ellwood & McGraw, 2009).

New Age Spirituality. The **New Age** movement began in the 1970s and the early 1980s as a reaction by some to the perceived failure of Christianity and secular humanism to provide ethical and spiritual guidance for the future. New Age has roots in nineteenth-century spiritualism and in the counterculture movement of the 1960s, rejecting materialism and favoring spiritual experience to organized religion. The movement emphasizes reincarnation, biofeedback, shamanism, the occult, psychic healing, and extraterrestrial life. It is a movement that is difficult to define, as evidenced by the multitude of the movement's publications on a wide range of topics, viewpoints, and paraphernalia, from crystals to tarot cards. Much of the emphasis of the various groups is on the paranormal or parapsychology. It involves such experiences as meditation, visualization, dream interpretation, self-improvement, extrasensory perception, telepathy, clairvoyance, divination, precognition, out-of-body experiences, channeling spirit guides, angels, regression analysis of past lives, and so forth. It has influences from Eastern religions such as Buddhism and Hinduism (Fisher, 2011; Brown, 2008; Robinson, 2006b).

Some New Agers believe Christianity to be a thing of the past. New Agers tend to reject highly structured, institutionalized religion, such as the organized Christian religious authority of the Roman Catholic Church. There is no formal institutional structure for the New Age movement, nor is there any agreed-upon creed. There is no authoritative hierarchy, and it is unclear precisely what the New Age groups are and what they are not (Fisher, 2011; Brown, 2008; Robinson, 2006e).

Wicca. Wicca, considered by some to be a neo-pagan religion, is sometimes referred to as witchcraft. Although its numbers are still relatively small compared to mainstream religions, it is by percentage of growth the fastest-growing religion in the United States. Adherents (referred to as Wiccans) increased from 8,000 in 1990 to 134,000 in 2001 (City University of New York, 2001). Wiccans have experienced comparable growth in Australia, Canada, and elsewhere in the world.

Wicca is a modern revival of the old religion of witchcraft. Wiccans believe that all nature is alive with the sacred and that humans are interconnected with nature, as is all else in the world. Member Wiccans form their own small groups, or covens, of 12 or 13 members, with no hierarchy or authoritarian priesthood. All members are witches. Rituals generally focus on the goddess, who appears in triple form. The Wiccan movement has focused on feminist spirituality and the sacred meaning of women's lives. The movement has attracted adolescents as well as adults and both men and women (Fisher, 2010; Hemeyer, 2010).

Cults. The term "cult" evokes a wide variety of reactions, from approval to contempt, on the part of members of mainstream religious groups. Ellwood and McGraw (2009) define cults as "minority religions characteristically centered on a charismatic leader, who requires strict adherence to beliefs and practices of the group. Generally, the cult contains teachings and practices from several sources and often requires adherents to sever ties with people who are not a part of the cult" (p. 494). Johnstone (2007) further suggests that cults tend to be transitory and short-lived. When the cult's charismatic leader dies, leaves, or is discredited, the cult usually disbands or disappears. In some instances the cult grows, develops a structure, and forms a leadership succession. The cult may then assume a denominational status. In this sense, during its early years, Christianity might have been characterized as a cult. Likewise, the Mormon Church could have been considered a cult in its early years, prior to becoming a sizable denomination.

Young people in many communities practice religions based on an Eastern religious tradition. This grouping includes the Hare Krishna, the Divine Light Mission, and the Unification Church.

During the past 25 or so years, there have been a number of highly publicized mass suicides among the so-called suicide cults. Among those involving Americans were the People's Temple, the Branch Davidians, and the Heaven's Gate group.

Interaction of Religion with Gender, Homosexuality, and Race

Religion can significantly influence one's perceptions, attitudes, and values. Religion is much like any other culture. One who lives in and with a religion absorbs the values of that religious culture and often integrates it into his or her personal value system. Religion influences attitudes toward issues such as gender, homosexuality, and race.

RELIGION AND GENDER

In an era of gender equality in the general society of the United States, issues of gender equality are often raised in religious institutions. In many of the more conservative religious bodies, the role of women is clearly defined and limited. There are no female priests in the Roman Catholic Church or Eastern Orthodox Churches, no woman can attain the priesthood in the Mormon Church, and very few fundamentalist churches or denominations have ordained or are willing to ordain women ministers. The same can be said about many other religious groups. At the 2000 annual Southern Baptist Convention, the 16,000 delegates voted on an explicit ban on women pastors. This action followed an earlier one by the Baptists to support the submission of women to their husbands.

Although, as Gomes (1996) notes, Lydia, Phoebe, and Priscilla were women mentioned in the New Testament as having prominent roles in the formative days of early Christianity, other biblical passages are used to delimit the participation of women in leadership roles in religious activity. In supporting the limitations of female leadership and wifely submission, these groups cite the fact that Jesus did not call on women to serve as his disciples. Biblical verses (e.g., I Corinthians 14:34–35) admonish women to submit themselves to their husbands and indicate that the husband is the head of the wife.

Van Leeuwen (1990) suggests that some biblical interpreters believe that God gave men, through Adam (Genesis 1:26–27), dominion over Eve and, therefore, men dominance over women. Other biblical scholars argue that such an interpretation is incorrect and that both Adam and Eve (man and woman) were given dominion over every other living thing. Groothuis (1997) indicates that in addition to the examples provided by Gomes (1996), there are numerous other biblical examples of women who were leaders or prophets (e.g., Deborah; see Judges 4–5).

The participation of women in leadership roles in both Protestantism and Judaism is a function of where the particular denomination falls on the liberal to conservative continuum. Liberal Protestants (e.g., Episcopalians) ordain women as priests. Likewise, the Reform Jewish movement has ordained women as rabbis since 1972. The Conservative Jewish seminaries began ordaining women as rabbis in 1985, but the Orthodox Jewish movement has not embraced this policy.

Limitations on the participation of females in religious activities are by no means the sole province of Judeo-Christian groups. Islam and other religions either limit the participation of females or typically rest leadership in the hands of men. Islam views women as equal to but different from men. They do not worship alongside the men in their mosques, but in separate areas. They are expected to observe all pillars of Islam, including the five daily prayers and fasts during Ramadan.

Women in some Middle Eastern countries have severe limitations placed on them (e.g., rules against working, attending school, or driving a car, and requiring face covering). These limitations are more a function of the culture of the country or region than they are mandates of Islam.

Due to the diversity of the backgrounds of adherents as well as the society in which they live, many Islamic women in the United States function differently than Islamic women in other parts of the world. Differences include the extent to which they are allowed to work outside the home, assume active roles in Islamic centers and community life, and interact with the non-Muslim community (Peach, 2002).

In addition to defining the parameters of religious participation of males and females, religion may also be used to prescribe male and female roles outside the religious context. Such prescriptions may be done either directly or indirectly. In religious groups in which women are given a less prominent status, this may carry over into general family life and other aspects of society as a natural course. In other instances, the pronouncements may be more direct. Religious writings of great importance, such as the Bible, are continuously interpreted, studied, and analyzed. In the United States, the Bible is viewed as sacred by most citizens who claim Christian church membership. Consequently, the Bible and other religious writings, such as the Koran, have a profound influence on many Americans.

Issues related to gender equality are treated extensively in Chapter 4. It is important for educators to be aware that many of society's attitudes toward gender equality or inequality may be rooted in religious practices. If religious practices dictate that wives are to be subservient to their husbands, or if women are prohibited from the highest or even high levels of leadership within a faith, then this practice often carries over into other aspects of everyday life. Educators who themselves observe gender limitations in their religious life or in their marriage have every right to do so. However, they must not draw inferences from these beliefs to impose limits on the potential for leadership in the classroom, the school, or the future for their female students. It is important that female students at an early age be encouraged and given the opportunity to develop leadership skills. This will enable them to pursue their future careers and personal choices and enable them to maximize their full potential.

RELIGION AND HOMOSEXUALITY

Homosexuality is one of the most controversial issues in religious institutions today. Attacks on homosexuality in the religious context are often justified through biblical interpretation or from other religious writings. Some argue that the textual interpretation and, in some cases, translation of biblical passages regarding homosexuality are not clear and may be subject to influence by misguided beliefs. Others argue that the Bible is clear on the issue of homosexuality, as in the book of Genesis, where God destroyed Sodom and Gomorrah because of the sinful behaviors, including homosexuality, of the inhabitants. The debate is serious, as are the consequences. Conservative Christians and conservatives of other religious groups tend to view homosexuality as a matter of choice—a sin and an abomination. More liberal religious groups tend to believe that the only choice is whether the individual engages in homosexual behavior. They contend that the individual is born homosexual.

California's 2008 Proposition 8, a voter initiative, banned gay marriage. It was strongly supported by the Roman Catholic Church, the Church of Jesus Christ of Latter-Day Saints (Mormon), evangelical Christian groups, Orthodox Jewish, Eastern Orthodox, and other religious groups (Advocate.com, 2008; Pirah, 2008; Helfand, 2008). Nearly $40 million was raised to support this initiative, which passed with a margin of 52.24% (Statement of Vote, 2008). However, all six of the Episcopal diocesan bishops in California, the Board of Rabbis of Southern California, various Jewish groups, the California Council of Churches, and certain other religious groups voiced their opposition to Prop 8.

Because some conservative Christians, as well as members of other religious bodies, view homosexuality as a sin, they believe the AIDS epidemic is God's retribution for the gay life. Other Christian groups have willingly accepted gays and lesbians into their congregations, and some have even ordained them into leadership positions, often creating controversy within the respective churches or denominations.

Views toward homosexuality vary considerably among other religious groups. There are often intergroup as well as intragroup differences. The Roman Catholic position on homosexuality is in keeping with that of many other conservative groups. These groups view homosexuality as "objectively disordered" and view homosexual practices as very serious "sins gravely contrary to chastity" (Robinson, 2010a).

The Catholic Church, however, has had to address the issues related to homosexuality among its own clergy. The unfortunate clergy abuse scandals involving young males in the United States and abroad that surfaced in recent years have caused great spiritual and economic turmoil in various dioceses and resulted in deep emotional scarring among many of the victims. Even though the abuses have been linked to a minority of priests, the scandal has caused immense problems for the Church.

The 2004 elevation of Rev. V. Gene Robinson to bishop in the Episcopal Diocese of New Hampshire, the first openly gay Episcopal bishop, has created considerable divisiveness among Episcopalians. In 2010 Rev. Mary Glasspool became the first openly gay female bishop in the Episcopal Church (Landsberg, 2010). These actions have severely strained relations between the parent Anglican Church and the American Episcopal Church, and have resulted in a schism in some Episcopal congregations over what they consider excessively liberal practices.

The views toward homosexuality among Jewish groups tend to mirror those of Christians and are typically a function of where the group lies on the continuum of liberal to conservative. Reform Judaism tends to view homosexuality as the normal behavior of a minority of adults. Orthodox Judaism views it as abnormal and condemned by God (Robinson, 2010f).

Homosexuality in Islam is viewed as lewd and sinful. There are two primary references to homosexuality in the Qur'an (Qur'an 7:80–81 and 26:165). Both address homosexuality negatively. In South and East Asian Islamic countries, no physical punishment for homosexuality is considered warranted. However, some Middle Eastern Islamic countries tend to deal with it harshly, especially Iran and Afghanistan when it was under the rule of the Taliban (Robinson, 2011).

Robinson (2010d) indicates that with the many schools and sects within Buddhism, there is, as with Christianity, no consensus regarding homosexuality within the religion. Buddha did not provide any teachings regarding homosexuality. Buddhism, Robinson states, is more concerned with good intentions and good actions. Because of the relative lack of homophobia in some sects of Buddhism, it has attracted some gay men and lesbian women.

Young (2010) indicates that the mention of homosexuality is rare in classical Hindu texts, and where it does occur, the practice is not viewed positively. Homosexuality is seen as fundamentally incompatible with the goals of duty and material well-being among Hindus. Young further states that the major Hindu deities (e.g., Shiva) have both masculine and feminine aspects, which contributes to a more tolerant attitude toward homosexuality and bisexual orientation in India, which has the world's largest Hindu population.

Religion and political affiliation are closely interwoven in the United States. Religious conservatives, particularly evangelical Christians, have closely aligned themselves with the Republican Party, whose leadership has generally opposed same-sex marriage and gay relationships (GOP, 2008). While 66% of Democrats supported same-sex marriage in a recent survey, only 35% of Republicans did (Saad, 2009). National and some state GOP platforms have opposed same-sex marriage, and the Texas GOP has proposed its criminalization (GOP, 2008; Siegel, 2010). When religion and politics become closely entwined, there is a concern that legislators will attempt to mandate, through legislation, who is and is not allowed to teach, what curriculum is permissible, and what material in textbooks should be censored. It is essential to bear this in mind in deciding what individuals and platforms to support in elections.

Religious views toward homosexuality have considerable implications for the educational setting. Educators have a right to their personal views toward homosexuality. They do not have a right to impose their views in the public school setting. They cannot allow students to harass or bully one another, and they cannot allow students to voice their personal opinions and attack other students verbally or otherwise in the classroom or on school grounds. It is the responsibility of every educator, including staff members, to provide a safe and accepting environment for every student.

PAUSE TO REFLECT 8.1

Historically, many religions have treated men and women differently. Today many religions still do not allow women to assume the highest leadership positions. This pattern often carries over into society in general. In 1966 Indira Gandhi became the first female Prime Minister of India, a predominantly Hindu country. In 1988 Pakistan's Benazir Bhutto made history by becoming the first woman to head the government of a Muslim-majority state in modern times. While women have held the highest elected office in predominantly Christian countries (e.g., Margaret Thatcher of Great Britain), no woman has to date been elected President of the United States. On January 4, 2007, history was made in the United States Congress when Representative Nancy Pelosi (D-CA) assumed the position of Speaker of the U.S. House of Representatives. This made Pelosi second in line to the presidency and arguably the highest-ranking woman ever in the United States government.

- If you teach in a public school setting, what is your responsibility to your male and female students?

- Are there any differences in the way you can or should treat gender bias in private, church-related schools?

- What should you do if a student makes inappropriate gender-biased statements in your class?

RELIGION AND RACE

In the United States, as in many other countries, religion has had a profound impact on race and ethnic diversity issues. When individuals misinterpret biblical scriptures or interpret them to justify aberrant behavior, the consequences can be severe. Gomes (1996) points out that at their 1995 meeting, the Southern Baptist Convention, the country's largest Protestant denomination, in an unprecedented act of contrition, apologized for the role it had played in the justification of slavery and in the maintenance of a culture of racism in the United States.

Slavery and Racism.   The Bible does not condemn slavery, and its practice can be found throughout both the Old and New Testaments. In the New Testament, there is no record of either Jesus or Paul specifically condemning the practice of slavery, which was a common practice during that period. Paul returned a slave to his master rather than provide refuge, as was required by Jewish law (Deuteronomy 23:15–16). Therefore, proponents of slavery believed that this institution had a solid biblical foundation.

Gomes (1996) suggests that the Catholic king of Spain and his ministers viewed it as their divine right and obligation to enslave and Christianize or slaughter the natives of Latin America. Both Cortés and Pizarro operated under papal and governmental authority as they enslaved or killed thousands of natives and justified their behavior with biblical texts.

Anti-Semitism also finds many of its historical roots in the Bible and other religious works. Gomes (1996) further suggests that Bach's *Passion of St. John*, though musically beautiful and inspiring, is filled with strong anti-Semitic German lyrics. Biblical passages are often used to justify anti-Semitic behaviors (e.g., Matthew 27:25–26, Romans 3:1). It is ironic that those individuals, especially Christians, who justify their anti-Semitic behaviors through religious doctrines and sacred writings tend to ignore the fact that Jesus and his earliest followers were themselves Jews.

PAUSE TO REFLECT 8.2

The first European settlers in what was to become the United States were primarily devout Christians. Likewise, the Founding Fathers of the country were primarily Christians. Until recent years, school prayer was permitted in our schools and at school athletic and other events.

In recent years, there has been a perception among some religious groups that moral decay is rampant in our society. Many of these individuals would like prayer returned to the schools and for the schools to instill in the students the basic morality reflected in the Ten Commandments.

- If the majority of the individuals living in your community are Christians, and the parents of students want the return of school prayer and want the Ten Commandments posted on every classroom wall, how can that harm any child in the school?

- What would be the harm of daily prayer if the prayers did not make mention of God or Jesus?

- While most families in the community where you teach favor school prayer and the posting of the Ten Commandments, families who do not share their religious beliefs or practices claim that the school is not upholding the separation of church and state and they are fighting to keep religion out of the schools. Who's right and what should be done?

Role of Black Religious Groups.

Historically, African Americans often organized their own religious institutions due to racism, which either prohibited or limited their membership, participation, or attendance in mainstream denominations. Black churches and religious institutions have served their communities in different ways. Some provide food, shelter, and occasional employment opportunities. Others, such as the Black Muslims, have provided a sense of Black Nationalism, pride, and a self-help philosophy. They have encouraged education and black entrepreneurship (Johnstone, 2007).

Civil Rights Movement and Black Churches.

The modern civil rights movement was centered in the South's African American churches. Many of the civil rights leaders were or are ministers or church leaders (e.g., Martin Luther King, Jr., Ralph Abernathy, Andrew Young, and Jesse Jackson). From their pulpits, these religious leaders were able to direct boycotts and organize civil disobedience and nonviolent confrontations. Prior to the successful 1955 Montgomery, Alabama, bus boycott, seating for black bus riders was segregated. Civil disobedience included sit-ins at segregated public places such as restaurants, where black individuals refused to leave when asked or ordered to do so. In these protests, church leaders instructed participants to respond to confrontations nonviolently.

African American churches deserve much of the credit for bringing about the civil rights gained in the last four or five decades. Alienated and disillusioned by mainstream politics, few African Americans registered to vote in the past. African American clergy nationwide have advocated church involvement in social and political issues. In recent years, black churches have been extremely successful in registering millions of voters and thereby becoming an important voice in the electoral process.

Disenchantment Among Younger Generations.

Johnstone (2007) suggests that some young African Americans have become increasingly disenchanted with their black churches. They have turned to secular organizations, which they feel deal more directly with their life situations and with the social problems they face. Johnstone emphasizes that this situation does not mean the demise of the black church. While some will remain out of habit, others are unwilling to give up the important associations and relationships available to them in their respective churches. The historical nature of the black church as the center of black community life makes it unlikely that the masses will abandon it.

In some religious groups, African Americans were permitted membership but prohibited from attaining the higher positions of church leadership. These prohibitions were justified through biblical interpretations or through divine revelations claimed by church leaders. Although nearly all such racial limitations on membership and church leadership have been removed in recent years, the long-term effects of these religious prohibitions remain to be seen.

Like the gender issues that have become the focus of religious debate, racial issues have been debated for decades. As the courts and society have turned their backs on segregation and racially limiting practices, most religious bodies have also taken an official position of openness. Although the official position and the actual position may differ somewhat, in churches that stress brotherly love, at least, the two may be moving to a higher level of congruence.

It is important to understand that clergy and other church and religious authorities have considerable influence on the people they lead. They, the writers and theologians who influence others, often find their inspiration or the justification for their positions in religious scriptures and writings. These writings are then interpreted for laypersons and may be used to shape their perceptions of self and others.

Children may learn that homosexuality is an abomination, or they may learn to believe that homosexuality is an innate and natural sexual orientation for some. They learn that if females have limitations within the religious institution, they are meant to carry over into school and society. However, they may instead learn to believe in gender equity and that girls can become leaders in their classroom, excel academically, and pursue their career dreams. They may learn to believe that some races are superior to others, or that all men and women are created equal without regard to race or ethnicity. Hopefully they will learn to respect all individuals as valued members of society.

Individual Religious Identity

Most Americans are born into the religion of their parents, later joining that same body. Within the context of the religious freedom espoused in the United States, however, individuals are always free to change their religion or to choose no religion. The greatest pressure to retain membership in the religious group in which one was born usually comes from the family and from other members of that same religious group. Often, it is more difficult for individuals to break away from their religious origins than to break from any of the other cultural groups of which they are members.

Although a person's ethnicity, class, or gender may have a considerable influence on behavior or values, religion may well be the primary microculture with which individuals identify. When ethnic identity is very important to an individual, it is often combined with a religious identification such as Irish Catholic, Russian Jew, or Norwegian Lutheran. The region of the United States in which one lives also affects the strength of identification with a specific religious group. For example, in parts of Alabama, many people will have the same or similar views; religious diversity may be limited. In some areas of the country, deviation from the common religious beliefs and practices may be considered heretical, making it very difficult for the nonadherent to be accepted by most members of the community. In other areas, the traditionally religious individual may not be accepted as a part of a community that is religiously liberal. Educators, as well as students, are usually expected to believe and behave according to the mores of the community—mores that are often determined by the prevailing religious values.

Most communities have some degree of religious diversity, although the degree of difference depends on the community. Students whose beliefs are different from those of the majority in the community may be ostracized in school and social settings. Educators must be careful that their own religious beliefs and memberships do not interfere with their ability to provide equal educational opportunity to all students, regardless of their religious identification.

Separating Church and State and Other Issues

School districts and various state legislators who seek to circumvent the principle of Separation of Church and State continually test the First Amendment. It is difficult to believe that state legislators, many of whom are attorneys, are not aware that laws requiring a form of religion are not intended to create a government-sponsored religious activity. It is likely that these legislators or school officials believe it their responsibility to infuse morality and ethics into the school's activities or curriculum. The Supreme Court, however, has the responsibility of ruling on the constitutionality of such directives. The following are examples of Supreme Court rulings related to education, the First Amendment, and the principle of the separation of church and state:

- *Engel v. Vitale*, 82 S. Ct. 1261 (1962) [New York]. The Court ruled that any type of prayer, even that which is nondenominational, is unconstitutional government sponsorship of religion.
- *Abington School District v. Schempp*, 374 U.S. 203 (1963) [Pennsylvania]. The Court found that Bible reading over the school intercom was unconstitutional, and in *Murray v. Curlett*, 374 U.S. 203 (1963), the Court found that forcing a child to participate in Bible reading and prayer was unconstitutional.
- *Epperson v. Arkansas*, 89 S. Ct. 266 (1968). The Court ruled that a State statute banning the teaching of evolution was unconstitutional. A state cannot set a course of study in order to promote a religious point of view.
- *Stone v. Graham*, 449 U.S. 39 (1980) [Kentucky]. The Court ruled that the posting of the Ten Commandments in schools was unconstitutional.
- *Wallace v. Jaffree*, 105 S. Ct. 2479 (1985) [Alabama]. The Court ruled that the State's moment of silence in a public school statute was unconstitutional, as a legislative record revealed that the motivation for the statute was the encouragement of prayer.
- *Edwards v. Aquillard*, 107 S. Ct. 2573 (1987) [Louisiana]. The Court found it unconstitutional for the state to require the teaching of "creation science" in all instances in which evolution is taught. The statute had a clear religious motivation.
- *Lee v. Weisman*, 112 S. Ct. 2649 (1992) [Rhode Island]. The Court ruled it unconstitutional for a school district to provide any clergy to perform nondenominational prayer at elementary or secondary school graduations. It involves government sponsorship of worship.

Nationally, adherence to the principle of separation of church and state has been schizophrenic at best. Oaths are typically made on Bibles and often end with the phrase "so help me God." U.S. coins and currency state "In God We Trust." We have military chaplains and congressional chaplains, and we hold congressional prayer breakfasts. The Pledge of Allegiance includes the words "under God." This has been interpreted by some to mean that the separation of church and state simply means that there will be no state church.

Complete separation of church and state, as defined by strict constitutionalists, would have a profound effect on social-religious life. It is likely that the American public want some degree of separation of these two institutions, but it is equally likely that some would be outraged if total separation were imposed. Total separation would mean no direct or indirect aid to religious groups, no tax-free status, no tax deductions for contributions to religious groups, no national Christmas tree, no government-paid chaplains, no religious holidays, no blue laws, and so on. The list of religious activities, rights, and privileges that could be eliminated seems almost endless.

Public schools are supposed to be free of religious doctrine and perspective, but many people believe that schools without such a perspective do not provide desirable values orientation for students. Debate about the public school's responsibility in fostering student morality and social responsibility is constant. A major point of disagreement focuses on who should determine the morals that will provide the context of the educational program in a school. Because religious diversity is so great in this country, that task is nearly impossible. Therefore, most public schools incorporate commonly accepted American values that largely transcend religions.

Although schools should be secular, they are greatly influenced by the predominant values of the community. Educators must be cognizant of this influence before introducing certain readings and ideas that stray far from what the community is willing to accept within their belief and value structure. Teachers face difficult choices when school administrators give in to parental demands to violate the principles of separation of church and state by infusing school prayer or religious instruction into the curriculum.

SCHOOL PRAYER

There are several controversial issues in the schools that challenge the principle of separation of church and state. In many instances the majority in a given community may support an issue, which may already have been ruled against by the courts. Among the controversial issues that are often on the agenda of the evangelical Christians and fundamentalist religious groups are school prayer, school vouchers, and censorship. Despite the 1962 and 1963 Supreme Court decisions regarding school prayer, conservative groups have persisted in their efforts to revive prayer in the schools.

The law in no way forbids private prayer in school. The Supreme Court decisions do not prevent teachers or students from praying privately in a school. Any teacher or student can offer his or her own private prayer before the noon meal or praying alone between classes and before and after school. The law forbids public group prayer. Advocates of school prayer sometime advance their efforts under the term "voluntary prayer." The interpretation of what constitutes voluntary school prayer has become a main issue in the prayer controversy. Some proponents of school prayer advocate mandated school prayer, with individuals voluntarily choosing to participate or not participate. It is likely that if such laws were ever enacted, the considerable social pressure to participate would make it difficult for some to refuse participation.

In 2000 the Supreme Court ruled against a Texas school district that had permitted prayer over the public address system at a football game, maintaining that the football games are extracurricular. Students were not required to attend and be a part of the prayer (*Santa Fe Independent School District v. DOE*, 2000). Seldom had this practice been challenged in the past, as it had the support of the majority of students and parents. However, the Court ruled that this is a violation of the separation of church and state.

SCHOOL VOUCHERS

Various groups raise school voucher initiatives periodically. **Vouchers** are intended to provide parents with a choice of schools, public or private, for their children. The funds for vouchers come from tax monies and usually range between $2,500 and $5,000, with around $3,000 being typical. Voucher initiatives are often strongly supported by religious factions, particularly those who send their children to private religious schools. It is for this reason that school vouchers are included in this chapter as a controversial issue.

Parents and others who support these initiatives point to the failure of the public schools to educate their children adequately. They point to the states' low national rankings in student math proficiency, reading proficiency, SAT scores, class sizes, and teacher/student ratios. They also point to falling systemwide test scores and to the moral decline in schools as evidenced by school violence, drugs, and teen pregnancies. They believe that school vouchers will make it possible to send their children to the schools of their choice.

Proponents of voucher programs argue that vouchers will not require any further appropriations since school districts can provide vouchers to students who are not using their services, thereby decreasing their expenses. They argue that when parents redeem a school voucher, part of the expense that would otherwise cost the school to educate the student can remain in the

Debate / School Prayer

In 1647 the first American school system was established in Massachusetts to ensure that children would grow up with the ability to read the Bible. Many, if not most, schools had some form of school prayer until 1962, when the U.S. Supreme Court ruled in *Engle v. Vitale* to affirm the separation of church and state by ruling against school prayer. The U.S. general public overwhelmingly supports some form of school prayer, and there have been organized efforts to either have the Supreme Court reverse its decision or have a Constitutional Amendment that would make school-sponsored prayer permissible.

FOR

■ The country was founded on religious principles by people who believed in freedom to practice one's religion openly. Our students should be able to participate in this heritage and seek the strength and support from God as they begin each day.

■ Voluntary prayer does not constitute government establishment of religion. The school prayer ban is not freedom of religion, but a ban against observing religion.

■ Voluntary prayer does not require the participation of all students. Those who do not wish to participate would have the freedoom not to.

■ The vast majority of Americans want school prayer. Banning prayer is undemocratic and allows the minority to rule.

■ Since school prayer was banned, the nation has been in a moral decline. Divorce rates have climbed, as have the rates of drug use, pornography, out-of-wedlock births, violent crime, street gang membership, abortion, and open homosexuality. School prayer would help restore moral values in America's youth.

AGAINST

■ School prayer has never been outlawed by the Supreme Court. Students have never been banned from reading the Bible, the Koran, or any other religious work. Schools can provide classes that study religions, compare religions, or discuss religions in an objective manner. Students are not barred from praying before their meals or in their own private moments. Public schools are government funded and as such are prohibited from the sponsoring or promoting of religion or providing formal school prayer.

■ School-sponsored prayer is a clear violation of the principle of the separation of church and state.

■ Religious upbringing is the responsibility of the parents and family, not the schools and government.

■ The argument that students would not be required to participate in school-sponsored prayer is invalid. Students who leave or protest prayer are subject to being ostracized by their peers.

■ There is no evidence that school-sponsored prayer would solve society's problems.

| QUESTIONS |

1. Should the majority opinion always rule? What if the majority in a given community wanted to ban African Americans or Asians or whites from attending public schools? Should the majority rule? Does the majority opinion necessarily represent the morally correct opinion?

2. Can students learn and maintain sound moral values if these values are not taught in schools?

3. Should prayer also be banned in private schools?

PAUSE TO REFLECT 8.3

Evangelical Christians and other conservative religious groups formed effective political alliances, which enabled them to elect a conservative president and gain control of both houses of Congress for the Republican Party. This in turn allowed for the appointments of conservatives to the federal courts and for control of the Supreme Court, which will have a lasting impact on how the laws are interpreted. The separation of church and state has had numerous challenges over the decades by groups seeking to include school prayer, the teaching of creationism, and school vouchers for students attending private church schools. Federal and state courts make important decisions on these matters, and these decisions are typically made by those individuals appointed to these courts by elected officials.

- What role should religion play in politics?

- Why do some people think that religious groups should not be involved in political elections?

- How do religious politics influence curriculum and instruction in schools?

public schools. Supporters of the voucher program believe that it will enable the school system to ensure the quality education that all parents wish for their children.

Opponents to voucher initiatives maintain that vouchers will indeed take away needed funds from the public schools. School districts have many fixed costs and already are suffering from inadequate funding. Opponents also suggest that voucher systems will exacerbate the fiscal crisis in the public schools. They further state that the $3,000 or $4,000 provided by the vouchers will not enable most children to go to any school of choice. Many private schools have annual tuitions of $15,000 to $25,000 or more, and the $3,000 or $4,000 vouchers will not even begin to cover the cost of the full tuition. While some schools may grant partial scholarships to deserving students with financial need, it is not possible to provide support to all. Private schools tend to be located in the more affluent areas of the community. Transportation will be a major problem for students who live in areas distant from the preferred schools. Opponents also contend that the primary beneficiaries of the school voucher programs will be the wealthy, who can afford the private schools and already enroll their children in them, and the few financially borderline families who can send their children to private schools only with the help of vouchers.

CENSORSHIP

Censorship occurs when expressive materials such as books, magazines, films, videos, or works of art are removed or kept from public access, including the removal of materials from textbook adoption lists. Censorship may be based on the age of or other characteristics of the potential user. Targets for the censors are books and materials that are identified as disrespectful of authority and religion, destructive to social and cultural values, obscene, pornographic, unpatriotic, or in violation of individual and familial rights of privacy.

Books may be banned for a multitude of reasons (Kelly, 2010). These include the use of profanity (e.g., *To Kill a Mockingbird* and *The Color Purple*), the use of racial slurs (*Adventures of Huckleberry Finn*, *Of Mice and Men*), the use of witchcraft (e.g., the Harry Potter series), and violence (*The Color Purple, Slaughterhouse Five*). Books written by gays and lesbians are also frequently attacked.

In a conservative community, teachers may be surprised to find that magazines such as *Time, Newsweek*, and *U.S. News and World Report* are sometimes attacked because they publish stories about war, crime, death, violence, and sex. Dictionaries with words and definitions described as offensive have been forced off book adoption lists. Other sources of concern include books written for adolescents about subjects objectionable to some parents, and those including language deemed objectionable. The emergence of African American literature, sometimes written in the black vernacular, is sometimes targeted by censors.

Individuals or groups may be self-appointed and pressure school districts or libraries, video stores, publishers, art galleries, and other venues not to stock or show, publish, or distribute the targeted materials. Censorship may also come from groups appointed by a state or school district as textbook selection committees. Censorship of textbooks, library books, and other learning materials in education has become another major battleground in education for the fundamentalist groups.

The Texas State Board of Education gained national attention in 2010 when it approved major changes in the requirements for the state's textbooks. Conservatives on the board were successful in strengthening the requirements on teaching the Judeo-Christian influences of the nation's Founding Fathers. New standards will require the U.S. government to be described as a "constitutional republic," rather than "democratic." They successfully rejected the modernization of the classification of historic periods from the traditional B.C. and A.D. (Before Christ and Anno Domini , or year of the Lord) to the corresponding B.C.E. and C.E. (Before the Common Era and Common Era).

The board also watered down the teaching of the civil rights movement, slavery, America's relationship with the United Nations, and many other items (Castro, 2010). Attempts to include the contributions of important Hispanic historical figures were denied by the board (Castro, 2010; Associated Press, 2010).

The impact of censorship in the public schools cannot be underestimated. It is a serious matter. Censorship or attempts at censorship have resulted in the dismissal or resignation of administrators and teachers. It has split communities and has the potential to create as much controversy as did the desegregation of schools. Few can doubt the sincerity of censors and their proponents. They feel passionately that the cause they support is just and morally right. Censors believe that they are obligated to continue their fight to rid schools of objectionable materials that in their opinion contaminate supple minds and contribute to the moral decay of society.

At the other end of the continuum, opponents of the censors also share the conviction that they are the ones in the right and that censors infringe on academic freedom as they seek to destroy meaningful education. Opponents to the censors believe that their antagonists thrive on hard times, such as when schools come under fire because of declining Scholastic Aptitude Test (SAT) scores and in the midst of rising illiteracy rates, escalating costs of education, and increasing concern about violence and vandalism in the schools. Other factors that motivate the activities of censors are the removal of school prayer; teaching methods that they brand as secular humanism; and programs such as values clarification, drug education, and sex education.

The failure to communicate effectively with parents is a contributing source of alienation between educators and parents. Teachers need to communicate the objectives of new curricula and to explain how these programs enrich the educational experience. Many administrators and librarians indicate that communication with parents is more crisis-oriented than continuous.

Information about programs, policies, and procedures tends to be offered in response to inquiries or challenges rather than as part of an ongoing public relations effort.

Showing parents how the curriculum will support rather than conflict with basic family values can avoid potential conflict.

SECULAR HUMANISM

Secular humanism has been a direct target of the censors, particularly those affiliated with fundamentalist religious groups. The emphasis in secular humanism is a respect for human beings, rather than a belief in the supernatural. Its objectives include the full development of every human being, the universal use of the scientific method, affirmation of the preciousness and dignity of the individual person, personal freedom combined with social responsibility, and fulfillment through the development of ethical and creative living (Robinson, 2010e).

Because many secular humanists feel that the effect of religion throughout history has been profoundly counterproductive, and because some humanists regard God as the creation of mankind rather than the reverse, they are often targets of conservative Christians. Secular humanism is not an organized religion like Roman Catholicism, Protestantism, or Judaism. It does not have rituals, a church, or any professed doctrines. Its existence is in the minds of individuals who align themselves with its perspectives. The specific beliefs and their manifestations vary from one believer to another.

Conservative Christians tend to view secular humanism as a religion, and one that has taken over the public school systems. This is unlikely since the majority of teachers in the public schools are from Christian backgrounds. The principle of separation of church and state requires public schools to base their curricula on secular or nonreligious foundations. In subjects such as human sex education, biology, sociology, and history, the secular approach often comes into conflict with conservative Christian theology. Consequently, books and materials viewed as secular humanist in orientation are often targets for censorship (Robinson, 2010d). Materials and topics infused into the curriculum that address issues such as abortion, corporal punishment of children, the death penalty, forced prayer in schools, homosexuality, and physician-assisted suicide will typically draw the attention of censors, who may view them as secular humanist and hence objectionable material.

Teachers are well advised to make certain that they have fully and accurately assessed the climate within the community before introducing new, innovative, or controversial materials, teaching strategies, or books. Experienced colleagues and supervisors can usually serve as barometers as to how students, parents, and the community will react to various new materials or teaching techniques.

Classroom Implications

Although religion and public schooling are to remain separate, religion can be taught in schools as a legitimate discipline for objective study. A comparative religions course is part of the curriculum offered in many secondary schools. In this approach, the students are not forced to practice a religion as part of their educational program. They can, however, study one or more religions.

The Fairfax County Schools in Virginia have provided teachers with a handout titled "Religion and Public Schools: The Path Between Too Much and Too Little." In the handout are guidelines for teaching about religions. This important advice will assist teachers in understanding how religion can be taught while maintaining the all-important separation of church and state (Becker, n.d.):

- The school may sponsor the study of religion but may not sponsor the practice of religion.
- The school may expose students to all religious views, but may not impose any particular view.
- The school's approach to religion is one of instruction, not one of indoctrination.
- The function of the school is to educate about all religions, not to convert students to any one religion.
- The school should study what all people believe, but should not teach a student what to believe.
- The school should strive for student awareness of all religions, but should not press for student acceptance of any one religion.
- The school should seek to inform the student about various beliefs, but should not seek to conform him or her to any one belief.

As part of the curriculum, students should learn that the United States (and indeed the world) is rich in religious diversity. Educators show their respect for religious differences by their interactions with students from different religious backgrounds. Understanding the importance of religion to students and their families is an advantage in developing effective teaching strategies for individual students. Instructional activities can build on students' religious experiences to help them learn concepts. This technique helps students recognize that their religious identity is valued in the classroom and encourages them to respect the religious diversity that exists.

At the same time, educators should avoid stereotyping all students from one denomination or church. Diversity is found within every religious group and denomination, as mentioned earlier in this chapter. Within each group are differences in attitudes and beliefs. For example, Southern Baptists may appear to be conservative to outsiders. Among Southern Baptists, however, some are considered part of a liberal or moderate group, whereas others would be identified as conservative.

Not only should educators understand the influences that drive the communities in which they teach; they should also periodically reexamine their own interactions with students to ensure that they are not discriminating against students because of differences in religious beliefs. It is imperative that educators recognize how influential membership in a religious microculture is in order to help students develop their potential.

Summary

Educators should never underestimate the importance that Americans place on religion. For some individuals, religion takes precedence over all other microcultures. We live in a society that has become increasingly diverse. Along with increasing ethnic diversity has come increasing religious diversity. The United States has operated under Judeo-Christian principles for more than two centuries. When new religions threaten established religions, controversies and challenges arise.

Educators, like many of their students, come from different religious backgrounds and may have differing values in relation to the importance of religion or what they believe. It is critical that the school provide a safe and accepting environment for every student and every educator and staff member. The Constitution of the United States guarantees religious freedom, and most of our leaders espouse a culture of religious tolerance and acceptance. If we are to make it a reality, it must begin in our schools as well as in the home.

Professional Practice

Questions for Discussion

1. What is the First Amendment to the Constitution? Explain the concept of separation of church and state. Does it mean that no religion can be taught in public schools?

2. In what ways do Americans manifest the significance of religion in their lives? Is the United States a religious country, and how does it compare to the rest of the world with respect to religion?

3. Discuss how the religious majority in a community can influence curriculum and instructional methodology. Can and should the majority religious group in a community determine what is taught in the schools?

4. What is the relationship of religion to public office? Why are some groups disproportionately represented in Congress, and how does this impact education within congressional districts, if at all?

5. What are the current trends with respect to membership in conservative, moderate, and liberal religious groups? What are the implications of these trends for the educational, political, and legal directions of the country?

6. How have Protestantism, Catholicism, and Judaism influenced American culture?

7. In what ways does gender affect religion and religion affect gender issues?

8. How do the perceptions about gay and homosexual individuals differ between religious conservatives and liberals? What are the responsibilities of the schools toward gay and lesbian students? How can tolerance and acceptance be promoted in the classroom?

9. What do laws permit with respect to school prayer? How and why do conservative Protestants want to change these laws? Do religious conservatives have valid concerns about our public schools?

10. What is secular humanism? What objections do the religious conservatives have against secular humanism in the schools?

Portfolio Activities

1. Form a group to study the multicultural curriculum or experiences provided in various private church schools. Divide your assignments so that the group can interview (if your community is large enough) a school administrator at a Roman Catholic school, a Protestant evangelical school, a Mainline Protestant church–related school, and an

Islamic school. If you are in a large metropolitan area a Jewish yeshiva may be available. Structure the assignments so that all of the schools interviewed have students at the same grade levels. Have students ask the school administrator what experiences or curriculum is provided to enhance their students' knowledge, sensitivity, and tolerance of other religious, ethnic, socioeconomic, and gender orientation groups. As a group, formulate a report looking at the similarities and differences between religious groups or denominations. (InTASC Standard 2: Learning Differences, Standard 4: Content Knowledge, and Standard 10: Leadership and Collaboration)

2. Utilizing various sources, including legal documents and search engines, find and summarize the court cases in your state in the last 25 years involving challenges to the First Amendment and public schools. (InTASC Standard 4: Content Knowledge)

3. Write a plan of action for meeting with parents and explaining to them how you will be addressing evolution in your class. Show what steps will be taken to avoid conflict with parental religious views. (InTASC Standard 2: Learning Differences, and Standard 10: Leadership and Collaboration)

Digital Resources for the Classroom

1. The Anti-Defamation League, founded by B'nai B'rith, a Jewish service organization, to combat anti-Semitism, has expanded its efforts against all forms of bigotry, including but not limited to that experienced by Christians and Muslims. The organization has been developing educational programs; see the web page on religious freedom: http://www.adl.org/main_Religious_Freedom/default.htm.

2. The Pew Forum on Religion and Public Life provides research, polls, surveys, and other information related to religion and public life: http://pewforum.org/.

3. The Tanenbaum Center for Interreligious Understanding promotes religious understanding between various religious groups: https://www.tanenbaum.org.

4. The American Religious Identification Survey (Kosmin & Keysar, 2009) provides insight into religion in the United States: http://www.americanreligionsurvey-aris.org/reports/ARIS_Report_2008.pdf.

5. The Pew Forum on Religion and Public Life-Religious Landscape Survey (2008), provides additional insights into religion in the United States: http://religions.pewforum.org/pdf/report2-religious-landscape-study-full.pdf.

MyEducationLab™

Go to the MyEducationLab (www.myeducationlab.com) for Multicultural Education and familiarize yourself with the topical content, which includes:

■ Assignments and Activities, tied to learning outcomes for the course, that can help you more deeply understand course content

- Building Teaching Skills and Dispositions learning units allow you to apply and practice your understanding of how to teach equitably in a multicultural education classroom
- Licensure Test Prep activities are available in the Book Resources to help you prepare for test taking
- A pretest with hints and feedback that tests your knowledge of this chapter's content
- Review, practice, and enrichment activities that will enhance your understanding of the chapter content
- A posttest with hints and feedback that allows you to test your knowledge again after having completed the enrichment activities

A Correlation Guide may be downloaded by instructors to show how MyEducationLab content aligns to this book.

Geography

The reality of any place is what its people remember of it.

Charles Kuralt, TV Journalist

| LEARNING OUTCOMES |

As you read the chapter, you should be able to:

- Explain what geography is and what the difference is between physical and human geography.

- Cite the primary characteristics of the South, New England and the Mid-Atlantic, Great Plains and Midwest, Southwest, and West regions of the United States.

- List some of the regional differences in education, religion, cuisine, health and well-being, and politics found in the United States.

- Differentiate characteristics of the rural versus urban areas of the United States.

- Examine how events in one part of the world affect the economics of other world regions.

- Articulate how to incorporate student geographical and cultural differences into the classroom.

278

In November a new student, Jack Williams, appeared at Mark Polaski's classroom door. Jack, whose family had moved to the neighborhood last week, appeared to be just another white student. Mr. Polaski assigned him a desk, asked him to introduce himself, and continued with the lesson.

Before a month had passed, Mr. Polaski noticed that other students had not accepted Jack. In fact, they were making fun of his mannerisms and dialect. He overheard a couple of the boys calling him a hillbilly. As he thought about Jack's involvement in the class up to that point, Mr. Polaski realized that Jack had been very quiet, not actively participating in the lively discussions that were encouraged. He was performing as well as most other students on the few tests that had been given, and he had turned in the required short paper on time just after Thanksgiving. Mr. Polaski tried to recall where Jack said he had last attended school. He was sure it was in a rural area of the state.

| REFLECTIONS |

1. Why was Jack not fitting into this diverse suburban school?

2. How does growing up in a different part of the country or world affect one's experiences in school?

3. How could Mr. Polaski learn more about Jack's cultural background?

4. If you were Mr. Polaski, how would you get the students to stop picking on Jack?

Geography and Culture

Our identities are closely linked to the geographic area in which we grew up and the places we later lived. One of the first questions we ask when meeting someone new is "Where are you from?" The answer will indicate whether we share a common background and experiences. Although our membership in other groups or microcultures may have a great impact on our identity, the place or places in which we have lived provide a cultural context for living.

Because we grew up in the same or a similar geographic area as our neighbors or friends does not mean we experienced the place in the same ways. Some members of a community have lived there much longer than others and have different histories and experiences that sometimes lead to conflict with more recent arrivals. The area takes on a different meaning based on a member's race, ethnicity, religion, age, and language, and how membership in those groups is viewed by other members of the community. One's job and educational background may take on different significance in one geographic area as compared to another. For example, almost all adults in one suburban neighborhood may have post-baccalaureate degrees and work as professionals or managers. Farming and related jobs are common in one area, logging and fishing in another, and manufacturing in yet another.

The natural surroundings and climate make a difference in the way we work, relax, and interact. People from Hawaii, Alaska, the mountains of Colorado, and the prairies of Nebraska adapt to their space in different ways. People in new environments may find that the "natives" use unfamiliar dialects and phrases and react to events somewhat differently than they are used to. Jack in the opening scenario, for instance, has a dialect and mannerisms that are different from those of other students in his new school. This strangeness is particularly noticeable when we travel outside the United States, but it also appears to some degree in different parts of the same city and from one region of the United States to another.

Different individuals and groups perceive places and events differently. Because their perceptions are different, their responses tend to be different. Some will find a given locale as the ideal place to live and raise a family; others will feel isolated, crowded, or entrapped. Mountains are critical to the well-being of some; others feel the need to be near bodies of water or the desert or greenery. Wide-open spaces in which one can live for a long period of time with little interaction with others provide freedom for some, but boredom and confinement for others. Cities can be exciting and stimulating places for some, but stifling and impersonal to others. Thus, the places in which to live provide complex multiple identities for the people who live in them. Understanding the place, including the particular part of the city or county, from which our students have come helps us know the context of their everyday experiences.

WHAT IS GEOGRAPHY?

You probably studied geography in elementary school as you learned about different parts of the world and memorized state capitals. We are enticed to learn more about a country when a disaster occurs, such as the 2010 earthquake in Haiti. Prior to the 2011 rebellions and conflicts in North African countries with continuous news coverage, many Americans would not have been able to locate Egypt, Tunisia, and Libya on a map. People who are fortunate enough to travel to other parts of the country and world become familiar with geographical, cultural, and language differences. People who are place-bound and unable to travel far beyond their own neighborhoods may have to learn about these differences in books, from the media, and on the Internet.

"Geography" comes from the Greek word *geographia,* which means a description of the earth's surface. It is the study of places, cities, countries, mountains, deserts, rural areas, oceans, continents, and communities. Geographers try to determine why places are the way they are. They not only explore the physical features of a place but they also examine the economic activities, human settlement patterns, and cultures of the people who live there. The place where one lives is the space or land area that is distinctive and has meaning or symbolism for the people who live there.

Physical geography is the study of the physical features of the earth such as the climate, soils, vegetation, water, and landforms. **Human geography,** on the other hand, is the study of the economic, social, and cultural systems that have evolved in a specific location. It encompasses many of the topics that are discussed in this book, such as classism, racism, ethnicity, poverty, language, sexual orientation, religion, exceptionalities, and age differences.

Geographers use a number of tools to record and track the physical and human geography of a place. Maps are the most common, as you probably remember from your study of geography. With today's technologies, geographers are able to understand an area in great and intricate detail through the use of computers, global positioning system (GPS) devices, and satellite images. Throughout this chapter we will use maps to understand the differences in the places our students live or used to live and the importance of location in one's everyday life.

OUR PLACE IN THE WORLD

Placing the United States within the world provides a context for understanding where we and others live. First, people are concentrated in certain areas since few choose to live in the earth's cold or dry areas. Three of every four people currently live in the Northern Hemisphere—the area north of the equator (Dahlman, Renwick & Bergman, 2011). Over half of the world's population of almost 7 billion live in Asia (Bremner, Frost, Haub, et al., 2010). China, with a population of over 1.3 billion and India, with almost 1.2 billion, are the two largest countries in the world in terms of population. The United States, the world's third largest country, had a population of around 313,232,044 in 2011 (U.S. Census Bureau, 2011d), or just less than 5% of the world's population.

North America has a culturally diverse population, most of whom emigrated from other parts of the world over the past 400 years. It is a resource-rich region that has undergone a great deal of economic development over the past 200 years. Its **metropolitan** areas are technology rich and oriented to a global economy, in which U.S. corporations have offices and employees

PAUSE TO REFLECT 9.1

Think about the geographic area in which you grew up (or one of them if you have moved from one area to another).

■ How would you describe the geographic landscape that influenced the way the people you know lived?

■ What stories were told when you were growing up that detailed someone's experience with the land or weather?

■ How do you think the place where you were raised has impacted your values and way of living?

in many parts of the world. The region is very consumer oriented, buying up the latest versions of the products its businesses produce. Although it is an affluent area, many of its citizens live in poverty.

Regional Diversity in the United States

Regional differences become apparent to educators as they move from one area to another to work. Sometimes local and regional differences will hardly be noticeable. At other times, they will lead to a number of adjustments in the way one lives, the content that can be taught in the classroom, and the manner in which one interacts with the community. For example, religion plays a more important role in some regions of the country than others, which could influence a teacher's approach to teaching sex education or evolution. Not only teachers move around the country and globe; so do students and their families, especially if they are in the military or on a fast track at a multinational corporation. Students such as Jack in the chapter-opening scenario may experience cultural shock, something that should be considered as they settle in a new school. To meet the needs of students, educators have to be aware of the influences of geography and space on the culture of the people who live in the area, especially school-age children.

Regional comparisons are at times difficult to make, with different sources utilizing different regional categories. The federal government tends to use four regions: Northeast, South, Midwest, and West. However, some of the reporting is broken down into smaller regions (e.g., New England, Appalachia, Southwest, Great Plains). In an attempt to minimize possible confusion, as we discuss each region we will provide examples of states in that region.

The 2010 Census revealed that the minority (non-white) population grew in every region of the United States. This was characterized by the 43% increase in Hispanics. Nearly half of the population in the West (47.2%) is made up of minorities. Minorities comprise 40% of the population in the South, 22% in the Midwest, and 31% in the Northeast regions of the United States (U.S. Census Bureau, 2011c).

The states with the highest minority percentages are primarily in the West, while those with the lowest are primarily in the Northeast. In four states—Hawaii, California, New Mexico, and Texas—and the District of Columbia, minorities comprise more than half of the population. In addition, Arizona, Florida, Maryland, Mississippi, Nevada, New Jersey, and New York had minority populations exceeding 40%. The states with the lowest percentages of minorities included Maine, Vermont, West Virginia, and New Hampshire. While the minority percentages in these four states were below 10%, all four of these states had increases in their minority population during the 2000 to 2010 census period, which far outpaced increases in the white population (U.S. Census Bureau, 2011c). Figure 9.1 shows the minority populations in the various regions of the United States.

From 1892 to 1954 immigrants entered the country by boat at Ellis Island on the East Coast. By the end of the twentieth century most were entering through airports in New York City, Los Angeles, and Seattle. They established or moved to ethnic enclaves that were similar to areas they had just left. In these communities they did not have to assimilate into the dominant culture and could continue to use their native languages. Examples can be found in the metropolitan Los Angeles area, where communities such as Little Saigon, Little Tokyo, Chinatown, and Koreatown have been established.

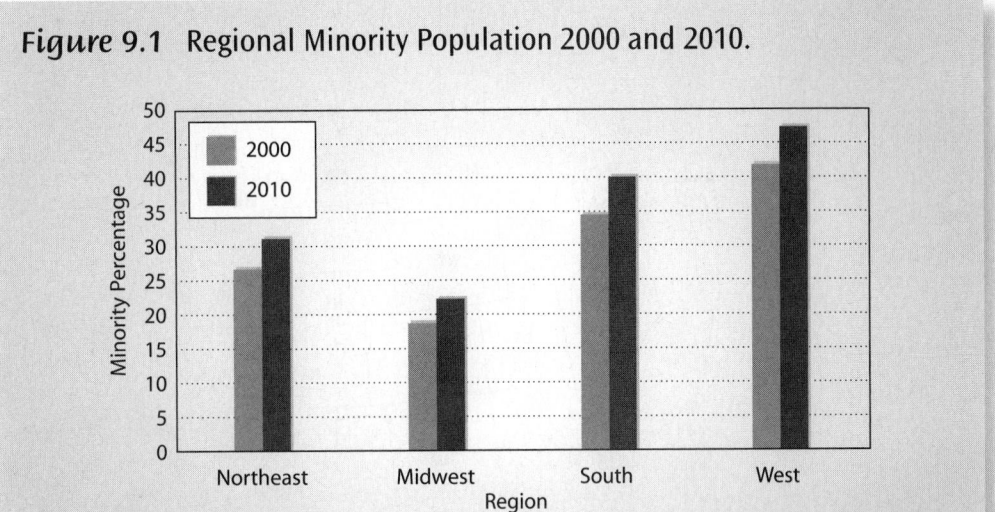

Figure 9.1 Regional Minority Population 2000 and 2010.

Source: U.S. Census Bureau. (2011). Adapted from: Overview of Race and Hispanic Origin: 2010, http://www.census.gov/prod/cen2010/briefs/c2010br-02.pdf.

A larger percentage of more recent immigrants are joining family members who live in the **suburbs** or in small towns. Some, especially refugees, have been sponsored by churches or community agencies in nonurban areas. Others have been attracted to the Midwest and South for jobs in the meatpacking and farming industries. Still others have chosen rural areas because they think the values and lifestyle are closer to their own there than in urban areas.

Whites represent many ethnic groups with different cultures and experiences, some who emigrated from Europe several centuries ago and others who are new immigrants. Whites in the South and New England are predominantly from Anglo backgrounds, but the ethnic diversity within the white population is increasing with migration from other states. The Mid-Atlantic and Midwest states have a greater mix of European ancestry from Great Britain, Ireland, Germany, Italy, Poland, and other Eastern European countries. A large portion of the population in the central Great Plains states is German American. Swedes and Norwegians settled in the northern states of this region (Johnson, Haarmann, Johnson & Clawson, 2010).

Characteristics of the population and land on which they live can be used to group geographic areas with similar landscapes and histories. The racial, ethnic, and religious diversity varies from one region to another. The interests and perspectives of those who live in various geographic regions often are reflected in their stands on state and federal issues, as reflected in national elections, which distinguish red (Republican) and blue (Democrat) states.

We will explore some of these regional differences in this section.

THE SOUTH

Outsiders identify Southerners by their distinctive dialect but may know little else about the region other than its involvement in the Civil War and the civil rights issues of the 1950s and 1960s. It is vibrant, rich in history and culture, and influenced by the many new and diverse individuals settling in the region. The area includes the 12 southeastern states shown in Figure 9.2, but the culture extends into the states that border them as well—into east Texas, east Oklahoma,

Figure 9.2 Map of the South.

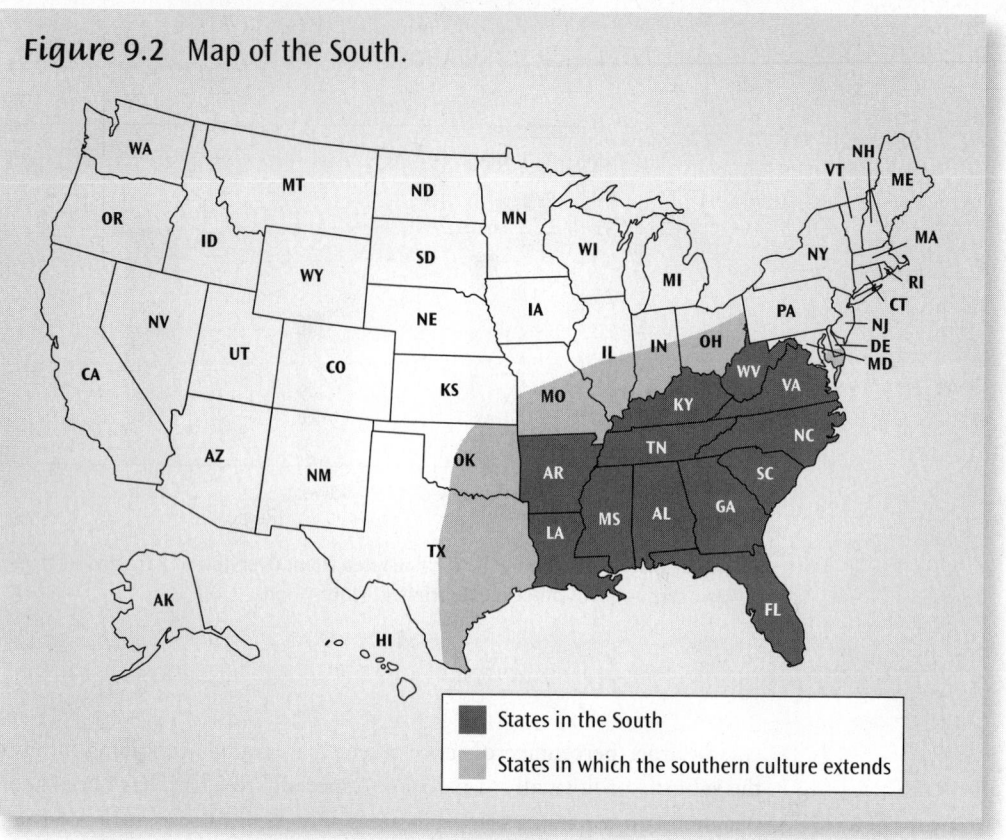

States in the South

States in which the southern culture extends

southern Missouri, southern Illinois, southern Indiana, southern Ohio, the eastern shore of Maryland, and southern Delaware. Not all states in the region share the same Southern culture. For example, south Florida, with its Cuban and Jewish populations, does not fit the traditional Southern culture and language patterns. Many northerners and others from outside the region have settled in Atlanta, one of the largest Southern cities. Others from northern states have found employment opportunities, have retired in the region, or spend the winter months there.

Nearly one of three of the nation's residents lives in the South (U.S. Census Bureau, 2011c). The region has a number of major cities: Atlanta, Nashville, Charlotte, Orlando, Miami, and New Orleans.

Characteristics of the South.   There is not a single Southern culture across the region. It includes many subregions, such as the Delta of Mississippi, the Low Country of South Carolina, south Florida, the Piedmonts of North Carolina and Georgia, the Ozarks of Arkansas, and the Bluegrass Country of Kentucky—all with their own distinctive cultures. Traditional cultures have been maintained by American Indian tribes and other groups, such as the Gullah of South Carolina and Georgia, and the Cajuns of Louisiana. The Southern culture has evolved from the mixing of its numerous American Indian, European, and African cultures—a process of **creolization.**

More African Americans continue to live in the South than in any other region of the United States. Fifty percent of U.S. African Americans live in that region (U.S. Census Bureau, 2011c). Until recently, most white Southerners were Protestants of English, Irish, or Scottish descent. The population is much more diverse today. The *Encyclopedia of Southern Culture* lists 34 American Indian and 54 other ethnic groups (Wilson & Ray, 2007). Since the 1970s, a growing number of Asian Americans have settled in the South, with the largest numbers being Filipino, Korean, Vietnamese, Hmong, and Asian Indian. Larger numbers of Latinos began to move into the Southern states in the 1990s. During this same period, the number of Middle Easterners increased in Florida, North Carolina, Texas, and Virginia.

Education in the South.   Schools were slow to develop in the South, and when they did, they were primarily for the children of landowners. It was illegal to teach slaves and their children. Most schools across the South were segregated by race until a decade or more after the 1954 *Brown* decision. During the period in which schools were being desegregated, many European American families established their own private schools—many of them Christian schools—or moved from cities to rural or suburban areas to avoid attending schools with African Americans. At the same time, many school districts did become more integrated, sometimes extending desegregation plans beyond city borders into the suburbs.

APPALACHIA

The region of the country called Appalachia follows the Appalachian Mountain chain, crossing many states from its northern projection into New York through northern Maryland and all of West Virginia; through western parts of Virginia, North Carolina, South Carolina, and Georgia along with eastern Kentucky and Tennessee; and into northern Mississippi and Alabama. Appalachia has been described in numerous fiction and nonfiction publications over the past century as mountainous and backward, not maintaining progress with other parts of the country. A commission convened by President John F. Kennedy in 1963 brought to public attention the severe poverty prevalent in the region at that time.

Characteristics of Appalachia.   The people of Appalachia have sometimes been stereotyped as mountaineers or hillbillies. The mountaineer is usually seen as a rugged and independent individual who has mastered the mountains. The hillbilly is a caricature of a person from the back country. These stereotypes have been promoted in popular cartoon strips like *Li'l Abner* and *Snuffy Smith* and television shows like *The Beverly Hillbillies* and *Dukes of Hazzard*. Appalachians have been projected as living in poverty, feuding with neighbors, operating moonshine stills, using violence to settle disputes, and being lazy. However, the poverty rate in Appalachia today is about the same as in other rural areas of the country, with the exception of eastern Kentucky, West Virginia, and northern Mississippi, where it remains below the national average (Johnson, Haarman, et al. 2010). While in 1964 one of three Appalachians lived in poverty, as of 2011 the poverty rate has been reduced to 18% (Appalachian Regional Commission, n.d.*a*).

Although bordered by Atlanta, Pittsburgh, and Cincinnati, Appalachia is primarily rural. Chattanooga and Knoxville (TN), Charleston (WV), and Asheville (NC) are its largest cities. Although more of the population live in rural areas than in most other parts of the country, the majority live in metropolitan areas and participate in the related commerce and labor markets.

Retirees and community activists have moved into the area, replacing some longtime residents and increasing the cost of living. Although coal mines still operate in the region, tourism leads its economic growth. It is home to the Blue Ridge Parkway and Shenandoah and Great Smoky Mountains National Parks. Appalachia has limited diversity. The population is predominantly white and reflects the general religious and ethnic background of the South.

Education in Appalachia. Historically, school attendance in the rural and mountain regions of Appalachia was lower than other parts of the country. The situation has improved dramatically since the 1960s. However, the percentage of the adult population in the most rural, isolated areas of the region who have finished high school and college are lower compared with the rest of the U.S. population (Appalachian Regional Commission, n.d.*b*).

NEW ENGLAND AND THE MID-ATLANTIC

The northeastern states that comprise New England and the Mid-Atlantic were home to the early political centers of the European settlers. As shown in Figure 9.3, the six states in New England include Connecticut, Maine, Massachusetts, New Hampshire, Rhode Island, and Vermont. Except in their major cities near the coast, such as Boston, Providence, and Hartford, residency is rather sparse. Dialects of New Englanders differ from area to area, but help distinguish them. The Mid-Atlantic area, with Delaware, Maryland, New Jersey, New York, and Pennsylvania plus the District of Columbia, is the more populated of these two areas, with major cities such as New York City, Philadelphia, Pittsburgh, Baltimore, and Washington, DC.

Characteristics of New England and the Mid-Atlantic. New England is among the least racially diverse areas of the country. For example, the total minority population in 2010 was 4.8% in Maine, 6.1% in New Hampshire, and 4.7% in Vermont (U.S. Census Bureau, 2011c).

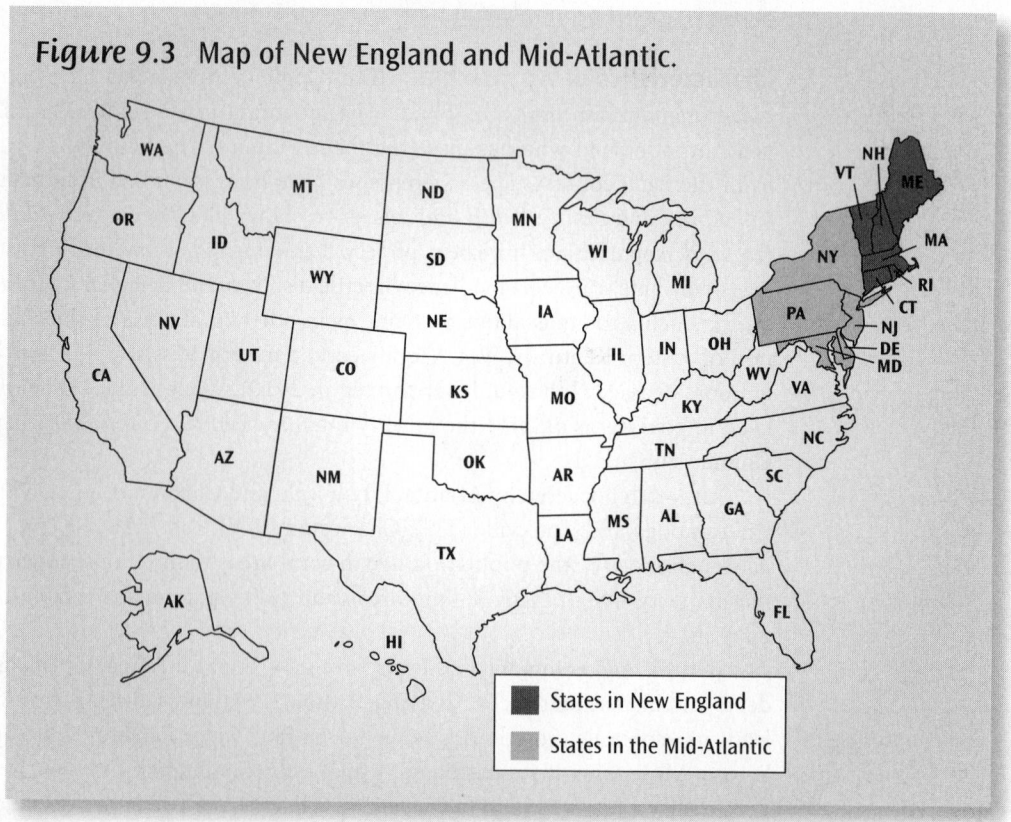

Figure 9.3 Map of New England and Mid-Atlantic.

Approximately 15% of the U.S. population live in the Mid-Atlantic. It is the most diverse region east of the Mississippi River. The population is 63% white and 37% minority (U.S. Census Bureau, 2011c). Most of the population in these two regions live in a metropolitan area. In contrast, Maine and Vermont are primarily rural. The Atlantic Coast is an important commerce center for these areas, and tourism flourishes. Companies with a high-technology focus have established roots in a number of these metropolitan areas.

Per capita income in 2008 was highest ($64,991) in the District of Columbia, which also had the highest poverty rate in the region, indicating a wide difference in the income and standard of living between the rich and poor in that city. Connecticut had the next highest per capita income, at $56,249. Incomes in Maine ($35,381) and Vermont ($38,880) are more similar to those in other rural states (U.S. Census Bureau, 2010i). Poverty rates in all New England states in 2009 were below the 14.3% national average. With the exception of the District of Columbia, which had a poverty rate 3.3% higher than the national average, all of the states in the Mid-Atlantic area had poverty rates below the national average (U.S. Census Bureau, 2010i).

Education in New England and the Mid-Atlantic. Cities in this region have been home to many new immigrants for centuries. Concerns were raised in colonial days about the cultures and language of German immigrants changing the Anglo culture. German was the language used in some schools and churches. By the mid-1880s, Catholics complained that the Protestant bible was used in public schools. These religious debates led to riots in some cities of this region and to the eventual move to the establishment of Catholic schools and a more secular curriculum in public schools.

New England and the Mid-Atlantic are home to some of the country's oldest and most prestigious colleges and universities. Harvard University was established in 1641, Yale University in 1701, and Princeton University in 1746. The first elementary and secondary schools were also established there, with the purpose of teaching the scriptures to develop moral citizens.

High school dropout rates for the five reporting New England states were fractionally lower than the national average. The dropout rates for the four reporting Mid-Atlantic states and the District of Columbia were fractionally higher than the national average (National Center for Education Statistics, 2007).

THE GREAT PLAINS AND MIDWEST

The Great Plains, sometimes remembered for the infamous dust bowl of the 1930s, lies between the Rocky Mountains and the Great Lakes as shown in Figure 9.4. They extend into central Texas on the south and into the Canadian provinces of Manitoba, Saskatchewan, and Alberta on the north. This region is often called the nation's breadbasket, producing enough grain to feed several nations. It is among the flattest surfaces on earth, interrupted only by the Black Hills of South Dakota and the Ozarks in Missouri.

The states of the Midwest connect the Mid-Atlantic and Great Plains regions. The five states of Illinois, Indiana, Michigan, Ohio, and Wisconsin are all connected to the Great Lakes and the rivers that lead to the Mississippi. This access to waterways, and later to the interstate highways that crossed them, allowed these states to develop industries whose products could easily be shipped to distant markets. As a result, these states are more populous, with their major industrial cities of Chicago, Detroit, Milwaukee, Cleveland, Columbus, and Indianapolis. Less than one of four residents in the Midwest lives outside of a metropolitan area.

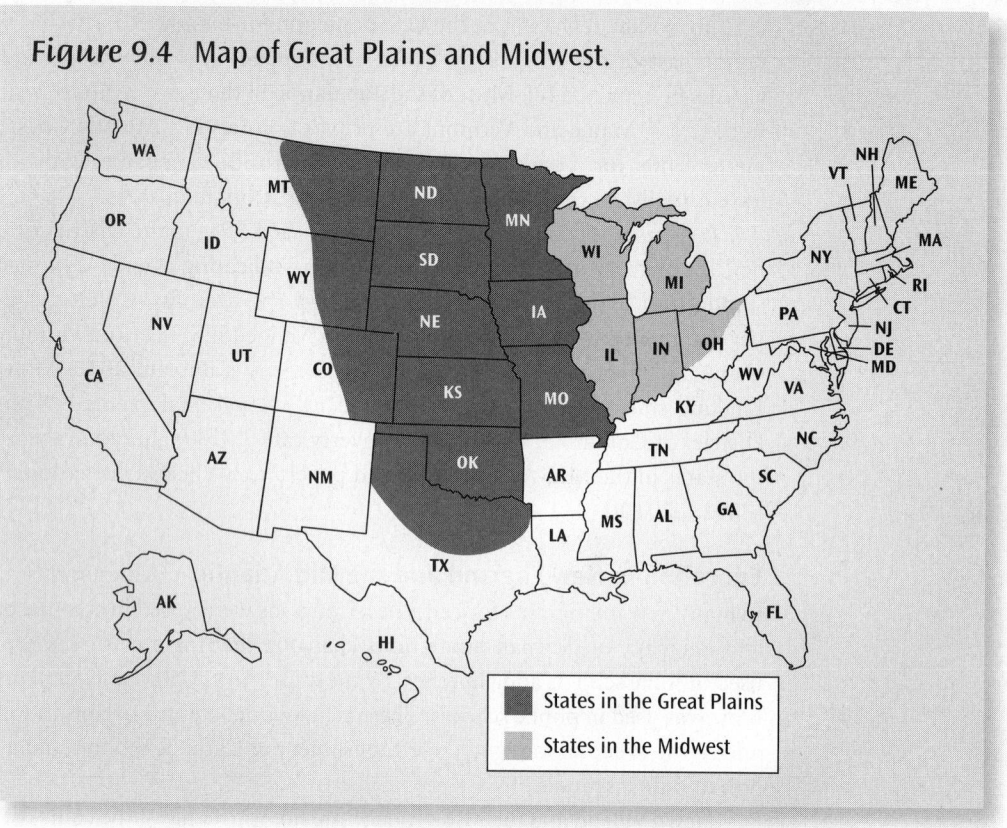

Figure 9.4 Map of Great Plains and Midwest.

States in the Great Plains

States in the Midwest

Characteristics of the Great Plains and Midwest. To the city dweller, the western Great Plains may appear uninhabitable. One-third of the people in this area live in rural areas of 2,500 people or less; Alaska is the only area that is more rural. Kansas City, St. Louis, and Oklahoma City are the area's urban areas; Dallas borders the area on the south. Smaller cities exist in the midst of farms, ranches, and small towns. A family may travel long distances to shop or visit neighbors. The population is sparse, with 30% of the region's population living in Missouri. The populations of North Dakota and South Dakota are each well under 1 million, which is less than those of a number of U.S. cities (U.S. Census Bureau, 2010h).

The Midwest states have greater diversity. Seventy-eight percent of the population is European American. The percentage of minorities ranges from 36.3% in Illinois to 16.7% in Wisconsin (U.S. Census Bureau, 2011c).

The Great Plains is home to a number of American Indian tribes. American Indians comprise 9.5% of South Dakota's population. In Oklahoma, Montana, and North Dakota they represent 8%, 6.4%, and 5.6%, respectively. Oklahoma has the greatest diversity in this region, with an overall 31.3% minority population (U.S. Census Bureau, 2010j).

As might be expected in a primarily rural area, the per capita income in the Great Plains is among the lowest in the country with the exception of Minnesota. The Midwest states are somewhat higher, but less than the national average in all states except Illinois. At the same time, most states in these two regions have a lower-than-average poverty rate.

Education in the Great Plains and Midwest. Although the region has less ethnic and racial diversity than other areas of the country, a growing number of school districts have implemented bilingual and ESL programs to serve students who speak an American Indian language, Spanish, Russian, Vietnamese or other Asian, African, or European language of recent immigrants. Communities strongly support the local control of schools and sometimes resent the perceived intrusion of the state or federal government in local school issues.

THE SOUTHWEST

Mexican and American Indian influences are prevalent in the culture, architecture, and commerce of the Southwest. The Southwest states, shown in Figure 9.5, include Arizona, New Mexico, Southern California, and West Texas.

By the beginning of 2011, the drug wars in Mexico had claimed lives at an unprecedented rate and showed no signs of easing. This problem, coupled with political and economic troubles in Mexico, has contributed to the flow of undocumented immigrants into the United States. The U.S. Customs and Border Patrol and Drug Enforcement Agents work continuously to secure the border by searching for undocumented immigrants and drug traffickers. Latinos from all walks of life, including U.S. citizens, are often stopped and questioned by government authorities. Power struggles between dominant and oppressed groups, landowners and migrant workers, and potential industries and the owners of water rights dominate the landscape.

Characteristics of the Southwest. Over half of the population in New Mexico and Texas (as well as California, in the West) have national origins other than a country in Europe. Forty-five percent of New Mexico's population are Latino, 10% American Indian. Thirty percent of Arizona's population are Latino, and 5% are American Indian. Around 37% of the population of Texas are Latino. The African American portion of the population across these states ranges

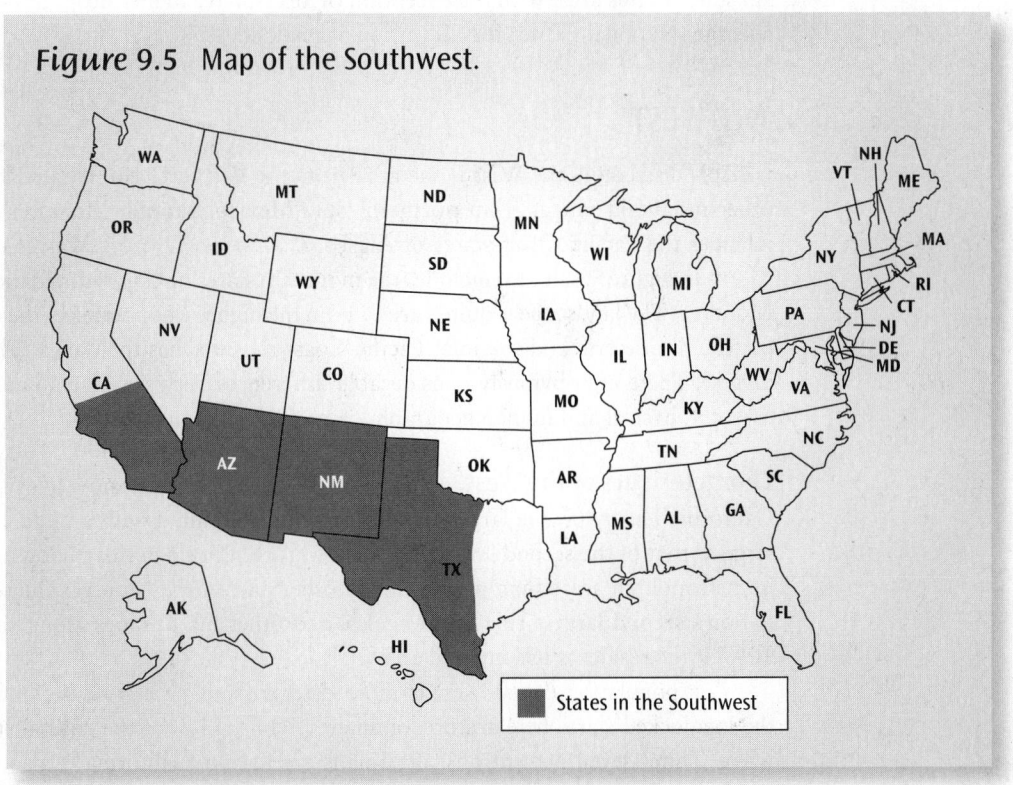

Figure 9.5 Map of the Southwest.

States in the Southwest

from 3% in New Mexico to 12% in Texas. The population in the Southwest are younger than in the rest of the country, which results in a growing number of students in schools (U.S. Census Bureau, 2010j).

The sun, dry climate, desert, and mountains attract retirees and working people looking for a change. Per capita income is low in the southwestern states, on par with the Great Plains. The percentage of people in poverty is higher in New Mexico, Arizona, and Texas than in the rest of the nation, with New Mexico the highest, at about 4% above the national average (U.S. Census Bureau, 2010i).

Education in the Southwest.   The use of Spanish and American Indian languages in instruction has been controversial for over 150 years. In 1855 California required that instruction be in English only. Texas soon followed, and by 1918 it had made the use of Spanish in schools a criminal offense. School segregation was common, especially in California and Texas, until midcentury. American Indian students in this and other regions were sometimes removed from their homes to attend boarding schools.

Bilingual education continues to be debated across the Southwest and other regions of the country. The public does not fully agree on the need for bilingual education, as shown in voter referenda (e.g., California Proposition 227 and Arizona Proposition 203) opposing it in some states, limiting its use in public schools. These state propositions are discussed in Chapter 6. Some local school boards have reprimanded teachers for teaching Mexican American history and the histories of other oppressed groups. The Navajo Reservation, however, operates its own educational system. Some schools in the region have been established to place American Indian history and traditions at the center of the curriculum rather than building on the traditional Eurocentric approach to schooling.

Teacher salaries are similar to those in the Great Plains, among the lowest in the country. All states in this area, with the exception of Texas, have higher dropout rates than the national average (National Center for Education Statistics, 2007).

THE WEST

For this discussion, the West is the area from the Pacific Ocean to the Rocky Mountains and other mountain ranges from northern New Mexico through Montana and into Canada. It includes the Pacific Coast states of Alaska, California, Oregon, Washington, and Hawaii, as shown in Figure 9.6. It also includes the mountain states of Colorado, Idaho, Nevada, Utah, and Montana. The landscape is quite varied, from the highest mountains in the country to mountain plateaus to deserts and the long Pacific Coast that reaches to Alaska. This area is extremely diverse. There are obviously considerable differences between Hawaii and Montana in terms of both physical and human geography.

Characteristics of the West.   Almost 20% of U.S. residents now live in these western states. California has by far the largest population in the country, with a population almost twice as large as that of the second largest state, New York. People in this region are more likely to live in metropolitan areas than people in any other part of the country. The region is home to the nation's second largest city, Los Angeles, and other major cities along the West Coast. Only 10% of the residents live in rural areas.

The population of the West is more diverse than the rest of the country. While 75% of the landlocked states here are predominantly white, 51% of the coastal states' population are white. Thirty-seven percent of Californians are Latino. California is also home to 4.6 million

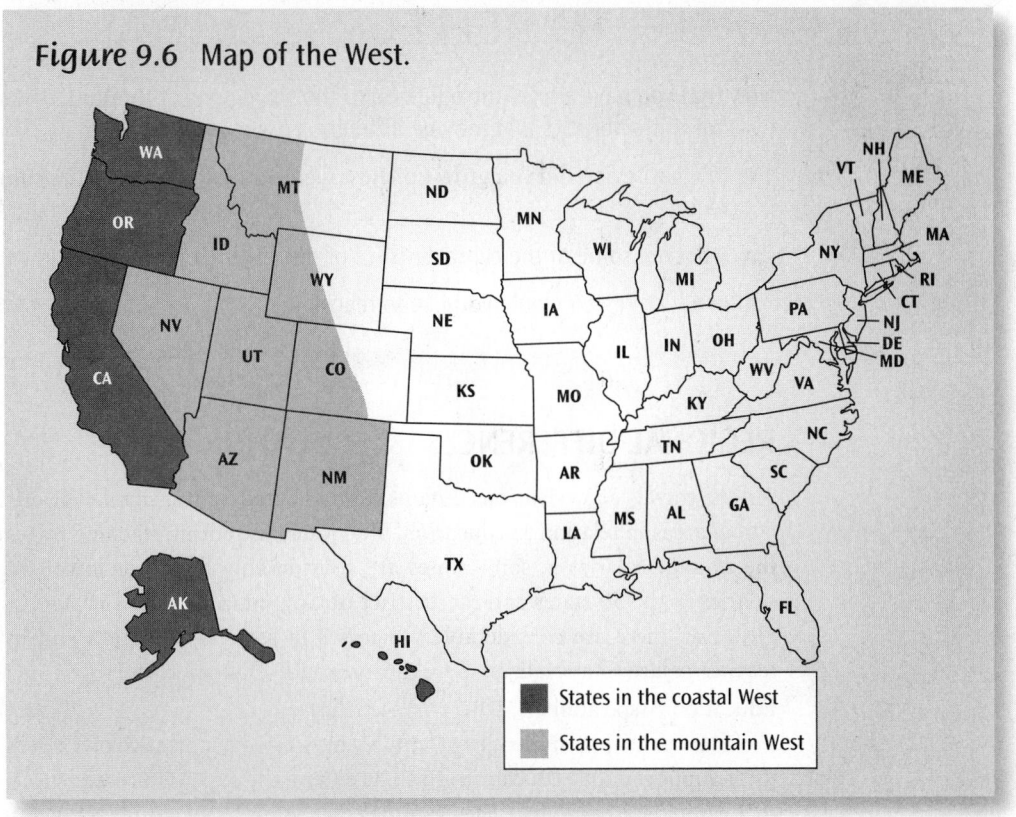

Figure 9.6 Map of the West.

Legend:
- States in the coastal West
- States in the mountain West

Asian Americans (U.S. Census Bureau, 2010j). The early sugar and pineapple plantation owners brought large numbers of Chinese, Japanese, Korean, and Filipino contract laborers to Hawaii. They also brought smaller numbers of Europeans and Latinos to fill their needs. Most of these workers and their families remained after completing their contracts, making Hawaii one of the most racially and ethnically diverse states. The other states in the region are not as diverse as California and Hawaii, with whites making up over 80% of the population. Poverty rates for states in this region were below the national average with the exception of Oregon, which was the same, and Idaho, which was 0.1 percentage point above average (U.S. Census Bureau, 2010i).

Education in the West. A number of Catholic mission schools, which had been established by Spanish priests, existed in California by the time of the Revolutionary War. The goal was to Christianize the local American Indian population, in the process teaching the converts the Spanish way of life. The Mexican government tried to secularize the missions in the early 1800s, but the influence of Catholicism on the culture remains in the cities that evolved from those early missions.

As in other regions of the country, American Indian, Mexican American, and Asian American students were categorized as non-white. In many communities they were required to attend segregated schools until the mid-twentieth century. As in the Southwest, the use of native languages for instruction continues to be debated. Along the Pacific Coast, language diversity is even greater than in the Southwest because of the large number of Asians and Latinos, many of them foreign-born or second-generation Americans. California, as discussed in the section on the Southwest, has implemented a voter referendum severely limiting the use of bilingual education. Dropout rates are higher than the national average in all states in this region.

PAUSE TO REFLECT 9.2

Now that you have a brief introduction to the six regions of the United States, think about cultural characteristics that may be different from your own.

- In what region did you grow up? How were you influenced by the culture of that region?

- What are some of the characteristics of the culture of the region in which you now live?

- In which region would you like to teach? Why?

REGIONAL DIFFERENCES IN EDUCATION

As one travels across various regions in the United States, significant differences can be found across areas in relation to education. Individuals exploring teaching opportunities will find that the average salaries in some states are considerably higher or lower than in others. Teacher salaries in the 50 states and the District of Columbia average $55,350, as shown in Table 9.1. However, there are considerable variations in salaries by region and by state. Average state teacher salaries range from $35,136 in South Dakota to $71,470 in New York (National Education Association, 2010).

State per capita student expenditures may also be indicative of a state's commitment or ability to support public education. To some extent, the expenditure variations may be a function of the regional cost of living. The National Education Association (NEA) found that expenditures varied considerable across states and reported that average per capita student expenditure in the United States was $10,586. New Jersey spent a high of $16,967 per student, while Arizona's expenditure was a low of $6,170 (NEA, 2011).

Educational attainment varies across regions. The percentage of individuals age 25 and above without a high school diploma varies across the different regions in the country. The Northeast and Midwest are at 11.8% and 10.2%, respectively, as of 2011. The South and West regions do not fare as favorably, with 15.0% and 14.8% (U.S. Census, 2011d) without secondary completion. The lack of high school completion could be a function of any of a number of variables (e.g., older immigrants without high school completion and higher dropout rates).

Regional Religious Differences. Religious differences are one of if not *the* most important of the regional differences in the United States, as well as other parts of the world. The daily behaviors and values of an individual may have a direct correlation to the individual's religious beliefs. Diet, values, and politics are often functions

Table 9.1 **Average Teacher Salaries by Region, 2008–10**

50 states and D.C.	$55,350
New England	$61,563
Mideast	$65,986
Southeast	$48,931
Great Lakes	$56,988
Plains	$47,754
Southwest	$46,806
R ocky Mountains	$47,649
Far West	$65,437

Source: Adapted from National Education Association. (2010). Summary Table G. Estimated Average Annual Salaries of Total Instructional Staff and Classroom Teachers, 2008-2009-10 In Rankings & Estimates of the States 2009 and Estimates of School Statistics 2010. Retrieved March 19, 2011, http://www.nea.org/assets/docs/010rankings.pdf.

of one's religion, as discussed in more detail in Chapter 8. Because values are often reflected in the platforms of political parties, individuals tend to support either liberal or conservative platforms, parties, and candidates. The Republican Party typically adopts the more conservative platforms and thus has tended to win the support of those states and regions where the residents are religious conservatives. Thus, in recent national elections the South and Midwest states along with the Mountain West have generally supported Republican candidates. The Northeast and the Pacific West, including Hawaii, have tended to support Democratic candidates.

Newport (2009a) found significant geographical differences in the religiosity of the American people. Based on responses to a question on the importance of religion in people's lives, the most religious segment of the population apparently reside in the South, supporting the contention tha the South is a major part of what is referred to as the Bible Belt. The six states with the highest responses on the importance of religion included Mississippi 85%, Alabama 82%, South Carolina 80%, Tennessee 79%, Louisiana 78%, and Arkansas 78%.

The states with the lowest religiosity responses are primarily in the Northeast and include Vermont, 42%; New Hampshire, 46%; Maine, 48%; Massachusetts, 48%; and Alaska, 51%.

Newport (2008) found the strongest belief in God among those living in the South (86%), followed by the Midwest (83%), the East (80%), and the West (59%). Newport (2010), in another, related survey, found that 9 of the 10 states with highest weekly religious service attendance were in the South. Mississippi ranked at the top, with 63%, and Utah, the only non-Southern state ranked in the middle of the top 10. At 23%, Vermont was the state with the lowest religious attendance and was joined by five other Northeast states in the bottom 10. Nevada joined far western states to round out the lowest 10 states in religious attendance. As might be expected from these findings, Newport (2009a) found that while 65% of Americans indicated that religion was important in their lives, the states with the highest percentages of residents indicating the importance of religion were in the South, led by Mississippi at 85%. The Northeast had 6 states ranked among the bottom 10 and the remaining 4 were western states.

The Pew survey (2008) also found that the South had the largest number of evangelicals, while the largest concentration of Catholics was in the Northeast. The Northeast and Northwest, along with Hawaii (Pew, 2008; Newport, 2009b), had the largest representation of unaffiliated individuals, including the largest numbers of atheists and agnostics. Newport (2009b) reported that the largest concentration of non-Catholics is in the South and nearby states. Catholics are heavily represented in Mid-Atlantic and New England states. As might be expected, the largest concentration of Latter-Day Saints (Mormons) is found in Utah and surrounding states, while the largest concentration of Jews is found in the Mid-Atlantic states. Other concentrations of Jews are found in Florida and California.

Regional Cuisine. Next to religion, for many individuals the most important factor associated with geography is the food. The mention of Philly cheese steak sandwiches, tamales and enchiladas, New England clam chowder, barbecued ribs, sushi, deep dish pizza, or country ham and red-eye gravy quickly brings a warm smile to the face of an individual from the region associated with the particular food. One person's feast, however, may bring a frown to one unfamiliar with that cuisine. American regional cuisines are as different as regional dialects and regional religious and political values.

As individuals migrated to the United States from different parts of the world, they brought with them their cuisines. Different groups of immigrants settled in different regions of the country, and each regional cuisine developed over time, influenced by the natural ingredients of the region and the historical cuisines of the settlers. New England cooking is heavily influenced by the local ingredients, such as seafood, apples, and cranberries, and by the cooking styles of the early English settlers.

Midwest cuisine relies heavily on beef, corn, dairy products, and the influence of German and Scandinavian settlers. Cuisine of the South is influenced by Spanish, English, and French settlers and the African slaves who served as the family cooks. We often see ingredients such as black-eyed peas, okra, and turnip greens served with Southern meals. The Southwest has been heavily influenced by the Spanish and Mexicans. The Northwest cuisine has much of its influence from local ingredients such as fish and game.

Hawaii plantation owners brought in contract workers from China, Japan, Korea, the Philippines, Portugal, Puerto Rico, and Europe. The Hawaiian cuisine is perhaps one of the most eclectic of all cuisines, reflecting not only the influence of the native Hawaiians, but also that of the many immigrant groups that settled in the islands.

Regional Health and Well-Being.
Health issues are closely associated with regional diets. Some Southern states are known for their tasty fried foods such as fried chicken, country (or chicken) fried steaks, fried catfish, barbecue, and delicious desserts. While these foods may be a culinary delight, excessive amounts may contribute to health risks.

The traditional native Hawaiian diet is one of the healthiest in the world. It is high in starch and fiber and is low in saturated fat, sodium, and cholesterol. It includes poi (made from the taro root), seafood, seaweed, leafy vegetables, fruit, chicken, hunted game, yams, and breadfruit. These foods were the staples of the early Hawaiians, and physicians in Hawaii to this day prescribe such a diet to individuals with health risks such as obesity and heart disease.

Hawaii tops the nation in overall well-being (Mendes, 2010) as determined by six indices: life evaluation, emotional health, work environment, physical health, healthy behaviors, and access to basic necessities. Among the top 10 states, 5 are in the West and Mountain West regions; for the states with the lowest well-being, 7 of the bottom 11 are Southern states. In addition to diet, there are socioeconomic and planned physical activity factors that may influence these findings.

In a related study, Witters (2010) also found a correlation between obesity and one's region of the country. Nationally 26.6% of adults are obese, but 29.4% in the South, 29.0% in the Midwest, 25.8% in the East, and 23.3% in the West were found to be obese. Associated health risks were also more prevalent in the higher-obesity states. These health risks include high blood pressure, high cholesterol, diabetes, and heart attack. These findings have important instructional implications for the classroom. From the time students enter kindergarten until they graduate, a strong emphasis on healthy living should be an integral part of the curriculum.

Regional Political Differences.
During and at the conclusion of every national election, maps of election results are posted in the media in the form of color-coded maps of all of the states. The maps use the traditional red for states won by Republicans and blue for those won by Democrats. In the 2008 presidential election, and both the 2008 and 2010 congressional and gubernatorial elections, many of the results were somewhat predictable. The states in the northeastern and far western United States were mostly shaded in blue, with the notable exception of Alaska, which is typically Republican. The South, Midwest, and Southwest are primarily Republican and red, as are most of the Mountain West states, such as Utah, Idaho, Wyoming, and Montana. Many of the states around the Great Lakes, such as Ohio, Michigan, Minnesota, and Wisconsin, are sometimes considered "battleground" or "swing" states, in which neither major political party has such overwhelming public support that election results can be taken for granted. The electorate in one of these states may switch political preferences from one election

to another, depending on the major issues at the time of the election (e.g., unemployment, the economy, war).

There are many other regional differences, too many to include here. However, this sampling of some of the important differences may help one understand how diverse the United States is. Understanding the diversity of one's own country should lead to the realization that other countries must also be diverse.

Rural, Urban, and Suburban Areas

Now that we have explored regions of the United States, let's examine differences within each region that also influence our lives. The way we experience life and our culture is greatly influenced by the people who share the space and place in which we live. We become very familiar with the place in which we live and know what is expected of us and others. This comfortableness is a reason why many teacher candidates indicate that they want to teach in or near the area in which they grew up.

Seventy-nine percent of the U.S. population live in towns, cities, and metropolitan areas with 2,500 people or more (U.S. Census Bureau, 2010j). Teaching in an isolated rural area hundreds of miles from a shopping center is very different from teaching in a wealthy suburban area with access to a wide range of cultural and sporting events. Let's examine the characteristics of rural, urban, and suburban areas that may help you determine where you would like to teach.

RURAL AREAS

In 1900 a majority of Americans lived in rural areas. Beginning early in the twentieth century, large numbers of rural workers migrated to cities for employment. Today rural areas are the location of choice for 21% of the U.S. population (U.S. Census Bureau, 2010j) and many people around the world. They may choose to live in rural areas because they enjoy the wide open space, the stars in the sky, as well as fishing, hunting, and other outdoor activities. In rural areas, there are fewer people with whom to contend and the freedom to have more control of one's life. Many of us have grown up in rural areas, but a growing number have moved from cities to escape the crowding, traffic, crime, pollution, and bureaucracies of city life—to recapture a quality of life that they believe provides a healthier environment for their families.

While there may be a tendency to think of rural areas as populated primarily by individuals involved in farming, less than 2% of Americans farm for a living today (U.S. Department of Agriculture, n.d.). The massive areas of rural land are dotted with small towns, some of which serve as the county seats for government purposes. The residents of these towns may work in a nearby city or in local manufacturing establishments. They may provide services to the farming communities as the managers and laborers at grain elevators, where the process of distributing grain to national and world markets begins. Businesses sell supplies needed to raise crops or animals, buy and sell meat products at the stockyards, and produce and deliver gas and oil required for farming. Grocery stores and other retail stores serve farm and small town residents, although some must drive many miles to the nearest mall to access larger stores and more options.

Populations of Rural Areas. The states with the largest rural populations are California, Texas, and New York, in that order (U.S. Census Bureau, 2010j). The rural population across the country is predominantly of European background. However, the majority of the 1.9 million American Indians and Alaskan Natives who receive services from the Department of the Interior through the 564 federally recognized tribes live in rural areas (U.S. Department of Interior, n.d.*a*).

In recent decades, increasing numbers of foreign-born Latinos and some African Americans have moved into rural areas. They are attracted to jobs in meatpacking, food processing plants, and agriculture.

Economics in Rural Areas.

Not all is idyllic in rural living. The rural workforce earns less than its urban counterparts, and the poverty rate is higher than in other places. While children have the highest poverty rates of any age group in both rural and urban America, poverty among rural children is higher, at 22%, than urban children, at 17% (O'Hare, 2009). O'Hare also reports that the band of southern-most states (excluding Florida) from South Carolina west to Arizona, plus Oklahoma, Arkansas, Tennessee, Kentucky, and West Virginia, has the highest regional rural child poverty rate, which exceeds 25% in each of these states. The rural economy is sensitive to fluctuations in manufacturing and export rates. Farm production can fluctuate with the weather and crop prices, which are controlled by the world economy.

Successful farmers today use technology and business principles, as well as their knowledge about agriculture, to manage a farm. In addition to watching the weather, they monitor the market to determine the best time to sell. They must have the resources to store products during times of low prices, including storage facilities and adequate finances to sustain them. The nature of the business is making it difficult for small farmers to survive. In this environment, the number of individual and family farmers has decreased over the past few decades. Although families still own the majority of farms in the country, corporation ownership is growing.

Multinational corporations have outsourced many of the manufacturing jobs that were once available in rural areas to lower-cost labor markets in other parts of the country or world. Processing plants for meat and fish continue to be located near the source of the raw product, but the work is often dangerous and laborers are poorly paid. Immigrants have been filling a number of these jobs in areas that previously had little racial or ethnic diversity.

Rural Schools and Their Issues.

Are you interested in teaching in a rural area? There are advantages and limitations. Schools in rural areas are smaller than those in suburban and urban areas, meaning that there are fewer students to manage and a better opportunity to get to know students' families.

The lower enrollment in rural schools usually results in a relatively low student-to-teacher ratio, allowing more individual attention for students. One of the problems in small schools is that teachers often must teach subjects for which they are not prepared (such as physics, chemistry, and biology). Schools often do not have sufficient resources for students to offer foreign language classes, technology education, music, art, or advanced placement courses. However, satellite connections in some rural areas allow students to take these courses via distance learning.

School consolidation can be a contentious issue in rural communities. In rural and even some urban schools, enrollments are very small. Debates about the value and implications of closing a school can be expected. Moving students to a school located many miles away will limit the participation of parents in school activities. Long bus rides to and from the consolidated school may cause hardship for some families.

Proponents for consolidation argue that the curriculum could be expanded to include subjects not available in a small school, buildings upgraded with educational equipment and technology, and students better served when small schools are combined.

Approximately 42,000 American Indian and Alaska Native children are educated by the Bureau of Indian Educaton at 164 elementary and secondary schools on 64 reservations in 23 states (U.S. Department of Interior, n.d.*b*).

URBAN AREAS

Some people choose to live in urban areas because of the excitement and access to the symphony, theater, opera, and other amenities. Large cities offer abundant professional jobs as well as sports complexes, numerous libraries, colleges and universities, recreational activities, restaurants that vary greatly in cuisine and price, and clubs with entertainment. Other people live in the city because they grew up or accepted a job there. They may choose to remain in the city because they like it or because it adequately meets their needs. Others have no choice because of family or economic obligations or just don't have the opportunity to break loose from the grip of the city. Many who live in the city have never taken advantage of the activities that attract people to the city, mainly because of limited income.

Geography plays a role in defining the conditions of a city. The upper middle class and the wealthy live together in one or more particular areas of the city; the middle-class and low-income families live in other areas of the city. The homeless are usually shepherded into specific areas where most others will not see them. Housing in the city is more expensive than in other places and the cost of living is usually high. A small two-bedroom condominium can cost over $500,000 in or very near the city. Low-rent housing is limited and often in disrepair. Most cities do not have enough public housing to meet their needs. The cost of owning a car and paying for the insurance may be exorbitant. Public buses and subway systems serve as major means of transportation.

Some people like the city because they can live their lives free from the prying eyes of neighbors. Neighbors in the city often don't know each other, let alone details about the families or roots of those who live around them. One is able to live alone within a great mass of humanity. On the other hand, there are communities within cities in which people do know their neighbors and work together on community projects. The city does not allow for a single stereotype that fits all of its residents. Economic conditions, ethnicity, race, and language sometimes divide cities into neighborhoods, such as Little Italy and Chinatown, that clearly distinguish one group from another.

Population of a City.   One-half of the world's population live in megacities. New York City is the largest city in the United States, with a population of around 9.3 million, which grows to 20.9 million when extended into the metropolitan area that includes its suburbs (City Mayors, 2011). Figure 9.7 shows how New York City, Los Angeles, and Chicago compare in size to other major cities around the world.

The power relations in these cities differ greatly. Cities in **developing nations** have limited means or resources to provide housing, sanitation, and a healthy environment for their growing populations. Not all new immigrants and migrants in the United States have access to adequate and inexpensive housing, leading to multiple families sharing very small homes or apartments, usually in violation of city ordinances. Some families end up homeless.

Fifty-two metropolitan areas in the United States have over 1 million residents (U.S. Census Bureau, 2010j). They range in size from metropolitan New York, with nearly 21 million, to Tucson, Arizona, with just over 1 million. The ethnic and racial diversity is usually greater in cities than in other areas, in part because many new immigrants from around the world initially settle in urban areas.

Figure 9.7 Population of Selected Large World Cities.*

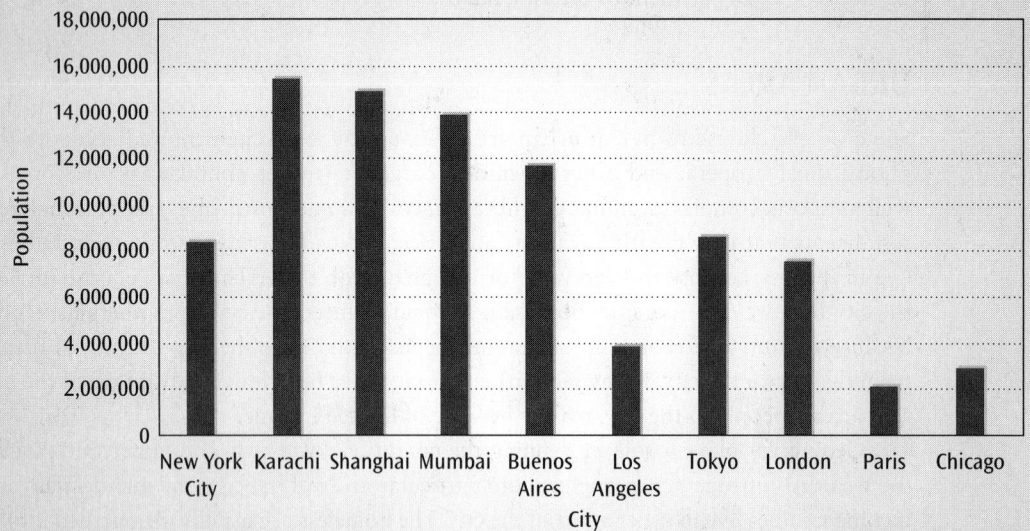

*Does not include metropolitan area. Karachi, Shanghai, and Mumbai are the world's largest cities. Tokyo is the largest metropolitan area world city, with 31,036,000.
Source: City Mayors. http://www.citymayors.com/statistics/largest-cities-mayors-1.html.

Contradictions of Cities. Cities are centers of extremes and contradictions. They are places where people from different cultural backgrounds intermingle. An expensive, elite restaurant may be found on one block and a food kitchen on the street behind it. Some of the highest salaries in the world are earned in the corporate headquarters housed in or near a city while large numbers of African Americans, Puerto Ricans, Mexican Americans, and women workers in the city are paid so little that their families live in poverty. The unemployment rate for young people of color is also high.

While the city provides the creative energy for many, it becomes oppressive and dangerous for others. Many city residents live in safe and comfortable environments with good schools, parks, and recreational facilities. Others live near waste dumps that have contributed to a disproportionately high incidence of asthma and other diseases. The night—and sometimes the daylight—may be interrupted by the sounds of gunshots, ambulances, and police raids in some sections of the city.

Our nation's capital, Washington, D.C., the seat of power and home to many of the country's elite, is also home to countless individuals living in poverty, and residents in some neighborhoods are in constant danger from daily violence. Infant mortality here is the highest in the nation and twice the national average (Annie E. Casey Foundation, 2010).

Some new immigrants may try to become American as defined by the dominant culture, but others strive to maintain their culture within the American context. Immigrant parents may raise their children in the cultural context with which they are most familiar, using their native language or their developing English. Children may try to shed their immigrant ways to be accepted by their American counterparts, which often leads to conflict between children and parents.

For oppressed people in the city the dominant values may not be serving them effectively. The hope, joy, and freedom associated with living in cities have not been the experience for many. Those who are better advantaged and living comfortably view the poorer sections of the city as places of chaos and immorality. City leaders find it difficult to raise the resources necessary to improve city services, ensure adequate housing and food, provide schools of the same quality across the city, and also pay enough to attract and retain highly qualified teachers. Low-income and public housing almost never is built in or near the economically advantaged areas of the city.

Urban Schools. Over 40% of the nation's students attend schools in the largest 500 school districts. Enrollment in the largest 100 school districts ranges from 47,260 in Wichita, Kansas, to 981,690 in New York City schools. Students of color are the majority in 60% of these school districts. Students in these largest school districts represent diverse ethnic, racial, and language characteristics, with over more than two of three coming from minority groups. Nearly half of them are eligible for free lunch and 12% are enrolled in English language programs (Proximity, 2010; Dalton et al., 2006).

Not all schools in a city are equal. Parents in upper-middle-class neighborhoods are able to donate funds to hire teachers of art and music. They can pay for tutors to ensure that their children have the knowledge and skills necessary for entry into desirable colleges and universities. California has a system of private foundations that support local school districts. The school districts in affluent areas benefit from fund-raising events, coordinated by parents and local citizens, that enhance the programs in the district. The less affluent school districts may not have a supporting foundation, or the funds their foundations raise may be limited. This can contribute to great disparity between school districts.

A number of low-income parents are engaged actively in their children's education. They talk with teachers; they try to ensure that their children are in classes with the best teachers; they encourage their children to be involved in extracurricular activities; and they monitor their children's performance to ensure that they are performing well on standardized tests. Most low-income parents do not have a great deal of cultural capital. They do not have the income that allows them to support school activities (e.g., paying the fees for extra-curricular activities), and their work situations may inhibit participation in school activities and meetings. Limited English skills on the part of some parents or their lack of education may lead to reluctance to interact with the educational system. One means of enhancing the involvement of immigrant parents is to meet with them in an environment that is perceived as less threatening, such as a local church or parish.

Urban schools are sometimes characterized as highly centralized, authoritative, and bureaucratic. However, a number of urban school districts now elect their school boards, have reduced the bureaucracy, decentralized, and have allowed the establishment of alternative schools. At the same time, mayors have taken over the management of schools in cities such as New York and Washington.

Magnet schools, in which the curriculum emphasizes a particular subject or field such as performing arts or mathematics and science, are popular in urban areas. Six percent of the schools in the 100 largest school districts are magnet schools, enrolling 9% of their districts' students (Dalton et al., 2006). Advantaged and well-educated families seek admission to select magnet schools, especially if their neighborhood school does not meet their standards.

A number of school districts allow parents, teachers, community groups, and entrepreneurs to establish **charter schools.** Charter schools are public schools of choice that operate free from many of the regulations that apply to traditional public schools. The "charter" includes a performance contract detailing the school's mission, program, goals, students served, methods of assessment, and ways to measure success.

PAUSE TO REFLECT 9.3

A 2009 U.S. government report (U. S. Global Change Research Program, 2009) contained several alarming warnings, which included, but were not limited to:

- Global warming is unequivocal and primarily human induced.
- Widespread climate impacts are occurring now and are expected to increase.
- Climate change will stress water resources.
- Crop and livestock production will be increasingly challenged.
- Threats to human health will increase.

Not everyone, including all scientists, agrees with the report.

- Why do some people disagree with the scientists' description of global warming?
- Why has the United States not provided leadership in acknowledging global warming and other environmental destruction?
- How do indigenous groups define their responsibility for the environment? How is this in conflict with the policies of most world leaders?

Some urban school students have family responsibilities and demands placed on them that children from more affluent areas do not. In some instances there is a lack of a supporting parental figure.

Some inner-city schools are in disrepair, and the economic problems of many communities and states have forced extreme cuts in school budgets. This has resulted in massive teacher and staff layoffs and cutbacks in resources for students.

SUBURBAN AREAS

In the 1930s a relatively small number of Americans lived in the suburbs. Today over half of the population live there. After World War II, the suburbs offered an opportunity to own a single-family house with a yard in an area that seemed safer than the city and more desirable for raising children. The wage earner—usually the father at that time—commuted to the city daily to work. Most wives stayed at home to care for children and became involved in developing a community.

Development of the Suburbs. The desire for home ownership was one of the primary reasons for the development of suburbia. With a minority of families unable to afford homes in many U.S. cities in the mid-twentieth century, lower-cost suburban developments became an attractive alternative. Low-interest loans to returning veterans enhanced the opportunities for many more families.

Most of the suburbs during the 1920s were racially and economically homogeneous. While African Americans established their own suburbs in a few places, neither they nor members of other ethnic groups of color were encouraged to settle in the suburbs. Racist governmental policies and business practices at the time exacerbated racial and class inequalities and guaranteed that suburbia was almost exclusively white. At the same time, programs for public housing, urban renewal, and replacement of homes with highways were undermining the stability and

Teacher Expectations

Apryl, a petite African American teenager, walks into an urban school's Spanish class 15 minutes late. The teacher, Mr. Roth, informs her that she cannot sit with her friends. Apryl proceeds to seat herself in the corner with her friends. Mr. Roth declares that he is going to call Apryl's counselor to come to class and talk to Apryl, and that he will give Apryl none of the worksheets the class is required to complete until Apryl moves to her seat. As Mr. Roth circulates the room, he makes no eye contact with Apryl. Apryl freezes any time Mr. Roth comes within earshot of her desk. Otherwise, she leans back in her chair, engages in conversation with the boys around her, and rearranges the papers in her backpack.

Apryl raises her hand to ask for the worksheets about 30 minutes into class, but is told she cannot have the worksheets until she moves. Apryl's conversation with the boys around her gets louder and more animated. She pulls food and drink out of her bag and starts eating and drinking. She gets out of her seat every 5 or 10 minutes to stand at the window to see what is going on outside. She starts a couple of exchanges with students across the room. Every once in a while, Mr. Roth shouts at Apryl, "You cannot talk in class." Apryl replies either that she "ain't talking, give me the work" or that she is "waiting for her counselor," and Mr. Roth starts ignoring Apryl again.

Fifty minutes into the 110-minute class, a boy near Apryl gets so disruptive that Mr. Roth starts filling out the paperwork to have security remove him from the classroom. Apryl starts packing her backpack. When security shows up at the door 10 minutes later, Apryl runs toward the door and begs the guard to remove her from the classroom. The guard cannot remove Apryl without a teacher request. Mr. Roth finally tells the guard to take both of them.

| QUESTIONS FOR CLASSROOM DISCUSSION |

- What are some reasons why Apryl may not be engaged in the assigned work?
- How is the worksheet assignment, which was the assignment for the full 110-minute period, related to Apryl's world?
- How did Mr. Roth's interactions with Apryl support or not support her learning of Spanish?
- Do Mr. Roth's responses to Apryl suggest that he has high expectations for her? Why or why not?
- Based on this limited information, would you say that Mr. Roth has a caring relationship with Apryl? Why or why not?

Adapted from Anderson, L. (2003). Ain't doin' that: Why "doing good in school" can be so hard. In L. Darling-Hammond, J. French, & P. Garcia-Lopez, *Learning to teach for social justice* (pp. 103–115). New York: Teachers College Press.

vibrancy of African American neighborhoods in the cities. In addition, African Americans were being denied mortgages to buy their own homes (Watkins, 2011; Rothacker & Mellnik, 2009; Freund, 2006).

Although racist official policies were dismantled years ago, zoning policies and homeowner association building requirements and restrictions can limit loans to the more economically advantaged.

Suburbia did not last long as just a bedroom community for people who worked in the city. Soon grocery stores, gas stations, parks, community services, schools, and churches were built to support the needs of suburban families. These were followed by malls and the emergence of a variety of retail stores. In time, more upscale suburban developments were built to meet the needs of affluent families wanting to escape the problems of the cities.

Shopping malls were joined by office complexes, high-tech and landscaped industrial parks, and an extensive network of highways. Wage earners no longer had to go to the city for work; factories and other businesses existed in their own backyards. Along with these changes came the problems that others had tried to escape by leaving the city—unemployment, homelessness, drugs, and crime. Most suburbs are economically, racially, ethnically, linguistically, and religiously diverse. Diversity within some communities is actively solicited and celebrated. In others, little is done to encourage it.

Software, electronic, and biotechnology companies found the suburban business centers to be ideal for their development and research. They attracted entrepreneurs and professionals, who moved into upscale housing developments near their jobs. These office and research parks began to interact academically and economically with research universities and both public and private groups to develop and use their products. Silicon Valley, south of San Francisco, is the center of much of the U.S. high-tech industry and an example of a suburban business and research complex.

Suburban Schools. The quality of schools is often one of the reasons that families move from cities to the suburbs. Because the suburbs are fairly new, their schools are not in disrepair as are many in urban areas. Wealthy suburbs are more likely to have beautiful schools with the latest technology, qualified teachers, advanced placement courses, gifted and talented programs, and numerous extracurricular activities.

However, not all suburban schools are of this high quality. Those that predominantly serve students with limited English skills, from low-income families, and from backgrounds other than Europe are likely to be the older schools in the region. Lacking in facilities, new equipment, and advanced technology, these schools may find the recruitment of teachers challenging.

The problems of urban schools affect many suburban schools as well, especially drugs, student-on-student harassment, and lack of attention to students who may need it the most. Not all suburban schools have the resources to adequately support counselors, social workers, and others who can help students deal with the complexity of today's life. Additionally, not all suburban schools have the computers and technology that are important in preparing students for their future work world.

Migration

The diversity of a geographic area varies because of history, immigration, and **migration**. Although the United States annually receives more immigrants than any other country, immigration is not a uniquely U.S. phenomenon; it occurs worldwide. About half of the world's immigrants have migrated to countries in the developed world. The other half have moved to countries with industrial, mining, and oil economies in the less developed world (Rowntree, Lewis, Price, & Wyckoff, 2009). For example, the majority of the population in oil-rich Kuwait and the United Arab Emirates are foreign-born (Ueda, 2007).

Migration refers to movement from one place to another, while immigration indicates that a person has moved to a country with the goal of permanently settling there. Political and religious persecution drives people out of the countries of their birth. Economic conditions that lead to the lack of jobs, inadequate wages, and hunger are other common reasons for leaving. What factors are considered in determining the country to move to? Sometimes people have no choice. The best they can do to escape oppression or threats to their lives is to cross into a contiguous country. When they have a choice, they are likely to choose a country with job opportunities or religious and political liberty.

While in years past, Americans tended to live their entire lives within a few miles from the place of their birth and their family home, this is no longer always the case. There are an increasing number of reasons why individuals and families are moving to different regions of the country and the world.

Travel has become increasingly accessible for most Americans. Air travel, though expensive, is still within the means of most. The interstate highway system is a vast improvement from the old highway system of 50-plus years ago, making travel to other regions of the country available to almost anyone who has access to a car.

An increasing number of women are joining men in higher education and in the military and the civilian work force. As these individuals pursue their educational opportunities, some may matriculate to colleges and universities in other areas of the country and abroad. Exposure to new regions could lead them to seek employment in areas away from their homes. Career opportunities and advancements may involve moving to other areas of the country or even the world, causing families to be uprooted and relocated. While most of these relocations may be temporary, some individuals will prefer the changes and make their relocation permanent.

School districts, private schools, and government agencies from foreign countries often send recruiters to job fairs and conferences to recruit teachers, just as national and international businesses recruit promising individuals to work in new, interesting, and sometimes distant regions. If you are interested in teaching outside of your area or even abroad, check for scheduled job fairs on the Internet.

In 1820 permanent legal U.S. resident status was given to 8,385 immigrants. By 1900 the number with new permanent resident status had grown to 448,572, and by 2009 to 1,130,819. In addition, another 1,703,697 temporary foreign workers and their families entered the United States in 2009, one-fifth of whom were intra-company transfers (U.S. Department of Homeland Security, 2010).

In addition to the legal immigration, large numbers of undocumented immigrants enter the country annually. Since there is no accurate means to determine the exact number

Much of the world's population live in squalid conditions. Educational opportunities may be minimal or nonexistent for most of these children.
© Jake Lyell/Water Aid/Alamy

entering or residing in the United States, only educated estimates are available. Between 2000 and 2005, it is estimated that that as many as 850,000 undocumented immigrants entered the country annually. The Pew Hispanic Center estimated that by March 2009, the annual number had dropped significantly, to 300,000 (Passel & Cohn, 2010a). The recession that began in 2008 likely had an effect on these numbers.

Passel and Cohn also estimate that approximate 9.4 million undocumented immigrants lived in the United States in 2000, and that figure climbed steadily to 12,000,000 in 2007. By 2010, during the U.S. recession, the number had dropped to 11,200,000 (Passel & Cohn, 2010b).

In 2010 there were 39.5 million foreign-born individuals living in the United States. This represents 12.5% of the total population. A majority of these immigrants were born in Latin America, and over one-fourth were from Asia. Mexico provided the largest percentage of the foreign-born population (29.8%). China (5.2%), the Philippines (4.5%), and India (4.3%) were the next largest groups (U.S. Census Bureau, 2010f).

MIGRATION WORLDWIDE

In much of the world, migration refers to people crossing borders temporarily. The host country views them as temporary guest workers who will eventually return to their homeland. They sometimes have been forced out of their homelands because of civil war, persecution, or economic depression, and may be living in refugee camps rather than working in the new country. They may later return home once economic and political conditions are stable. However, many migrants never return to their homelands. The United Nations reported that nearly 33 million people were forced migrants or refugees at the end of 2006, fleeing for many reasons. The most compelling reasons are war, famine, life-threatening disasters, and government coercion or oppression (Knox & Marston, 2010).

International examples of forced migration include the conflict and displacement of millions in Darfur and the 2011 earthquake, tsunami, and nuclear disaster in Japan.

The worldwide trend is migration from rural to urban areas. This trend is particularly salient in less developed countries where families can no longer sustain themselves in rural areas. They hope to find jobs and greater economic stability in an urban area. The problem is that most cities in developing countries are unable to provide necessary services for a rapidly growing population. Housing, food, water, waste treatment, and jobs do not exist. As a result, large numbers of migrants are living in shanty villages on city borders without clean water and sanitation. When they can find work, it is often in the informal economy of selling wares on the street, gathering items to sell from garbage dumps, or participating in illegal activities. Death rates are high, and life expectancy is low. Schooling for children in these areas is very limited or nonexistent.

MIGRATION IN THE UNITED STATES

As the government expanded its territory in the nineteenth century, the population of the early colonies migrated west. Some groups like the Cherokees and other American Indian tribes were forced by the government to move to lands west of the Mississippi River. In the 1920s, the 1940s, and the 1950s, large numbers of African Americans moved from the South to northern and western industrial areas to fill jobs that were then open to them. Today, migration within the United States takes place continuously and is discussed in Chapter 2, Ethnicity and Race.

Globalization

The realities of the twenty-first century call for us to know not only the places where we live, but also the places where others live. We are connected to other countries through economic, political, environmental, and cultural systems. One of five students in our schools has a foreign-born parent. We live in a global world that is becoming more controlled by international conglomerates.

We think and respond globally for different reasons and in different ways. When major world events occur, responses from the international community are often a function of a number of variables. If countries have a vested political or economic interest in the country affected, the response may be swift and decisive. If no action can be identified that is in the best interest of a country, then inaction may be the option of choice.

The U.S. and international response was prompt to the devastating Indian Ocean tsunami in 2004, the Haitian earthquake in 2010, and the New Zealand and Japanese earthquakes in 2011. However, the results for responding to political unrest are mixed. For example, the decision by the United States to intervene or not to intervene in the 2011 internal rebellions within various North African and Middle Eastern countries was determined in part by the political ties the United States had with each country's leadership, and what our economic and political interests were with regard to the individual country. The United States and the United Nations were slow to respond to the genocides in Bosnia and Rwanda in the 1990s and more recently in Darfur. However, the United States and the United Nations were relatively quick to respond to the 2011 political and civil unrest in Libya.

The early stages of **globalization** occurred when European nations began to colonize the Americas, Africa, and India in the late fifteenth century. Europeans wanted both the raw materials and the labor of these countries, usually taking them by force and sending them back to their home countries. The colonizers followed a policy of **manifest destiny,** in which they saw their own cultures as superior to all others and destined to rule over others. After the United States became independent of England, it became a colonizer itself, making and breaking treaties with American Indian tribes and gaining land by annexing it or winning it in wars with Mexico and Spain. By the mid-1800s the Europeans had colonized Indonesia, Indochina, and all of Africa except for Ethiopia and Liberia. They controlled the crops that would be produced and limited industrial development. Globalization during this period moved resources primarily in one direction—from the colonized country to Europe or America.

It wasn't until after World War II that these countries were able to become independent from their colonizers. However, the colonizers quickly centralized their power in 1948 by establishing GATT (General Agreement on Tariffs and Taxes), which later became the World Trade Organization (WTO). With a membership beyond the European colonizers, the goal of the WTO was to reduce barriers of trade so that goods and labor could move more easily across national borders. The International Monetary Fund and World Bank were established to help defend the world's monetary system and make investments through loans in the infrastructure of developing countries. Not to give up their control of global economic and political issues, the old colonizing countries (Germany, Great Britain, France, and Italy) joined the other economically and politically powerful countries (United States, Canada, Japan, and Russia) to form the Group of Eight (G-8) to oversee the world's future development, which will affect the lives of both the richest and poorest people of the world.

Globalization also impacts the ability of the world's population to live without famine, debilitating and killing diseases, and brutality brought on by poverty, religious beliefs, or war.

The United Nations Educational, Scientific and Cultural Organization (UNESCO) and other international organizations see the education of children and women as critical to changing their economic status and ability to be self-sufficient. The 1989 United Nations Convention on the Rights of the Child identified early childhood care and education, especially for the neediest children, as its top goal and collects data to track the progress of countries in meeting this goal (UNESCO, 2011).

ECONOMICS

Events in one country can affect other countries around the world. For example, when adjustments are made to the stock market in China, the stock markets drop or rise in Japan, Europe, and the United States. When rainforests are depleted in Ecuador, the natural production of oxygen for the world is reduced, and the indigenous groups depending on the rainforests lose their livelihood. When the 2011 earthquake, tsunami, and nuclear disaster struck Japan, much of their business infrastructure from manufacturing to shipping was severely compromised. Few Americans realized initially how this would impact U.S. manufacturing. However, many components that go into the assembly of American automobiles (e.g., pigment for red and black auto paint) and into high-tech equipment are manufactured in Japan, and shipments to the United States were affected. Worldwide, there is so much interdependence that no country can operate in isolation from others.

Hungry for a quick fix of American food while traveling overseas? You will have little difficulty finding a McDonald's cheeseburger in Zermatt, Switzerland, or in Xian, China. McDonald's has tens of thousands of locations in over 100 countries, including a Kosher site in Buenos Aires. If you prefer fried chicken, KFC, which has its imprint in over 100 countries, has over 2,000 locations in 400 cities in China. Need cash in Iguaçu, Brazil, or Barcelona, Spain? Your Bank of America ATM card in those locations will likely provide access to your own bank account at home. There are many U.S. brands that have become international and many foreign brands so prevalent, that many believe them to be U.S. companies. These are all examples of globalization and how the countries of the world have become increasingly interdependent.

Do you need technical support for a problem with your computer? If you call your U.S. computer manufacturer, your call may be routed to a technical support call center in Delhi, India. Someone who has recently been given the Western work name of "Kevin" will literally take control of your computer and correct your problem. Many U.S. factories and assembly plants have moved their production to Mexico, Vietnam, China, and other overseas locations. There are no longer pineapple canneries in Hawaii, as American companies are now growing their products in countries with lower labor costs, such as Costa Rica. Financial globalization usually involves the goal of profitability, either from reaching new markets or saving capital against higher U.S. labor costs. The latter may or may not lower consumer costs, but may result in loss of American jobs.

It would be difficult to complete a wardrobe with clothing made entirely in the United States. Even the most expensive designer labels typically indicate that they are made overseas. Products are sometimes produced by children or women in sweatshops under conditions that would be illegal in this country. Consumerism of U.S. products is promoted around the world, and cheaper products from other countries are consumed here as imports grow. The managers and owners of large corporations have profited greatly from their global connections.

Although economic growth remains strong in the old industrialized countries and is becoming strong in developing countries such as India and China, many people in the world are struggling to live from day to day. Absolute poverty in developing countries is defined as having a daily income of $1 or less. Over one-fifth of the people in these countries live in absolute poverty, many undernourished and without clean water and sanitation. In developed nations such as the United States and in Europe, many groups of color and new immigrants have not benefited from the economic growth of their countries, living in poverty and sometimes in conditions similar to those in developing countries. Across the world, the disparities between the rich and poor continue to increase.

Technology is both changing the job market and opening communications across national borders. It provides the opportunity to connect people around the world. The use of computers and cellular phones around the globe has increased dramatically over the past decade. The Internet is allowing direct communications across national, political, and geographical boundaries. Individuals are able to communicate with each other around the world instantaneously via e-mail and video conferencing. However, the digital revolution is not reaching the majority of the world's population, especially people in developing nations.

ENVIRONMENT

The environment is also greatly influenced by global conditions, changes, and decisions. A volcano, explosion, fire, or oil spill in one country can impact the environment and economy of many other countries as ash or pollutants are spread by wind or water around the earth. A number of factors contribute to the degradation of the environment and the world's **ecosystem.** As the world's population increases, the need for food, clean water, sanitation, and jobs also increases. Rapid economic growth, which draws on natural resources, is expected to continue in countries such as China and India. Another factor is the increased consumption of natural resources and produced goods by the populations of industrialized countries.

Although the destruction of the environment is a global problem, some countries contribute much more to the problem than others. Industrialized nations are the greatest offenders, using more than their equitable proportion of natural resources and adding more than their share of pollutants to the environment. The United States is among the leading consumers and environmental polluters. Although the U.S. population is only 5% of the world, we consume one fourth of the oil produced (Caspian Oil, 2011; Reuters, 2011) and emit disproportionately high amounts of carbon dioxide. The United States is also the third largest consumer of water, behind China and India (Rowntree et al., 2009).

Most scientists believe that the damage can be halted and steps taken to dramatically improve the environment. Such a change in direction requires a global commitment from multinational corporations, local companies, policymakers, and the public to do things differently. Industrial leaders have traditionally argued against environmental control because it may cost more money, hurting their competitiveness and profits. However, the tide may be turning. A number of companies are marketing sustainable development. A growing number of cities are enforcing their own greening policies to support a sustainable environment. In 2006 the state of California adopted the strictest control on carbon dioxide in the United States; it plans to cut emissions 25% by 2020.

RESISTANCE BY INDIGENOUS PEOPLE

Not all people are excited about the globalization that is opening up the world to the interests of corporations, investors, and politicians. Skeptics do not believe that these groups have the best interests of the people and the environment in mind as they make decisions that consider only their profits and their own economic and social well-being. Indigenous people are the most severely affected by global decisions, but they have had limited or no voice in the decisions that dramatically change their lives.

Indigenous people may be a small fraction of the world population, but some are living on the natural resources that others desire. At least 375 million people live in an estimated 5,000 indigenous societies around the world. They are spread around the world: in the Amazon jungles; the mountains of the Andes; the tundras of the far north; the forests of Canada, Siberia, and Indonesia; the islands of the Pacific; the agricultural lands of the Philippines, Guatemala, Mexico, and the United States; and the grasslands and deserts of Africa (Hall & Fenelon, 2009; Mander, 2006). They face immediate threats to their cultures and lives as others seek to acquire their natural resources.

Community values are central in the lives of an indigenous people. Those in the dominant group, on the other hand, value individual freedom and the right of the individual to accumulate his or her own wealth and power.

Another core value of indigenous peoples is their reciprocal relationship with nature (Mander, 2006). As the earth gives them the gifts of water, food, and protection, they must give back to the earth and take care of it. To them, globalization has given the powerful the ability to dominate both people and the earth for the purpose of making money with no commitment to take care of either. These strangers who want to destroy the land on which the natives have lived for thousands of years do not have a relationship with the land. The land and its produce have much more meaning to the natives than providing the substance for living. Winona LaDuke of the Anishinabeg (Ojibwe) people describes the contradiction: "For us, rice is a source of food and also wisdom. For the globalizers, it is just a commodity to be exploited for profit" (LaDuke, 2006, p. 25). In 2011 the Ojibwe were once again faced with threats from individuals outside their community. Lawmakers and business interests were working to loosen Minnesota's water quality standards. While relaxing water standards will make copper mining easier, it will put the wild rice used for food and medicine at risk. Most indigenous groups practice **subsistence living,** in which they produce enough food for their communities to survive, but do not accumulate food or money for private use. The wild rice is viewed as sacred, a gift from their creator, and central to their identity (Karnowski, 2011).

Many of the world's indigenous peoples struggle to protect their languages, cultures, religions, artifacts, and traditional knowledge and sciences.
© Karin Duthie/Alamy

Collective ownership is another core value of indigenous groups (Mander, 2006). European settlers in the 1830s tried to convince the Cherokees to divide their lands in the southeastern United States into private plots that would be owned by individual Cherokees. The intent of the European settlers was to buy the property plot by plot from the owners, thus removing the Cherokees from the land that the new settlers desired. The Cherokees resisted individual ownership, which resulted in their being moved forcibly from their homes by federal troops. Indigenous peoples are constantly confronted with others trying to exploit their collective ownership.

Many indigenous groups have suffered from the invasion of their lands by highways and pipelines. They have been relocated to make way for hydroelectric dam projects that flood their lands and destroy their livelihoods. Some have become ill because of contamination from the dumping of oil and chemicals into the water. They are not immune to diseases and problems such as alcohol abuse that arrive with industrial development. When people are removed from their land and subsistence living, they are forced to enter the capitalist economy, in which they have to sell their products to buy the necessities for life. The indigenous society begins to fall apart as family members are forced to find jobs away from their native lands (Lloyd, Soltani, & Koenig, 2006).

Today groups of indigenous people are fighting in the courts and public forums for their rights to sovereignty, self-governance, and collective ownership (e.g., the Hawaiian sovereignty movement). Many do not want to assimilate into the dominant society. They desperately want to protect their languages, cultures, religions, artifacts, and traditional knowledge and sciences (Mander, 2006). They fight against the deforestation that will destroy their environment and many of the living organisms that have made the ecosystem work effectively for them. They fight the globalization that could destroy their families and communities.

Incorporating Students' Cultural and Geographical Differences into the Classroom

Students and their families may have lived in the community served by the school for all their lives like the generations before. But some may have recently moved from another part of the city, another area of the state, or another state or country, as in the chapter's opening scenario. The local protocols for behavior in schools and social settings may be strange to these newcomers. Students may speak a language or dialect for which they are teased or harassed. Teachers should recognize that these differences are not shortcomings on the part of students. Instead they are an outgrowth of their own histories and experiences outside of the local community. Educators may have to become acquainted with other cultures to serve the new students effectively. Meeting with parents and listening to the students' own narratives of their lived experiences will help in providing a context for effective teaching and learning.

One area in which local and regional differences are reflected is the school traditions that develop over time. The mascots and slogans of schools distinguish a group of students from others. The sports valued and supported in communities vary. Rivalries develop across schools and communities that last for some graduates far into adulthood. Students and adults display symbols connected to their group memberships and locale. Many thrive on the connections to school and community. Others escape as soon as possible to a place where they can establish their own identities outside the confines of the dominant and powerful groups in their community.

TEACHING IMMIGRANT STUDENTS

Immigrant students, especially at the high school level, tend to be overlooked by their teachers and other officials. Their education is affected by a number of factors that impact their families. A large number of immigrant students are living in segregated, low-income communities. The parents of some Latino students are undocumented immigrants who worry about being deported and separated from their families. Some students in rural areas will be in the school a short time as their parents participate in seasonal agricultural work and then move to another area of the country where they can be employed. Many immigrant students will be English language learners who are participating in one of the language programs discussed in Chapter 6.

Older students in urban areas may be assigned to a special newcomer school or program that is designed to help them learn English and adjust to the U.S. school culture. Younger students are more likely to be assigned to a class where the majority of students are native-born. Most rural schools and many urban and suburban school districts will not have special schools or programs for older immigrant students. Instead, the students will be integrated into current classrooms with or without support to help them adjust to their new settings.

Where should you begin if an immigrant student is assigned to your class? First, you should be welcoming and supportive of the student. Second, you should find out from a school administrator what support the school district offers for immigrant students. You should learn whether the district has translators or student advocates who can assist you in working with the student and his or her parents. If the student is an English language learner and you have no background in ESL or bilingual education, enroll in a staff development or local university course. Courses may be available online to provide you with assistance. Talk with other teachers in your building or school district who have been successful at integrating immigrant students into their classrooms and helping them be academically successful. In some cases, a school district will not have support systems for either the student or the teacher. You will have to learn on your own.

Most immigrant parents strongly believe that education is critical to their children's future success and will be supportive of the teacher's efforts to help their children learn. In many cultures, the parents respect the role of teachers and trust them to have the best interest of their children in mind. You should consider the family an ally.

As you work with immigrant students, you should make it clear that you have high expectations for them and do everything you can to help them meet those expectations. While parents may have hopes for their children attending college, the children do not always have the appropriate academic preparation for college. They may not have a full understanding of college requirements, admissions procedures, and how they might access financial aid, even if this has been communicated to them in writing or verbally. With the professional staff cutbacks that are occurring in schools, guidance counselors and advisors may be overwhelmed and may not be able to give adequate attention to all students in need. Teachers should be alert to such students and be prepared to obtain assistance for them.

You should be conscious of the ethnic identification of immigrant students. They may be at very different stages of assimilation, which means that they cannot be thought of as a homogeneous group. Some students will identify strongly with the dominant group. Others will be transcultural or successful in figuring out how to fuse the culture of the dominant society with their native culture. Still other students will strongly identify with their native cultures and even resist or develop opposition to the dominant culture. A number of researchers have found that the longer immigrant students are in school, the more negative about the value of education they become (Suárez-Orozco & Suárez-Orozco, 2007). If you understand where they are, you can better understand how to use their native cultures to help them learn and possibly counter their opposition to academic achievement.

HONORING FAMILY CULTURES

Students' cultural backgrounds should be reflected in the examples used to teach. Rural students do not relate to riding a subway to school or work, nor do inner-city students easily relate to single-family homes with large yards and no other houses around them. If students seldom see representations of themselves, their families, or their communities in the curriculum, it becomes difficult to believe that the academic content has any meaning or usefulness for them. It will appear to them that the subject matter has been written and delivered for someone else. At the same time, they can still learn about other lifestyles based on different cultural backgrounds and experiences, but not if they are the only ones to which they are ever exposed. The teacher's repertoire of instructional strategies should relate content to the realities of the lives of students.

The teacher who understands the experiences of students from different cultural backgrounds can use that knowledge to help students learn subject matter. A teacher's sensitivity to those differences can be used to make students from oppressed groups feel as comfortable in the class as those from the dominant culture.

INCORPORATING GLOBAL PERSPECTIVES

Because our world has become so interdependent and will become even more so in the future, it is important that students have an understanding of global connections and how they impact their lives. As you plan lessons, think about how you can integrate worldwide events and actions. A natural disaster such as a tsunami, earthquake, or volcanic eruption provides an opportunity to learn about the part of the world in which the disaster occurred, the people affected, and its implications for the United States and even for them. Students can learn more about the areas in which the United States is at war or involved in peacekeeping missions, who lives there, and how they are affected. A lesson on manufacturing should investigate where around the world products are being made and who is working in the factories or sweatshops. Students could study child labor laws and how children are involved in the manufacture of products that they buy. A lesson on music could explore the influence of U.S. music around the world and the influence of music from other countries on the United States. How could you bring other parts of the world into the subject that you plan to teach?

Another strategy for incorporating global issues into the curriculum is to help your students think about topics from the perspective of different classes of people in another country. Their perspectives on an issue could be the same or quite different from those of students in your classroom. Globalization itself will look quite different from the perspective of a less developed nation than from a developed nation. Indigenous people look at the environment in a very different way than oil companies. Presenting different perspectives will help students clarify the issues and understand why different people think quite differently about the same issue.

With the Internet your students can connect to students in classrooms around the world. Some schools connect their students as pen pals to students in other countries. Students in different countries could work on projects together to learn more about each other or on an issue or project in which both countries are engaged. Students from all kinds of schools participate in exchange programs with families around the world. Teachers sometimes sponsor trips for students to visit other countries. The possibilities for interacting with people from other countries will continue to expand as we learn how to use technology to work together.

WORKING WITH FAMILIES AND COMMUNITIES

Not all parents feel welcome in schools, in part because most schools reflect the dominant culture and language rather than their own. Therefore, school personnel may need to reach out to parents, rather than simply wait for them to show up at a meeting. A true collaboration requires that parents and teachers become partners in the teaching process. Teachers need to listen to parents and participate in the community to develop a range of teaching strategies that

Debate / Incorporating Global Perspectives in the Curriculum

When a number of teachers in John F. Kennedy High School began to realize the impact that globalization was having on their community, they began to talk to their colleagues about more systematically incorporating global perspectives across the curriculum. Some of the other teachers agreed. They clearly saw that a number of parents had lost their jobs when several factories relocated to Southeast Asian cities. And all around them they could see that they and their students were wearing clothing and buying goods that were made outside the United States. The latest threats to food were due to imports from China.

Other teachers thought it was nonsense to change their curriculum to integrate global issues and perspectives. One teacher was overheard saying, "Who do these young radicals think they are? All they want to do is convince these kids that the United States is an imperialist country that only cares about filling corporate pockets. The country will be ruined with such talk." The principal, however, likes the idea of students developing a greater global awareness. She thinks that it might gain community support and provide a unique branding for the school.

FOR

- The study of globalization will help students understand how different nations are connected.
- It will help students understand which people are benefited by globalization and which ones lose as a result.
- Students will learn to think more critically about the changes that are occurring in the country as a result of globalization.
- Projects in some classes could help students become more involved in their communities by organizing to fight against inequalities.

AGAINST

- Social studies courses already cover global issues.
- The approach must present a balanced view of the importance of globalization for our economy.
- Including global perspectives in the curriculum will politicize the curriculum.
- The curriculum should concentrate on preparing students for college or jobs.

| QUESTIONS |

1. Why do faculty members disagree about how globalization should be addressed in the curriculum?

2. Why do the proponents feel that it is important to help students not only to understand globalization, but to understand the negative impact it is having on many of them students as well as children around the world?

3. Where do you stand on including global perspectives throughout the curriculum? How could they be integrated into the subject that you will be teaching?

are congruent with the home cultures of students. Parents can learn to support their children's learning at home but may need concrete suggestions, which they will seek from teachers who they believe care about their children.

Educators must know the community to understand the cultures of families. In a school in which a prayer is said every morning regardless of the Supreme Court's decision forbidding prayer in public schools, a teacher should not discuss evolution in the first week of classes. In that school setting, one may not be able to teach sex education in the same way it is taught in many urban and suburban schools. In another school, Islamic parents may be upset with the attire that their daughters are expected to wear in physical education classes and may not approve of coed physical education courses. Jewish and Muslim students often wonder why the school celebrates or at least acknowledges Christian holidays, but never their religious holidays.

Because members of the community may revolt against the content and activities in the curriculum does not mean that educators cannot teach multiculturally. It does suggest that they know the sentiments of the community before introducing concepts that may be foreign and unacceptable. Only then can educators develop strategies for effectively introducing such concepts. The introduction of controversial issues should be accompanied by the education of parents and by the presentation of multiple perspectives that place value on the community's mores.

In addition, the community becomes a resource in a multicultural classroom. We can learn much about cultures in the community through participation in activities and by inviting community members into the school. Community speakers and helpers should represent the diversity of the community. Speakers also should be selected from different roles and age groups. Not only will students learn about other cultural groups, but so will you.

Summary

The places in which we live influence our culture and our experiences. We have common understandings of everyday life and events with people who attended the same school and lived in the same neighborhood as we did. When we are in another country, we share a culture and understanding with other U.S. citizens who are there.

Within the United States, people live in six regions of the country that help define who they are. The regions have different historical contexts, characteristics, and populations that impact their culture and education. Educational issues differ across regions, as do student populations and teacher salaries.

Each region has rural, urban, and suburban areas that provide different experiences for families and their children. Schools in rural areas usually have fewer students, contributing to a lower teacher to student ratio. Urban schools vary in size and quality across a city with a large number of students of color, English language learners, and students from low-income families. Overall, suburban schools have students of a higher socioeconomic level and teachers who are better qualified than schools in the nearby city.

Families around the world move not only from school to school, but from state to state and from one country to another. In most of the rest of the world, more people move from rural to urban areas, placing stress on cities in developing nations. In the United States, people are more likely to move from an urban to a rural or suburban area.

The world today is very interdependent, with events in one country having an impact on many other countries. For example, globalization affects the economics of U.S. citizens as jobs move from this country to one with lower wages and fewer regulations. It also affects the environment. Not all people support globalization that can dramatically change their economic status and quality of living. For example, indigenous populations have been destroyed as their lands are taken over by international conglomerates.

Schools and teachers must determine how they will integrate students from around the world into their educational environment. These strategies include honoring the cultures of new families and drawing on them to help you teach. Because the families of most of these students understand the importance of their children becoming educated, teachers need to become their allies. Finally, teachers should bring the world to the classroom, introducing students to global perspectives from around the world.

Professional Practice

Questions for Discussion

1. How does where one lives (geography) help determine one's cultural identity?
2. What historical events have had a great impact on the education of students in the South?
3. How would you describe the geographic landscape of Appalachia? How has it impacted its families and children over the past 50 years?
4. What influence have educators in New England had on education in the United States?
5. Why do you think students in the Great Plains finish high school at higher rates than students in other regions of the country?
6. What are the major educational issues debated at the political level in the West and Southwest?
7. What are the major differences in teaching in a rural, urban, and suburban school district?
8. What impact does a family's moving from one school district to another have on their children? How can teachers provide a welcoming environment to a new student?
9. Why should global perspectives be included in the P–12 curriculum?
10. How should a teacher integrate immigrant students into the classroom and assist them in learning at a level similar to that of other students?

Portfolio Activities

1. Observe teachers several times in a rural and in an urban or suburban school. As you observe, make notes of the diversity of students and teachers in the different schools, the relationship of students and teachers, and the interactions of students across groups. Contrast the two schools in a paper or matrix and discuss your findings. (InTASC Standard 2: Learning Differences, and InTASC Standard 3: Learning Environments)
2. Visit a school with a number of immigrant students to determine the approaches being used to integrate the students and help them learn. Talk with teachers about the instructional strategies they are using to most effectively serve these students and their families. Write a summary of your findings for your portfolio with recommendations about how you will work with new immigrant students when you begin teaching. (InTASC Standard 2: Learning Differences, and InTASC Standard 8: Instructional Strategies)

Digital Resources

1. The U.S. Census Bureau provides extensive information on U.S. demographics: http://www.census.gov/.

2. The National Center for Education Statistics provides extensive information on educational statistics in the United States, including the most current report on "the condition of education": http://nces.ed.gov/.

3. The U.S. Department of Homeland Security provides information on immigration statistics: http://www.dhs.gov.

4. The Gallup organization provides frequent information related to demographic differences from religion to health and politics: http://www.gallup.com/Home.aspx.

MyEducationLab™

Go to the MyEducationLab (www.myeducationlab.com) for Multicultural Education and familiarize yourself with the topical content, which includes:

- Assignments and Activities, tied to learning outcomes for the course, that can help you more deeply understand course content

- Building Teaching Skills and Dispositions learning units allow you to apply and practice your understanding of how to teach equitably in a multicultural education classroom

- Licensure Test Prep activities are available in the Book Resources to help you prepare for test taking

- A pretest with hints and feedback that tests your knowledge of this chapter's content

- Review, practice, and enrichment activities that will enhance your understanding of the chapter content

- A posttest with hints and feedback that allows you to test your knowledge again after having completed the enrichment activities

A Correlation Guide may be downloaded by instructors to show how MyEducationLab content aligns to this book.

10
The Youth Culture

If people learn to love and learn to share in early adulthood, they will be able to care for and guide the next generation effectively.

Fergus P. Hughes and Lloyd D. Noppe (1991)

| LEARNING OUTCOMES |

As you read this chapter, you should be able to:

- Provide examples of how an individual's age and culture can impact the way he or she functions in daily life.

- Characterize young adulthood and differentiate between generations Y and Z.

- List the many issues and concerns that influence children's lives.

- Recognize the teacher's role in understanding how children's age, culture, and life circumstances impact their ability to learn and interact with others.

Due to the economic downturn, 16-year-old Sean Thornton had moved across the country with his family to an area where his grandfather found a job for his father. Sean had lived in a medium-size city on the East Coast, where he had a few friends at school, and he was now living in a small southwestern town of 30,000, where he had no friends. Sean was gay but had never openly discussed it with his parents, who had uncomfortable feelings about some of his behaviors but tried to ignore them.

His speech patterns and mannerisms, which his parents tried to ignore, were very much noticed by his new classmates. It was not long after he arrived that his classmates began to talk about him. At first they made comments behind his back, but then they began to make them to his face. The comments were cruel and involved name-calling and continuous teasing. They then escalated to threats. Several of the teachers had noticed Sean's mannerisms and speech, but they chose to ignore them. One teacher had actually overheard some of the teasing but, having strong negative feelings about gays, did nothing and said nothing to anyone.

Sean told his parents that he wanted to drop out of school, and he pleaded with them to allow him to do so. When asked why, he said that he missed his old school and that the teachers and students in his new school were unfriendly. They told him that he had to stick it out and finish high school and college. They assured him that things would get better. They did not. Physical intimidation took place at school, with shoving and name calling, and with some of the larger boys shoving him against his locker, knocking his books to the floor, grabbing at his rear end, and laughing. Some of the girls would watch and join in with the laughing.

Sean did not tell his parents that some students had made a video of him from clips taken from their cell phones. The video, which ridiculed him on everything from the bullying episodes to his clothing, his speech, and his mannerisms, had just been posted on the web. It had gone viral in his school, and students laughed at him when he walked by. Sean then told his parents that he was dropping out of school. This time he was not asking for permission. Angered, his father swore at him and told him to suck it up and to get over it. He stated that no one in his family had ever failed to finish high school and most had graduated from college. Sean was not to be the family failure. A week later, Sean's body was found in a wooded area behind his grandparent's home. He was dead from a gunshot wound to the head from his grandfather's hunting rifle. Sean had become another statistic and one of the 2,000-plus teenagers in the United States who would take their own lives that year.

| REFLECTIONS |

1. Who was at fault in Sean's death?
2. What should Sean's parents have done when they first noticed mannerisms that they thought atypical for a teenage boy?
3. Should the teachers have done anything if they only observed mannerisms they thought might suggest that he was gay?
4. Was the teacher who observed some of the bullying and chose to ignore it guilty of negligence or unprofessional behavior?
5. What is the responsibility of the school toward gay and lesbian students?

Age and Culture

Each person who lives long enough will become a part of every age group. Without choice, we must all go through the various stages in life and eventually join the ranks of the aged. Like other cultural groups, we feel, think, perceive, and behave, in part, based on the age group to which we belong. In this edition, we are focusing on school-age groups and the age cohort that many young pre-service students and beginning teachers belong to: young adulthood. We include young adults to demonstrate how many in this age group tend to function or are perceived to function by others. We examine how ethnicity, gender, social status, and other determinants of culture interface with the periods in an individual's life. We examine how peer pressure affects behavior in some age groups. Critical issues such as child abuse, childhood obesity, adolescent substance abuse, and adolescent suicide are examined. Finally, we examine how an understanding of age groups can affect the educational process.

An understanding of the various age groups is helpful in understanding and providing appropriately for the needs of students. A student's classroom behavior may be a function of his or her relationships with parents, siblings, and significant others. As these family members and significant others move through various age stages in their lives, their behavior, as well as their relationship to the student, may change. Consequently, the student's behavior may, in part, be influenced by the age changes of the significant people in his or her life.

How we behave is often a function of age. Although many adolescents behave differently from one another, the ways they think, feel, and behave is at least partly the result of their being adolescents. At the same time, age is not alone in affecting the way a person behaves or functions. Ethnicity, socioeconomic status, religion, and gender interact with age to influence a person's behavior and attitudes.

A Fort Worth, Texas, child in her preschool years, for example, may eat the type of food she does partly because her age and a related health condition require eliminating certain foods from her diet. But her socioeconomic status may determine, to some extent, the foods her parents can afford to buy, and her ethnicity and the fact that she lives in Texas may determine her choices in foods. Her gender, language, disability/nondisability status, and religious background may not influence her eating habits to any significant degree, unless she belongs to a religious group with dietary restrictions. These other cultural variables, however, along with her age, may influence other types of behavior and functioning. From the time of birth through the last days of life, a person's age may influence perceptions, attitudes, values, and behavior.

In this chapter, we do not attempt to examine all developmental stages and age groups. This information can be obtained through a human development text. Instead, we examine some critical issues related to various age groups. Because it is impossible to address all critical issues affecting each age group, we selectively address issues affecting schools directly or indirectly.

Young Adulthood

Young adulthood, comprising more than 30 million in the United States (U.S. Census Bureau, 2009a), is typically defined as ages 18 to 22 or 18 to 25 (Simpson, 2008). Young adulthood is a critical period in the life of an individual because it is the time when one's hopes and aspirations begin to take shape or, for some, when one's dreams are shattered. The latter is often the case for the millions of low-income and disenfranchised young Americans. This is the period when many who seek careers in education begin their pre-service preparation and some others begin their teaching careers. We begin our discussion of age groups with young adults because this is the target age group for K–12 educators as they prepare their students for the world of work, including military service, or higher education.

The young adult years represent an exciting time—a time of important decision making coupled with stress and sometimes pain. Young adults are under pressure to make some of the most important decisions they will ever make, which may have an impact on the rest of their lives. Decisions must be made about education beyond high school; vocational choices must be made; and decisions regarding a mate, marriage, and children may also be made during this period.

At the same time, unwise choices in education or vocation along with frustration in courtship and in relationships can bring frustration and emotional pain. To many Americans in poverty, young adulthood brings the reality that they are among the disenfranchised in this country. If they are among the minority groups frequently targeted for discriminatory practices, life can be particularly difficult. Lack of financial resources may make the reality of a higher education elusive. Good jobs are particularly difficult to find because preference is often given to members of the dominant group and to individuals from more favored minority groups. During a recession, these individuals tend to be the most affected. They may suffer from abject poverty, unemployment, and poor living conditions and find it difficult to escape from this way of life. Frustration and anger appear to be inevitable, along with an intense feeling of impotence.

Those with strong family support and connections are often able to gain entrance to prestigious colleges and universities and upon graduation receive generous and sometimes highly satisfying employment options. While we hear examples of the individuals who succeed in spite of their humble backgrounds, they are more often the exception rather than the rule.

GENERATION Y

Generation Y (Gen Y-ers), sometimes referred to as the Net Generation, Echo Boomers, Millennials, or Digital Natives, are the children of baby boomers and the younger siblings of

Generation X. Tulgen (2009) indicates that those who belong to this generation were born between 1978 and 2000. However, he divides the group into two cohorts: 1978 to 1990, which he labels Generation Y, and the younger group, born between 1991 and 2000, Generation Z. Comments here will pertain to the entire 1978 to 2000 cohort group. More specific descriptions of Generation Z will follow in the next section. This group, with at least 70 million Americans, includes some who have completed college, some who are in graduate school, and some who have already entered an increasingly diverse and multigenerational workplace.

The older members of this cohort witnessed on TV the Los Angeles riots following the Rodney King incident, and they also have experienced, with their younger cohort, the wars in Afghanistan and Iraq, and the aftermath of Hurricane Katrina and the Virginia Tech shootings. Important personalities they have grown up with include Tiger Woods, Bono, Princess Diana, and Bill and Hillary Clinton (Tapscott, 2009). A Russian nuclear attack has never been a concern to them, but they are aware of possible Iranian and North Korean nuclear capabilities. They have had to learn to avoid areas of known street gang banging (activity), go through tightened airport security, and consider the threat of a terrorist attack.

This is a generation defined by technology and globalization, and they have never known the world any other way. They have been described as the most technologically advanced generation educators have ever seen. Born around the time when the PC came on the scene, they have grown up with technology, and learning to use it came as naturally as learning to walk. Most have access to computers in their homes, and some have their own websites. However, one should not assume that this description fits all students in this generation. Some have no computers in their homes and only limited online access elsewhere, and their computer literacy may be only superficial (The Economist, 2010).

They have grown up with the ability to access people worldwide through their computers. iPods and social media (e.g., MySpace, Facebook, and YouTube) are an everyday part of their lives. Generation Y-ers are plugged in 24 hours a day, 7 days a week. They are heavily immersed in the digital world and prefer e-mail and text messaging, webinars, and other online technology. Social networking is now the most popular medium of communication, and Generation Y-ers have fully embraced this new technology. Social networking sites are popular because they allow immediate, easy, and wide interaction (Miller, 2011).

While highly adept at utilizing social networking, some in this age group have realized too late the consequences of placing inappropriate information about themselves on the Internet. College admissions officers and potential employers often access the information from social media sites, and they may base admissions and hiring decisions on their findings.

Tulgan (2009) refers to Generation Y as "Generation X on fast forward with self-esteem on steroids." He emphasizes how parents and educators have continually reinforced these individuals' self-esteem. Even when their accomplishments are minimal, they are commonly praised for their efforts by their parents (and often by their schools) and have been awarded and rewarded all of their lives. Consequently, many have a very positive image of themselves, even when that image is unrealistic. They have learned to be themselves and that it is fine to walk to their own beat. They are sometimes described as the most challenging group to prepare for the workforce, in part because of their high opinion of themselves and their expectations of positive responses from others.

Their parents believed that they needed structure, so they were heavily programmed with organized activities. Because, as a group, they have been so highly valued by their parents, they view themselves as special. They in turn tend to be very close to their parents, and many consider their parents to be their best friends. Unlike some earlier generations, they prefer rules to rebellion and choose teamwork over individualism (Tulgan, 2009).

One of the most encouraging characteristics of Generation Y-ers is that they are perhaps the most tolerant generation in this country's history. Because they themselves are products of interracial or multicultural marriages or are friends of those who are, they tend to rail against racism, sexism, and homophobia. Generation Y has much to learn from the older generation, and the latter have much to learn from this new generation. Both age groups have much to offer and much they can share with each other.

GENERATION Z

Generation Z is the younger cohort of Generation Y. This group is just now being addressed in the literature, and includes those born between 1991 and 2000, which includes some adolescents. While they share proficiency in the available technology with the older (1978–1990) cohort, they were born and grew up with much more advanced technology. The high-tech world the young teens in the United States are entering is one that some of their parents and grandparents cannot even comprehend. Facebook, Skype, Facetime, and iChat allow this generation of young people to communicate in real time with friends and family across the country, or around the world. In addition, they witnessed the amazing impact of mass social networking technology on the election of the President of the United States in 2008.

Many adults from older generations do not even know of the existence of YouTube and MySpace, websites where individuals, many of whom are teens, post their own materials and information. Anyone with a computer connected to the Internet can access MySpace either to place their own materials or to see what others have on their pages. These sites allow an estimated 1.5 billion people to access the Internet globally and interact with each other (Dolgin, 2011).

These websites are extremely popular with teenagers and some young adults, and they can be a means of sharing excellent information and ideas—and, unfortunately, an avenue by which sexual predators seek out potential victims. This has been particularly problematic with MySpace and Facebook, in which individuals have been known to falsify information, use bogus photographs, and make contact with children and teens while posing as younger individuals.

Astute in the use of cell phones, the Internet, and other means of staying connected, the Z generation will pose a challenge for both educators and parents. While familiar with the Internet and knowing how to utilize search engines such as Google, these young students are not always astute enough to evaluate the quality of sources and to determine if the information they have found on the Internet is valid. Often seeking the most expedient way to obtain answers or information to complete their reports, they lack the background to ask the right questions to determine if data should be utilized. Even college students and professors are sometimes led astray by the Internet. While some of the information in the online encyclopedia Wikipedia is accurate, not all of the material is. There is no close scrutiny to verify the accuracy of materials, which are submitted voluntarily by individuals who are not all qualified to

Utilizing social networks is a major means of communication with this generation.
© Annie Fuller/Pearson

do so. Unfamiliar with their sources of information, some may be unable to determine the qualitative difference between popular publications such as *People* and scholarly journals.

While we as educators are often in awe at the computer skills of our young students, it is incumbent on us to provide our students with the necessary skills in effective library and research use of the Internet. Without these skills, it is unlikely that they will develop into effective scholars.

Twenge, Konrath, Foster, Campbell, and Bushman (2008) suggest that parental efforts to boost the self-esteem of their children may have backfired. Generation Y, as a group, have become more narcissistic than their older, Generation X siblings ever were. Twenge, with other researchers across the country, studied 16,000 college students who were given psychological surveys to determine if they had narcissistic personalities. The study found that almost two-thirds of recent college students had narcissism scores above the 1982 average. These researchers suggest that the findings may in part be due to the self-esteem programs many schools adopted 20 years ago. They further state that nursery schools had children sing songs with lyrics such as "I am special. I am special. Look at me." As a group, they appear to be used to instant gratification and grade inflation. Some may see themselves as the "now" generation and will enter the real world of work dangerously naïve.

Beloit College Mindset List.   Since 1998 Beloit College in Wisconsin has distributed its Mindset List to both school faculty and staff. The list identifies some of the characteristics—the mindset, or the facts of life—that distinguish the incoming freshmen class from the students of years past who preceded them. The class of 2014 entered Beloit in 2010. Most were 17 or 18 years old and were born in 1988. The complete Mindset List can be accessed online at: http://www.beloit.edu/mindset. A sampling of the 75 items on the Mindset List follows:

- Fergie is a pop singer, and not a princess.
- Russians and Americans have always been living together in space.
- Czechoslovakia has never existed.

PAUSE TO REFLECT 10.1

We have often seen children from Generation Y and now Generation Z with highly structured lives. Parents are involving their children in one organized activity after another, from weekly matches during soccer season to basketball leagues for both boys and girls. We also see parents freer with their praise than in earlier generations. University professors frequently complain of grade inflation and about students expecting an A and certainly no less than a B simply because they attend a class. If some of the literature is accurate, indicating that these young people are naïve and entering the workplace with unrealistic expectations, are we doing our children a disservice?

- Do we need to temper our praise to a more realistic level?

- Are we indeed witnessing grade inflation?

- Do we need to prepare our children better for the real world of hard work and competition?

- Ruth Bader Ginsburg has always sat on the Supreme Court.
- Leno and Letterman have always been trading insults on opposing networks.

While most undergraduate students can easily relate to this mindset, their baby boomer professors will be continuously reminded that they belong to another generation.

Childhood

Childhood is an especially critical time in the life of an individual. This is a time when the individual begins school, where he or she will be socialized and exposed to cultures other than that of the home, family, and neighborhood. The educational setting can have a profound influence on the young child. Teachers can provide support to the parents' efforts toward appropriate rearing practices or to try to counter that which negatively affects the child.

The child's response to these new cultural experiences may be influenced by the home and the school. Children will develop habits during this time that can affect their health throughout life. The school should assist them in making sound choices. Signs related to child maltreatment may be observable in the school. Educators should always be vigilant, with a concern for the overall well-being of their students.

SOCIAL CLASS AND POVERTY

Teachers in the inner city and in some other communities may find that nearly all of the children in their classrooms live in poverty. Poverty creates numerous problems for children. In many instances, children live with a single parent, typically the mother. When the father is absent, children often lack adequate male role models, and the mother often bears the entire burden of discipline and financial support. Single mothers living in poverty must often work outside the home to provide for their families. Appropriate child care is often difficult, if not impossible, for working mothers to provide.

Mothers from middle and upper socioeconomic groups may not need to work outside the home. Those who choose to do so can often be selective in their choice of a day care setting to obtain an environment congruent with their family values. Day care settings are often important in the socialization process because many of a child's early behaviors are learned from peers and caregivers. Parents from less affluent groups, however, may have limited choices for their children's day care environment. In some instances older siblings, themselves children, may be required to assume family child care responsibilities with the parent(s) working outside the home. Inadequate child care may compromise the child's socialization and development processes.

CHILDREN, ETHNIC AWARENESS, AND PREJUDICE

After years of work in improving race relations in this country, the 1980s and 1990s saw growing optimism that the United States had turned the corner on race relations. The hate crimes and racial violence that have emerged in recent years, however, remind us that the ugliness of racism remains with us. Although we as educators may expect to see racism among adults and, to some extent, adolescents, we are sometimes shocked and often dismayed when it is evidenced in the behavior of young children. Attention by educators to signs of developing prejudice in young children can, in some instances, have a positive effect in countering its influence.

CHILD ABUSE

Each year hundreds of thousands of child abuse cases are reported. Child abuse is the physical or psychological mistreatment of a child. In the United States, a report of child abuse is made every 10 seconds. Almost five children die every day as a result of child abuse. Three out of four victims are under the age of 4.

According to the Centers for Disease Control and Prevention (CDC), over 772,000 children in the United States were identified as victims of child abuse and neglect in 2008, and 1,740 children died as a result. Seventy-one percent were victims of neglect, 9% sexual abuse, 16% physical abuse, and 7% emotional or psychological abuse (some may have been reported in more than one category). Most maltreatment came at the hands of parents. Of the 1,740 children who died in 2008 from abuse or neglect, 80% were under the age of 4, 10% ages 4 to 7, and 4% ages 8 to 11 (CDC, 2010a).

Abuse-induced stress can disrupt early brain development in young children. Abused children may experience serious problems in school, in terms of both disruptive behavior and academic achievement. Maltreatment can have a long-lasting effect on an individual. Extreme stress can have a negative effect on the nervous and immune systems, resulting in higher risks for health problems as an adult. These problems include alcoholism, depression, drug abuse, eating disorders, obesity, high-risk sexual behaviors, smoking, suicide, and certain chronic diseases (CDC, 2010b). Bartollas and Miller (2011) assert that research continues to demonstrate that children who are victims of maltreatment are placed at a greater risk for arrest. Abused children are 59% more likely to be arrested as juveniles and 30% more likely to commit a violent crime. More than 36% of women in prisons reported being abused as children, as compared to 12% to 17% of women in the general population. Fourteen percent of male prison inmates reported abuse as children, as compared to 5% to 8% of men in the general population (CDC, 2010b).

Abused children are 25% more likely to experience teen pregnancy. Sixty percent of individuals in drug rehabilitation centers indicate that they were child abuse victims. The cost of child abuse and neglect in the United States was estimated to be $104 billion in 2007 (Childhelp Inc., 2008).

Child abuse or maltreatment is usually categorized as physical abuse, physical neglect, sexual abuse, or emotional abuse. The Federal Child Abuse Prevention and Treatment Act (U.S. Code Title 42, 5106g: Definitions) defines child abuse as:

- Any recent act or failure to act on the part of a parent or caretaker, which results in death, serious physical or emotional harm, sexual abuse or exploitation; or
- An act or failure to act, which presents an imminent risk of serious harm (Childhelp Inc., n.d.).

Physical Abuse. **Physical abuse** refers to nonaccidental injury inflicted by a caretaker. There is often a fine line between physical abuse and discipline through physical punishment. In the United States, physical punishment is common in many families as a child-rearing practice. Physical abuse ranges from minor bruises to severe fractures or even death as a result of punching, beating, kicking, biting, shaking, throwing, stabbing, choking, hitting (with a hand, stick, strap, or other object), burning, or otherwise harming a child. These injuries are considered abuse whether or not the caregiver intended to injure the child (Child Welfare Information Gateway, n.d.).

Neglect. **Neglect** involves the failure of the parents, guardian, or caregiver to provide for the basic needs of a child. Neglect may be:

- Physical (e.g., failure to provide necessary food, shelter, or supervision)
- Medical (e.g., failure to provide medical or mental health treatment)
- Educational (e.g., failure to educate a child or tend to special education needs)
- Emotional (e.g., inattention to a child's emotional needs, failure to provide psychological needs, or permitting a child to engage in substance abuse) (Child Welfare Information Gateway, n.d.).

At times older siblings may be required to assume child care responsibilities. When these siblings are considered by authorities to be too young to provide responsible care, this may be considered neglect. This is particularly problematic in cities with large immigrant populations, especially when parents cannot afford child care when they work. Some children who suffer from neglect may exhibit poor hygiene, may be inappropriately dressed for weather conditions, may suffer from hunger, or may have inadequate medical or dental care. At times, the practices of some religious groups come into conflict with the law regarding parental decisions for addressing illness and refusing conventional medical care. The courts have, in some instances, intervened and overturned parental rights when children were considered to be at extreme risk.

Sexual Abuse. **Sexual abuse** refers to the involvement of children or underage adolescents in sexual activities. It also includes practices that violate the social mores of one's culture as they relate to family roles. Sexual abuse is usually found in the form of familial abuse or incest; extrafamilial molestation or rape; exploitation through pornography, prostitution, sex rings, or cults; or institutional abuse (e.g., day care centers). Sixty thousand cases of child sexual abuse were reported in the United States during 2009 (Berk, 2012).

Emotional Abuse. Children who are emotionally abused are chronically belittled, humiliated, rejected, or they have their self-esteem attacked. **Emotional abuse** "is a pattern of behavior that impairs a child's emotional development or sense of worth. This may include constant criticism, threats, or rejection, as well as withholding love, support, or guidance" (Child Welfare Information Gateway, 2008, p. 3).

Figure 10.1 provides some of the key signs of child abuse. Child abuse is everyone's problem. It is the responsibility of each teacher to report known or suspected cases of child abuse to the school supervisor. The supervisor, in turn, is responsible for reporting these problems or concerns to professionals who are mandated by state and federal laws to bring the matter to the attention of appropriate protective agencies. These professionals are referred to as "mandated reporters." Every state has mandated laws requiring the reporting of child abuse. State laws differ in that one state may have no penalties for failure to report, whereas others impose fines and even jail terms. Some states stipulate that a report must be made if there is suspicion of abuse; others stipulate accountability for failure to report if there is "reasonable cause to believe." Beyond the legal mandates, educators have a professional and ethical obligation to make reports to protect children from abuse.

All states have a legal requirement that educators, care providers, and others must report suspected child abuse. If you suspect child abuse of one of your students you must report it to a supervisor.

Figure 10.1   Recognizing Child Abuse

The following signs may be indicative of child abuse or neglect:

The Child

- Shows sudden changes in behavior or school performance.
- Has not received help for physical or medical problems brought to the parent's attention.
- Has learning problems (or difficulty concentrating) that cannot be attributed to specific physical or psychological causes.
- Is always watchful, as though preparing for something bad to happen.
- Lacks adult supervision.
- Is overly compliant, passive, or withdrawn.
- Comes to school or other activities early, stays late, and does not want to go home.

The Parent

- Asks teachers or other caretakers to use harsh physical discipline if the child misbehaves.
- Sees the child as entirely bad, worthless, or burdensome.
- Demands a level of physical or academic performance the child cannot possibly achieve.
- Looks primarily to the child for care, attention, and satisfaction of emotional needs.

The Parent and Child

- Rarely touch or look at each other.
- Consider their relationship entirely negative.
- State that they do not like each other.

Source: Child Welfare Information Gateway. (2008). Recognizing child abuse and neglect: Signs and symptoms. Washington, DC: U.S. Department of Health and Human Services, http://www.childwelfare.gov/pubs/can_info_packet.pdf.

CHILDHOOD OBESITY

The Centers for Disease Control and Prevention (2010c) reported the prevalence of childhood obesity in the United States has more than tripled in the last 30 years. Increased rates of overweight and obese children have affected all levels from preschool through high school. The prevalence among children 6 to 11 years old increased from 6.5% to 19.6% in 2008. In the 12 to 19 age group it increased from 5.0% to 18.1%. Today, 32% of children in the United States are overweight; 17% are obese (Berk, 2012).

Bad nutrition habits are often formed during youth. Nearly a third of U.S. adults are overweight or obese. In addition to facing emotional and social problems, obese children are likely to have lifelong health issues (Berk, 2012). Overweight adolescents have up to an 80% chance of becoming overweight or obese adults. It is estimated that obesity has a $117 billion impact in health care costs and loss of productivity. Childhood obesity alone is costing as much as $14 billion a year in direct health care costs (U.S. Newswire, 2007).

The CDC suggests that being overweight or obese can have serious consequences. It increases the risk for numerous diseases and health conditions, including (CDC, 2010c):

- Cardiovascular disease (e.g., high cholesterol and high blood pressure)
- Bone and joint problems

- Sleep apnea
- Social and psychological problems (e.g., stigmatization and low self-esteem)
- Likelihood of becoming obese adults, with associated health problems

The physical consequences of overweight and obesity are often obvious; however, there are other consequences that may not be as easy to identify. Prejudice and discrimination toward overweight children may be another consequence, which may have serious implications for children. Obese children frequently feel socially isolated and experience teasing by their peers, low self-esteem, depression, and suicidal thoughts (Berk, 2012).

While parents may view their "chubby" child as cute with "just baby fat," the evidence is fairly conclusive that infants who are overweight tend to remain overweight as they grow older. The cause of overweight problems in both children and adults is multifaceted. There is probably no single cause we can attribute to the problem. Among the contributing factors are:

- Food and marketing
- Parental influences on eating behavior
- Dietary intake
- Lack of physical activity or exercise

Unfortunately for many individuals, the foods that seem to taste the best are the ones that are often unhealthy. The youth in the United States (and other parts of the world) have grown up in a culture where fast food is an integral part of daily life. Much of it may be tasty but it is often high in saturated fats. Until recent harsh criticism aired against the fast-food industry, many in the industry encouraged consumers to "supersize" or to increase the portions of their food orders for a modest additional cost. In addition to the prevalence of these fast-food establishments throughout the community, many schools have included these foods in their offerings. Many of the foods considered unhealthy by nutritionists have been referred to as "junk" foods. Some school cafeterias and school vending machines readily dispense sugar-filled soft drinks, chips, cookies, and other unhealthy items. While only one-fourth of elementary schools in the United States allow vending machines, the proportion rises in middle schools and is nearly 100% for high schools (Arnett, 2010).

Parents may exacerbate the problem by encouraging or even forcing their children to eat all of their food and clean their plates, even if they are already satiated. Other parents, also hooked on unhealthy foods, purchase unhealthy food items and serve them in their homes. Both quality and quantity are clearly issues of concern.

Another concern is the sedentary lifestyle that many of our youth have adopted. Again, parental modeling is often flawed. Today's youth have more entertainment options than earlier generations with no or limited access to television, video games, and computers. The lack of physical activity among much of today's youth is a major contributor to their obesity and lack of physical conditioning.

Health care professionals, state legislatures, and even the U.S. Congress are beginning to address the

Schools have moved to healthy options to combat obesity and other childhood health problems.
© Jim West/Alamy

The variables that contribute to childhood obesity are obvious. Many of our children do not get enough exercise, their eating habits are terrible, and many are addicted to junk foods, which taste good to them but are filled with saturated fats and calories. Many of our schools contribute to the problem by selling sodas and junk foods.

- What can you do in your classroom to help reduce the problem?

- Is there anything you can do to help educate parents as to the steps they can take to help their children choose healthier and more nutritious foods?

- Is there any way you can voice your concern to the school authorities without seriously jeopardizing your position?

problem. The Institute of Medicine, a part of the National Academy of Sciences, recommended that junk foods such as potato chips, doughnuts, chocolate-covered ice cream, and sugary drinks be banned from K–12 schools. Efforts have and are being made at the federal level to ban junk foods in schools (Gardiner, 2010; Dunham, 2007).

Many states have now enacted laws specifying what can and cannot be served in schools. For example, in Alabama the sale of foods with minimal nutritional value during meal service time is prohibited. An Arkansas law bans elementary school students' access to vending machines offering food and soda (School Nutrition Association, 2008). These are some positive steps. However, faced with very difficult budgetary situations, some schools are having difficulty letting go of highly profitable sales of junk food. If educators, administrators, and school boards are sincere in advocating for the welfare of their students, they will not place profit over health.

In 2010 First Lady Michelle Obama launched a campaign (Let's Move) to address the childhood obesity epidemic. Let's Move emphasizes eating healthier and moving more (at least 60 minutes of vigorous physical activity). This initiative proposes the creation of partnerships among schools, businesses, communities, and federal and state governments to assist in that effort (Let's Move, 2011).

Adolescence

Adolescence, approximately ages 13 through 18, is perhaps one of the most challenging times in the life of an individual and the family. It is a long transitional period (6 years or so) during which the individual is "suspended" between childhood and adulthood. During adolescence, emancipation from the primary family unit is the central task of the individual. It is a difficult period for the young person, who is attempting to be free from the role of a child but is not fully equipped to assume the responsibilities of adulthood.

RELATIONSHIP WITH PARENTS

As the adolescent shifts emotional ties from the family to peers, a restructuring may take place in the parent-adolescent relationship. Parents may be viewed more objectively. Parents may become more concerned about peer influence as they experience increasingly less interaction with their child. These changes have the potential to turn the period of adolescence into one of dissonance and alienation from parents and other members of the family. One need only observe a few adolescent-family situations, however, to realize that the degree of dissonance and alienation varies greatly.

The attitude of the parents may contribute to the alienation. Parents who expect problems with their children in the adolescent period sometimes fall into the trap of a self-fulfilling prophecy. Their expectation of alienation generates a hostile attitude on their part. In contrast, parents who have confidence in their children may promote a feeling of confidence and trust. These children often develop sufficient self-confidence to resist peer pressure when resistance is appropriate.

Alienation is disturbing to families, to adult members of the community, and to the adolescents themselves. In their efforts to achieve autonomy, sexual functioning, and identity in order to become productive, self-sufficient individuals, some adolescents think they must turn away from the family. As adolescents assert their rights to assume adult behaviors, they sometimes are unable to assume complementary adult-like responsibilities. Recognizing this shortcoming, parents are understandably reluctant to grant adolescents adult privileges; this further adds to the alienation.

AT-RISK YOUTH AND HIGH-RISK BEHAVIOR

It is important to differentiate between the terms "at risk" and "high risk." At-risk youth are those with a disadvantaged living status. This may be due to conditions such as poverty, discrimination, family instability, genetic or constitutional factors, parental neglect or abuse, or major traumatic events. High-risk behaviors are those that youth engage in that make them or others vulnerable to physical, social, or psychological harm or negative outcomes. Youth deemed "at risk" do not necessarily engage in high-risk behaviors. High-risk behaviors include the use of harmful substances such as alcohol or other drugs, and sexual behaviors leading to unwanted pregnancies or sexually transmitted diseases. These behaviors are initiated during adolescence, are frequently interrelated, and often extend into adulthood.

SUBSTANCE ABUSE

The use of harmful substances, primarily by children and adolescents, has been one of the most problematic areas faced by parents, schools, communities, and law enforcement agencies in the past two decades. It will inevitably continue to be a major problem in the next decade. Substance abuse is the use of banned or illegal drugs and substances or the overuse of legal substances. The problem is a national phenomenon, and many of the problems of adult substance abuse have their roots in adolescence.

Substances are abused to produce altered states of consciousness. The adolescents who use them often seek relief, escape, or comfort from stress. The social institutions to which the adolescents must relate, including family and particularly the educational system, may be perceived as unresponsive or openly hostile. Their inability to focus on long-range goals, their desire for immediate gratification, and their lack of appreciation for the consequences of their behavior may contribute to some adolescents' misuse of substances.

There are two broad categories of adolescent drug users: the experimenters and the compulsive users. Experimenters make up the majority of adolescent drug users. A few progress from experimenters to compulsive users. Although most experimenters eventually abandon such use, the possibility of progression to compulsive use is a serious concern of parents and authorities. Recreational users fall somewhere between experimenters and compulsive users.

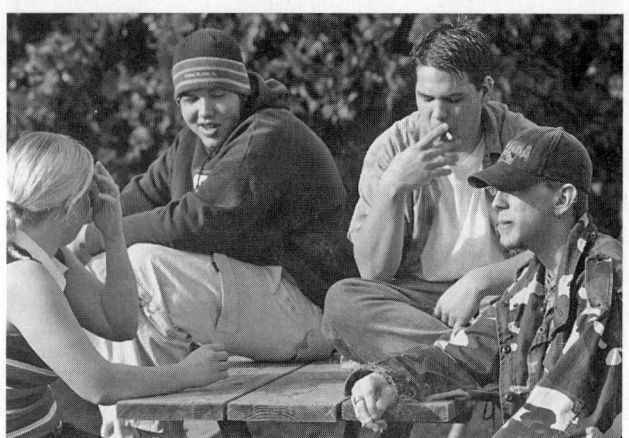

Experimentation with smoking, alcohol, and drugs often occurs during adolescence at the urging of peers.
© George Dodson/PH College

For them, alcohol and marijuana are often the drugs of choice. Use is primarily to achieve relaxation and is typically intermittent. For a few, however, the goal is intoxication, and these individuals pose a threat to themselves and others.

The national Youth Risk Behavior Survey (YRBS) monitors priority health risk behaviors among youth and young adults. These include tobacco, alcohol and other drug use, as well as sexual behaviors that contribute to unwanted pregnancy and sexually transmitted diseases (STDs). The 2009 YRBS provided disturbing statistics: 72.5% of students had at least one drink of alcohol; 24.2% had five or more drinks in a row within a couple of hours (binge drinking); 36.8% had used marijuana; 2.8% had used cocaine; 11.7% had sniffed glue, or inhaled paints or sprays; 4.1% of students had used methamphetamines; and 3.3% had taken steroid pills (CDC, 2010d).

Most Americans seem to understand the detrimental effects of smoking; nationally nearly 20% of youth and young adults smoke on a daily basis. Comparing youth from different ethnic racial groups, whites lead the daily smoker list, followed by Hispanics, and African Americans at a distant third. White female cigarette use exceeds white male use slightly. Many or most of these tobacco users believe that they can quit when they want to. Unfortunately for these young smokers, when they finally internalize the health hazards of smoking, many are already addicted, and smoking cessation is then extremely difficult and sometimes impossible. In addition to the health risks to the individual, smokers risk the well-being of those close to them with secondhand smoke. Adding smokeless tobacco (i.e., snuff, chewing tobacco) and cigars into the mix, current tobacco use increases to 26% of youth.

The CDC (2010d) reports some decline in substance abuse. Alcohol use among high school students has decreased from 50% in 1999 to 42% in 2009. However, the incidence of binge drinking is a concern. Binge drinking involves five or more drinks of alcohol in a row, usually within two hours. Twenty-four percent of students have engaged in this activity, and it is particularly alarming that 15.3% of ninth-graders have done so.

Marijuana use decreased from 27% in 1999 to 3% in 2009 and ecstasy use from 11% in 2003 to 7% in 2009. Heroin use, however, remained steady at 2%, while methamphetamine use decreased from 10% in 2001 to 4% in 2009 (CDC, 2010d).

Adolescent substance abuse may have serious long-term consequences. Berk (2012) suggests that youth who rely on alcohol and drugs do not learn healthy coping techniques and responsible decision-making skills. As a result, they may suffer from anxiety, depression, and antisocial behavior.

Numerous problems related to substance abuse affect the community at large. Intravenous drug users are one group at high risk for AIDS. The spread of the deadly human immunodeficiency virus (HIV) among adolescents had, by the 1990s, affected thousands of the country's youth.

It is a complex problem that deserves more attention by educators than the brief coverage here. The problem can and must be dealt with through the home, school, and law enforcement authorities, as well as through social agencies and responsible media.

ADOLESCENT SEXUAL BEHAVIORS

The 2009 Youth Risk Behavior Survey (CDC, 2010d) indicates that 46.0% of high school students have had sexual intercourse at least once. Nationwide, 5.9% of students indicated that they had had sexual intercourse before the age of 13. Apparently, the majority of these individuals are using some form of birth control. Slightly over 60 percent reported that they had used a condom, while nearly 20% indicated that they or their partner had used birth control pills to prevent pregnancy during their previous sexual activity. These statistics clearly suggest that America's high school students are involved in activities that can lead to pregnancy and STDs, including HIV infection. While some are utilizing birth control measures, there are still some who are not and some are exposing themselves to the possibility of developing STDs, some of which can have lethal consequences.

Table 10.1 indicates the percentages of high school students who are sexually active by racial group. This high-risk behavior and the resulting teen pregnancies often have a high correlation with poverty and with states and regions with high levels of poverty (e.g., Washington, D.C.). Consequently, there is a higher birth rate among teens of color who are significantly impacted by poverty. Compared across poverty groups, teen birth rates among poor whites and poor African Americans, Hispanics, and American Indians/Alaskan Natives are more uniform.

The poverty rates are disproportionately high for these three groups, and Johnson, Musial, Hall, and Gollnick (2011) suggest that poverty appears to be the most important factor contributing to teen pregnancy. They state that many teens associate sex with the freedom and sophistication of adulthood, and that girls and women often connect sex with being accepted, being attractive, and being loved. This may be more pronounced among adolescents living in poverty. Their problems are often exacerbated by limited supervision due to parents working long hours or being absent for other reasons. They may also lack access to adequate medical care and advice.

After increases in 2006 and 2007, teen birth rates declined slightly in 2008 to 41.5 births per 1,000 women ages 15 to 19. The birth rate for the older (ages 18 and 19) teens was 70.6 per 1,000 in 2008 (Martin, Hamilton, Sutton, et al., 2010).

As might be expected, birth rates among adolescent women tend to parallel the level of sexual activity of the various ethnic racial groups. While the precise statistics vary by age group, in all age groups except for the 10–14 group, the highest birth rate is among Hispanic females, followed by black, American Indian or Alaskan Native, white, and Asian or Pacific Islanders. Table 10.2 shows the birth rates for the 15–19 age group per 1,000 women. Adolescent females from ethnic minority backgrounds, particularly Hispanic, black, and American Indian or Alaskan Native, have considerably higher pregnancy rates than their white or Asian/Pacific Islander peers.

In 2008 there were 1,901 young people ages 13–19 who were diagnosed with HIV infections and another 556 diagnosed with AIDS. At 75%, the largest percentage of infected HIV adolescents were African American, as were those (71%) infected by AIDS. Infected Hispanic youth comprised 13% of the HIV-infected adolescents and 17% of the AIDS group, while white youth comprised 11% of the HIV and 10% of the diagnosed AIDs individuals. Asian and

Table 10.1 Sexually Active High School Students

Racial Groups	Percent Sexually Active
African Americans	47.7%
Hispanics	34.6%
Whites	32.0%

Source: Centers for Disease Control and Prevention (2010). National Youth Risk Behavior Survey, United States, 2009. Retrieved from www.cdc.gov/mmwr/preview/mmwrhtml/ss5505al.htm.

Table 10.2 Birth Rates for U.S. Women Ages 15 to 19 Years (per 1,000).

All Races	41.5%
White	26.7%
Black	62.8%
American Indian or Alaskan Native	58.4%
Asian or Pacific Islander	16.2%
Hispanic	17.5%

Source: Martin, Hamilton, et al. (2010), Births: Final data for 2008. CDC: National Vital Statistics Reports, http://www.cdc.gov/nchs/data/nvsr/nvsr59/nvsr59_01.pdf.

Pacific Islander youth and American Indian or Alaskan Native comprise less than 1% of each of these categories (CDC, 2010e). These findings provide an indication for health care and school personnel as to which groups should be targeted for sex education and HIV/AIDS awareness and prevention.

Although there has been a decline in STDs, the rate in the United States remains much higher than that of Canada and Western Europe. Of all age groups, adolescents have the highest rate of STDs. If untreated, adolescents are at risk for serious lifelong complications (Berk, 2012).

As many as 20% of teenagers have been engaging is a disturbing practice referred to as **sexting**, which involves the sending of nude or semi-nude pictures from cell phone to cell phone (CBS News, 2009). It typically involves sending a picture to a boyfriend or girlfriend. Child pornography laws are very strict, and the distribution or possession of nude photos of underage individuals, even of oneself, may be a serious felony subject to imprisonment and registration as a sex offender. Problems are exacerbated when photos are shared with friends who in turn upload the pictures to social network sites. Parents and educators need to impress on teens the seriousness and consequences of such activities (Stone, 2009).

ADOLESCENT SUICIDE

Many of America's youth are apparently troubled, some depressed to the point of thoughts of suicide and some who actually carry through with the act. During the 12-month period preceding the 2009 CDC Youth Surveillance Survey, 13.8% of students nationwide indicated that they had seriously considered suicide, and 6.3% indicated that they had made plans as to how they would attempt suicide. Among young adults, ages 15 to 24, there are approximately 100 to 200 attempts for every completed suicide (CDC, 2010d). Although the overall rate among teenagers

PAUSE TO REFLECT 10.3

It is quite obvious, whether we approve or not, that half or more of our nation's teenagers are involved in sexual activity. The problems are at least twofold. They are risking the possibility of pregnancies, and many are having unprotected sex and risking the possibility of contracting sexually transmitted diseases (STDs).

- Whose responsibility is it to deal with this? The students? The parents? The school? Public health agencies?

- Does providing free condoms to junior high and high school students encourage them to be sexually promiscuous?

- If they are going to be involved in sexual activity anyway, should we protect both them and society?

has declined since 1992, suicide remains the third leading cause of death among young people, surpassed only by car accidents and homicide. It is estimated that annually in the United States nearly 4,500 young people ages 15 to 24 commit suicide each year (CDC, 2008). In all likelihood, the actual number of adolescent deaths due to suicide is higher than that reported. Some suicides are likely reported as accidents, especially high-speed automobile crashes where no suicide notes are recovered. Likewise, some gunshot deaths may be reported as accidents.

Numerous theories have been advanced for the adolescent suicide phenomenon. Among the reasons offered are the decline in religiosity, tension between parents, the breakup of the nuclear family, family tensions and conflict, substance abuse, and the competitiveness of school. A disproportionate number of gay and lesbian youth have attempted or committed suicide. In recent years attention has been drawn to students who have been bullied, including cyberbullying, and who have resorted to suicide.

Because of their lack of experience in making accurate judgments, depressed adolescents may be more prone to respond to the suggestion of suicide than an adult. Adolescent depression is a function of a wide range of situations, perhaps involving failure, loss of a love object, or rejection. It can also be a function of biochemical imbalances in the brain or the loss of a parent through death, divorce, separation, or extended absence. The widespread availability and use of both legal prescription and illegal drugs may be another contributing factor.

There are a number of warning signs adolescents may manifest when contemplating suicide. The observant educator can often catch these signs and solicit appropriate intervention. Some of these signs are listed in Figure 10.2.

There are considerable ethnic differences in the adolescent suicide rates. Hispanic and African Americans have slightly lower suicide rates than Caucasian Americans, whereas Native American rates are twice the national average (Berk, 2012). This alarming statistic is partly a result of the history of cultural disintegration forced on Native Americans by flawed public policy (Berk, 2012).

Adolescents who do not to conform to expected sexual behavior patterns are at considerable risk. Malley, Posner, and Potter (2008) suggest that lesbian, gay, and bisexual youth display more suicidal behaviors than other youth groups. They report, using various sources, that this group is one and a half to seven times more likely to attempt suicide. They further suggest that while mortality reporting generally does not indicate sexual orientation, the higher suicide attempts likely lead to more completed suicides among this youth group.

Suicide attempts are often more of a desperate attempt to be heard and understood than an act whose true intent is to end one's life. Those who contemplate suicide but do not follow through with an attempt often report that their plans were changed by someone's simple act of concern.

ADOLESCENT SELF-INJURY

Because self-injury is done in private, most educators are unaware of its prevalence and its seriousness. Self-injury or self-mutilation is the deliberate act of harming one's own body. This may include cutting or burning oneself. It may also include behaviors such as pulling one's skin or hair, swallowing toxic substances, self-bruising, or the breaking of bones. Tattoos and body piercing are not considered self-injury unless done deliberately to harm oneself.

Self-injury may begin as early as age 7, although most such behaviors tend to begin between the ages of 12 and 15. The reported prevalence of this behavior varies considerably, ranging from 4% to 38%, with the most consistent reports of high school students in the United States and Canada indicating between 13% and 24%.

Figure 10.2 Warning Signs of Adolescents Contemplating Suicide

- Sleep changes
- Withdrawal from others and routine activities
- Aggressive and hostile behaviors, including running away
- Unusual passive behavior
- Substance abuse
- Neglecting personal appearance
- Personality changes
- Persistent boredom, difficulty concentrating, or a decline in the quality of schoolwork
- Frequent complaints about physical symptoms, often related to emotions (e.g., stomachaches, headaches)
- Loss of interest in pleasurable activities
- Loss of interest in schoolwork and activities
- Complaints of being a bad person or feeling bad inside
- Providing verbal hints, with statements suggesting that they will no longer be a problem, that things no longer matter, or that they will not be around much longer
- Giving away or throwing away valued possessions and other behaviors suggesting that the individual is putting affairs in order
- Exhibiting euphoria following depression
- Expressions of hopelessness and helplessness
- Unusual reckless, life-endangering behaviors (e.g., speeding)

Sources: **Teen Suicide. (2008). The American Academy of Child and Adolescent Psychiatry, No. 10. Updated May 2008, from http://www.aacap.org/galleries/FactsForFamilies/10_teen_suicide.pdf ; Teen Suicide U. S. http://www.teensuicide.us/articles2.html; MedicineNet.com, Teen Suicide Warning Signs, http://www.medicinenet.com/script/main/art.asp?articlekey=55145.**

Individuals suggest that they engage in this behavior because it provides a means to manage painful feelings, cope with anxiety, and relieve stress and pressure. It is considered a means of avoiding suicide. It is linked to childhood abuse, especially sexual abuse. It is also linked to eating disorders, substance abuse, borderline personality disorder, depression, and anxiety disorders.

Symptoms include, but are not limited to, scars, fresh cuts, frequent claims of accidents, broken bones, and wearing long sleeves or long pants in hot weather. Because the behavior is done secretly and in private, many parents and educators are unfamiliar with this practice. If you observe or suspect symptoms, report to appropriate school authorities so that help can be provided in developing more appropriate behaviors for coping with problems that have contributed to the problem (Mayo Clinic Health Manager, 2010; Cornell, n.d.).

BULLYING

Almost everyone can remember the popular kids in school and those who were treated as social outcasts. From an early age children can be incredibly cruel. Bullying may involve teasing, taunting, verbal abuse, shoving, hitting, spreading rumors, or deliberately excluding someone. Bullying by peers can have serious long-term consequences for young children. It takes a considerable toll on their physical and mental health. An estimated 20% of high school students reported being bullied on school property in 2009, with a higher prevalence among females than males (CDC, 2010g).

Perhaps the most notorious case of bullying involved Phoebe Prince, a 15-year old who emigrated from Ireland to South Hadley, Massachusetts, with her mother and siblings in the fall of 2009. Prince was bullied by students in her school for months. She was reportedly called a whore, and an Irish slut, on Twitter, Facebook, and other forms of social media. She was threatened and harassed in the school hallways and library. In January 2010 an empty drink can was thrown at her from a car while she walked home from school. She continued walking home, where she hung herself. Her tormentors then used Facebook to mock her death. They told police investigators that they had nothing to do with Prince's death and then went back to school, where they allegedly continued to mock her.

The case drew international media attention and put the focus on bullying in American schools. Eventually nine teens, seven girls and two boys, were indicted on charges ranging from criminal harassment to stalking to civil rights violations. One of the girls was charged with assault by means of a dangerous weapon: the drink can she had thrown at Prince. The two males, ages 17 and 18, were charged with statutory rape. The district attorney in charge of the case said that numerous faculty members, staff members, and administrators at South Hadley High School were aware of the bullying—some even witnessed physical abuse—and did nothing (Kennedy, 2010; Cullen, 2010). Following this, the Massachusetts legislature passed antibullying legislation. Although this occurred too late for Phoebe Prince, later that year a South Hadley school committee adopted a more comprehensive anti-bullying policy.

With the popularity of social networking, cyber bullying has become extremely problematic in recent years. Attacks on individuals, with truths and untruths, innuendos, and rumors, cyberbullying can have serious consequences.

In 2011, there were shocking suicides of a young Canadian and a New York teen. Eleven year-old Mitchell Wilson of Ontario, Canada, suffocated himself after being beaten and bullied. Wilson suffered with muscular dystrophy. While he was allegedly beaten for a cell phone, his father indicated that he was bullied as well because of his disability and became extremely fearful of going outside the home and to school (Duell, 2011).

Fourteen-year-old Jamey Rodemeyer, of Buffalo, NY, was bullied and tormented because he was gay. Cyberbullies made posts such as, "Jamie is stupid, gay, fat, and ugly. He must die." Another read, "I wouldn't care if you died. No one would. So just do it" (Stump, 2011).

Following Rodemeyer's suicide, Lady Gaga dedicated a concert to him. When a Lady Gaga song was played at his Buffalo school dance, the bullies started chanting, "You're better off dead!" and "We're glad you're dead." Educators cannot lose sight of the fact that much of the bullying begins in the early school years. Sensitivity training must begin in the early grades and continue through high school. As with the carrying of weapons to school, there should be no tolerance for such behaviors.

YOUTH VIOLENCE

Violence is one of the greatest problems facing young Americans today. Although the violent crime rate in the United States has declined in recent years, this trend has not been evident in the juvenile violent crime rate. In 2008, 17.5% of students nationally carried a weapon (e.g., gun, knife, or club) in the 30 days prior to the survey (CDC, 2010e). In that same survey, 5.6% had carried a weapon (gun, knife, or club) onto school property. During the 12 months prior to the survey, 7.7% of students had been threatened or injured with a weapon on school property.

The CDC (2010f) reported that in 2007 there were 5,764 homicides among young people ages 10 to 24. The increase in violent deaths among young people accounts for the fact that their mortality rate has not improved over the past 30 years (Dolgin, 2011). In 2008 there were over 656,000 reports of violence-related injuries in young people ages 10 to 24 (CDC, 2010f).

Due to media coverage, the nation has become well conditioned to school violence. In reality, less than 1% of all homicides among school-age children (5 to 19 years of age) occur in or around school grounds or on the way to or from school (CDC, 2010g). However, the occurrence of multiple-victim school shooting incidents never ceases to disturb us.

Everyone in the United States was shocked and stunned when the images of the April 1999 shootings at Colorado's Columbine High School reached their TV screens, and by the shooting rampage at Virginia Tech University eight years later. In the first incident, in a few brief moments two outcast students shot and killed 12 of their classmates and a popular teacher/coach at Columbine High School, then killed themselves. On the Blacksburg, Virginia, campus a solitary, troubled student gunman took 32 lives, wounding many more before taking his own life. The odds were certainly against such a scenario taking place at either of the schools serving these comfortable and otherwise peaceful communities.

Columbine students are overwhelmingly white, and only one of the victims was black. The school served the affluent community of Littleton. Perhaps even more alarming was the intent of the two assailants, who had planted at least 30 bombs in the school with the intention of killing even more of their classmates. Fortunately, the bombs never detonated.

While the Columbine incident involved high school students, the Virginia Tech incident involved a 23-year-old. His emotional problems were said to have been diagnosed as early as middle school.

In 2007, 3,042 children and adolescents in the United States were killed by gunfire, almost equal to the number of U.S. combat deaths in Iraq through May 2010. Between 1979 and 2010, more than 100,000 children and youth were killed in the United States by gun violence (Children's Defense Fund, 2010).

The Littleton incident was but one of a string of violent attacks against students and teachers across the United States in recent years. Most of these high-profile shootings involved young males, most of whom are depicted as alienated individuals or outcasts. Often, their peers had ridiculed them, and consequently they associated with other disaffected individuals in outcast groups.

The Columbine assailants had provided ample warning signs of their troubled lives and potential to do harm. Authorities apparently ignored or paid little heed when advised of a hate-filled website and death threats against another student. The two students intensely disliked the school athletes, who allegedly mocked and harassed them. Not unlike other suicidal teens, these were individuals who were troubled and who broadcast warning signs to those who would pay heed. Unfortunately, no one who might have prevented the tragedy in this instance, and in so many other situations, paid heed.

Many of these warning signs of potentially aggressive behavior overlap with the warning signs of individuals considering suicide (e.g., depression). Whether or not the presence of these signs is indicative of suicide consideration or imminent danger to others, it is a warning of a potentially troubled individual. Parents, teachers, and school authorities cannot risk taking such warnings lightly.

Depression does not necessarily indicate the likelihood of violent behaviors; however, violent behavior is often a function of depression. If you have reason to suspect that a student is depressed, refer the individual to a school counselor or to another appropriate authority.

Debate / Zero Tolerance

Because of the increasing violence in the schools, officials have instituted zero tolerance regulations in which specific behaviors and items are banned from the school. In general, violators are dealt with immediately and sometimes harshly (e.g., immediate expulsion) regardless of the intent, the age of the offender, or the severity of the offense. Often administrators have no discretionary powers to make exceptions. The tough rules are designed to ensure that the schools will be safer, with every violation having a mandatory punishment.

FOR	**AGAINST**
■ Seemingly harsh punishment for infractions is a small price to pay for keeping our schools and children safe.	■ Young children are expelled simply for forgetting some minor item.
■ Students and their parents know what the rules are. If they break the rules, then they must suffer the consequences.	■ Zero tolerance has gone too far. Innocent children are treated like criminals, scarring them for life.
■ Zero tolerance means that there are consequences for every infraction.	■ Unless administrators are given more discretion, these ridiculous laws need to be scrapped.
■ Good zero tolerance policies do not require the maximum punishment for every offense.	

| QUESTIONS |

1. If we don't institute zero tolerance policies, what can the schools do to make students and parents realize that they are serious about curbing violence?

2. Should there be more flexibility for administrators in dealing with grade school offenders than with older students?

3. Is zero tolerance really zero tolerance if administrators have discretionary powers and can make exceptions?

Educators must not allow such behavior to go on without intervention. The stakes are far too high. The problems associated with school violence actually extend beyond the reported incidents.

The CDC 2009 Youth Risk Surveillance Survey reported some very disturbing findings. Nationally 5% of students had stayed home from school one or more times during the 30-day period preceding the survey because they felt unsafe at school or on the way to or from school. As troubling as this finding may be, it should not be surprising given the results from the CDC survey. During the 12 months preceding the survey:

- 7.7% of students nationwide had been threatened or injured with a weapon (e.g., a gun, knife, or club) on school property one or more times.
- 15.6% of male students and 6.7% of female students had been in a physical fight on school property one or more times.
- 5.6% of students had carried a weapon (e.g., a gun, knife, or club) on school property one or more times (in the 30 days preceding the survey).

The reasons for such untoward violent behaviors are varied. By the age of 18 the average American child will have viewed about 200,000 acts of violence, including 16,000 murders, on television alone (Dolgin, 2011; Beresin, 2008). The level of violence on Saturday morning cartoons exceeds that of prime time. There are 20 to 25 acts of violence an hour on Saturday morning as compared with 3 to 5 during prime time. Some of the most popular prime-time network shows are crime shows (e.g., *CSI, Law and Order,* etc.). The crime scenes on some of these shows are now so realistic and graphic that viewers are becoming desensitized to viewing mutilated bodies of murder victims. Though highly entertaining to some viewers, these graphic scenes of violence are unsuitable for young children and perhaps even for younger adolescents. However, many children have a television in their own rooms, and when left unsupervised may be watching these programs.

Beresin (2008) suggests that very young children may imitate the aggressive acts they view on TV in their play activities with peers. Before the age of 4, children are unable to distinguish fact from fiction, and may perceive the violent acts they see on TV as everyday occurrences. In movies and on TV, the good guys often eradicate the bad guys with acts of violence and become heroes as they punish the victimizers.

Newer sources of violence to which children and adolescents are exposed are the Internet and video games. These games often involve violent attacks with graphic and realistic scenes of shootings, knifings, and even decapitation. In these forms of entertainment, individuals are able to act out their own violence rather than just passively observing as with movies and TV. Unfortunately, some children live in violent environments, and the violent media they experience is too often reinforced by real-life events. Producers of such movies, TV programs, and video games are often more concerned with profit than with the effects on our youth. Consequently, the responsibility to control the viewing by children rests with parents. Programming decisions rest with government agencies that rate or censor films and games for younger viewers, and government agencies who enforce standards and viewer restrictions.

The reality is that much of what is supposed to take place to protect children never happens. Schools may be a last resort for educating children about the negative consequence of violence and for teaching children how to interpret what they see in the media, including the intent and content of commercials. In this way children may become increasingly able to discern right from wrong and identify which media messages are valid (Beresin, 2008).

Parents should use considerable discretion before allowing children to view such violent programming. With such continuous exposure to violence, is it possible that our children have become desensitized to senseless violent acts?

Adolescents in poverty, especially those of color, are more likely to live in neighborhoods with conditions that contribute to criminal activity. The literature also suggests that African American youth receive differential treatment from the juvenile justice system. They are more likely to be arrested, convicted, and incarcerated than white youth for similar offenses. The poor typically have court-appointed attorneys, and the trial and subsequent incarceration often seem a mere formality. Youth from middle-class backgrounds may have the benefit of privately retained attorneys who may be able to secure probation or a reduced sentence. Incarceration severely impacts the future of these individuals, limiting educational opportunities, employment opportunities, and income (Drakeford & Garfinkel, 2007; Justice Policy Institute, 2010).

STREET GANGS

Prior to the 1980s middle-class white Americans had few concerns with respect to street gangs. By the mid-1980s street gangs composed primarily of adolescents and young adults were engaged in drug distribution and protected their interests from their rivals with violence. Problems were exacerbated by the use of sophisticated weapons, including high-capacity semi-automatic pistols and assault weapons, injuring and killing not only their rivals but also innocent bystanders, including children. Gang members consider guns essential for passing through the turf of other gangs, avenging an insult, or retaliating for a rival gang's previous assault. Of the 27,302 homicides in Los Angeles County between 1979 and 1994, 7,288 were gang related (Violence Policy Center, 2009).

Individuals are attracted to street gangs because of family stress, protection against victimization, the money they receive through illicit dealings, and the sense of family the gang offers (Gangs and At-Risk Kids, 2010; Los Angeles Police Department, n.d.). For many, affiliation with a gang is the means of achieving status in a community. The gangs acquire power in a community through violent acts and the fear that such behavior generates.

Gang membership is usually structured by race or national origin. The most visible are Hispanic, African American, and Asian gangs and Jamaican posses. Predominantly or exclusively white gangs have been in existence for decades. Some of them are white supremacist in nature (e.g., Skinheads). Some gang members belong to the same gangs that their fathers joined before them. Among the best-known gangs are the African American Bloods and Crips. The Crips began in the Los Angeles area as high schoolers who extorted money from classmates and were involved in other violence. Both gangs have extended well beyond Los Angeles, spreading as far north as Alaska and as far east as Washington, D.C, making inroads in communities across the country.

Asian gangs are most prominent in Chinese, Vietnamese, Cambodian, and Filipino communities. Asian gangs are, by their own choice, less visible but capable of the same levels of violence as the other ethnic gangs. It is believed that some Asian gangs have ties to organized crime groups in Asia, such as the Hong Kong and Mainland China triads. They also have spread across the United States and Canada (Streetgangs.com, n.d.). These Asian gangs typically target other Asians who are distrustful of law enforcement and reluctant to participate in attempts to prosecute violators. Their typical activities include gambling, extortion, theft of luxury cars to be shipped overseas, and smuggling of illegal immigrants.

Gang members are usually identifiable by their clothing, communication, graffiti, and tattoos. Bloods and Crips often wear bandannas on their heads. The color of the Bloods is red, the Crips blue. Clothing may identify individuals as gang members. Gang-specific clothing may include jackets or sweatshirts bearing gang names. Tattoos on the hands, arms, and shoulders are common among Latino gang members but are not usually displayed by African American gang members. Hand signs may identify an individual with a specific gang.

Graffiti used by gangs can provide considerable information. African American and Latino gang graffiti differ from one another: Black gang graffiti often contains profanity and other expressions that are absent from Latino gang graffiti. Latino gang graffiti has more flair and more attention to detail. Gangs use graffiti to stake a claim to turf. If the graffiti is crossed out and new graffiti written over it, another gang is challenging the former's claim to the turf. Through

Graffiti may be an indication of street gangs marking their turf.
© Scott Cunningham/Merrill

careful observation, law enforcement can determine a gang's sphere of influence. Graffiti will indicate where the gang has unchallenged influence and where challenges are posed and by whom.

The emergence of street gangs over the past three decades has become a major challenge for educators. Their purpose in attending school may involve the distribution of drugs, recruitment, extortion, or intimidation. Their presence in a classroom is challenging for the teacher, especially when untoward behavior is manifested. In some instances, schools have become scenes of violence, resulting in the installation of metal detectors and the hiring of security guards at the schools.

Either the solutions for ending gang membership have not yet been found, or the will to solve the problems has not yet been sufficient. If law enforcement is unable to stem the growth of gang violence, it is unlikely that educators are any better equipped to do so. As with other issues related to youth, gang participation is often a function of poverty, disproportionately affecting individuals of color. Somehow society has failed to provide better alternatives to gang membership. Perhaps that is one of the major challenges for education.

THE HIP-HOP CULTURE

Already accounting for billions of dollars in sales, music, clothing, and related goods, industry giants seek to entice hip-hop enthusiasts into buying their products. Rap and rap music are a major part of the **hip-hop culture.** Rap may be described as a rhythmic delivery of rhymes, with or without music. It is now the most popular music genre among American adolescents. While rap is certainly very popular among black and Hispanic adolescents, it is also the most popular music genre among white adolescents (Arnett, 2010). Snoop Dogg, Eminem, Kanye West, and Jay-Z are among the better-known rap artists. Rap artists have been under increasing criticism for their frequent use of sexist, racist, and violence-laced lyrics. Another aspect of the rap music culture is **break dancing** (also referred to as b-boying, b-girling), an improvised form of dancing with intricate and sometimes acrobatic moves. Michael Jackson used break dancing in some of his music videos.

Honor Student and Star Athlete

Kevin Johnson is a senior in a top-rated suburban high school and is in his last term of the school year. He was the co-captain of the football team and an all-conference running back. He has excelled academically as well, and has been offered a full scholarship to an Ivy League university. An important physics exam is coming up in Ms. O'Leary's physics class, where Kevin has maintained a grade average between an A minus and an A. Two days before the scheduled exam, Tony Morris, also a senior in the physics class, enters Ms. O'Leary room shortly after school is out. He asks if he can speak with her briefly. She responds affirmatively, and he then tells her that Kevin and Earl Swenson, who sits next to him in the back of the class, have been cheating on exams the entire year. He states that he has observed them doing this repeatedly. He describes how it is done and tells Ms. O'Leary that if she watches them carefully, she will see what he has described about their cheating process. He states that he is fed up with the two because he and others have had to work so hard for their grades and Kevin and Earl have been cheating their way through school.

On the day of the exam, Ms. O'Leary watches all of the students carefully, but especially Kevin and Earl. Then she sees exactly what Tony had described about the cheating process. She has some important decisions to make.

If Ms. O'Leary takes decisive action, it will create a major scandal. Kevin is no ordinary senior student. He is among the top five students in the senior class, and exposing him will have serious consequences. If he is severely disciplined and his Ivy League school learns of his cheating, he may lose the scholarship and even forfeit his admission.

| QUESTIONS FOR CLASSROOM DISCUSSION |

- Should Ms. O'Leary confront Earl and Kevin on the spot in front of the class?
- Should she wait until after the exam and risk the evidence disappearing?
- Should she confront them privately and administer her own punishment?
- Should she report the incident to the principal?
- If it is proven that Kevin and Earl have been cheating, should the school put into question all of Kevin's previous high grades?

CELL PHONES AND TEXTING

They do it during breakfast, annoying their parents; at restaurants; while at the movies; in class, against school rules; in bed at night; and worst of all, while driving. Their parents complain that they seldom see their teenagers' faces because they are too busy texting on their cell phones. Teenagers' love for their cell phones and for texting goes without saying. Averaging almost 80 messages a day, reports of texting messages in the hundreds each day are not uncommon. Hafner (2009) cites an example of a 13-year-old girl who was associated with 14,458 text messages in one month.

Lister (2010) identified subcultures among adolescents in which communication is primarily through texting. Lister also found:

- Twenty-three percent of teens report that they send or receive over 100 text messages daily.
- Many teens prefer texting to talking on their cell phones.
- Forty-two percent of parents contacted their teens daily using cell phones.
- Twenty-seven percent of pre-teens ages 9 to 12 owned cell phones.
- Seventy-five percent of teens ages 13 to 17 own cell phones.
- Eighty-seven percent of teens use text messaging.

Mobile messaging has shown its value to society in recent years. It has provided needed assistance in emergency situations and allowed individuals to stay in contact when necessary. However, there have been some negative outcomes from mobile messaging devices. There are reports of individuals becoming addicted to their use. Perhaps one of the most frightening aspects of these devices is their continued use to communicate while driving. Many auto deaths have been attributed to drivers using their cell phones and being distracted while driving. Many more individuals have been injured because of this behavior.

In spite of the increasing number of states that have banned the use of hand-held cell phones while driving, and 31 states plus the District of Columbia and Guam prohibiting texting while driving (as of May 2011), individuals continue to do so. Adolescents have always shown themselves to be more prone to auto accidents that most other age groups. They place themselves and others at greater risk with these behaviors. Parents and educators cannot emphasize enough the dangers of ignoring the laws against texting while driving. Other concerns over excessive and compulsive texting include anxiety, distraction in school, failing grades, repetitive stress injury (thumbs), and sleep deprivation (Hafner, 2009).

In this section, we have deliberately focused on some of the critical and problematic issues facing adolescents today. We should emphasize, however, that most adolescents go through this period of their life in a productive manner and that this can be one of the happiest and most memorable periods in one's life.

America's Youth in Today's Classrooms

Like other cultural groups, the various age groups of the U.S. population contribute greatly to the pluralistic nature of this society. Some basic educational considerations should be examined in the study of age groups as a function of culture. American society in general has not always been viewed as particularly supportive or positive in its perceptions of all age groups. The discussion on adolescence noted that this period is often viewed as a time of storm and stress, although in some cultures this period passes with few crises. In American society, the former view tends to prevail. In addition, the elderly are not viewed in U.S. culture with the respect or reverence that is found in many other cultures. While we did not address the elderly in this chapter, we would like to acknowledge here that ageism, discriminatory attitudes toward the elderly, does exist and is, regretfully, as much a part of our social system as racism, sexism, and discrimination against those with disabilities. With the advances in medical science, the elderly are living longer, which may be positive but at the same time will require those working to assume a greater tax burden to support them through social services.

For these reasons, it is critically important that students learn to understand and value the contributions of all age groups and cultures. Moreover, studying age and its relation to culture is important because students, if they live to their full life expectancy, will become members of each age group in turn, including that of the elderly. Thus, unlike the study of different ethnic groups, students can learn to understand and appreciate cultural groups of which they have been members, are presently members, or will eventually become members. By addressing the issues of various age groups in the classroom, educators can help students to better understand their siblings, parents, and other important people in their lives. Knowledge can eliminate fear of the unknown as students begin to move into different age groups at different times in their lives. It is important that issues related to age groups be appropriately introduced into the curriculum because students need to understand the concept of ageism. Just as the school assists students in understanding the problem of racism, the school should be responsible for helping students understand the aged and dispel the myths related to this group. Field trips to retirement homes or visits to the class by senior citizens may provide useful experiences. As students become aware of the nature and characteristics of each age group, they will develop the perception of each individual, regardless of age, as being an important and integral part of society.

It is critically important for educators to understand age as it relates to both students and their parents. Understanding the particular age group characteristics and needs of students can assist the educator in better understanding and managing age-related behavior, such as reactions or responses to peer group pressure. Understanding the nature of parents, siblings, and other important individuals (e.g., grandparents) will assist the educator in parent-teacher relationships and in helping students cope with their interactions with others. For example, when an elderly grandparent moves into the family setting, this event may affect a child and his or her classroom behavior.

The school is perhaps in the best position of any agency in the community to observe the effects of child abuse. The classroom teacher is an important agent in detecting and reporting abuse and in all states is required by law to do so. To do this, the teacher must be aware of the problem of abuse, the manifestations of abuse, and the proper authorities to which abuse is reported. If the teacher's immediate supervisor is unresponsive to the reporting of a potential abuse problem, the teacher should continue to seek help until competent and concerned individuals in positions of authority provide it.

The single most important factor in recognizing possible child abuse is the physical condition of the child. Telltale marks, bruises, and abrasions that cannot be adequately explained may provide reason to suspect abuse. Unusual changes in the child's behavior patterns, such as extreme fatigue, may be reason to suspect problems. The parents' behavior and their ability or lack of ability to explain the child's condition and the social features of the family may be reason to suspect abuse. Although physical abuse or neglect may tend to have observable indicators, sexual abuse may occur with few, if any, obvious indicators. Adults may be unwilling to believe what a child says and may be hesitant to report alleged incidents. There is no typical profile of the victim, and the physical signs vary. Behavioral manifestations are usually exhibited by the victims but are often viewed as insignificant or are attributed to typical childhood stress. Chronic depression, isolation from peers, apathy, and suicide attempts are some of the more serious behavioral manifestations of the problem.

The number of children and youth infected by the HIV virus and other sexually transmitted diseases is a national tragedy. An estimated 2.5 million children worldwide were living with an HIV diagnosis in 2009, with 2,244 diagnosed cases in youth age 19 and younger in the United States (Avert.org, n.d.). Prevention efforts must be multifaceted if these diseases are to be eradicated. The school has a major role to play, and there are specific steps that can be taken. School-based programs are critical in reaching youth before they engage in risky behaviors. Topics such as HIV, STDs, unintended pregnancy, and tobacco and other drug abuse should be integrated into the curriculum and should be an ongoing program for all students, kindergarten through high school. The development of these programs should be done carefully and should take into consideration parental and community values.

The majority of suicides are planned and not committed on impulse, and most suicide victims mention their intentions to someone. Often, a number of warning signs can alert teachers, other professionals, and parents. Educators should take these signs seriously (see Figure 10.3).

If teachers or other school personnel suspect trouble, friendly, low-key questions or statements may provide an appropriate opening: "You seem down today" or "It seems like something is bothering you." If an affirmative response is given, a more direct and probing (but supportive) question may be asked. If there is any reason whatsoever to suspect a possible suicide attempt, teachers and other school staff should alert the appropriate school personnel. Teachers should recognize their limitations and avoid making judgments. The matter should be referred to the school psychologist, who should, in turn, alert a competent medical authority (psychiatrist) and the child's parents. Assistance can also be obtained from local mental health clinics and suicide prevention centers. Prompt action may save a life.

Our coverage of adolescent substance abuse has been brief. But the importance of the problem is such that every educator should be aware of the problem and work toward providing children at an early age with appropriate drug education. No agency, group, or individual can wage an effective campaign against substance abuse alone. Only with a united effort can an effective battle be waged. Possible symptoms of alcohol or drug abuse among adolescents often overlap with those of individuals who are at risk for suicide. The Partnership for a Drug Free America (2006) provides some possible physical symptoms of individuals involved in substance abuse:

- Change in sleeping patterns
- Bloodshot eyes
- Slurred or agitated speech
- Sudden or dramatic weight loss or gain
- Skin abrasions/bruises
- Neglected appearance/poor hygiene
- Sick more frequently
- Accidents or injuries

Some possible behavioral symptoms of substance abuse include (Dorsey, Jaffe, Slotnick, Smith, & Segal, 2007):

- Negative schoolwork changes
- Increased secrecy about possessions or activities

- Use of incense, room deodorant, or perfume (to hide smoke or chemical odors)
- Subtle changes in conversations with friends (more secretive, using "coded" language)
- "New friends"
- Increase in borrowing money
- Frequent use of mouthwash or breath mints (covering up alcohol)

In the event these signs are observed in the classroom, the school nurse should be notified immediately. If none is available, then someone trained in CPR should be summoned. It would be advisable for a list of all personnel with CPR training to be made available to all teachers and other staff.

As parents hurry their children into adulthood, educators may contribute to the hurrying process. Teachers, administrators, and support personnel should be cognizant of the fact that the children they teach and work with are children, and not miniature adults. Children have but one opportunity to experience the wonders of childhood. In comparison with adulthood, childhood and adolescence are relatively short periods of time, and these young people should have every opportunity to enjoy these stages of their lives to the fullest extent possible.

Summary

The study of age as a function of culture is important to educators because it helps them understand how the child or adolescent struggles to win peer acceptance and to balance this effort with the need for parental approval. In some instances, the pressures from peers are not congruent with those from the home.

As each child develops into adolescence, we observe a growing need for independence. Adolescence for some is a time of storm and stress; for others, it passes with little or no trauma.

Young adulthood is one of the most exciting times in life. It is a time for courtship, marriage, having children, and career choices. It is a time when individuals reach their physical and occupational prime. Young adulthood can also be a threatening time because choices made at this time often have a lifelong impact on the individual.

Professional Practice

Questions for Discussion

1. Explain why child abuse is a problem, and cite some of the signs of child abuse.
2. When does ethnic identification begin in children, and how is it manifested?
3. Describe some variables that contribute to prejudice in children.
4. What are the variables that contribute to childhood obesity, why is it a problem, and what can the schools do to address the problem?
5. What are the sources of alienation between adolescents and their families?

6. What is the extent of substance abuse among adolescents, and what are some of the underlying causes of substance use in this age group?

7. What are the causes of adolescent suicide, and what are the warning signs?

8. How does Generation Y differ from Generation Z?

Portfolio Activities

1. Interview three teachers from three different schools and ask them what their school policy is for reporting suspected abuse of their students. (InTASC Standard 9: Learning and Ethical Practice)

2. Interview teachers or administrators from schools to find out what their policy is on zero tolerance or, if there is no zero tolerance policy, what measures are taken for students who carry weapons or drugs to school. (InTASC Standard 9: Learning and Ethical Practice)

Digital Resources for the Classroom

1. The Anti-Defamation League's website includes resources and strategies for anti-bullying and anti-cyberbullying measures: http://www.adl.org/combatbullying/.

2. The Child Welfare Information Gateway provides information on child abuse : http://www.childwelfare.gov/pubs/can_info_packet.pdf.

3. Teen Suicide U.S. provides information on teen suicide prevention, a list of suicide prevention organizations, and direct links to other resources: http://www.teensuicide.us/.

4. Teen Pregnancy Help provides useful information and links concerning teen pregnancies: http://www.teenpregnancyhelp.net/.

5. The Beloit College Mindset List provides the world view of each year's entering freshman class: http://www.beloit.edu/mindset/.

6. The Adolescent Substance Abuse Knowledge Base is a website provided by CRC Health Group, a health care provider: http://www.adolescent-substance-abuse.com/.

MyEducationLab™

Go to the MyEducationLab (www.myeducationlab.com) for Multicultural Education and familiarize yourself with the topical content, which includes:

- Assignments and Activities, tied to learning outcomes for the course, that can help you more deeply understand course content

- Building Teaching Skills and Dispositions learning units allow you to apply and practice your understanding of how to teach equitably in a multicultural education classroom

- Licensure Test Prep activities are available in the Book Resources to help you prepare for test taking

- A pretest with hints and feedback that tests your knowledge of this chapter's content

- Review, practice, and enrichment activities that will enhance your understanding of the chapter content
- A posttest with hints and feedback that allows you to test your knowledge again after having completed the enrichment activities

A Correlation Guide may be downloaded by instructors to show how MyEducationLab content aligns to this book.

11 Education That Is Multicultural

We must be the change we wish to see in the world.

Mahatma Gandhi

As you read this chapter, you should be able to:

- Identify the characteristics and purpose of education that is multicultural.

- Understand the importance of placing students at the center of teaching and learning by incorporating student knowledge and voices in the dialogue of the classroom and engaging them in the process of learning.

- Recognize that a classroom climate can be established to promote human rights and respect for the cultures of students and their families.

- Develop confidence that all students can learn as demonstrated by holding high expectations for their academic achievement and pushing them to develop their potentials.

- Acknowledge and build on the life histories and experiences of students and their families through the use of culturally responsive teaching.

- Address inequity and power relationships in the classroom to help students understand them and be able to take action that supports equity.
- Model social justice and equality in the classroom by helping students think critically and by fostering learning communities in which students work together to promote learning.
- Develop a plan to expand your knowledge and skills so you can deliver education that is multicultural.

Natisha Loftis had not said a word to any of her teachers since the beginning of the school year. It's not that she was a "bad" student; she turned in assignments and made B's. She certainly didn't cause her teachers trouble. Therefore, the high school counselor, Mr. Williams, was somewhat surprised to hear that she was dropping out of school. He had been Natisha's advisor for more than two years, but he couldn't really remember her. Nevertheless, it was his job to conduct interviews with students who were leaving school.

Natisha described her daily experience as coming to school, listening to teachers, and going home. School was boring and not at all connected to her real life, in which she had the responsibility to help her father raise her five brothers and sisters. She might even be able to get a job with the same cleaning firm that her dad worked for. Certainly, nothing she was learning in school could help her get a job. And she knew from more than 10 years of listening to teachers and reading textbooks that her chances of becoming a news anchorwoman or even a teacher were about the same as winning the lottery. The last time a teacher had even asked about her family was in the sixth grade, when her mom left. The only place anyone paid attention to her was in church.

School had helped silence Natisha. Classes provided no meaningful experience for her. The content may have been important to the teachers, but she could find no relationship between it and her own world.

| REFLECTIONS |

1. Why has Natisha decided to drop out of school?

2. How can the curriculum be made more meaningful to students who are not middle-class and white?

3. How can teachers engage a student like Natisha and help her become excited about learning?

Education That Is Multicultural

After learning the sociopolitical aspects that provide the framework for multicultural education in the earlier chapters of this book, you are probably wondering how to put it all together to provide education that is multicultural. There is no recipe for how to respond to students from different cultural groups. For one thing, differences within groups can be as great as differences among groups. Therefore, the recipe would work for some students, but not all of them. This chapter is designed to provide some suggestions for delivering multicultural education, incorporating the multiple identities of your students into your teaching, and becoming more multicultural yourself.

It is no easy task to incorporate cultural knowledge throughout teaching. In the beginning, you must consciously think about multiculturalism as you interact with students and plan lessons and assignments. You should approach multicultural teaching as an enthusiastic learner with much knowledge to gain from students and community members who have cultural identities different from your own. You may need to remind yourself that your way of believing, thinking, and acting evolved from your own culture and experiences, which may vary greatly from those of the students in your school. You will need to listen to the histories and experiences of students and their families and integrate them into your teaching. Students' lives will need to be validated within both their in-school and out-of-school realities—a process that is authentic only if you value the cultures of your students.

Educators are often at a disadvantage because they do not live, and have never lived, in the community in which their students live. Too often, the only parents with whom they interact are those who are able to attend parent-teacher meetings or who have scheduled conferences with them. In many cases, they have not been in their students' homes nor been active participants in the community. How do we begin to learn the cultures of other people? Using the tools of an anthropologist or ethnographer, we can observe children in classrooms and on playgrounds. We can listen carefully to students and their parents as they discuss their life experiences. We can study other cultures. We can learn about the perspectives of others by reading articles and books written by men and women from different ethnic, racial, socioeconomic, and religious groups. Participation in community, religious, and ethnic activities can provide additional perspectives on students' cultures.

Our knowledge about our students' cultures will allow us to make the academic content of our teaching more meaningful to students by relating it to their own experiences and building on their prior knowledge. It should help us make them and their histories the center of the education process in our effort to help them reach their academic, vocational, and social potentials. In the process, students should learn to believe in their own abilities and become active participants in their own learning. Students should be able to achieve academically without adopting the dominant culture as their own. They should be able to maintain their own cultural identities inside and outside the school.

Teaching multiculturally requires the incorporation of diversity throughout the learning process. If race, ethnicity, class, and gender are not interrelated in the curriculum, students do not learn that these are interrelated parts of a whole called self. Although the multiple cultural groups of which we are members are separate and distinct, they should be interwoven throughout our teaching. For example, if activities are developed to fight sexism but continue to perpetuate racism, we are not providing multicultural education. At the same time, we must integrate the experiences of women of color and women in poverty when discussing the impact of sexism and other women's issues.

All teaching should be multicultural and all classrooms should be models of democracy, equity, and social justice. To accomplish this goal, educators must:

1. Place the student at the center of teaching and learning.
2. Establish a classroom climate that promotes human rights.
3. Believe that all students can learn.
4. Acknowledge and build on the life histories and experiences of students and their families through culturally responsive teaching.
5. Analyze oppression and power relationships in schools and society to understand racism, sexism, classism, heterosexism, ableism, and ageism.
6. Model social justice and equality in the classroom and in interactions with students, families, and the community.

Teachers and other school professionals can make a difference. Making our teaching and classroom multicultural is an essential step in empowerment for both teachers and students. Now that you know about the multiple groups to which you and your students belong, how can you put it all together to help students learn? Education that is multicultural is a holistic approach to teaching all students and confronting the barriers that prevent many students from being able to access the education that is so critical to their future.

Remember that multicultural education is for all students, not just English language learners or students of color. European American students also belong to racial and ethnic groups and need to understand how their race and ethnicity have been privileged in schools. A strength of multicultural education is that we learn about our similarities and differences as we struggle to provide equity for all people. Students who are in segregated classrooms or in communities with little religious, language, ethnic, and racial diversity need to learn about the pluralistic world in which they live and the role they can play in providing social justice in their communities and beyond. Social justice and equity are an integral part of our commitment to a democratic society.

Place the Student at the Center of Teaching and Learning

Our children are the foundation of our future. They are among the most powerless groups in the country, especially if they were born into a low-income family. Over one-fifth of the nation's children live in poverty; over 8 million of them are living in extreme poverty. Too many of them are abused or neglected by their parents or caregivers. Nearly as many children are killed by guns in a year as the total number of troops killed in combat in Iraq (Children's Defense Fund, 2010). These figures suggest a crisis among our children that deserves immediate attention by policymakers. Nevertheless, states spend almost three times as much on a prisoner as they do on a public school student. Don't our children deserve better? Next to parents, educators should be the major advocates for children, especially for their right to an education that helps them reach their potential.

The major purpose of education is to help students learn the concepts and skills that we are teaching. However, teaching is so much more than knowing the content that we are teaching. We have to know and understand our students. Who are they? What is important to them? What do they like? How can we engage them in learning? Teaching should be all about our students and moving them to their highest potential academically, socially, physically, and emotionally. Helping them develop their potential in these areas at the same time that they are learning to read and compute well enough to pass standardized tests at the proficient level is our challenge as teachers. How can we as teachers ensure that students and their learning are the primary focus of our work in schools? How do we make education work effectively for students?

ENCOURAGING STUDENT VOICES

Multicultural teachers seek, listen to, and incorporate the voices of students, their families, and communities. Students are encouraged to speak from their own experiences, to do more than regurgitate the answers that the teacher would like to hear. Teaching that incorporates the student voice allows students to make sense of subject matter within their own lived experiences and the realities they know because they themselves have experienced them. Listening to students helps the teacher understand their prior knowledge of the subject matter, including any misinformation or lack of information that may suggest future instructional strategies. Student voices also provide important information about students' cultures.

Most schools today legitimate only the voice of the dominant culture—Standard English and the world perspective of the European American middle class. Many students, especially those from oppressed groups, learn to be silent or disruptive, or they drop out, in part because their voices are not accepted as legitimate in the classroom. **Culturally responsive teaching** requires educators to recognize the incongruence between the voice of the school and the voices of students. Success in school should not be dependent on the adoption of the school's voice.

Teachers could use an approach in which instruction occurs as a dialogue between teacher and students. Rather than depend on a textbook and lecture format, the teacher listens to students and directs them in the learning of the discipline through dialogue. This approach requires discarding the traditional authoritarian classroom to establish a democratic one in which both teacher and students are active participants.

Too often, teachers ignore students' attempts to engage in dialogue and, as a result, halt further learning by many students. However, introducing student voices to the instructional process can be difficult, especially when the teacher and students are from different cultural backgrounds. The teacher may face both anger and silence, which in time will be overcome by the use of dialogue that develops in students' tolerance, patience, and a willingness to listen. Although this strategy increases the participation of students in the learning process, some teachers are not comfortable with handling the issues that are likely to be raised.

In addition to dialogue between students and teacher, student voices can be encouraged through written and artistic expression. Some teachers ask students to keep journals in which they write their reactions to what is occurring in class. The journals make the teacher aware of the learning that is occurring over time. To be effective, students must feel comfortable writing whatever they want without the threat of reprisal from the teacher. The dialogues developed through these approaches can help students understand the perspectives brought to the classroom by students from different cultures. The resulting dialogues can help students relate subject matter to their real world, encouraging them to take an interest in studying and learning it.

ENGAGING STUDENTS

Culturally responsive teaching encourages student participation, critical analysis, and action. Classroom projects focus on areas of interest to students and the communities in which they live. As they participate in these activities, they apply and extend the mathematics, science, language arts, and social studies that they have been learning. Teachers and students in these classrooms have developed a vision for a more egalitarian and socially just society. Projects often engage students in collective action to improve their communities.

After conducting research and collecting and analyzing data, students sometimes move their recommendations through the democratic processes of their local communities to make changes toward improving conditions. In one Nebraska school, students and their teacher became very concerned about the treatment of new immigrants in the local community and businesses. They drafted legislation requiring the study of race in social studies classes across the state. Facing opposition from some, they lobbied the state legislature on behalf of the bill and were successful in having it adopted. These students not only were able to affect school curriculum through their actions, but also learned about the legislative process of their state through hands-on experience.

A group of teenagers from across the country shared their views of how teachers can keep students engaged, motivated, and challenged in the book *Fires in the Bathroom: Advice for Teachers from High School Students* (Cushman & the Students of What Kids Can Do, Inc., 2003). These students from diverse populations suggest that teachers get and keep students motivated by:

- Being passionate about their subjects and work.
- Connecting to issues that students care about outside school.
- Giving students choices on things that matter.
- Making learning a social thing.
- Making sure students understand.
- Responding with interest when students show interest.
- Caring about students and their progress.
- Helping students keep on top of their workload.
- Showing your pride in students' good work.
- Providing role models to inspire students.

Establish a Classroom Climate That Promotes Human Rights

Over 10 years before the civil rights movement had taken hold in the 1960s, the United Nations adopted a Universal Declaration of Human Rights (UDHR) that called on countries around the world to provide human rights and social justice to their populations. It "declared the equality of all humans by guaranteeing the right to self-determination and freedom from tyranny, oppression, and exploitation" (Grant & Gibson, 2010, p. 14). It called for the right to an education; social security; equitable wages; an adequate standard of living allowing one to be able to afford housing, food, clothing, and medical care; and participation in the cultural life of the community. The United States and a number of other Western countries supported the civil and political rights that were incorporated into the UDHR, but resisted the inclusion of social and economic rights that were part of the Eastern tradition. In addition, the countries were expected to guarantee these rights and be responsible for ensuring the economic and social welfare of their citizens (Grant & Gibson, 2010). Nevertheless, the UDHR was adopted by the United Nations General Assembly in 1948.

The UDHR views education as a basic human right for all people. It also expected schools to teach about human rights with the goal of eliminating poverty, discrimination, and exploitation—conditions that often have led to conflicts that threaten world peace (Grant & Gibson, 2010). These world leaders called on educators to model human rights and provide social justice for the most economically disadvantaged members of society.

Since the adoption of the UDHR, the United States made great strides in the human rights area, with the passage of the Voting Rights Act, the Civil Rights Act, and the Equal Pay Act. Congress created Head Start for preschool services and Title I to support the education of children from low-income families. It passed legislation for bilingual education, IDEA for students with disabilities, Title IX for sex equity in schools, and technical assistance related to race, national origin, and sex equity. Today, 60 years after UDHR, members of the U.S. Congress continue to debate the role of the government in enforcing social and economic rights for the population. With governmental support for public education waning during this recession recovery period, many multiculturalists are questioning the countries' commitment to human rights, especially with respect to the nation's children. Under these economic and social conditions, how can you model human relations in your classroom?

THE SCHOOL CLIMATE

Visitors entering a school can usually feel the tension that exists when cross-cultural communications are poor. They can observe whether diversity is a positive and appreciated factor at the school. If only students of color or only males are waiting to be seen by the assistant principal in charge of discipline, visitors should wonder whether the school is providing effectively for the needs of all of its students. If bulletin boards in classrooms are covered only with the pictures of European Americans, visitors should question the appreciation of diversity in the school. If the football team is composed primarily of African Americans and the chess club of European Americans, they should wonder about the inclusive nature of extracurricular activities. If school administrators are primarily men and most teachers are women, or if the teachers are European American and the teacher aides are Latino, the visitors could suspect discriminatory practices in hiring and promotion of staff. These are examples of a school climate that does not reflect a commitment to multicultural education.

Staffing composition and patterns should reflect the diversity of the country. At a minimum, they should reflect the diversity of the geographic area. Women, as well as men, should be school administrators; men, as well as women, should teach at the preschool and primary levels. Persons of color should be found in the administration and teaching ranks, not concentrated in custodial and clerical positions. Faculty, administrators, and other staff see themselves as learners enhanced and changed by understanding, affirming, and reflecting cultural diversity. Teachers and administrators are able to deal with questions of race, intergroup relations, and controversial realities on an objective, frank, and professional basis.

When diversity is valued within a school, student government and extracurricular activities include students from different cultural groups. Students should not be segregated on the basis of their membership in a certain group. In a school where multiculturalism is valued, students from various cultural backgrounds hold leadership positions. Those roles are not automatically delegated to students from the dominant group in the school.

If the school climate is multicultural, then multiculturalism is reflected in every aspect of the educational program. In addition to those areas already mentioned, assembly programs will reflect multiculturalism in their content as well as in the choice of speakers. Bulletin boards and displays will reflect the diversity of the nation, even if the community is not rich in diversity.

Effective cross-cultural communications between students and teachers promote student learning. When the cultural cues between students and teachers are not understood, communications and learning often are affected adversely.
© Pearson Learning Photo Studio

Cross-cultural communications among students and between students and teachers are positive. Different languages and dialects used by students are respected. Both girls and boys are found in technology education, family science, calculus, bookkeeping, physics, and vocational classes. Students from different groups participate in college preparatory classes, advanced placement classes, special education, and gifted education at rates equal to their representation in the schools. Differences in academic achievement levels disappear between males and females, white students and students of color, and upper-middle-class and low-income students. Instructional materials are free of biases, omissions, and stereotypes.

In a school climate that promotes human rights, discrimination against students from different cultural groups is not tolerated. Students respect the cultural differences within the school population, and harassment of students does not exist. Students assist each other in the learning process, helping students who are struggling to understand a concept or a problem. Students are not afraid to let teachers and other students know that they need assistance, because they know they won't be labeled as academically challenged or lazy. Students and teachers work together to learn and support each other in that process.

The school climate must be supportive of multicultural education. When respect for cultural differences is reflected in all aspects of students' educational programs, the goals of multicultural education are being attained. Educators are the key to developing this climate.

HIDDEN CURRICULUM

In addition to a formal curriculum, schools have a hidden curriculum that consists of the unstated norms, values, and beliefs about the social relations of school and classroom life that are transmitted to students. Because the hidden curriculum includes the norms and values that support the formal curriculum, it must also reflect diversity if education is to become multicultural. Although the hidden curriculum is not taught directly or included in the objectives of the formal curriculum, it has a great impact on students and teachers alike. It includes the organizational structures of the classroom and the school, as well as the interactions of students and teachers.

MESSAGES SENT TO STUDENTS

Unknowingly, educators transmit biased messages to students. Most educators do not consciously or intentionally stereotype students or discriminate against them. They usually try to treat all students fairly and equitably. We have learned our attitudes and behaviors, however, in a society that is ageist, ableist, racist, sexist, and heterosexist. Some biases have been internalized

PAUSE TO REFLECT 11.1

The school climate is an indicator of whether diversity and equality are respected and promoted in a school. Take an inventory of (a) a school that you may be observing; (b) the school, college, or department of education that is responsible for preparing teachers at your college or university; or (c) the college or university itself.

- What is the diversity of the faculty? How diverse is the student body?

- How does the diversity differ between administrators and faculty? How reflective of diversity are displays on the walls and in display cases?

- What is the diversity of students on the honor roll or dean's list? The diversity of the students who are suspended? That of the students who are performing below grade level on standardized tests?

to such a degree that we do not realize we have them. When educators are able to recognize the subtle and unintentional biases in their behavior, positive changes can be made in the classroom.

Students of color are often treated significantly differently than white students. Because many white students share the middle-class culture of the teacher, they also share the cultural cues that foster success in the classroom. Students who ask appropriate questions at appropriate times or who smile and seek attention from the teacher at times when the teacher is open to such gestures are likely to receive encouragement and reinforcement from the teacher. In contrast, students who interrupt class or seek attention from the teacher when the teacher is not open to providing it do not receive the necessary reinforcement.

As a result of the teacher's misreading of the cultural cues, ethnic or racial boundaries are established within the classroom. This situation is exacerbated when students from the dominant group receive more opportunities to participate in instructional interactions and get more praise and encouragement. Low-income students and students of color receive fewer opportunities to participate, and the opportunities usually are of a less substantive nature. They also may be criticized or disciplined more frequently than European American students for breaking the rules.

Unless teachers can critically examine their treatment of students in the classroom, they will not know whether they are treating students inequitably because of cultural differences. Once that self-examination has been undertaken, changes can be initiated to ensure that cultural identity will not be a basis for automatically relating differently to students. Teachers may need to become more proactive in initiating interactions and in providing encouragement, praise, and reinforcement to students from cultural groups different from their own.

Teachers usually evaluate students' academic performance through tests and written and oral work. Much more than academic performance is evaluated by teachers, however. Student misbehavior occurs when classroom rules are not adequately obeyed, and usually results in some sort of punishment. Discipline varies with the infraction and student, but sometimes is influenced by the gender, race, and class of the student. Similarly, students who have been assigned low-ability status often receive negative attention from the teacher because they are not following the rules, rather than because they are not performing adequately on academic tasks. Our interactions with students should be evaluated to ensure that we are actually supporting learning rather than preventing it.

In addition to evaluations based on academic performance and institutional rules, teachers make evaluations based on personal qualities. Students are sometimes categorized according to their clothes, family income, cleanliness, and personality rather than assessed based on their academic abilities. This practice is particularly dangerous because most tracking perpetuates inequities.

Another aspect of the hidden curriculum is unequal power. In many ways, this is a dilemma of childhood. By the time students enter kindergarten, they have learned that power is in the hands of adults. The teacher and other school officials require that their rules be followed. In addition to enforcing the institutional rules, teachers may require that students give up their home languages or dialects to be successful academically or at least to receive the teacher's approval. Instead, students should be encouraged to be bicultural, practicing both their home and dominant cultural language and patterns. They will be well served by knowing more than one language in an increasingly interdependent world.

STUDENT AND TEACHER RELATIONSHIPS

Although the development and use of culturally responsive materials and curricula are important and necessary steps toward providing multicultural education, alone they are not enough. Relationships among teachers and students determine the quality of education (Nieto, 2010). Teachers send messages that tell students about their potential and whether they can learn or cannot learn. They can make students feel either very special or incompetent and worthless. Teachers who know their subject matter, believe that all students can learn, and care about students as individuals can have a great impact on students and their learning. Unfortunately, researchers find that "close connections between students and their teachers are most markedly absent in the large urban schools most low-income students of color attend" (Darling-Hammond, 2010, p. 63).

Gloria Ladson-Billings (2009) observed elementary school teachers who were able to help their African American students learn at high levels. She found that these teachers were able to interact easily with their students, giving them individual attention as needed. When a student was struggling, one teacher sat at the student's desk and asked him to explain the problem to her. The student became the teacher, which required him to explain the process or help the teacher perform the task. Many of the successful teachers expected the students to help each other learn by working together to solve problems while the teacher monitored their progress. The classroom was like an extended family that would not let anyone fail.

Who knows the most about effective teaching? Students themselves can tell you which teachers are caring and which teachers have helped them learn. Teenagers recommend that teachers show respect, trust, and fairness by:

- Being clear about what they should expect from you and what you expect from them.
- Knowing the subject that you are teaching.
- Having high expectations for each of them and encouraging them to do their best.
- Being prepared to teach every day.
- Making sure each student is learning.
- Grading fairly, not giving advantages to some students.
- Admitting when you have made a mistake.
- Not denigrating them.
- Not showing your biases in the classroom.

- Treating them like they are mature young people.
- Listening to them and asking what they think.
- Caring about their lives and what's happening to them.
- Not betraying their confidences. (Cushman, et al., 2003)

To provide the greatest assistance to all students, teachers cannot apply the same treatment to each student; they should work toward meeting individual needs and differences. Teachers must be sure they are not treating students differently, however, based solely on student group membership. With the elimination of bias from the teaching process and the emergence of proactive teachers who seek the most effective strategies to meet the needs of individual students, the classroom can become a stimulating place for most students, regardless of their cultural identities, abilities, and experiences.

How can teachers analyze their own classroom interactions and teaching styles? If the equipment is available, teachers can videotape or audiotape a class and then systematically record the interactions as they view or listen to the tape later. An outside observer could be asked to record a teacher's interactions with students. An analysis of the data would show teachers how much class time they spend interacting with students and the nature of the interactions. These data would reveal any differences in interaction based on gender, ethnicity, or other characteristics of students. Such an analysis would be an excellent starting point for teachers who want to ensure that they do not discriminate against male or female students or students from different ethnic or socioeconomic groups.

Every effort must be made to ensure that a teacher's prejudices are not reflected in his or her interactions with students. Teachers must continually assess their interactions with boys as opposed to girls, and with students from dominant and oppressed groups, to determine whether the interactions involve different types of praise, criticism, encouragement, and reinforcement based on the culture of the student. Only then can steps be taken to equalize treatment.

STUDENT AND TEACHER COMMUNICATIONS

Lack of skill in cross-cultural communications between students and teachers can prevent learning in the classroom. This problem is usually the result of misunderstanding cultural cues of students with cultural identities different from that of the teacher.

Just as cultures differ in the structure of their language, they also differ in the structure of oral discourse. The moves made in teaching-learning discourse, who is supposed to make them, and the sequence in which they should be made varies from culture to culture. These rules are not absolute laws governing behavior; in fact, students learn them in their interactions within our own cultural groups. But when these patterns differ between the culture of the teacher and the culture of the child, serious misunderstandings can occur as the two participants use different patterns and assign different social meanings to the same actions.

These differences are likely to prevail in schools with large numbers of students from oppressed groups. Miscommunication occurs when the same words and actions mean something different to the individuals involved. When students are not responding appropriately in the classroom, teachers should consider the possibility that their communication cues do not match those of their students.

One of the characteristics of teachers who are successful in working with students from diverse populations is caring. As part of their caring, they have high expectations for academic achievement and push students to achieve at those levels.
© Anne Vega/Merrill

Direct and continuous participation in cultures that are different from our own can improve our competency in other communication systems and help us be more sensitive to differences in cultures with which we are not familiar. Teachers who are aware of these differences can redirect their instruction to use the communications that work most effectively with students. At the same time, the teacher can begin to teach students how to interact effectively in situations that make them uncomfortable. This approach will assist all students in responding appropriately in classroom situations that are dominated by unfamiliar interactions.

Believe That All Students Can Learn

Education that is multicultural requires teachers and other school professionals to possess dispositions that support learning by students from diverse populations. **Dispositions** are made up of the values, beliefs, attitudes, behaviors, commitments, and professional ethics of educators. They influence our teaching and interactions with students, families, colleagues, and communities. They affect our view of student learning, student motivation, and student development as well as our own professional growth. They include values such as caring, fairness, honesty, responsibility, and social justice. Multicultural educator Sonia Nieto (2010) indicates that one of the purposes of schools is "to provide all students with an equal and high quality education," which requires that we "begin with the belief that all students are capable and worthy of learning to high levels of achievement" (p. 30). It is not just multiculturalists who believe that this disposition is important for all teachers. The InTASC standards (2011), which are used for licensure

Adults in the community can be valuable resources in discussions of cultural differences. When community members trust school officials, they become partners with teachers in improving students' learning.
© Scott Cunningham/Merrill

by many states, also call for new teachers to believe that all students can learn. This section will explore ways that teachers can implement the belief that all students can learn in their classrooms.

FOCUS ON LEARNING

It is important to multicultural teachers that all of their students learn regardless of the obstacles they face because of their disabilities or economic conditions that limit their social capital. These teachers recognize when some students are not learning, reach out to them, and try different pedagogical strategies to help them learn. They do not allow students to sit in their classrooms without being engaged with the content. They do not ignore the students who are withdrawn, depressed, or resistant to classroom work. They do everything they can to help students see themselves as learners and to value learning.

The focus on learning is not limited to the basic literacy and numeracy skills that all people need to function effectively in society. Multicultural educators help students understand the **big ideas**, the concepts that undergird a subject. They encourage students to question what is written in textbooks and the newspaper and what they see on television and in movies. They do not treat students as receptacles into which knowledge is poured. They help students learn by doing, involving them in hands-on activities and community projects, collecting data from their neighborhoods, and testing their ideas.

The Center for Research on Education, Diversity, and Excellence (CREDE) at the University of California, Berkeley, has identified the following five standards as critical to improving the learning of diverse students:

1. **Joint productive activity.** Teachers and students producing together facilitate learning, especially when the teacher and students are from different cultural groups. To realize this goal, the teacher and students must work together on projects. Depending on the project, students should be organized into groups by different criteria, such as interests, cross-ethnic groups, or cross-ability groups. The teacher monitors and encourages interactions among students and him- or herself as they work to solve a problem, develop a product, or complete a project.

2. **Language development.** Developing language across the curriculum improves competency in the language and literacy of instruction. Because literacy is the most fundamental skill necessary for academic access, all teachers must assist students in becoming literate. Teachers should respect students' native languages and dialects and build on them to teach students the patterns of discourse in schools. Teachers help students connect their language with the subjects they are teaching though speaking, writing, reading, and listening activities that help students develop their literacy skills.

3. **Contextualization.** Connecting teaching and curriculum to students' lives gives meaning to the subjects being taught. Students who are not from middle-class families may not see

how a subject has any meaning to their everyday lives. Teachers need to design instruction that will make these relationships clear. It means connecting new knowledge to the past experiences of the students, not the past experiences of the teacher. By being involved in the school community and working closely with parents, teachers can develop their knowledge bases about the cultures and experiences of their students, which may be very different from those of the teacher.

4. **Challenging activities**. Teaching complex thinking challenges students to develop cognitive complexity. Some teachers mistakenly do not provide the same academic challenges to English language learners, students with disabilities, students from low-income families, or students of color because they think that these students already face too many challenges or perhaps are not as capable of handling academic challenges as their peers. Too often, these students are engaged in repetitive, rote drill activities that are uninteresting and boring. Teachers should maintain standards for student performance that challenge all students, which requires designing activities that advance understanding at deeper levels.

5. **Instructional conversation**. Teaching through conversation engages students through dialogue. Sharing and questioning ideas and knowledge are critical components of instructional conversation among students and the teacher. In this method, teachers use teacher-student dialogue with a clear academic goal to explore the topics and concepts being taught, rather than lecturing about them. They guide student conversation, building on students' prior experiences and knowledge to help them learn. (CREDE, n.d.)

A key to helping students learn is to connect the curriculum to their culture and real-world experiences. They should be able to see themselves in the curriculum to provide meaning for their own lives. Otherwise, they may resist the curriculum and learning, which are seen as the dominant culture's way of denigrating their culture. Researchers at CREDE have tested and refined these standards in a number of schools with diverse populations. Lesson plans and multimedia resources for using the standards, as well as research reports, can be found at CREDE's website at www.crede.org.

HOLD HIGH EXPECTATIONS

Some teachers respond differently to students on the basis of their group identities. They may have low expectations for the academic achievement of students of color and students from low-income families based on negative generalizations about a group and its members' ability to learn at high levels. When these generalizations are applied to all or most students from those groups, grave damage can be done. Students tend to meet the expectations of the teacher, no matter what their actual abilities are. Self-fulfilling prophecies about how well a student will perform in the classroom are often established early in the school year, and both student and teacher unconsciously fulfill those prophecies. Thus, educators should develop strategies to overcome negative expectations they may have for certain students and plan classroom instruction and activities to ensure success for all students.

Cultural group membership cannot become an excuse for students' lack of academic achievement. Empathy with a student's situation (for example, being homeless) is appropriate, but we must prevent it from subsequently lowering our expectations for her or his academic achievement.

Not all expectations are low. Teachers often expect high achievement from Asian American students. Upper-middle-class students are placed disproportionately in high academic tracks, whereas low-income students are disproportionately placed in low academic tracks. Even when students have no differences in ability, academic tracks often reflect race, gender, language, and

PAUSE TO REFLECT 11.2

The most important goal of teaching is to help students learn. The problem is that some teachers do not accept this challenge, encouraging some students to learn at high levels while allowing other students to learn little.

■ How will you know that students are learning?

■ Do you believe that all students can learn? Why or why not?

■ How will you relate the subject that you are teaching to the lives of your students?

class differences (Darling-Hammond, 2010). Students who end up in the low-ability classes have limited academic mobility; they rarely are perceived as capable of achieving at a level high enough to move them to the next level (Ladson-Billings, 2009; Nieto, 2010). Teaching behavior for high-ability groups is much different than for low-ability groups. Middle-ability groups usually receive treatment more similar to that of high-ability groups. Students in the lowest tracks are often subject to practice and review drills. At the high end of the track, students are engaged in interesting and motivating intellectual activities.

To a large degree, students learn to behave in the manner that is expected of the group in which they are placed (Ladson-Billings, 2009). Through tracking, educators have a great influence not only on directing a student's potential but also on determining it by their initial expectations for that student. The sad reality is that tracking does not appear to work, especially if the goal is to improve learning.

Heterogeneous grouping is more helpful in improving academic achievement for students from low-income and oppressed groups (Nieto, 2010). Contrary to popular belief, such grouping does not limit the academic achievement of the most academically talented students, especially when the instruction is geared to challenging all students. The students who suffer the most from tracking practices are those from groups who are disproportionately placed in the low-ability groups. Compared with students in other tracks, these students develop more negative feelings about their academic potential and future aspirations (Gay, 2010). Educational equity demands a different strategy. It requires that all students be academically challenged with stimulating instruction that involves them actively in their own learning.

CREATE CARING RELATIONSHIPS

One of the complaints of students is that their teachers don't know them and don't care about them. Students are more willing to work and their performance improves when they feel the teachers care about them (Gay, 2010). However, caring does not mean going easy on students or being permissive, letting students do what they want. It is not enough to just like the students. A caring teacher has high expectations for students, and pushes students to meet those high expectations.

Caring means honoring students and their families. Caring teachers have overcome their racial biases and do not stereotype students just because they do not know their father, their parents are gay, their mother is on drugs, or a student wears the same clothes day after day. They do not punish students because they do not conform to the dominant culture's expectations for normalcy. They do not label students or "find them unlovable, problematic, and difficult to honor or embrace without equivocation" (Gay, 2010, p. 49) because they are from different cultural groups than the teacher.

What are the characteristics of caring teachers? They are patient, persistent, and supportive of students. They listen to students and validate their culture. They respond to students' personal lives and the institutional barriers they encounter (Nieto, 2010). They empower their students to engage in their own education. Caring teachers don't give up on their students. They understand why students may not feel well on some days or may be having a difficult time outside of school. Nevertheless, these teachers do not accept failure.

"Caring interpersonal relationships are characterized by patience, persistence, facilitation, validation, and empowerment for the participants" (Gay, 2010, p. 49). It is more than being nice (Nieto, 2010). Caring teachers have all of these characteristics and demand that students perform at academically high levels (Gay, 2010). Natisha, whose story began this chapter, did not have teachers who tried to learn why she was silent. Her teachers did not care enough about her to reach out and engage her in her education.

Acknowledge Life Histories and Experiences of Students and Their Families Through Culturally Responsive Teaching

Culturally responsive teaching is an essential component of education that is multicultural. This pedagogy affirms the cultures of students, views the cultures and experiences of students as strengths, and reflects the students' cultures in the teaching process. It is based on the premise that culture influences the way students learn (Nieto, 2010; Hollins, 2011; Gay, 2010). It moves beyond the dominant **canon** of knowledge and ways of knowing. "Students are taught to be proud of their ethnic identities and cultural backgrounds instead of being apologetic or ashamed of them" (Gay, 2010, p. 36).

In this section we will explore elements of the teaching-learning process that you should consider and develop if you wish to become a culturally responsive teacher. Begin now to incorporate these practices into your own lesson plans and work in classrooms. Look for evidence of these practices as you observe teachers in schools and identify other practices that support culturally responsive teaching.

IMPLEMENTING A MULTICULTURAL CURRICULUM

The curriculum should define the knowledge and skills that students are expected to learn in a course or program. It is also political. Whose story, whose culture, and whose values will be reflected in the curriculum being taught and the textbooks and readings that are assigned? Will students be pushed to assimilate the dominant culture, making its stories their own? Or will the curriculum value the students' cultures and teach them their histories and experiences along with those of the dominant culture? A **multicultural curriculum** supports and celebrates our diversity in the broadest sense; it includes the histories, experiences, traditions, and cultures of students in the classroom. In classrooms with limited diversity, the curriculum introduces them to the major cultural groups in the state or nation.

Regardless of the grade level or subject being taught, the curriculum should be multicultural. All students should be able to acknowledge and understand the diversity in the United

States and the world. Students in settings with limited diversity may have few opportunities to interact with persons from other cultural groups. However, they can learn to value diversity rather than fear it. They should come to know that others have different perspectives on the world and events that are based on different experiences.

Although communities are not always rich in ethnic diversity, they all are diverse. Educators need to know the cultural groups that exist in the community. Schools on or near American Indian reservations will include students from the tribes in the area as well as non-American Indians. Urban schools typically include multiethnic populations and students from different socioeconomic levels and religions; inner-city schools have a high proportion of low-income and immigrant students. Rural schools include low-income and middle-class families. Teachers who enter schools attended by students from diverse groups will need to learn about the cultures in the community. Otherwise, both students and teachers could suffer.

The current traditional curriculum is very good at incorporating the histories, experiences, and perspectives of the dominant group. The problem is that the experiences of other groups are often marginalized or ignored, either not appearing at all or appearing as an afterthought, not an integrated, important part of society. Multicultural teaching should tell it as it is. Diversity existed in the United States when Europeans arrived and it became greater with each passing century. To teach as if only one group is worthy of inclusion in the curriculum is not to tell the truth. Instructional materials and information about different groups are available to students and teachers. It may be more difficult to find resources on groups where the membership is small or somewhat new to the United States, but it is not impossible. Both students and teachers can use the Internet to locate information, including personal narratives, art, music, and family histories. Although teachers cannot possibly address each of the hundreds of ethnic and religious groups in this country, they should attempt to include the groups represented in the school community, whether or not all of them are represented in the school.

In western Pennsylvania, a teacher should include information about and examples from the Amish. This approach will signal to other students that the diversity in their community is valued. In schools in the Southwest, the culture of Mexican Americans and American Indians should be integrated throughout the curriculum. In other areas of the country, the curriculum should reflect the histories, experiences, and perspectives of Mormons, Muslims, Vietnamese Americans, Lakotas, Jamaican Americans, African Americans, Chinese Americans, Puerto Ricans, or whatever groups are appropriate. It will be important for students to see the experiences of their relatives and ancestors. If they are not included in the textbook, you will have to find other resources.

Educators are cautioned against giving superficial attention to groups. Hosting an international festival where immigrant groups wear native dress, share native foods, and teach native dances acknowledges the diversity in the community. However, it will not ensure their inclusion in the curriculum or the academic achievement of their children. Multicultural education is much more than food, festivals, and fun, or heroes and holidays. Even celebrating African American history only during February or women's history during March is not multicultural education. It is much more complex and pervasive than setting aside an hour, a unit, or a month. It should become the lens through which the curriculum is presented.

The amount of specific content about diverse groups will vary according to the course taught, but awareness and incorporation of the nation's diversity can be reflected in all classroom experiences and courses. No matter how assimilated students in a classroom are, it is the teacher's responsibility to ensure that they understand diversity, know the contributions of members of both dominant and other groups, and hear the voices of individuals and groups who are from cultural backgrounds different from their own.

Multiculturalism is not a compensatory process to make others more like the dominant group. As an educator integrates diversity into the curriculum, the differences across groups must *not* become deficits to be overcome. Teachers who believe that their own culture is superior to students' cultures will not be able to build the trust necessary to help all students learn. When you begin to teach multiculturally, allow extra planning time to discover ways to make the curriculum and instruction reflect diversity. With experience, this process will become internalized. You will begin to recognize immediately what materials are not multicultural and will be able to expand the standard curriculum to reflect diversity and multiple perspectives.

REFLECTING CULTURE IN ACADEMIC SUBJECTS

Knowledge about students' cultures is important in teaching subject matter in a way that students can learn it. Culturally responsive teaching increases academic achievement because the subject matter is taught within the cultural context and experiences of the students and the communities served. In this approach, the subject begins to have meaning for students because it relates to their lives and experiences. Today's students are not satisfied with passively listening to a teacher tell them what they need to know. They need to be involved in their learning. They learn from hands-on activities. They like to explore, experiment, and test new ideas. If they can use technology to learn, all the better to spark their interest.

Teachers must know a subject well to help students learn it. Subject matter competence alone, however, does not automatically translate into student learning. Without an understanding of students' cultures, teachers are unable to develop instructional strategies related to students' life experiences. You will have to pay attention to the stories being read by students to ensure that they see themselves in some of the stories while learning about people and families from other cultures in other stories. You will need to pay attention to the projects you assign and classroom activities to determine whether some students' cultures are being privileged over others. You may need to substitute word problems used in math and science to better reflect the cultures of the students you are teaching. For example, a problem that focuses on the number of milk cans needed by a farmer has little or no meaning to students who have lived in the city all of their lives. A problem asking them to figure out how much money would be needed to buy a leather jacket would be more meaningful in view of their realities (Delpit, 2006).

INCORPORATING MULTIPLE PERSPECTIVES

It is important for students to learn that individuals from other ethnic, religious, and socioeconomic groups may have perspectives on issues and events that are different from their own. Movies, books, and music provide different perspectives on local, national, and world issues that expand our knowledge about the way others live and how events are experienced by them. Comedians from diverse groups also provide different views of the world from their own and others' experiences. The more we listen to others, the more we can expand our cultural knowledge.

Most members of the dominant group have not had to face the negative, discriminatory experiences that people of color have in schools, with the police, in government offices, or in shopping centers. They may not understand the privilege they enjoy based solely on their skin color. These experiences and the histories of our own group provide a lens for viewing the world. Perspectives vary for good reasons. Understanding the reasons makes it easier to accept that most other perspectives are just as valid as our own. At the same time, perspectives and behaviors that degrade and harm members of specific groups are unacceptable.

Teaching About Thanksgiving

Michele Johnson was observing a kindergarten class in a school near her campus during the fall semester of her junior year. She was taking a class in multicultural education at the same time and was expanding her knowledge base regarding groups of color. The week before Thanksgiving, the teacher she was observing gave her materials for students to color as a part of their study of the meaning of Thanksgiving. When she looked through the materials, she discovered that the kindergartners were to cut out and decorate headbands that they would wear with feathers while presenting gifts to the pilgrims for Thanksgiving. She was appalled that the teacher was perpetuating stereotypes of First Americans and their relationships with the European settlers. She worried that the students were already learning stories about cultural groups that were inaccurate.

| QUESTIONS FOR CLASSROOM DISCUSSION |

- Why does Michele think the project to teach about Thanksgiving is not appropriate?
- How would you teach kindergartners about Thanksgiving? What images would you use to project First Americans and pilgrims in relation to each other?
- Should Michele say something to the teacher who might later be evaluating her performance? Why or why not?

Culturally responsive teaching requires examining sensitive issues and topics. It requires looking at historical and contemporary events from the perspective of European American men, African American women, Puerto Ricans, Japanese Americans, Central American immigrants, Jewish Americans, and Southern Baptists. Reading books, poems, and articles by authors from diverse cultures is helpful because it exposes students to the perspectives of those from other groups.

The community and students may view as untrustworthy teachers and others who are unable to accept alternative perspectives to an issue or event. An example is the inability of whites to see the racism inherent in almost everything experienced by African Americans. Even when African American students point out a racist action, many white teachers and students cannot see it, in part because they have no experience of knowing or being subjected to racism. Instead of acknowledging it, they will often argue that the reporter misinterpreted the action or that the action was not meant to be racist. As a result, many African Americans learn that whites do not recognize racism and are indifferent about it (Tatum, 2011). Immigrant students, other students of color, students with disabilities, and girls and young women have similar narratives that are given little or no credence by many members of the dominant group.

Children ask questions that often make adults uncomfortable. "Why is that man's skin so black?" "Why does Johnny always get to mow the yard while I do the dishes?" "What's a fag?" "Why does that person talk funny?" "Why is Susie in that chair [wheel-chair]?" "Why are those women wearing scarves?" Although these questions are often asked of parents when they are with their children in a public place like a shopping center or grocery store, they are also asked in classrooms. The answers help those who are asking determine "right" and "wrong" behavior. The answers can clarify or confuse the issues. Children may learn that they shouldn't ask those questions. Adults sometimes answer their questions directly and honestly; at other times they aren't truthful or forthright in their responses. For teachers, these questions in the classroom and on the playground provide opportunities to discuss issues related to diversity, equity, and social justice. They provide the opportunity to denounce name calling and harassment against other students. They are "teachable moments" that allow the correction of myths or misperceptions students have about people who are different from themselves.

ADDRESSING INEQUITY AND POWER

Teachers are sometimes reluctant to answer or address the questions raised above, and the questions and issues become even more complex and controversial as students move from elementary school to middle school to high school. Young people of color begin to ask why so many of them are not learning, why teachers do not care about them, and why they are disciplined more often than other students. Young women are struggling with the mixed messages they are receiving about their expected behavior, sexuality, potential, and self-actualization. Students from low-income families may be asking what school is doing for them or wondering how they could possibly afford to attend college. At base, many of these students are questioning the power relationships and inequity that they are experiencing in their lives, although they may not be able to frame their questions and concerns in those terms. Many of them are feeling their powerlessness; others are beginning to rebel against the inequities they are feeling.

Teachers may be uncomfortable in addressing these serious but sometimes controversial issues (Sapon-Shevin, 2010). They may be confused about the issues themselves. They may feel that they don't know enough about the topic to discuss it with students or that talking about the topic would just "rock the boat." They may worry that a discussion of the topic might get them in trouble with parents, the principal, or their colleagues. With the focus on preparing students for upcoming standardized testing, some teachers decide they don't have time to address issues such as poverty, homelessness, abuse, sexual identity, disabilities, or religious diversity.

Some educators might think that it is inappropriate to address topics related to social and economic inequities in the classroom, especially with younger children. Preschool and elementary teachers can address these topics in developmentally appropriate ways, relating the topic to the realities of their students' lives (Sapon-Shevin, 2010). Not only can teachers help students understand why something happens, they can also help a student know what to do when another student is called "gay," when a Jewish student doesn't understand why she has to participate in Christmas activities, or when a student in a wheelchair can't go on a field trip. Students at any age can learn that they can make a difference and that they can speak up when they see an inequity (Sapon-Shevin, 2010).

Race is one of those issues that some teachers find difficult to address in the classroom. Yet it affects the work of schools. Most European American students probably don't believe that

Debate / At What Age Should We Teach About the War?

The School Board in one school district passed a resolution that all middle-level and high schools dedicate one class period and one after-school event to studying the war in Afghanistan. The resolution indicates that age-appropriate materials should be used by teachers and diverse perspectives presented. When the resolution was adopted, one teacher in the district was already discussing the war with her fourth-grade students. As part of social studies, these students were studying Afghanistan and why U.S. troops were fighting a war there. They were examining the war from the perspectives of people around the globe. They were not limiting their discussion to one class period. Is it appropriate to discuss political issues such as war with young children?

FOR

- Young children need to know the critical issues that affect the lives of their families (e.g., they or their classmates may have family members serving in Afghanistan).

- Young children should be helped to understand different perspectives on the political issues they see covered on television.

- Without a critical discussion of war with younger students, they may conclude that war is an acceptable response to conflict.

- A critical discussion of war may help young students understand why they should not hate the Afghans, other Arabs, or Arab Americans.

AGAINST

- Talking about war may scare young children.

- Young children are not able to understand the complexity of war and other controversial political issues.

- Discussing war contributes to the development of extreme patriotism and feelings of hate against the citizens of another nation.

- Teachers should not be influencing students' perspectives on the Afghanistan war. It is the role of parents to help their children understand the war.

| QUESTIONS |

1. Should teachers help students see the war with Afghanistan from the perspective of the Afghan people and their leaders as well as that of the United States and its allies? Why or why not?

2. How old should students be to begin the critical study of political issues?

3. Thinking critically about issues fits naturally into social studies. How can teachers help students think critically about mathematics, science, and literacy?

Adapted from Dawson, K. (2003, Summer). Learning from the past, talking about the present: A fourth-grade teacher reflects on her own schooling and poses hard questions to her students about the war. Rethinking Schools, 17(4), 17.

racism is a factor in their lives; they may even question its existence. Most people of color, on the other hand, feel the pressure of racism all around them. They don't understand how their white peers and teachers could possibly miss it. To ignore the impact of racism on society and our everyday world is to negate the experiences of students and families who suffer from its impact. Can we afford to ignore it because it is complex, emotional, and hard for some students to understand and handle? As teachers incorporate diversity throughout the curriculum, there should be opportunities to discuss the meaning of race in this country and the debilitating effect racism (as well as sexism, classism, etc.) has on large numbers of people in this country and the world.

There is value in racial and ethnic groups working together to overcome fears and correct myths and misperceptions. This healing can begin with educators who are willing to facilitate the dialogue about race. Discussions of race often challenge the teachers' and students' deeply held beliefs about the topic. Some students react with anger and despair; others are defensive and feel shame or guilt (Tatum, 2011). At the beginning, many white students will resist reexamining their worldviews, acknowledging the privilege of whiteness, and accepting the existence of discrimination. These changes do not occur overnight. They take months, and sometimes years, of study and self-reflection. Some people never accept that racism exists and needs to be eliminated.

Another difficult topic to analyze critically is poverty, especially its causes. Too often, families and individuals are blamed for their own poverty. It is difficult for many, especially those advantaged by the current economic conditions, to acknowledge that our system does not provide the same opportunities for all people.

Teachers can help students explore the contributions of the labor class as well as the rich and powerful. They can examine various perspectives on eliminating jobs in one area of the country and moving them to cheaper labor markets in another part of the country or world. Students could examine the changing job markets to determine the skills needed for future work. They could discuss why companies are seeking labor outside the United States for high-tech jobs as well as low-paying jobs in meat processing companies and agriculture. They could critique different perspectives on seeking labor outside the country and its impact on U.S. workers and families.

Model Social Justice and Equality

Social justice is "a philosophy, an approach, and actions that embody treating all people with fairness, respect, dignity, and generosity" (Nieto, 2010, p. 46). Teaching for social justice requires a disposition of caring and social responsibility for those who are not advantaged. But it is much more than a disposition. Teachers who practice social justice confront untruths and stereotypes that contribute to inequality and discrimination against groups. Social justice requires the provision of resources to all students equitably to promote their learning. It means believing in students, having high expectations for them, and providing rigorous and meaningful curriculum and instruction to assist them in developing the social and cultural capital to meet their potential. It requires teachers to build on students' languages, cultures, and experiences to nurture their talents and strengths. Socially just teachers provide a learning environment that encourages **critical thinking** and prepares students to be active citizens in a democracy (Nieto, 2010).

Socially just classrooms are democratic, engaging students and teachers in learning together. Establishing a democratic classroom helps overcome the power inequities that exist between students and teachers. Students become active participants in governing classrooms and in critically analyzing school and societal practices related to equity and social justice.

As part of social justice education, teachers establish learning communities among students to encourage them to work together in the learning process. The learning communities with members from different cultural groups can also promote cross-cultural interactions and understandings.
© Jeff Greenberg 4 of 6/Alamy

A socially just curriculum helps students recognize the biases and discrimination that prevent some students and families from taking advantage of society's benefits. To provide social justice education requires a "safe, caring, equitable learning environment where all students experience success" (Russo & Fairbrother, 2009, p. 12). In this environment students learn to identify discrimination and inequities in the school and the community and become involved in projects working for the elimination of these inequities. Within the school, students work

PAUSE TO REFLECT 11.3

Many teacher education programs claim that social justice is part of their conceptual framework. As a result, they expect teacher candidates to develop proficiencies related to social justice.

- What is a conceptual framework? What is the conceptual framework for the program in which you are enrolled?

- Does your program's conceptual framework include social justice or some aspect of social justice? What are you expected to know and be able to do in relation to social justice?

- What does social justice mean to you?

toward the elimination of bullying and harassment of lesbian, gay, bisexual, transgender, and queer (LGBTQ) students. High school students could choose to tutor younger students to improve their chances for academic success. In the community, they could work with community leaders to improve the environment, establish better services for the young and elderly, and create youth centers to promote the physical and intellectual development of young people.

DEVELOPING CRITICAL THINKING

As a result of being taught multiculturally, students learn to think critically about what they are learning and experiencing. **Critical thinking** challenges the status quo, encourages questioning of the dominant canon and culture, and considers alternatives to the inequitable structure of society. Students should be supported in questioning the validity of the knowledge presented in textbooks and other resources. They should be encouraged to explore other perspectives. Developing the skills to think critically about issues helps students make sense of the events and conditions that affect their lives.

Multicultural teaching requires students to investigate racism, classism, and sexism and how societal institutions have served different populations in discriminatory ways. Even though we may overcome our own prejudices and eliminate our own discriminatory practices against members of other cultural groups, the problem is not solved; it goes beyond what we individually control. The problem is societal and is imbedded in historical and contemporary contexts that students should be helped to understand.

Most students accept the information written in their textbooks as the absolute truth. However, critical thinkers do not automatically accept the content of textbooks as truth. They understand that authors write from their own perspectives, with their own biases. The presentation is usually from the perspective of the dominant culture rather than that of persons who have been oppressed because of events and practices supportive of the dominant culture. Teaching for social justice encourages students to question what is written in textbooks or appears in multimedia materials. Students are expected to conduct research that provides other facts and perspectives to balance the content in the textbook.

Educators can help students examine their own biases and stereotypes related to different cultural groups. These biases often surface during class discussions or incidents outside the classroom. They should not be ignored by the teacher. Instead, they should become one of those teachable moments in which issues are confronted and discussed. Accurate information can begin to displace the myths that many hold about people who are from cultural groups different from their own.

FOSTERING LEARNING COMMUNITIES

Numerous studies show that interactions and understandings among people from different racial and ethnic groups increase as they work together on **meaningful projects** inside and outside the classroom. In social justice education, meaningful projects address equity, democratic practices, and critical social issues in the community.

Teachers should ensure that students are integrated in cooperative groups and group work. **Cooperative learning** is a popular strategy for supporting learning communities. It involves grouping students to work together on a project to support and learn from each other. It minimizes competition among students and encourages them to share the work necessary to learn. They can establish opportunities for cross-cultural communications and learning from each other, but teachers should ensure that groups are racially mixed.

TEACHING AS A POLITICAL ACTIVITY

Teachers who have made their teaching multicultural confront and fight racism, sexism, and other discrimination in schools and society. They develop strategies to recognize their own biases and overcome them. They use their knowledge and skills to support a democratic and equitable society.

Politically active teachers are advocates for children who have been marginalized by society. They may be active in political campaigns, supporting candidates who are positive advocates for children and for adults with the greatest needs. They become involved in local political action to improve conditions in the community. They are teachers who work for equity, democracy, and social justice.

Preparing to Teach Multiculturally

Educators should undertake a number of actions to prepare to deliver education that is multicultural. First, they should know their own cultural identity and the degree to which they identify with the various groups of which they are members. Second, they should accept the fact that they have prejudices that may affect the way they react to students in the classroom. When they recognize these biases, they can develop strategies to overcome or compensate for them in the classroom.

KNOW YOURSELF AND OTHERS

One of the first steps to becoming multicultural is knowing your own cultural identity. Many European American students have never identified themselves as ethnic or racial (Carr & Lund, 2009). They have not thought about their privilege in society. Students of color may have thought little about their own multiple identities because their race or ethnicity has been the center of their identity.

In addition to knowing yourself, you need to learn about groups other than your own. You can read about them, attend ethnic movies or plays, participate in ethnic celebrations, visit different churches and ethnic community gatherings, and interact with members of different groups in a variety of settings. If you enjoy reading novels, you should select authors from different cultures. The perspective presented may be very different from your own. Novels may help you understand that other people's experiences lead them to react to situations differently from the way you would. It is often an advantage to discuss one's reactions to such new experiences with someone else to clarify and confront your own prejudices or stereotypes.

You should make an effort to interact with people who are culturally different from you. Long-term cultural experiences are probably the most effective means of overcoming fear and misconceptions about a group. You must remember, however, that there is much diversity within a group. You cannot generalize about an entire group on the basis of the characteristics of a few persons. In direct cross-cultural contacts, you can learn to be open to the traditions and ways of the other culture in order to learn from the experience. Otherwise, your own traditions, habits, and perspectives are likely to be projected as better, rather than as just different. If you can learn to understand, empathize with, and participate in a second culture, you will have a valuable experience. If you learn to live multiculturally, you are indeed fortunate.

Teachers also should take a critical look at their own interactions with students and communities of color. Many teachers have not critically examined the meaning of race and racism and their role in maintaining the status quo. If educators are unable to acknowledge the existence of racism and understand the effect it has on their students, it will be difficult to serve communities of color effectively, and nearly impossible to eliminate racism in either schools or society.

REFLECT ON YOUR PRACTICE

To provide education that is multicultural, professional educators need to continually reflect on their practice in the classroom. Multicultural educators care that the content of textbooks and district-wide curriculum accurately portray diversity and perspectives beyond the dominant culture. They ask questions about school practices that lead to a disproportionate number of students of color being suspended from school; disproportionate numbers of Asian Americans and upper-middle-class white students in gifted and talented programs; and disproportionate numbers of low-income males and English language learners in low-ability classes. They recognize racism, sexism, homophobia, and ableism and confront students and colleagues who are not treating others with respect. They correct their own behavior when they learn that their prejudices are showing.

As you begin working with students and other professional educators in schools, continue to observe how you and others interact with students, parents, and colleagues of cultures different from your own. Think about ways you can use the students' cultures to help them learn the subjects and skills you are teaching. By reflecting on what works and does not work in the classroom, you can continuously improve your teaching for all students.

Summary

Education that is multicultural respects the cultural diversity of students and supports equity and social justice with the goal of helping students reach their academic, social, physical, and emotional potentials. Teachers are the major ingredient in ensuring that students learn. They can make a difference in students' lives.

The voices of students and the community are valued and validated in classrooms that are multicultural. Teachers should make an effort to know all of their students, to build on their strengths, and to help them overcome their weaknesses.

Positive student relationships can support academic achievement, regardless of gender, ethnicity, age, religion, language, sexual orientation, exceptionality, or where one lives. Oral and nonverbal communication patterns between students and teachers can be analyzed and adjusted to increase the involvement of students in the learning process. Teachers must be sure, however, that they do not treat students differently solely on the basis of group membership.

An important teacher disposition is the belief that all students can learn. Teachers with this belief do not give up on students. They take on the challenge of finding a way to help a struggling student learn a concept, solve a problem, or develop a skill. Teachers should regularly evaluate their academic expectations for students and their own biases to ensure that they are helping all students learn.

Culturally responsive teachers help students increase their academic achievement levels in all areas through the use of teaching approaches and materials that are sensitive and relevant to students' cultures and experiences. A multicultural curriculum incorporates the culture of the community and students in the classroom. Multicultural education starts where people are, builds on the histories and experiences of the community, and incorporates multicultural resources from the local community.

Teachers introduce students to the social and historical realities of U.S. society. They need to help them gain a better understanding of the causes of oppression and inequality, including racism, classism, sexism, ableism, heterosexism, and ageism. In the process, students explore the roots of inequities and oppression and learn how to take action against them.

By teaching social justice, teachers encourage students to think critically by considering multiple perspectives on a topic or event. They are encouraged to question the content of text-books, news reports, movies, and other media as they develop their own knowledge bases and ideas. Teachers establish democratic classrooms in which students are active participants in their own learning and in helping their peers learn.

One of the first steps in becoming a multicultural educator is examining and clarifying your own cultural identity. In addition, you should become familiar with the cultures of other groups, especially those in the area in which you will be teaching. Teaching multiculturally will require continuous reflection to determine what is working and what needs to be changed to help all students learn.

Professional Practice

Questions for Discussion

1. What criteria would you use to determine if a school is providing education that is multicultural?

2. How can you incorporate student voices into the subject that you plan to teach? What will you do if a student refuses to participate in classroom dialogues?

3. What characteristics determine that a school is committed to human rights? What components of the hidden curriculum do you want to address in your classroom?

4. How will you know if you have higher expectations for students in your classroom from specific groups? What events in the classroom could alert you to inequities that may be occurring?

5. If the textbook you have been assigned includes no information or examples pertaining to groups other than European Americans, what can you do to provide a balanced and realistic view of society to students?

6. What will you do if students in your classroom resist the open and frank discussion of racism, classism, or sexism? How will you handle students who are belligerent because of the way they have been treated on the basis of their race, economic conditions, or sex?

7. What are the characteristics of socially just classrooms? How do they differ from most classrooms? Why is teaching for social justice controversial in some school systems?

8. What do you need to do to prepare yourself to understand and use the culture of students in your own teaching?

Portfolio Activities

1. Select a school and write a case study about its multicultural orientation. Describe the diversity of the students and teachers in the school. Describe the climate in terms of its reflection of the school's commitment to diversity, equity, and social justice. Describe how the school addresses multicultural education based on interviews with selected teachers and students. (InTASC Standard 2: Learning Differences)

2. Develop a lesson plan in your subject area that relates the subject to a real-life community issue (for example, social services, care of the elderly, or environment issues). (InTASC Standard 3: Learning Differences, Standard 7: Planning for Instruction, and Standard 10: Leadership and Collaboration)

3. Develop a personal plan for increasing your knowledge about and experiences with groups that are different from your own. How will you assess your progress at becoming more aware of cultural differences? (InTASC Standard 3: Learning Differences, and Standard 9: Professional Learning and Ethical Practice)

Digital Resources for the Classroom

1. The Southern Poverty Law Center's magazine Teaching Tolerance includes many resources for culturally relevant pedagogy. They can be accessed at http://www.tolerance.org/tdsi/crp.

MyEducationLab™

Go to the MyEducationLab (www.myeducationlab.com) for Multicultural Education and familiarize yourself with the topical content, which includes:

- Assignments and Activities, tied to learning outcomes for the course, that can help you more deeply understand course content
- Building Teaching Skills and Dispositions learning units allow you to apply and practice your understanding of how to teach equitably in a multicultural education classroom
- Licensure Test Prep activities are available in the Book Resources to help you prepare for test taking
- A pretest with hints and feedback that tests your knowledge of this chapter's content
- Review, practice, and enrichment activities that will enhance your understanding of the chapter content
- A posttest with hints and feedback that allows you to test your knowledge again after having completed the enrichment activities

A Correlation Guide may be downloaded by instructors to show how MyEducationLab content aligns to this book.

Accent. How an individual pronounces words.

Acculturation. Adoption of the dominant group's cultural patterns by a new or oppressed group.

Acting white. The taking on of the behaviors, values, and attitudes of the dominant white culture by a student of color.

Additive bilingualism. The development or addition of a second language with no detriment to the first language.

Adequate yearly progress (AYP). A minimum level of improvement—measurable in terms of student performance—that school districts and schools must achieve within a specific time frame, as specified in the federal law No Child Left Behind.

Adolescence. Approximately ages 13 through 19.

African American English. Another term for Black English, Vernacular Black English, or Ebonics. A dialect used by many African Americans, primarily those in working-class families.

Afrocentric curriculum. A curriculum centered on or derived from Africa.

Alienation. Estrangement or disconnectedness from oneself or others.

Allah. God in Arabic. It is the term used for God by Muslims and Arab Christians.

American Sign Language (ASL). A natural language that has been developed and used by people who are deaf that is based a system of manual gestures.

Americans with Disabilities Act (ADA). Public Law 101-336, passed on January 26, 1990, designed to end discrimination against individuals with disabilities in private-sector employment, public services, public accommodations, transportation, and telecommunications. It was intended to complete what Section 504 was unable to. The increased accessibility in buildings, public transportation, at sidewalk curbs, for example, can to a great extent be credited to ADA.

Argot. A somewhat secret vocabulary of a coculture group.

Arizona Proposition 203. Voter initiative passed in 2000 and patterned after California's Proposition 227. Designed to eliminate bilingual education and to require sheltered English immersion programs for English language learners (ELLs).

Assimilation. Process by which groups adopt and change the dominant culture.

Asylees. Individuals who travel to the United States from another country and request asylum or protection from persecution in their native country.

At risk. Refers to children and youth who are economically disadvantaged to a degree that can affect their educational opportunities.

Attention deficit hyperactive disorder (ADHD). A chronic disorder that interferes with an individual's ability to regulate activity level, control behavior, and attend to tasks in developmentally appropriate ways.

Authenticity. An approach that relates the curriculum and activities to real-world applications with meaning in the lives of students.

Authoritarian. The concentration of power in one figure, usually the teacher or principal in schools.

Barna group. An evangelical Christian polling organization focusing on faith and culture.

Basic interpersonal communications skills (BICS). Everyday conversational skills, which English language learners can develop in approximately two years.

Biased assessments. Assessments that favor one group over another group. One example is tests that, in the past, were typically developed and normed on white middle-class children. Children of color, particularly African Americans and Latinos, have been and often still are at a disadvantage in testing because the content and context of test items are more familiar to white middle-class children. The bias may lie in the instrument, the administration of the assessment, or the interpretation of test results.

Bicultural. Ability to function effectively in two distinct cultures.

Bidialectical. Refers to an individual who has the ability to speak or utilize two or more dialects.

Big ideas. The major concepts that support a subject such as mathematics or English language arts.

Bilingual education. The use of two languages as media of instruction. The system accepts and develops native language and culture in the instructional process to help students learn English and learn academic subject matter. Bilingual education may use the native language, as well as English, as the medium of instruction.

Bilingualism. The ability to function in two languages. While some contend that bilingualism implies native-like fluency, others measure competency in two languages as adequate to be considered bilingual.

Bisexual. Having a sexual attraction to both members of the same sex and those of the opposite sex.

Black English. Another term for African American English, Vernacular Black English, or Ebonics. A dialect used by many African Americans, primarily those in working-class families.

Black Muslims. A group of African Americans who now align themselves primarily with the Sunni form of Islam. Black Muslims in the United States likely had their beginnings in the late 1800s, but at that time had little in common with traditional Islam. In the 1970s Elijah Muhammad led them into national visibility.

Blue-collar. Designation for jobs or workers characterized by manual labor that is usually mechanical and routine.

Born again. Refers to Christians who have had a conversion experience with a spiritual rebirth into a new life.

Break dancing. A form of dancing involving fast acrobatic moves in which different parts of the body touch the ground; typically done solo with rap music (also referred to as B-boying or breaking).

Buddhism. The fourth largest religion in the world. Founded in 535 B.C. by Siddhartha Gautama, who was believed to be a prince of India. Buddhists believe in reincarnation and emphasize virtue, good conduct, morality, concentration, meditation, mental development, discernment, insight, wisdom, and enlightenment.

Canon. The principles, rules, standards, values, or norms that guide a Western European education.

Case law. Published opinions of judges, which are used to interpret statutes, regulations, and constitutional provisions.

Castilian Spanish. The variety of Spanish spoken in north and central Spain or as the Spanish language standard for radio and TV.

Catholic. Members of the Roman Catholic Church who believe that the Pope in Rome is God's visible lieutenant on earth and the rightful leader of Christianity.

Charter schools. Public schools that are exempt from many of the bureaucratic regulations of traditional public schools.

Child abuse. The physical or psychological mistreatment of a child.

Civil rights. The rights of personal liberty guaranteed by the Thirteenth and Fourteenth Amendments to the U.S. Constitution and by acts of Congress.

Class. A group sharing a particular economic and social status.

Classism. The view that one's class level (e.g., middle or upper class) makes one superior to members of classes perceived as below one's own.

Cocultures. Groups of people who exist and function apart from the dominant culture (e.g., street gangs, drug dealers, prostitutes).

Cognitive academic language proficiency (CALP). The higher levels of proficiency required in highly structured academic situations.

Colloquialisms. The informal or conversational speech in a community. An example of a Texas colloquialism is "I like to got hit by that car," meaning "I was almost struck by that car."

Color blindness. The claim that one does not see a person's race and treats everyone equally, regardless of race.

Compensatory education. The provision of special services to students who have limited economic or educational advantages.

Composition index. An index that compares the percentage of a group in a program with the percentage that group represents in the overall population. It gives us the answers to two questions, such as: What is the percentage of African American students in classes for students with intellectual disabilities, and what is the percentage of African Americans in the school-age population?

Conservative Protestants. Protestants who believe in the virgin birth of Jesus, the inerrancy of the Bible, and Jesus as the son of God being essential to salvation.

Cooperative learning. Strategy for grouping students to work together on a project or activity to support and learn from each other.

Creation science. The designation advocated by conservative Protestants who support the teaching of the biblical account of creation.

Creolization. The result of European Americans, African Americans, and American Indians intermarrying and developing unique cultures, languages, and dialects.

Critical thinking. An effort to see an issue clearly and accurately in order to judge it fairly without a preset bias.

Cultural borders. Boundaries between groups based on cultural differences that may limit an individual's understanding of people from a different cultural background.

Cultural capital. Endowments such as academic competence, language competence, and wealth that provide an advantage to an individual, family, or group.

Cultural pluralism. The maintenance of cultures as parallel and equal in status to the dominant culture in a society.

Culturally responsive teaching. A pedagogy that affirms the cultures of students, views the cultures and experiences of students as strengths, and reflects the students' cultures in the teaching process.

Culture. Socially transmitted ways of thinking, believing, feeling, and acting within a group. These patterns are transmitted from one generation to the next.

Curriculum. A sequence of courses offered by an educational institution.

De facto segregation. Separation of people by race that occurs by the choice of the people involved.

De jure segregation. State-mandated separation of people by race.

Deductive. A way of thinking and reasoning where one begins with general principles to reach conclusions about particular details.

Democracy. A government in which power is vested in the people and exercised directly or indirectly through elected representatives.

Developing nations. Countries that have lower per capita income, greater poverty, and much less capital development than the nations that wield global economic power such as the United States, Japan, and some European countries.

Developmental disabilities. Mental or physical impairments that occur during birth or by the adolescent years. Typically, functional limitations are seen in at least three areas of major life activities, such as self-care, language, learning, mobility, and independent living.

Dialects. Variations of a language usually determined by region or social class (e.g., Southern drawl).

Discrimination. The arbitrary denial of the privileges and rewards of society to members of a particular group.

Dispositions. Values, attitudes, and commitments that guide the work of teachers and other school professionals.

Dominant group. The cultural group whose values and behaviors have been adopted by most institutions in society, including schools. In the United States, this group is the middle-class, white, English-speaking, heterosexual Christian culture with its historical roots in Europe.

Dual language immersion programs. Programs that include students with an English background and usually an equal number of students with one other language background.

Ebonics. Another term for Black English, Vernacular Black English, or African American English. A dialect used by many African Americans, primarily those in working-class families.

Ecosystem. The natural system of animals, plants, and microorganisms functioning together in the physical and chemical environment in which they are located.

Egalitarianism. A belief in the guaranteeing of social, political, and economic rights and privileges for all people.

Emotional abuse. A pattern of behavior that impairs a child's emotional development or sense of worth.

Enchiladas. A Mexican dish consisting of a rolled tortilla (flat cornmeal pancake) with a filling of meat or cheese and served with a chili sauce.

Enculturation. The process of acquiring the characteristics of a given culture and becoming competent in its language and ways of behaving and learning.

Endogamy. Marriage within a single ethnic, cultural, or religious group.

English as a Second Language (ESL). Educational strategy that relies exclusively on English for teaching or learning the English language. ESL programs are used extensively in this country as a primary medium to assimilate English language learners (ELLs) into the linguistic mainstream as quickly as possible.

English language learners (ELLs). Students who have limited or no English skills and are in the process of learning English.

English only. Used interchangeably with "official English."

Equality. The state in which one cultural group is not inferior or superior to another and all individuals have access to the same benefits of society regardless of their group memberships.

Ethnic group. Membership based on one's national origin or the national origin of one's ancestors when they immigrated to the United States.

Ethnocentrism. The view that one's cultural group is superior to all others.

Evangelicals. Conservative Christians who fall under a broad umbrella. Some are considered more moderate within the group and focus on social action agendas in addition to their religious agenda. Another group tends to be more conservative and focus on issues such as pro-life and an anti-gay agenda. Evangelicals generally agree in three areas: (1) one must have a "born again" conversion experience, (2) one must encourage others to believe in Jesus Christ as the son of God, and (3) the Bible is the actual word of God.

Exceptional children. Children with learning and/or behavior problems, children with physical disabilities or sensory impairments, and children who are intellectually gifted or have special talents.

Feminists. People who actively support the rights of women.

Formal standard. The acceptable written language that is typically found in grammar books.

Freedom. Not being unduly hampered or constrained in choice or action by others.

Full inclusion. Serving students with disabilities and other special needs entirely within the general classroom. This is an important difference from inclusion, as students in full inclusion do not receive any of their education in segregated settings.

Fundamentalist Christians. Conservative Christians who advocate the teaching of creation as presented in the Bible as opposed to the theory of evolution. There are many different groups of fundamentalist Christians. Each has its own unique set of distinctions to set it apart from other groups.

Gay. Refers to males who are sexually attracted to other males. The term is sometimes used to refer to all people who are not heterosexual.

Gay-straight alliance (GSA). A student-initiated club of LGBTQ and straight students that provides a safe place for students to discuss issues and meet others with similar interests.

Gender. The respective characteristics associated with femininity and masculinity as determined by culture.

Generation X. The generation born between 1965 and 1976.

Generation Y. The children of baby boomers, and the younger siblings of Generation X, who were born between the early 1980s and 1994.

Generation Z. The age cohort of individuals born after 1990.

Gifted and talented. Refers to students with very high intelligence or such unusual gifts and talents in the arts that they require special educational programming to reach their full potential.

Globalization. A system that connects countries economically, politically, environmentally, and culturally through a global economy supported by free trade, international corporations, and worldwide labor markets.

Hajj. Pilgrimage to Mecca, Saudi Arabia, which every adult Muslim is supposed to make at least once in his or her lifetime.

Heteronormativity. The assumption that heterosexuality is normal and any other sexual identity is abnormal.

Heterosexism. An irrational fear of or aversion to homosexuals that leads to prejudice, discrimination, and sometimes violence against gays, lesbians, bisexuals, and transgendered individuals. Although "heterosexism" is the more accurate term, "homophobia" is more commonly used.

Heterosexual. Having a sexual attraction to members of the opposite sex.

Hidden curriculum. The unwritten and informal rules that guide the behaviors and attitudes expected of students in school.

High-risk behaviors. Actions such as drug use or premarital sex, which could lead to alcohol or drug dependency, teenage pregnancy, sexually transmitted diseases, or some other undesirable outcome.

Hinduism. The major religion of India and the third largest religion in the world, with over 750,000 adherents and as many as 1 million in the United States. Unlike Christianity and Islam, Hinduism does not limit itself to a single religious book of writings, or to one God. Hinduism relies on a number of sacred writings and a number of gods. They believe that the goodness of an individual's life will determine how he or she will be reincarnated.

Hip-hop culture. Popular urban youth culture closely associated with rap music and with the style and fashions of African American inner-city youth.

Homophobia. An irrational fear of or aversion to homosexuals that leads to prejudice, discrimination, and sometimes violence against gays, lesbians, bisexuals, and transgendered individuals.

Homosexual. Sexual attraction to people of the same sex.

Human geography. The study of the economic, social, and cultural systems that have evolved in a specific location of the world.

Immigrated. Entered into a country other than that in which one was born for the purpose of becoming a permanent resident.

Immigration. The process of entering into a country other than that in which one was born for the purpose of becoming a permanent resident.

Inclusion. The placement of special education students in general education settings. (See also *full inclusion*.)

Income. Money earned in wages or salaries.

Indigenous. Refers to a population that is native to a country or region. In the United States, Native Americans, Hawaiians, and Alaska Natives are indigenous populations.

Individualism. A dominant feature of Western culture that stresses the rights, freedom, and importance of the individual versus groups.

Individualized Education Program (IEP). A written program required for all children with disabilities under IDEA. It includes statements concerning the student's present performance, annual goals, short-term objectives, specific educational services needed, relevant dates, participation in regular education, and evaluation procedures. Parents should participate in the development of the IEP and sign the document.

Individuals with Disabilities Education Act (IDEA). Public Law 101-476, which emphasizes the individual over the disability, forever changing how individuals with disabilities are referred to in the literature (e.g., "students with mental retardation" took the place of "mentally retarded students").

Individuals with Disabilities Education Improvement Act (P.L. 108-446). Passed in 2004 and sometimes referred to as IDEA 2004, this law added new language about "academic and functional goals." IEPs are required to include "a statement of measurable annual goals," including academic and functional goals. It aligned IDEA with the No Child Left Behind requirement of "highly qualified teachers." Emergency or provisional certificates do not qualify an individual.

Inductive. A way of thinking and reasoning where one begins with specific facts or details to reach a general conclusion.

Inequality. A condition marked by distinctions in economic success, educational achievement, educational credentials, and power among groups of people.

Informal standard. The language considered proper in a community.

Intellectual disabilities. Impaired intellectual functioning with limited adaptive behavior. Also referred to as "cognitive disabilities" and "mental retardation."

Intelligent design. The theory that only an intelligent being could have created a natural world so complex and well ordered as ours. Some if not most supporters of the evolution theory view intelligent design as a new term for creationism or creation science.

Intersex. Refers to people born with the sexual organs of both men and women.

Involuntary immigrants. People who did not choose to emigrate from their native countries, but were forced to leave or were conquered by the dominant group.

Islam. The second largest religion in the world, which is still growing in numbers and influence. "Islam" means to submit to the will of Allah or God and is derived from the same Arabic word as "peace." Islam offers hope and salvation to the righteous and God-fearing individuals of all religions. Muslims believe that the Qur'an (Koran) is the final message delivered to his prophet Muhammad. The holy writing contains laws, moral precepts, and narratives guiding the lives of nearly one fifth of the world's population.

Islamaphobia. Extreme or irrational fear of all Muslims.

Jim Crow laws. Legal restrictions on people of color sharing public accommodations with whites.

Koran. The holy writings of Islam, believed by Muslims to be the exact words revealed by God or Allah to the prophet Muhammad. It is also written as Qur'an in English.

Kosher. Usually refers to food prepared in accordance with Jewish dietary laws.

Language. Written or spoken human speech. It is a system that enables people to communicate with one another and to share their thoughts and ideas with one another.

Learning disability (LD). A disability of unexpected underachievement, typically involving reading, that is resistant to treatment.

Least restrictive environment (LRE). The educational setting closest to a regular school or general education setting in which the child with a disability can be educated. For many children, this may mean a general education classroom. Others may require a less inclusive setting to best meet their needs.

Lesbian. Woman who is sexually attracted to other women.

LGBT. Lesbian, gay, bisexual, or transgender.

LGBTIQ. Lesbian, gay, bisexual, transgender, intersex, or queer/questioning.

LGBTQ. Lesbian, gay, bisexual, transgender, or queer/questioning.

Liberal Protestants. Protestants, considered to be on the liberal end of the religious continuum, who view Christianity in ways that are meaningful in a world of science and continual change. They stress the right of the individual to determine what is true in religion. They may or may not believe in the virgin birth of Jesus and may or may not believe the Bible to be inerrant.

Magnet schools. Schools in which the curriculum emphasizes a particular subject or field, such as performing arts or mathematics and science. Generally, students from anywhere in a school district can apply to attend these schools.

Mainline Protestants. Identified as liberal, this was once the largest group of Protestants but now has a lower membership than evangelical groups. Includes United Methodists, Evangelical Lutherans, Presbyterians, Episcopalians, American Baptists, United Church of Christ, and the Christian Church.

Manifest destiny. A policy in which a nation or culture believes itself superior to all others and that it is destined to rule over other nations and cultures.

Marginalization. Relegation to a position that is not part of the mainstream or accepted by most people.

McKinney-Vento Homeless Assistance Act. The federal legislation that outlines the education rights of and protections for homeless children and youth.

Meaningful projects. Student projects that address equity, democratic, and social justice issues in the community.

Median income. An income value such that the number of persons, families, or households who earn more than this income is the same as the number who earn less than this income.

Meritocracy. A system based on the belief that an individual's achievements are based on his or her own personal merits and hard work and that the people who achieve at the highest levels deserve the greatest social and financial rewards.

Metropolitan. A geographic area thdensely populated city with its less populated suburbs.

Microcultural. Pertaining to subcultures such as religion, gender, and ethnicity.

Middle class. Group whose members earn annual incomes that allow them to have a standard of living that includes owning a home and a car. Members include blue-collar workers, white-collar workers, professionals, and managers.

Miscegenation. Marriage between people of different races.

Monolingualism. The ability to speak only one language.

Multicultural curriculum. An educational concept that addresses cultural diversity and equity in schools. It incorporates the different cultural groups to which individuals belong with an emphasis on the interaction of race, ethnicity, class, and gender in students' lives.

Multicultural education. An educational concept that addresses cultural diversity and equity in schools. It incorporates the different cultural groups to which individuals belong, with an emphasis on the interaction of race, ethnicity, class, and gender in students' lives.

Multiculturalism. The condition in which different cultural groups can maintain their unique cultural identities while participating equally in the dominant culture.

Multiethnic curriculum. A curriculum that incorporates accurate and positive information about the history, experiences, contributions, and perspectives of the ethnic groups that comprise the U.S. population.

Muslims. Believers and followers of Islam.

MySpace. Social networking website that allows users to create web pages and interact with other users. Users of the service are able to create blogs, upload videos and photos, and design profiles to showcase their interests and talents.

Nativism. Policy favoring assimilated ethnic groups in a country over immigrants.

Net worth. The amount of money remaining if all owned property were converted to cash and all debts paid.

New Age. A spiritualistic movement that began in the early 1980s. New Age has roots in nineteenth-century spiritualism and in the counterculture movement of the 1960s, rejecting materialism and favoring spiritual experience to organized religion. New Age emphasizes reincarnation, biofeedback, shamanism, the occult, psychic healing, and extraterrestrial life. The movement is difficult to define, as there are so many variations of followers.

Nonsexist education. Education that attends to the needs of girls and boys equitably by incorporating females as well as males in the curriculum, ensuring that girls and boys achieve at the same levels in all subjects, and encouraging girls and boys to choose subjects which they traditionally would not have selected.

Nonstandard dialect. A dialect of a given language (e.g., English) that is not considered standard (e.g., Black English).

Nordic race. Germanic people of northern Europe who are white with a tall stature, long head, light skin and hair, and blue eyes.

Normalization. Making available to all persons with disabilities or other handicapping conditions patterns of life and conditions of everyday living that are as close as possible to—or, indeed, the same as—the regular circumstances and ways of life of society.

Official English. A position supported by U.S. English, a citizen's action group that is seeking to have English declared the official language of the United States by Congress. Individuals who support this movement believe that all public documents, records, legislation, and regulations, as well as hearings, official ceremonies, and public meetings should be conducted solely in English.

Orthodox Jews. The oldest, most conservative, and most diverse form of Judaism. Orthodox Jews look upon every word in their sacred texts as being divinely inspired. They adhere to a strict dietary law (kosher), which requires the use of special ingredients and preparation. Kosher usually refers to food, but may refer to anything ritually fit or proper by Jewish law.

Otherness. Emphasis on the differences between other cultural groups and our own.

Overreferrals. In special education, typically the excessive referrals by teachers of students or groups of students to classes for students with disabilities.

Patriarchal. Social organization in which the father controls the family and the wife and children are legally dependent on him. It also refers to men having a disproportionately large share of power in society.

Prejudice. Negative attitudes about a general group of people.

Privilege. Advantages and power over others in society because of one's socioeconomic status, race, native language, gender, or other group membership.

Proficiencies. Knowledge, skills, or dispositions that students or teachers must acquire to meet standards.

Proposition 227. An initiative passed by California voters in 1998 requiring all language minority students to be educated in sheltered English immersion programs, not normally intended to exceed one year. Proposition 227 was designed to eliminate bilingual education from California's schools.

Proposition 8. A California ballot initiative passed in 2008 that eliminated the right of same-sex couples to marry. It was the most heavily funded initiative (over $80 million total on both sides), with much of the support coming from religious groups.

Public Law 94-142, Education for All Handicapped Children Act. Comprehensive legislation signed into law in 1975 that guarantees all children ages 3 to 21 with disabilities a free and appropriate education in the least restrictive environment.

Q. A Christian organization founded by Gabe Lyons.

Queer. General term for all non-heterosexuals. It is a more political way to connote nonconformity.

Queer theory. Theory that challenges the categories of man/woman and gay/straight.

Qur'an. The same as the Koran.

Racism. The belief that one race is inherently superior to all other groups and therefore has a right to dominance.

Ramadan. The ninth and most sacred month of the Islamic calendar, lasting 30 days, during which strict fasting is observed from sunrise to sunset.

Red eye gravy. Popular gravy in the southern United States made from the drippings of pan-fried country ham, bacon, or other pork, sometimes mixed with black coffee.

Refugees. Persons recognized by the U.S. government as being persecuted or legitimately bearing persecution in their home country because of race, religion, nationality, or membership in a specific social or political group.

Regression to the mean. A statistical phenomenon implying that scores at the extreme ends of the statistical distribution move toward the population average (mean), with low scores moving higher and high scores moving lower.

Response to intervention (RTI). A multi-tiered pre-referral method involving increasingly intensive interventions. Usually associated with learning disabilities, RTI has the primary aim of providing intervention to students who are not achieving at comparable rates with their peers.

Risk index. A measure of the percentage of a group in a program compared to other groups. It provides us the answer to a question such as: What percentage of African American students are in classes for students with intellectual disabilities as compared to white students?

Sabbath (Shabbat). A day of rest and holiness observed by Jews and a minority of Christian denominations (e.g., Seventh Day Adventists). It is observed from sunset on Friday night until nightfall on Saturday. Most Christian groups observe Sunday as the Sabbath.

Section 504 of Public Law 93-112. Part of the Rehabilitation Act of 1973 designed as a counterpart law for individuals with disabilities to the Civil Rights Act of 1964. It requires reasonable accommodations for those with disabilities, and prohibits the denial of participation in any program receiving federal funds solely on the basis of one's disability.

Secular humanism. A non–religiously based philosophy promoting man as the measure of all things. It typically rejects the concept of a personal God and regards humans as supreme. Secular humanists tend to see God as the creation of man, rather than man being a creation of God.

Self-fulfilling prophecy. A teacher's prediction of a student's academic achievement that becomes true as the student progresses through the education process. This is often the result of socioeconomic, social, and cultural factors that lead to placement in an academic track that may or may not match the student's academic potential.

Sexism. The conscious or unconscious belief that men are superior to women, resulting in behavior and action to maintain the position of power by males in society and families.

Sexting. Sending sexually explicit messages or photos electronically, primarily between mobile phones.

Sexual abuse. Sexual activity among males and females or members of the same sex that is unwelcome. The abuse can be among peers or on the part of adults involved with children or underage adolescents.

Sexual harassment. Unwanted and unwelcome sexual behavior that includes verbal, visual, or physical abuse that interferes with the victim's normal life.

Sexual identity. The sexual orientation with which one identifies.

Sexual orientation. One's sexual attraction to persons of the same or the opposite sex or to both sexes.

Shaman. A medicine man or priest found in certain tribes of North American Indians.

Sheltered English immersion. A process of English language acquisition structured so that nearly all instruction is in English. This is the instructional method mandated by California Proposition 227 and is normally limited to one year.

Signed English. A system that translates an English oral or written word into a sign.

Sikhism. A religion founded by Guru Nanak during the fifteenth or sixteenth century B.C.E. in India. He drew from the elements of Hinduism and Islam, and stressed a universal single God. Union with God, he said, is accomplished through meditation and surrender to divine will. He believed in reincarnation, karma, and the destruction and rebuilding of the universe, but he rejected the Hindu belief in the caste system.

Social justice. A philosophy calling for citizens to provide for those in society who are less advantaged.

Social media. Media designed to be disseminated through social interaction, including online technology tools enabling people to communicate via the Internet to share information and resources.

Social role valorization. Giving value to individuals with intellectual disabilities.

Social stratification. Ranking of people and families based on specific characteristics such as income, education, occupation, wealth, and power.

Socialization. The process of learning the social norms and expectations of the culture and society.

Socioeconomic status. Composite of the economic status of families or individuals on the basis of occupation, educational attainment, income, and wealth.

Spanglish. A hybrid language combining words and idioms from Spanish and English, notably Spanish speech that borrows many English words and expressions.

Standard English. The English spoken by a particular group of individuals in a community. Typically this group is the professional educated middle class, the group with a high degree of influence and prestige in the community.

Stereotyping. The application of generalizations, many of which are negative and inaccurate, about a group with no consideration of individual differences within the group.

Structural assimilation. The assimilation of groups to the point where they share primary relationships, intermarry, and maintain equality with the dominant group.

Subcultures. Groups within a society that are connected to cultural group memberships such as gender, sexual orientation, race, ethnicity, socioeconomic status, religion, exceptionalities, language, and age.

Subsocieties. Groups within a society, such as punks, gangs, skinheads, or hippies, that have developed their own values, attitudes, and behaviors, which are different from the norm and often not acceptable to the dominant cultural group.

Substance abuse. Use of drugs or alcohol to the level of addiction or other at-risk behaviors.

Subtractive bilingualism. The situation where a second language replaces the first.

Suburbs. The communities that surround a city and are home to many of the city's workers.

Tamales. Mexican dish comprised of chopped meat or cheese and crushed peppers, highly seasoned and wrapped in cornhusks spread with masa (dough made of dried corn), and then steamed.

Title IX. Legislation passed by Congress in 1972 to provide females equal access to all aspects of education, including the curriculum and athletics.

Tracking. Assignment of students to a specific class or program (e.g., gifted) based on their perceived academic abilities, educational potential, or vocational interests.

Transgender. Refers to people who have a psychological sense that their gender does not match their biological sex.

Transition plan. A needs assessment and planning tool for the transition from student into adulthood. Transition plans became a requirement for all children with disabilities by age 14 in IDEA 1990.

Transitional programs. Programs emphasizing bilingual education as a means of moving from the culture and language most commonly used for communication in the home to the mainstream of U.S. language and culture. The native language of the home is used to help the student make the transition to the English language. The native language is gradually phased out as the student becomes more proficient in English.

Transsexuals. Those who have surgically changed their genitals and characteristics to match their gender identity.

Transvestites. People, especially males, who adopt the dress and behaviors of the opposite sex.

Unchurched. Individuals who are not a part of an organized church or religious group. It does not necessarily mean that the individual is without religion or spiritual values.

Underreferrals. Disproportionately low referrals by teachers of children for specific programs or activities. These often include the disproportionately low numbers of children of color (particularly African American, Latino, and American Indian) in classes for the gifted and talented or advanced placement classes.

Unification Church. A religion founded in Korea in 1954 by the Reverend Sun Myung Moon. Individuals outside of the faith refer to the group's adherents as "Moonies," a label considered derogatory by its members, who refer to themselves as Unificationists. Rev. Moon moved to the United States in 1972 and began a major effort to proselytize members into his church.

Upper class. Group whose members earn the highest annual incomes and have the greatest wealth.

Upper middle class. Affluent group in the middle class whose members are highly educated professionals, managers, and administrators.

Values. Qualities or principles that are considered desirable and important.

Vernacular Black English. Another term for Black English, African American English, or Ebonics. A dialect used by many African Americans, primarily those in working-class families.

Vouchers. For the purposes of this text, certificates issued by a government to parents to be applied toward the cost of private school education.

Wealth. Accumulated money and property such as stocks, homes, and cars that can be turned into cash.

White-collar. Designation for jobs or workers characterized by nonmanual labor in offices, retail stores, and sales.

Working class. Group whose members hold manual jobs that do not generally require postsecondary education, except for the more skilled jobs.

Yiddish. The language of Jews from Central and Eastern Europe and their descendants, resulting from a fusion of elements derived principally from a High German language written in Hebrew characters.

YouTube. A website where users can upload, view, and share videos.

Abbott, G., Bievenue, L., Damarin, S., Kramarae, C., Jepkemboi, G., & Strawn, C. (2007). Gender equity in the use of educational technology. In S. S. Klein, *Handbook for achieving gender equity through education* (2nd ed.). Mahwah, NJ: Lawrence Erlbaum.

Adger, C. T., Wolfram, W., & Christian, D. (2007). *Dialects in schools and communities* (2nd ed.). Mahwah, NJ: Lawrence Erlbaum.

Adherents.com. (2011). Largest religious groups in America. Retrieved March 10, 2011, from http://www.adherents.com/rel_USA.html.

Advocate.com. (2008, August 8). Catholic bishops endorse Prop. 8. Retrieved from http://www.advocate.com/article.aspx?id=42173.

American Academy of Pediatrics. (2011). How can we help our children learn to deal with prejudice? Retrieved May 30, 2011, from http://www.healthychildren.org/English/family-life/family-dynamics/pages/Children-and-Prejudice.aspx?nfstatus=401&nftoken=00000000-0000-0000-0000-000000000000&nfstatus description=ERROR%3a+No+local+token.

American Political Science Associatio n. (2004). *American democracy in an age of rising inequality*. Washington, DC: Author.

American Psychological Association (n.d.). Facing the school dropout dilemma. Retrieved May 14, 2011, from http://www.apa.org/pi/families/resources/school-dropout-revention.aspx.

American Psychological Association. (2006). *Answers to your questions about transgender individuals and gender identity*. Washington, DC: Author.

American Psychological Association. (2008). Answers to your questions: For a better understanding of sexual orientation and homosexuality. Retrieved March 28, 2011, from www.apa.org/topics/sorientation.pdf.

Americans with Disabilities Act of 1990, 42 U.S.C. 12101 *et seq.* (P.L. 101-336).

Amour, S. (2005, November 6). Generation Y: They've arrived at work with a new attitude. *USA Today*. Retrieved from www.usatoday.com/money/workplace/2005-11-06-gen-y_x.htm.

Andersen, M. L., & Collins, P. H. (2010). *Race, class, and gender: An anthology* (7th ed.). Belmont, CA: Thomson Wadsworth.

Anderson, S., Collins, C., Pizzigati, S., & Shih, K. (2010). *CEO pay and the great recession* (17th Annual Executive Compensation Survey). Washington, DC: Institute for Policy Studies.

Annie E. Casey Foundation. (2010). 2010 Kids count data book. Retrieved from http://datacenter.kidscount.org/DataBook/2010/OnlineBooks/2010DataBook.pdf.

Anti-Defamation League. (n.d.). What to tell your child about prejudice and discrimination. Retrieved April 5, 2011, from http://www.adl.org/what_to_tell/whattotell_learning.asp.

Appalachian Regional Commission. (n.d.*a*). Appalachian region: Economic overview. Retrieved March 26, 2011, from www.arc.gov/index.do?nodeId=26.

Appalachian Regional Commission. (n.d.*b*). *Education: High school and college completion rates in Appalachia, 2000*. Washington, DC: Author.

Arnett, J. J. (2010). *Adolescence and emerging adulthood: A cultural approach*. Upper Saddle River, NJ: Prentice-Hall.

Artiles, A. J., & Bal, A. (2008). The next generation of disproportionality research. *Journal of Special Education, 42*(1), 4–14.

Associated Press. (2010, March 12). Texas schools to drop "Democratic" from textbooks.Retrieved from http://abclocal.go.com/kgo/story?section=news/education&id=7328517.

Aud, S., Hussar, W., Planty, M., Snyder, T., Bianco, K., Fox, M., Frohlich, L., Kemp, J., & Drake, L. (2010). *The condition of education 2010* (NCES 2010-028). Washington, DC: U.S. Department of Education, National Center for Education Statistics, Institute of Education Sciences.

August, D., Goldenberg, C., & Rueda, R. (2010). Restrictive state language policies: Are they scientifically based? In P. Gandara & M. Hopkins (Eds.), *Forbidden languages: English learners and restrictive language policies*. New York, NY: Teachers College Press.

Avert.org. (n.d.*a*). United States HIV & AIDS statistics summary. Retrieved April 5, 2011, from http://www.avert.org//.

Banks, C. A. M. (2004). Intercultural and intergroup education, 1929–1959: Linking schools and communities. In J. A. Banks & C. A. M. Banks (Eds.), *Handbook of research on multicultural education* (2nd ed., pp. 753–781). San Francisco, CA: Jossey-Bass.

Banks, J. A. (2004). Multicultural education: Historical development, dimensions, and practice. In J. A. Banks & C. A. M. Banks (Eds.), *Handbook of research on multicultural education* (2nd ed., pp. 3–29). San Francisco, CA: Jossey-Bass.

Bartollas, C., & Miller, S. (2011). *Juvenile justice in America* (6th ed.). Upper Saddle River, NJ: Prentice Hall.

Baum, S., & Ma, J. (2010). *Trends in college pricing.* New York: College Board.

Becker, B. (n.d.). *Religion and public schools: The path between too much and too little.* Springfield, VA: Fairfax County Schools.

Bellah, R. N., Madsen, R., Sullivan, W. M., Swidler, A., & Tipton, S. M. (2008). *Habits of the heart: Individualism and commitment in American life.* Berkeley, CA: University of California Press.

Beloit College. (2010). Mindset list for the class of 2014. Retrieved April 11, 2011, from http://www.beloit.edu/mindset/2014.php.

Beresin, E. V. (2008). The impact of media violence on children and adolescents: Opportunities for clinical interventions. Retrieved April 11, 2011, from http://www.aacap.org/cs/root/developmentor/the_impact_of_media_violence_on_children_and_adolescents_opportunities_for_clinical_interventions.

Berg, B. J. (2009). *Sexism in America: Alive, well, and ruining our future.* Chicago, IL: Lawrence Hill Books.

Berk, L. D. (2012). *Infants, children, and adolescents.* Boston, MA: Allyn & Bacon.

Berk, L. E. (2012). *Infants and children: Prenatal though middle childhood.* Boston, MA: Allyn & Bacon.

Berk, L. E. (2012). Infants and children: Prenatal through middle childhood. Boston, MA: Allyn & Bacon.

Berk, L. E. (2012). *Infants and children: Prenatal through middle childhood.* Boston, MA: Allyn & Bacon.

Biddle, R. (2009). Special education abuse. *American Spectator.* Retrieved April 24, 2011, from http://spectator.org/archives/2009/12/10/special-education-abuse.

Biegel, S. (2010). The right to be out: Sexual orientation and gender identity in America's public schools. Minneapolis, MN: University of Minnesota Press.

Board of Education of the Hendrick Hudson School District v. Rowley, 458 U.S. 176 (1982).

Boys in K–12 education, 1994 to 2009. (2011, September). *Postsecondary Education Opportunity,* No. 231.

Bremner, J., Frost, A., Haub, C., Mather, M., Ringheim, K., & Zuehlke, E. (2010). World population highlights: Key findings from PRB's 2010 World Population Data Sheet. Retrieved March 22, 2011, from http://www.prb.org/pdf10/65.2highlights.pdf.

Brown, F., Gerber, S., & Oliva, C. M. (2011). Characteristics of Children with Autism. PBS Parents. Retrieved October 6, 2011, http://www.pbs.org/parents/inclusivecommunities/autism2.html

Brown v. Board of Education of Topeka, 347 U.S. 483, 74 S. Ct. 686, 91 L. Ed. 873 (1954).

Brown v. Board of Education, 349 U.S. 294, at 300 (1955).

Brown, K. (2010). Top ten wealthiest members of Congress. Retrieved from http://politics.blogs.foxnews.com/2010/08/31/top-ten-wealthiest-members-congress#.

Brown, M. F. (2008). The New Age and related forms of contemporary spirituality. In R. Scupin (Ed.), *Religion and culture: An anthropological focus* (2nd ed.). Upper Saddle River, NJ: Prentice Hall.

Bureau of Indian Affairs. (2010). Who we are. Retrieved April 28, 2011, from http://www.bia.gov/FAQs/index.htm.

Bureau of Labor Statistics. (2011). America's young adults at 23: School enrollment, training, and employment transitions between ages 22 and 23 summary. Retrieved April 2, 2011, from http://www.bls.gov/news.release/nlsyth.nr0.htm.

Burris, C. C., Wiley, E., Welner, K., & Murphy, J. (2008, March). Accountability, rigor, and detracking: Achievement effects of embracing a challenging curriculum as a universal good for all students. *Teachers College Record, 110*(3), 571–608.

Burros, M. (2007, April 26). Panel suggests junk food ban in schools to help fight obesity. *New York Times,* A22.

Carlson, D. K. (2005, May 24). Americans weigh in on evolution vs. creationism in schools. Retrieved from www.galluppoll.com/content/?ci=16462&pg=1.

Carr, P. R., & Lund, D. E. (2009). The unspoken color of diversity: Whiteness, privilege, and critical engagement in education. In S. R. Steinberg (Ed.),

Diversity and multiculturalism: A reader (pp. 45–55). New York, NY: Peter Lang.

Caspian Energy. (2011). World daily oil production in February 2011 reached new historic high. Retrieved March 31, 2011, from http://caspenergy.com/index_en.shtml?id_node=68&id_file=24058&lang=en.

Castro, A. (2010, May 21). Texas board OKs big changes to textbooks. Retrieved from http://www.aolnews.com/nation/article/texas-board-oks-big-changes-to-textbooks/19487377.

Cauthen, N. K., & Fass, S. (2007). Measuring income and poverty in the United States. Retrieved from www.nccp.org/publications/show.php?id=707.

CBS News. (2009). Sexting shockingly common among teens. Retrieved April 12, 2011, from http://www.cbsnews.com/stories/2009/01/15/national/main4723161.shtml.

Center for Research on Education, Diversity, & Excellence. (n.d.). The five standards for effective pedagogy. Retrieved July 10, 2011, from http://gse.berkeley.edu/research/crede/archive/standards.html.

Centers for Disease Control and Prevention. (2008). Youth suicide. Retrieved March 26, 2011, from http://www.cdc.gov/ncipc/dvp/suicide/youthsuicide.htm.

Centers for Disease Control and Prevention. (2009). Prevalence of Autism Spectrum Disorders. Retrieved October 6, 2011, http://www.cdc.gov/mmwr/preview/mmwrhtml/ss5810a1.htm

Centers for Disease Control and Prevention. (2010). Advisory committee on childhood lead poisoning prevention recommends a work group to investigate lowering limits on elevated blood lead levels. Retrieved April 22, 2011, from http://www.cdc.gov/nceh/lead/lower_blood_levels.htm.

Centers for Disease Control and Prevention. (2010a). Child maltreatment: Facts at a glance. Retrieved April 6, 2011, from http://www.cdc.gov/violenceprevention/pdf/CM-DataSheet-a.pdf.

Centers for Disease Control and Prevention. (2010b). Understanding child maltreatment: Fact sheet. Retrieved April 6, 2011, from http://www.cdc.gov/violenceprevention/pdf/CM-FactSheet-a.pdf.

Centers for Disease Control and Prevention. (2010c). Childhood obesity. Retrieved April 6, 2011, from http://www.cdc.gov/healthyyouth/obesity/.

Centers for Disease Control and Prevention. (2010d). Youth risk surveillance, United States—2009. Retrieved April 7, 2011, from http://www.cdc.gov/mmwr/pdf/ss/ss5905.pdf.

Centers for Disease Control and Prevention. (2010e). HIV surveillance in adolescents and young adults. Retrieved April 9, 2011, from http://www.cdc.gov/hiv/topics/surveillance/resources/slides/adolescents/.

Centers for Disease Control and Prevention. (2010f). Youth violence: Fact sheet. Retrieved April 11, 2011, from http://www.cdc.gov/violenceprevention/pdf/YV-FactSheet-a.pdf.

Centers for Disease Control and Prevention. (2010g). Youth violence: Facts at a glance. Retrieved April 11, 2011, from http://www.cdc.gov/violenceprevention/pdf/YV-DataSheet-a.pdf.

Chambers v. Babbitt, 145 F. Supp. 2d 1068, 1073 (District of Minn. 2001).

Child Welfare Information Gateway. (n.d.). Definitions of child abuse and neglect in federal law. Retrieved April 6, 2011, from http://www.childwelfare.gov/can/defining/federal.cfm.

Child Welfare Information Gateway. (2008). What is child abuse and neglect? Retrieved April 5, 2011, from http://www.childwelfare.gov/pubs/can_info_packet.pdf.

Childhelp, Inc. (2008). National child abuse statistics: Child abuse in America. Scottscale, AZ: Author. Retrieved from http://www.childhelp.org/pages/statistics.

Children's Defense Fund. (2010). The state of America's children: Gun violence. Retrieved March 12, 2011, from http://www.childrensdefense.org/child-research-data-publications/data/state-of-americas-children-2010-gun-violence.pdf.

City Mayors. (2011). The largest cities in the world and their mayors. Retrieved March 29, 2011, from http://www.citymayors.com/statistics/largest-cities-mayors-1.html.

City University of New York (CUNY). (2001). American religious identification survey 2001. Retrieved from www.gc.cuny.edu/faculty/research_studies.htm#aris_1.

Cleveland, K. P. (2011). *Teaching boys who struggle in school: Strategies that turn underachievers into successful learners*. Alexandria, VA: Association for Supervision & Curriculum Development.

Cloud, J. (2009, September 3). Problem with close-talking? Blame the brain. *Time*. Retrieved May 15, 2011, from http://www.time.com/time/health/article/0,8599,1919910,00.html.

CNN. (2010). Home and away: Iraq and Afghanistan war casualties. Retrieved September 1, 2010, from http://www.cnn.com/SPECIALS/war.casualties/.

Committee on Education Funding (2010). Appropriations tracker: Special education. Retrieved April 17, 2011, from http://www.cef.org/resources/appropriations/.

Connell, R. (2009). *Gender in world perspective* (2nd ed.). Malden, MA: Polity Press.

Conroy, T., Yell, M., Katsiyannis, A., & Collins, T. (2010). The U. S. Supreme Court and parental rights under the Individuals with Disabilities Education Act. *Focus on Exceptional Children, 43*(2), 1–16.

Cook, B. G., Tankersley, M., & Landrum, T. J. (2009). Determining evidence-based practices in special education. *Exceptional Children, 75*(3), 365–383.

Corbett, C., Hill, C., & St. Rose, A. (2008). *Where the girls are: The facts about gender equity in education.* Washington, DC: American Association of University Women.

Cornell Research Program. (n.d.). Self-injurious behavior in adolescents and young adults. Retrieved April 10, 2011, from http://www.crpsib.com/whatissi.asp.

Corrigan, J., & Hudson, W. S. (2010). *Religion in America* (8th ed.). Upper Saddle River, NJ: Prentice Hall.

Cox, K. M. (2011, April 21). Blaine school audit finds problem with special education funds. *Bellingham Herald.* Retrieved April 24, 2011, from http://www.bellinghamherald.com/2011/04/21/1978152/blaine-school-audit-finds-problem.html.

Crabtree. S. (2010, August 31). Religiosity highest in world's poorest nations. Retrieved from http://www.gallup.com/poll/142727/Religiosity-Highest-World-Poorest-Nations.aspx.

Craig, T. (2007, February 2). House proposes tough laws; Senate objects to some. *Washington Post,* p. B5.

Crawford, J. (2007). The decline of bilingual education: How to reverse a troubling trend. *International Multilingual Research Journal, 1*(1) 33–37.

Crawford, J., & Krashen, S. (2007). *English learners in American classrooms: 101 questions, 101 answers.* New York, NY: Scholastic.

Cross, W. E., Jr. (1992). *Shades of black: Diversity in African American identity.* Philadelphia, PA: Temple University Press.

Crowley, M. S. (2010). Defining themselves: LGBQS youth online. In C. C. Bertram, M. S. Crowley, & S. G. Massey (Eds.), *Beyond progress and marginalization: LGBTQ youth in educational contexts* (pp. 250–279). New York, NY: Peter Lang.

Cullen, K. (2010, January 24,). The untouchable Mean Girls. *Boston Globe.* Retrieved April 10, 2011, from http://www.boston.com/news/local/massachusetts/articles/2010/01/24/the_untouchable_mean_girls/.

Cummins, J. (1984). *Bilingualism and special education: Issues in assessment and pedagogy.* San Diego, CA: College Hill Press.

Cummins, J. (1996). *Negotiating identities: Education of empowerment in a diverse society.* Los Angeles, CA: California Association for Bilingual Education.

Cummins, J. (2000). *Language, power and pedagogy: Bilingual children in the crossfire.* Clevedon, England: Multicultural Matters.

Cushman, K., & Students of What Kids Can Do. (2003). *Fires in the bathroom: Advice for teachers from high school students.* New York, NY: New Press.

Dahlman, C., Renwick, W. H., & Bergman, E. F. (2011). *Introduction to geography: People, places, and environment* (5th ed.). Upper Saddle River, NJ: Pearson Prentice Hall.

Dalton, B., Sable, J., & Hoffman, L. (2006). *Characteristics of the 100 largest public elementary and secondary school districts in the United States: 2003–2004* (NCES 2006-329). Washington, DC: U.S. Department of Education, National Center for Education Statistics.

Darling-Hammond, L. (2010). *The flat world and education: How America's commitment to equity will determine our future.* New York, NY: Teachers College Press.

Davis, G., Rimm, S., & Siegle, D. (2011). *Education of the gifted and talented.* Upper Saddle River, NJ: Pearson Education.

Davis, T. (2007, February 4). Lead poisoning in kids a persistent problem. *Arizona Daily Star.*

Delpit, L. (2006). *Other people's children: Cultural conflict in the classroom.* New York, NY: New Press.

DeNavas-Walt, C., Proctor, B. D., & Smith, J. C. (2010). *Income, poverty, and health insurance coverage in the United States: 2009* (Current Population Reports P60-238). Washington, DC: U.S. Census Bureau.

Denny, F. M. (2011). *An introduction to Islam* (4th ed.). Upper Saddle River, NJ: Prentice Hall.

Dewey, J. (1966). *Democracy and education: An introduction to the philosophy of education.* New York, NY: Free Press. (Original work published 1916.)

Diana v. State Board of Education, Civil Action No. C-7037 RFP (N.D. Cal. Jan. 7, 1970, and June 18, 1973).

Diaz, E. M., & Kosciw, J. G. (2009). *Shared differences: The experiences of lesbian, gay, bisexual, and transgender students of color in our nation's schools.* New York, NY: GLSEN.

Dolgin, K. G. (2011). *The adolescent: Development, relationships, and culture.* Boston, MA: Allyn & Bacon.

Douglas, S. J. (2010). *Enlightened sexism: The seductive message that feminism's work is done.* New York, NY: Times, Henry Holt.

Dowd, N. E. (2010). *The man question: Male subordination and privilege.* New York, NY: New York University Press.

Drakeford, W., & Garfinkel, L. F. (n.d.). Differential treatment of African American youth. Retrieved May 2007, from http://www.edjj.org/Publications/pub_06_13_00_2.html.

Drew, C. J., & Hardman, M. L. (2007). *Intellectual disabilities across the lifespan* (9th ed.). Upper Saddle River, NJ: Pearson Education.

Duell, M. (2011). Another victory for the bullies: Disabled boy, 11, commits suicide after 'thug punched him to the ground for iPhone.' Retrieved from http://www.dailymail.co.uk/news/article-2043480/Disabled-Mitchell-Wilson-11-commits-suicide-thug-punched-iPhone.html.

Dunham, W. (2007). Expert panel urges junk food ban in schools. Retrieved April 13, 2011, from http://www.reuters.com/article/2007/04/25/us-usa-schools-food-idUSN2528576820070425.

Dunn, L. (1968). Special education for the mildly retarded: Is much of it justifiable? *Exceptional Children, 7,* 5–24.

Eagan, P. J., & Sherrill, K. (2009, January). *California's Proposition 8: What happened and what does the future hold?* Washington, DC: National Gay and Lesbian Task Force.

Eaklor, V. L. (2008). *Queer America: A people's GLBT history of the United States.* New York, NY: New Press.

Eckes, S. E., & McCarthy, M. M. (2008, September). GLBT teachers: The evolving legal protections. *American Educational Research Journal, 45*(3), 530–554.

Edgerton, R. B. (1967). *The cloak of competence.* Berkeley, CA: University of California Press.

Education for All Handicapped Children Act of 1975, 20 U.S.C. 1401 *et seq.* (P.L. 94-142).

Education Trust. (n.d.). *African American achievement in America.* Washington, DC: Author.

Education Trust. (2008, November). *Core problems: Out-of-field teaching persists in key academic courses and high-poverty schools.* Washington, DC: Author.

Education Trust. (2009, April). Who makes it through high school on time? In *Education watch: National report.* Washington, DC: Author.

Eliot, Lise. (2009). *Pink brain, blue brain: How small differences grow into troublesome gaps—and what we can do about it.* Boston, MA: Mariner, Houghton Mifflin Harcourt.

Ellwood, R. S., & McGraw, B. A. (2009). *Many people, many faiths* (9th ed.). Upper Saddle River, NJ: Prentice Hall.

Equal Rights Advocates. (2011). Sexual harassment at school: Know your rights. Retrieved June 28, 2011, from http://www.equalrights.org/publications/kyr/shschool.asp.

Escamilla, K., Shannon, S., Carlos, S., & Garcia, J. (2003). Breaking the code: Colorado's defeat of the Anti–Bilingual Education Initiative (Amendment 31). *Bilingual Research Journal, 27*(3), 357–382.

Faltis, C. J. (2006). *Teaching English language learners in elementary school communities: A joint fostering approach* (4th ed.). Upper Saddle River, NJ: Pearson Prentice Hall.

Family Income and Educational Attainment: 1970 to 2009. (2010, November). *Postsecondary Education Opportunity,* No. 221.

Federal Bureau of Investigation. (2010, November 22). *Hate crime statistics, 2009.* Washington, DC: Author.

Federal Child Abuse and Treatment Act, 1972 (amended 1978, 1984, 1988, 1992, 1996, 2003). U.S. Code Title 42, 5106g. Retrieved from http://www.acf.hhs.gov/programs/cb/laws_policies/cblaws/capta03/capta_manual.pdf.

Federal Register. (2011). Annual update of the HHS poverty guidelines. Retrieved March 23, 2011, from http://www.federalregister.gov/articles/2011/01/20/2011-1237/annual-update-of-the-hhs-poverty-guidelines.

Fine, C. (2010). *Delusions of gender: How our minds, society, and neurosexism create difference.* New York, NY: W. W. Norton.

Fisher, M. P. (2011). *Living religions* (8th ed.). Upper Saddle River, NJ: Pearson Education.

Ford, D. Y. (2010). *Reversing underachievement among gifted black students—again!* The Update. Reston, VA: The Association for the Gifted (Winter 2011).

Freund, D. M. P. (2006). Marketing the free market. In K. M. Kruse & T. J. Sugrue (Eds.), *The new suburban history* (pp. 11–32). Chicago, IL: University of Chicago Press.

Gallagher, C. A. (2010). Color-blind privilege: The social and political functions of erasing the color line in post race America. In M. L. Andersen & P. H. Collins, *Race, class, and gender: An anthology* (7th ed., pp. 95–98). Belmont, CA: Wadsworth.

Gallup Poll. (2006). Religion. Retrieved December 28, 2006, from www.galluppoll.com/content/?ci=1690&pg=1.

Gallup. (2010). Religion. Retrieved September 12, 2010, from http://www.gallup.com/poll/1690/Religion.aspx.

Gallup. (2011). Race relations. Retrieved April 29, 2011, from http://www.gallup.com/poll/1687/Race-Relations.aspx?version=print.

Gangs and At-Risk Kids. (2010). Website. Retrieved April 13, 2011, from http://www.gangsandkids.com/.

Gay, G. (2010). *Culturally responsive teaching: Theory, research, and practice* (2nd ed.). New York, NY: Teachers College Press.

Geck, C. (2006, February). The generation Z connection: Teaching information literacy to the newest net generation. *Teacher Librarian, 33*(3), 19(5).

Gliedman, J., & Roth, W. (1980). *The unexpected minority.* New York, NY: Harcourt Brace Jovanovich.

Goldberg, A., Collins, C., Pizzigati, S., & Klinger, S. (2011, April). *Unnecessary austerity, unnecessary shutdown.* Washington, DC: Institute for Policy Studies, Program on Inequality and the Common Good.

Goldenberg, C. (2008, Summer). Teaching English language learners: What the research does—and does not say. *American Educator.* Retrieved May 23, 2011, from http://www.aft.org/pdfs/americaneducator/summer2008/goldenberg.pdf.

Gomes, P. (1996). *The good book.* New York: Morrow.

GOP. (2008). Preserving traditional marriage (2008 Republican Party platform). Retrieved from http://www.gop.com/2008Platform/Values.htm.

Gorski, P. (2008, April). The myth of the "culture of poverty." *Educational Leadership, 65*(7): 32–36.

Grant, C. A., & Gibson, M. L. (2010). "These are revolutionary times": Human rights, social justice, and popular protest. In T. K. Chapman & N. Hobbel, *Social justice pedagogy across the curriculum: The practice of freedom.* New York, NY: Routledge.

Grinberg, J., Price, J., & Naiditch, F. (2009). Schooling and social class. In S. R. Steinberg (Ed.), *Diversity and multiculturalism: A reader.* New York, NY: Peter Lang.

Groothuis, R. M. (1997). *Good news for women: A biblical picture of gender equality.* Grand Rapids, MI: Baker Books.

Gruber, J. E., & Fineran, S. (2008, April 5). Comparing the impact of bullying and sexual harassment victimization on the mental and physical health of adolescents, *Sex Roles, 5,* 1–13.

Grutter v. Bollinger, 123 S. Ct. 2325 (2003).

Guadalupe Organization, Inc. v. Tempe Elementary School District No. 3, 587 F.2d 1022, 1030 (9th Cir. 1978).

Gurian, M., & Stevens, K. (2005). *The minds of boys: Saving our sons from falling behind in school and life.* San Francisco, CA: Jossey-Bass.

Hacker, J. S., & Pierson, P. (2010). *Winner-take-all politics: How Washington made the rich richer—and turned its back on the middle class.* New York, NY: Simon & Schuster.

Hafner, K. (2009). Texting may be taking a toll. *New York Times.* Retrieved May 4, 2011, from http://www.nytimes.com/2009/05/26/health/26teen.html.

Hakuta, K. (2001a). Silence from Oceanside and the future of bilingual education. Retrieved May 23, 2011, from http://faculty.ucmerced.edu/khakuta/research/SAT9/silence1.html.

Hakuta, K. (2001b). Follow-up on Oceanside: Communications with Ron Unz. Retrieved May 23, 2011, from http://faculty.ucmerced.edu/khakuta/research/SAT9/silence2.html.

Hakuta, K., Butler, Y. G., & Bousquet, M. (1999). What legitimate inferences can be made from the 1999 release of SAT-9 scores with respect to the impact of California's Proposition 227 on the performance of LEP students. Retrieved May 23, 2011, from http://www.stanford.edu/~hakuta/www/research/SAT9/sat9_1999.html.

Hallahan, D., Kauffman, J., & Pullen, P. (2012). *Exceptional learners: An introduction to special education.* Upper Saddle River, NJ: Pearson Education.

Hanson, K., Guilfoy, V., & Pillai, S. (2009). *More than Title IX: How equity in education has shaped the nation.* New York: Rowman & Littlefield.

Harlow, C. W. (2005). *Hate crimes reported by victims and police: Special report* (NCJ 209911). Washington, DC: U.S. Department of Justice, Bureau of Justice Statistics.

Harris, G. (2010, February 7). A federal effort to push junk food out of schools. *New York Times.* Retrieved April 13, 2011, from http://www.nytimes.com/2010/02/08/health/nutrition/08junk.html?_r=1.

Hartz, P. R. (2009). Native American religions (3rd. ed.). New York, NY: Chelsea House.

Helfand, D. (2008). Bishops in state oppose Prop. 8. *Los Angeles Times.* Retrieved from http://articles.latimes.com/2008/sep/11/local/me-gaymarriage11.

Helms, J. A. (Ed.). (1990). *Black and white racial identity development: Theory, research, and practice.* Westport, CT: Praeger.

Hemeyer, J. C. (2010). *Religion in America* (6th ed.). Upper Saddle River, NJ: Prentice Hall.

Hernandez, D. J. (2011, April). *Double jeopardy: How third-grade reading skills and poverty influence high school graduation.* Baltimore, MD: Annie E. Casey Foundation.

Herrera, S. G., and Murry, K. G. (2011). *Mastering ESL and bilingual methods* (2nd ed.). Boston, MA: Pearson Education.

Heward, W. L. (2009). *Exceptional children* (9th ed.). Upper Saddle River, NJ: Merrill/Prentice Hall.

Himmelstein, K. E. W., & Brückner, H. (2011, January). Criminal-justice and school sanctions against nonheterosexual youth: A national longitudinal study. *Pediatrics, 127*(1), 49–57.

Hollins, E. R. (2011). The meaning of culture in learning to teach: The power of socialization and identity formation. In A. F. Ball & C A. Tyson, *Studying diversity in teacher education* (pp. 105–132). New York, NY: Rowman & Littlefield.

Hopfe, L. M., & Woodward, M. R. (2009). *Religions of the world* (11th ed.). Upper Saddle River, NJ: Pearson Education.

Howard, T. C. (2010). *Why race and culture matter in schools: Closing the achievement gap in America's classrooms.* New York, NY: Teachers College Press.

Hudley, A. H., & Mallison, C. (2011). *Understanding English language variation in U.S.* New York, NY: Teachers College Press

Huget, J. L. (2011). Is that right? News photos of obese people create bias. *Washington Post.* Retrieved May 15, 2011, from http://www.washingtonpost.com/blogs/the-checkup/post/is-that-right-news-photos-of-obese-people-create-bias/2011/05/13/AFbD9Z2G_blog.html.

Human Rights Campaign. (2010). Washington, DC: Author. Adoption stories. Retrieved on October 14, 2011, from http://www.hrc.org/resources/entry/adoption-stories.

Individuals with Disabilities Education Act Amendments of 1997, 20 U.S.C. 1400 *et seq.* (P.L. 105-17).

Individuals with Disabilities Education Act of 1990, 20 U.S.C. 1400 *et seq.* (P.L. 101-476).

Individuals with Disabilities Education Improvement Act of 2004, 118 Stat. 2647, 601 *et seq.* (P.L. 108-446).

Interstate Teacher Assessment and Support Consortium (InTASC). (2011). *InTASC model core teaching standards: A resource for state dialogue.* Washington, DC: Council of Chief State School Officers.

Iraq Casualty Count. (2010). Operation Iraqi Freedom. Retrieved September 1, 2010, from http://www.icasualties.org/Iraq/index.aspx.

Irving Independent School District v. Tatro, 468 U.S. 883 (1984).

James, S., & Thomas, D. (2009). *Wild things: The art of nurturing boys.* Carol Stream, IL: Tyndale House.

Jamil, O. B., & Harper, G. W. (2010). School for the self: Examining the role of educational settings in identity development among gay, bisexual, and questioning male youth of color. In C. C. Bertram, M. S. Crowley, & S. G. Massey (Eds.), *Beyond progress and marginalization: LGBTQ youth in educational contexts* (pp. 175–202). New York, NY: Peter Lang.

Jennings, K. (Ed.). (2005). *One teacher in 10: LGBT educators share their stories* (2nd ed.). Los Angeles, CA: Alyson Books.

Jewish Virtual Library. (2011). Fiorello LaGuardia. Retrieved May 15, 2011, from http://www.jewishvirtuallibrary.org/jsource/biography/LaGuardia.html.

Jiménez, T. R. (2010). *Replenished ethnicity: Mexican Americans, immigration, and identity.* Berkeley, CA: University of California Press.

Johnson, D. K. (2004). *The lavender scare: The cold war persecution of gays and lesbians in the federal government.* Chicago, IL: University of Chicago Press.

Johnson, D. L, Haarmann, V., Johnson, M. L., & Clawson, D. L. (2010). *World regional geography: A development approach* (10th ed.). Upper Saddle River, NJ: Pearson Prentice Hall.

Johnson, J. A., Musial, D. L., Hall, G. E., & Gollnick, D. M. (2011). *Foundations of American education: Perspectives on education in a changing world* (15th ed.). Saddle River, NJ: Merrill.

Johnstone, R. L. (2007). *Religion in society: A sociology of religion* (8th ed.). Upper Saddle River, NJ: Prentice Hall.

Joint Center for Housing Studies of Harvard University. (2010). *The state of the nation's housing: 2010.* Cambridge, MA: Author.

Jones, J. M. (2008, August 4). Majority of Americans say racism against blacks widespread. Retrieved April 30, 2011, from http://www.gallup.com/poll/109258/Majority-Americans-Say-Racism-Against-Blacks-Widespread.aspx?version=print.

Jones, J. M. (2011a, May 20). For first time, majority of Americans favor legal gay marriage. Retrieved June 1, 2011, from http://www.gallup.com/poll/147662/First-Time-Majority-Americans-Favor-Legal-Gay-Marriage.aspx.

Jones, J. M. (2011b, May 26). Support for legal gay relations hits new high. Retrieved May 26, 2011, from http://www.gallup.com/poll/147785/Support-Legal-Gay-Relations-Hits-New-High.aspx.

Jordan-Young, R. M. (2010). *Brainstorm: The flaws in the science of sex differences*. Cambridge, MA: Harvard University Press.

Joyce, J. A., O'Neil, M. E., & McWhirter, E. H. (2010). Aspirations, inspirations, and obstacles: LGBTQ youth and processes of career development. In C. C. Bertram, M. S. Crowley, & S. G. Massey (Eds.), *Beyond progress and marginalization: LGBTQ youth in educational contexts* (pp. 126–148). New York, NY: Peter Lang.

Justice Policy Institute. (2010). Racial disparities. Retrieved April 11, 2011, from http://www.justicepolicy.org/research/category/.

Karnowski, S. (2011, April 15). In Minnesota, copper mining runs afoul of wild rice. Retrieved April 17, 2011, from http://www.businessweek.com/ap/financialnews/D9MK0P980.htm.

Kavale, K. A., & Spaulding, L. S. (2008). Is response to intervention good policy for specific learning disability? *Learning Disabilities Research and Practice, 23*(4), 169–179.

Keen, L. (2011, April 8). LGBTs comprise 3.5 percent of U.S. adult population. Retrieved April 10, 2011, from http://www.keennewservice.com/2011/04/08/lgbts-comprise-3-5-percent-of-u-s-adult-population/.

Kelley, M. (2000, September 8). Indian Affairs head makes apology. Washington, DC: Associated Press.

Kelly, M. (2010). Censorship and book banning in America: Top 10 banned books. Retrieved from http://712educators.about.com/cs/bannedbooks/a/bookbanning.htm.

Kennedy, H. (2010, March 29). Phoebe Prince, South Hadley High School's "new girl," driven to suicide by teenage cyber bullies. *New York Daily News*. Retrieved April 10, 2010, from http://articles.nydailynews.com/2010-03-29/news/27060348_1_facebook-town-hall-meetings-school-library.

Kimmel, M. (2008). *Guyland: The perilous world where boys become men*. New York, NY: Harper.

Kincheloe, J. L., Steinberg, S. R., & Stonebanks, C. D. (2010). *Teaching against Islamaphobia*. New York, NY: Peter Lang.

Kinnaman, D., & Lyons, G. (n.d.). "Q" ideas that create a better world. Retrieved June 27, 2010, from http://qideas.org/essays/unchristian-change-the-perception.aspx.

Kinsey Institute. (2011). Data from Alfred Kinsey's studies. Retrieved March 24, 2011, from http://www.kinseyinstitute.org/research/ak-data.html#homosexuality.

Knox, P. L., & Marston, S. A. (2010). *Human geography: Places and regions in a global context* (5th ed.). Upper Saddle River, NJ: Pearson Education.

Kosciw, J. G., Greytak, E. A., Diaz, E. M., & Bartkiewicz, M. J. (2010). *The 2009 national school climate survey: The experiences of lesbian, gay, bisexual and transgender youth in our nation's schools*. New York, NY: Gay, Lesbian and Straight Education Network.

Kosmin, B. A., & Keysar, A. (2009). American religious identification survey, summary report. Retrieved from http://www.americanreligionsurvey-aris.org/reports/ARIS_Report_2008.pdf.

Kosmin, B. A., & Lachman, S. P. (1993). *One nation under God: Religion in contemporary American society*. New York, NY: Harmony.

Krashen, S., & Mc Field, G. (2005) What works? Reviewing the latest evidence on bilingual education. *Language Learner, 1*(2), 7–10, 34.

Ladson-Billings G. (2004). New directions in multicultural education: Complexities, boundaries, and critical race theory. In J. A. Banks & C. A. M. Banks (Eds.), *Handbook of research on multicultural education* (2nd ed., pp. 50–65). San Francisco, CA: Jossey-Bass.

Ladson-Billings, G. (2009). *The dream keepers: Successful teachers of African American children*. San Francisco, CA: Jossey-Bass, Wiley.

LaDuke, W. (2006). The people belong to the land. In J. Mander, V. Tauli-Corpuz, & International Forum on Globalization. *Paradigm wars: Indigenous peoples' resistance to globalization* (pp. 23–25). San Francisco, CA: Sierra Club Books.

Landsberg, M. (2010, May 15). L.A. region's first two female Episcopal bishops are ordained. *Los Angeles Times*. Retrieved from http://articles.latimes.com/2010/may/15/local/la-me-bishops-20100516.

Larry P. v. Riles, C-71-2270, FRP. Dist. Ct. (1979).

Lau v. Nichols, 414 U.S., 563–572 (Jan. 21, 1974).

Lawrence v. Texas, 539 U.S. 558 (2003).

Lee, J., & Bean, F. D. (2010). *The diversity paradox: Immigration and the color line in 21st century America*. New York, NY: Russell Sage Foundation.

Legal Momentum. (2008). *Legal resource kit: Sexual harassment in the schools*. New York, NY: Author.

Lehr, J. I. (2007). Beyond nature: Critically engaging science to queer straight teachers.

In N. M. Rodriguez & W. F. Pinar (Eds.), *Queering straight teachers: Discourse and identity in education* (pp 33–64). New York, NY: Peter Lang.

Leonardo, Z. (2009). *Race, whiteness, and education.* New York, NY: Routledge.

Let's Move. (2011). Website. Retrieved April 13, 2011, from http://www.letsmove.gov/.

LeVay, S. (2011). *Gay, straight, and the reason why.* New York, NY: Oxford University Press.

Lewis, J. (2008). *Cultural studies: The basics* (2nd ed.). Los Angeles, CA: Sage.

Lewis, M. P. (Ed.). (2009). *Ethnologue: Languages of the world* (16th ed.). Dallas, TX: SIL International.

LGBTQ Nation. (2010, October 1). Two more gay teen suicide victims—Raymond Chase, Cody Barker, mark 6 deaths in September. Retrieved April 10, 2011, from http://www.lgbtqnation.com/2010/10/two-more-gay-teen-suicide-victims-raymond-chase-cody-barker-mark-6-deaths-in-september/.

Lister, K. M.(2010) Compulsive text messaging: Do youth need to kick the habit? Bowling Green State University doctoral dissertation. Retrieved May 4, 2011, from http://etd.ohiolink.edu/send-pdf.cgi/Lister%20Kelly%20M.pdf?bgsu1276915835.

Lloyd, J., Soltani, A., & Koenig, K. (2006). Infrastructure development in the South American Amazon. In J. Mander, V. Tauli-Corpuz, & International Forum on Globalization. *Paradigm wars: Indigenous peoples' resistance to globalization* (pp. 89–94). San Francisco, CA: Sierra Club Books.

Los Angeles Almanac. (2011). Retrieved May 23, 2011, from http://www.laalmanac.com/LA/la10b.htm.

Los Angeles Police Department. (n.d.). Gangs. Retrieved April 11, 2011, from http://www.lapdonline.org/get_informed/content_basic_view/1396.

Lovell v. Comsewogue School District, 214 F. Supp. 2d 319 (E.D.N.Y. 2002).

Macgillivray, I. K. (2007). *Gay-straight alliances: A handbook for students, educators, and parents.* New York, NY: Routledge.

Macgillivray, I. K. (2008). Developing teacher leadership on lesbian, gay, bisexual, and transgender issues in education: New challenges for the 21st century. In J. C. Lee & L. Shiu (Eds.), *Developing teachers and developing schools in changing contexts* (pp. 291–312). Hong Kong: Chinese University of Hong Kong Press.

Mahoney, K., MacSwan, J., Haladyna, T., & Garcia, D. (2010). Castaneda's third prong: Evaluating the achievement of Arizona's English learners under restrictive language policy. In P. Gandera &

M. Hopkins (Eds.), *Forbidden languages: English learners and restrictive language policies..* New York, NY: Teachers College Press.

Malley, E., Posner, M., & Potter, L. (2008). *Suicide risk and prevention for lesbian, gay, bisexual, and transgender youth.* Newton, MA: Suicide Prevention Resource Center.

Mander, J. (2006). Introduction: Globalization and the assault on indigenous resources. In J. Mander, V. Tauli-Corpuz, & International Forum on Globalization. *Paradigm wars: Indigenous peoples' resistance to globalization* (pp. 3–10). San Francisco, CA: Sierra Club Books.

Marsden, G. M. (2006). *Fundamentalism and American culture* (2nd ed.). New York, NY: Oxford University Press.

Martin, J. A., Hamilton, B. E., Sutton, P. D., Ventura, S. J., Matthews, T. J., & Osterman, M. J. K. (2010). Births: Final data for 2008. Retrieved April 9, 2011, from http://www.cdc.gov/nchs/data/nvsr/nvsr59/nvsr59_01.pdf.

Maslow, A. (1954). *Motivation and personality.* New York, NY: Harper.

Mastropieri, M. A., & Scruggs, T. E. (2007). *The inclusive classroom: Strategies for effective instruction* (3rd ed.). Upper Saddle River, NJ: Pearson Education.

Mather, M. (2009, February). *Reports on America: Children in immigrant families chart new path.* Washington, DC: Population Reference Bureau.

Mayo Clinic Health Manager. (2010). Self-injury/cutting. Retrieved April 10, 2011, from http://www.mayoclinic.com/health/self-injury/DS00775.

McCready, L. T. (2010). *Making space for diverse masculinities: Difference, intersectionality, and engagement in an urban high school.* New York, NY: Peter Lang.

McFeat, I. (2005, Summer). Tackling tracking. *Rethinking Schools, 29*(4), 38–42.

McIntosh, P. (2010). White privilege: Unpacking the invisible knapsack. In M. L. Andersen & P. H. Collins, *Race, class, and gender: An anthology* (7th ed., pp. 99–103). Belmont, CA: Wadsworth.

Meacham, J. (2009, April 4). The end of Christian America. *Newsweek.* Retrieved from www.newsweek.com/id/192583.

Mendes, E. (2010) Well-being: Hawaii tops Utah for nation's best. Retrieved from http://www.gallup.com/poll/125849/Hawaii-Tops-Utah-Nation-Best.aspx.

Mercer, J. (1973). *Labeling the mentally retarded.* Los Angeles, CA: University of California Press.

Meyer, E. J. (2007). "But I'm not gay": What straight teachers need to know about queer theory. In N. M. Rodriguez & W. F. Pinar (Eds.), *Queering straight teachers: Discourse and identity in education* (pp. 15–32). New York, NY: Peter Lang.

Meyer, E. J. (2010). *Gender and sexual diversity in schools*. New York, NY: Springer.

Mickelson, R. A., & Smith, S. S. (2010). Can education eliminate race, class, and gender inequality? In M. L. Andersen & P. H. Collins, *Race, class, & gender: An anthology* (7th ed., pp. 407–415). Belmont, CA: Wadsworth.

Miller, M. (2011). *Social networking*. Upper Saddle River, NJ: Prentice Hall.

Miller, N. (2006). *Out of the past: Gay and lesbian history from 1869 to the present*. New York, NY: Alyson Books.

Mills v. Board of Education, 348 F. Supp. 866 (D.D.C 1972).

Mock, B. (2007, Spring). Face right: Black religious opposition to gays rising. *Intelligence Report, 125,* 19–23.

Monger, R., & Yankay, J. (2011, March). *U.S. legal permanent residents: 2010*. Washington, DC: U.S. Department of Homeland Security, Office of Immigration Statistics.

Mooney, N. (2008). *(Not) keeping up with our parents: The decline of the professional middle class*. Boston, MA: Beacon.

Morrison v. Board of Education, 461 P.2d 375 (Cal. 1969).

Morse, A. & Birnbach, K. (2011, July 8). In-state tuition and unauthorized immigrant students. Washington, DC: National Conference of State Legislatures. Retrieved on October 7, 2011, from http://www.ncsl.org/default.aspx?tabid=13100.

Murdick, N., Gartin, B., & Crabtree, T. (2007). *Special education law* (2nd ed.). Upper Saddle River, NJ: Merrill/Prentice Hall.

Murphy, J., & Tobin, K. (2011). *Homelessness comes to school*. Thousand Oaks, CA: Corwin.

Nabozny v. Mary Podlesny, William Davis, Thomas Blauert, et al., 92 F.3d 446 (2004).

National Alliance of Black School Educators. (2008). Education is a civil right. Retrieved May 30, 2011, from http://www.nabse.org/civilright.htm.

National Assessment of Educational Progress. (2011). NAEP data explorer. Retrieved May 27, 2011, from http://nces.ed.gov/nationsreportcard/naepdata/.

National Association for Bilingual Education. (n.d.). What is bilingual education? Retrieved May 16, 2011, from http://www.nabe.org/bilingualed.html.

National Board for Professional Teaching Standards. (2001). *The impact of national board certification on teachers: A survey of national board certified teachers and assessors*. Arlington, VA: Author.

National Center for Education Statistics. (2007). Public high school number of dropouts. Retrieved March 26, 2011, from http://nces.ed.gov/ccd/tables/2010313_04.asp.

National Center for Education Statistics. (2008). Digest of education statistics: Percentage of gifted and talented students in public elementary and secondary schools by sex, race/ethnicity, and state. Retrieved April 22, 2011, from http://nces.ed.gov/programs/digest/d09/tables/dt09_054.asp.

National Center on Family Homelessness. (2010). Children. Retrieved May 22, 2011, from http://www.familyhomelessness.org/children.php?p=ts .

National Clearinghouse for English Language Acquisition (NCELA). (2006). Growing numbers of limited English proficient students. Retrieved from www.ncela.gwu.edu/policy/states/reports/statedata/2004LEP/GrowingLEP_0405_Nov06.pdf.

National Clearinghouse on Child Abuse and Neglect Information. (2004). *Child maltreatment 2002: Summary of key findings*.

National Coalition for the Homeless. (2009, July). Rural homelessness. Retrieved May 22, 2011, from http://www.nationalhomeless.org/factsheets/rural.html.

National Coalition for Women and Girls in Education. (2008). *Title IX at 35*. Washington, DC: Author.

National Collegiate Athletic Association. (2009). NCAA sports sponsorship and participation rates report: 1981-82–2007-08. Retrieved January 10, 2011, from http://www.ncaa.org/wps/portal/ncaahome?WCM_GLOBAL_CONTEXT=/ncaa/NCAA/Research/Participation+and+Demographics/Sponsorship_and_Participation.html.

National Education Association. (2010). Summary Table G. Estimated average annual salaries of total instructional staff and classroom teachers, 2008–2009-10. In *Rankings & estimates of the states 2009, and estimates of school statistics 2010*. Retrieved March 19, 2011, from http://www.nea.org/assets/docs/010rankings.pdf.

National Education Association. (2011). *Ranking of states 2011, and estimates of school statistics 2011*. H-11: Current expenditures for public K–12 schools per student in fall enrollment, 2009–2010. Retrieved from http://www.nea.org/assets/docs/HE/NEA_Rankings_and_Estimates010711.pdf.

National Federation of State High School Associations. (2010). Athletics participation survey totals. Retrieved January 10, 2011, from http://www.nfhs.org/content.aspx?id=3282&linkidentifier=id&itemid=3282.

National Institute of Justice. (2010, December 22). Hate crime prevalence and victimization. Retrieved April 30, 2011, from http://www.nij.gov/nij/topics/crime/hate-crime/prevalence-victimization.htm.

National Law Center on Homelessness and Poverty. (2010). Homelessness & poverty in America. Retrieved May 22, 2011, from http://www.nlchp.org/hapia.cfm.

National Women's Law Center. (2007, October). *How to protect students from sexual harassment: A primer for schools.* Washington, DC: Author.

Neu, T. W., & Weinfeld, R. (2007). *Helping boys succeed in school: A practical guide for parents and teachers.* Waco, TX: Prufrock.

New America Foundation. (n.d.). Individuals with Disabilities Education Act: Funding distribution. Retrieved April 23, 2011, from http://febp.newamerica.net/background-analysis/individuals-disabilities-education-act-funding-distribution.

Newport, F. (2006, June 5). Almost half of Americans believe humans did not evolve. Retrieved from www.galluppoll.com/content/?ci=23200&pg=1.

Newport, F. (2008). Belief in God far lower in Western U.S. Retrieved from http://www.gallup.com/poll/109108/Belief-God-Far-Lower-Western-US.aspx.

Newport, F. (2009a). State of the states: Importance of religion. Retrieved from http://www.gallup.com/poll/114022/State-States-Importance-Religion.aspx.

Newport, F. (2009b). Religious identity: States differ widely. Retrieved from http://www.gallup.com/poll/122075/Religious-Identity-States-Differ-Widely.aspx#1.

Newport, F. (2010a). Americans' church attendance inches up in 2010. Retrieved March 18, 2011, from www.gallup.com/poll/141044/Americans-Church-Attendance-Inches-2010.aspx.

Newport, F. (2010b). Mississippians go to church the most; Vermonters, least. Retrieved from http://www.gallup.com/poll/125999/Mississippians-Go-Church-Most-Vermonters-Least.aspx?CSTS=alert.

Nieto, S. (2008). Nice is not enough: Defining caring for students of color. In M. Pollock (Ed.), *Everyday antiracism: Getting real about race in school* (pp. 28–31). New York, NY: New Press.

Nieto, S. (2010). *Language, culture, and teaching: Critical perspectives.* New York, NY: Routledge.

Nirje, B. (1985). The basis and logic of the normalization principle. *Australia and New Zealand Journal of Developmental Disabilities, 11,* 65–68.

Nuxoll v. Indian Prairie Sch. Dist. No. 204 Bd. of Educ., 523 F.3d 668 (7th Cir. 2008).

NYC Mayors. (2011). Fiorello Henry LaGuardia. Retrieved May 15, 2011, from www.nyc.gov/html/nyc100/html/classroom/hist_info/mayors.html#laguardia.O'Hare, W. P. (2009). The forgotten fifth: Child poverty in rural America. Retrieved March 28, 2011, from http://www.carseyinstitute.unh.edu/publications/Report-OHare-ForgottenFifth.pdf.

O'Hare, W. P., & Savage, S. (2006, Summer). *Child poverty in rural America: New data show increase in 41 states* (Fact Sheet No. 1). Durham, NH: University of New Hampshire, Carsey Institute.

Orenstein, P. (2011). *Cinderella ate my daughter: Dispatches from the front lines of the new girlie-girl culture.* New York: Harpers.

Orfield, G., & Frankenberg, E. (2004, Spring). Where are we now? *Teaching Tolerance, 25,* 57–59.

Orfield, G., & Lee, C. (2010). Why segregation matters: Poverty and education inequality. In M. L. Andersen & P. H. Collins, *Race, class, and gender: An anthology* (7th ed., pp. 416–425). Belmont, CA: Wadsworth.

Organisation for Economic Co-operation & Development. (2008). *Growing unequal? Income distribution and poverty in OECD countries.* Paris, France: Author.

Organisation for Economic Co-operation & Development. (2011a). *Education at a glance 2011.* Paris, France: Author.

Organisation for Economic Co-operation & Development. (2011b). Five family facts. Retrieved May 24, 2011, from http://www.oecd.org/dataoecd/8/10/47710686.pdf.

Orr, J. E., Butler, Y. G., Bousquet, M., & Hakuta, K. (2000). What can we learn about the impact of Proposition 227 from SAT-9 scores? An analysis of results from 2000. Retrieved May 23, 2011, from http://faculty.ucmerced.edu/khakuta/research/SAT9/SAT9_2000/analysis2000.html.

Owens, R. E., Jr. (2005). *Language development* (6th ed.). Needham Heights, MA: Allyn & Bacon.

Page, B. I., & Jacobs, L. R. (2009). *Class war? What Americans really think about economic inequality.* Chicago, IL: University of Chicago Press.

Paquette, K. (2010, April). Current statistics on the prevalence and characteristics of people experiencing homelessness in the United States. Retrieved May 22, 2011, from http://homelessness.samhsa.gov/resource/current-statistics-on-the-prevalence-and-characteristics-of-people-experiencing-homelessness-in-the-united-states-48841.aspx.

Parents Involved in Community Schools v. Seattle School District #1, 127 S. Ct. 2738 (2007), 2821.

Passel, J., & Cohn, D. (2010a). U.S. unauthorized immigration flows are down sharply since mid-decade. Retrieved March 30, 2011, from http://pewhispanic.org/reports/report.php?ReportID=126.

Passel, J., & Cohn, D. (2010b). Unauthorized immigrant population: National and state trends, 2010. Retrieved from http://pewhispanic.org/reports/report.php?ReportID=133.

Passel, J., & Cohn, D. (2011, February). Unauthorized immigrant population: National and state trends, 2010. Washington, DC: Pew Hispanic Center.

Passell, J. S., and Cohn, D. (2008). U. S. population projections: 2005–2050. Retrieved May 16, 2011, from http://pewhispanic.org/files/reports/85.pdf.

Peach, L. J. (2002). *Women and world religions*. Upper Saddle River, NJ: Prentice Hall.

Pence, K., & Justice, L. (2008). *Language development from theory to practice*. Upper Saddle River, NJ: Pearson/Merrill Prentice Hall.

Pennsylvania Association for Retarded Citizens v. Commonwealth of Pennsylvania, 343 F. Supp. 279 (E.D. Pa. 1972).

Pew Forum. (2008, June 24). Pew Forum on Religion and Public Life. Religious Landscape Survey, Report 1: Religious Affiliation. Retrieved from http://religions.pewforum.org/reports#.

Pew Forum. (2009). Pew Forum on Religion and Public Life. Global Restrictions on Religion. Retrieved from http://pewforum.org/uploadedFiles/Topics/Issues/Government/restrictions-fullreport.pdf.

Pew Forum. (2009, June 24). Pew Forum on Religion and Public Life. Religious Landscape Survey, Report 1: Religious Affiliation. Retrieved from http://religions.pewforum.org/reports#.

Pew Forum. (2009, October 7). Pew Forum on Religion and Public Life. Mapping the global Muslim population: Executive summary. Retrieved from http://pewforum.org/Muslim/Mapping-the-Global-Muslim-Population.aspx.

Pew Forum. (2010, September 15). Pew Forum on Religion and Public Life. Muslim networks and movements in Western Europe. Retrieved from http://features.pewforum.org/muslim/number-of-muslims-in-western-europe.html.

Pew Forum. (2010b). Controversies over mosques and Islamic centers across the U.S. Retrieved from http://features.pewforum.org/muslim/assets/mosque-map-all-text-10-5.pdf.

Pew Forum. (2011). Pew Forum on Religion and Public Life. How the 112th Congress (2011–2012) compares with the American public.Retrieved from http://pewforum.org/Government/Faith-on-the-Hill-The-Religious-Composition-of-the-112th-Congress.aspx.

Pimpare, S. (2008). *A people's history of poverty in America*. New York, NY: New Press.

Pirah, J. (2008). LDS donate millions to fight gay marriage. *Daily Herald*. Retrieved from http://www.heraldextra.com/news/local/article_84a8a9bf-6851-56a1-8c36-f170e8cd9f13.html.

Plessy v. Ferguson, 163 U.S. 537 (1896). U.S. Supreme Court, caselaw.1p.findlaw.com/scripts/printer_friendly.pl?page=us/163/537.html.

Plyler v. Doe, 457 U.S. 202 (1982).

Pollock, M. (2008). Introduction: Defining everyday antiracism. In M. Pollock (Ed.), *Everyday antiracism: Getting real about race in school* (pp. xvii–xxii). New York, NY: New Press.

Population Reference Bureau. (2010). Total fertility rate (TFR). Retrieved April 30, 2011, from http://www.prb.org/Datafinder/Topic/Rankings.aspx?sort=r&order=a&variable=93.

Portes, A., & Rumbaut, R. G. (2001). *Legacies: The story of the immigrant second generation*. Berkeley, CA: University of California Press.

Potok, M. (2010, Winter). Under attack: The religious anti-gay right has been knocked back on its heels by gay rights advances. But its hardest core angrily press on. *Intelligence Report, 140*, 26–30.

Potok, M. (2011, Spring). The year in hate & extremism. *Intelligence Report, 141*, 41–68.

Proximity. (2010). Largest 100 U.S. school districts. Retrieved March 29, 2011, from http://www.proximityone.com/lgsd.htm.

Ratcliffe, C., & McKernan, S. (2010, June). Childhood poverty persistence: Facts and consequences. Retrieved May 24, 2011, from http://www.urban.org/UploadedPDF/412126-child-poverty-persistence.pdf.

Rehabilitation Act of 1973, 29 U.S.C. 794, Section 504.

Renn, K. A. (2010, March). LGBT and queer research in higher education: The state and status of the field. *Educational Researcher, 39*(2), 132–141. Retrieved

September 7, 2010, from http://712educators.about .com/cs/bannedbooks/a/bookbanning.htm.

Reuters. (2011). Update2: US Jan oil demand up 3.2 percent from year ago. Retrieved March 31, 2011, from http://af.reuters.com/article/energyOilNews/ idAFN3018942820110330.

Riggle, E. D. B., Whitman, J., Olson, A., Rostosky, S. S., & Strong, S. (2008). The positive aspects of being a lesbian or gay man. *Professional Psychology: Research and Practice, 39*(2), 210–217.

Rivera, C. (2008, May 12). Are gifted students getting left out? *Los Angeles Times*.

Roberts, R. (2010, September 10). Faith and fear: Islam in America. Retrieved from http://abcnews .go.com/GMA/video/faith-fear-islam-americas -muslims-11697044&tab=9482930&section =1206852&playlist=11128084&page=1.

Robinson, B. A. (2006a). Eastern Orthodox churches. Retrieved March 7, 2007, from www .religioustolerance.org/orthodox.htm.

Robinson, B. A. (2006b). New age spirituality. Retrieved September 28, 2010, from: http://www .religioustolerance.org/newage.htm.

Robinson, B. A. (2010a). The Roman Catholic Church and homosexuality . Retrieved September 3, 2010, from www.religioustolerance.org/hom_rom.htm.

Robinson, B. A. (2010b). Hinduism, the world's third largest religion. Retrieved March 16, 2011, from www.religioustolerance.org/hinduism.htm.

Robinson, B. A. (2010c). Policies and teachings about homosexuality in Judaism. Retrieved March 16, 2011, from www.religioustolerance.org/hom_ judaism.htm.

Robinson, B. A. (2010d). The Buddhist religion and homosexuality. Retrieved March 16, 2011, from www.religioustolerance.org/hom_ budd.htm.

Robinson, B. A. (2010e). Humanism and the humanist manifestos. Retrieved March 15, 2011, from www .religioustolerance.org/humanism.htm.

Robinson, B. A. (2010f). Policies and teachings of Jewish groups about homosexuality. Retrieved October 19, 2011, from http://www.religioustolerance.org/ hom_jover.htm (Ontario Consultants on Religious Tolerance)

Robinson, B. A. (2011). Islam and homosexuality. Retrieved March 16, 2011, from www .religioustolerance.org/hom_isla1.htm.

Rose, S. J. (2007). *Social stratification in the United States: The American profile poster*. New York, NY: New Press.

Rothacker, R., & Mellnik, T. Lenders reject minority mortgage loans twice as often as whites. *Charlotte*

Observer. Retrieved April 2, 2011, from http://www .greenchange.org/article.php?id=4662.

Rothstein, R. (2008). Whose problem is poverty? *Educational Leadership, 65*(7), 8–13.

Rowntree, L., Lewis, M., Price, M., & Wyckoff, W. (2009). *Diversity amid globalization: World regions, environment, development* (4th ed.). Upper Saddle River, NJ: Pearson Prentice Hall.

Roxas, K. (2010, April–June). Who really wants "the tired, the poor, and the huddled masses" anyway? Teachers' use of cultural scripts with refugee students in public schools. *Multicultural Perspectives, 12*(2): 65–73.

Rudolph, D. (2010, October 3). Bullied to death: New cases shine light on old problem. Retrieved April 10, 2011, from http://www.keennewsservice.com/ 2010/10/03/bullied-to-death-new-cases-shine -light-on-old-problem/.

Rueda, R., Artiles, A. J., Salazar, J., & Higareda, I. (2002). An analysis of special education as a response to the diminished academic achievement of Chicano/Latino students: An update. In R.R. Valencia (Ed.), *Chicano school failure and success: Past, present, and future* (2nd ed.) (pp. 310-332). London: Routledge/Falmer.

Russo, P., & Fairbrother, A. (2009). Teaching for social justice Pre-K–12: What are we talking about? In R. D. Davis, A. London, & B. Beyerbach, *How do we know they know? A conversation about pre-service teachers learning about culture and social justice* (pp. 9–26). New York, NY: Peter Lang.

Ryan, M. (2010). *Cultural studies: A practical introduction*. Malden, MA: Wiley-Blackwell.

Saad, L. (2009, May 20). Republicans move to the right on several moral issues. Retrieved from http://www .gallup.com/poll/118546/Republicans-Veer-Right -Several-Moral-Issues.aspx/

Saad, L. (2009, November 9). U.S. waiting for race relations to improve under Obama. Retrieved April 29, 2011, from http://www.gallup.com/ poll/124181/U.S.-Waiting-Race-Relations-Improve -Obama.aspx.

Saad, L. (2010, July 6). Americans closely divided over immigration reform priority. Retrieved April 30, 2011, from http://www.gallup.com/poll/141113/ Americans-Closely-Divided-Immigration-Reform -Priority.aspx.

Sable, J., Plotts, C., & Mitchell, L. (2010). *Characteristics of the 100 largest public elementary and secondary school districts in the United States: 2008–09* (NCES 2011-301). Washington, DC: U.S. Department of Education, National Center for Education Statistics.

Sadker, D. Sadker, M. & Zittleman, K. R. (2009). *Still failing at fairness: How gender bias cheats girls and boys in school and what we can do about it.* New York, NY: Scribner.

Samovar, L. A., Porter, R. E., & McDaniel, E. R. (2010). *Communication between cultures* (7th ed.). Boston, MA: Wadsworth.

Sanders, W. I., & Rivers, J. C. (1996). *Cumulative and residual effects of teachers on future student academic achievement.* Knoxville, TN: University of Tennessee Value-Added Research and Assessment Center.

Santa Fe Independent School District v. DOE (99–62) 16 F.3d 806 (June 19, 2000).

Sapon-Shevin, M. (2010). *Because we can change the world: A practical guide to building cooperative, inclusive classroom communities* (2nd ed.). Thousand Oaks, CA: Corwin.

Savage, T. A., & Harley, D. A. (2009, Summer). A place at the blackboard: LGBTIQ. *Multicultural Education, 16*(4), 2–9.

Schlatter, E. (2010, Winter). The hard-liners: A small coterie of groups now comprise the hard core of the anti-gay movement. *Intelligence Report, 140,* 35–43.

School Nutrition Association. (2008). Summary of state school nutrition standards. Retrieved April 7, 2011, from http://www.schoolnutrition.org/uploadedFiles/School_Nutrition/16_LegislativeAction/Summary_of_State_Nutrition_Standards_April_2008.pdf.

Schroeder v. Hamilton School District, 282 F.3d 946 (7th Cir. 2002).

Shapka, J. D., & Keating, D. P. (2003, Winter). Effects of a girls-only curriculum during adolescence: Performance, persistence, and engagement in mathematics and science. *American Educational Research Journal, 40*(4), 929–960.

Shaw, S. M., & Lee, J. (Eds.). (2007). *Women's voices, feminist visions: Classic and contemporary readings.* New York, NY: McGraw-Hill.

Siegel, E. (2010, June 22). Texas GOP advocates criminalizing gay marriage, banning strip clubs, pornography. *Huffington Post.* Retrieved from http://www.huffingtonpost.com/2010/06/22/texas-gop-platform-advoca_n_619601.html.

Silicon Valley Daily. (2009, December 26). Median California home price $304,520 in November. Retrieved March 23, 2011, from http://www.svdaily.com/realestateprices.html.

Simpson, R. (2008). Massachusetts Institute of Technology Young Adult Development Project.

Retrieved April 1, 2011, from http://hrweb.mit.edu/worklife/youngadult/youngadult.pdf.

Singleton, G. E., & Hays, C. (2008). Beginning courageous conversations about race. In M. Pollock (Ed.), *Everyday antiracism: Getting real about race in school* (pp. 18–23). New York, NY: New Press.

Siperstein, G. N., Parker, R. C., Bardon. J. N., & Widaman, K. F. (2007). A national study of youth attitudes toward the inclusion of students with intellectual disabilities. *Exceptional Children, 73*(4), 435–455.

Skiba, R. J., Simmons, A. D., Ritter, S., Gibb, A. C., Rausch, M. K., Cuadrado, J., & Chung, C. (2008). Achieving equity in special education: History, status, and current challenges. *Exceptional Children, 74*(3), 264–288.

Sleeter, C. E., & Bernal, D. D. (2004). Critical pedagogy, critical race theory, and antiracist education. In J. A. Banks & C. A. M. Banks (Eds.), *Handbook of research on multicultural education* (2nd ed., pp. 240–258). San Francisco, CA: Jossey-Bass.

Sleeter, C. E., & Grant, C. A. (2009). *Making choices for multicultural education: Five approaches to race, class, and gender* (6th ed.). New York, NY: Wiley.

Smith, D. (2008). *The Penguin state of the world atlas* (8th ed.). New York, NY: Penguin.

Smith, D., & Tyler, N. (2010). Introduction. In *Special education: Making a difference* (7th ed.). Upper Saddle River, NJ: Pearson Education.

Snyder, T. D., & Dillow, S. A. (2011). *Digest of education statistics 2010* (NCES 2011-015). Washington, DC: U.S. Department of Education, National Center for Education Statistics, Institute of Education Sciences.

Soss, J., & Jacobs, L. R. (2009). The place of inequality: Non-participation in the American polity. *Political Science Quarterly, 124*(1), 95–125.

SoundVision. (2004). Education, educating our future! Retrieved July 15, 2004, from www.soundvision.com/info/education/.

Southern Poverty Law Center. (2011). *When Mr. Kobach comes to town: Nativist laws and the communities they damage.* Montgomery, AL: Author.

Stahl, L. (2010, July 25). The narrative. *60 Minutes,* CBS.

Statement of Vote. (2008, November 4). California General Election. Retrieved from http://www.sos.ca.gov/elections/sov/2008_general/sov_complete.pdf.

Stein, M. (2010). *Sexual injustice: Supreme Court decisions from Griswold to Roe.* Chapel Hill, NC: University of North Carolina Press.

Stone, G. (2009, March 13). Sexting teens can go too far. Retrieved April 12, 2011, from http://abcnews .go.com/Technology/WorldNews/sexting-teens/ story?id=6456834.

Streetgangs.com. (n.d.). Asian gangs. Retrieved April 11, 2011, from http://www.streetgangs.com/asian.

Stump, S. (2011). Teen's parents: After suicide, he's stil being bullied. TODAY.com., http://today .msnbc.msn.com/id/44684938/ns/today-today_ people/t/teens-parents-after-suicide-hes-still-being -bullied./

Suárez-Orozco, C., & Suárez-Orozco, M. (2007). Education. In M. C. Waters & R. Ueda (Eds.), *The new Americans: A guide to immigration since 1965* (pp. 243–257). Cambridge, MA: Harvard University Press.

Swanson, C. B. (2009). *Perspectives on a population: English language learners in American schools.* Bethesda, MD: Editorial Projects in Education.

Symcox, L. (2002). *Whose history? The struggle for national standards in American classrooms.* New York, NY: Teachers College Press.

Taggar, S. V. (2006). Headscarves in the headlines! What does this mean for educators? *Multicultural Perspectives, 8*(3), 3–10.

Takaki, R. (1993). *A different mirror: A history of multicultural America.* Boston, MA: Little, Brown.

Tapscott, D. (2009). *Grown up digital.* New York, NY: McGraw-Hill.

Tatum, B. D. (2003). *"Why are all the black kids sitting together in the cafeteria?" And other conversations about race.* New York, NY: Basic Books.

Tatum, B. D. (2009). Teaching white students about racism: The search for white allies and the restoration of hope. In E. Taylor, D. Gillborn, & G. Ladson-Billings (Eds.), *Foundations of critical race theory in education* (pp. 277–288). New York, NY: Routledge.

Tatum, B. D. (2011). Talking about race, learning about racism: The application of racial identity development theory in the classroom. In K. P. Afolabi, C. Bocala, R. C. DiAquoi, J. M. Hayden, I. A. Liefshitz, & S. S. Oh (Eds.), *Education for a multicultural society* (pp. 267–293). Cambridge, MA: Harvard University Press.

The Economist. (2010). The Net generation, unplugged. Retrieved April 15, 2011, from http://www .economist.com/node/15582279.

Tulgan, B. (2009). *Not everyone gets a trophy.* San Francisco, CA: Jossey-Bass.

Turnbull, R., Turnbull, A., & Wehmeyer, M. L. (2010). *Exceptional lives* (6th ed.). Upper Saddle River, NJ: Pearson Education.

Twenge, J. M., Konrath, S., Foster, J. D., Campbell, W. K., & Bushman, B. J. (2008). Egos inflating over time: A cross-temporal analysis of the narcissistic personality inventory. *Journal of Personality, 76*(4), 875–901.

Tyack, D. (2003). *Seeking common ground: Public schools in a diverse society.* Cambridge, MA: Harvard University Press.

Tyre, P. (2010). Foreword. In M. Reichert & R. Hawley, *Reaching boys, teaching boys: Strategies that work—and why.* San Francisco, CA: Jossey-Bass, Wiley.

U.S. Bureau of Labor Statistics. (2010, June). *Highlights of women's earnings in 2009* (Report 1025). Washington, DC: U.S. Department of Labor.

U.S. Bureau of Labor Statistics. (2011a, May 6). The employment situation—April 2011. Retrieved May 22, 2011, from http://www.bls.gov/news .release/pdf/empsit.pdf.

U.S. Bureau of Labor Statistics. (2011b, March). A profile of the working poor, 2009. Retrieved May 22, 2011, from http://www.bls.gov/cps/ cpswp2009.pdf.

U.S. Census Bureau. (2006). *Statistical abstract of the United States: 2007* (126th ed.). Washington, DC: Author.

U.S. Census Bureau. (2009a). American community survey. Retrieved April 4, 2011, from http://www .census.gov/acs/www//.

U.S. Census Bureau. (2009b). *Statistical abstract of the United States: 2010* (129th ed.). Washington, DC: Author.

U.S. Census Bureau. (2010a). 2005–2009 American community survey. Retrieved January 2, 2011, from http://factfinder.census.gov/servlet/ DatasetTableListServlet?_ds_name=ACS_ 2009_5YR_G00_&_type=table&_program=ACS&_ lang=en&_ts=312166909367.

U.S. Census Bureau. (2010b). Facts for features: American Indian and Alaska Native heritage month: November 2010. *U.S. Census Bureau News.* Retrieved April 28, 2011, from http://www.census .gov/newsroom/releases/archives/facts_for_features_ special_editions/cb10ff22.html.

U.S. Census Bureau. (2010c). Income distribution to $250,000 or more for families: 2009. Retrieved May 22, 2011, from http://www.census.gov/hhes/ www/cpstables/032010/faminc/new07_000.htm.

U.S. Census Bureau. (2010d). Income, poverty and health insurance coverage in the United States: 2009. Retrieved March 23, 2011, from http://www.census.gov/prod/2010pubs/p60-238.pdf.

U.S. Census Bureau. (2010e). New Census Bureau report analyzes nation's linguistic diversity. Retrieved May 16, 2011, from http://www.census.gov/newsroom/releases/archives/american_community_survey_acs/cb10-cn58.html.

U.S. Census Bureau. (2010f). Place of birth of foreign born population. Retrieved April 2, 2011, from http://www.census.gov/prod/2010pubs/acsbr09-15.pdf.

U.S. Census Bureau. (2010g). Poverty data. Retrieved May 24, 2011, from http://www.census.gov/hhes/www/poverty/data/index.html.

U.S. Census Bureau. (2010h). Resident population data. Retrieved March 22, 2011, from http://2010.census.gov/2010census/data/apportionment-pop-text.php.

U.S. Census Bureau. (2010i). Small area income and poverty estimates. Retrieved March 26, 2011, from http://www.census.gov/did/www/saipe/county.html.

U.S. Census Bureau. (2010j). *Statistical abstract of the United States: 2010* (129th ed.). Washington, DC: Author.

U.S. Census Bureau. (2010k). *Statistical abstract of the United States: 2011* (130th ed.). Washington, DC: Author.

U.S. Census Bureau. (2010l). The 2010 statistical abstract: Educational attainment. Retrieved from http://www.census.gov/compendia/statab/2010/tables/10s0226.pdf.

U.S. Census Bureau. (2010m). U.S. census data. Retrieved March 28, 2011, from http://2010.census.gov/2010census/data/.

U.S. Census Bureau. (2011a). *Statistical abstract of the United States: 2012* (131st ed.). Washington, DC: Author.

U.S. Census Bureau. (2011b). The 2011 statistical abstract: Population. Retrieved April 3, 2011, from http://www.census.gov/compendia/statab/cats/population.html.

U.S. Census Bureau. (2011c). Overview of race and Hispanic origin: 2010. Retrieved March 25, 2011, from http://www.census.gov/prod/cen2010/briefs/c2010br-02.pdf.

U.S. Census Bureau. (2011d). The 2011 statistical abstract. Retrieved from http://www.census.gov/compendia/statab/.

U.S. Census Bureau. (2011e). U.S. Census Bureau releases data on population distribution and change in the U.S. Based on analysis of 2010 census results. Retrieved April 1, 2011, from http://www.census.gov/newsroom/releases/archives/2010_census/cb11-cn124.html.

U.S. Census Bureau. (2011f). International data base: Country rankings. Retrieved March 22, 2011, from http://www.census.gov/ipc/www/idb/rank.php.

U.S. Department of Agriculture. (n.d.). Introduction. Retrieved March 28, 2011, from http://www.csrees.usda.gov/qlinks/extension.html#intro.

U.S. Department of Education. (2001). *No Child Left Behind Act of 2001* (www.ed.gov/nclb/overview/intro/presidentplan/proposal.pdf). Washington, DC: U.S. Government Printing Office.

U.S. Department of Education, National Center for Education Statistics. (2007). *The condition of education 2007* (NCES 2007-064). Washington, DC: U.S. Government Printing Office.

U.S. Department of Education, Office of Civil Rights. (2006). 2006 Civil Rights Data Collection. Retrieved April 23, 2011, from http://ocrdata.ed.gov/downloads/projections/2006/2006-nation-projection.xls.

U.S. Department of Homeland Security. (2010). 2009 yearbook of immigration statistics. Retrieved, March 30, 2011, from http://www.dhs.gov/xlibrary/assets/statistics/yearbook/2009/ois_yb_2009.pdf.

U.S. Department of Interior. (n.d.*a*). American Indians and Alaska Natives. Retrieved March 28, 2011, from http://www.doi.gov/tribes/index.cfm.

U.S. Department of Interior. (n.d.*b*). Education. Retrieved March 28, 2011, from http://www.doi.gov/tribes/education.cfm.

U.S. English. (2011). States with official English laws. Retrieved May 16, 2011, from www.us_english.org/inc/.

U.S. Global Change Research Program. (2009). Global climate change impacts the United States. Retrieved March 31, 2011, from http://downloads.globalchange.gov/usimpacts/pdfs/climate-impacts-report.pdf.

U.S. Newswire. (2007, April 4). Robert Wood Johnson Foundation announces $500 million commitment to reverse childhood obesity in U.S.

Ueda, R. (2007). Immigration in global historical perspective. In M. C. Waters & R. Ueda (Eds.), *The new Americans: A guide to immigration since 1965* (pp. 14–28). Cambridge, MA: Harvard University Press.

United Nations Educational, Scientific and Cultural Organization. (2011). Education for all global monitoring report 2011. Retrieved March 31, 2011, from http://unesdoc.unesco.org/images/0019/001907/190743e.pdf.

Unz, R. K., & Tuchman, G. M. (1998). *Initiative statute: English language education for children in public schools* (www.nabe.org/unz/text). Palo Alto, CA: Author.

Van Leeuwen, M. S. (1990). *Gender and grace*. Downers Grove, IL: InterVarsity Press.

Violence Policy Center. (2009). Youth gang violence and guns: Data collection in California. Retrieved April 10, 2011, from http://www.vpc.org/studies/CAgang.pdf.

Vyas, S. (2004). "We are not all terrorists!" Listening to the voices of Muslim high school students in the post September 11 era. *Ejournal/Ejournal, 1*(2). Retrieved from vyas.pdf, www.subr.edu/coeducation/ejournal/EJournal.

Waitoller, F. R., Artilles, A. J., & Chaney, D. A. (2010). The miner's canary: A review of overrepresentation research and explanations. *Journal of Special Education, 44*(1), 29–49.

Watanabe, T. (2011, May 8). Dual-language immersion programs growing in popularity. *Los Angeles Times*. Retrieved May 8, 2011, from http://www.latimes.com/news/local/la-me-bilingual-20110508,0,3841220.story.

Watkins, S. (2011). Minorities struggle to get mortgage loans in Ohio. *Business Courier*. Retrieved April 2, 2011, from http://www.bizjournals.com/cincinnati/blog/2011/01/minorities-struggle-to-get-mortgage.html#.

Weishaar, M. K. (2007). *Case studies in special education law: No Child Left Behind Act and Individuals with Disabilities Education Improvement Act*. Upper Saddle River, NJ: Pearson Education.

Welner, K. G. (2002). Ability tracking: What role for the courts? *Educational Law Reporter, 163*(2), 565–571.

Wentworth, L., Pellegrin, N. Thompson, K., & Hakuta, K. (2010). Proposition 227 in California: A long-term appraisal of its impact on English learner student achievement. In P. Gandera & M. Hopkins (Eds.), *Forbidden languages: English learners and restrictive language policies*. New York, NY: Teachers College Press.

Whitlock, R. U. (2007). Queerly fundamental: Surviving straightness in a rural southern high school. In N. M. Rodriguez & W. F. Pinar (Eds.), *Queering straight teachers: Discourse and identity in education* (pp. 65–94). New York, NY: Peter Lang.

Williams, L. (2011, January 11). Meg Whitman campaign spending: Meg lost, but payday was sweet for many. *Huffington Post*. Retrieved from http://www.huffingtonpost.com/2011/02/10/meg-whitman-campaign-spen_0_n_821678.html.

Wilson, C. R., & Ray, C. (2007). Ethnicity. In *The new encyclopedia of Southern culture, Vol. 6*. Chapel Hill, NC: University of North Carolina Press.

Wilson, G., & Rahman, Q. (2008). *Born gay: The psychobiology of sex orientation*. London, UK: Peter Owen.

Witters, D. (2010). One in three adults obese in America's most obese states. Retrieved from http://www.gallup.com/poll/141734/One-Three-Adults-Obese-America-Three-Obese-States.aspx.

Wolfensberger, W. (1972). *Normalization: The principle of normalization in human services*. Toronto: National Institute on Mental Retardation.

Wolfensberger, W. (1983). Social role valorization: Proposed new form for the principle of normalization. *Mental Retardation, 21*(6), 234–239.

Wolfensberger, W. (2000). A brief overview of social role valorization. *Mental Retardation, 38*(2), 105–123.

Wolters, R. (2008). *Race and education: 1954–2007*. Columbia, MO: University of Missouri Press.

Wright, V. R., Chau, M., & Aratami, Y. (2011). Who are America's poor children? Retrieved March 23, 2011, from http://www.nccp.org/publications/pdf/text_1001.pdf.

Wright, V. R., Chau, M., & Aratani, Y. (2011, March). *Who are America's poor children? The official story*. New York, NY: National Center for Children in Poverty.

Yell, M. L. (2012). *The law and special education*. Upper Saddle River, NJ: Pearson Education.

Young, W. A. (2010). *The world's religions* (3rd ed.). Upper Saddle River, NJ: Pearson Prentice Hall.

Zhou, L. (2010). *Revenues and expenditures for public elementary and secondary education: School year 2007–08 (fiscal year 2008)* (NCES 2010-326). Washington, DC: U.S. Department of Education, National Center for Education Statistics.

Ellwood, R. S., 253, 256, 258, 259, 260
Equal Rights Advocates, 128
Escamilla, K., 231

Fairbrother, A., 370
Faltis, C. J., 225
Family Income and Educational Attainment, 83, 93
Federal Bureau of Investigation, 61
Federal Child Abuse Prevention and Treatment Act, 324
Fine, C., 111, 114
Fineran, S., 128
Fisher, M. P., 256, 257, 258, 260
Ford, D. Y., 192, 218
Foster, J. D., 322
Fox, M., 2, 52, 53, 96, 124, 131
Freund, D. M. P., 302
Frohlich, L., 2, 52, 53, 96, 124, 131
Frost, A., 281

Gallagher, C. A., 63
Gallup, 61, 240, 241, 243, 246, 247, 250, 251
Gallup Poll, 241
Gandhi, M., 348
Gangs and At-Risk Kids, 339
Garcia, D., 231
Garcia, J., 231
Garfinkle, L. F., 339
Gartin, B., 179, 180, 181, 182, 185
Gay, G., 362
Gay, Lesbian, and Straight Education Network (GLSEN), 157
Gerber, 197
Gibb, A. C., 189, 190, 191
Gibson, M. L., 353, 354
Gliedman, J., 187
Goldberg, A., 79
Goldenberg, C., 213, 222, 225
Gollnick, D. M., 13, 331
Gomes, P., 261, 265
GOP, 264
Gorski, P., 87
Grant, C. A., 26, 353, 354
Greytak, E. A., 157, 159, 162, 166, 167
Grinberg, J., 17
Groothuis, R. M., 261
Gruber, J. E., 128
Guilfoy, V., 132
Gurian, M., 110, 112, 135, 138

Haarmann, V., 283, 285
Hacker, J. S., 76, 78, 89, 90, 91

Hafner, K., 342
Hakuta, K., 230, 231
Haladyna, T., 231
Hall, G. E., 13, 331
Hallahan, D., 174, 183
Hamer, D., 145
Hamilton, B. E., 331, 332
Hanson, K., 132
Hardman, M. L., 176, 191, 199
Harley, D. A., 145, 146, 156, 159, 163, 164
Harlow, C. W., 62
Harper, B. W., 148
Hartz, P. R., 259
Haub, C., 281
Hays, C., 64
Helfand, D., 263
Helms, J. A., 54
Hemeyer, J. C., 247, 248, 253, 258, 259, 260
Hernandez, D. J., 96
Herrera, S. G., 213
Heward, W. L., 174, 219
Higareda, I., 194
Hill, C., 111, 131
Himmelstein, K. E. W., 156
Hoffman, L., 299
Hollins, E. R., 14, 363
Hopfe, L. M., 255, 257, 258, 259
Howard, T. C., 28, 39
Hudley, A. H., 211
Hudson, W. S., 247, 248, 249, 250, 260
Huget, J. L., 219
Hughes, F. P., 316
Human Rights Campaign, 155
Humes, K. R., 51
Hussar, W., 2, 52, 53, 96, 124, 131

Institute of Medicine, 328
Interstate Teacher Assessment and Support Consortium, 30
Iraq Coalition Casualty Count, 254
Ivanov, V., 212

Jacobs, L. R., 18, 80, 84
James, S., 115
Jamil, O. B., 148
Jefferys, K., 45
Jepkemboi, G., 134
Jewish Virtual Library, 210
Jiménez, T. R., 49
Johnson, D. K., 149, 153
Johnson, D. L., 283, 285
Johnson, J. A., 13, 331
Johnson, M. L., 283, 285

Johnstone, R. L., 252, 256, 261, 266
Joint Center for Housing Studies of Harvard University, 86
Jones, J. M., 61, 154
Jones, N. A., 51
Jordan-Young, R. M., 111, 112
Joyce, J. A., 147
Justice, L., 225
Justice Policy Institute, 339

Kalita, S. M., 7
Karnowski, S., 308
Katsiyannis, A., 185
Kauffman, J., 174, 183
Kavale, K. A., 183
Keating, D. P., 138
Keen, L., 144
Kelley, M., 38
Kemp, J., 2, 52, 53, 96, 124, 131
Kennedy, H., 335
Keysar, A., 243, 244, 247, 250, 251, 253, 257, 258
Kimmel, M., 113, 114, 116, 121, 128, 130, 131
Kincheloe, J. L., 255
Kinnaman, D., 245
Kinsey Institute, 144
Klinger, S., 79
Knox, P. L., 304
Konrath, S., 322
Kosciw, J. G., 148, 157, 159, 162, 166, 167
Kosmin, B. A., 243, 244, 247, 250, 251, 253, 256, 257, 258
Kramarae, C., 134
Krashen, S., 223, 232
Kuralt, C., 278

Lachman, S. P., 256
Ladson-Billings, G., 357, 362
LaDuke, W., 308
Landrum, T. J., 182
Landsberg, M., 263
Lee, J., 11, 115
Legal Momentum, 128
Lehr, J. I., 145
Leonardo, Z., 52
Let's Move, 328
LeVay, S., 145
Lewis, J., 12, 212
Lewis, M., 303, 307
LGBTQ Nation, 157
Lister, K. M., 342
Los Angeles Almanac, 212
Los Angeles Police Department, 339

Lund, D. E., 372
Lyons, G., 245

Ma, J., 84
Macgillivray, I. K., 148, 167
MacSwan, J., 231
Madsen, R., 9
Mahoney, K., 231
Malley, E., 333
Mallison, C., 211
Mander, J., 308, 309
Marsden, G. M., 247
Marston, S. A., 304
Martin, J. A., 331, 332
Maslow, A., 195
Mastropieri, M. A., 199
Mather, M., 40, 45, 52, 53, 281
Matthews, T. J., 331, 332
Mayo Clinic Health Manager, 334
McCarthy, M. M., 160
McCready, L. T., 167
McDaniel, E. R., 211, 219, 220
McField, G., 232
McGraw, B. A., 253, 256, 258, 259, 260
McIntosh, P., 23, 51
McKernan, S., 85
McWhirter, E. H., 147
Meacham, J., 245
Mellnik, T., 302
Mendes, E., 294
Mercer, J., 189
Meyer, E. J., 146, 161, 162, 163, 164, 165, 167
Mickelson, R. A., 57
Miller, M., 320
Miller, N., 149, 153
Miller, S., 324
Mitchell, L., 2
Mock, B., 155
Monger, R., 40, 41, 45, 52
Mooney, N., 89
Morse, A., 44
Murdick, N., 179, 180, 181, 182, 185
Murphy, J., 87, 100
Murry, K. G., 213
Musial, D. L., 13, 331

Naiditch, F., 17
National Academy of Sciences, 328
National Alliance of Black School Educators, 28
National Assessment of Educational Progress, 67, 96, 133

National Association for Bilingual Education, 226
National Center for Education Statistics, 174, 287, 290
National Center on Family Homelessness, 86
National Centers for Disease Control (CDC), 152
National Clearinghouse for English Language Acquisition, 222
National Coalition for the Homeless, 85
National Coalition for Women and Girls in Education, 132
National Collegiate Athletic Association, 133
National Education Association, 292
National Federation of State High School Associations, 133
National Institute of Justice, 62
National Institute of Mental Health, 197
National Institutes of Health, 198
National Law Center on Homelessness and Poverty, 85
National Women's Law Center, 128, 130
Neu, T. W., 116
New America Foundation, 175
Newport, F., 248, 293
Nguyen, M. L., 36
Nieto, S., 67, 357, 359, 362, 363, 369
Nirje, B., 199
Noppe, L. D., 316
NYC Mayors, 210

Office of Civil Rights (OCR), 190
O'Hare, W. P., 296
Oliva, 197
Olson, A., 148
O'Neil, M. E., 147
Orenstein, P., 113, 114, 135
Orfield, G., 57
Organisation for Economic Co-operation & Development, 91, 95, 104
Orr, J. E., 230
Osterman, M. J. K., 331, 332

Page, B. I., 18, 80
Paquette, K., 86

Parker, R. C., 175
Partnership for a Drug Free America, 344
Passel, J., 44, 225, 304
Peach, L. J., 262
Pellegrin, N., 231
Pence, K., 225
Pew Forum, 225, 242, 243, 244, 249, 253, 257, 258, 293
Pew Hispanic Center, 304
Pierson, P., 76, 78, 89, 90, 91
Pillai, S., 132
Pimpare, S., 85, 87
Pirah, J., 263
Pizzigati, S., 79, 91
Planty, M., 2, 52, 53, 96, 124, 131
Plotts, C., 2
Pollack, W., 116
Pollock, M., 64
Population Reference Bureau, 52
Porter, R. E., 211, 219, 220
Portes, A., 45
Posner, M., 333
Potok, M., 43, 62, 155
Potter, L., 333
Price, J., 17
Price, M., 303, 307
Proctor, B. D., 92, 93, 94
Proximity, 299
Pullen, P., 174, 183

Rahman, Q., 145
Ramirez, R. R., 51
Randolph, A. P., 1
Ratcliffe, C., 85
Rausch, M. K., 189, 190, 191
Ray, C., 285
Renn, K. A., 159
Renwick, W. H., 281
Reuters, 307
Riggle, E. D. B., 148
Rimm, S., 192
Ringheim, K., 281
Ritter, S., 189, 190, 191
Rivera, C., 192
Rivers, J. C., 69
Roberts, R., 255, 256
Robinson, B. A., 257, 258, 260, 263, 273
Rose, S. J., 80
Rostosky, S. S., 148
Roth, W., 187
Rothacker, R., 302
Rothstein, R., 97
Rowntree, L., 303, 307
Roxas, K., 44

SUBJECT INDEX

Al Jazeera, 255
Allah, 253
American Indians
  Bureau of Indian Education, 297
  cultural pluralism of, 12
  demographic data, 2, 38, 46
  dialects, 215
  European immigrants and, 38
  gender and work, 125
  geography and, 288
  gifted and talented underrepresentation, 190
  globalization and, 307–309
  HIV/AIDS and, 332
  income inequality, 94
  migration and, 304
  religion, 259
  sexual orientation and, 148
  suicide, 333
  teen birth rates, 331
American Muslim Mission, 256
American Psychiatric Association, 149
American Religious Identification Survey, 244–245,
    250, 259
American Sign Language (ASL), 218–219
Americans with Disabilities Act (ADA; 1990),
    181–182
Amish, 238, 246
Antiracist education, 28, 64
Anti-Semitism, 252–253, 265
Appalachia, 285–286
Appropriate education, 180, 183, 184–185
Argot, 211
Ashkenazim, 251
Asian Americans
  assimilation of, 11
  demographic data, 2
  HIV/AIDS and, 331–332
  immigrant history, 40
  immigration data, 45
  income inequality, 92–94
  language and, 211
  Lau v. Nichols (1974), 227
  Naturalization Act (1790), 55
  pan-ethnic classification of, 51
  sexual orientation and, 148
  special education placement and, 193
  street gangs, 339
Assessment
  achievement gap and, 67–69
  in InTASC standards, 29, 30
  language and, 225–226
  purpose of, 69
  special education placement and, 193, 225
Assimilation
  acculturation and, 10, 49, 60
  cultural identity and, 14

definition, 11
dominant culture and, 11–12, 14
education level and, 45–46
of immigrant students, 310
of indigenous people, 309
and instructional strategies, 12
intergroup teachers, 25
language and, 222
of people with disabilities, 175, 176
of upper class, 91
Asylees, 41, 42
Atheists, 239, 243, 245, 293
Athletics
  people with disabilities, 189
  Title IX, 132–133
At-risk youth, 329
Audio recording of interactions, 358
Autism Spectrum Disorders (ASD), 197–198

Bach, Johann Sebastian, 265
Baha'ism, 260
Banning books, 271–273
Basic interpersonal communicative skills (BICS),
    223–224, 230
Battleground states, 294
Behavioral disorders, 174, 175
Beloit College (Wisconsin), 322
"Berdache" people, 116–117
Biased assessment, 193, 225–226
Bible, 246, 247, 248, 259, 261, 262, 265, 268, 270
BICS (basic interpersonal communicative skills),
    223–224, 230
Biculturalism, 15–16
Bidialectalism, 215–216
Big ideas, 360
Bilingual education
  definition, 226
  as differentiated instruction, 226–229
  effectiveness of, 213, 232
  English as a second language versus, 229
  English Only, 224–225
  geography and, 288–289, 290
  as multicultural education, 24
  Proposition 227 and, 194
  special education placement and, 193
Bilingualism, 213, 224–225
Binet, Alfred, 111
Binge drinking, 116, 330
Birth control, 162, 250, 331
Birth rates, 52, 331–332
Bisexual, 145, 146
Black churches, 266
Black English, 208, 212, 216–218
Black Muslims, 256, 266
Blacksburg, Virginia, 336
Bloods (gang), 339

Cleveland, Grover, 38
Clinton, Bill, 153
Clothing and street gangs, 339
Co-cultures, 211
Cognitive academic language proficiency (CALP),
    223–224, 230
Collaboration, in InTASC standards, 29, 30, 31
Collective ownership, 308–309
Colloquialisms, 209
Color blindness, 63
Columbine High School, 336
Coming out, 147–148, 157
Communication
    cell phones, 134, 307, 317, 332, 342
    cross-cultural, 37, 70, 355, 358
    dialog, teacher-student, 352, 358, 361, 367, 369
    exceptional students, 196
    globalization of, 307
    in InTASC standards, 29, 31
    messages to students, 355–357
    nonverbal. *See* Nonverbal communication
    teachers and parents, 272–273, 299
    texting, 342
    in U.S. dominant group, 9
Compensatory education, 26, 97
Composition index, 190
Conflict
    intergroup conflict, 60–61
    status and, 10, 15
Confucianism, 257
Conservative Judaism, 251
Conservative Protestants, 246
Content, teaching of
    in InTASC standards, 29–31
    small schools, 296
Contextualization, 360–361, 365
Cooperative learning, 360, 365, 371
Corporations
    environmental issues, 307
    farming and, 296
    globalization of, 306
    and gross national incomes, 80
Cost of living, 79
Co-teaching, 183
Council for Exceptional Children, 179
Covens, 260
CPR, 345
Creationism, 246, 248–249, 268
CREDE (Center for Research on Education, Diversity,
    and Excellence), 360–361
Creolization, 284
Crime, 324, 335–336
Crips (gang), 339
Critical pedagogy, 28
Critical race theory, 28
Critical thinking

about media, 338
    multicultural education and, 28, 104, 371
    tracking and, 100
Criticism and gender, 114
Cross-cultural communication, 37, 70, 355, 358
Cross-dressers, 117, 146
Cults, religious, 260–261
Cultural borders, 15–16, 356
Cultural capital, 26, 299
Cultural encapsulation, 12
Cultural identity, 13–16, 350, 372–373
Culturally deprived, 26
Culturally responsive teaching, 352–353, 363–369
Cultural pluralism, 11–12, 240
Cultural relativism, 8
Culture, 3–10
    age and, 318–319, 342–343
    biculturism, 15–16
    characteristics of, 4–5
    in the classroom, 350
    communication and, 6, 219–221, 358–359
    dominant. *See* Dominant culture
    geography and, 280–282
    home–school dissonance, 3
    of immigrant families, 310–311
    influencing learning, 363
    in InTASC standards, 29
    language and, 6, 208–210
    learning about, 350, 352, 359, 364, 372
    lenses of culture, 6, 8
    manifestations of, 5–6
    multiculturalism, 12–13
    nonverbal communication and, 6, 219–221
    norms, 3–4
    oral discourse and, 358
    pluralism, 10–13
    religion and, 238–239, 240, 261, 267
Culture of poverty, 87
Curriculum
    ageism and, 343
    assimilation and, 11
    culturally responsive teaching and, 363–365
    gender in, 113–115, 134, 138
    globalization in, 311, 312
    hidden, 14, 23–24, 134, 355
    high-risk behaviors in, 344
    magnet schools, 299
    multicultural, 364
    privileged, 23–24
    queering of, 146, 162–165
    race and ethnicity in, 65–67
    religion and, 3, 239–240, 268–269, 273–274
    school consolidation and, 296
    sexual orientation in, 153, 156, 158, 162–165
    students in, 361
    teaching for equality, 101, 103–104

Dropping out
  demographic data, 63, 226
  geography and, 287, 290, 291
  Latinos, 45, 226
  poverty and, 93
  school disconnect, 349
  sexual orientation and, 162
Drug use, 324, 329–330, 344–345
Drug war, 289
Dual-language immersion programs, 228–229

Eastern Orthodoxy, 258–259, 261
Ebonics, 208, 212, 216–218
Echo Boomers, 319
Economics
  globalization and, 296, 306–307
  rural areas, 296
  suburban areas, 302
Ecosystem, 307
Education
  civil rights cases, 55–57
  English language learners and, 222
  gender and, 127, 133
  geography and, 285, 286, 287, 288–289, 290, 291,
    292–295
  immigrant students and, 310
  poverty and, 93
  power and, 83–84
  race and, 125
  religion and, 246, 248–249, 250, 252, 256, 287
  right to seek, 44, 59, 86–87, 178, 180
  self-sufficiency and, 306
  single-sex, 136, 137–138
  U.S. Supreme Court decisions, 44, 56–59, 177–178,
    184–185, 227, 232, 268
Education for All Handicapped Children Act (1975),
    180–181, 227
Educators. *See* Teachers
Edwards v. Aquillard (1987), 268
Egalitarianism, 16. *See also* Equality
Eisenhower, Dwight D., 149
Elementary and Secondary Education Act, 29
Emotional abuse, 325
Emotional disturbance, 174, 175, 192
Enculturation, 4
Endogamy, 11, 46, 50, 91, 219
Engaging students, 352–353
Engel v. Vitale (1962), 268, 270
English as a Second Language (ESL)
  academic English, 223–224
  bilingual education and, 227–228, 229
  as differentiated instruction, 229–233
  special education placement and, 193
English language
  ability and success, 45–46
  English Only, 224–225, 231

as official language, 42
  sheltered English immersion, 194
  signed English, 219
  Standard English, 208, 211, 213, 215–216, 218
English language learners (ELL)
  academic English, 223–224
  definition, 221
  demographic data, 221, 222
  English Only, 224
  in high-poverty schools, 96
  standardized test performance, 45
English Only, 224–225, 231
Enrollment demographic data, 299
Environment and globalization, 307
Epperson v. Arkansas (1968), 268
Equal Pay Act (1963), 119, 354
Equal Rights Amendment (ERA), 120, 152
Equality
  and educational opportunity, 19
  in educational opportunity, 18, 57, 69
  gender, 118–121
  individualism versus, 16–17, 18–19
  obstacles to, 20–24
  teaching for, 97–104
  treatment versus accessibility, 22
ESL. *See* English as a Second Language (ESL)
Establishment clause, 239–240, 267–273
Ethnic groups
  definition, 46
  in immigrant groups, 38
  racial groups versus, 49
Ethnic identities, 25
Ethnicity, 36–70
  achievement gap, 67–69
  acknowledging, 63–64, 366, 367
  communication styles, 210
  demographic data, 2–3
  ethnic group definition, 46
  ethnic identity, 47–49
  food and, 293–294, 319
  gender identity and, 117
  geography and, 283, 284–285
  identity stages, 54
  income and, 92–94, 125
  race versus, 49
  religion and, 243, 250, 267
  sexual activity and, 331–332
  sexual orientation and, 148
  special education placement and, 192
  street gangs and, 339
  suicide and, 333
  tracking and, 101
Ethnic studies
  banned, 11
  civil rights movement and, 26, 55
  as multicultural education, 24

Judaism
demographic data, 243, 244, 249
gender and, 262
geography and, 293
overview, 250–253
Sabbath and school, 237
sexual orientation and, 263
Junk food, 327–328

Karma, 258, 259
Kennedy, John F., 250, 285
Khalsa, 259
King, Lawrence, 156
King, Martin Luther, Jr., 55, 150
Kinsey, Alfred, 144, 146, 149
Kinsey scale, 146
Koran, 253, 255, 262, 263
Ku Klux Klan, 252

Lady Gaga, 335
La Guardia, Fiorello, 209–210
Language, 206–233
American Sign Language, 218–219
culture and, 6, 208–210
definition, 208
development as critical, 360
differences, 212–219
differentiated instruction for, 225–233
distance, conversational, 220
diversity of, 209, 210, 212, 291
English as official, 42
in InTASC standards, 29, 31
learning of, 209
nature of, 211–212
nonverbal communication. *See* Nonverbal communication
person-first, 182
respect for, 355
second language acquisition, 221–225
sheltered English immersion, 194, 224, 229–230
as socializing agent, 209–210
Larry P. v. Riles (1979), 193
Latinos. *See also* Mexican Americans
assimilation of, 11
definition of term, 39
demographic data, 2, 40, 53
dropping out, 45, 226
drug war and, 289
ethnic identity of, 47
gender and work, 125
geography and, 296
HIV/AIDS and, 331
immigration data, 45
income inequality, 92–94
pan-ethnic classification of, 50
religion and, 242

sexual activity, 331
special education, 190, 193, 218
street gangs, 339
suicide, 333
Latter-Day Saints. *See* Mormons
Lau v. Nichols (1974), 227, 232
Lavender Scare, 149
Lawrence v. Texas (2003), 155, 160
Lead poisoning, 191–192
Learning communities, 371
Learning disabilities, 174, 175
Learning environment, in InTASC standards, 30
Learning styles and gender, 131
Least restrictive environment (LRE), 180, 200, 201
Lee v. Weisman (1992), 268
Lesbian, as term, 145
Let's Move, 328
LGBTQ (lesbian, gay, bisexual, transgender, and queer), 144, 146
Liberal Protestants, 246
Licensure, 29, 31
Literacy, 360–361
Littleton, Colorado, 336
Longfellow, Henry Wadsworth, 259
Lovell v. Comsewogue School District (2002), 160
Low-ability students
and discipline, 100
limited education of, 100, 362
socioeconomic status and, 101, 102
teacher attention, 357
teacher expectations, 99

Magnet schools, 299
Mainline Protestants, 244, 246, 247
Mainstreaming, as term, 199
Male. *See* Gender; Masculinity
Manifest destiny, 305
March on Washington (1963), 150
Marginalization. *See* Alienation
Marriage
disabilities and, 176
endogamy, 11, 46, 50, 91, 219
race and, 50
sexual orientation and, 151, 152, 153–154, 263, 264
socioeconomic status and, 117
Masculinity, 115–117, 128, 130, 135, 146, 148, 161, 187
Maslow, Abraham, 195
McKinney-Vento Homeless Assistance Act (1987), 86–87
Meaningful projects, 371
Mecca, 253
Media
gender perception, 113
prejudice and, 21
Mennonite students, 238
Meritocracy, 17–18
Metropolitan, 281

Pink Scare, 149
Plessy v. Ferguson (1896), 58, 177
Pluralism, 10–13
Plyler v. Doe (1982), 44
Political action committee (PAC), 152
Politics
   foreign intervention and, 305
   geography and, 293, 294–295
   money and, 249
   religion and, 248, 249, 250, 252, 264, 266
   sexual orientation and, 152, 153
   socioeconomic status and, 84
   teaching as political, 372
   women in, 121
Polygamy, 258
Poole, Elijah, 256
Portfolio, InTASC artifacts, 31
Poverty
   absolute poverty, 306–307
   children in, 85, 95–97, 296, 323, 351
   criminal activity and, 338
   culture of, 87
   discussions about, 369
   ethnicity and, 191
   gender and, 94
   geography and, 285, 287, 290, 291, 296
   pregnancy and, 191, 331
   reading skills and, 96
   special education and, 191
   unemployed and homeless, 85–87
   U.S. versus world, 91–92
   working poor, 88–89
Power
   culture and, 5, 10–11, 13
   democracy and, 16
   discussions about, 135, 367, 369
   group relationships, 20
   hidden curriculum and, 357
   language and, 211
   religion and, 266
   socioeconomic status and, 84
   street gangs and, 339
   wealth and, 80, 91
Praise and gender, 114
Prayer in schools, 239, 246, 248, 268, 269, 270
Pregnancy
   child abuse and, 324
   poverty and, 191, 331
   preterm births, 191
   teen pregnancies, 191, 331
Prejudice, 20–21, 22
Prince, Phoebe, 335
Privilege
   color blindness and, 62
   of hetersexuality, 155
   overview, 23–24

of whiteness, 11, 23, 28, 51–52, 53–54
Pro-choice, 118, 247, 248, 250
Professional development, in InTASC standards, 30
Proficiencies, multicultural, InTASC standards,
   29–31
Proposition 8 (California), 263
Proposition 227 (California), 194, 228, 229–231
Proselytizing, 258
Protestantism, 246–249. *See also* Christianity
Public Law 93-112, 180
Public Law 94-142. *See* Education for All Handicapped
   Children Act (1975)
Public Law 101-336. *See* Americans with Disabilities
   Act (ADA; 1990)
Public Law 101-476. *See* Individuals with Disabilities
   Education Act (IDEA; 1990)
Public Law 105-17. *See* IDEA Amendments
   (1997)
Public Law 108-446. *See* Individuals with Disabilities
   Education Improvement Act (2004)
Punishment. *See* Discipline

Queer, as term, 145, 146
Queering the curriculum, 146, 162–165
Queer theory, 146
Questioning (sexual orientation), 146
Qur'an, 253, 255, 262, 263

Race, 36–70
   achievement gap, 67–69
   acknowledging, 63–64
   definition, 49
   demographic data, 2
   discussions about, 369
   ethnicity versus, 49
   geography and, 286–287
   identification of, 50–51
   identity stages, 54
   income and, 92–94, 125
   racial diversity, 52–53
   racial identity, 53–54
   religion and, 265–267
   sexual activity and, 331–332
   sexual orientation and, 148
   smoking and, 330
   special education and, 192
   street gangs and, 339
   suicide and, 333
   tracking and, 101
Racism
   children displaying, 323–324
   confronting, 64
   demographic data, 61
   multicultural education and, 24
   sexual orientation and, 148
   slavery and, 265

Sexual harassment, 128, 130
Sexual orientation, 142–167
  bullying, 147, 148, 157, 159, 161, 166, 317, 335
  cause of, 145
  coming out, 147–148, 157
  in curriculum, 153, 156, 158, 162–165
  definition, 144, 145
  equality struggles, 149–155
  First Amendment and, 165, 166
  heterosexism, 155–159
  identity stages, 147
  intergroup relations, 148
  LGBTQ teachers, 159–161
  mannerisms, 317
  marriage and, 151, 152, 153–154, 263, 264
  milestones in gay rights, 151
  multiple, 147
  publications, 161
  religion and, 247, 262–264
  reparative therapy, 147
  sexual identity, 144–148, 162–164
  student support, 165–167, 264
  suicide and, 147, 157, 333
  terms for, 145–146
Sexually transmitted diseases (STDs), 330, 331, 332
Shamans, 259, 260
Sheltered English immersion, 194, 224, 229–230
Shepard, Matthew, 156
Shi'i (Shi'ite) Muslims, 255
Signed English, 219
Sign language, 208, 218–219
Sikhism, 259–260
Single-sex education, 136, 137–138
Skinheads, 339
Slavery, 265, 285, 305
Smith, Alfred, 250
Smith, Joseph, 258
Smoking, 330
Socialization, 4
Social justice
  definition, 19, 369
  obstacles to, 20–24
  in schools, 20, 369–372
Social networking, 134, 320, 321
Social role valorization, 199
Social stratification, 77–78
Socioeconomic status (SES), 74–104. *See also* Class
  of African Americans, 39
  childhood and, 323
  demographic data, 2
  disabilities and, 175
  disparities in, 20
  education, 82–83, 271, 299
  English language learners, 222

income, 78–80
justice system and, 338
occupation, 80–82
power, 83–84
religion and, 241
special education and, 192
tracking and, 101
urban areas and, 297
wealth, 80, 84, 90–91, 241, 249, 250
Sodomy laws, 151, 153, 155
South (U.S.), 283–285
Southern Poverty Law Center, 70
The Southwest, 289–290
Spanish language, as Latino identity, 50
Special education
  demographic data, 174
  development of, 26
  disproportionate placement, 189–194
  gender and, 137
  as multicultural education, 25
  placements, 200
  referrals, 183, 191–193
Speech impairment, 174
Sports. *See* Athletics
Standard English
  accents and, 213
  as artificial, 211, 216
  definition, 208
  dialects and, 215–216, 218
Standardized tests
  achievement gap and, 64, 67–68
  gender and, 131
  language and, 225–226
Standards
  fundamental versus multicultural, 28
  InTASC multicultural standards, 29–31
  for learning improvement, 360–361
States
  Arizona immigration law, 43
  bilingual education, 194, 224, 228, 229–231, 290
  cell phone usage, 342
  censorship, 272
  child abuse, 325
  child poverty, 95, 296
  diversity demographics, 2, 38, 52–53
  English language learners, 221–222
  environmental issues, 307
  expenditures per pupil, 104, 292
  food, 293–294
  health, 294
  immigration data, 40, 45
  minority populations of, 282
  obesity, 328
  politics and, 294–295
  religion and, 293

Television, 113, 338

Test scores. *See also* Assessment; Standardized tests
    age and, 133
    assimilation and, 68
    gender and, 110, 131
    No Child Left Behind and, 28
    Proposition 227 and, 230
    tracking and, 100

Textbooks, 25–26, 55, 59, 66, 101, 114–115, 272
Texting, 342
Time, as U.S. value, 9
Title I, 97, 354
Title IX, 108, 121, 130, 131–133, 354
Tobacco use, 330
Tracking
    antiracist education and, 28
    socioeconomic status and, 362
    teaching for equality, 100–101, 102, 357
Transgender identity, 115, 116–117, 145–146, 160
Transition plan, 182
Transitional programs (bilingual education), 228
Transportation
    desegregation of, 55, 266
    migration and, 303
    Plessy v. Ferguson (1896), 177
    to school, 87, 271, 296
Transsexuals, 146, 160
Transvestites, 117, 146
"Two-souled" people, 116
Two-way bilingual immersion programs, 228–229

Unauthorized immigrants
    demographic data, 44, 304
    drug war and, 289
    ordinances against, 42
Unchurched, 245
Unemployed, 85–87, 93
UNESCO (United Nations Educational, Scientific
    and Cultural Organization), 306
Unification Church, 242, 243, 261
Unions and working poor, 88–89
Unitarian Universalists, 259
United Nations, 304, 306, 353
United Nations Convention on the Rights of the
    Child (1989), 306
United Nations Educational, Scientific and Cultural
    Organization (UNESCO), 306
U.S. Census Bureau, religion data, 242
U.S. Department of Education, 157
U.S. Department of Health and Human Services,
    157
U.S. Office of Bilingual Education and Minority
    Language Affairs, 232
U.S. Supreme Court decisions
    desegregation, 56–59, 177–178

education, 44, 56–59, 177–178, 184–185, 227, 232,
    268
    miscegenation laws, 50
    religion, 7, 239, 246, 268, 269, 270
    sexual orientation, 151, 155, 160
Universal Declaration of Human Rights (UDHR),
    353–354
Universities
    geography and, 287
    religion and, 246, 250, 252
Unz, Ron, 229–231
Upper class, 90–91
Upper middle class, 89–90
Urban areas
    contradictions of, 298–299
    environmental issues, 307
    immigrants in, 40, 41
    migration and, 304
    populations of, 297, 298
    schools, 70, 299–300
    socioeconomic status, 297
    U.S. population, 295

Values
    community, of indigenous people, 308
    culture and, 6
    definition, 3
    religious, 238, 239, 240, 244, 245, 246, 261, 267,
        272
    of U.S. dominant culture, 8–10
Vending machines, 327, 328
Vernacular Black English, 208, 212, 216–218
Video games, 338
Video recording of interactions, 358
Violent crime, 335–339
Virginia Tech University, 336
Visual impairment, 174, 175, 188
Vocational Rehabilitation Act (1993), 172, 180
Voluntary prayer, 269
Voting, 84, 266
Voting Rights Act (1965), 55, 150, 354
Vouchers, school, 269, 271

Wallace v. Jaffree (1985), 268
War on Poverty, 97
Washington, D.C.
    desegration, 58
    March on Washington (1963), 55, 150
    March on Washington, gay and lesbian, 151
    One Million Man March (1996), 256
    poverty, 298
WASP (white, Anglo-Saxon, Protestant), 8
Wealth, 80, 84, 90–91, 241, 249, 250
Weapons, 335, 338, 339
Well-being and geography, 294

West (U.S.), 290–291
Western canon, 23, 363
Western worldview
  in curriculum, 65, 84, 161
  individualism, 9
  U.S. dominant culture, 8
White European Americans
  assimilation and, 11, 40
  demographic data, 2
  as dominant culture, 8
  dropping out, 226
  ethnic identities, 47
  HIV/AIDS and, 331
  holidays and, 239
  immigrant history, 39, 40
  Passing of the Great Race, The (Grant), 50
  in poverty, 93
  as raceless, 51–52, 369, 372
  racial development stages, 54
  racism and, 367
  sexual activity, 331
  street gangs, 339
  suicide, 333
White supremacists, 62, 339
White-collar workers, 81, 84, 88, 89
Wicca, 260
Witchcraft, 260
Women's studies, 25, 138

Woodson, Carter G., 25
Work
  bilingualism and, 229
  class and, 84–91
  discussions about, 369
  employer sponsorship of immigrants, 41
  gender and, 123–128
  globalization and, 296, 306
  intergroup conflict and, 60, 62
  Internet postings and, 320
  sexual orientation and, 155
  in U.S. values, 9
  young adults and, 320, 322
Working class, 85, 87–89, 214
Working poor, 88–89
World Bank, 305
World Trade Organization (WTO), 305
World Wide Web. *See* Internet

X, Malcolm, 256

Yiddish, 209, 210
Young, Brigham, 258
Young adulthood, 319–323
Youth Risk Behavior Survey (YRBS), 330, 331,
  332, 337

Zero tolerance of violence, 337